A HANDBOOK OF COMMUNICATION SKILLS

A Handbook of Communication Skills

Edited by Owen Hargie

NEW YORK UNIVERSITY PRESS
Washington Square, New York

© 1986 Owen Hargie

First published in 1986 in the United States of America by
NEW YORK UNIVERSITY PRESS, Washington Square,
New York, N.Y. 10003

Library of Congress Cataloging-in-Publication Data

A Handbook of Communication Skills.

    Bibliography: p.
    Includes index.
    1. Interpersonal relations. 2. Interpersonal
communication. 3. Social skills. I. Hargie, Owen.
HM132.H332 1986   302.3'4   86–8534
ISBN 0–8147–3440–5

Printed and bound in Great Britain

CONTENTS

Contents

DETAILS OF CONTRIBUTORS

Jerry Authier is associate professor of medical psychology in the Department of Family Practice at the University of Nebraska Medical Center in Omaha, Nebraska. He is also a practising psychotherapist in the community and provides therapy for patients using largely a psychoeducational model of treatment. He received his PhD in psychology from the University of Portland, Portland, Oregon. His professional interests include the areas of (1) characteristics which differentiate the effective from the ineffective therapist; (2) the microcounselling paradigm; and (3) psychoeducation. He has written several articles, book chapters, and is co-author with Dr Allen Ivey in the second edition of the text *Microcounseling Innovations in Interviewing Counseling Psychotherapy and Psychoeducation* (CC Thomas, 1978).

James C. Baxter is professor of psychology at the Univesity of Houston. He received a PhD in clinical psychology from the University of Texas at Austin. His primary research interests are in person perception, self-presentation, personality theory, proxemics and statistical methodologies.

Herbert H. Blumberg lectures in psychology at the University of London Goldsmith's College. He received his doctorate from the Johns Hopkins University and has authored or co-authored over 30 articles and chapters in social psychology and social research methods. He is on the advisory panel of the Center for Intercultural Communication. With A. Paul Hare, he has co-edited several volumes about nonviolent direct action.

George Brown is reader in University Teaching Methods at the University of Nottingham and national co-ordinator of academic staff training in universities for the UK Committee of Vice Chancellors and Principals. He has been an active researcher in the field of higher education and in classroom research. He has written texts on statistics, teaching and lecturing and articles on higher education and medical and health education. Dr Brown has acted as a consultant for the British Council, UNESCO and the WHO. He is currently preparing a practical text on teaching in higher education and completing a research project on the consultation in general practice.

Leonard G. Cairns is senior lecturer in education and chairman of the school of teaching and curriculum studies at the University of Sydney. After a career as a primary school teacher, he studied social psychology, with a particular interest in interpersonal interaction and the use of unobtrusive measures in attitude research. In the last few years he has researched microteaching, classroom management, and supervision of the practicum in teacher education. Recently, he has turned his attention to language in education as an area that combines many of these fields of research interest.

Martin F. Davies received his BA and MA in natural sciences from the University of Cambridge, his PhD in psychology from the University of London, and is currently senior lecturer in psychology at Goldsmiths' College, University of London, where he specialises in social psychology. His original interest in groups he derived from research at the Communication Studies Group, University College London, into group problem-solving via telecommunications media. Current research interests centre on cognitive processes in social interaction sequences.

David A. Dickson is a lecturer in the Department of Communication, University of Ulster. After reading for a joint honours degree in psychology and philosophy at Queen's University, Belfast, he proceeded to train as a teacher at the same institution gaining a diploma in education. He then studied for a masters degree in education at the New University of Ulster, before obtaining his PhD in applied social psychology at Ulster Polytechnic. Election to Associate Membership of the British Psychological Society took place in 1982. His research interests lie in the field of social skills training, particularly in the identification of interpersonal skills in professional contexts and in the generalisation of training effects. He has published various articles and is co-author (with O. Hargie and C. Saunders) of *Social Skills in Interpersonal Communication* (Croom Helm, 1981).

J. T. Dillon edits *Questioning Exchange* a multidisciplinary review (twice yearly) encompassing all aspects of questioning in all fields of endeavour; and he has published several dozen studies on questioning in various contexts, such as classrooms and scholarly inquiry. After receiving a PhD in educational psychology from the University of Chicago, he treated himself to an MA in history and currently teaches curriculum at the University of California, Riverside.

Daniel Druckman received a PhD in social psychology from Northwestern University, Illinois, USA. In addition to nonverbal communication, his primary interests are in the areas of interparty conflict resolution, policy decision-making, negotiations, political stability and regional politics and modelling methodologies, including simulation. He has published numerous book chapters in these areas. He has also written, with Rozelle and Baxter, the 1982 Sage volume, *Nonverbal Communication: Survey, Theory, and Research,* and edited the volume *Negotiations: Social-Psychological Perspectives,* also published by Sage. He is now principal study director at the National Research Council in Washington DC. Previously, he was a scientist at Mathematica, Inc., and at Booz. Allen & Hamilton in Bethesda, Maryland.

Hugh Foot is senior lecturer in the Department of Applied Psychology, University of Wales Institute of Science and Technology, Cardiff. He received his PhD in psychology from St Andrews in 1966, and is a Fellow of the British Psychological Society. He has written numerous articles and book chapters on the subject of humour and laughter, and co-organised the First International Conference on Humour and Laughter held in Cardiff in 1976. He has co-edited with A. Chapman two books on humour and laughter: *Humour and Laughter: Theory Research and Application* (Wiley, 1976) and *It's a Funny Thing, Humour* (Pergamon, 1977). He has also produced four books on other topics.

Maryanne Galvin is clinical director of the School Consultation Program at Tufts-New England Medical Center in Boston, Massachusetts. Dr Galvin is a licensed psychologist in private practice and has written numerous articles pertaining to communication skills development for professionals and creative problem-solving strategies.

Owen D.W. Hargie is senior lecturer in the Department of Communication and head of the Social Skills Centre at the University of Ulster, Jordanstown. After graduating from Queen's University, Belfast, he was awarded a PhD in psychology from the CNAA (Ulster Polytechnic). He has published numerous articles and book chapters on interpersonal communication, and co-authored *Microteaching in Perspective* (Blackstaff Press, 1979) and *Social Skills in Interpersonal Communication* (Croom Helm, 1981). He has also produced (with P.McCartan) *Social Skills Training and Psychiatric Nursing* (Croom Helm, 1986). He has considerable experience in planning, implementing and evaluating programmes of communication skills training for professional groups.

Allen E. Ivey is director of the counselling psychology programme at the University of Massachusetts in Amherst. He is the author of over 150 articles and several books encompassing the spectrum of topics in counselling psychology, training and cognition.

Valerie Kent is senior lecturer in psychology at the University of London, Goldsmiths' College. Her two principal areas of interest are social influence processes and the social development of pre-school children. Her current research analyses the social interaction of mothers and young children, and takes an intersubjective approach to the development of pro-social behaviour. She is a co-editor of *Small Groups and Social Interaction.*

Peter Marshall is lecturer in communication at the University of Ulster. After serving in the Royal Navy he went to Westhill College of Education, Birmingham, and was awarded the diploma in youth work. He then spent a number of years working as training officer for the NI Association of Youth Clubs, and entered the Careers Service, studying for the diploma in careers guidance and practising as an area careers officer for six years. Following this, he joined the Ulster

Polytechnic as senior lecturer in vocational guidance. He has considerable experience in communication and interactive skills and has written a number of training manuals for firms and public bodies. He also acts as consultant in this subject to a variety of organisations.

John McGregor McMaster is chief executive of the Boys' and Girls' Welfare Society, Cheadle, Cheshire. He was formerly a senior lecturer in educational psychology at Preston Polytechnic and a lecturer in behavioural science at the University of Newcastle-upon-Tyne. He is a master of education and has diplomas in physical and primary education, and in the education of the physically and mentally handicapped. He is author of *Towards an Educational Theory for the Mentally Handicapped* (Edward Arnold, 1973), and editor of *Methods in Social and Educational Caring* (Gower, 1982) and *Skills in Social and Educational Caring* (Gower, 1982). He is consultant to a number of statutory authorities and voluntary organisations, and has a special interest in an integrated and multidisciplinary approach for the caring professions.

Ian Morley is senior lecturer and chairman of the Department of Psychology, University of Warwick. His research interests include social psychology, especially cognitive social psychology and the study of group performance, leadership, self-fulfilling prophecies, psychology and the law, social factors in memory and interviewing. Recently, the SSRC awarded him a grant to study (with A. Sherr) the effects of experience on the initial interview between a lawyer and a client. He has written extensively on bargaining and negotiation, including (with G.M. Stephenson) *The Social Psychology of Bargaining*.

R. Glynn Owens is lecturer in clinical psychology at the University of Liverpool. After taking a first-class honour's degree in psychology at the University of Brunel, he was awarded a DPhil from Oxford University and diploma in clinical psychology of the British Psychological Society. Following this, he spent a number of years working for the Prison Department and in special hospitals before moving to the University of Liverpool in 1980. He has considerable experience of working with violent individuals, both in institutional settings and, latterly, in outpatient groups. He has published a number of articles in the area of forensic psychology and is co-author (with J.B. Ashcroft) of *Violence: A Guide for the Caring Professions* (Croom Helm, 1985).

Richard F. Rakos received his PhD from Kent State University, Ohio, USA in 1978. He is a behaviour therapist who has focused his research and clinical interests on assertiveness and social skills training and behavioural self-management programmes. Professor Rakos' publications on assertion include numerous articles in scientific journals, one book chapter, and a self-administered audiocassette training programme. Most recently, he has conducted a series of studies investigating the social response to assertion. Professor Rakos is now an associate professor of psychology at Cleveland State University where he teaches graduate courses in behaviour modification, clinical interviewing and ethical and legal issues.

Richard M. Rozelle is professor of psychology and director of graduate education in social psychology in the Department of Psychology at the University of Houston. He received a PhD in social psychology from Northwestern University. His research interests include impression formation and management, attitude—behaviour change, bargaining behaviour, behavioural medicine, organisational climate and programme evaluation.

Christine Y.M. Saunders is lecturer in the Department of Communication at the University of Ulster. The first ten years of her career were spent teaching in a range of schools in Scotland and England. Between 1973 and 1976 she studied and was awarded the diploma in advanced studies in education (with distinction) and an MPhil from the New University of Ulster, Coleraine. Following this, she spent two years working as a research officer in the Department of Education at Ulster Polytechnic before moving to her present post in 1979. Her main research interest is in the area of social skills, with particular reference to the identification and analysis of communication skills in specific professional contexts. She has co-authored two books: *The Assessment of Teaching Practice* (with E.D. Saunders), University of Ulster, 1980, and *Social Skills in Interpersonal Communication* (with O.D.W. Hargie and D.A. Dickson), Croom Helm, 1981. In addition, she has contributed a number of chapters to readers in social skills, presented papers at national and international conferences and published widely in academic and professional journals.

Voncile M. Smith is professor communication at Florida Atlantic University. She received her BA, MA, and PhD from the University of Florida. Her research and teaching interests are in interpersonal and public communication, phonology and communication theory. She is a member of the Speech Communication Association, the International Listening Association and the International Communication Association. She has written a number of articles and papers on various communication topics and a book on *Communication for the Health Care Team* (Lippincott, 1979). She is now under contract to complete a book on speaking and listening for college students.

Dorothy Whittington is senior lecturer in psychology in the University of Ulster. She began her career as an infant school teacher then lectured in educational psychology at Callendar Park College, Falkirk. Since moving to Ulster Polytechnic (now part of the University of Ulster) she has been a member of the Departments of Educational Studies, Communication Studies and Psychology. She has considerable experience of social skill training and has provided pre-service, in-service and workshop courses for a very wide range of professional groups including teachers, careers officers, health visitors, district nurses, speech therapists, social workers and psychologists. She has written several articles on aspects of social skill training and is co-author (with Roger Ellis) of *A Guide to Social Skill Training* (Croom Helm, 1981) and *New Directions in Social Skill Training* (Croom Helm, 1983).

EDITORIAL INTRODUCTION

As society develops and becomes more complex, there seems to be a need for a greater number of what Ellis (1980) has referred to as 'interpersonal professionals' who spend a large part of their working lives in face-to-face interaction with others. Such professionals include doctors, teachers, speech therapists, social workers, psychologists, nurses, careers advisers, counsellors and marketing executives, to name but a few.

Until recently, the training of many of these professionals has focused almost entirely upon the acquisition of specialised knowledge but included little or no direct reference to or study of interpersonal communication. However, professional competence in many types of profession involves the effective implementation of three main sets of skills, namely:

1. *Cognitive skills:* the knowledge base of the profession, that which characterises it and sets it apart from other groups of professionals;
2. *Technical skills:* the manipulative skills inherent within a profession. Thus, a surgeon must be able to utilise a scalpel skilfully, a nurse must be able to dress a wound and a surveyor needs to know how to use a theodolite;
3. *Social or communication skills:* the ability of the individual to interact effectively with others in the professional context.

Traditionally, the education and training of most professional groups has placed emphasis upon the former two sets of skills at the expense of social or communication skills. This is somewhat surprising, given that it has long been recognised that the ability to communicate effectively is central to success in many walks of life. McCroskey (1984), in emphasising this fact, points out that: 'The importance of competence in communication has been recognized for thousands of years. The oldest essay ever discovered, written about 3,000 BC consists of advice on how to speak effectively. This essay was inscribed on a fragment of parchment addressed to Kagemni, the eldest son of Pharoah Huni. Similarly, the oldest extant book is a treatise on effective communication. This book, known as the Precepts, was composed in Egypt about 2,675BC by Ptah-Hotep.'

However, this emphasis upon communication seems to have been overlooked in the education and training of many professional groups, despite the fact that the ability to communicate effectively is vital in their professional roles. Given the central importance of effective communication, it is reasonable to expect that these professionals should have knowledge of, and expertise in, communication skills. Indeed, as Ellis and Whittington (1981) state, 'all but the most isolated occupations demand interaction with others at times, but some jobs have skilled interaction as a primary focus'. Therefore, it is hardly surprising that in the past

1

few years increasing attention has been devoted to the study of social skills in professional contexts. Hargie and Saunders (1983) list a total of 16 separate professions wherein programmes of training in interpersonal communication have been implemented and evaluated in the literature.

Increasing attention, in fact, has been devoted to the entire spectrum of socially skilled interaction. The fairly obvious observation that some individuals are more socially skilled than others has led to carefully formulated and systematic investigations into the nature and functions of social skills. Ellis and Whittington (1981) have identified three discrete contexts within which such investigations have taken place:

1. *Developmental*. Here the concern is with the development of socially skilled behaviour in children; with how, and at what stages, children acquire, refine and extend their repertoire of social skills;

2. *Remedial*. In this context, the focus of attention is upon those individuals who, for whatever reason, fail to develop an adequate repertoire of social skills. Investigators are interested in attempting to determine the nature and causes of social inadequacy, and in ascertaining to what extent social skill deficits can be remediated;

3. *Specialised*. Attention is devoted to the study of social skills in professional encounters. Most professions will involve interaction of a specialised nature either with clients or with other professionals. Therefore, it is important to chart the types of communication skills which are effective in professional situations.

It is with the latter context that this book is concerned. While interest in the field of specialised social skills has developed rapidly, relatively few books have attempted to provide systematic descriptions of such skills or to evaluate research which has investigated their efficacy. This book is intended to help rectify the situation by bringing together, for the first time, original contributions from international authorities in the field of interpersonal communication. As such, it incorporates a comprehensive study of those communication skill areas central to effective interpersonal functioning in a range of professional contexts.

The book has five separate sections; Part 1 provides a theoretical framework for the study of communication skills, examines the concept of communication as skilled behaviour (Chapter 1), and presents a theoretical model of interpersonal communication (Chapter 2). Part 2 focuses upon eight core communication skills, namely, nonverbal communication, questioning, reinforcement, reflecting, opening and closing, explaining, self-disclosure and listening. While these are not entirely mutually exclusive (for example, aspects of nonverbal communication are referred to in each of these chapters), each chapter deals with a discrete and important component of communication.

In Part 3, different aspects of group skills are highlighted. This section incorporates a study of factors which impinge upon the individual working in a group

(Chapter 11), an analysis of the skills necessary for effective group leadership (Chapter 12), negotiating and bargaining skills (Chapter 13), and skills essential in the preparation and presentation of a case to a group (Chapter 14).

Part 4 deals with four important dimensions of communication which have applications in a range of situations, including the use of humour and laughter (Chapter 15), the ability to deal with people who are displaying strong emotions (Chapter 16), asserting and confronting skills (Chapter 17) and demonstrating a capacity for warmth and empathy (Chapter 18). The final section (Part 5) provides an overview that brings together the main issues arising from the study of communication skills.

The information about interpersonal communication provided in this book should be regarded as providing resource material. How these resources are applied will depend upon the personality of the reader and the situation in which he or she is operating. It is impossible to legislate in advance for every possible social situation, and decisions about what approach could best be employed can only be made in the light of all the available background information. As such, this book certainly does not provide a preordained set of responses for given situations. Rather, it offers a selection of communication perspectives which should inform the reader, and facilitate the interactive process.

Thus the contents of this book provide an overview of the central skills and dimensions of communication which have been identified to date. As such, it offers valuable information which should enable the reader to refine and extend his or her own pattern and style of interaction. However, it should be realised that research in the field of social interaction is progressing rapidly, and it is anticipated that other skills will be identified as our knowledge of this area increases. Finally, although the aspects contained in this book are presented separately, it is recognised that, in practice they overlap, are interdependent and often complement one another. However, for the purposes of analysis and evaluation it is valuable to identify separately those elements of communication which seem to 'hang together', and thereby attempt to understand and make sense of what is a complex field of study.

(It should be noted that where either the masculine or feminine gender is referred to throughout this text, this should be taken as encompassing both genders as appropriate.)

References

Ellis, R. (1980) 'Simulated Social Skill Training for the Interpersonal Professions' in W. Singleton, P. Spurgeon and R. Stammers (eds), *The Analysis of Social Skill*, Plenum, New York

Ellis, R. and Whittington, D. (1981) *A Guide to Social Skill Training*, Croom Helm, Beckenham

Hargie, O. and Saunders, C. (1983) 'Training Professional Skills' in P. Dowrick and S. Biggs (eds), *'Using Video'*, Wiley, Chichester

McCroskey, J. (1984) 'Communicative Competence: The Elusive Construct' in R. Bostrom (ed.), *'Competence in Communication: A Multidisciplinary Approach'*, Sage, Beverly Hills

Part 1:
BACKGROUND

1　COMMUNICATION AS SKILLED BEHAVIOUR

Owen Hargie

This chapter is concerned with an examination of the nature of skilled behaviour, and in particular with the perspective that interpersonal communication can be viewed in terms of socially skilled behaviour. In order to evaluate this perspective, it is necessary to relate the history of the study of social skill directly to the study of motor skill, since it was from the latter source that the concept of communication as skill eventually emerged. The extent to which this analogy between motor skill and social skill can be pursued is then discussed, together with an analysis of the nature of social skill *per se*. Overall, therefore, this chapter provides a reference point for the entire book, by investigating the nature, and defining features, of social skill.

Motor Skills

The study of skill and skilled performance has a long and rich tradition within psychology, in relation to the analysis of perceptual–motor skills. Perceptual–motor skills refer to those skills which involve co-ordinated physical movements of the body. Such skills are obviously widely employed in human performance and include, for example, walking, writing, playing tennis or driving a car. Welford (1968) has traced the scientific study of motor skill back to 1820, when the astronomer Bessel investigated differences between individuals on a task that involved the recording of star-transit times. However, direct psychological interest in the nature of motor skill really began with studies by Bryan and Harter (1897) into the learning of Morse code, followed by studies on movement by Woodworth (1899), and the investigations by Book (1908) into the learning of typewriting skills. Since these early studies, the literature on perceptual–motor skill analysis has become voluminous, and indeed this area still remains an important focus of study for psychologists.

A number of definitions of motor skill have been put forward. Marteniuk (1976) states that 'a perceptual–motor skill refers to those activities involved in moving the body or body parts to accomplish a specified objective', while Kerr (1982), in similar vein, iterates that 'a motor skill is any muscular activity which is directed to a specific objective'. These definitions emphasise the goal-directed nature of skilled behaviour, which is regarded as intentional, rather than chance or unintentional. As Whiting (1975) points out: 'Whatever processes may be involved in *human* skill learning and performance, the concern is with *intentional* attempts to carry out motor acts, which will bring about pre-determined results'.

A further distinction has been made between innate behaviour, such as breathing and coughing, and learnt behaviour. For behaviour to be regarded as skilled it must be behaviour which has been learnt. This feature is highlighted by a number of theorists. Thus motor skill is defined by Knapp (1964) as 'the learned ability to bring about predetermined results with maximum certainty', and by Magill (1980) as 'acts or tasks that require movement and must be learned in order to be properly performed'.

Other aspects of skilled performance are covered by Cratty (1964) who describes motor skill as 'reasonably complex motor performance . . . (denoting) . . . that some learning has taken place and that a smoothing or integration of behaviour has resulted'. Skilled behaviour is therefore more complex than instinctive or reflexive movements, and usually consists of a hierarchy of smaller component behaviours, each of which contributes in part to the overall performance of the skill. In this respect, Summers (1981) describes skilled performance as requiring 'the organisation of highly refined patterns of movement in relation to some specific goal'.

As these definitions indicate, while there are commonalities within definitions, different theorists tend to emphasise different features of skill. Irion (1966), in tracing the history of research into motor skills, points out that: 'The field of motor skills does not suffer from a lack of variety of approach. Indeed, the approaches and methods are so extremely various that there is some difficulty in defining, in a sensible way, what the field of motor skills is.' Robb (1972), in discussing the acquisition of motor skill, reached a similar conclusion, stating that: 'The problems associated with how one acquires skill are numerous and complex. For that matter, the term *skill* is itself an illusive and confusing word.'

However, Welford (1958) has summarised the interest of psychologists in this field as being encapsulated in the question: 'When we look at a man working, by what criteria in his performance can we tell whether he is skilled and competent or clumsy and ignorant?' In other words, the basic distinction to be made is between skilled and unskilled behaviour, although, in fact, these two concepts represent opposite ends of a continuum of skilled performance, with individuals being more or less skilled in relation to one another. In his investigations into the nature of skill, Welford (1958) has identified three main characteristics common to all skills:

1. They consist of an organised, co-ordinated activity in relation to an object or a situation and, therefore, involve a whole chain of sensory, central and motor mechanisms which underlie performance;
2. They are learnt, in that the understanding of the event or performance is built up gradually with repeated experience;
3. They are serial in nature, involving the ordering and co-ordination of many different processes or actions in sequence. Thus, the skill of driving involves

a pre-set repertoire of behaviours which must be carried out in temporal sequence (put gear into neutral, switch on ignition, and so on).

Social Skills

Given the vast amount of attention which has been devoted to the analysis and evaluation of motor skill performance, it is rather surprising that psychologists have only comparatively recently begun to investigate seriously the nature of social skill. Welford (1980) attributes the recent growth of interest in this field to the initial work of Crossman (1960) who, in a report on the effects of automation on management and social relations in industry, noted that a crucial feature in the work of the operator of an automatic plant was his ability 'to communicate easily with his fellows, understand their points of view and put his own across. In other words, they must exercise *social skills*. As yet no serious attempt has been made to identify or analyse these skills further.' Crossman subsequently contacted Michael Argyle, a social psychologist at the University of Oxford: together they carried out a study of social skill, explicitly designed to investigate the similarities between man–machine and man–man interactions. In this way, the first parallels were drawn between motor skills and social skills.

In 1967 Fitts and Posner, in discussing technical skills, emphasised that: 'Social skills are also important. In particular, man must learn to communicate with others and must acquire the complex social patterns of his group.' In the same year, Argyle and Kendon published a paper on social skills in which they related the features of motor skill, as identified by Welford, directly to the analysis of social skill. They proposed a definition of skill as comprising . . . 'an organized, co-ordinated activity in relation to an object or a situation, that involves a whole chain of sensory, central and motor mechanisms . . . the performance or stream of action is continuously under the control of the sensory input . . . and the outcomes of action are continuously matched against some criterion of achievement or degree of approach to a goal' (Argyle and Kendon, 1967). While recognising some of the important differences between motor and social performance, they argued that this definition could be applied in large part to the study of social skill. (The extent to which this application can be made will be examined in more depth in Chapter 2.)

The intervening years since the publication of Argyle and Kendon's paper have witnessed a veritable flood of literature in the field of social skills. However, quite often researchers and theorists in this area have been working in differing contexts, with little cross-fertilisation between those involved in clinical, professional and developmental settings. The result has been a plethora of different approaches to the analysis and evaluation of social skill. Therefore, it is useful to examine the existing degree of consensus as to what exactly is meant by the term 'social skill'. In one sense, this is a term which is widely used and generally understood, since the term has already been used, and presumably understood, by the reader. In this global sense, social skills are the skills employed when interacting at an interpersonal level with other people. This definition of social skill is not very illuminating, however, since it describes what social skills are *used for* rather than what they *are*. It is rather like defining a bicycle as something which gets you from one place to another! Attempts to provide a more technical, insightful definition of social skill proliferate within psychology. Thus it is useful to examine some of these definitions in order to ascertain the extent to which common elements emerge.

Definitions of Social Skill

Phillips (1978) in reviewing a number of approaches to the analysis of social skill, concludes that a person is socially skilled according to: 'The extent to which he or she can communicate with others, in a manner that fulfils one's rights, requirements, satisfactions, or obligations to a reasonable degree without damaging the other person's similar rights, satisfactions or obligations, and hopefully shares these rights, etc. with others in free and open exchange.'

This definition emphasises the macro elements of social encounters, in terms of reciprocation between participants, and focuses upon the outcome of social skills rather than the skills *per se* (although Phillips does point out that 'knowing how to behave in a variety of situations' is part of social skill). A similar approach is adopted by Combs and Slaby (1977) who define social skill as: 'The ability to interact with others in a given social context in specific ways that are socially acceptable or valued and at the same time personally beneficial, mutually beneficial, or beneficial primarily to others.'

Although again highlighting *outcome,* this definition differs from that of Phillips in that it is less clear about to whom the skilled performance should be of benefit. Both definitions view social skill as an *ability* which the individual may possess to a greater or lesser extent. A slightly different focus has been put forward by other theorists. Spence (1980) encompasses both the outcome or goals of social interaction and the *behaviour* of the interactors when she defines social skills as '. . . those components of social behaviour which are necessary to ensure that individuals achieve their desired outcome from a social interaction'. In like vein, Argyle (1981) clearly states: 'By socially skilled behaviour, I mean social behaviour which is effective in realising the goals of the interactors.'

Other definitions of social skill, while focusing upon behaviour, include the concept of positive or negative reactions (reinforcement) by the other person as an element of skilled behaviour. Thus Libet and Lewinsohn (1973) define social skill as: '. . . the complex ability to maximise the rate of positive reinforcement and to minimise the strength of punishment from others'.

The problem with this definition is that it does not address the social dimension of behaviour and, as Curran (1979) points out, an adroit boxer beating his opponent in the ring, while receiving the adulation of the crowd, could be regarded as socially skilled using these rather general terms of reference. Kelly (1982), while retaining the central thrust of this definition, overcame this problem by iterating: 'We can define social skills as those identifiable, learned behaviours that individuals use in interpersonal situations to obtain or maintain reinforcement from their environment.'

This definition introduces the notion of the *situation* in which the behaviours occur, and also emphasises the *learned* aspect of behaviours which comprise social skill. The aspect of situational features is also taken up by Cartledge and Milburn (1980) who view social skills as: '. . . behaviours that are emitted in response to environmental events presented by another person or persons (for example, cues, demands, or other communications) and are followed by positive environmental responses'.

Ellis (1980) combines both the goal-directed nature of social skill and the interactive component when he points out: 'By social skills I refer to sequences of individual behaviour which are integrated in some way with the behaviour of one or more others and which measure up to some pre-determined criterion or criteria.'

Finally, a number of theorists define social skill solely in relation to its behavioural determinants. McGuire and Priestley (1981) regard social skills as: '. . . those kinds of behaviour which are basic to effective face-to-face communication between individuals'. Rinn and Markle (1979) define social skill as 'a repertoire of verbal and nonverbal behaviours', as do Wilkinson and Canter (1982) who state that: 'Verbal and nonverbal behaviour are therefore the means by which people communicate with others and they constitute the basic elements of social skill.' Curran (1979), in discussing the problems involved in defining social skills, goes so far as to argue that one should 'limit the construct of social skill to motoric behaviour'. He bases his argument on the fact that the behavioural domain is still being charted and that this task should be completed before expanding the analysis of social skill into other domains. However, this emphasis on behaviourism would not be acceptable to many of those involved in research, theory and practice in social skills, who regard other aspects of human performance (such as cognition and emotion) as being important both in determining behaviour and understanding the process of interpersonal communication.

An analysis of these definitions reveals a remarkable similarity with the position relating to motor skill definitions, in that, again, there are common elements across definitions, but no uniform agreement about the exact nature of social skill. Phillips (1980) sums up the state of affairs which still exists when he says: 'The simple facts about all social skills definitions are these: they are ubiquitous, varied, often simple, located in the social/interpersonal exchange, are the stuff out of which temporal and/or long-range social interactions are made, underlie and exemplify normative social behaviour and, in their absence, are what we loosely call psychopathology.'

However, Furnham (1983) does not regard the lack of consensus in social skills definitions as a major problem, since as he points out: 'there also exists no agreed-upon definition of psychology itself', and this has not retarded the development of psychology as a social science. Indeed, progress in all areas is a cycle in which initially less precise terms are sharpened and redefined in the light of empirical enquiry. Futhermore, social interaction is such a rapidly changing, complex process involving a myriad of impinging variables, that an understanding of even a small part of the process can be difficult to achieve. It is hardly surprising therefore that definitions of what constitutes social skill have proliferated within the literature. Any definition, however all-embracing, must, of necessity, be a simplification. This is not to say that global definitions are without value: at the very least, a definition sets parameters as to what should be included in the study of social skill and, therefore, acts as a guideline as to what should constitute legitimate investigation in this field.

Van Hasselt *et al.* (1979), in evaluating existing definitions of social skill, identified three main elements which they regard as being central to the concept:

1. Social skills are situation-specific. Few, if any, interpersonal behaviours will have the same significance across situations and cultures. The meaning of any particular behaviour will vary according to the situation in which it occurs. Thus, prolonged eye contact may indicate great affection between two young lovers, or a prelude to physical violence between two young males;
2. Interpersonal effectiveness is judged on the basis of verbal and nonverbal response components displayed by an individual. These responses are learned, and failure to learn social skills can result in social inadequacy;
3. The role of the other person is important, and interpersonal effectiveness should include the ability to behave without causing harm (verbal or physical) to others.

These three elements constitute the core dimensions of social skill. A socially skilled individual will possess the ability to behave in an appropriate manner in any given situation. However, he or she can only be judged as being socially skilled on the basis of overt behavioural performance. It is possible for someone to be *au fait* with the requirements needed to function successfully in a social context, in terms of being able to describe these requirements, and yet still fail to put this knowledge into practice (through, for example, a high level of anxiety). Such an individual would not be described as socially skilled. Thus, social skills refer to behaviour displayed by an individual. The definition adopted in this book, which is an extension of the one given by Hargie, Saunders and Dickson (1981), is that a social skill is *a set of goal-directed, inter-related situationally appropriate social behaviours which can be learned and which are under the control of the individual*.

This definition emphasises six main features of social skills. These are as follows:

1. Socially skilled behaviours are *goal-directed* and intentional. They are those behaviours which the individual employs in order to achieve a desired outcome, and are therefore purposeful behaviours, as opposed to chance or unintentional behaviours. These goals may be subconscious during social interaction, and indeed this is a feature of skilled action. The skilled car driver is not consciously aware of his or her goals when driving the car, yet these goals nevertheless guide his or her behaviour. Thus, just as the skilled driver does not consciously think 'I want to slow down; I must brake', so the skilled interviewer does not consciously think 'I want to know more about X; I must ask an open question'. At the stage of skill-learning, such conscious thoughts may be present, but these become more subconscious with practice and increased competence. If person A is skilled and wishes to encourage person B to talk freely, she will ask open questions, look at B, nod her head when B speaks, refrain from interrupting B, and guggle ('mm hum', 'uh hu') periodically. In this case, these *behaviours* are *directed* towards the goal of encouraging participation.

2. Socially skilled behaviours are *inter-related*, in that they are synchronised behaviours which are employed in order to achieve a common goal. One of the elements of skill is that it involves a repertoire of inter-related behaviours. The car driver needs to synchronise the clutch, accelerator, gear lever and steering wheel simultaneously. Similarly, in the previous example, when encouraging B to talk, A may guggle, nod, look directly at B and pause — all at the same time, and these signals will be interpreted by B as signs of encouragement to continue speaking. However, if A guggles, nods, yawns and looks away from B, then these behaviours are contradictory rather than inter-related and will not be seen as clear indicators of encouragement. If A adopts this pattern of mixed response over a prolonged period, she will be judged to be low in social skills.

3. Social skills must be *appropriate* to the *situation* in which they are employed. While certain behaviours will be appropriate when displayed in one situation, they may be unacceptable if applied in another context. Thus it may be acceptable for a rugby player drinking with his team-mates in a pub the evening after a match to leap onto a table, take off his trousers and wave them round his head. It most certainly would not be acceptable for him to do so in church on Sunday morning! Therefore, knowing the rules of the social situation is an important aspect of social skill, in order to successfully relate behaviours to the context in which they are employed. Having a very strong serve in tennis is of no value if it is always sent directly into the crowd. Similarly, being a fluent speaker may be of little value if the speaker always dominates the interaction and refuses to listen to the other person. Being able to apply the skill appropriately to the person with whom one is interacting is also important. For example, different forms of reward are used with young children, teenagers, and members of the same sex and opposite sex. Thus, 'You look really gorgeous'; 'Who's a clever little girl'; 'You have really matured'; and 'Your stomach has disappeared' may be appropriate for some of the aforementioned groups but not for others!

4. Social skills are defined in terms of identifiable units of *behaviour* which

the individual displays. In a sense, all that is ever really known about a person during social interaction is how they actually behave. All kinds of judgements are inferred about people from such behaviours (boring, humorous, warm, cold and so on). Skilled behaviour is regarded as hierarchical in nature with small elements (such as depressing the clutch) combining to form larger skill areas (such as driving). Similarly, large social skill areas (such as interviewing) can be regarded as being composed of smaller components (such as asking questions, giving reinforcement). This viewpoint has guided training in social skills, whereby the emphasis is upon encouraging the trainee to acquire separately smaller units of behaviour before integrating them to form the larger elements of social responses. This technique has been employed in the learning of many motor skills (this issue of skills training is further discussed in Chapter 19).

5. The fifth aspect of the definition is that social skills are comprised of behaviours which can be *learned*. It is now generally accepted that most forms of behaviour displayed in social contexts are learned. This is evidenced by the finding that children reared in isolation from other humans display distorted, socially unacceptable behaviour patterns and do not acquire a language. At a less extreme level, there is evidence to suggest that children from a socially deprived home environment may also develop unacceptable social behaviours, while children from a culturally richer home environment tend to develop more appropriate social behaviours (Rutter, 1972).

Bandura (1971) has developed a social learning theory in which he purports that all repertoires of behaviour, with the exception of elementary reflexes (such as eye blinks or coughing), are learned. This social learning process involves the *modelling* and *imitation* of significant others, such as parents, peers, siblings and teachers, whereby behaviour is acquired by watching others and then carrying out similar responses. By this process, from an early age, children may walk, talk and act like their same-sex parent. At a later stage, however, they will begin to adopt the accent of peers (if different from parents) who become more significant in their lives. The second major element in social learning theory is the *reinforcement* of behaviours which the person displays. As a general rule, people tend to employ more frequently those behaviours which are positively reinforced or rewarded, and to display less often those behaviours which are punished or ignored.

6. The final element of social skill, which is also a feature of social learning theory, is the degree of cognitive *control* which the individual has over his or her behaviour. Thus, a socially inadequate individual may have learned the basic behavioural elements of social skill but may not have developed the appropriate thought processes necessary to control the utilisation of these behaviours. If a social skill is to have its desired effect, then the timing of its implementation is a crucial consideration. For instance, verbal statements of encouragement need to be given immediately following the action they are intended to encourage, otherwise the reward will lose its effect. Similarly, highly personal questions are not usually asked of someone who has just been met for the first time. Learning *when*

to employ socially skilled behaviours is every bit as important as learning *what* these behaviours are and *how* to use them. Indeed, saying the right thing at the wrong time is a characteristic of some social inadequates.

This aspect of control is also important in the learning of motor skills, which are regarded as sequential in nature. Thus, the skill of driving involves a pre-set sequence of behaviours which must be carried out in the correct order (put gear into neutral, switch on ignition, depress clutch, engage first gear). In social interaction there are usually stages in social episodes which tend to be followed sequentially. For instance Morris (1971) has identified the following sequence for courtship: eye to body; eye to eye; voice to voice; hand to hand; arm to shoulder; arm to waist; mouth to mouth; hand to head; hand to body; mouth to breast; hand to genitals; genitals to genitals. This sequence is obviously different from the motor skills sequence in that it is not always necessary to go through all of these steps, depending upon the situation and the person. Elements may be removed if, for example, the first meeting is at a dance or if the other person is willing.

There are many social situations where a certain sequence of behaviour is expected. Checking into a hotel usually involves interacting in a set way with the receptionist, being shown to your room by a porter and finally giving a tip. Likewise, when going to a restaurant, the doctor, the dentist or church, there are sequences of behaviour which are expected and which can be more or less formalised, depending upon the setting. Indeed, it can be disconcerting and embarrassing if one is in a situation where the sequence is not as expected or has not been learned (for example attending a church service of a different religious denomination). In such situations, however, we will usually cope and, unlike the sequence of behaviours in driving a car, these behaviours are expected rather than essential. It is only in certain rituals or ceremonies that a pre-set sequence is essential (for example, weddings in church) and responses are demanded in a fixed temporal order. Social skills are usually more fluid and individualised than most motor skills in that people can, and do, break the sequential 'rules' without necessarily being social failures. In this sense, social skills are more open and free-flowing than motor skills. Different people will employ different combinations of behaviours (often with equal success) in professional contexts such as interviewing, teaching or counselling. What does seem to be the case is that there are common stages in social episodes (for example, opening, discussion, closing), but the behaviours used within each stage will vary from one person to another.

Social Skills and Motor Skills

From the above analysis of social skill, it is obvious that there are similarities and differences between social skills and motor skills. The main similarities include the goal-directed or intentional nature of the behaviour, the fact that it is learned, that skill is identified as a set of synchronised behaviours and that cognitive control is necessary for success. The main difference is that social skill always involves another person whereas motor skill may not. Thus, the social operator must be capable of responding and adapting to the responses and feelings of the other person. The machine operator, on the other hand, knows how the machine will respond (barring mechanical failure) and is not usually worried about hurting its feelings! However, closer parallels can be drawn with social skills where motor skill operation involves the participation of others. Thus, an analogy can be drawn between a game such as tennis and a social encounter such as negotiating. Both players make moves, try to anticipate the actions of their opponent, try to score 'points' and win the 'game'.

However, such an analogy would be rejected by some theorists. For example, Plum (1981) argues that the meaning of 'good' tennis playing can be easily measured by widely agreed criteria such as accuracy and points scored, whereas the meaning of social acts cannot be so judged. Yet, presumably, the skilled negotiator can also be judged upon specified outcomes (percentage pay increase, price of goods, and so on). Plum further argues that good motor skill equals success, yet good social skill is purely subjective; for example, what is judged as an act of empathy by one person could be viewed as an insensitive intrusion by someone else. However, similar disputes exist regarding motor skill operators. The author has often stood on the terraces at soccer games and debated with fellow spectators whether a forward was attempting to shoot or pass, whether a goal was the result of a great striker or a terrible goalkeeper, and whether the midfielder was capable of playing for his country or incapable even of playing for his club side. Equally, it is agreed that often the most skilful sides do not win the trophies — if they are lacking in fitness, determination and work-rate, or have not had 'the luck'.

Both Plum (1981) and Yardley (1979) argue that social skills are unique in that only the people involved in interpersonal interaction understand the real meaning of that interaction. This is certainly true in that no one else can experience exactly what another person is experiencing. However, the same is also true of motor skill operators. Television commentators frequently ask sportsmen following a competition, 'What were you trying to do at this point?' or 'What was going through your mind here?' as they watch a video-replay of the action. This is to gain some further insight into the event, and how it was perceived by the participants. However, while such personal evaluations are important, so too are the evaluations of others. When people are not selected at job interviews, do not succeed in dating or fail teaching practice, their personal perspective does not help. In such situations they are usually regarded as lacking in skill, just as is the youth who fails to get picked for a sports team or the car driver who fails the driving test.

Another argument put forward by Yardley (1979) is that social skills are not goal-directed in the same way as motor skills. She states that few individuals could verbalise their superordinate goals during social interaction and that, furthermore, social interaction is often valued in its own right rather than as a means to an end. Again, however, these arguments can be disputed. It seems very probable that the negotiator will be able to state his or her superordinate goal during negotiations, while the doctor will be able to do likewise when making a diagnosis. Furthermore, although social interaction is often valued *per se*, it is likely that individuals could give reasons for engaging in such interactions (to share ideas, pass the time, avoid loneliness, and so on). In addition, motor skill operators often engage in seemingly aimless activities, as when two people on the beach kick or throw a ball back and forth to one another, for which they would probably find difficulty in providing superordinate goals.

Thus, although there are differences between motor and social skills, it would appear that there exists enough similarities to allow useful parallels to be drawn between the two, and to employ methods and techniques used to identify and analyse the former in the examination of the latter. In this way, interpersonal communication can be viewed as a form of skilled behaviour. In order to exemplify how this can be achieved in practice, it is necessary to look at an actual social skill in more detail.

Example of Social Skill

A brief analysis of the skill of reinforcement will serve to illustrate how this aspect of communication can be regarded as skilled behaviour. Reinforcement is basically the process whereby reward and encouragement for others is provided during social interaction (this skill is reviewed in more depth in Chapter 5). The first distinction which can be made is between verbal and nonverbal reinforcement. In turn, these two subdivisions are analysed in terms of the operational behaviours which are used to define and chart the use of the skill itself (Figure 1.1).

Verbal Reinforcers

These are the utterances made by individuals which encourage another person to continue with a certain behaviour or activity. There are four main categories of verbal reinforcement:

Acknowledgement. This refers to words or phrases used to acknowledge or agree with what has been said or done by another. Examples of such reinforcers include: 'Thank you'; 'OK'; 'That's right'. This is not a strong form of reinforcement, but it is expected and people often get annoyed if it is not given (for example, when someone holds open a door for another who does not acknowledge it).

Evaluative. This is a strong form of reinforcement in which the individual is praised for some effort he has made, with the reinforcement being in the form of a positive evaluation. Examples include: 'You have put a lot of work into this'; 'Well done'; 'That was a great speech'. Evaluative reinforcers are commonly used by teachers,

Figure 1.1: The Social Skill of Reinforcement

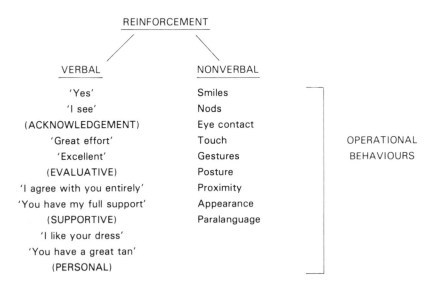

nurses, physiotherapists and a host of other professionals to encourage clients to continue to work hard.

Supportive. This is used to convey support or encouragement for others, and to indicate that they are quite justified to think or feel as they do. Examples include: 'I understand how you must feel'; 'You were right to do that'; 'That must be very difficult for you'. These reinforcers are widely used in counselling or helping situations where a client needs sympathy and understanding.

Personal. Commonly referred to as compliments, personal reinforcers differ from evaluative reinforcers in that they evaluate some aspect of the individual, rather than some activity the individual has performed. Examples would include: 'You haven't changed a bit'; 'You're looking well today'; 'Your new hairstyle really suits you'.

Nonverbal Reinforcers

These include most of the features of nonverbal behaviour (see Chapter 3) when used in a positive or encouraging fashion. Thus *smiles, head nods,* and *looking* at the other person are usually signs of reinforcement. Similarly, certain forms of *touch* can be used to provide encouragement (patting a child's head or hugging a fellow member of a sports team), as can certain *gestures* ('thumbs-up') or a forward-learning attentive *posture* when seated. Likewise, *body proximity* is often used as a reinforcer since we normally stand or sit closer to those we like or have an interest in. *Appearance* can also be reinforcing, as when we dress up for a date or a selection interview to demonstrate that we view the other person as being worthy of attention. Finally, the whole area of *paralanguage* is important — how something is said as opposed to what is said. For example, saying 'that is very interesting' in a dull, flat monotone will serve to negate the reinforcing value of the statement, and so oral statements should always be accompanied by apposite paralanguage in order to enhance the verbal content.

Reinforcement as a Social Skill

The above verbal and nonverbal responses represent the central behavioural elements of reinforcement. In relation to the definition of social skill given on page 12, reinforcement as a social skill can be regarded as:

1. Goal-related. It is used to provide reward during social interaction. There may, of course, be ulterior motives behind the provision of reward, as when a salesman uses reinforcement as a means of encouraging someone to make a purchase, and different forms of reinforcement will be used to attain different goals.

2. Inter-related behaviour. A number of inter-related verbal and nonverbal behaviours will be employed simultaneously to provide reinforcement, as when A smiles, looks at B and says, 'It's really good to see you again'. Each of these behaviours is related to the goal of rewarding B.

3. Situationally appropriate. The reinforcers used should be appropriate both to the person and the situation. This is the qualitative dimension of skill, since judgements about what is appropriate, or how well a skill is employed, are subjective and differ both within and across cultures. Thus, for example, the term 'Stickin' out' is often used in Belfast to mean 'Very good' but will not be taken to mean this in New York or London!

4. Learned. The value of reinforcement as a social skill is evidenced in interactions between a mother and her infant at a very early age. The mother will give a lot of verbal and nonverbal reinforcement to the child, and in turn will be rewarded by eye contact and smiles from the child. As the child grows it will learn the value of reinforcement as a means of giving and receiving reward.

5. Under the control of the individual. An individual who is highly skilled will be able to use reinforcement in a controlled, fluent fashion. One of the features of many social inadequates is their inability to provide reward during social interaction which, in turn, leads to greater social isolation since individuals who are unrewarding tend to be avoided.

Overview

This chapter has examined the core elements of skilled performance as identified in the analysis of perceptual–motor skill, and has related them directly to the analysis of social skill. While certain differences exist between the two sets of skills, there are also a number of features of skilled performance which are central to both, namely the intentionality, learning, control and synchronisation of behaviour. The realisation that such similarities exist has facilitated during the past few years a systematic and coherent evaluation of social or communication skill. This has resulted both in concerted efforts to determine the nature and types of communication skills in professional contexts, and in attempts to encourage professionals to develop and refine their own repertoire of socially skilled behaviours. However, both of these facets are dependent upon a sound theoretical foundation. This chapter has provided a background to such theory, and this will be extended in Chapter 2, where an in-depth evaluation will be made of the extent to which the apparent similarities between motor and social skills actually hold in practice.

References

Argyle, M. (1981) *Social Skills and Health*, Methuen, London
———— and Kendon, A. (1967) 'The Experimental Analysis of Social Performance' in L. Berkowitz (ed.), *Advances in Experimental Social Psychology: Volume 3'* Academic Press, New York
Bandura, A. (1971) *Social Learning Theory*, General Learning Press, New Jersey
Book, W. (1908) *The Psychology of Skill*, Univ. of Montana, Studies in Psychology, vol. 1 (republished 1925), Gregg, New York
Bryan, W. and Harter, N. (1897) 'Studies in Physiology and Psychology of the Telegraphic Language', *Psychol. Rev, 4*, 27–53
———— (1899) 'Studies on the Telegraphic Language: The Acquisition of a Hierarchy of Habits', *Psychol. Rev, 6*, 345–75
Cartledge, G. and Milburn, J. (1980) *'Teaching Social Skills to Children'*, Pergamon Press, New York
Combs, M. and Slaby, D. (1977) 'Social Skills Training with Children' in B.B. Lahey and A.E. Kazdin (eds), *Advances in Clinical Child Psychology'*, Plenum Press, New York
Cratty, B. (1964) *Movement Behaviour and Motor Learning'*, Lea and Febiger, Philadelphia
Crossman, E.R. (1960) *Automation and Skill*, DSIR Problems of Progress in Industry, No. 9, HMSO, London
Curran, J. (1979) 'Social Skills: Methodological Issues and Future Directions' in A. Bellack and M. Hersen (eds) *'Research and Practice in Social Skills Training'*, Plenum Press, New York
Ellis, R. (1980) 'Simulated Social Skill Training for Interpersonal Professions' in W.T. Singleton, P. Spurgeon and R. Stammers (eds), *'The Analysis of Social Skill'*, Plenum Press, New York
Fitts, P. and Posner, M. (1967) *Human Performance*, Brooks-Cole, Belmont
Furnham, A. (1983) 'Research in Social Skills Training: A Critique' in R. Ellis and D. Whittington (eds), *New Directions in Social Skill Training*, Croom Helm, Beckenham
Hargie, O., Saunders, C. and Dickson, D. (1981) *Social Skills in Interpersonal Communication*, Croom Helm, Beckenham
Irion, A. (1966) 'A Brief History of Research on the Acquisition of Skill' in E.A. Bilodeau (ed.), *Acquisition of Skill*, Academic Press, New York
Kelly, J. (1982) *Social Skills Training: A Practical Guide for Interventions*, Springer, New York
Kerr, P. (1982) *Psychomotor Learning*, CBS College Publishing, New York
Knapp, B. (1964) *Skill in Sport*, Routledge and Kegan Paul, London
Libet, J. and Lewinsohn, P. (1973) 'The Concept of Social Skill with Special Reference to the Behaviour of Depressed Persons', *Journal of Consulting and Clinical Psychology, 40*, 304–12.
Magill, R. (1980) *Motor Learning: Concepts and Applications*, W.C. Brown, Iowa
Marteniuk, R. (1976) *Information Processing in Motor Skills*, Holt, Rinehart and Winston, New York
McGuire, J. and Priestley, P. (1981) *Life After School: A Social Skills Curriculum*, Pergamon, Oxford

Morris, D. (1971) *Intimate Behaviour,* Cape, London

Phillips, E. (1978) *The Social Skills Basis of Psychopathology,* Grune and Stratton, New York

———— (1980) 'Social Skills Instruction as Adjunctive/Alternative to Psychotherapy' in W. Singleton, P. Spurgeon and R. Stammers (eds), *The Analysis of Social Skills,* Plenum, New York

Plum, A. (1981) 'Communication as Skill: A Critique and Alternative Proposal', *Journal of Humanistic Psychology, 21,* 3–19

Rinn, R. and Markle, A. (1979) 'Modification of Skill Deficits in Children' in A. Bellack and M. Hersen (eds), *Research and Practice in Social Skills Training* Plenum Press, New York

Robb, M. (1972) *The Dynamics of Motor Skill Acquisition,* Prentice-Hall, Englewood Cliffs

Rutter, M. (1972) *Maternal Deprivation Reassessed,* Penguin, Harmondsworth

Spence, S. (1980) *Social Skills Training with Children and Adolescents,* NFER, Windsor

Summers, J. (1981) 'Motor Programs' in D. Holding (ed.) *Human Skills,* Wiley, New York

Van Hasselt, V., Hersen, M., Whitehill, M. and Bellack, A. (1979) 'Social Skill Assessment and Training for Children: An Evaluative Review', *Behaviour Research and Therapy, 17,* 413–37

Welford, A. (1958) *Ageing and Human Skill,* Oxford University Press, London (reprinted 1973 by Greenwood Press, Connecticut)

———— (1968) *Fundamentals of Skill,* Methuen, London

———— (1980) 'The Concept of Skill and its Application to Performance' in W. Singleton, P. Spurgeon and R. Stammers (eds), *The Analysis of Social Skill,* Plenum, New York

Whiting, H. (1975) *Concepts in Skill Learning,* Lepus Books, London

Wilkinson, J. and Canter, S. (1982) *Social Skills Training Manual,* Wiley, Chichester

Woodworth, R.S. (1899) 'The Accuracy of Voluntary Movement', *Psychol. Rev. Monogr. Suppl.* 3, no. 3

Yardley, K. (1979) 'Social Skills Training: A Critique', *British Journal of Medical Psychology, 52,* 55–62

2 INTERPERSONAL COMMUNICATION: A THEORETICAL FRAMEWORK

Owen Hargie and Peter Marshall

This chapter is concerned with an analysis of the extent to which the analogy between motor skill and social skill, as discussed in Chapter 1, actually holds in practice. As such, it incorporates an examination of the central processes involved in skilled behaviour, and an evaluation of how far the application of a motor skill model of performance can be adopted in the study of interpersonal communication. Differences between these two areas are investigated, and an extended model of interpersonal interaction is presented. This extended model is based upon the motor skill model, but is adapted to account for those features which are peculiar to social encounters.

The Motor Skill Model

A variety of models of motor skill have been put forward by different theorists, all of which have central areas of commonality. A good example of this type of model is the one presented by Welford (1965), in the shape of a block diagram representing the operation of perceptual motor skills, in which the need for the co-ordination of a number of processes in the performance of skilled behaviour is highlighted. As shown in Figure 2.1, this model represents the individual as receiving information about the outside world via his or her sense organs (eyes, ears, nose, hands, and so on). In this way, a range of such perceptions is received, and this incoming information is held in the short-term memory store until sufficient data have been obtained to enable a decision to be made about an appropriate response. Such a decision is also facilitated by using information already retained in the long-term memory store. Having sifted through all the data from these sources, a response is then carried out by the effector system (hands, feet, voice, and so on). In turn, the outcome of this response is monitored by the sense organs and perceived by the individual, thereby providing feedback which can be used to adjust future responses. Thus, a golfer will observe the position of the ball in relation to the hole, the lie of the land between ball and hole and prevailing weather conditions. All of this information will be held in short-term memory and compared with information from long-term memory regarding previous experience of similar putts in the past. As a result, decisions will be made about which putter to use and exactly how the ball should be struck. The success of the putt will be observed and used to guide future decisions.

Figure 2.1: Welford's Model of the Human Sensory–Motor System

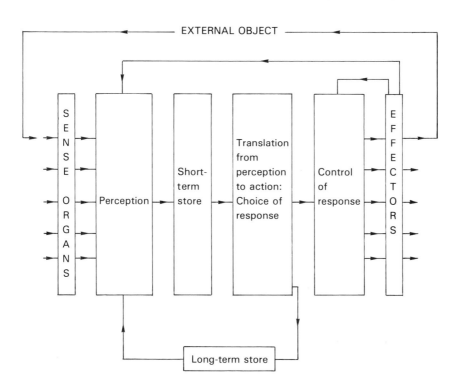

Argyle and Kendon (1967), in noting the degree of similarity which seemed to exist between motor and social skill, applied this model to the analysis of social skill (Figure 2.2). Their model was a slightly modified version of Welford's, in which they simplified the flow diagram by removing the memory store blocks, combining sense organs and perception, control of responses and effectors, and adding the elements of motivation and goal. An example of how this model can be applied to the analysis of motor performance would be where someone is sitting in a room in which the temperature has become too warm (motivation), and therefore wants to cool down (goal). This can be achieved by thinking up a range of alternative plans of action, such as: opening a window, removing some clothing or adjusting the heating system (translation). Eventually, one of these plans will be carried out: a window will be opened (response), and the situation monitored: cool air then enters the room, making the temperature more pleasant (change in outside world). This change in temperature will be perceived by the individual and the goal deemed to have been achieved. Another goal will then be pursued.

A simple example of the application of this motor skill model to a social context would be meeting a member of the opposite sex whom we like very much

Figure 2.2: Argyle and Kendon's Motor Skill Model

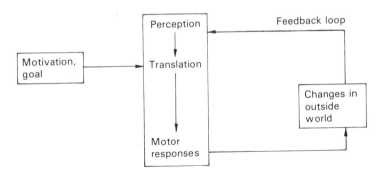

(motivation), and wanting to find out their name (immediate goal). To do so, various plans of action can be translated (ask directly, give own name and pause), and carried out, for example asking: 'What's your name?' (response). This will then result in some response from the other person: 'Joan' (change in the outside world), which we hear while observing how they react towards us (perception). We can then move on to the next goal.

At first sight, then, it would appear that this motor skill model can be applied directly to the analysis of social skill. However, there are a number of differences between these two sets of skills which are not really catered for in the basic motor skill model. In fact, many of these differences were recognised by Argyle (1967) in the first edition of *The Psychology of Interpersonal Behaviour* when he attempted to extend the basic model to take account of the responses of the other person in the social situation, and of the different types of feedback which accrue in interpersonal encounters. However, this extension did not really succeed and was dropped by Argyle in later editions.

Subsequently, few attempts have been made to expand the basic model to account for the interactive nature of social encounters. Pendleton and Furnham (1980), in critically examining the relationship between motor and social skill, did put forward an expanded model, albeit applied directly to doctor–patient interchanges. Furnham (1983) later pointed out that, although there were problems with this interactive model, it was a 'step in the right direction'. In this chapter a model is presented which builds upon the Pendleton and Furnham extension, in an attempt to cater for many of the special features of social skill (see Figure 2.3). This model attempts to account for the following differences between social and motor performance:

1. Social interaction, by definition, involves other people, whereas certain motor skills, such as operating a machine, do not. The goals of the others involved in interaction are of vital import. Not only do we pursue our own goals, but we also try to interpret what the goals of the other person are. If these goals concur,

Figure 2.3: Extended Model of Interpersonal Interaction

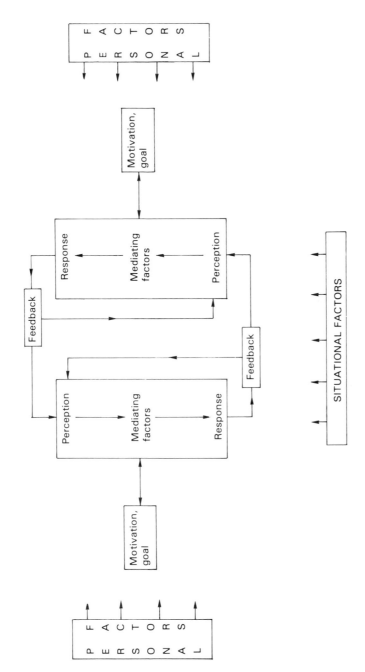

then this will facilitate social interaction, but if they conflict, interaction can become much more difficult. It is much easier for a teacher to teach pupils who want to learn, as opposed to those who do not even want to be in the classroom! Similarly, it is easier to help someone who wants to be helped, than someone who does not even want to talk to you.

2. Feelings and emotions are important in interpersonal interaction. The way we feel will affect the way others are perceived and responded to. Furthermore, we are often concerned about the feelings of other people, but rarely worry about the feelings of machines!

3. There are three forms of perception in social interaction: first, we perceive our own responses (we hear what we say and how we say it, and may be aware of our nonverbal behaviour), and will be concerned about the impression being made on others; secondly, we perceive the responses of others; thirdly, there is the field of metaperception, wherein we attempt to perceive how the other person is perceiving us and to make judgements about how the other person thinks we are perceiving him.

4. Personal factors relating to those involved in social interaction will have an important bearing upon the responses of participants. This would include the age, sex and appearance of those involved. For example, two members of the opposite sex will usually engage in more eye contact than two males.

5. Situational factors are also important in social encounters. The roles and cultural background of the interactors, the environment in which interaction is taking place and the nature of the task will all affect the behaviour of the inter-actors.

Each of these elements must be taken into consideration in any analysis of interpersonal communication. However, it is difficult to devise a model which would provide an in-depth representation of each of these facets, in addition to the core processes. Such a model would be extremely complicated and cumbersome. As a result, a relatively straightforward, yet robust, extension has been produced. This model, as illustrated in Figure 2.3, takes into account the goals of both interactors, the influence of personal and situational factors, and the fact that feedback comes from our own as well as the other person's responses. In addition, the term 'translation' has been replaced by 'mediating factors', to allow for the influence of emotions, as well as cognitions, on performance. This model can best be explained by providing an analysis of each of the separate components.

Goals and Motivation

The starting point in this model of social interaction is the goal being sought by the individual, and his or her related motivation to achieve the goal. The importance of goals in determining behaviour has long been recognised within psychology. McDougall (1912) pointed out that 'the manifestation of purpose or the striving to achieve an end is, then, the mark of behaviour'. In like vein, Vernon (1969) noted that 'much human behaviour . . . is characterised by its organised, highly motivated, goal-directed nature'.

The goals which someone decides to pursue will be directly influenced by the degree of motivation which they have for each goal. This will, in turn, be influenced by their needs. There are a number of needs which must be met in order for someone to live their life to the fullest possible extent. Different psychologists have posited differing categorisations of needs, but the best known hierarchy of human needs remains the one put forward by Maslow (1954), as exemplified in Figure 2.4.

Figure 2.4: Maslow's Hierarchy of Human Needs

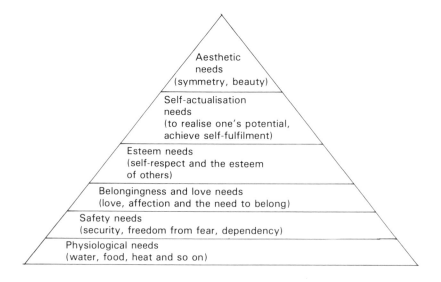

At the bottom of this hierarchy, and therefore most important, are the physiological needs which are essential for the survival of the individual, including the need for water, food, heat and so on. Once these needs have been met, the next most important needs are those connected with the safety of the individual, including protection from physical harm, freedom from fear and the need for security. These needs are met in society by various methods, including the establishment of police forces, by security chains on doors or by the purchase of insurance policies. At the next level are the belonging and love needs, such as the need for a mate, wanting to be accepted by others and to avoid loneliness or rejection. Getting married, having a family or joining a club, society or some form of group, are all means whereby these needs are met. Belonging and love needs can be closely related to esteem needs as, for example, when a woman marries a man of high status partly in order to achieve status herself (although increasingly, of course, women are being given the opportunity to achieve their own status through careers). Esteem needs are met in a number of ways through, for instance, occupational status, achievement in sports or success in some other sphere. At a higher level is the need for self-actualisation, by fulfilling one's true potential. People seek new challenges, feeling the need to be 'stretched' and to develop themselves fully. Thus, someone may give up secure salaried employment in order to study at college or enter into their own business venture. Finally, once all of these needs have been attained, there are aesthetic needs, such as the pursuit of beauty. Individuals who have achieved the five lower needs often seek the 'finer things in life' such as beautiful paintings, designer clothes or exquisite jewellery.

Maslow argues that only when basic needs have been achieved will the individual seek higher needs. The person who is suffering from hunger will usually seek food at all costs, even risking personal safety, and will not worry about being held in high esteem. At a higher level, someone deeply in love may publicly beg their partner not to leave them, thereby foregoing their own self-esteem. However, it should be recognised that this hierarchy does not hold in all cases. Needs can also be influenced directly by individual goals. One example of this is where political prisoners starve themselves to death in order to achieve particular political goals. But for the most part this hierarchy of needs will hold true, and the behaviour of an individual can be related to his or her existing level of need. Similarly, people can be manipulated either by promises that their needs will be met, or threats that they will not be met. Politicians promise to meet safety needs by reducing the crime rate and improving law and order, computer dating firms offer to meet love needs by providing a partner, while company management may threaten various needs by warning workers that if they go on strike the company will close and they will lose their jobs.

Theories of Motivation

There are three main theories of motivation which have been put forward to explain human behaviour. The earliest of these, 'drive theory', purported that humans possess drives which are activated by the need to attain certain goals. When we are hungry, it is argued, we have a drive to behave in such a way as to obtain food; when we are cold we are driven to seek heat, and so on. Drive reduction is said to occur when the goal of the drive is attained, and this results in a pleasant internal state. While drive theory satisfactorily accounts for much human behaviour it does not explain some behaviours, like going on frightening rides at an amusement park, climbing a mountain or sailing round the world single-handedly. In all of these cases drives are increased rather than decreased. Furthermore, drive theory tends to over-emphasise internal states while failing to take account of the influence of external events and stimuli. Someone who is not initially hungry may be tempted to eat by the sight of cakes in a cafe window. In this instance, the cakes can be seen as an incentive to eat.

As a result, an alternative theory of motivation, 'incentive theory', has been postulated, emphasising the importance of external incentives as motivation for behaviour. A central tenet of this theory is that we will seek positive incentives and avoid negative incentives. If we are hungry, food will be a positive incentive and approached, whereas the sight of a bully at school will be a negative incentive and avoided. Bindra and Stewart (1971), in recognising the importance of both theories, point out that 'any goal-directed action is instigated by a central motivational state, which itself is created by an interaction within the brain between the neural consequences of bodily organismic states ('drives') and neural consequences of environmental incentives ('reinforcers')'.

Arousal is an important element of both drive (where it is viewed as being caused by deprivation) and incentive (where it is regarded as the result of external stimuli) theories. A recognition of the central role of arousal has led to a third theory of motivation, 'arousal theory', wherein motivation is seen as being one among a number of causes of arousal (the others being: environmental factors such as noise and other people; novel events; drugs). The level of arousal has a direct effect upon the performance of the individual, in that if someone is under- or over-aroused then their performance will be adversely affected (Figure 2.5). Someone who is extremely nervous about speaking in public will usually perform poorly, as will the person who couldn't care less about the speech. Optimum performance occurs when there is a medium degree of arousal.

Figure 2.5: The Relationship Between Arousal and Performance

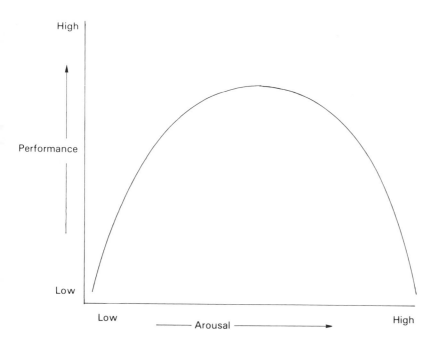

Arousal levels vary from one person to another. Some people need a lot of stimulation and become bored easily, whereas others prefer a minimum amount of stimulation to perform effectively. Individual levels of arousal will influence the behaviour of the individual in many ways, ranging from type of job to choice of marriage partner. Those with low levels of arousal will prefer safe, quiet jobs, whereas others with high levels of arousal need occupations in which danger and excitement are prevalent. The level of arousal which can be tolerated is also affected by the time of day, with lower levels being prevalent early in the morning and increasing throughout the day. A knowledge of the effects of arousal on performance should be recognised by many professionals. Teachers may need to increase the arousal level of pupils during the first class of the day, whereas they may have to decrease arousal in the first class after lunch in order to encourage concentration. Similarly, doctors and dentists often deal with people in high states of arousal and should pay attention to environmental stimuli (waiting room, surgery) and their own behaviour, in an effort to reduce this arousal. A dentist who is clearly nervous will certainly serve to increase the arousal level of the patient!

Goals and Behaviour

Motivation is therefore important in determining the goals which we seek in social interaction. Our behaviour, in turn, is judged on the basis of the goals which are being pursued. Judgements about an individual's goals, based on his or her behaviour, however, can prove inaccurate and we can be deceived by others in terms of the reasons for their behaviour. Someone may be friendly with us in order to obtain extraneous benefit, rather than for the sake of friendship or their liking for us. In other words, they may have an ulterior motive for their behaviour. Nevertheless, our judgement about the goals of others, based upon their responses to us, are frequently made and are generally accurate. This is why we are surprised or shocked if we discover that someone who was trusted as having honourable goals, turns out to have deceived us by having hidden goals. In certain cases, judgements about the goals of behaviour are of crucial importance, for example when a courtroom jury has to decide whether a killing by a defendant was accidental or pre-meditated.

Boden (1972) describes behaviour which is being carried out to achieve a conscious goal as 'being actively attended to; it is guided by precise foresight of the goal; and it is open to introspection in the sense that its component features are discriminable (and verbally describable)'. The individual will be aware of his or her own behaviour and of the reasons why it is being employed, will have planned to carry it out, and will be able readily to explain and justify the behaviour in terms of the goals being pursued. A young man who has arranged a date with a young woman may plan, for example, a sequence of behaviour in order to achieve a particular goal (honourable or otherwise!) and be aware of his goals as he carries out his dating behaviour. Similarly, a skilled negotiator will usually have decided his or her goals before negotiation and will be conscious of these when attempting to attain them by employing various behaviours in the negotiating encounter.

Often, however, people operate at a more subconscious level in terms of goals. Indeed, this is a feature of skilled behaviour in that the experienced interviewer will ask questions and provide reward without consciously thinking about so doing, just as an experienced driver will turn on the ignition, engage gear and so on without being consciously aware of the goals of the behaviour. An important aspect of skilled performance is the ability to act and react quickly at a subconscious level. An extreme example of this is given by Argyle (1983) who reports a lecturer who claimed the ability to 'arise before an audience, turn his mouth loose, and go to sleep'!

A final distinction which needs to be made is between long-term and short-term goals. Actions are generally guided by short-term, immediate goals, although the long-term or superordinate goal will be taken into account (Von Cranach *et al.*, 1982). In order to achieve the long-term goal, a number of short-term goals will need to be devised and executed. For example, a personnel officer may want to appoint an appropriate person for a job vacancy (long-term goal). In order to do so, there are a range of sub-goals which must be carried out; advertising the position, drawing up a short-list of candidates, interviewing each one, and so on. These subgoals can be further subdivided. At the interview stage the chief goal will be to assess the suitability of the candidate, which, in turn, involves subgoals including welcoming the candidate, making introductions and asking relevant questions. Usually, the short-term goals will contribute to the achievement of the long-term goal. However, goal conflict may occur occasionally where the short- and long-term goals may not concur. Telling a good friend that they have an annoying habit, while maintaining the same level of friendship, would be one example of conflicting goals. Encounters such as this obviously require skill and tact.

Regardless of whether goals are conscious or subconscious, short-term or long-term, they play a vital role in determining behaviour. Once appropriate goals have been decided upon, these will have an important bearing on our perceptions, behaviour and on the intervening mediating factors.

Mediating Factors

The term 'mediating factors' refers to those internal states, activities or processes within the individual which mediate between the feedback which is perceived, the goal which is being pursued and the responses that are made. These factors influence the way in which people and events are perceived, and determine the capacity of the individual to assimilate, process and respond to, the social information received during interpersonal encounters. It is at this stage that the person makes decisions about the likelihood of goals being achieved, given the existing situation, and then decides upon an appropriate course of action. Two main mediating factors, namely cognition and emotion, will be focused upon.

Cognition

Neisser (1967) has defined cognition as 'all the processes by which the sensory input is transformed, reduced, elaborated, stored, recovered and used'. This definition encompasses the main functions of cognition, which involves *transforming*, or decoding and making use of the sensory information which is received. To do so, it is often necessary to *reduce* the amount of information which is attended to, in order to avoid overloading the system. Conversely, at times it will be necessary to *elaborate* upon minimal information by making interpretations, judgements or evaluations (for example, 'He is not speaking to me because I have upset him'). Some of the information will be *stored* either in short-term or long-term memory.

Short-term memory refers to the retention of information over a brief interval of time (no more than a few minutes), while long-term memory refers to retention over long intervals (weeks, months or years). Information stored in short-term memory will quickly be lost unless it is transferred to the long-term memory store. Thus, we can usually still remember the name of our first teacher at school, yet ten minutes after meeting someone for the first time may have forgotten their name. One theory which has been put forward to account for memory is that we use a process of *context-dependent coding*. Remembering occurs by recalling the context of the original event. When we meet someone we recognise but cannot place, we try to think where or when we met them before — in other words, we try to put them in a particular context. A similar process occurs in social situations, whereby we evaluate people and situations in terms of our experience of previous similar encounters.

Information that is stored can be *recovered* or retrieved to facilitate the process of decision-making and problem-solving. Existing circumstances will be compared with previous knowledge and experience. There is evidence to suggest that conceptual 'schemas' are used to faciltate the process of decision-making (Carroll, 1980; McIntyre, 1983). For example, an experienced teacher will have a number of schemas, such as 'class getting bored' and 'noise level too high', each with accompanying action plans — 'introduce a new activity', 'call for order'. These schemas are used both to evaluate situations and to enable appropriate responses to be made. Experienced teachers will have built up a greater store of such schemas, and so will be able to cope more successfully than novices. The same is true in other professions. Experienced doctors, nurses, social workers or salesmen will have developed a range of schemas to enable them to respond quickly and confidently in the professional context. This ability to respond quickly and appropriately is, in turn, a feature of skilled perfomance. Thus, the skilled professional will have developed his or her cognitive ability to analyse and evaluate available information and make decisions about how best to respond. He or she will also have formulated a number of contingency plans which can be implemented immediately should the initial response fail.

As Shaw (1979) points out, however, 'some thinking and remembering is purposeful and goal-oriented while other mental activity is less controlled and has an automatic, involuntary nature'. The extent to which these 'automatic thoughts' interrupt the main direction of mental activity varies from one person to another, but is highest in certain pathological states, such as schizophrenia, where a large number of unrelated thoughts may 'flood through' the mind. The socially skilled individual will have greater control over his or her thought processes and will use these to facilitate social interaction. Snyder (1974) regards this as a system of 'self-monitoring', whereby skilled individuals have a capacity for monitoring and regulating their own behaviour in relation to the responses of others. This process of regulation necessitates an awareness of the ability level of the person with whom one is interacting and of the 'way they think', since, as Wessler (1984) points out, 'in order to interact successfully and repeatedly with the same persons, one must have the capacity to form cognitive conceptions of the others' cognitive conceptions; such capacity, it may be hypothesised, depends on both ability and previous experience'.

Therefore, cognition plays a very important role in interpersonal communication. The socially skilled individual will have an ability to 'size up' people and situations more rapidly, and respond in a more appropriate fashion, than the individual who is low in social skills. Such an ability is dependent upon the capacity of the individual to cognitively process the information received during social interaction.

Emotion

Differing theoretical perspectives exist within psychology concerning the nature and cause of emotion. An early viewpoint put forward by James (1884) was that emotions were simply a category of physiological phenomena resulting from the perception of an external stimulus. Thus, James argued, you see a bear, the muscles tense and glands secrete hormones to facilitate escape; as a result fear is experienced. However, this view was undermined by later research which demonstrated that patients who have had glands and muscles removed from the nervous system by surgery, nevertheless reported the feeling of emotions. More recent theorists emphasise the link between cognition and emotions, and highlight two main elements involved in the subjective experience of emotion: first, the perception of physiological arousal; and, second, the cognitive evaluation of that arousal to arrive at an emotional 'label' for the experience (Berscheid, 1983).

However, differences persist about the nature of the relationship between cognition and emotion. Some theorists argue that a direct causal relationship exists between thought processes and emotions, with the latter being caused by the former (for example, Ellis, 1962). Within this model, irrational beliefs would be seen as causing fear or anxiety, which, in turn, could be controlled by helping the individual to become more rational about his or her beliefs. This perspective is regarded by others as being an over-simplification of the relationship between cognition and affect. It is argued that emotional states can also cause changes in cognition, so that an individual who is very angry may not be able to 'think straight'; it is also possible to be 'out of your mind' with worry. In this sense, there does seem to be a reciprocal relationship between cognitions and emotions (Meichenbaum and Butler, 1980). The way someone thinks can influence how they feel and *vice versa.*

There are three main components of emotion: first, there is the direct conscious experience or feeling of emotion; second there are the physiological processes which accompany emotions; and third, there are the observable behavioural actions which are used to express and convey the emotions. Izard (1977), in noting these three processes, points out that 'virtually all of the neurophysiological systems and subsystems of the body are involved in greater or lesser degree in emotional states. Such changes inevitably affect the perceptions, thoughts and actions of the person'. As a result, the individual who is in love may be 'blind' to the faults of another and fail to perceive negative cues, while someone who is very depressed will be inclined to pick up negative cues and miss the positive ones. Similarly, the happy person will display signs of happiness by smiling, being lively and joining in social interaction, while the sad person will adopt a slouched posture, flat tone of voice and will generally avoid interaction with others.

Emotional states are, therefore, very important both in terms of our perception of the outside world and how we respond to it. The fact that emotions are important is evidenced by the vast array of words and terms used to describe the variety of emotional states which are experienced. Averill (1975) carried out an investigation in which the objective was 'to obtain a fairly complete list of emotional concepts within the English language'. Starting with previous lists compiled by Allport and Odbert (1936), Lindauer (1968) and Nowlis (1965), he eventually compiled a total of 717 terms for analysis. These concepts were rated by 173 undergraduate students at the University of California, Berkeley, on the extent to which each represented an emotional state. Two main criteria were applied to these ratings, namely that (1) the term was familiar to at least three-quarters of the undergraduates, and (2) these undergraduates believed that many ordinary people would consider the term representative of an emotional state. By this process, a final total of 558 discrete emotional labels were identified, ranging from 'abandoned' and 'abashed' to 'zealous' and 'zestful'. While some of these emotions seem to be expressed in a common fashion across cultures (interest, joy, surprise, distress, disgust, anger, shame and fear), there are also differences between cultures. For example, Levy (1974) reports that the Tahitian language has no word which signifies anything like a sense of guilt. In addition, the factors which provoke emotion will differ across cultures, in that great anxiety may be caused in one society by an eclipse of the sun and in another by the threat of nuclear war.

Although emotion and cognition are the two main aspects focused upon in this chapter, there are other mediating factors which influence how we process information. The values and beliefs which we hold will affect our perceptions, actions, cognitions and emotions. The devout Christian may view the death of a close relative as an act of God and a cause for celebration, since the deceased has 'gone to a better place', while the atheist may regard this as a time of sorrow at the termination of a life. Our political, moral and religious beliefs and values will therefore influence our actions and reactions to others. These will also influence our attitudes towards other people, which, in turn, will affect our thoughts, feelings and behaviour as we interact with them.

Our attitudes are affected not only by our beliefs and values, but by previous experiences of the person with whom we are interacting, and also by our experiences of similar people. Finally, the disposition of an individual will play an important part in determining social responses. Whether we are co-operative or competitive, extroverted or introverted, dominant or submissive, and so on, will influence both how we perceive situations and how they are responded to.

All of these factors come into play at the decision-making stage during interpersonal encounters. For the most part, this process of translating perceptions into actions will take place at a subconscious level, thereby enabling faster, smoother responses to be made. Just as the skilled car driver does not have to consciously think about depressing the clutch and putting the gear lever into neutral, so the skilled counsellor does not have to consciously think about encouraging the client to speak freely. A feature of skilled performance is the ability to operate at this subconscious level, while monitoring the situation to ensure a successful outcome.

Responses

Once a goal has been decided upon and an action plan has been devised to achieve the goal, the next step is to implement this plan in terms of social responses. It is the function of the response system to carry out the plan by employing a range of behaviours. As Figure 2.6 indicates, an initial distinction can be made between linguistic and non-linguistic behaviour. Linguistic behaviour refers to all aspects of speech, including the actual verbal content (the words used), and the paralinguistic message associated with it (pitch, tone, speed, volume of voice, accent, pauses, speech dysfluencies, and so on). Non-linguistic communication encompasses all bodily communication and is concerned with the study of what a person does rather than what he says. It can be subdivided into tacesics, which is the systematic study of bodily contact; proxemics, the systematic study of the spatial features of social presentation (interpersonal distance, orientation, territoriality etc.); and kinesics, the systematic study of body motion (facial expressions, head movements, posture, gestures, gaze, and so on).

These aspects of social behaviour are discussed fully throughout the remaining chapters of this book, with one chapter being devoted to the study of non-verbal communication (Chapter 3). In all of the other chapters, the linguistic and non-linguistic elements of behaviour are presented in an integrated fashion. In this sense, the entire book is devoted to a study of the response component of the interpersonal interaction model; this section concentrates on some of the aspects of the response domain which influence skilled performance.

Figure 2.6: Classifications of Social Behaviour

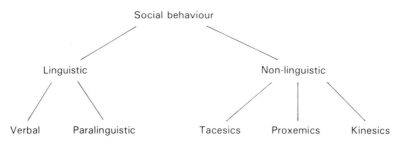

As discussed in Chapter 1, skilled behaviour is hierarchically organised, with larger tasks being made up of smaller component units. An example of this is given by McFall (1982) in discussing the task of 'finding a spouse', when he points out that: 'Nested within that global task would be smaller tasks, like ''meeting potential spouses'', ''dating'', and ''developing an intimate relationship''. Dating, in turn, might be broken into sub-tasks, such as initiating, conversing, parting etc. Each of these could be subdivided further into component tasks, for example, initiating a date may be segmented into smaller task units such as selecting a person to approach, arranging for the opportunity to make the overture, and proposing the date. Conceivably, each of these might be decomposed into even smaller units.'

Behavioural Style

A task such as finding a spouse involves a long-term goal and numerous short-term goals. Different strategies may have to be employed in order to achieve each short-term goal. A strategy in this sense can be regarded as elements of various social skills which are combined and employed to attain a specific goal. Therefore, strategies are situation or goal-specific. A more permanent aspect of individual behaviour is the concept of style, which is defined by Norton (1983) as 'the relatively enduring pattern of human interaction associated with the individual . . . it is an accumulation of ''microbehaviours'' . . . that add up to a ''macrojudgement'' about a person's style of communicating'. Norton identifies nine main communicative styles, which can be interpreted as continuums, as follows:

1. Dominant/submissive. Dominant people like to control social interactions, give orders and be the centre of attention; they use behaviours such as loud volume of voice, interruptions, prolonged eye contact and fewer pauses to achieve dominance. At the opposite end of this continuum, submissive people prefer to keep quiet, stay out of the limelight and take orders.

2. Dramatic/reserved. Exaggeration, story-telling and use of nonverbal communication are techniques used by the dramatic individual who will tend to overstate his or her message. The other end of the continuum is characterised by the reserved type of person who is more quiet and modest.

3. Contentious/affiliative. The contentious person will be argumentative, provocative or contrary, as opposed to the agreeable, peace-loving, affiliative individual.

4. Animated/inexpressive. An animate style involves making use of hands, arms, eyes, facial expressions, posture and overall body movement to gain attention or convey enthusiasm. The converse here is the dull, slow-moving, inexpressive person.

5. Relaxed/frenetic. This continuum ranges from people who do not get over-excited, always seem in control and are never flustered, to people who are tense, quickly lose self-control, get excited easily and behave frenetically.

6. Attentive/inattentive. Attentive individuals will listen carefully to others and will display overt signs of listening such as eye contact, appropriate facial expression and posture. Inattentive individuals, on the other hand, are poor listeners who do not make any attempt to express interest in what others are saying.

7. Impression-leaving/insignificant. The impression-leaving style is characterised by flamboyant individuals who display a visible or memorable style of communicating and leave an impression on those whom they meet. They are people who, for example, wear loud clothes, have unusual hair styles or controversial verbal styles. The opposite of this is the insignificant individual who 'fades into the fabric' of buildings, is non-controversial and dresses conservatively.

8. Open/closed. Open people will talk about themselves freely, are approachable, unreserved, unsecretive, frank and conversational. At the opposite end of this continuum are very closed individuals who will disclose no personal information, are secretive, loth to express opinions and 'keep themselves to themselves'.

9. Friendly/hostile. This style continuum covers a range of perspectives, from the friendly person who will smile frequently, be happy, very rewarding and generally non-competitive, through to the sad person who is miserable and discontented, and on to the hostile person who is overtly aggressive, highly competitive and very unrewarding.

Most people can be evaluated overall in terms of these style continuums, although style of communication can also be affected by situations. A dominant teacher in the classroom may be submissive during staff meetings, while a normally friendly individual may become hostile when engaging in team sports. Nevertheless, there will be elements of style which will endure across situations, and these will have a bearing on a number of facets of the individual. For example, someone who tends to be dominant, frenetic, inattentive or hostile will probably not make a good counsellor. Similarly, a very dominant male is unlikely to marry a very dominant female, and *vice versa*.

Learning

Much of the behaviour that one displays is learned through a process of modelling and imitation of significant others. This begins at an early age since, as Bandura (1967) points out: 'The pervasiveness of this form of learning is also clearly evident in naturalistic observation of children's play in which they frequently reproduce the entire parental role, including the appropriate mannerisms, voice inflections and attitudes, much to the parents' surprise and embarrassment.'

As the child develops he or she will then model others, including peers, pop stars, film actors or sports personalities. Various behaviours will be tried out, until eventually the individual builds up patterns of responses which suit his or her personality, and eventually evolves a personal style of communication. A similar process occurs when an individual enters a new profession, resulting in a professional style of interacting.

Behavioural style also seems to be affected by class differences and 'it has frequently been shown that indices of social class, e.g., occupation, are good predictors of many forms of social behaviour, especially communication skills' (Wheldall, 1975). This is especially marked in relation to the use of language. Bernstein (1971) has made a distinction between two language codes: a restricted code which is used predominantly by the 'working class' (unskilled and semi-skilled workers) and an elaborated code which is used predominantly by the 'middle class'. The main differences between the two codes are that the restricted compared to the elaborated code involves:

1. Shorter and simpler sentences;
2. A more limited vocabulary with frequent use of traditional, idiomatic expressions;
3. Greater use of personal pronouns (I, we, you) as opposed to impersonal pronouns (one, it);
4. Repetitive use of conjunctions (because, so then, but);
5. 'Sympathetic circularity': this involves the use of statements phrased as questions ('. . . know what I mean?', '. . . you know?', '. . . isn't it?', 'It wouldn't be right, would it?');
6. Increased tendency to replace reason by command: Bernstein (1961) exemplifies this with reference to a mother–child interaction on a bus, beginning with the working class example:
   Mother: 'Hold on tight'.
   Child: 'Why?'
   Mother: 'You'll fall'.
   Child: 'Why?'
   Mother: 'I told you to hold on tight, didn't I?'
This contrasts with the middle class example:
   Mother: 'Hold on tight.'
   Child: 'Why?'
   Mother: 'If you don't, you will be thrown forward and you'll fall.'
   Child: 'Why?'
   Mother: 'Because if the bus suddenly stops you'll jerk forward on to the seat in front.'

The elaborated code will be utilised in interactions between professionals, usually to the extent where a set of new terms, or jargon, is introduced within a profession. At the same time, it is important for professionals to be able to apply the restricted code where necessary when interacting with certain clients. On occasions, failure to do so may lead to alienation, lack of comprehension or increased anxiety on the part of the client. Doctors and pharmacists should certainly bear this in mind when providing instructions and information to patients, since it is a common finding that patients either fail to remember, or misunderstand, such guidance (Ley, 1977).

These are some of the elements of social behaviour which should be borne in mind during interpersonal interaction. A knowledge of such behaviour is important, not only in controlling our own responses, but also in interpreting the behaviour of others.

Feedback

Once a response has been carried out, the individual will look for feedback in order to determine the effects of the response. This feedback thereby enables the person to alter subsequent responses in the light of this information. In order to perform any task efficiently, it is necessary to receive such feedback in terms of 'knowledge of results' of performance (Annett, 1969), so that corrective actions can be taken when required. Thus, we could not effectively drive a car, throw darts or even walk along a straight line if we could not see the results of our movements. In social interaction, we also require feedback in terms of an awareness of our own actions, and the reactions of other people towards us.

Wiener (1954) gives a technical definition of feedback as 'a method of controlling a system by reinserting into it the results of its past performance'. Wiener considered communication and control as virtually identical terms, so his discussion of cybernetic systems was 'to all intents and purposes, a discussion of the communication systems that govern or control the functions of the mechanical systems' (Fisher, 1978). Cybernetics as a theory of control or mechanisms for control, remains central to virtually all the various uses of the term 'feedback'. The elementary concept of feedback as a control process stipulates that the output of a system is 'fed back', into the system as additional input, which, in turn, serves to regulate further output.

Within the sphere of social interaction, feedback may be viewed as a response given by one person to a stimulus received from another. Seen from this simple viewpoint, then, the difference between one-way and two-way communication is whether feedback takes place or not. In the dyadic situation, messages are received and transmitted from one person to the other in a continuous return loop. At the same time, however, the transmitting person is getting 'internal' feedback on his own behaviour (see Figure 2.3). This internal feedback process provides information about the individual's own performance. For example, if we ask a question which we immediately perceive to be poorly worded, we will often rephrase the question before the listener has had an opportunity to respond to the initial one.

In relation to these internal aspects of feedback, the sender needs to have a full understanding of the message being communicated. In this context, his own feedback acts as an internal control mechanism. This control is influenced by the role being played in any given situation. Within the context of the particular role chosen, or forced upon him by the situation, so certain levels of feedback will be expected. Should he be in the position of leadership, so it will be expected that he will present to the other members of the group a level and style of behaviour associated with their expectations and the type of leadership he has adopted. If the person then perceives that he is 'doing well' in terms of his own performance, his confidence will be boosted; whereas if he perceives that he is not performing well, his behaviour may deteriorate even further.

Feedback Channels

During interaction between two people the available feedback can vary, in the same way as the flow of messages can also change. Leavitt and Mueller (1951) in their study on feedback found that the difference in feedback was related to the message barriers that are erected to restrain the flow of communication. The more limited the messages, the less feedback will be provided.

As the number of channels open for messages to be transmitted varies, so also does the potential for feedback. In terms of communication, a written message denies any immediate interactional feedback, while a telephone limits the visual feedback but enhances the paralinguistic channel. Even in face-to-face situations channels can be limited or enhanced by the apparent status of the interactors. A child meeting an important adult for the first time may become tongue-tied. However, the adult may be able to relax the situation and thereby open up new channels to enhance the feedback.

The more relaxed a social situation becomes, the more channels may become opened, thereby increasing the degree of feedback that can take place. Conversely, the more tense a situation becomes, the chances are that the level of feedback will be reduced, since people may not have the confidence to emit their normal behaviours. Thus, a very nervous candidate at a selection interview may give a poor impression of himself, owing to the stressful nature of the situation, and may provide the interviewers with poor feedback accordingly.

Another clearly recognised restriction of feedback is that caused by the behaviour of the other interactor. When a 'closed' question is asked, the response tends to be limited to a simple 'Yes' or 'No'; had an 'open' question been posed, then the possible amount of feedback would have been greatly enhanced (see Chapter 4).

Feedback as Reinforcement

Within social interaction, feedback can be obtained from the verbal and nonverbal messages emitted by others. Over and above basic acknowledgement of a response from one person contained in such messages, 'any additional elements can be seen as reinforcement' (Berger and Lambert, 1968). Feedback, in this sense, includes reinforcers, whether of a positive or negative nature. So, during an interaction, such comments as 'Good', 'I agree', and 'You are right', not only include the message reply but also include a positive reinforcement towards the other person. These verbal messages may well be accompanied by smiles, nods or hand gestures, such nonverbal signs supporting the reinforcement. Conversely, of course, negative signs may also be transmitted.

In a normal conversational situation each person will indicate to the other that he is listening by the eye contact given to the speaker. Generally, the listener will give more eye contact to the speaker than the speaker needs to give to the listener. During such an exchange, the eyes also indicate when each person can contribute, when, in fact, it is their turn to speak. The eyes control and provide feedback to the speaker and, should the listener stop giving sufficient eye contact, the speaker may speak with more emphasis, or even ask if the other person is listening. In the end, if positive feedback is still denied, he will usually stop speaking altogether.

This aspect of feedback is important, since when negative feedback is supplied during interpersonal interaction, there tends to be a lowering in the interactor's behaviour and confidence level. However, the converse does not seem to apply so readily, in that positive feedback does not always appear to improve a person's performance during social interaction (Blubaugh, 1969; Vlandis, 1964).

Using Feedback

Each person is bombarded by a constant stream of sensory stimulation during a social encounter. These are noises, sights, smells, tastes and tactile sensations. In the social situation we receive perceptual inputs through our eyes, ears and tactile senses. While smell may also affect the relationship we develop with others, in western society it tends to play a smaller part than other senses, since bodily odours are often camouflaged by wearing various types of artificial scents. With such a barrage of information attacking our senses, and without the development of mechanisms to cope, we would become saturated and hopelessly confused.

As Hargie, Saunders and Dickson (1981) point out, it is necessary, therefore, for the individual to filter out some of the available stimuli, so that he can deal more effectively with the remainder. In this sense, a selective perception filter is operative, and its main function is to filter a limited amount of information into the conscious, while storing the remainder at a subconscious level (Figure 2.7). Consider an office situation with two people talking together about a subject both find interesting and engrossing, while at the same time a third person is typing a letter. Neither of the two talkers hears the typing noises, due to their concentration and their involvement with each other: the noise has been filtered out.

Should the typist then stop typing, both people may well identify that this has happened.

Figure 2.7: Selective Perception Process

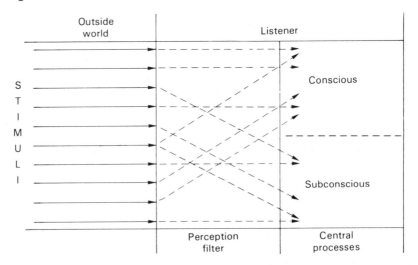

Unfortunately, vital information from another person may be filtered out during social interaction and less important cues consciously perceived. In other words, from all the social stimuli available to us, we may focus upon less relevant stimuli and miss important verbal or nonverbal signals. Thus, it is crucial that professionals learn to make appropriate use of the feedback available during interactions with clients, by perceiving the central messages and filtering out the peripheral ones.

Perception

Our perceptions provide us with information concerning our environment, in terms of physical objects and events, and other people. Mitchell (1978) defined perception as 'those processes that shape and produce what we actually experience', while Gergen and Gergen (1981) state that, in the perception of other people, the 'perceiver must conceptualize the behaviour he or she observes'. This latter type of perception is referred to as 'person perception', which 'not only involves the judgements we make about people as objects (tall, bald, wearing brown shoes, etc) but is primarily concerned with the impressions we form of people as people (impulsive, religious, tired, happy, anxious and so on)' (Warr and Knapper, 1968). The crucial role played by person perception in social interaction is emphasised by Cook (1979), who points out that: 'The way people see each other determines the way they behave towards each other, so the study of "person perception" is one of the keys to understanding social behaviour.'

One of the most common observations made concerning the nature of humans is that 'people are all different'. They differ in terms of physical characteristics such as size, weight and colour. They differ in sex; they differ according to their family background, cultural inheritance, educational standard, peer group influences and personality traits. One particular way people differ is in the way they perceive the world around them. This is influenced by other individual characteristics that go towards making each person unique. In order to understand why and how people differ in the way they receive information, we need to understand some of the factors which influence the perceptual process.

Aspects of Perception

Roth (1976) has identified four important elements of perception. First, our perceptions enable us to structure and organise the world. The incoming information that is received is structured and organised into an acceptable order to enable the receiver to give it meaning. Thus we respond to people as people, rather than as a series of different shapes and colours. Second, we integrate a number of perceptual cues in order to make judgements. During social encounters the verbal and nonverbal signals received are combined to produce an overall perceptual message. When we meet people we notice their dress, body shape, age, sex, verbal and vocal messages and so on, and integrate all of this information into a meaningful whole. Third, we make associations and causal links between perceptions: if we see a brick being hurled at a window we expect the glass to shatter, and attribute this breakage as being caused by the brick. Similarly, if we shout at someone who then begins to cry, we will assume that our behaviour has caused the tears. Fourth, we attribute stability and constancy to our perceptions. For example, as people walk away from us, they actually 'appear' to be getting smaller, but we do not believe that they are slowly shrinking — but will interpret the decreased size as being due to the fact that they are moving further away from us. In other words, the viewer perceives them to be still the same height. Constancy and stability in the behaviour of other people, is also looked for and we are surprised if they deviate markedly from the way we expect them to behave.

Another factor which influences our perceptions is the familiarity of the incoming stimuli. The more familiar the signal, the faster we are to receive and conceptualise the message. Within social interaction such elements as a common understandable language, recognised dialect and phrasing, influence perceptual capacity. So our speed of perception drops, if a person uses technical terms with which we are unfamiliar or speaks at too fast a rate. In a similar vein, if the nonverbal signals do not register as understandable, or are distracting, then our perceptual reception is hampered. In either situation, we may selectively filter out the unfamiliar or unacceptable and thus receive a distorted or inaccurate message.

Our perceptions are also affected by our attitudes or emotions towards the person with whom we are interacting. If we hold positive feelings towards the other person then we are likely to perceive more of their behaviours because more signals are filtered in; but if we do not like the person we are likely to receive fewer signals or to distort them in an unfavourable manner. Someone renowned for grumbling may well be avoided despite the interest the subject might hold. A girl meeting a boy whose appearance she likes will be able to describe more of his characteristics than those of a boy she found less appealing.

Linked to this are the emotions concerned with a situation. If we expect an unpleasant situation, we are less likely to pay as much attention to the people involved: the situation is perceived more vividly than the people. A person involved in an accident tends to remember the accident but has only a hazy recollection of the people. Someone experiencing a very enjoyable activity will remember the activity and those involved much more clearly.

Another important aspect of perception relates to accuracy. As Cook (1979) points out, there is a great deal of evidence to indicate that we are often very inaccurate in our perceptions and can be deceived in terms of what we appear to see. For example, a series of bulbs lit in quick succession will appear as the flowing movement of light. Another example of how perception can be distorted is shown in the 'impossible object' in Figure 2.8. This object is meaningful if we look at either end of it, but when viewed in its entirety it is, in fact, an optical illusion.

Figure 2.8: Impossible Figure

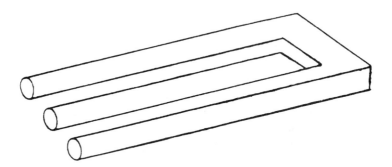

Likewise in person perception one can be deceived by appearances. Family and friends are often shocked when someone commits suicide without seeming to be at all unhappy. Similarly, initial impressions of people we meet for the first time will influence how we respond to them, despite the fact that such impressions can be misleading. Indeed, important decisions, such as whether or not to give someone a job, are highly influenced by the first impressions of the candidate gleaned by the interviewer (Arvey and Campion, 1984).

Labelling

Labels are used during person perception to enable people to be categorised and dealt with more readily. Such labels are influenced by a person's age, physical appearance, sex, mode of dress, posture and other nonverbal behaviour, as well as the verbal message they may send. Judgements and inferences are made according to the 'picture' received. Consider a quiet, pretty child sitting at a table: in terms of past experience of children, and expectations of how a child should behave in such a situation, the child may be categorised as a 'good child'. The observed behaviour has been thus labelled under a familiar heading.

This labelling is a complex process derived from past experience, expectations and interpretation of the situation. It also arises from the need to classify and categorise others. The function of labelling is to simplify complex information, which would otherwise become unmanageable. Labelling is also influenced by the private 'persona' established for the other person. According to the other person's appearance and behaviour in the present observed situation, a personality for that person is predicted. Should the expected behaviour not then manifest itself, the unacceptable tends to be filtered out, or the behaviour attributed to situational rather than personal factors.

One type of label which has been identified is that of the social stereotype, whereby once a person is identified as belonging to a particular group of people then he is attributed with the characteristics of that group, irrespective of his individual characteristics (Trower, 1979). In this way, set patterns of behaviour are anticipated in someone belonging to a specific group (racial, class, religious and so on). A person belonging to a professional group is also likely to evoke a set of behavioural expectations. Thus, policemen will be associated with one set of expectations, while social workers will be associated with a different set. The stereotype an individual holds of a professional group will tend to influence how he perceives, and interprets, the behaviour of any particular member of that group.

Theories of Perception

There are two main theories of perception, namely intuitive and inference (Cook, 1979). Intuitive theories regard perception as being innate, purporting that people instinctively recognise and interpret the behaviour and feelings of others. There is some evidence to support the existence of such an innate capacity. It has been found, for example, that monkeys reared in isolation are able to recognise and respond to the emotions displayed by other monkeys. Furthermore, humans blind from birth are able to display facial expressions of emotions (albeit of a more restricted range as compared to sighted people), while a number of facial expressions of emotion seem to be common across different cultures. However, although there may be elements of emotion which are perceived intuitively, it is unlikely that many of the perceptual judgements people make are innate (for example, warm, intelligent, sophisticated). Such detailed judgements are culture-specific and dependent upon learning.

Indeed, if perception was innate and instinctive, then we should be very accurate in our perceptions. Yet this is patently not the case, and we are often very inaccurate. It has also been demonstrated that it is possible to improve perceptual abilities, thereby supporting the view that there is a degree of learning involved. Thus, while intuition plays a role in our perceptions of others, it cannot fully account for the entire perceptual process.

The second theory purports that judgements of others are based on inferences made as a result of past experiences. An example of how such inferences are arrived at is: fat people are usually happy (generalisation based upon past experience); this woman is fat (this person is perceived as fitting the generalisation); therefore she is probably happy (inference).

Bruner and Tagiuri (1954) emphasised the importance of what they referred to as 'implicit personality theories' which influence the judgements people make about others. These theories are dependent on three types of inference rules: first, there are *identification rules,* which involve the perception of overt cues (dress, shape, physical appearance) in order to identify and 'place' people in certain ways; second, *association rules* enable another person to be associated with a certain set of beliefs or stereotypes, once they have been categorised and identified as belonging to a particular group; third, *combination rules* involve the combination of a number of perceptual cues in order to allow an overall picture to be built up. Thus, perceptual judgements are made as the result of the identification, association and combination of a number of cues.

It would seem, therefore, that both intuition and inference play a part in person perception. The innate perception of certain basic emotions in others is probably important for the survival of the individual, but in a complex society, learned inferences will enable one to recognise and interpret a range of social messages, and respond to these more readily. The more socially skilled individual will have a greater perceptual ability than someone less socially adept.

Metaperception

There are three main types of perception: first, we perceive the responses of other people; second, we perceive our own responses, in that we hear what we say and may be aware of some of our own nonverbal responses. Indeed, the socially skilled person will have a good awareness of his own behaviour during social interaction, and will monitor and regulate his performance in relation to the responses of others. However, it would seem that a curvilinear relationship exists between social performance and self-perception, in that being excessively aware of our own behaviour can be just as detrimental as being totally unaware.

Metaperception is the third type of perception, and this refers to perception of the perception process itself. As we interact with others, we attempt to evaluate how they are perceiving us, and to ascertain how they think we are perceiving them. Both of these factors play an important role in social interaction. It has been shown that if A likes B, he will judge that B likes him. Also, if A thinks B dislikes him, he will tend to behave as if B does not like him, with the result that B will probably end up not liking A (regardless of initial feelings), and in this way a self-fulfilling prophecy occurs.

Person perception, therefore, is concerned with the impressions people form of one another, and how interpretations are made concerning the behaviour of others. It is concerned with the 'external' world coming into contact with the 'internal' world of expectations, hopes, fears, needs, memories and so on. Professionals need to develop an ability to perceive accurately the cues being emitted by clients, while also being aware of their own responses. To be effective in social interaction it is necessary to be sensitive to relevant social feedback, in terms of the verbal and nonverbal behaviour being displayed both by oneself and by others. If such perceptions are inaccurate, then decisions about future responses will be based upon invalid information, and the resulting responses are therefore likely to be less appropriate.

Therefore, perception is the final central process involved in the dyadic model of social interaction, as outlined in Figure 2.3, and together with the processes of motivation and goal, mediating factors, response and feedback, comprises the core of such interaction. However, in order to attempt to fully comprehend the nature of interpersonal communication, we must take account of two other aspects, namely personal and situational factors, which impinge upon, and influence, such communication.

Personal Factors

Before we actually interact with other people, we make a number of judgements about them based upon their physical appearance. Such judgements can markedly affect the goals which one may wish to pursue, our motivation to open an interaction with them, the way in which we perceive them, and how we respond to them. Therefore, it is necessary to take account of those aspects of the individual which are immediately visible to others; it is these aspects which are referred to here as personal factors. Four main personal factors are analysed which have a bearing upon interpersonal communication.

Sex

During social interaction we tend to respond differently to, and have differing expectations about, the behaviour of people depending upon whether they are males or females. Indeed, as Mayo and Henley (1981) point out: 'Sex as signaled by cues of appearance is a powerful force in human interaction . . . and often the first aspect of another to which we respond.' From an early age, sexual differences are emphasised by the ways in which infants are dressed, and responded to, by adults. Such early influences inevitably contribute towards later differences in behaviour, and expectations thereof. The extent to which these differences are innate or learned remains unclear, although it is likely that both nature and nurture play a part in shaping later gender differences in behaviour (Haviland and

Malatesta, 1981).

In western society, males are more likely to be viewed positively if they are regarded as being competent, assertive and rational; females are generally more likely to be highly valued if they display traits such as gentleness, warmth and tact. With increasing emphasis upon equal opportunities for men and women, and the growing strength of various women's movements, it will be interesting to note to what degree such values change during the next decade. At present, however, research tends to indicate marked differences in social responses between the sexes.

Clear differences can be observed in nonverbal behaviour. Females tend to smile more frequently, require less interpersonal space, are touched more, use a greater number of head nods and engage in more eye contact than males. In addition, women are more skilled than men in interpreting the nonverbal behaviour of others. It has been hypothesised that these attention-giving, encoding, non-verbal skills, and the greater ability to decode nonverbal cues, may be associated with the child-rearing role of women in our society. However, regardless of the causes of different behaviour patterns between the genders, it still remains true that males or females who deviate markedly from their expected sex role behaviour are likely to encounter problems during social interaction.

Age

The age of those with whom we interact will also influence both our behaviour and expectations. Although we may attempt to camouflage our actual age, this is something which will generally be fairly accurately judged by others, certainly within the main 'stages' of life (infancy, childhood, adolescence, early adulthood, middle age, old age). Generally, more mature professionals are often viewed as being more competent, whereas the newly qualified professional may find difficulty in inspiring confidence in clients. In this way, expectations are held about others based upon age; an older person wearing trendy fashions may be seen as an 'old fool', while 'act your age' is an instruction given to even very young children!

The problem age for most individuals would appear to be late adolescence and early adulthood. At this stage, the individual is still developing a self-image, going through the transition from adolescence into adulthood, trying to establish a career and position in society, searching for a mate or coping with the demands of a young family. It is at this stage that problems such as drug addiction, schizophrenia and anorexia nervosa are most prevalent. Indeed, despite the often publicised problems of the elderly, Gergen and Gergen (1981), in considering research in this field, conclude that: 'The greatest life satisfaction is experienced by individuals who are approximately 70 years old. Although satisfaction declines after the age of 70, it never reaches the low experienced by people in their 20s and 30s.'

Physical Appearance

The physical appearance of other people, in terms of body size, shape and attractiveness, will also affect our behaviour and expectations. As Stewart, Powell and Chetwynd (1979) illustrate, people are judged upon their appearance from a very early age, so that nursery school children have been shown to exhibit an aversion to chubby individuals and a greater liking for physically attractive peers.

Attractiveness is a very important feature in interpersonal communication. An individual who is regarded as being attractive will also be seen as being more popular, friendly and interesting to talk to. Such expectations inevitably affect the way in which attractive people are responded to, and their behaviour interpreted, thereby creating a self-fulfilling prophecy. Ratings of physical attractiveness seem to be fairly consistent across variations in age, sex, socioeconomic status and geographical location, with most people agreeing about the attractiveness of particular individuals. Furthermore, cross-cultural agreement about ratings of attractiveness are likely to be increasingly influenced (and westernised) by the ever-expanding role of the mass media (soap operas, worldwide beauty contests and so on).

Cook (1977), in an analysis of interpersonal attraction, points out that: 'In most but not all relationships people look for someone who is attracted to them . . . A relatively unattractive or unpopular person who tries to make friends with — or a sexual partner of — someone much more attractive or popular is likely to suffer a rebuff.' One example of this is the finding that we tend to marry those who are at the same level of attractiveness as ourselves. Attractiveness, however, involves more than physical features, since other factors such as personality, competence, cleanliness and dress are used in judging attractiveness. The former two characteristics will be relevant in terms of the establishment of long-term relationships; a physically unattractive professional may be successful and popular with clients by ensuring that he or she has a good interactive style and a professional approach.

Physique can also influence how others are perceived and reacted to. Some tentative conclusions can be gleaned from research findings in this area. For females, ectomorphs (thin figure) tend to be rated most favourably, being seen as clean, tidy, quiet and conscientious, although nervous. Mesomorphic (muscular) females are regarded as strong and healthy with a forceful personality, while endomorphs (fat) are often perceived as being untidy, sloppy and lazy, although happy. With males, mesomorphs tend to be most popular, followed by ectomorphs, and once again, endomorphs are least popular. However, studies which have reported these findings usually concentrate on extreme stereotypes of body shape, without taking into account variations between these three body types. For example, a female with large breasts but a slim waist would not easily fit within any of these categories. Thus, more detailed research is needed into the social effects of specific aspects of body shape.

Height is another significant element, particularly in relation to judgements of males. Taller men tend to achieve more in our society in terms of occupational indices such as promotion and salary, and social indices such as dating. Furthermore, higher status males tend to be viewed as taller in direct proportion to their status (regardless of actual height). While research evidence in relation to the effects of height of females is rather scanty, it does seem that, for many women, being tall is often regarded as a deficit, since 'short men and tall women have problems in date or mate selection . . . when adolescent boys are worried about their height, they are worried by their shortness, whereas adolescent girls who worry about height are concerned by their tallness' (Stewart *et al.*, 1979).

Dress

Although one of the main functions of clothing is to protect the wearer from cold or injury, it is obvious that dress also serves a social function. This is evidenced by the amount of money spent annually on clothes, especially in western society. The clothes people wear can serve to indicate group membership, individual identity, occupation, status, sex and personality. Most professionals will have either a formal or informal uniform, which can enable others to identify the professional (for example the nurse in hospital), or one that is chosen as a symbol of professional image (the businessman's three-piece suit). In addition, we also employ other embellishments such as fine jewellery, expensive watches or appropriate spectacles, to enhance our overall image. Since so much attention is devoted to the choice of dress, it is hardly surprising that we make judgements about others based upon this dimension. Thus, Eicher and Kelley (1972), in a study of high school girls, found that 'it is dress first, then personality, then common interests that lead to pursual of friendships'. Therefore, it would appear that the way we dress can act as a powerful signal, providing information to others about the types of people we are.

Situational Factors

The influence of situational factors plays an important part in determining the behaviour of people during interpersonal encounters. Magnusson (1981) argues that such factors are important for three reasons: first, we learn about the world and form conceptions of it, in terms of the situations which are experienced; second, all behaviour occurs within a given situation and so can only be fully understood through a knowledge of situational variables; and third, by increasing knowledge of situations we can thereby increase their understanding of the behaviour of individuals.

Argyle, Furnham and Graham (1981) define a social situation as 'the sum of the features of a social occasion that impinge on an individual'. They have identified nine main features of social situations.

Goal Structure

The goals which we seek will be influenced by the situation in which we are interacting, while, conversely, the goals which we seek will also influence the situations in which we choose to interact. Thus, the doctor in her surgery will have goals directly related to dealing with patients. However, if the doctor has a 'social' goal of finding a mate, she will seek out social situations in which she is likely to encounter available males. In this way, goals and situations are intertwined.

Most professional contexts will have specific goal structures, with each primary goal having a number of related secondary, or subgoals. In the case of the doctor who wishes to make a diagnosis (overall goal), this will often involve ascertaining a set of answers to structured questions (subgoals). Thus, knowing the correct goal structure for a range of professional situations is an important aspect of professional interaction.

Roles

In any given situation, people will play, and be expected to play, different roles. These roles carry with them sets of expectations about behaviour, attitudes, feelings and values. Thus, a doctor is expected to behave in a thorough, caring fashion, to be concerned about patients' health and to treat their problems in confidence. A central feature of training in any profession is that the trainee is expected to learn in detail the duties and behaviour associated with the role of that particular profession. We will, of course, play different roles from one situation to another, for example, from that of teacher in school to mother at home. We can also play more than one role in the same situation: if we are entertaining friends at home we may be expected to play the roles of host, husband, friend and father. The roles of those involved will affect both the goals and behaviour of participants. For example, a teacher will behave differently, and have different goals, as he moves from teaching pupils in the classroom to attending a staff meeting at lunch time, and then an interview with the headmaster about possible promotion.

Rules

Social interaction has been likened to a game, in that both involve specific rules which must be followed if a successful outcome is to be achieved. The main difference is that games involve explicit rules whereas, for the most part, social interaction involves implicit rules (although in more formal interactions, such as debates, there may be explicit rules). Examples of breaking the implicit rules would include refusing to answer any questions at all at a selection interview, singing loudly in the cinema or wearing swimwear in church. Professionals must be aware not only of the rules of the situations which they will encounter, but also how to deal with clients who break the rules (for example, pupils misbehaving in the classroom).

Repertoire of Elements

Different types of behaviour will be more or less appropriate in different situations and, therefore, it is important for professionals to develop a range of behavioural repertoires. By developing as wide a repertoire of behavioural elements as possible, the professional will more readily cope with a variety of clients. Thus, in one situation fact-finding may be crucial and the skill of questioning will be central, while in another situation it may be necessary to explain carefully certain facts to a client. This book is devoted to charting a large number of such behavioural elements in terms of communication skills; for this reason it is obviously of value to professionals.

Sequences of Behaviour

The elements of behaviour relevant to particular social situations usually occur in an expected sequence. An example of this was given in Chapter 1 in relation to the sequence associated with courtship. In the case of a doctor's surgery, the sequence will be:

1. Patient enters the surgery;
2. Doctor makes a greeting;
3. Patient responds and sits down;
4. Doctor seeks information about the patient's health;
5. Patient responds and gives information;
6. Doctor makes a diagnosis;
7. Doctor prescribes and explains treatment;
8. Doctor makes closing comments;
9. Patient responds, stands up and leaves the surgery.

This sequence will also be expected by the patient who would be most unhappy if the doctor moved straight from (1) to (7) without going through the intervening steps! Different professional situations will have different behavioural sequences.

Situational Concepts

A certain amount of conceptual information will be necessary for effective participation in any given situation. In order to play the game of poker, one must be aware of the concepts of 'full house', 'flush' and 'run'. Similarly, a patient visiting the dentist may need to be aware of the concepts of 'filling', 'crown' or 'bridge'. However, a common error which many professionals make is to assume that patients are familiar with concepts when in fact, they are not aware of their meaning. Indeed, most professionals will have developed a jargon of specific terminology for various concepts, and must ensure that it is avoided, or fully explained, when dealing with clients.

Skills and Difficulties

The nature of the task is another central consideration: if it is simple and pleasant then it can be executed with ease. However, it is likely to cause difficulties in terms of social interaction if the task is unpleasant or complex. Within any particular profession there will be some tasks which are more difficult than others. Indeed, it is likely that certain professional situations will cause specific difficulties that require specific skills. Thus, dealing with aggressive clients, counselling terminally ill patients and their relatives or teaching mentally handicapped children, are all situations which require detailed preparation, in terms of the difficulties that these situations present and the skills and strategies appropriate for handling them.

Language and Speech

There are linguistic variations associated with social situations; some situations require a higher degree of language formality than others. Giving a lecture, being interviewed on television or chairing a committee meeting will all usually involve a more formal, deliberate, elaborated use of language than, for example, having a chat with a friend over coffee. Equally, changes in tone, pitch and volume of voice will change across situations: there are vocal patterns associated with evangelical clergymen addressing religious gatherings, barristers summing up in court and sports commentators describing ball games. Professionals will need to develop and refine their language and speech to suit a particular context. Thus, a teacher who cannot project his voice in an authoritative manner is not likely to be successful in the classroom.

Physical Environment

The nature of the environment will influence the behaviour of individuals. People feel more secure on 'home territory' than in new environments. Thus, a social worker will tend to find clients more at ease in their own homes than in their office, whereas the social worker will probably be more comfortable in the latter situation. People also tend to feel more comfortable, and will therefore talk more freely, in 'warm' environments (soft seats, concealed lights, carpets, curtains, pot plants). The physical lay-out of rooms is also important in either encouraging or discouraging interaction. This can be exemplified in relation to the organisation of seats at a table, where different seating arrangements can convey different messages:

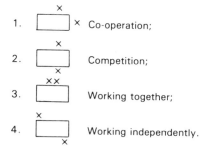

1. Co-operation;

2. Competition;

3. Working together;

4. Working independently.

The organisation and preparation of the physical environment is, therefore, a feature of situations which professionals should consider in relation to interactions with clients. Thus, for example, (1) above would usually be the most appropriate seating arrangement in a doctor's surgery.

Overview

The model described in this chapter attempts to account for the central facets of interpersonal interaction. It will be apparent from this brief review that inter-action between people is a complex process involving a myriad of variables, some or all of which may be operative at any given time. Although each of these has been discussed in isolation, it should be realised that in reality these processes occur simultaneously. Thus, as information is perceived it is immediately dealt with and responded to so quickly that we are not usually aware that these processes are occurring. As has been pointed out, we behave for the most part at a sub-conscious level and, indeed, this is a feature of skilled performance.

Given the number of factors which influence the behaviour of individuals during social interaction, it is extremely difficult to make judgements or interpretations about the exact reasons why certain behaviours are, or are not, displayed. Never-theless, the model as presented does provide a systematic structure for analysing human behaviour. It has taken account of: the goals which people pursue, and their motiviation to pursue them; the cognitive and affective processes which influence the processing of information; the feedback available during social encounters; the perception of this feedback; personal and situational factors; and the social responses which people make.

While some of the features of the extended model of interpersonal interaction (Figure 2.3) are the same as those contained in the motor skills model (Figure 2.2), there are also a large number of differences. In particular, the reciprocal nature of social interaction, the role of emotions, the nature of person perception and personal and situational factors, must be emphasised during social, as opposed to motor, skill performance. However, it can be argued that the analogy between motor and social skills has proved to be useful in providing a basic foundation upon which to build a theoretical framework for interpreting interpersonal in-teraction.

Finally, the model presented has focused upon the application of the main interactive processes involved in dyadic (two-person) interaction. When more than two people are involved, then, although the same processes are involved inter-action becomes even more complex and certainly much more difficult to repre-sent diagrammatically. Despite the increased complexity (in terms of differing goals, motivation and so on), a knowledge of these central processes will facilitate attempts to understand, and make sense of, group and dyadic interaction.

Acknowledgements

We would like to thank our colleagues Dr David Dickson and Christine Saunders for their advice and suggestions during the formulation of this chapter.

References

Allport, G. and Odbert, H. (1936) 'Trait-names: A Psycho-lexical Study', *Psychological Monographs,* *47* (1, whole No. 211)

Annett, J. (1969) *Feedback and Human Behaviour,* Penguin, Harmondsworth

Argyle, M. (1967) *The Psychology of Interpersonal Behaviour,* Penguin, Harmondsworth

———— (1983) *The Psychology of Interpersonal Behaviour,* 4th edn, Penguin, Harmondsworth

———— Furnham, A. and Graham, J. (1981) *Social Situations,* Cambridge University Press, Cambridge

———— and Kendon, A. (1967) 'The Experimental Analysis of Social Performance' in L. Berkowitz (ed.) *Advances in Experimental Social Psychology: Volume 3,* Academic Press, New York

Arvey, R. and Campion, J. (1984) 'Person Perception in the Employment Interview' in M. Cook (ed.), *Issues in Person Perception,* Methuen, London and New York

Averill, J. (1975) 'A Semantic Atlas of Emotional Concepts', *JSAS Catalogue of Selected Documents in Psychology, 5,* 330

Bandura, A. (1967) The Role of Modelling Processes in Personality Development' in T. Foley, R. Lockhart, and D. Merrick (eds), *Contemporary Readings in Psychology,* Harper and Row, New York

Berger, S. and Lambert, W. (1968) 'Stimulus-Response Theory in Contemporary Social Psychology' in G. Lindzey and E. Aronson (eds), *The Handbook of Social Psychology,* 2nd edn, Vol. 1, Addison-Wesley, Reading, Massachusetts

Bernstein, B. (1961) 'Social Structure, Language and Learning', *Educational Research, 3,* 163–76

———— (1971) *Class, Codes and Control* Routledge and Kegan Paul, London

Berscheid, E. (1983) 'Emotion' in H. Kelley, E. Berscheid, A. Christensen, *et al.* (eds), *Close Relationships,* W.H. Freeman, New York

Bindra, D. and Stewart, J. (eds) (1971) *Motivation,* 2nd edn, Penguin, Harmondsworth

Blubaugh, J. (1969) 'Effects of Positive and Negative Audience Feedback on Selected Variables of Speech Behaviour', *Speech Monographs, 36,* 131–37.

Boden, M. (1972) *Purposive Explanation in Psychology,* Harvard University Press, Massachusetts

Bruner, J. and Tagiuri, R. (1954) 'The Perception of People' in G. Lindzey (ed.), *Handbook of Social Psychology,* Addison-Wesley, Reading, Massachusetts

Carroll, J. (1980) 'Analysing Decision Behaviour: The Magician's Audience' in T. Wallsten (ed.), *Cognitive Processes in Choice and Decision Behaviour,* Lawrence Erlbaum, Hillsdale

Cook, M. (1977) 'The Social Skill Model and Interpersonal Attraction' in S. Duck (ed.), *Theory and Practice in Interpersonal Attraction,* Academic Press, London

———— (1979) *Perceiving Others,* Methuen, London

Eicher, J. and Kelley, J. (1972) 'High School as a Meeting Place', *Michigan Journal of Secondary Education, 13,* 12–16

Ellis, A. (1962) *Reason and Emotion in Psychotherapy,* Lyle Stuart, New York

Fisher, B. (1978) *Perspectives on Human Communication,* Macmillan, London

Furnham, A. (1983) 'Research in Social Skills Training: A Critique' in R. Ellis and D. Whittington (eds) *New Directions in Social Skill Training,* Croom Helm, Beckenham

Gergen, K. and Gergen, M. (1981) *Social Psychology,* Harcourt Brace Jovanovich, New York

Hargie, O., Saunders, C. and Dickson, D. (1981) *Social Skills in Interpersonal Communication,* Croom Helm, Beckenham

Haviland, J. and Malatesta, C. (1981) 'The Development of Sex Differences in Nonverbal Signals: Fallacies, Facts and Fantasies' in C. Mayo and N. Henley (eds), *Gender and Nonverbal Behaviour,* Springer-Verlag, New York

Izard, C.E. (1977) *Human Emotions,* Plenum Press, New York

James, W. (1884) 'What is Emotion?', *Mind, 4,* 188–204

Leavitt, H. and Mueller, R. (1951) 'Some Effects of Feedback on Communications', *Human Relations Journal, 4,* 401–10

Levy, R. (1974) 'Tahiti, Sin and the Question of Integration between Personality and Sociocultural Systems' in R.A. Le Vine (ed.), *Culture and Personality,* Aldine, Chicago

Ley, P. (1977) 'Psychological Studies of Doctor — Patient Communication' in J. Rachman (ed.), *Contributions of Medical Psychology, Vol. 1* Pergamon Press, Oxford

Lindauer, M. (1968) 'Pleasant and Unpleasant Emotions in Literature: A Comparison With the Affective Tone of Psychology', *The Journal of Psychology, 70,* 55–67

Magnusson, D. (ed.) (1981) *Towards a Psychology of Situations,* Lawrence Erlbaum, Hillsdale, New Jersey

Maslow, A. (1954) *Motivation and Personality,* Harper and Row, New York

Mayo, C. and Henley, N. (1981) 'Nonverbal Behaviour: Barrier or Agent for Sex Role Change' in C. Mayo and N. Henley (eds), *Gender and Nonverbal Behaviour,* Springer-Verlag, New York

McDougall, W. (1912) *Psychology: The Study of Behaviour,* Williams and Norgate, London

McFall, A. (1982) 'A Review and Reformulation of the Concept of Social Skills', *Behavioural Assessment, 4,* 1–33

McIntyre, D. (1983) 'Social Skills Training for Teaching' in Ellis, R. and D. Whittington (eds), *New Directions in Social Skill Training,* Croom Helm, Beckenham

Meichenbaum, D. and Butler, L. (1980) 'Cognitive Ethology: Assessing the Streams of Cognition and Emotion' in K. Blankstein, P. Piner and J. Polivy (eds), *Advances in the Study of Communication and Affect: Volume 6,* Plenum Press, New York

Mitchell, T. (1978) *People in Organizations,* McGraw-Hill, New York

Neisser, U. (1967) *Cognitive Psychology,* Appleton-Century-Crofts, New York

Norton, R. (1983) *Communicator Style: Theory Application and Measures,* Sage, Beverly Hills

Nowlis, V. (1965) 'Research with Mood Adjective Check List' in S.S. Tompkins and C. Izard (eds), *Affect, Cognition and Personality,* Springer, New York

Pendleton, D. and Furnham, A. (1980) 'A Paradigm for Applied Social Psychological Research' in W. Singleton, P. Spurgeon and R. Stammers (eds), *The Analysis of Social Skill,* Plenum Press, New York

Roth, I. (1976) *Social Perception,* Open University Press, Milton Keynes

Shaw, B. (1979) 'The Theoretical and Experimental Foundations of a Cognitive Model for Depression' in P. Pliner, K. Blankstein and I. Spigel (eds), *Advances in the Study of Communication and Affect: Volume 5,* Plenum Press, New York

Snyder, M. (1974) 'The Self-Monitoring of Expressive Behaviour,' *Journal of Personality and Social Psychology, 30,* 526–37.

Stewart, R., Powell, G. and Chetwynd, S. (1979) *Person Perception and Stereotyping,* Saxon House, Farnborough

Trower, P. (1979) 'Fundamentals of Interpersonal Behaviour' in A. Bellack and M. Hersen (eds), *Research and Practice in Social Skills Training,* Plenum Press, New York

Vernon, M. (1969) *Human Motivation,* Cambridge University Press, Cambridge

Vlandis, J. (1964) 'Variations in the Verbal Behaviour of a Speaker as the Function of Varied Reinforcing Conditions', *Speech Monographs, 31,* 116–19.

Von Cranach, M., Kalbermatten, U., Indermuhle, K. and Gugler, B. (1982) *'Goal-Directed Action',* *European Monographs in Social Psychology, 30,* Academic Press, London

Warr, P. and Knapper, C. (1968) *The Perception of People and Events,* Wiley, London

Welford, A. (1965) 'Performance, Biological Mechanisms and Age: A Theoretical Sketch' in A. Welford and J. Birren (eds), *Behaviour, Aging and the Nervous System,* C.C. Thomas, Illinois

Wessler, R. (1984) 'Cognitive-Social Psychological Theories and Social Skills: A Review' in P. Trower (ed.), *Radical Approaches to Social Skills Training,* Croom Helm, Beckenham

Wheldall, K. (1975) *Social Behaviour,* Methuen, London

Wiener, N. (1954) *The Human Use of Human Beings,* Houghton Mifflin, Boston

Part 2:

CORE SOCIAL SKILLS

3 NONVERBAL COMMUNICATION

Richard M. Rozelle, Daniel Druckman and James C. Baxter

Nonverbal Behaviour in Perspective

In recent years, it has become increasingly recognised that investigators in a field of inquiry — any field — bring personal perspectives and figurative comparisons to bear on their work. Such perspectives have been called paradigms, metaphors or fundamental analogies, but their influence has been thought to be pervasive. Indeed, both philosophers and working scientists acknowledge the value and necessity of such processes in the realm of creative thought (Glashow, 1980; Koestler, 1964; Oppenheimer, 1956; Pepper, 1942).

Examples of this phenomenon abound. In psychology a recent example has been provided by Gentner and Grudin (1985). They undertook a review of a sample of theoretical contributions to the field published in *Psychological Review* between the years 1894 and 1975. From the 68 theoretical articles they reviewed, they were able to identify 265 distinct mental metaphors. They defined a mental metaphor '. . . as a nonliteral comparison in which either the mind as a whole or some particular aspect of the mind (ideas, processes, etc.) is likened to or explained in terms of a nonliteral domain (p. 182)'. These metaphors were all introduced by their contributors as ways of understanding the field. They were often based on explicit comparisons, such as James' 'stream of consciousness', (Gentner and Grudin, 1985), but were also frequently based on subtly implied, extended comparisons only identifiable from broad sections of text. Gentner and Grudin identified four categories of analogy which characterised the period; spatial, animate-being, neutral and systems metaphors, and found clear trends in metaphor preference and rates of usage over time.

Such an examination of the field of psychology is illuminating and provocative. Recognising that the use of different metaphors places different aspects of the field in relief and inter-relation, and introduces different explanatory and predictive emphasis, one can recognise remarkable shifts in the ways in which psychologists have thought about their subject matter. For example, the recent emphasis on sytems metaphors suggests a focus on lawfully constrained interaction among elements where organisation, precision and mutuality of influence are stressed. Predictions are complex but specific, analysis is multifacted and hierarchic.

Nonverbal Behaviour as Communication

A comparable examination of contributions to the field of nonverbal behaviour may be meaningful. To this end, it is interesting to note that attention has been directed at the meaningfulness of gesture and nonverbal behaviour since earliest recorded Western history. According to Kendon (1981), Classical and Medieval works on rhetoric frequently focused on the actual conduct of the orator as he delivered his speech. They occasionally defined many forms of particular gestures and provided instructions for their use in creating planned effects in the audience.

At least as early as 1605, gesture as a medium of communication co-ordinate with vocal and written language was recognised by Francis Bacon. He suggested that '. . . as the tongue speaketh to the ear, so the hand speaketh to the eye' (quoted in Kendon, 1981, p. 155). Subsequent analyses, inspired by Bacon's proposal, were undertaken to examine chirologia (manual language) as both a rhetorical and natural language form (Bulwer, 1644/1974). During the eighteenth and nineteenth centuries, scholars argued that emotional expression and gesture, the so-called natural languages, surely provided the foundation for the more refined and artificial verbal symbolic communication (for example, Lavater, 1789; Taylor, 1878; Wundt, 1973). Spiegel and Machotka (1974) have identified a collateral history in dance, mime and dramatic staging beginning in the late eighteenth century. Body movement as communication has been an analogy of broad and continuing interest.

In examining the focus on nonverbal behaviour as communication, a number of somewhat different analogies can be identified. Darwin (1872) focused on facial behaviour as neuromuscular expression of emotion, vestiges of the past and informative of an inner affective state. A number of investigators have extended this approach and elaborated the *affective expression* metaphor (for example, Ekman, Friesen and Ellsworth, 1972; Izard, 1971; Tomkins, 1962, 1963; Woodworth and Schlosberg, 1954). In delineating bodily movement, gesture, vocalisation and particularly facial movement as expressive of affect, an emphasis is placed on the rapid, automatic, serviceable, universal aspects of behaviour. Indeed, consciousness, intention and guile are ordinarily not central to such an analysis, although experiential overlays and culturally modified forms of expression are of interest. In examining how readily people recognise affective displays in others (Ekman and Oster, 1979; Hager and Ekman, 1979) or how rules of expression are acquired (Cole, 1984), an emphasis is placed on the plastic nature of neuromuscular form.

A related metaphor comparing nonverbal actions, especially accidents and parapraxes to a *riddle* or *obscure text,* has been employed by psychodynamic investigators. Indeed, Freud (1905/1938, 1924) argued that such actions are usually meaningful and can often be recognised as such by the patient. At the same time, Freud recognised that patients frequently deny the significance of gestural–parapraxic actions, leaving the analyst in a quandry with respect to the validity of his interpretation. Freud offered a number of interpretive strategies, including articulation with the patient's life context and delayed verification as approaches to this problem.

In dealing with the problem of patient denial, Freud seems to have foreshadowed the more recent concerns about the questions of consciousness and intention in determining expressive actions. In any event, Freud's approach to the investigation of nonverbal behaviour as communication appears to have taken the analogies of the riddle or perhaps the obscure text which can be made meaningful by the application of accepted interpretive (for example, hermeneutic) principles. Many psychoanalytic investigators have utilised the broad interpretive analysis of behavioural text (Deutsch, 1952, 1959; Feldman, 1959). Feldman's examination of the significance of such speech mannerisms as 'by the way', 'incidentally', 'honest', 'before I forget', 'believe me', 'curiously enough', and many others provides an illustration of the fruitfulness of regarding speech and gesture as complex, subtle, multi-levelled communication.

Certainly, the reliance on an affective expression as opposed to an obscure text analogy places the process of communciation in different perspectives. In the first instance, the automatic, universal, perhaps unintended and other features identified above are taken as relevant issues, while the articulation with context, uniqueness, obfuscation and necessity of prolonged scholarly examination by trained and skilful interpreters are equally clearly emphasised by the behaviour as riddle analogy.

A third general approach to the behaviour as communication analogy has been provided by the careful explication of *nonverbal behaviour as code* metaphor. Developed most extensively by Birdwhistell's (1952, 1970) analogy with structural linguistics and the Weiner, Devoe, Runbinow *et al.* (1972) comparison with communication engineering, the central concern rests with the detailed, molecular examination of the structure of the code itself, modes (that is, channels) of transmission and accuracy-utility of communication. Levels of communication (for instance, messages and meta-messages), channel comparisons, sending and receiving strategies and accessibility of the intention–code–channel–code–interpretation sequence as an orderly, linear process are all designed to emphasise the systematic, objective and mechanistic features of the metaphor (cf. Druckman, Rozelle and Baxter, 1982).

Certainly the boundaries of the particular variations in the behaviour as communication analogies which have been identified are fuzzy, and the explicit categories of the metaphors as employed by particular investigators are difficult to fully articulate; yet the three variations of the communication analogy seem valid as the history and current investigation in nonverbal behaviour as communication is examined. In this spirit, a fourth general communication metaphor can also be identified — *nonverbal behaviour as dramatic presentation.*

While this analogy clearly descends from mime, dance and dramatic stage direction (Poyatos, 1983; Spiegel and Machotaka, 1974; Stanislavski, 1936), the approach has been most skilfully developed by Goffman (1959, 1969) as both expressive form (that is, identity and situation presentation) and rhetorical form (that is, persuasion, impression management and tactical position). The particularly fruitful features of this analogy appear to be the crafted, holistic, completely situated, forward-flowing nature of expression, with emphasis on recognisable skill, authenticity and purpose. Strategy, guile and deception are important aspects of this analogy, and subtlety and complexity abound (Scheibe,

1979; Schlenker, 1980).

Nonverbal Behaviour as Style

While the nonverbal behaviour as communication analogies hold historical precedence in the area, two additional analogies can be identified: *nonverbal behaviour as personal idiom* (Allport, 1961; Allport and Vernon, 1933) and *nonverbal behaviour as skill* (Argyle, 1967, 1969; Argyle and Kendon, 1967). Allport introduced the important distinction between the instrumental aspects of action and the expressive aspects, the latter being personalised and stylistic ways of accomplishing the tasks of life.

Comparisons with one's signature, voice or thumb prints are offered. This perspective emphasises holism, consistency and configural uniqueness, while de-emphasising complexity, skill and authenticity. Demonstrations of the application of the analogy have been offered, but the richness and fruitfulness of the metaphor have not yet been fully exploited.

Perhaps the most inviting metaphor of nonverbal behaviour has been the emphasis on skilled performance. The fruitfulness of the analogy of acquired skills as a way of thinking about nonverbal behaviour has been recognised for some time (Bartlett, 1958; Polanyi, 1958). However, its extension to nonverbal behaviour has been rather recent (Argyle, 1967; Argyle and Kendon, 1967; DePaulo, Stone and Lassiter, 1984; Friedman, 1979; Hargie, Saunders and Dickson, 1981; Knapp, 1972, 1984; Rosenthal, 1979; Rosenthal, Hall, DiMatteo, *et al.*, 1979; Snyder, 1974). The analogy has directed attention to both the expressive or sending (encoding) and interpretive or receiving (decoding) aspects of nonverbal exchanges, and has begun to highlight aspects of face-to-face interaction previously not investigated.

The skilled performance analogy. Since the introduction of the skilled perform-ance metaphor is somewhat recent in the area of nonverbal behaviour analysis, it might prove useful to attempt to explain some of the categories of such an analogy. As Bartlett (1958) points out, in the general case and in every known form of skill, there are acknowledged experts in whom much of the expertness, though perhaps never all of it, has been acquired by well-informed practice. The skill is based upon evidence picked up directly or indirectly from the environ-ment, and it is used for the attempted achievement of whatever issue may be required at the time of the performance. Examples of such performance would include the sports player, the operator engaged at his work bench, the surgeon conducting an operation, the telegrapher deciphering a message, the pilot controlling an airplane and many more (see Chapter 2 for full discussion).

Initial examination of the comparison suggests a number of important features of skilled performance which are relevant to the investigation of nonverbal behaviour. First, skilled performances usually imply complex, highly co-ordinated motor acts which may be present in unrefined form at the outset of training, but in many cases are not, and which only emerge gradually with training and development. Thus, final performances may be quite different from untutored performances. Also, the recognisability of individuality in the crafting of skilful expression seems clearly implied. A second feature of such performance is that it is based on perceptually differentiating environmental properties or conditions often unrecognised by the untutored. A quality of 'informed seeing' or 'connoisseurship' develops which serves to guide and structure refined action.

A third feature of skilled performances is their dependence on practice, usually distributed over extended periods of time. The importance of combinations of both practice and rest as aids in acquiring desired performance levels and the occurrence of marked irregularities in progress during the attainment of desired levels are recognisable, as are the influences of age and many physical condition factors (Bilodeau, 1966). A fourth important feature of skilled performances is their persistence and resistance to decay, interference and effects of disuse. While comparisons are difficult, the general belief is that skilled actions remain viable after verbal information has been lost to recovery.

A fifth area of importance is the general assumption that individuals vary in their potential or ability to acquire highly refined levels of performance, that is, individual differences are particularly striking. A sixth characteristic of skilled actions is that they typically are ineffable, acquired best by modelling and described only imprecisely by linguistic means.

Finally, the expression of skilled performances usually entails the incorporation of internalised standards of the quality of expression. Performers can recognise inadequacies or refinements in their performance which serve to guide both practice and performance styles.

The development of the skilled performance metaphor in the investigation of nonverbal behaviour as expression seems to have suggested several areas of development and possible advance in the field. Training strategies, individual differences, the role of practice, the importance of performance feedback and internalised criteria of achievement represent a few areas of investigation of nonverbal behaviour implied by this analogy which have not been fully exploited to this point.

The Scientific Study of Nonverbal Behaviour

Literature dealing with nonverbal behaviour as communication has increased dramatically both in volume and complexity, particularly during the last several decades. Wolfgang and Bhardway (1984) list 170 booklength volumes published during the last 100 years that contain nonverbal communication materials, the vast majority of which have appeared within the last 15 years.

The topic is usually presented with two different emphases: (1) theoretical–research orientation, and (2) application–demonstration orientation. Because of its relation to the subtle and interpretative aspects of communication, there is a tendency on the part of popular lay-texts to emphasise application without a balanced presentation of the theory and research which examines validity and reliability aspects necessary for proper understanding of nonverbal behaviour as one form of communication. The challenge of the present chapter is to discuss nonverbal behaviour as a communication skill, while maintaining the scientific integrity needed to critically evaluate the degree to which application is appropriate for any particular reader. It is hoped that the reader will assume a critical, scientific perspective in treating nonverbal behaviour as a meaningful yet complex topic for research and application.

Behavioural Dimensions

Knapp (1972) has suggested seven dimensions which describe the major categories of nonverbal behaviour research as related to communication, and are useful for placing this chapter in perspective. The first category is kinesics and is commonly referred to as 'body language', including movements of the hand, arm, head, foot, leg, postural shifts, gestures, eye movements and facial expressions. A second category is paralanguage and is defined as content-free vocalisations and patterns associated with speech such as voice pitch, volume, frequency, stuttering, filled pauses (for example, 'ah'), silent pauses, interruptions and measures of speech rate and number of words spoken in a given unit of time. A third category involves physical contact in the form of touching.

Another category is proxemics which involves interpersonal spacing and norms of territoriality. A fifth category of nonverbal communication concerns the physical characteristics of people such as skin colour, body shape, body odour and attractiveness. Related to physical characteristics is the category of artifacts or adornments. Examples include perfume, clothes, jewellery and wigs. Environmental factors make up the last category and deal with the influences of the physical setting in which the behaviour occurs, such as a classroom, office, hallway or street corner.

There are numerous examples in the literature that detail these categories, either individually or in combinations (Argyle and Cook, 1976; Duncan and Fiske, 1977; Ekman, Friese and Ellsworth, 1972; Harper, Weins and Matarazzo, 1978; LaFrance and Mayo, 1978; Mahl and Schulze, 1964), and the reader is referred to these for detailed discussion.

This chapter will present these categories in various combinations as they pertain to nonverbal behaviour as a communication skill. It is important to stress that nonverbal behaviour is dependent upon all of these factors for meaningful communication to take place. Some of these categories are covered in the theoretical and empirical presentation; others are not, but are nevertheless important and should always be considered as part of the 'universe' comprising nonverbal communication.

Setting and Role Influences on Nonverbal Behaviour

One of the major problems in focusing on the interpretation of nonverbal behaviour is to treat it as a separate, independent and absolute form of communication. This view of the topic is much too simplistic. The meaning of nonverbal behaviour must be considered in the context in which it occurs. Several types of contextual factors will be used to guide this discussion of nonverbal communication and the behaviours associated with it.

One involves the environmental setting of the behaviour. Both the physical and social aspects of the environment must be described in sufficient detail to assess possible contributing factors to nonverbal behaviour as meaningful communication. For example, the furniture arrangement in an office can be a major factor influencing the nonverbal behaviours exhibited. Body movements are different depending upon whether the person is sitting behind a desk or openly in a chair. The proximity and angle of seating arrangements has been shown to serve different functions during interaction and affect such behaviour as eye contact, gazing and head rotation (Argyle and Dean, 1965; Manning, 1965).

Nonverbal behaviour may have very different meanings when exhibited on the street than in a classroom. Background noise level in a work setting may produce exaggerated nonverbal communication patterns that would have very different meaning in more quiet settings such as a library. The influence of ecological factors on behaviour has become an increasingly important focus in the study of human behaviour (McArthur and Baron, 1983; Stokols and Shumaker, 1981; Willems, 1985). Most research in nonverbal communication dealing with physical-environmental factors has focused on interpersonal spacing, proxemics and cultural differences in interaction patterns (Baxter, 1970; Collett, 1971; Hall, 1966).

The social climate of the environment is also an important factor in the consideration of nonverbal behaviour (Jones, Rozelle and Svyantek, 1985). Research has demonstrated that different behaviours are produced in stressful versus unstressful situations (Rozelle and Baxter, 1975). The formality of a setting will determine the degree to which many nonverbal behaviours are suppressed or performed. Competitive versus co-operative interaction settings will also produce different types, levels and frequencies of nonverbal behaviours. These are just several examples of factors affecting the communicative meaning of nonverbal behaviour. The reader is encouraged to systematically survey factors that may be of importance in settings more familiar to her or him.

Nonverbal Behaviour as Communication: Process and Outcome Factors of the Interaction Episode

Many communication models as applied to nonverbal behaviour have concentrated on the interpersonal level and have not elaborated to the same degree the role and situational levels of communication. An important distinction in viewing nonverbal behaviour as communication is that between the encoder and the decoder. The encoder is analogous to an actor or impression manager, producing and 'sending' the behaviours to be interpreted. The decoder is analogous to an observer 'receiving' the presented behaviours and interpreting them in some fashion. Within the context of the encoder–decoder distinction, a major concern is that of intention and whether intended and unintended messages obey the same rules and principles of communication (Dittmann, 1978).

Ekman and Friesen (1969) have provided two general classifications for behavioural messages. The first is the 'informative act' which results in certain interpretations on the part of a receiver without any active or conscious intent on the part of the sender. Thus, an individual's nonverbal behaviour is unintentionally 'giving off' signals that may either be correctly or incorrectly interpreted by a decoder (Goffman, 1959). The important point is that an impression is being formed without the encoder's knowledge or intention. A second classification is termed the 'communicative act'. In this case, the encoder in intentionally attempting to send a specific message to a receiver. A difficulty lies in distinguishing varying degrees of conscious intent as opposed to 'accidental' or nonspecifically motivated behaviour. Extreme examples of communicative behaviours intended to convey such emotions as anger, approval or disagreement are usually described in the literature (for example, Jones and Wortman, 1973). Similarly, informative acts such as fidgeting and gaze aversion are presented as examples of informative behaviour indicating unintended guilt, anxiety or discomfort.

As will be discussed later in this chapter, role and situational considerations can lead to gross misinterpretations of what is considered 'informative' or 'communicative' behaviour on the part of both encoder and decoder in an interaction. Most interactions among people involve less extreme emotion and a complexity of intentions. Also, many social interactions involve changing roles between encoder and decoder as the participants take turns in speaking and listening (for example, Duncan, 1969; Jones and Thibaut, 1958).

A useful model dealing with the issues of social influence in nonverbal communication is presented by MacKay (1972). The distinction is made between two types of nonverbal signals exhibited by the encoder: (1) goal-directed and, (2) non-goal-directed. The receiver or decoder then interprets either of these signals as being (3) goal-directed or, (4) non-goal-directed. Thus the signal and the interpretation may be similar: (1) goal-directed signal being interpreted as goal-directed, (2) non-goal-directed signal being interpreted as non-goal-directed, or dissimilar, (3) goal-directed signal being interpreted as non-goal-directed, and (4) non-goal-directed signal being interpreted as goal-directed.

When considering goal-directed signalling, MacKay's model assumes that the encoder is behaviourally attempting to communicate a specific internal state or presence and that the intended communication has a desired effect on the encoder. If, in the encoder's judgement, the intended effect has not been achieved, the goal-directed, nonverbal behaviour is modified to achieve the desired effect. Thus, the encoder actively evaluates the reaction of the decoder and proceeds accordingly.

Requiring communicative behaviour to be explicitly goal-directed, with an immediate adjustment on the part of the encoder depending upon the decoder's response, limits the number of behaviours that can be considered communicative. In typical conversations, many nonverbal behaviours become automatic responses and are performed at low levels of awareness or involve no awareness at all. What was once a specifically defined goal-directed behaviour becomes habitual and is no longer a product of conscious intention. The degree to which nonverbal behaviours involve varying levels of awareness then becomes difficult to determine.

Another consideration for the understanding of nonverbal communication is whether or not the encoder and decoder share a common, socially defined signal system. Weiner *et al.* (1972) argue that this is a crucial requirement for communication to occur, regardless of the degree to which any behaviour is intentional. This represents a limited perspective on what is considered communication. One of the more pervasive problems in the use of nonverbal behaviour in both the encoding and decoding process is when a common system is *not* shared and misinterpretation of behaviour results.

Certain encoded behaviours may have unintended effects, especially when contextual factors such as cultural, role and spatial factors are inappropriately considered during an interaction. The misinterpretation of behaviour that results can lead to profound consequences and must be considered a type of communication.

Current Approaches to Nonverbal Behaviour as Communication

Ekman and Friesen

Perhaps the most useful model of nonverbal communication that encompasses these issues (but does not resolve them) is one originally presented by Ekman and Friesen (1969). They begin with distinguishing between three characteristics of nonverbal behaviour; (1) usage, (2) origin and (3) coding.

Usage refers to the circumstances that exist at the time of the nonverbal act. It includes consideration of the external condition that affects the act, such as the physical setting, role relationship and emotional tone of the interaction. For example, the encoder and decoder may be communicating in an office, home, car or street. The role relationship may involve that of an interviewer–interviewee, therapist–client, supervisor–employee, husband–wife or teacher–student. The emotional tone may be formal or informal, stressful or relaxed, friendly or hostile, warm or cold, competitive or co-operative. Usage also involves the relationship between verbal and nonverbal behaviour. For example, nonverbal acts may serve to accent, duplicate, support, substitute for or be unrelated to verbal behaviours.

Usage is the characteristic Ekman and Friesen choose to employ in dealing with awareness and intentionality on the part of the encoder, as discussed previously. In addition, usage involves external feedback which is defined as the receiver's verbal or nonverbal reactions to the encoder's nonverbal behaviours as interpreted by the encoder. This does not involve the receiver's actual interpretations of the sender's behaviour, but is only information to the sender that his nonverbal behaviours have been received and evaluated.

Finally, usage refers to the type of information conveyed in terms of being informative, communicative or interactive. Informative and communicative acts have been discussed. Interactive acts are those that detectably influence or modify the behaviour of the other participants in an interaction. Thus, these three information types involve the degree to which nonverbal messages are understood, provide information and influence the behaviour of other people.

The second characteristic of nonverbal behaviour discussed by Ekman and Friesen is its origin. Some nonverbal behaviours are rooted in the nervous system, such as reflex actions; other nonverbal behaviours are commonly learned and used in dealing with the environment. For example, human beings use their feet for transportation in one form or another. A third source of nonverbal behaviour refers to culture, family or any other instrumental or socially distinguishable form of behaviour. Thus, some people behave in such ways as to drive a car, eat in certain manners and clean themselves in various ways. Different social customs dictate nonverbal patterns of greeting one another, expressing approval or disapproval and appropriate distances from each other depending upon the type of interaction involved.

The last characteristic of nonverbal behaviour is coding, that is, the meaning attached to a nonverbal act. The primary distinction is between extrinsic and intrinsic codes. Extrinsically coded acts signify something else and may be either arbitrarily or iconically coded. Arbitrarily coded acts bear no visual resemblance to what they represent. A thumbs-up sign for signalling that everything is okay would be an arbitrarily coded act since it conveys no meaning 'by itself'. An iconically coded act tends to resemble what it signifies, as in the example of a throat-cutting movement with a finger. Intrinsically coded movements are what they signify. Playfully hitting a person, say on the upper arm, is an intrinsically coded act in that it is actually a form of aggression.

With usage, origin and coding as a basis for defining nonverbal behaviour, Ekman and Friesen distinguish among five categories of behavioural acts:

1. Emblems. These are nonverbal acts that have direct verbal translation and can substitute for words, the meaning of which is well understood by a particular group, class or culture. Emblems originate through learning, most of which is culture-specific, and may be shown in any area of the body. Examples include waving the hands in a greeting and frowning to indicate disapproval;

2. Illustrators. These are movements that are tied directly to speech and serve to illustrate what is verbalised. Illustrators are socially learned, usually through imitation by a child of a person he wishes to resemble. An example of an illustrator is holding the hands a certain distance apart to indicate the length of an object;

3. Regulators. These nonverbal acts serve to regulate conversation flow between people. Regulators are often culture-specific and may be subtle indicators

to direct verbal interaction such as head nods, body position shifts, and eye contact. Because of their subtle nature, regulators are often involved in miscommunication and inappropriate responses among people of different cultures or ethnic backgrounds. This will be examined in greater detail when the authors' police–citizen research is described;

4. Adaptors. These are object or self-manipulations. The specific behaviours are first learned as efforts to satisfy bodily needs, usually during childhood. In adult expression, only a fragment of the original adaptive behaviour is exhibited. Adaptors are behavioural habits and are triggered by some feature of the setting that relates to the original need. There are three types of adaptors: (a) self-adaptors such as scratching the head or clasping the hands; (b) alter-adaptors which may include protective hand movements and arm-folding intended to protect oneself from attack or represent intimacy, withdrawal or flight; (c) object adaptors, which were originally learned to perform instrumental tasks and may include tapping a pencil on the table or smoking behaviours;

5. Affect displays. These consist primarily of facial expressions of emotions. There is evidence that the basic emotions of happiness, anger, surprise, fear, disgust, sadness and interest are similar across a wide variety of cultures (Ekman *et al.*, 1972; Izard, 1971). However, these expressions are usually modified and often hidden by cultural display rules learned as 'appropriate' behaviour. Thus, affect displays may be masked in social settings in order to show socially acceptable behaviour.

The nonverbal characteristic-category system of Ekman and Friesen has provided a useful means of analysing and organising nonverbal behaviours used in communication and is readily applicable in describing processes of information expression-exchange in normal, social interactions.

Dittman

Another way of organising nonverbal acts in terms of their communicative nature is by focusing on the 'communication specificity' and channel capability of message transmission. These concepts have been presented by Dittman (1972, 1978) as part of a larger model of the communication of emotions and are an important aspect of using nonverbal behaviour as a communication skill.

Dittman focuses primarily on four major channels of communication: (1) language, (2) facial expression, (3) vocalisations, and (4) body movements. These four channels can be discussed in terms of their 'capacity', defined as the amount of information each may transmit at any given moment. Channel capacity can be described along two dimensions: (1) communication specificity (communicative–expressive) and (2) information value (discrete–continuous). Table 3.1 summarises the relationships among the four communication channels and the two dimensions of information conveying potential or capacity.

The closer a channel is to the communicative end of the continuum, the more discrete its information value will be in terms of containing distinguishable units

Table 3.1: Transmission of Messages

Channel of communication	Channel capacity	
	Specificity	Information value
Language	Communicative	Discrete
Facial expression	↑	↑
Vocalisations	↓	↓
Body movements	Expressive	Continuous

with identifiable meanings (for instance, words). The more discrete a communication is, the greater the communication specificity it will usually have. These channels have the greatest capacity for conveying the largest number of messages with a wide variety of emotional meaning.

Channels at the other end of the capacity dimension are described as being relatively more expressive and continuous. For example, foot movements or changes in posture are more continuous behaviours than are spoken words, and are more expressive than specifically communicative in their emotional content. These channels have a lower capacity for conveying information regarding how a person is feeling. Facial expressions and vocalisations (paralanguage) may vary in their capacity to convey emotional expression depending on their delivery, the role the person is playing, the setting of the behaviour and the characteristics of the decoders (for example, family, friends or strangers).

Dittman also discussed the degree to which a message varies in intentional control on the part of the encoder, and awareness on the part of the decoder. Intentional control refers to the degree to which an encoder is in control of allowing his or her emotions to be expressed. Level of awareness refers to a decoder either being aware of, repressing or not noticing a message being sent by an encoder.

The most useful contribution by Dittman to the nonverbal communication area is his analysis of channels of communication. A major challenge in nonverbal behaviour research is to examine the degree to which single versus multiple channels of transmission provides more meaningful communication in human interaction.

Mehrabian

An influential approach that uses multiple nonverbal categories and attempts to organise them in terms of three dimensions is that of Mehrabian (1972). These dimensions, described as social orientations, are positiveness, potency and responsiveness. Positiveness involves the evaluation of other persons or objects that relate to approach–avoidance tendencies, usually described in terms of liking. Nonverbal behaviours associated with positiveness represent 'immediacy' cues such as eye contact, forward-lean, touching, distance and orientation.

Potency represents status or social control and is demonstrated through 'relaxation' cues of posture such as hand and neck relaxation, sideways lean, reclining angle and arm–leg position asymmetry. Responsiveness is expressed through 'activity' cues that relate to orientating behaviour and involves the relative importance of the interaction participants. Such nonverbal behaviour as vocal activity, speech rate, speech volume and facial activity are indices of responsiveness. Mehrabian's system of nonverbal expression is thus organised into (1) dimensions, (2) associated cues, and (3) specific nonverbal indicators of the cues.

Mehrabian's system places nonverbal behaviour in socially meaningful contexts and is especially useful for nonverbal behaviour as a communication skill. The dimensions of nonverbal behaviour can be applied equally to encoding or decoding roles and are supported by numerous experimental results. For example, data collected by Mehrabian and others indicate that the positiveness dimension, with its immediacy cues, is primarily concerned with deceptive or truthful communication. The potency dimension as expressed by relaxation cues is useful in understanding situations where social or professional status is salient, such as military rank, corporate power, teacher–student relations and therapist–client interactions.

The responsiveness dimension as expressed by activity cues relates to persuasion, either as intended (encoding) or perceived (decoding). Thus, Mehrabian organised a complex set of nonverbal behaviours into manageable proportions, which are readily testable and applicable to social situations experienced daily, particularly by professionals whose judgement and influence are important to those with whom they communicate.

Patterson

A more recent attempt to organise nonverbal behaviour into basic functions or purposes of communication is presented by Patterson (1983). He argues that as social communication, nonverbal behaviour is only meaningful when considered in terms of an exchange of expressions between participants in an interaction. It is this relational nature of behaviours that must be considered and 'requires sensitivity to the behavioural context each person constructs for the other' (1983). The basic functions of nonverbal behaviour are related to the management (and interpretation) of those acts primarily involved in social interaction.

There are five basic functions suggested: (1) providing information, (2) regulating interaction, (3) expressing intimacy, (4) expressing social control, and (5) facilitating service or task goals. Nonverbal behaviour is best considered as 'co-ordinated exchanges' and configurations of multi-channel combinations as related to the five functions. Thus, presenting nonverbal behaviour in terms of separate channels (for instance, facial expressions, arm movements, paralanguage and so on), does not properly emphasise the interdependent and co-ordinated relationship among channels that are meaningfully involved in the functions. This configural approach is important for application to the development of communication skills.

The reader should be constantly aware that if nonverbal behaviour is discussed separately by channel, then it is primarily for organisational clarity; neither should any one channel be considered at the exclusion of others in either managing or interpreting social behaviour. This, of course, results in a more complex task in using nonverbal behaviour as a communication skill, yet it places the topic in a more appropriate perspective *vis-à-vis* communication in general.

The information function is considered to be most basic and is seen primarily from an impression formation or decoder perspective. When observing an encoder's (actor's) behaviour patterns, the decoder may infer aspects of the encoder's more permanent dispositions, temporary states or the meaning of a verbal interaction. Facial cues are emphasised (Ekman and Friesen, 1975) usually to infer emotional expressions. However, other channels of nonverbal behaviour such as postural, paralinguistics, and visual are also important in formulating the impression.

The function of regulating interaction deals with the development, maintenance and termination of a communicative exchange. These nonverbal behaviours are usually 'automatic' or operate at low levels of awareness. Two types of behaviours are involved in regulating interactions: the first are structural aspects that remain relatively stable over the course of an interaction and include posture, body orientation and interpersonal distance; the second type of behaviour is dynamic and affects momentary changes in conversational exchange, such as facial expression, gaze, tone and pitch of voice and change in voice volume (Argyle and Kendon, 1967; Duncan, 1972). Both the information and regulating functions are 'molecular' in form and represent communicative aspects of more isolated and specific nonverbal behaviours.

The last three functional categories represent broader purposes of communication and are molar descriptions of more extended interactions. These are of greater importance in understanding and predicting the nature of nonverbal acts during an interaction. Intimacy refers to liking, attraction or, generally, the degree of 'union' or 'openness toward another person'. Extended mutual gazing into another's eyes, closer interpersonal spacing and mutual touching are examples of communicating intimacy.

Social control functions to persuade others and establish status differences related to the roles of the interaction participants. Examples of nonverbal behaviours involved in social control are gaze patterns and touch to clarify status differences; and eye contact, direct body orientation and vocal intonation to attempt to persuade someone to accept another's point of view. Much of the authors' research relates to this function and will be discussed later in the chapter.

The service–task function involves nonverbal behaviours that are relatively impersonal in nature. Role and situational factors are particularly important here since many of the same nonverbal behaviours involved in intimacy are also present in service–task functions. A good example is close interpersonal spacing and touching behaviour on the part of a physician toward a patient or between hairdresser and customer. The distinguishing feature of service–task behaviours is that they function to service the needs of individuals.

Patterson's functional approach to nonverbal behaviour is similar to Mehrabian's in its application to social–communicative processes. Both stress the importance of the multi-channel use of configurative aspects of nonverbal communication. However, Patterson provides a broader framework in which to view nonverbal behaviour in role- and setting-specific conditions, by emphasising the degree of overlap in multi-channel expression among the functions and the importance of interpreting these expressions in light of the psychological, social and environmental context.

Nonverbal Communication in Context

This chapter has stressed that nonverbal behaviour, as a communication skill, is most usefully understood when discussed in role- and setting-defined contexts. With the possible exception of facial expressions subject to display rules, nonverbal communication cannot be discussed adequately by presenting absolute principles that have universal application. Perhaps a useful way of presenting research results as applied to communication skills is to provide a sampling of findings in selected contexts. At present, research on nonverbal communication is incomplete and asks more questions than it provides answers, yet it is hoped that the reader will better appreciate scientific attempts to study meaningfully this communication skill.

In a recent review, Knapp (1984) discusses the relevance of nonverbal behaviour to communication in general and suggests several assumptions from which nonverbal research can be viewed. Among these are that human communication consists primarily of combinations of channel signals such as spatial, facial and vocal signals operating together. Another assumption is that communication is composed of 'multi-level signals' and deals with broader interpretations of interactions such as general labelling (for example, a social or professional encounter) and inferences about longer term relationships among the interactants. His last assumption is most crucial for the present discussion since it points out the critical importance of context for generating meanings from human communication encounters.

Setting and Role Applications

A major limitation of much nonverbal behaviour research is that it is conducted in a laboratory setting devoid of contextually relevant environmental and social features which are present in real life interactions (Davis, 1984; Druckman, *et al.*, 1982; Knapp, 1984). This is a serious problem in generalising techniques of impression management and processes of impression formation to specific role-defined settings such as the psychotherapeutic or counselling session, health professional–patient interactions, the employment interview and police–citizen encounters.

Professionals in areas such as these have a special interest in nonverbal behaviour since accurate and effective communication is crucial to the participants and the purposes of the interaction. One series of studies conducted over a number of years is illustrative of setting- and role-defined research and reveals the importance of the interplay among the categories of kinesics, paralanguage, proxemics, physical characteristics, adornments and environmental factors mentioned earlier as describing major categories of nonverbal behaviour.

The specific role-defined setting was that of a standing, face-to-face police–citizen interaction. In the initial study (Rozelle and Baxter, 1975), police officers were asked to indicate the 'traits, characteristics and features they look for when interacting with a citizen while in the role of a police officer'. They were also asked to indicate cues they used in forming these impressions of the citizen. These cues or information items were classified as either behavioural (that is, the other person's verbal and nonverbal behaviour) or situational (that is, aspects of the environment, such as number of other people present, inside a room or on the street, lighting conditions). The officers were asked to compare a 'dangerous' versus 'non-dangerous' situation. Under conditions of danger, the officers indicated a broadened perceptual scan and were more likely to utilise behavioural (mainly nonverbal) and situation–environmental cues (for instance, area of town, size of room, activities on the street) in forming an impression of the citizen.

Under the non-dangerous conditions, the officers concentrated almost exclusively on specific facial and vocal cues, eye contact, arm and hand movements, dress and behavioural sequences such as body orientation and postural positions. Under these less stressful conditions, police officers indicated an impression formed that described the citizen primarily in terms of dispositional characteristics such as guilty, suspicious, deceptive, honest or law-abiding.

Dispositional causes of observed behaviour are contrasted with situational causes such as attributing one's behaviour to momentary discomfort or confusion, crowding, responding to another's actions or other events in the immediate environment. Thus, in the more typical police–citizen interaction, which is nonstressful for the police officer (for instance, obtaining information from a witness to an accident or crime), the officer focused predominantly on the citizen's nonverbal behaviours and dispositional attributions, rather than situational attributions, to explain the citizen's behaviour (for example, guilty or innocent).

Actor and Observer Bias in Explaining Nonverbal Behaviour

An important feature of impression–management (encoding) and formation (decoding) processes deals with differences arising out of the perspectives of the interaction participants (Jones and Nisbett, 1972). In most role-defined interactions, the person in the encoding role is considered to be the actor, whereas the decoder is the observer. It has been proposed that unless otherwise trained or sensitised (Watson, 1982), observers over-emphasise dispositional qualities in inferring the causes of the actor's behaviour, while ignoring the more immediate situational factors related to the observed behaviour. Actors, on the other hand, usually over-emphasise situational factors at the expense of dispositional ones in explaining their own behaviour.

From the Rozelle and Baxter (1975) study, it was concluded that police officers see themselves as observers, evaluating and judging the behaviours of the citizen with whom they are interacting. As a result, the officer makes predominantly dispositional interpretations, ignoring situational causes of the observed behaviour. Of particular importance in this type of face-to-face interaction is that the officer himself is probably one of the more distinguishable features of the situation and that his or her own behaviour is an important situational determinant of the citizen's behaviour. Thus, the officer underestimates or completely ignores his or her own behaviour as a contributing, situational determinant of the citizen's behaviour. This can lead to misinterpretations of behaviour, particularly when judgements must be made on the basis of a relatively brief, initial encounter. It should be noted that the citizen also may be misinterpreting his or her own behaviour in terms of reacting to the situation, including the officer's behaviour; thus nonverbal cues are not 'managed' properly to avoid expressing or concealing appropriate behaviour for desired evaluation on the part of the officer. Other types of role-defined interactions resemble this condition in various degrees.

Interpersonal Distance, Roles and Problems of Interpretation

A more dramatic example of how this observer bias can lead to clear, yet inaccurate interpretations of behaviour was obtained when the category of proxemics was included in the police–citizen interaction. Based on his observations of North American behaviour in a variety of settings, Hall (1959, 1966) proposed four categories of interpersonal distance that describe different types of communications in face-to-face interactions:

1. Intimate distances in which interactants stand from six to 18 inches from each other. Types of interactions expressing intimacy are 'love-making and wrestling, comforting and protecting';
2. Personal distances of 1.5 to four feet and usually reflect close, personal relationships;
3. Social or consultative distances of four to seven feet that are typical of business and professional–client interactions;
4. Public distances that range from twelve to 20 feet and involve public speaking in which recognition of others spoken to is not required.

Hall stipulated that these distances are appropriate only for North American and possibly Northern European cultures and that other cultures have different definitions of interpersonal spacing (1966).

A study by Baxter and Rozelle (1975) focused on a simulated police–citizen interview between white male undergraduates at a North American university and an interviewer playing the role of a police officer questioning the student–citizen about various items in his wallet. The interview consisted of four, two-minute phases in which the distance between the officer and citizen was systematically varied according to Hall's first three distance classes.

For both the experimental and control groups, the role-played officer stood four feet away from the student during the first two-minute phase. At the beginning of the second two-minute phase, the officer casually moved within two feet (personal distance) of the subject for both groups. For the experimental group only the intimate or 'severe crowding' condition (due to the inappropriate roles being played) occurred during the third two-minute phase: the officer moved to an eight-inch nose-to-nose distance from the subject, and then returned to the two-foot distance during the fourth two-minute phase. The two-foot distance was maintained throughout phases two, three and four for the control group. The police interviewer was instructed to maintain eye contact during all phases of the interaction. The student was positioned next to a wall which prevented him from moving back or escaping during the crowding condition.

The nonverbal behaviours exhibited by the subjects during the crowding condition were consistent with typical reactions of people experiencing inappropriate, intimate, interpersonal spacing. As the subject was increasingly crowded during the interview, his speech time and frequency became disrupted and disorganised, with an uneven, staccato pattern developing. Eye movements and gaze aversion increased, while few other facial reactions were displayed. Small, discrete head movements occurred, and head rotation/elevation movements increased. Subjects adopted positions to place their arms and hands between themselves and the interviewer, and there was a noticeable increase in hands-at-crotch positioning. Brief rotating head movements increased, while foot movements decreased.

These nonverbal behaviours were produced by a situational manipulation (that is, crowding) but were strikingly similar to those emphasised by Rozelle and Baxter's real police officers as the described behaviours indicating dispositional characteristics of guilt, suspicion and deception. Officers in the earlier study specified facial and vocal cues, arm and hand behaviour, posture and body orientation; they related nonverbal behaviours as being particularly reliable indices of these dispositions. At that time, the training course (at the police academy) required of all officers included instructions to stand close to the citizen and maintain maximal eye contact during such an interview. Thus, reliance on nonverbal behaviour has, in this role-specific setting, a high probability of miscommunicating intention, motivations and other dispositions from actor to observer. The observer, by not properly including his or her own behaviour as a significant part of the situation influencing the actor's nonverbal behaviour, inaccurately forms an impression of the actor in a highly reliable and confident manner.

Nonverbal Behaviour in Professional Settings: A Sample of Research Findings

Interviewing. Although the police–citizen encounter was brief, and involved rather extreme situational–proxemic variations with only a moderate amount of verbal exchange, it has elements similar to many professional, role-defined interactions. For example, the actor–observer distinction could be applied to the employment interview. In such an interaction, the interviewer could be considered the 'observer' or decoder evaluating the verbal and nonverbal acts of the interviewee who is the 'actor' or encoder.

In the authors' experience with the professional interview setting, the interviewer often makes an important, job-related decision regarding the interviewee based on dispositional attributions occurring as a result of behaviour observed during a 30- minute interview. Although the employment interview may be a typical experience for the interviewer during the working day, it is usually an infrequent and stressful one for the interviewee. This could increase the observer-dispositional bias, actor-situational-bias effect. The interviewer, in the role of observer, proceeds 'as usual', while the interviewee reacts in a highly sensitive manner to every verbal and nonverbal behaviour of the interviewer. Unaware that the very role of the interviewer is an important, immediate–situational cause of the interviewee's behaviours, the interviewer uses these same behaviours to infer long-term dispositional qualities to the interviewee–actor and may make a job-related decision on the basis of the impression formed. Thus, from a nonverbal communication perspective, the impression formed is, to varying degrees, inadvertently encoded by the interviewee–actor, and possibly misinterpreted in the decoding process on the part of the interviewer.

This miscommunication process may be particularly important during the initial stages of an interaction, since expectancies may be created that bias the remaining interaction patterns. Research indicates that first impressions are important in creating expectancies and evaluative judgements (and sometimes diagnoses) of people in interviewing, counselling, teaching, therapeutic and other professionally role-related interactions.

Zajonc (1980) states that evaluative judgements are often made in a fraction of a second on the basis of nonverbal cues in an initial encounter. Others have shown that a well-organised judgemental impression may be made in as little as four minutes. People who are in professional roles such as interviewing, counselling and teaching should constantly remind themselves of the influence they have on clients' nonverbal behaviour and not to rely on 'favourite' nonverbal behaviours as flawless indicators of dispositional characteristics.

Knowledge of potential effects of verbal and nonverbal behaviour can be useful in impression management techniques to create more effective communication in face-to-face interactions. For example, in a simulated employment interview setting, Washburn and Hakel (1973) demonstrated that when applicants were given a high level of nonverbal 'enthusiasm' by the interviewer (for instance, gazing, gesturing and smiling), the applicants were judged more favourably than those given a low level of interviewer enthusiasm.

Another study showed that when candidates received nonverbal approval during an employment interview, they were judged by objective observers to be more relaxed, more at ease and more comfortable than candidates who received nonverbal disapproval from the interviewer (Keenan, 1976).

Impression management strategies may also be utilised by the interviewee. For example, the American Psychological Association gives specific suggestions, based on research, to graduate school applicants to nonverbally communicate favourable qualities during an interview (Fretz and Stang, 1982). Research studies generally show that such nonverbal behaviours as high levels of gaze, combinations of paralinguistic cues, frequent head movement, frequent smiling, posture, voice loudness and personal appearance, affect impressions formed and evaluative judgements made by employment interviewers (Forbes and Jackson, 1980; Hollandsworth, Kazelskis, Stevens *et al.*, 1979; Young and Beier, 1977).

Caution should be advised before applying these specific behaviours, since qualifying factors have been reported. For example, one study reported that if an applicant avoids gazing at the interviewer, an applicant of high status will be evaluated more negatively than one of low status (Tessler and Sushelsky, 1978). Evidently, gaze aversion was expected, on the part of the interviewer, from a low-status applicant but not from a higher status one. Status differences and associated nonverbal behaviours have also been recognised in the military setting where physical appearance such as uniform markings clearly identify varying rank of the interactants (Hall, 1966).

Counselling and Therapy. Nonverbal impression management strategies also have been studied in counselling setting interactions. One study reported that counsellors who initiated more gestures and more actively changed posture, gaze and facial expression were judged to be more warm, agreeable, casual and energetic than those counsellors who restrained most of their nonverbal movements (Strong, Taylor, Bratton, *et al.*, 1971). However, these results were complicated by the finding that the attributes on the friendly–attractive dimension were associated with judgements of the counsellor being less serious, controlled and orderly.

Another study showed that, compared to a restrained nonverbal expression condition, counsellor smiling, gazing and pleasant tone of voice increased the effectiveness of the counsellor's verbal reinforcement (Bourget, 1977). Clients receiving these nonverbal behaviours reported relatively stronger feelings about themselves and their interest in relating to others. This impression management strategy (which was labelled 'delight'), also resulted in clients rating the counsellor's comments as being more informative and sensitive, while also remembering more of the counsellor's verbal feedback a week after the session.

Several studies have demonstrated that nonverbal communication skills are important in maximising the effectiveness of other factors in the counselling setting. Siegel (1980) found that the client's perceptions of the counsellor were most favourable when nonverbal expertise (defined as hand gestures, forward body lean and increased gaze) was combined with objective evidence, such as visibly displayed diplomas and certificates. Claiborn (1979) reported that nonverbal responsiveness (defined as paralinguistic cues, facial expressiveness, gaze, head nodding and gestures) combined with an interpretation mode of verbal intervention (as opposed to a restatement mode) produced the highest client ratings of counsellor expertise, trustworthiness and attractiveness.

Goss (1984) investigated the effects of a male therapists' attire and seating arrangement in observer's ratings of attractiveness, expertise and trustworthiness during an initial, pre-therapy interview. The therapist was judged most attractive when dressed casually and not seated behind a desk. Female judges rated the therapist lower on all three characteristics when he was seated behind the desk. These initial impressions were highly related to the judges' willingness to consult further with the therapist. Focusing on patient behaviour, Fisch, Frey and Hirsbrunner (1983) found relationships between nonverbal behaviour and severely depressed versus nearly recovered patients during doctor–patient interviews.

Another study showed that proxemics are important in the effectiveness of positive verbal versus neutral feedback on the part of the counsellor in a diet clinic (Greene, 1977). Clients complied with the counsellor's recommendations to diet for five weeks to a greater degree when positive verbal feedback (in the form of acceptance) was given in close proximity; neutral feedback in close proximity resulted in less adherence to recommendations. It should be noted that clients had to lose at least five pounds (2.2kg) to be included in the compliance group. The results were interpreted in terms of positive verbal feedback at close proximity being consistent with the counsellor role, whereas the neutral feedback under such proxemic conditions is inconsistent with this role. Inconsistency produced client suspiciousness regarding the integrity of the counsellor's behaviour and reduced the counsellor's influence. These results parallel the findings of Rozelle and Baxter (1978) in which encoded, inappropriate (as opposed to appropriate) nonverbal behaviours on the part of a citizen at either close or distant proximity to a police officer produced ratings of greater citizen deceptiveness and suspiciousness on the part of the observers.

In addition to the counselling area, a number of studies have investigated nonverbal behaviour in the physician–patient interaction setting (DiMatteo, 1979; Friedman, 1979). Results parallel those in counselling and therapeutic studies in that they demonstrate the significant impact of a variety of nonverbal behaviour categories, especially in how the physician is perceived by patients and/or observers (DiMatteo, Taranta, Friedman *et al.*, 1980; DiMatteo and Taranta, 1979; Harrigan and Rosenthal, 1983; Rand, 1981; Smith and Larsen, 1984).

Profile of Nonverbal Sensitivity. Rosenthal and his colleagues (Rosenthal, 1979; Rosenthal *et al.*, 1979) have provided an extensive set of investigations of nonverbal behaviour as skilled performance that apply to a variety of professional and social factors, both from an encoding and decoding perspective. They have developed an audiovisual procedure known as the PONS (Profile of Nonverbal Sensitivity) test by filming a young white female actress (a colleague) instructed to express 20 specific social emotional messages each falling in one of four categories: positive-dominant, positive-submissive, negative-dominant and negative-submissive.

Video recordings focused on the face only, the trunk only or the face and trunk, while the auditory position of the expressions were made 'content-free' either by randomly combining short segments of sound tracks or electronically by eliminating high-frequency sounds. Thus, 220 different two-second exposures were obtained by presenting each of the three body and two vocal channels alone and in combination (a total of 11) for each of the 20 expressions. Using the PONS test, administered to over 200 samples in the United States and other countries, these investigations have demonstrated the presence of stable individual variation in decoding ability (that is, matching interpretations with intended expressions) associated with age (younger samples are generally more accurate in interpreting vocal than visual cues), gender (women are more accurate), personality dimension (for instance, cognitively complex subjects perform better), profession (for instance, actors are better than clinicians), professional effectiveness (physicians and teachers judged more effective do better) and many other variables.

They have also examined encoding effectiveness by recording several groups as they expressed intended messages. These recordings were then decoded, either by other members of the same sample (for example, physician groups) or by standard raters. Encoding effectiveness has also been shown to reflect individual differences and to vary with many of the variables associated with decoding effectiveness, although the correlation between encoding and decoding skill often varies, and self-reported effectiveness appears to relate poorly with performance measures.

Perhaps most interesting, Rosenthal *et al.* (1979) have found that in eight samples where re-testing was done, performance on the second decoding test was substantially improved over initial performance. Beyond this, improvement scores were shown to relate to self-reports of interpersonal effectiveness, especially with the opposite sex.

This brief sampling of empirical results provides impressive evidence for the importance of nonverbal behaviour in managing and forming impressions in role-defined settings. However, these results also reveal that nonverbal behaviour in the form of kinesics interacts with other nonverbal categories such as proxemics, paralanguage, physical characteristics and environmental factors. For example, although this creates a rather complex formula for applications, all of Knapp's seven dimensions are important to consider in developing communication skills in the various contexts of role-defined interactions that one experiences.

A Specific Example of Current Research and Application: International Politics

In the final section of this chapter, a programme of research will be presented briefly that illustrates an attempt to identify systematically certain nonverbal behaviours associated with specific intentions of the communicator (encoder), and to then apply these findings to develop better skills in interpreting (decoding) observed behaviour of others (Druckman *et al.*, 1982). The context selected for this research is international politics. This is an area that encompasses a broad range of situational, cultural, personal and social factors and thus attempts to deal with the complexity of nonverbal expression and interpretation. It is also an area which contains elements similar to a variety of everyday experiences encountered by a broad range of people in professional and social interactions.

Laboratory Research

The initial research project involved a role-playing study in which upper-level university students were instructed to play the role of a foreign ambassador being interviewed in a press conference setting. A set of pertinent issues were derived from United Nations transcripts and were presented to the subjects in detail. After studying the issues, subjects were randomly assigned to one of three intention conditions which directed them to express their country's position on the issues in either an honest, deceptive or evasive fashion. Examples of honest, deceptive and evasive arguments and discussion points were presented to the subjects to help prepare them for the interview.

A formal 15-minute video-taped interview was conducted between the 'ambassador' and a trained actor playing the role of a press interviewer. An informal seven-minute post-interview discussion was also video-taped in which the subject was asked to be 'himself' and discuss his activities at the university. It is important to note that the subject-ambassadors were not aware that the purpose of the study was to assess nonverbal behaviour exhibited by them during the interview. Thus, the study dealt with 'informative' rather than consciously controlled 'communication' acts as described by Ekman and Friesen (1969) and discussed by Dittman (1978). Also, the interviewer was unaware of whether the subject was in the honest, deceptive or evasive intention condition. Ten subjects served in each of the conditions.

The video-taped interviews were coded by an elaborate process involving 200 student volunteers carefully trained to reliably observe specific channels of nonverbal behaviour patterns produced by subjects in the honest, deceptive and evasive conditions.

Research findings. Among the detailed results presented by Druckman *et al.* (1982), several general findings are appropriate for this discussion. One set of analyses revealed that honest, deceptive and evasive subjects could be classified accurately solely on the basis of their nonverbal behaviours. Using ten nonverbal behaviours (for instance, head-shaking, gaze time at interviewer, leg movements and so on), 96.6 per cent of the subjects were classified correctly as being honest, deceptive or evasive. In another segment of the interview, three nonverbal behaviours (for instance, leg movements, gaze time at interviewer and object-fidgeting) were accurate in 77 per cent of the cases in detecting honest, deceptive or evasive intentions of the subject.

These computer-generated results were in striking contrast to another set of judgements produced by three corporate executives selected on the basis of their experience and expertise in 'dealing effectively with people'. These executives viewed the tapes and then guessed if the subject had been in the honest, deceptive or evasive condition. Results indicated that the experts correctly classified the subject–ambassadors in only 43, 30 and 27 per cent of the cases, respectively. Thus, even 'experts' would appear to benefit from further training and skill development in interpreting nonverbal behaviours — and actually may be in special need of such training (DePaulo *et al.*, 1984).

Another set of analyses revealed significant shifts in nonverbal behaviour patterns when the subject changed from the ambassador role to being 'himself' during the informal post-interview period. Generally, subjects showed more suppressed, constrained behaviour when playing the role of ambassador: for example, significantly fewer facial displays, less head-nodding, fewer body swivels and less frequent statements occurred during the interview than in the post-interview period. It would appear that the same person displays different patterns and levels of nonverbal behaviour depending upon the role that is being communicated. Also, different patterns of behaviour occurred in the three, five-minute segments of the formal interview. Thus, even when a person is playing the same role, different behaviours emerge during the course of an interaction. These may be due to factors of adaptation, stress, familiarity, relaxation or fatigue.

Yet another set of analyses using subjects' responses to a set of post-interview questions indicated that certain patterns of nonverbal behaviours were related to feelings the subject had during the interview (for example, stress, relaxation, confidence, apprehension), and that these patterns were related to the intention condition assigned to the subject. Evasive and honest subjects displayed behaviours indicating involvement, while evasive and deceptive subjects displayed nonverbal indication of stress and tension. Subjects in all three conditions displayed behaviour patterns related to expressed feelings of confidence and effectiveness.

Training the Decoder. Even though the results of this study were complex, they were organised into a training programme designed to improve the observer's ability to distinguish among honest, deceptive and evasive intentions of subjects playing this role. Three basic programmes were presented to different groups of decoders and represented three levels of instruction, ranging from general to specific information regarding nonverbal indicators of intention. Results showed that accuracy of judgement in distinguishing between honest, deceptive and evasive presentations improved as the specificity and applied organisation of the instructional materials increased.

Strategies for Interpreting Nonverbal Behaviour: An Application of Experimental Results

The studies reviewed above support the assumption that gestures, facial expressions and other nonverbal behaviours convey meaning. However, while adding value to interpretation in general, an understanding of the nonverbal aspects of behaviour may not transfer directly to specific settings. Meaning must be established within the context of interest: for example, the nonverbal behaviour observed during the course of a speech, interview or informal conversation.

Building on the earlier laboratory work, a plan has been developed for deriving plausible inferences about intentions and psychological or physical states of political leaders. The plan is a structure for interpretation: it is a valuable *tool* for the professional policy analyst; it is a useful *framework* for the interested observer of significant events. In the following sections, themes and techniques for analysis are discussed, and the special features of one particular context, that of international politics, is emphasised.

Themes for Analysis

Moving pictures shown on video or film are panoramas of quickly changing actions, sounds and expressions. Just where to focus one's attention is a basic analytical problem. Several leads are suggested by frameworks constructed to guide the research cited above. Providing a structure for analysis, the frameworks emphasise two general themes, namely, focus on combinations of nonverbal behaviours and take contextual features into account.

While coded separately, the nonverbal behaviours can be combined for analysis of total displays. Patterns of behaviours then provide a basis for inferences about feelings or intentions. The patterns may take several forms: one consists of linear combinations of constituent behaviours, as when gaze time, leg movements and object fidgeting are used in equations to identify probable intentions; a second form is correlated indicators or clusters, such as the pattern of trunk swivels, rocking movements, headshaking and head-nodding shown by subjects attempting to withhold information about their 'nation's' policy; another form is behaviours that co-occur within the same time period as was observed for deceivers in the study presented above — for example, a rocking/nodding/shaking cluster was observed during interviews with deceptive 'ambassadors'.

Patterned movements are an important part of the total situation. By anchoring the movements to feelings and intentions, one can get an idea of their meaning. But there are other sources of explanation for what is observed. These sources may be referred to as context. Included as context are the semi-fixed objects in the setting (for instance, furniture), the other people with whom the subject interacts and the nature of the discourse that transpires. The proposition that context greatly influences social interaction/behaviour comes alive in Rapoport's (1982) recent treatment of the meaning of the built environment.

Constraining influences of other people on exhibited expressions are made apparent in Duncan's (1983) detailed analyses of conversational turntaking. Relationships between verbal statements and nonverbal behaviour are the central concern in the analyses of stylised enactments provided by Druckman *et al.* (1982). Each of these works is a state-of-the-art analysis. Together, they are the background for developing systems that address the questions of *what* to look for and *how* to use the observations/codes for interpretation. Highlighted here is a structure for interpreting material on the tapes.

It is obvious that the particular intention–interpretation relationships of interest vary with particular circumstances. Several issues are particularly salient within the area of international politics. Of interest might be questions like: what is the state of health of the leader (or spokesman), to what degree are his (her) statements honestly expressive of his (her) true beliefs (or actual policy), how committed is the person to the position expressed, how fully consolidated and secure is the person's political position?

Knowing where to focus attention is a first step in assessment. A particular theme is emphasised in each of the political issues mentioned above. Signs of failing health are suggested by incongruities or inconsistencies in verbal and nonverbal behaviours, as well as between different nonverbal channels. Deception is suggested by excessive body activity, as well as deviations from baseline data. Strong commitment to policy is revealed in increased intensity of behaviours expressed in a variety of channels. The careful recording of proxemic activity or spatial relationships provides clues to political status. Biographical profiles summarise co-varying clusters of facial expressions and body movements. Each of these themes serves to direct an analyst's attention to *relationships* (for health indicators and profiles), to *particular nonverbal channels* (for deception and status indicators) or to *amount* as in the case of commitment.

Knowing specifically what to look at is the second step in assessment. Results of a number of experiments suggest particular behaviours. These provide multiple signs whose meaning is revealed in conjunction with the themes noted above. Illustrative indicators and references in each category are the following:

1. Health indicators:

(a) Pain: furrowed brow and raised eyelids; change in vocal tone and higher pitch (Ekman and Friesen, 1975);

(b) Depression: hand to body motions, increased self-references and extended periods of silence (Aronson and Weintraub, 1972);

(c) Irritability: more forced smiling (McClintock and Hunt, 1975), fewer positive head nods (Mehrabian, 1971);

(d) Tension: increased spontaneous movement (Mehrabian and Ksionzky, 1972), faster eyeblinking, self-adaptive gestures (for body tension) (McClintock and Hunt, 1975);

(e) Stress: flustered speech as indicated by repetitions, corrections, use of 'ah' or 'you know', rhythm disturbances (Baxter and Rozelle, 1975; Kasl and Mahl, 1965), abrupt changes in behaviour (Hermann, 1979), increased eye movements and gaze aversion in an otherwise immobile facial display, increased head rotation/elevation, increased placement of hands in front of the body (Baxter and Rozelle, 1975);

(f) General state: verbal/nonverbal inconsistencies where different messages are sent in the two channels (Mehrabian, 1972).

2. Deception indicators:

(a) Direct deception: speech errors as deviations from baseline data (Mehrabian, 1971), tone of voice (DePaulo, Zuckerman and Rosenthal, 1980), fidgeting with objects, less time spent looking at other than during a baseline period, patterns of rocking, head-shaking and nodding movements varying together (co-ordinated body movements) (Druckman *et al.*, 1982);

(b) Indirect deception (evasion): more leg movements during periods of silence (when subject feels less assertive), frequent gazes elsewhere especially during periods of stress, frequent headshaking during early periods in the interaction, increasing trend of self-fidgeting throughout the interaction (Druckman *et al.*, 1982; McClintock and Hunt, 1975).

3. Commitment to policies:

(a) Commitment: increased use of 'allness' terms (Hermann, 1977), increased redundancy, more trunk swivels, more time spent looking at (versus looking away from) the other (Druckman *et al.*, 1982);

(b) Persuasiveness (impact on others): increased intensity in voice, increased object (other) — focused movements (Freedman, 1972), more facial activity and gesturing, increased headnodding, fewer self-manipulations, reduced reclining angles (Mehrabian, 1972; Washburn and Hakel, 1973);

(c) Credibility (impact on others): sustained gazing at short distances (Exline and Eldridge, 1967; Hemsley and Doob, 1975), relaxed vocalisations (Addington, 1971)

4. Political status:

(a) Relative status: non-reciprocated touching, eye contact at closer distances for higher-status members, more frequent use of words suggesting distance from people and objects (Frank, 1977) hand and neck relaxation, sideways lean, reclining posture, arm-leg position asymmetry (Mehrabian, 1972);

(b) Changes in status: increased physical distance from colleagues (Dosey and Meisels, 1969), increased signs of psychological withdrawal from situations (outward-directed gestures, changed postures) for reduced status (Mehrabian, 1968), more frequent appearances at State functions for enhanced status.

Techniques for Analysis

Whereas patterns of nonverbal behaviour are the basis for interpretation, it is the separate behaviours which are the constitutents of the displays. A first step is to code specific, well-defined movements and expressions. Advances in technique make possible the efficient coding of a large variety of behaviours. Particularly relevant is a subset of nonverbal behaviours chosen on the basis of high reliability, as determined by independent coders, and importance, in terms of distinguishing among intentions and emotional states. Included in this list are the following: gaze time at interviewer or other person, leg movements, object fidgeting, speech errors, speaking frequency, rocking movements, head nodding, illustrator gestures and foot movements. These are some of the movements or vocalisations coded directly from videotapes of laboratory subjects (experiments cited above) and world leaders.

Efficiency is gained by training coders to be channel specialists. Small groups are trained to focus their attention on one channel — vocalisations, eyes, face, body, legs or spatial arrangements. Frequencies are recorded for some measures (for instance, leg movements); for others, the coder records time (for example, gaze at interviewer, speaking time). Further specialisation is obtained by assigning the different groups to specific segments of the tapes. Such a division of labour speeds the process, increases reliability and preserves the coders for other tasks. A set of 25 nonverbal behaviours shown by subjects in 30, 20-minute tapes was coded in about three weeks, each individual coder contributing only two hours of effort.

The procedures define a coding scheme or notation system for processing video material. Computer-assisted analysis would facilitate the transforming of nonverbal measures into profiles of selected world leaders. Here, one becomes more interested in characteristic postures or movements than in particular psychological or physical states. The emphasis is on idiosyncratic styles of leaders, condition-ed as they are by situational factors. Using the nonverbal notation system, these styles can be represented as animated displays. New developments in interactive videodisc technologies expand the range of programming options (Currier, 1983). They also contribute tools for creative exploration of movement and expression control, such as manipulating the display to depict styles in different situations (Badler and Smoliar, 1979).

The list of behaviours is one basis for structuring the analysis. Another basis is a more general category system that encompasses a range of situations, pur-poses and verbal statements, as well as types of displayed nonverbal behaviours. Sufficient footage in each category makes possible the tasks of charting trends, making comparisons and developing profiles. It also contributes to inventory management: systematic categorising and indexing of materials aids in the task of retrieving relevant types from archival collections.

Multiple measurements provide alternative indicators that may be useful when all channels are not available to the observer (such as leg and feet movements for a speaker who stands behind a podium, eye movements for an actor seen from a distance). They also provide complementary indicators, bolstering one's con-fidence in the inferences made. And, for the time-sensitive analyst, a manageable subset of nonverbal behaviours can be identified for 'on the spot' commentary.

Systematic Comparisons. Focusing on the individual foreign leader, the nonver-bal indicators can be used to build profiles. It is evident that such an approach emphasises Allport's (1961) concept of morphogenic analysis and stresses the analogy of expressive behaviour as personal idiom. This strategy of systematic comparison is designed to increase an analyst's understanding of his 'subject'. This is done by tracking the displays exhibited by selected personalities across situations and in conjunction with verbal statements.

Comparisons would be made in several ways: (1) examine deviations from baseline data established for each personality (for instance, speech errors); (2) compare nonverbal displays for the same personality in different situations (for example, within or outside home country; formal or informal settings); and (3) compare displays for different types of verbal statements (for example, defence of position, policy commitment). These analyses highlight consistencies and inconsistencies at several levels — between situations, between verbal and non-verbal channels, and within different nonverbal channels. They also alert the analyst to changes in nonverbal activity: being aware of changes from a baseline period would give one a better understanding of relatively unique expressive behaviour. Further analysis consists of comparing different personalities in similar situations or dealing with similar subject matter.

The value of these comparisons is that they contribute to the development of a system of movement representation similar to the notation and animation systems described by Badler and Smoliar (1979). Extracted from the data are sets of co-ordinated movements which may change over time and situations. The co-ordinated movements can be represented in animated graphic displays. Illuminated by such displays are 'postural' differences within actors across time and between actors. When associated with events and context, the observations turn on the issue of how the feelings and intentions which are evoked by different situations are represented in body movement. When compared to displays by actors in other cultural settings, the observations are relevant to the question: what is the contribution of culture to observed nonverbal displays?

Several analytical strategies enable an investigator to get to know his subject or group. Each strategy formalises the idea of 'following a subject around'. Extended coverage provides an opportunity to assemble baseline data for comparisons. It also permits execution of within-subject analytic designs for systematic comparison of displays observed in different situations and occasions, as well as when addressing different topics. These strategies enable an analyst to discriminate more precisely the meaning of various nonverbal displays.

Extensive video footage makes possible quite sophisticated analyses of leaders' behaviours. Relationships are highlighted from comparisons of responses to questions intended to arouse varying levels of stress. Profiles are constructed from the combinations of expressions and movements seen over time. Predictive accuracy of the form 'is he telling the truth?' is estimated from behaviours coded in situations where a subject's intentions are known; namely, does the subset of behaviours discriminate between an honest, evasive and deceptive statement? Contributing to an enhanced analytical capability, these results reduce dependence on notation systems developed in settings removed from the critical situations of interest. They would also contribute information relevant to time-sensitive requests.

Time-sensitive Requests. Demand for current assessments often place the analyst on the spot. He is frequently asked to provide interpretations without the benefits of penetrating analysis, extensive video footage or hindsight. Indeed, these are the conditions often present for both technical specialist and layman. Scheibe (1979) notes that the informed observer (whom he calls the sagacious observer) relies on good memory for past characteristic patterns and astute observation of departure from the 'typical'. Under these conditions, notation systems are especially useful. They provide the analyst with a structure for focusing attention on relevant details. Determined largely on the basis of what is known, the relevant details are part of a larger coding system whose validity is previously established.

Serving to increase the analyst's confidence in his judgements, the codes (relevant details) highlight where to focus attention and what to look at. Examples include the following.

Abrupt Changes. Readily detectable from limited data, abrupt changes may take the form of incongruities between different nonverbal channels (face and body) or increased intensity of behaviours expressed in a number of channels. The former may be construed as signs of failing health; the latter often indicates a strong commitment to policies.

Leaks. Regarded as signs of deception, leaks take the form of excessive activity in one channel (body) combined with reduced activity in another (face) (Ekman and Friesen, 1974). Based on an 'hydraulic model' analogy, the concept of leakage describes the consequences of attempts by a subject to control his facial expressions during deception — to wit, the poker face.

A study designed by the authors was intended as a test of the leakage hypothesis. Subjects in one condition were asked to control their facial expressions during a deceptive communication; those in another condition were asked to control their body movements. Both conditions were compared to an earlier session where subjects were not instructed to control expressions or movements during deception. More body movements in the 'control-face' condition and more facial expressions in the 'control-body' condition than in the earlier session would support the leakage hypothesis.

Micro-momentary Expressions (MMEs). Regarded as universal expressions, MMEs are the muscle activities that underlie primary emotions (happiness, sadness, surprise, anger, fear, disgust, interest) and information-processing stages (informative seeking, pre-articulation processing, response selection). With the aid of special instrumentation, workers have been able to identify quite precisely the muscle clusters associated with particular emotions (Ekman, Friesen and Ancoli, 1980) or processing stages (Druckman, Karis and Donchin, 1983; Karis, Druckman, Lissak, *et al.,* 1984).

Illustrated above are the kinds of observations that can be used for inferences from limited data; for example, behaviours that change quickly (MMEs) or obviously (incongruities), and those that occur within the time frame of a statement (leaks). However, useful as these indicators are, they are only a part of the story. Missing are the cultural and contextual influences that shape what is observed. These influences are discovered through careful analysis of leaders' behaviour in the settings of interest.

Context for Nonverbal Displays

The comparisons described above emphasise the value of learning about people as they move through space and time. Added to these emphases is information about context, particularly how individuals respond to others. Of special interest are responses to direct questions asked usually by interviewers. Interviewers can determine the atmosphere of a situation, as the authors discovered in a preliminary analysis of tapes showing Castro being interviewed at the Havana Conference of Nonaligned Nations.

Three types of questions were shown to arouse different levels of tension in the person being interviewed: building rapport or 'breaking the ice' (for instance, 'Are you considering writing your memoirs?'), nonchallenging policy-related questions (for instance, 'In what form would you welcome United States investment in Cuba?'), and challenging or provocative questions such as 'Are you (Castro) now sending troops into Rhodesia?'

Having isolated different levels of arousal, a next step would consist of coding the nonverbal behaviours seen in response to the questions. Results could provide nonverbal indicators of stress: differences within a leader in response to varying levels of tension, and differences between leaders in their response to stress. These indicators would be incorporated in the notation and animation systems described above.

The example discussed above emphasises the interpretation of expressive nonverbal behaviour as a social skill. This approach focuses upon 'knowing' where to direct attention, 'what' to look for, and 'how to apply' heuristics of interpretation which prove useful. As with other types of skills, it assumes that 'practice perfects' and 'internalised standards evolve'. Perhaps one of the most problematic aspects of the example, however, is the need for observational opportunities and materials, especially audiovisual recordings, to be available for analysis — and, perhaps above all, reasonable means of external corroboration and feedback.

Systematic analysis of foreign video can be designed to fill gaps in one's understanding. Most notable is the way that culture shapes the nonverbal displays shown by national leaders. Culture has strong effects on facial expressions, namely, what is allowed, where and when. Referred to as 'display rules', effects include amplifying, deamplifying, neutralising, blending or masking the feelings aroused in certain situations. These regulating effects have been demonstrated for members of Western European, Middle Eastern, Latin American and some Oriental societies. While showing the importance of culture, the results do not yet address distinctive expressions manifested by members of other cultures. (A review of these and other findings can be found in Druckman *et al.*, 1982; and Harper *et al.*, 1978.)

Televised international conferences provide an excellent opportunity for exploring cultural effects. Leaders from different societies often appear in similar situations. They may even appear simultaneously at the same conference. These situations can be exploited for comparison by focusing attention on those facial expressions (or gazes, distance, touching) found to reflect cultural learning. Going a step further, attempts to separate cultural from idiosyncratic expressions would be useful in establishing two types of baselines, one for the culture, another for the person. Being able to distinguish among universal, cultural, and idiosyncratic expressions or movements enhances one's interpretive skills, especially in situations where on-the-spot commentary is required.

Summary and Conclusions

Considering the large number of full-length books published on nonverbal behaviour, the present chapter has only sampled highlights of this important form of communication. Beginning with an organisational overview and historical perspective, the discussion covered general issues, theoretical and methodological frameworks, and provided more specific examples of research findings and applications. As the chapter has demonstrated, there is a wealth of information generated from scientific inquiry which reveals the significant impact of nonverbal behaviour on communication, yet this body of knowledge is incomplete and often complex.

The authors have argued that nonverbal behaviour, as a communication skill, is meaningful only if the context of behaviour is taken into account. Incomplete or narrow perspectives regarding others' or one's own behaviour may lead to misinterpretation of actions observed or performed. On the other hand, careful and reliable applications of nonverbal behaviour can enrich and enlighten one's understanding and control of communication in a variety of situation, role and cultural settings.

In addition to further experimental work and replication of results, one direction for future research may be to study, in greater detail, the accomplishments and strategies of proven experts in both performance and interpretation of nonverbal behaviour in the communication process. For example, when considering nonverbal behaviour as skilled performance, aspects of style, expertise and expression are stressed. The ways in which such crafted performances are accomplished and their effects assessed should aid in the training and development processes as well as in directing future experimental research. However, regardless of the specific approach, nonverbal behaviour must be examined rigorously by a variety of laboratory and real-life perspectives designed to provide a systematic convergence of valid, reliable and useful information for more meaningful understanding and application of this important form of communication.

References

Addington, D.W. (1971) 'The Effect of Vocal Variation on Ratings of Source Credibility', *Speech Mono.*, *35*, 242–7

Allport, G. (1961) *Pattern and Growth in Personality*, Holt, Rinehart and Winston, New York
—— and Vernon, P. (1933) *Studies in Expressive Movement*, Macmillan, New York

Argyle, M (1967) *The Psychology of Interpersonal Behaviour*, Penguin, London
—— (1969) *Social Interaction*, Aldine-Atherton, New York
—— and Cook, M. (1976) *Gaze and Mutual Gaze*, Cambridge University Press, New York
—— and Dean, J. (1965) 'Eye-Contact, Distance and Affiliation', *Sociometry, 28*, 289–304
—— and Kendon, A. (1967) 'The Experimental Analysis of Social Performance', in L. Berkowitz (ed.), *Advances in Experimental Social Psychology.*, Academic Press, New York

Aronson, H. and Weintraub, W. (1972) 'Personal Adaptation as Reflected in Verbal Behaviour' in A.W. Siegman and B. Pope (eds.), *Studies in Dyadic Communication*, Pergamon, New York

Badler, N.I. and Smoliar, S.W. (1979) 'Digital Representation of Human Movement', *Computing*

Surveys, 11, 19–38

Bartlett, F. (1958) *Thinking: An Experimental and Social Study,* Basic Books, New York

Baxter, J.C. (1970) 'Interpersonal Spacing in Natural Settings', *Sociometry, 33,* 444–56

——— and Rozelle, R.M. (1975) 'Nonverbal Expression as a Function of Crowding During a Simulated Police-citizen Encounter', *J. of Per. and Soc. Psy., 32,* 40–54

Bilodeau, E. (ed.) (1966) *Acquisition of Skill,* Academic Press, New York

Birdwhistell, R. (1952) *Introduction to Kinesics,* Foreign Service Institute, Washington DC

——— (1970) *Kinesics and Context,* University of Pennsylvania Press, Philadelphia

Bourget, L.G.C. (1977) 'Delight and Information Specificity as Elements of Positive Interpersonal Feedback (doctoral dissertation, Boston University Graduate School), *Dissertation Abstracts International, 38,* 1946B–1947B, (University Microfilms no. 77-21, p. 580)

Bulwer, J. (1644/1974) *Chirologia,* Southern Illinois University Press, Carbondale, Illinois

Claiborn, C.D. (1979) 'Effects of Counselor Interpretation, Restatement, and Nonverbal Behaviour on Perceptions of the Counselor and the Counselor's Ability to Influence, (doctoral dissertation, University of Missouri-Columbia) *Dissertation Abstracts International, 39,* 505B, University Microfilms no. 7906855(b)

Cole, P. (1984) 'Display Rules and the Socialisation of Affect Displays' in G. Ziven (ed.), *The Development of Expressive Behaviour Biology-Environment Interactions,* Academic Press, New York

Collett, P. (1971) 'Training Englishmen in the Nonverbal Behaviour of Arabs', *Inter'l. J. of Psy., 6,* 209–15

Currier, R.L. (1983) 'Interactive Videodisc Learning Systems', *High Tech., 3,* 51–9

Darwin, C. (1872) *The Expression of Emotion in Man and Animals,* John Murray, London

Davis, M. (1984) 'Nonverbal Behaviour and Psychotherapy: Process Research' in H. Wolfgang (ed.), *Nonverbal Behaviour: Perspectives, Applications, Intercultural Insights,* C.J. Hogrefe Inc., New York, pp. 203–29

DePaulo, B.M., Zuckerman, M. and Rosenthal, R. (1980) 'Detecting Deception: Modality Effects' in L. Wheeler (ed.), *Review of Personality and Social Psychology,* vol. 1., Sage, Beverly Hills

——— Stone, J.I. and Lassiter, G.D. (1984) 'Deceiving and Detecting Deceit' in B.R. Schlenker (ed.), *The Self in Social Life,* McGraw-Hill, New York

Deutsch, F. (1952) 'Analytic Posturology', *The Psychoa. Quar., 21,* 196–214

——— (1959) 'Correlations of Verbal and Nonverbal Communication in Interviews Elicited by Associative Anamnesis', *Psychoso. Med., 21,* 123–30

DiMatteo, M.R. (1979) 'Nonverbal Skill and the Physician-patient Relationship' in R. Rosenthal (ed.), *Skill in Nonverbal Behaviour,* Oelgeschlager, Gunn and Hain, Cambridge, Massachusetts

——— and Taranta, A. (1979) 'Nonverbal Communication and Physician-patient Rapport: An Empirical Study', *Professional Psychology, 10*(4), 540–7

——— Taranta, A., Friedman, H.S., *et al.* (1980) 'Predicting Patient Satisfaction From Physicians' Nonverbal Communication Skills', *Medical Care, 18,* 376–87

Dittman, A.T. (1972) *Interpersonal Messages of Emotion,* Springer, New York

——— (1978) 'The Role of Body Movement in Communication' in A.W. Siegman, and S. Feldstein (eds.), *Nonverbal Behaviour and Communication,* Lawrence Erlbaum Associates, Hilldale, New Jersey

Dorsey, M.A. and Meisels, M. (1969) 'Personal Space and Self Protection', *J. of Pers. and Soc. Psy., 11,* 93–7

Druckman, D., Rozelle, R. and Baxter, J. (1982) *Nonverbal Communication: Survey, Theory, and Research,* Sage Publications, Beverly Hills

——— Karis, D. and Donchin, E. (1983) 'Information-processing in Bargaining: Reactions to an Opponent's Shift in Concession Strategy' in R. Tietz (ed.), *Aspiration Levels in Bargaining and Economic Decisionmaking,* Springer-Verlag, Berlin

Duncan, S.D. (1969) 'Nonverbal Communication', *Psy. Bull., 72,* 118–37

——— (1972) 'Some Signals and Rules for Taking Speaking Turns in Conversations', *J. of Pers. and Soc. Psy., 23* 283–92

——— (1983) 'Speaking Turns: Studies in Structure and Individual Differences' in J.M. Wiemann and R.P Harrison (eds.), *Nonverbal Interaction,* Sage, Beverly Hills

——— and Fiske, D.W. (1977) *Face to Face Interaction: Research, Methods, and Theory,* Lawrence Erlbaum, Hillsdale, New Jersey

Ekman, P. and Friesen, W. (1969) 'The Repertoire of Nonverbal Behavior: Categories, Origins,

Usage, and Coding', *Semiotica, 1,* 49–98

———— (1974) 'Detecting Deception From the Body or Face', *J. of Pers. and Soc. Psy., 39,* 228–98

———— (1975) *Unmasking the Face: A Guide to Recognizing Emotions from Facial Clues,* Prentice-Hall, Englewood Cliffs, N.J.

———— Friesen, W., and Ellsworth, P. (1972) *Emotion in the Human Face,* Pergamon Press, New York

———— and Oster, H. (1979) 'Facial Expression of Emotion' in M. Rosenzweig (ed.), *Annual Review of Psychology,* Annual Reviews Inc., Standford, pp. 527–54

———— Friesen, W.V. and Ancoli, S. (1980) 'Facial Signs of Emotional Experience', *J. of Pers. and Soc. Psy., 39,* 1125–34

Exline, R.V. and Eldridge, C. (1967) 'Effects of Two Patterns of a Speaker's Visual Behavior Upon the Perception of the Authenticity of His Verbal Messsage', presented at the meeting of the Eastern Psychological Association, Boston

Feldman, S. (1959) *Mannerisms of Speech and Gestures in Everyday Life,* International Universities Press, New York

Fisch, H.U., Frey, S. and Hirsbrunner, H.P. (1983) 'Analyzing Nonverbal Behaviour in Depression', *J. Abn. Psy., 92*(3), 307–18

Forbes, R.J. and Jackson, P.R. (1980) 'Nonverbal Behaviour and the Outcome of Selection Interviews', *J. of Occup. Psy., 53,* 65–72

Frank, R.S. (1977) 'Nonverbal and Paralinguistic Analysis of Political Behaviour: The First McGovern-Humphrey California Primary Debate, in M.G. Hermann (ed.), *A Psychological Examination of Political Leaders,* John Wiley, New York

Freedman, R. (1972) 'The Analysis of Movement Behaviour During the Clinical Interview' in A.W. Siegman and B. Pope (eds.), *Studies in Dyadic Communication,* Pergamon, New York

Fretz, B.R. and Stang, D.J. (1982) *Preparing for Graduate Study in Psychology: Not for Seniors Only!* American Psychogical Association, Washington

Freud, S. (1905/1938) 'Psychopathology of Everyday Life' in A.A. Brill (ed.), *The Basic Writings of Sigmund Freud,* Modern Library, New York

———— (1924) *A General Introduction to Psychoanalysis.* Doubleday, Garden City

Friedman, H. (1979) 'The Concept of Skill in Nonverbal Communciation: Implications for Understanding Social Interaction' in R. Rosenthal (ed.), *Skill in Nonverbal Communication: Individual Differences,* Oelgeschlager, Gunn and Hain, Cambridge, Massachusetts

Gentner, D. and Grudin, J. (1985) 'The Evolution of Mental Metaphors in Psychology: A 90-year Perspective', *Amer. Psy, 40,* 181–92

Glashow, S., (1980) 'Toward a Unified Theory: Threads in a Tapestry', *Sci., 210,* 1319–23

Goffman, E. (1959) *The Presentation of Self in Everyday Life,* Doubleday Anchor Books, Garden City

———— (1969) *Strategic Interaction,* University of Pennsylvania Press, Philadelphia

Goss, C.S. (1984) 'Therapeutic Influence as a Function of Therapist Attire and the Seating Arrangement in an Initial Interview', *J. of Clin. Psy., 40*(1), 52–7

Greene, L.R. (1977) 'Effects of Verbal Evaluative Feedback and Interpersonal Distance on Behavioural Compliance', *J. of Coun. Psy., 24*(1), 10–14

Hager, J.C. and Ekman, P. (1979) 'Long-distance Transmission of Facial Affect Signals', *Etho. and Sociobiol., 1,* 77–82

Hall, E.T. (1959) *The Silent Language,* Doubleday, New York

———— (1966) *The Hidden Dimension,* Doubleday, New York

Hargie, O., Saunders, C. and Dickson, D. (1981) *Social Skills in Interpersonal Communication,* Croom Helm Ltd, Beckenham

Harper, R.G., Weins, A.N. and Matarazzo, J.D. (1978) *Nonverbal Communication: The State of the Art,* John Wiley, New York

Harrigan, J.A. and Rosenthal, R. (1983) 'Physicians' Head and Body Positions as Determinants of Perceived Rapport', *J. Appl. Soc. Psy., 13*(6), 496–509

Hemsley, G.D. and Doob, A.N. (1975) 'Effect of Looking Behavior on Perceptions of a Communicator's Credibility', presented at the meeting of the American Psychological Association, Chicago

Hermann, M.G. (1977) 'Verbal Behaviour of Negotiators in Periods of High and Low Stress' in M.G. Hermann (ed.) *A Psychological Examination of Political Leaders,* Free Press, New York

———— (1979) 'Indicators of Stress in Policymakers During Foreign Policy Crises', *Poli. Psy., 1,* 27–46

Hollandsworth, J.G., Jr., Kazelskis, R., Stevens, J., *et al.* (1979) 'Relative Contributions of Verbal, Articulative, and Nonverbal Communication to Employment Decisions in the Job Interview Setting',

Personnel Psy., *32*, 359–67

Izard, C. (1971) *The Face of Emotion*, Appleton-Century-Crofts, New York

Jones, A.P., Rozelle, R.M. and Svyantek, D.J. (1985) 'Organizational Climate: An Environmental Affordances Approach', unpublished manuscript, University of Houston

Jones, E.E. and Nisbett, R.E. (1972) 'The Actor and the Observer: Divergent Perceptions of the Causes of Behaviour' in E.E. Jones, D.E. Kanouse, H.H. Kelley, *et al.* (eds.), *Attribution: Perceiving the Causes of Behaviour*, General Learning Press, Morristown, New Jersey

────── and Thibaut, J. (1958) 'Interaction Goals as Bases of Influence in Interpersonal Perception' in R. Taguiri and L. Petrullo (eds.), *Person Perception and Interpersonal Behaviour*, Stanford University Press, Stanford

────── and Wortman, C. (1973) *Ingratiation: An Attributional Approach*, General Learning Press, Morristown, NJ

Karis, D., Druckman, D., Lissak, R., *et al.* (1984) 'A Psychophysiological Analysis of Bargaining: ERPs and Facial Expressions' in R. Karrer, J. Cohen and P. Tueting (eds.), *Brain and Information: Event-Related Potentials*, Annals of the New York Academy of Sciences, volume 425, New York Academy of Sciences, New York

Kasl, S.V. and Mahl, G.F. (1965) 'The Relationships of Disturbances and Hesitations in Spontaneous Speech to Anxiety', *J. of Per. and Soc. Psy.*, *1*, 425–33

Keenan, A. (1976) 'Effects of Nonverbal Behaviour of Interviewers on Candidates Performance', *J. of Occup. Psy.*, *49*, 171–6

Kendon, A. (1981) 'The Study of Gesture: Some Remarks on its History' in J.N. Deely and M.D. Lenhart (eds), *Semiotics* (1983), Plenum Press, New York

Knapp, M.L. (1972) *Nonverbal Communication in Human Interaction*, Holt, Rinehart and Winston, New York

────── (1984) 'The Study of Nonverbal Behaviour Vis-a-vis Human Communication Theory' in A. Wolfgang (ed.), *Nonverbal Behaviour: Perspective, Application, Intercultural Insights*, C.J. Hogrefe Inc., New York

Koestler, A. (1964) *The Act of Creation*, Hutchinson, London

LaFrance, M., and Mayo, C. (1978) *Moving Bodies: Nonverbal Communication in Social Relationships*, Brooks/Cole, Monterey, CA

Lavater, J. (1789) *Essays on Physiognomy, Vol. 1*, John Murray, London

MacKay, D.M. (1972) 'Formal Analysis of Communicative Processes' in R.A. Hinde (ed.), *Nonverbal Communication*, Cambridge University Press, Cambridge

Mahl, G.F., and Schulze, G. (1964) 'Psychological Research in the Extralinguistic Area' in T.H. Sebeok, A.S. Hayes and M.C. Bateson (eds.), *Approaches to Semiotics*, Mouton, The Hague

Manning, P. (ed.) (1965) *Office Design: A Study of Environment*, Rockliff Brothers Ltd, Liverpool

McArthur, L.Z., and Baron, R.M. (1983) 'Toward an Ecological Theory of Social Perception, *Psy. Rev.*, *90*, 215–38

McClintock, C.C. and Hunt, R.G. (1975) 'Nonverbal Indicators of Affect and Deception', *J. of Appl. Soc. Psy.*, *1*, 54–67

Mehrabian, A. (1968) 'Relationship of Attitude to Seated Posture, Orientation and Distance', *J. of Per. and Soc. Psy.*, *10*, 26–30

────── (1971) 'Nonverbal Betrayal of Feeling', *J. of Exp. Res. in Per.*, *5*, 64–73

────── (1972) *Nonverbal Communication*, Aldine, Chicago

────── and Ksionzky, S. (1972) 'Categories of Social Behaviour', *Comp. Gr. Stu.*, *3*, 425–36

Oppenheimer, R. (1956) 'Analogy in Science', *Am. Psychologist*, *11*, 127–35

Patterson, M.L. (1983) *Nonverbal Behaviour: A Functional Perspective*, Springer-Verlag, New York

Pepper, S. (1942) *World Hypotheses*, University of California Press, Berkeley

Polanyi, M. (1958) *Personal Knowledge*, Routledge and Kegan Paul, London

Poyatos, F. (1983) *New Perspectives in Nonverbal Communication*, Pergamon Press, New York

Rand, C.S. (1981) 'Communication of Affect Between Patient and Physician', *J. Health & Soc. Beh.*, *22*(1), 18–30

Rapoport, A. (1982) *The Meaning of the Built Environment: A Nonverbal Communication Approach*, Sage, Beverly Hills

Rosenthal, R. (ed.) (1979) *Skill in Nonverbal Communication: Individual Differences*, Oelgeschlager, Gunn and Hain, Cambridge, Massachusetts

────── Hall, J., DiMatteo, M., *et al.* (1979) *Sensitivity to Nonverbal Communication: The PONS Tests*, Johns Hopkins University Press, Baltimore

Rozelle, R.M. and Baxter, J.C. (1975) 'Impression Formation and Danger Recognition in Experienced Police Officers', *J. of Soc. Psy.*, *96*, 53–63

————— (1978) 'The Interpretation of Nonverbal Behaviour in a Role-defined Interaction Sequence: The Police Citizen Encounter', *Envir. Psy. and Nonv. Beh.*, *2*(3), 167–80

Scheibe, K. (1979) *Mirrors, Masks, Lies, and Secrets,* Praeger, New York

Schlenker, B. (1980) *Impression Management,* Brooks/Cole, Monterey

Siegel, J.C. (1980) 'Effects of Objective Evidence of Expertness, Nonverbal Behaviour, and Subject Sex on Client-Perceived Expertness', *J. of Coun. Psy.*, *27*, 117–21

Smith, C.K. and Larsen, K.M. (1984) 'Sequential Nonverbal Behaviour in the Patient-physician Interview', *J. Fam. Pract.*, *18*(2), 257–61

Snyder, M. (1974) 'Self-monitoring of Expressive Behaviour', *J. of Per. and Soc. Psy.*, *30*, 526–37

Spiegel, J. and Machotka, P. (1974) *Messages of the Body,* The Free Press, New York

Stanislavski, C. (1936) *An Actor Prepares,* Theater Arts Books, New York

Stokols, D. and Shumaker, S.A. (1981) 'People in places: A Transactional View of Settings' in John H. Harvey (ed.) *Cognitive, Social Behavior and the Environment,* Lawrence Erlbaum and Associates, Hillsdale, NJ

Strong, S.R., Taylor, R.G., Bratton, J.C., *et al.* (1971) 'Nonverbal Behavior and Perceived Counselor Characteristics', *J. of Coun. Psy.*, *18*, 554–61

Taylor, E.G. (1878) *Research Into the Early History of Mankind,* John Murray, London

Tessler, R., and Sushelsky, L. (1978) 'Effects of Eye Contact and Social Status on the Perception of a Job Applicant in an Employment Interviewing Situation', *J. of Voc. Beh.*, *13*, 338–47

Tomkins, S. (1962) *Affect, Imagery, and Consciousness: The Positive Affects, Vol. 1,* Springer, New York

————— (1963) *Affect, Imagery and Consciousness: The Negative Affects, Vol. 2,* Springer, New York

Washburn, P.V. and Hakel, M.D. (1973) 'Visual Cues and Verbal Content as Influences on Impressions Formed after Simulated Employment Interviews', *J. Appl. Psy.*, *58*, 137–41

Watson, D. (1982) The Actor and the Observer: How are Their Perceptions of Causality Divergent?', *Psy. Bull.*, *92*(3), 682–700

Weiner, M., Devoe, S., Runbinow, S. and Geller, J. (1972) 'Nonverbal Behavior and Nonverbal Communication', *Psy. Rev.*, *79*, 185–214

Willems, E.P. (1985) 'Behavioral Ecology as a Perspective for Research in Psychology Research' in C.W. Deckner (ed.), *Methodological Perspectives in Behavioral Research,* University Park Press, Baltimore MD

Wolfgang, A. and Bhardwa, A. (1984) '100 Years of Nonverbal Study', in A. Wolfgang (ed.), *Nonverbal Behaviour: Perspectives, Applications, Intercultural Insights,* C.J. Hogrefe Inc., New York

Woodworth, R. and Schlosberg, H. (1954) *Experimental Psychology,* Holt, Rinehart and Winston, New York

Wundt, W. (1973) *The Language of Gesture,* Mouton and Co., The Hague

Young, D.M. and Beier, E.G. (1977) 'The Role of Applicant Nonverbal Communication in the Employment Interview', *J. of Employ. Coun.*, *14*, 154–65

Zajonc, R.B. (1980) 'Feeling and Thinking: Preferences Need No Inferences', *Am. Psy.*, *35*, 151–75

4   QUESTIONING

J.T. Dillon

Everyone knows how to ask questions, and especially how to answer them. How may questions be used *skilfully* as a communicative device? In an approach to this question this chapter first notes the available literature, seeking to appreciate what is known about questioning. Next selected contexts of questioning are reviewed in order to understand what questioning skill must mean in practice. Then, in the major part of the chapter, the elements of questioning are identified, showing how they can turn this way or that to suit communicative purpose. Manipulating the elements according to purpose constitutes the communicative skill of questioning. Anything else is questioning, but no skill.

Literature on Questioning

A large and growing body of literature can be found in enterprises concerned with the study and practice of questioning. Table 4.1 provides a convenient reference to appreciate the kinds of literature available and the kinds of knowledge they permit one to have about questioning.

Kinds of Literature

Table 4.1 cites one representative book from each of a dozen disciplines of study, and one each from a dozen fields of practice. In some cases an extensive journal literature is also available, well summarised in review articles and chapters such as from logic (Harrah, 1985), linguistics (Kearsley, 1976), education (Dillon, 1982b) and survey research (Bradburn, 1982). A multidisciplinary overview is also available (Dillon, 1982a).

There are two important limitations to this literature. First, these are English-language sources only. The considerable literature in many other languages reminds one that both one's understanding and practice of questioning may be specific to English-language questions and restricted to one or two cultural contexts of questioning. Compared to this case, both the questions and the questioning differ in significant respects in other languages and cultures.

Moreover, there is no unified literature on questioning, but separate traditions within various disciplines and fields; and there is no one knowledge, but differing ways of knowing different things. All of these stand presently unrelated to one another — much as the books in Table 4.1 do not refer to one another. Relations among the traditions remain to be drawn and exhibited in a comprehensive, multidisciplinary study of questioning (for such relations, see Dillon, 1982a).

Table 4.1: Selected Literature on Questioning

Question-answer models		Question-answer practices	
Discipline	Book	Field	Book
Philosophy	Clark, 1972	Counselling	Long, Paradise and Long, 1981
Philosophy of science	Hintikka, 1981	Teaching	Hyman, 1979
Logic	Belnap and Steel, 1976	Law	Kestler, 1982
Linguistics	Chisholm, 1984	Private investigation	Buckwalter, 1983
Sociolinguistics	Stenstroem, 1984	Criminal interrogation (police)	Inbau and Reid, 1967
Discourse analysis	Carlson, 1983	Interviewing (varia)	Richardson, Dohrenwend and Klein, 1965
Anthropology	Goody, 1978	Survey research	Sudman and Bradburn, 1982
Hermeneutics	Meyer, 1983	Journalism	Metzler, 1977
Psychology	Graesser and Black, 1985	Medicine	Fisher and Todd, 1983
Artificial intelligence	Lehnert, 1978	Sales	Xerox Corp., 1976
Information science	Bolc, 1980	Library science	Slavens, 1978
Varia	Kiefer, 1983	Pastoral work	Robinson, 1980
		Parliament	Chester and Bowring, 1962
		Varia	Kaiser, 1979

As Table 4.1 suggests, knowledge of questioning lies in the question–answer models exhibited in the theoretical and empirical literature from the disciplines of study, and in the question–answer practices described by empirical reports and practitioner manuals in the fields of practice. There are, then, three kinds of literature yielding three kinds of knowledge.

Kinds of Knowledge

The theoretical, empirical and practitioner literatures afford knowledge in conception, observation and action. These are differing knowledges of questioning.

Conceptual Knowledge. This knowledge of questioning is just beginning to take form and is now the object of increasingly widening inquiries in one discipline after another. By far the major part of what is known in this way comes from logic, and quite recently so — within past decades; a lesser part, even more recent, comes from linguistics and information science. Conceptions are therefore restricted by the number and nature of the disciplines that formulate them. Logical models, for example, ordinarily exhibit certain relations among certain classes of questions. Knowledge is further restricted in the breadth of aspects that have been conceived. For example, the pragmatics of questioning is known least of all, in fact, almost nothing is known by contrast to syntax and semantics. This limitation of our knowledge is pointedly significant when it comes to 'practical' questions such as what questions are and how they operate.

Empirical Knowledge. This is the weakest of the three kinds. It is formed of observations from descriptive and experimental studies. Descriptive studies are lacking in the broadest areas, such as everyday question–answer exchanges, and in most fields of question–answer practice. For example, it is not known for a fact what kinds of questions journalists and interrogators ask. Experimental studies are lacking both overall and in many specific fields; and, where descriptive studies are relatively plentiful, experimental studies are comparatively rare. For example, there are numerous descriptive studies but few experiments on classroom questioning. Hence, knowledge grounded in experimental observations is the weaker part of the weakest part of knowledge about questioning. These limitations severely constrict the grounds available for supporting generalisations and recommendations for the practice of questioning.

Practical Knowledge. This knowledge of questioning consists of knowledge-in-action. It is a kind of prudential knowledge, knowing to choose and act in a circumstance where action is necessary but consequences are uncertain. This is the knowledge that is probably of most interest to most readers. Yet least of all can be said of it, in generalised propositional form. Manuals of practice are necessarily full of sentences about it, in the form of advice, anecdotes and assertions about strategies, skills, tactics, techniques and the supposed effect of each upon any respondent. Even in the best cases, some of the propositions sound silly: 'Ask the right questions, in the right order'; 'Facilitative questions are helpful, but inappropriate questions can be harmful'; 'If you want creative answers, ask creative questions.'

Even if all statements in all manuals were to be conceptually well-founded and empirically well-established in addition to being practically tried and true, two problems would be faced in coming to know that knowledge.

First, each manual refers to one field of practice. It is not known, but may be doubted, that this knowledge applies to another field, let alone to the dozen fields of practice in Table 4.1. Second, practical knowledge is particular both in circumstance and in knower. Knowledge-in-action is possessed and exhibited by an individual practitioner with a given purpose in a given situation. It is knowledge that everyone, but not all together, can hold — in one practice but not in another.

None of this, of course, is a fault of the manuals — which may or may not themselves be excellent — but merely a limitation of knowledge. As a consequence of this and other limitations in the three kinds of knowledge that one can have about questioning, few direct answers will be given here to the pressing and fascinating questions of practice: What is the skill of questioning for effective communication? What kinds of questions should be asked, and what strategies of questioning should be used?

For in this chapter, a direct answer to such questions would have to represent not only knowledge-in-action but also corrollary knowledge-in-conception-and-observation; and, in being given to an individual reader from one field of practice, the answer would have to represent knowledge of questioning that is general to all practitioners in all fields. No such knowledge is available. (The author can think of no useful generalisation that applies.)

To appreciate that this is the case and to get around it as best as possible, the rest of this chapter reviews the contexts of questioning and then the elements of questioning. The contexts will show the variety of questioning behaviours that are practised in different fields *and* within any single field. Here, a new sense will be gained of the general question of most interest: 'What constitutes skilful questioning for effective communication?' Next this question is addressed by gaining an understanding of the elements of questioning, particularly how each element can turn this way or that, and in this or that circumstance. Finally, the question is answered by each practitioner who uses this understanding to manipulate the elements of questioning according to purpose in circumstance. It is that, then, which constitutes practical knowledge and skill of questioning.

Contexts of Questioning

To understand the question, 'What might constitute skilful questioning?' questioning practices in three fields are examined — teaching, psychotherapy and law. These will be seen to differ both among themselves and, so to speak, within themselves. Not only are they three different contexts for questioning, but also each one exhibits a variety of contexts with different questioning behaviours within each context. That fact alone would rule out one entire class of expected answers to the general question: answers that describe any set of questioning behaviours. For the behaviours that constitute skilful questioning in one context may make only for fumbling in another, even within one and the same field of practice.

Teaching

The classroom may be a single place but it is a complex of multiple contexts. In elementary classrooms, Berliner (1983) observed eleven distinct 'activity structures' and Stodolsky, Ferguson and Wimpelberg (1981) observed 16 'instructional formats'. Among many other factors, the teacher's role was observed to differ in each of these structures and formats. It can be imagined that different sorts of questioning might be used in widely different classroom contexts, such as lecture and seatwork. But different questioning is also used in two quite similar contexts — discussion and recitation.

Discussion classes or episodes differ from recitation ones in the styles of questioning used and the frequencies and types of questions asked (Dillon, 1981, 1984a). Moreover, there are different types of discussion, providing different contexts for questioning. For example, Roby (1985) distinguished five models of discussion and, in analysing transcripts of high school discussion, he observed that each type was characterised by a particular rhetoric of questioning and predominant usage of given types of questions.

Questioning during recitation differs not only from discussion but also within various contexts of recitation. For example, Stodolsky *et al.* (1981) observed differences by purposes, subject-matters and socioeconomic status (SES) of pupils. The questioning served five different instructional purposes — to review, to introduce new material, to check answers to work, to practice and to check understanding (clarifying); furthermore, several purposes were commonly served during a single recitation segment. More questioning was observed in mathematics than in social studies classes, at each of three SES levels, while more questioning in both subject matters was observed in lower than in middle SES classrooms, and more in middle than in higher. Other studies have also found that teachers use different styles of questioning and ask contrasting types of questions in schools of different SES.

Manuals on classroom questioning recommend a multiplicity of questioning behaviours. For example, a recent manual (Hyman, 1979) specifies five general questioning strategies, 15 specific strategies and 25 questioning techniques. Other manuals specify yet other techniques for a dozen different types of questions (for instance, Hunkins, 1972), some techniques not only different but also divergent from those in other manuals (Dillon, 1983).

The skill of questioning in this context must be a complex matter. Classroom teaching is not a single process in a single context, but a variety of processes in multiple contexts. The questioning differs among these processes and contexts, even between closely related ones (recitation and discussion), as it does even among various forms of one process (discussion) and even within a single segment of one process (recitation). Pedagogical manuals differ and diverge on the multiplicitous questioning behaviours to be used. What, then, must 'questioning skill' consist of in the case of classroom teaching?

Psychotherapy

In addition to representing a different context of practice, this case describes divergent processes that afford different contexts for questioning. The differences in the questioning describe polar reversals.

In client-centred therapy (Rogers, 1951), the use of questions is fairly prohibited and the substitution of declarative statements is prescribed; in rational-emotive therapy (Ellis, 1977), the therapist is told to take a Socratic questioning stance rather than making declarative statements. In other, or eclectic, styles of therapy, manuals may either discourage the use of questions (Arbuckle, 1975), encourage it (Long *et al.*, 1981), or both (Benjamin, 1977).

The case in practice is not known, but published transcripts show no questions in client-centred sessions, and nothing but questions in rational–emotive sessions. When one or two therapist questions do appear in client-centred transcripts they are footnoted with criticism, on the grounds that the therapist is being directive (Curran, 1952, pp. 237–40; Rogers, 1942, pp. 272, 280). The questions in rational–emotive transcripts are noted with approval, on the grounds that frequent questions keep the therapist from being dominant (Wessler and Wessler, 1980).

Quite apart from these divergent processes in this 'one' context, each instance of any one process exhibits different phases or episodes, describing subcontexts. For example, Long *et al.* (1981) distinguish three consecutive phases in the course of a therapeutic treatment — exploration, integration and action. Each phase is marked by distinctive uses of questions, each of various types. The types of questions required for the second phase are inappropriate for use in the first phase.

In sum, the very use of questions, skilful or not, in one style of therapy marks untherapeutic behaviour, while, in another style, failure to use questions denotes lack of therapeutic behaviour. In still other cases, the course of therapy requires using certain types of questions during one phase but not another. 'Questioning skill' exhibited in various contexts of therapy, and in various subcontexts within a therapy, would denote blundering and effective communication. Thus there would seem to be no one set of behaviours that constitute questioning skill in counselling and psychotherapy.

Law

This is a classic case, because on the whole communication here is constrained to proceed only by questions and answers. As before, it is a case of multiple contexts with contrasting uses of questioning. First, several courtroom contexts are reviewed, both pre-trial and trial, then extra-courtroom contexts are looked at.

Initial appearance and *change of plea* are two courtroom pre-trial proceedings with different questions asked in each. Philips (in press) observed 'contextual variation' in the frequency and type of wh-questions asked. Expressed as proportions, twice as many wh-questions were asked during initial appearance (IA) as during change of plea (CP), and several times as many of the questions were in non-fronted and non-sequential form. As for types of wh-questions, in IA 'What?' predominated and 'How?' questions were negligible: the reverse was the case in CP. Further, more of the questions in CP — both 'What?' and 'How?' — were routinely asked than was the case in IA. Moreover, the question-types differed between themselves. Compared to 'What?' questions, more of the 'How?' were routinely asked, expressed in full sentences and given wh-fronting.

Thus, there were situational as well as functional differences in the questions asked. For example, the particular ways in which the 'What?' questions were asked — less routinised, less sentential, less fronted — led to greater diversity in the length and content of the response (longer and less predictable). These differences describe divergent patterns of question–answer usage, types and function in the two courtroom contexts.

Change of Plea. Here only one context and one set of questions are seen, but different askers and correspondingly different functions of the same question in this one situation. In examining the CP cases, Philips (1984) found systematic differences in the usage and function of the same question-forms, syntactic and semantic, according to the relative status of the questioner. First, the higher the status, the more the questions asked. Judges asked most of the questions, lawyers far fewer and defendants even fewer. (In still another context, lawyers ask most of the questions during a trial.) Second, the higher the status of the questioner, the more controlling the question — the same syntactic and semantic question. Seen from the respondent's viewpoint, the higher the status relative to the questioner, the less controlling the question. These functions can be seen in two characteristics of the answer: the extent to which it copies the form of the question and elaborates beyond a single utterance.

1. *Question-copy.* The higher the status, the less the copy. In answering questions, defendants copied the question-form in 95 per cent of the cases, lawyers in two-thirds of the cases and judges only half the time.

2. *Elaboration.* The higher the status, the greater the elaboration. In answering questions, defendants elaborated in only 2 per cent of the cases; lawyers elaborated in 20 per cent.

In sum, the same questions asked by different questioners in the same situation serve different functions.

Trial. Here is the case of one courtroom situation with different subcontexts and different questioners asking different questions in each of the different contexts. Woodbury (1984) studied a murder trial and found systematic differences in the types of questions asked by each questioner in each context. She distinguished seven grammatical types of questions (for instance, wh-, alternative, yes/no) and arranged them in a hierarchy from less to more controlling. The seven types were used differently during direct and cross-examination by lawyers for the prosecution and the defence.

The questions were less controlling during direct than during cross-examination. More wh-questions were asked by both prosecution and defence during direct than during cross-examination and in each case more of the prosecution's questions than the defence's were of these less-controlling types. More yes/no questions were asked on cross- than on direct-examination; and in each case more by the defence than by the prosecution.

On direct-examination, the *prosecutor* asked more wh-questions than yes/no questions, and on cross-examination, more yes/no than wh-questions; more of his questions on cross than on direct were yes/no; and on both direct and on cross, he asked more wh-questions than did the defence. The *defence* asked more yes/no than wh-questions both on direct and on cross-examination; more yes/no questions on cross than on direct; and more yes/no questions than the prosecutor on both direct and cross.

Summing up, the same questions were used differently in different contexts by the different questioners — although all transpired within the 'one' context of a courtroom trial, and although all describe 'the use of questions by lawyers'. A lawyer can: serve either for the prosecution or the defence; ask questions either on direct or on cross-examination; and question either an adversarial or a friendly witness. In each role, during each episode, with each witness, the same lawyer uses the same set of questions differently.

Extra-courtroom Contexts. Lawyers use questioning not only during courtroom trials and pre-trial proceedings, but also in extra-courtroom contexts. These might include discovery and depositions, interviewing one's witnesses and rehearsing one's witness (Kestler, 1982). The use of questions differs between the courtroom and the non-courtroom contexts, and differs further among these non-courtroom contexts, both by reason of legal constraints and strategic considerations.

The different questioning that is used in all of these different contexts (for example, courtroom and extra-courtroom), in the different situations within each context (courtroom pre-trial and trial proceedings, and IA and CP pre-trial proceedings), in the different episodes within each situation (direct and cross-examination), each of these compounded by the different roles that a lawyer can play (prosecution and defence), the different roles witnesses can play in relation to lawyer roles (adversary and not), and the different people who can ask and answer questions (judge, lawyers, witnesses) — this complex whole can entail polar reversals in the use of questions. The questions that should be used in the one context must altogether be avoided in the other, *and* the questions that must be avoided in the first case should positively be pursued in the second. For a small example, leading questions are judicially prohibited during direct examination but are permissible and strategically useful on cross, as for impeaching a witness or ruining an expert's standing.

Beyond the variety of contexts in which questions are used differently, there is a multiplicity of ways to use questions. A current manual on trial advocacy (Kestler, 1982) gives 33 principles of questioning strategy, 33 psychological aspects of questioning strategy and 44 questioning techniques and tactics. What is more, Wellman's (1903) classic manual details how using one and the same questioning technique proved to bring victory in one famous case and disaster in another.

What, then, can be 'the skill of questioning' in the field of law, or yet the skill of questioning in general? The general implication is that questioning skill is not a matter of asking a specifiable set of questions in a specifiable set of ways — even within any given field of practice, not to say for various fields. No type of question is a good or effective question to ask; no technique of questioning is a good or effective technique to use. No specific behaviours constitute questioning skill. Rather, it is something like an attribute of behaviour in context. The skill lies in knowing the elements of questioning and then manipulating them to purpose.

Elements of Questioning

Viewed simply, questioning is comprised of (1) expressing (2) a question — or, an act and a sentence. It also entails sentences just before, so to speak, and sentences just after — assumptions and answers. On this view, questioning has three ordered elements, each comprised of an act and a sentence:

1. Assumptions;
2. Question;
3. Answers.

A theoretical understanding of these three elements, above all the third one, is the best possible way to know how to manipulate them skilfully in practice.

Assumptions

Questioning entails two kinds of assumptions that, for being prior, are called presuppositions and presumptions. The first is a logical property of the question-sentence; the second is a pragmatic property of the act of uttering that sentence. Thus, when a person asks a question, he is communicating something in addition to the very question he asks; he communicates also what he assumes by (1) the question and (2) the asking of it — that is, his presuppositions and presumptions.

Presuppositions. Informally put, presuppositions are those sentences that (express propositions that) are entailed by the question–sentence. For a question to be valid, its presuppositions must be true. Then it can be validly answered. If the presuppositions are not true, the question cannot be truly answered, for the fact that an answer affirms the presupposition of the question. Thus any answer to a question with not-true presuppositions (whether false or indeterminate — not known to be true or false) itself re-assumes the not-true supposition that the question pre-assumes.

The implication for practice is that the questioner know (1) what the presuppositions are, and (2) whether they are true. Otherwise, the meaning and the worth of the answer cannot be known.

The implication is not that the questioner ask questions that are true, only that he know the truth of them. Most questioners do neither. Some questioners knowingly ask questions with false presuppositions, or with indeterminate ones. These might be called 'trick' questions, used as a strategy or tactic of questioning in some cases — most notoriously in such cases as, 'Have you stopped beating your wife?' Whether the answer is yes *or* no, *and* whether the answer is true *or* false, the answer communicates 'I did beat my wife'.

What the practitioner must do is to know the content and the truth of the presuppositions and then elect to ask the question or not, according to purpose. Some purposes are served only by questions with true presuppositions, other purposes are also served by false and indeterminate ones. It is part of the skill of questioning to use one presupposition and not another for one particular purpose and not another. Not to know which is which is already, by definition, lack of skill, even before asking any question at all.

For example, a deliberately false and serviceable presuppositon is as follows: an interrogator who believes that a criminal suspect is lying, as in giving the alibi that he was at the Hollywood Bowl at the crucial hour in question, may make up a fictitious event and then ask a question that presupposes the truth of this falsity: 'How did you react when one of the concert players had a heart attack?' (Buckwalter, 1983, p. 224). Whatever the answer, it will prove to be false because it affirms the truth of the false presupposition.

Cross-examiners, by contrast, may try to insert a *true* or indeterminate presupposition into a question in order that, whatever the answer, it be affirmed as true. 'Did you ever get those brakes fixed on that truck?' In that way the adversarial witness unwittingly testifies to something that damages his case, for the presupposition is now admitted into evidence. For that reason opposing counsel must be alert to the presuppositions of every question being asked by his counterpart, and speedily object to the question before *any* answer is given, that is before the presupposition of the question is affirmed.

With suspects whose guilt is reasonably known, the investigator's questions presuppose certain facts rather than question them. The questions are not 'Did you?' or 'Are you?', for these presuppose that *either* yes or no is true. The investigator does not believe in the truth of that presupposition, so he uses questions that presuppose the truth of 'you did' and the falsity of 'you didn't'. The questions are 'How did you?' and 'Why did you?', and so on (Buckwalter, 1983, p. 220).

Presumptions. This second kind of prior assumption (again, in this chapter's terms) attaches not to the question–sentence but to the act of uttering it. For a question to be valid, its presuppositions must be true. For the questioning to be genuine or sincere, its presumptions must be true — that is, they must describe accurately the conditions that hold in the question–situation.

When a person asks a question, he communicates his belief in certain conditions that obtain. These conditions describe such states as knowing the answer, desiring the answer, believing that there is an answer and one true answer, and estimating that the respondent can and will supply the answer. The respondent is invited to presume likewise or, at least, to believe that the questioner so presumes.

For example, here are the presumptions describing what is called the standard question-situation. The act of asking the question implies that the questioner:

1. Does not know the answer;
2. Desires to know it;
3. Believes there exists at least one true answer;
4. Thinks that the respondent can and will supply the/an answer;
5. Believes in the truth of the question's presuppositions.

That is called the standard case, but it is not the case in most situations. Most questioners and respondents do not presume that these conditions hold. They presume rather that the questioner already knows the answer. Indeed, the social norm is positively not to display ignorance, and few professional norms require or even permit such display behind the questioning.

For example, cross-examiners know the answers to the questions they ask. Their practice positively requires them not to ask a question to which they do not know the answer. The rule of thumb runs, 'Never ask a question unless you already know the answer'. Examiners in any field already know the answer, whereas the candidates are not presumed to know it. Media interviewers may not care what the answer is, nor whether it be true or not, rather that *an* answer be given that is of a certain quality — revealing, quotable, and so on.

In other cases the presumptions may vary according to context. Teachers might be viewed as already knowing the answers to their questions, but in practice teachers and students participate in a complex of shifting presumptions. Johnson (1979) has identified nine possible sets of teacher/student assumptions regarding knowledge of the matter in question, and belief in the truth of the question's presuppostions. Here are the presumptions in the three most common types of questioning observed in classrooms:

1. *Request for demonstration of information.* The teacher (T) knows the answer and does not assume that the student (S) does not know it. Similarly, T believes what the question presupposes and does not believe that S disbelieves it. Note that the presumption is not, 'T believes that S knows the answer'. This test-like

kind of question is insincere only when T assumes that S does not know the answer.

2. *Request for factual information.* T does not know the answer and thinks that S at least may know it; T at least does not disbelieve the presupposition, and believes that S does believe it.

3. *Request for opinion information.* Same as (2), save that, here S does know the answer.

This analysis describes shared beliefs — T believes, and S believes, and each believes the other believes; yet it should be evident that the beliefs, in practice, can be held by one party but not another. This introduces a further complexity in theory, and one that in certain fields is deliberately introduced into practice.

For example, interrogators of criminal suspects and reluctant witnesses or informants will at times communicate by their questioning that they already know the answer whereas in truth they are trying to find it out. The suspect is to believe in a condition that the interrogator believes not to hold in the question–answer situation. Thus the suspect comes to believe, 'He already knows more than I thought, I might as well confess'. The investigator in the earlier example, who asked a question with a deliberately false presupposition ('How did you react when one of the concert players had a heart attack?'), is involved in a situation with these presumptions:

1. The suspect believes in the truth of the question's presupposition, and the interrogator knows it to be false;

2. The interrogator does not believe that there exists any true answer, and the suspect presumes that some answer must be true (but which one?);

3. The suspect wants to give the true (correct, right) answer, but the interrogator does not want any true answer at all, rather he wants a false one;

4. The investigator does not care what the answer is, any answer will do, because all answers will be false.

The implication for practice is that the questioner must know just what conditions are being presumed, both by himself and by the respondent, and how accurately these presumptions describe the situation. Then the questioning can be pursued with skill — whether the situation is such as to require that the presumptions be accurate or that they be not, or that this or that presumption hold to such or such a degree, or be held by such or such a party to the exchange. Not to know these things is already to blunder.

Question

This second element, too, has two parts, the question-sentence and the act of uttering it. Of all the aspects under which these may be considered, only the formulation of the question and the manner of its expression are examined.

Formulation. Formulation refers to the verbal form in which the question in mind is couched. As is the case in general with language, most questioners find it difficult to put into words just what it is they want to know or to find out from the respondent. Apart from this enduring problem, the major point about the formulation of a question is that it defines the kind of answer possible and it affects several characteristics of the eventual answer given. Selected semantic and syntactic aspects of the question's formulation are examined — its vocabulary and structure.

1. Vocabulary. It is obvious that the wording of a question affects the answer. Here it is noted that the *choice* of words can influence the answer, as survey researchers especially have demonstrated long ago in a number of classic experiments (for instance, Blankenship, 1940; Payne, 1951). For example, more than twice as many American respondents will not 'allow' speeches against democracy as will 'forbid' them (Schuman and Presser, 1981, p. 277). Similarly , in trying to get reliable answers about the respondent's 'socially undesirable' behaviour (for example, intoxication, drug addiction), survey researchers discover that by using familiar rather than formally correct words in the question, people report having consumed twice as many cans of beer and masturbated thrice as often (Bradburn and Sudman, 1980).

For their part, investigators find that their choice of words affects the readiness of suspects to reveal information. The questioners *avoid* correct, precise terms like 'kill, steal, rape', and ask about 'shoot, take, sex'. A rapist may deny having raped the victim, but readily admit having sex with the woman. In assault-and-battery cases, the question 'Why did you hit him?' will be evaded, but 'Did you fight him?' affirmed. In case of murder, motives are revealed in answer to 'Why did you do it?' more than to 'Why did you murder the man?' In general, suspects are more forthcoming when asked to 'tell the truth' than to 'confess your crime' (Buckwalter, 1983, pp. 229–30).

The choice of words also affects answers about ordinary things that people have just seen. An observed person is reported to be 10 inches taller in answer to 'How tall?' than to 'How short?', and a film 30 minutes longer for 'How long?' than for 'How short?' Eyewitnesses to traffic collisions give systematically higher estimates of speed when asked 'How fast were the cars going when they contacted/hit/smashed?' — 31/34/41mph (Loftus, 1979, p. 96).

What is more, the wording of the question can influence people not only to over/under-report but also to give truly answers about non-existent things. A tradition of psychological experiments since Muscio (1916) has amply shown that people will witness to events that never took place, and aver having seen objects that were not present in the scene before them. They do so unwittingly via answering questions that assert that event or object in the wording of the question.

The classic case, and the simplest, is for the questioner to denote by 'the' instead of 'an' an object that was not present in the observed scene. Where there was no X, more people will say yes to 'Did you see the X?' than will say no to 'Did you see an X?' In the author's view, this result is attributable to the presuppositions marked by the wording. The first question presupposes the existence of X, while the second does not (that is, it presupposes that X either did or did not exist). Here it is seen again that answers affirm the presuppositions and that respondents tend to agree to the presuppositions in the course of answering in terms of the question.

This tendency appears attributable to both the logico–linguistic workings of presuppositions and to the social and pragmatic norms of agreeableness and co-operativeness. People will respond to questions, and most will respond agreeably (which is not to say, cheerfully). They agree to respond and they agree to the question. That can present a problem to the questioner who wants to get a reliable answer (for instance, an opinion pollster), and it presents an opportunity for the questioner who wants to outwit a respondent (for instance, a cross-examiner).

In general, respondents find it easier — even more desirable — to go along with the question as posed rather than to dispute it and complicate the exchange. For, where the X in question did not exist, a respondent would first have to reject the question, 'Did you see the X?'; deny and then correct the false presupposition ('There was an X'); next negotiate a new understanding with the questioner who, though the more authoritative speaker in the exchange, now stands awkwardly corrected; and last await and answer yet further questions about that one point. It is easier to say yes and let it go at that.

It is noted further that people say yes but *not* no in such cases. 'No' would reveal their ignorance or uncertainty about a commonplace event to which they are supposedly a witness and the occurrence of which the questioner has just affirmed. Hence a 'no' would call into question for the respondents themselves their own competence as an ordinary observer and knower. 'Be agreeable and say yes' seems to be the pragmatic motto.

Once having been so agreeably incorrect in their answer, respondents base their answers to subsequent questions upon the truth of the false presupposition that they had affirmed in their previous answer. In that way their 'eyewitness testimony' can build fiction upon fiction, without either the questioner or the answerer recognising it as fiction. Or, otherwise viewed, this is a case where the non-existent event, once heard in the question, passes into the respondent's memory and is retrieved therefrom in answer to subsequent questions (Loftus, 1982). For example, some witnesses who agreeably answer to 'How fast was the car going when it passed the barn?', at a scene where no barn stood, tend subsequently to answer yes to 'Did you see the barn?' (Loftus, 1982). Eyewitnesses asked the 'smashed' version of the question, 'How fast were the cars going when they . . .?' tend to answer yes to the subsequent question, 'Did you see any broken glass?', when no broken glass existed at the scene they had witnessed (Loftus, 1979).

It is noted that these witnesses are not making up answers. They are searching their memory for information that is indeed truly remembered. But it is false information. It is traceable to the false presupposition, the truth of which they had affirmed in agreeably answering the prior question. It is a false answer truly given.

In that way one returns to the usefulness for the questioner of knowing the presuppositions to his questions, and then of choosing, rightly *or* wrongly, to ask these questions, false *or* true. On that will depend the content and the worth of the answer, irrespective of whether the answer in turn be X or not-X, and true or not. The value of question–answer does not turn on its truth/falsity but on its suitableness to purpose in a particular circumstance of practice. True answers can be worthless, as can false answers truly given.

One principle that applies in all situations is to use words that the respondent understands and that have only the intended meaning. But who can formulate questions like that? According to the experts who recognise the principle (Sudman and Bradburn, 1982), formulating questions that satisfy it is difficult — for experts. After formulating questions for over 200 surveys, Schuman and Presser (1981) 'despaired of being able to construct questions immune from serious criticism' (p. 13). Payne's (1951) classic manual gives a checklist of 100 considerations in wording a question (pp. 228–37), and a list of 1,000 familiar words of which the 'problem words' range from 'about, all, always, any' through 'fair, most, see' to 'where, who, you' (pp. 151–7). These are the words *mis*understood or variably understood by respondents.

2. Structure. As a matter of logic, the syntactic structure of a question circumscribes the set of possible answers and, as a matter of pragmatics, it influences the answers actually given. Of the multiple aspects of structure, only the working of alternative-questions is examined and compared to questions without alternatives.

Alternative-questions. One class of questions is structured so as to specify the alternatives in answer. The two most useful points here about alternatives are that questioners rarely specify them correctly (for instance, the wrong ones or too few), and that the number and kind of alternatives in the question affects the content and worth of the answer.

Questions may frequently be structured for a yes/no, either/or answer when the case in fact is not one of yes or no, either X or Y, or even Z. In general, it is difficult to structure a question with correctly dichotomous alternatives or with mutually exclusive and jointly exhaustive ones. This difficulty describes a common intellectual deficiency that is exhibited in, but is not specific to, the formulation of questions. Of course, false-dichotomous questions can also be used as a deliberate ploy, as in asking a loaded question ('Would you rather be Red or dead?').

Both the number and the content of alternatives affect the answers. For example, shoppers report having tried more new products when asked 'How many — One? Five? Ten?' than for 'One? Two? Three?' (Loftus, 1982). In a series of experiments, Schuman and Presser (1981) have demonstrated particularly interesting effects of changing the alternatives in four different ways. The results are useful for showing how to formulate such questions in practice.

1. *Don't-know.* As a result of explicitly adding a 'don't-know' or no-opinion alternative to the basic 'agree-disagree' question, an average of 22 per cent more respondents (in 19 experiments) shifted from 'agree-disagree' to 'don't-know'. Thus a questioner might take care to provide in an explicit and permissive way for the alternative case that the respondent does not know the answer or has no answer to give. As noted earlier, people may tend to respond agreeably in terms of the question and/or avoid displaying ignorance or uncertainty. Where purpose benefits, 'don't-know' can be explicitly made to be perfectly acceptable.

2. *Counterargument.* Adding a consideration for the negative or opposite view in question resulted in a shift of 8 per cent to the negative (nine experiments). Without such a consideration, the respondent is faced with such a choice as 'X, or anti-X?' As noted, respondents may tend to agree with the proposition in question, especially when no balancing terms are provided for the opposite view: indeed, the opposite view may even remain unidentified in the question. A general way to provide balance is, 'Some people think X, some people think not-X, which do you think?' or 'X because of A, and not-X because of B; X or not-X?'

3. *Middle term.* Adding a logical middle term resulted in a shift of 15 per cent more respondents to the middle alternative (16 experiments). For example, 'strict, lenient, or about right?'

4. *Placement.* Whatever its content, the last-listed of two or three alternatives was chosen by 10 per cent more respondents than when this same alternative was in first or second place. For example, 14 per cent more respondents answered 'plenty' when asked if America is running out of oil or has plenty, than for plenty or running out. When asked if divorce should be made easier to obtain, more difficult, or stay as is, 10 per cent more respondents chose 'more difficult' when that was the last alternative (vs. when it was the second), and 12 per cent more chose 'as is' when that was last (vs. second).

The implication for practice is to appreciate the workings of alternatives and then manipulate them according to purpose. Far from benefiting from added alternatives, some purposes may require avoiding them altogether. For example, lawyers are advised: 'Avoid questions that offer alternatives' (Kestler, 1982, p. 74). In discovery proceedings, the witness might choose one of the two proffered alternatives instead of giving yet a third which would be more damaging; and there is no point to giving a choice on cross-examination: 'Pin the witness down to the answer you want' (p. 75).

'Open/closed' Questions. Questions can be structured without specified alternatives. These are sometimes called 'open/free' questions, in contrast to 'closed/fixed' ones, but it is important to adopt the notion and not these terms, for the terms uselessly refer to multiple divergent things in various fields and books.

The notion being described here (not as a definition of these terms) is that one generic form of question permits respondents to bespeak their own ideas in their own words, whereas the other generic form specifies ideas and words for them to choose. Both types constrain the response but in differing ways. The differences are shown in the only systematic research available on this point, the experiments of Schuman and Presser (1981). On every point of comparison investigated, the two generic forms of question differed importantly. Here are three examples:

1. *'What do you think is the most important problem facing this country at present?'* Only half as many respondents *identified* crime while giving their answer as did *choose* it from the specified alternatives in the other version of the question — 'Which do you think: (a) crime . . . (b) . . .' (p. 83).

2. *'What would you most prefer in a job?'* Only half as many people answered 'a feeling of accomplishment' as did select it from the alternatives. Good pay was mentioned by as many respondents in both cases, but it was the *least* frequently chosen alternative and the *most* frequently volunteered answer. In one experiment, 60 per cent of the responses to the open question fell outside of the five categories in the closed question.

3. *'What do you think is the most important thing for children to learn to prepare them for life?'* 'To think for themselves' was selected by two-thirds of the respondents but identified by only 5 per cent. 'To obey' was selected by one-fifth but identified by 2 per cent.

What is to be made of these differences? The implication for practice is altogether conceptual. It is to recognise that different answers are given to the two forms of question, and that the answers given to the one form may not even be given *at all* to the other form. The conceptual significance is that the questioner who asks alternative-questions may be specifying categories of thought that are unrepresentative of what respondents think, with the result that 'we risk having respondents confirm our own frame of reference without even being aware of it' (Schuman and Presser, 1981, p. 108).

Narrative/directive Questions. Here too the terms vary. The notion runs that the one structure permits the respondent to speak at some length about his knowledge of a topic, the other directs him to answer point for point. For example, a witness might be asked 'And then what happened?' and, after detailing the events, be asked any kind of question about specific points mentioned or omitted. The difference in the answers has long been known.

For example, Yamada (1913) had students read a geographical description of South America, and then asked a free-narrative question ('What do you know about the surface of South America?') followed by a series of 24 specific questions from the reading. On average, the students made three times more errors in answering the specific questions, even incorrectly answering about points that they had correctly reported during their narrative answer.

Apart from the accuracy of answer, there is its completeness or the exhaustiveness of detail. A number of studies have examined these two characteristics as they vary by three types of question (see Loftus, 1979):

1. Answers to the free-narrative or open question are the most accurate but least complete;
2. Answers to the controlled-narrative or specific questions are less accurate and more complete;
3. Answers to multiple-choice or alternative questions are the least accurate and the most complete.

The implication for practice is obviously that each of the different types of question has advantages and disadvantages. In some fields the implication is to use these types in a particular order. Investigators, for example, are advised to interview co-operative witnesses by first asking a free-narrative question, then a series of specific questions about the points mentioned, going from general to specific information and from known to unknown; next to ask some cross-questions to re-examine, test, verify or probe selected points; and lastly to ask some open, summary questions such as to see if anything important has been left out or remains to be clarified. But that is not the case when faced with a reluctant witness; then the interrogator is to use patient, persistent and probing questions (Buckwalter, 1983).

Finally, one practical implication may be emphasised that touches generally upon the formulation of questions (whether vocabulary, structure, topic and so on).

Practitioners in several fields are emphatically advised to prepare their questions with care, to formulate them in writing and to arrange them in some order — all beforehand. This advice is given to interviewers and interrogators (Buckwalter, 1983), survey-takers (Sudman and Bradburn, 1982), lawyers (Kestler, 1982), journalists (Metzler, 1977) and teachers (Dillon, 1983).

What is more, practitioners in some fields are advised to test the formulation of their questions before using them in practice. Teachers are urged to put their questions to family and friends on the eve of recitation, to find out if the questions mean to others what they mean to the teacher (Dillon, 1983). Survey researchers are urged to test and revise their questions no fewer than four times before asking them in a survey; and, if resources are lacking for a pilot-test, they are told in italics not to do the survey (Sudman and Bradburn, 1982).

This advice seems surprising to give to people whose daily practice consists almost entirely of asking questions. Another reason it may seem surprising is that asking questions is widely believed to be an easy thing to do (Sudman and Bradburn, 1982). Indeed, it is easy to ask questions in everyday situations. And it is easy to ask everyday questions in professional practice. But it takes *great care* to prepare an educative question, for example: to conceive of it requires thought, to formulate it requires labour, and to pose it requires tact (Dillon, 1983).

Nothing looks as effortless and spontaneous as the facile questioning by lawyers, journalists, teachers and the like seen on television or experienced in real life. They ask an impressive number of questions. Are the questions effective to purpose? Is the questioning skilful? One wonders, not knowing. That depends not only on the formulation of the question but also on the manner of expressing it.

Expression. Formulation refers to the question-sentence, expression refers to the act of putting the question. Here, too, there are multiple aspects to consider, and divergent ways that any one manner of questioning can affect responses. Only two aspects are considered — the flow of questions and the attitude expressed in the questioning. These seem useful enough to show the variety of manner and the necessity of adopting a manner suited to particular purpose.

1. Flow. Flow of questioning refers to such things as the frequency, rate and sequence of questions asked. The most useful generalisation is that people don't like to be asked a lot of questions, especially at a fast pace. At minimum the experience is vaguely uncomfortable; from there it can become actively stressful. According to purpose, then, the practitioner would adjust the flow of questioning.

One would think, for example, that where purposes include the stimulation of respondents' expressivity or enhancement of understanding, the questioning would be deliberate, measured and calm. And, where the purpose is to get respondents to disclose information that they do not wish to give, the questioning would be fast, urgent and hectic. Yet that is not the case, at least not in classrooms and interrogations.

Ever since the very start of research into classroom questioning (Stevens, 1912), observers have noted regularly and with some astonishment that teachers ask a great number of questions at a markedly high rate — too fast for pupils to think, let alone to express their thought. The average lapse of time between the pupil's answer and the teacher's next question has been measured at less than one second (Rowe, 1974). It has proven to take arduous training for teachers to increase their pausing or 'wait-time' even to two seconds (Swift and Gooding, 1983).

What purposes are served by this fast, continuous questioning? One of the purposes seems to be to maintain control over social and verbal behaviour in the classroom (for instance, Mishler, 1975), hence the understandably great difficulty of getting teachers to reduce the number or rate of questions asked — that is, seemingly to reduce their control over the classroom. This manner of questioning is manifestly effective for that purpose. On the other hand, it cannot be demonstrated to advance other purposes such as the enhancement of pupils' cognitive, affective, and expressive processes (Dillon, 1982b).

Interrogators, too, can be seen to use this manner of questioning — in police dramas and World War II films. But in practice, as far as is known, their manner of questioning is advisedly measured and calm. According to the manuals, the questions should be asked in a conversational tone, in a smooth, lower, relaxed voice (Buckwalter, 1983). The interrogator is to *avoid* all rapid-fire questions and rushing any answers; he is to wait for the full answer, as complete as the respondent wishes, and to give the respondent the opportunity to qualify it. What purpose is served? The intended purpose is to obtain true, factual information from someone who is reluctant to disclose it. Rapid, rough questioning seems to frustrate this purpose; it is better to use persistent yet patient questioning (see also Inbau and Reid, 1967; Royal and Schutt, 1976).

For some reason, physicians use a manner of questioning similar to that popularly thought to be used by interrogators but not actually used by them, and identical to that actually used by teachers but seemingly not expected to be used by them. In doctor–patient interviews, the doctor is observed (West, 1983) to speak almost nothing but questions, to ask numerous, response-constraining questions (yes/no, multiple-choice), at a staccato pace with incursions into patient turns, and with an even briefer pause between the patient's answer and the doctor's next question — as little as one-tenth of a second, 'demonstrating that a simple "yes" or "no" is all that he will listen to' (p. 91). Moreover, precisely as with students and teachers, patients ask remarkably few questions of doctors. What purposes are being served, and which ones frustrated, by this questioning?

Cross-examiners also use rapid-fire questioning, but advisedly so. It is relentless and intimidating, keeping pressure on the witness and keeping him off-balance, while enforcing his subordinate status (Kestler, 1982). The purpose is to give the witness no time to think, and no opportunity to formulate the answer carefully. 'There should be no gap between questions which would allow the witness time to think' (p. 46). As Wellman (1903) put it in his classic manual, 'He cannot invent answers as fast as you can invent questions' (p. 68). The sequencing of the questions is also according to purpose. In carefully preparing the questions, the examiner arranges them in logical order but he must not ask them in logical order (Wellman, 1903), rather eliminating any semblance of order at all, using 'the hop, skip, and jump approach' (Kestler, 1982, p. 123). The trick is not in using chaotic questioning but in creating order from it for the jury, not to mention for the examiner himself.

As these four cases show, the flow of questioning differs in various practices, as do the purposes that are served *and* that are not served by the manner of questioning in a given practice.

2. *Attitude.* Here, too, the practitioner may ask self, 'Just what am I questioning *for?*', and then adopt an attitude of questioning that achieves that purpose. There is no one attitude to adopt, and no point in adopting the attitude of successful questioners in other circumstances.

Again, the only generalisation that appears to hold is that people find it threatening or somehow diminishing to be asked questions, even when the questioner does not set out to be threatening. Great care must therefore be taken to see that the attitude that is received is the attitude that the questioner wishes to convey, and that both be suitable to purpose. A threatening manner is conducive to some purposes but not others, even in the same situation.

The questioner must be clear both as to what his purpose is, and which purposes are being served by his manner of questioning. The case is complicated because there are multiple purposes that can be held in any one situation, such that one purpose but not another may be served by the questioning.

For instance, one purpose in a classroom might be to stimulate student thought, and in a personnel interview, to get the applicant to talk about self; yet the teacher's questioning may serve rather the purpose of social and verbal control, and the interviewer's may cause the respondent to talk less and less with each successive question (see Dillon, 1978, 1982b; Drake, 1972). There is a therapeutic purpose in psychoanalysis that the analyst's questioning might not only not serve but actually contravene, both by reinforcing such things as dependency and defensiveness in the patient and by serving the therapist's pregenital desire to master and dominate in the relationship (Olinick, 1954).

Such are the purposes that are exactly appropriate, on the other hand, in cross-examination. But they are quite inappropriate to interrogation, and they are ruinous to survey interviewing. Interrogators and interviewers must deliberately adopt a non-judgemental manner of questioning, the first because they need all true information, the second because they need all reliable responses. The two cases form a surprising pair, for respondents in an opinion poll are not coerced into answering the questions and seemingly stand to lose nothing by answering them correctly, whereas suspects are in a coercive situation where they can lose a great deal by giving truthful answers.

As will be detailed in a subsequent section, survey respondents give distorted answers to apparently innocuous questions about everyday matters — when the matters are seen as socially desirable and when the questions are felt to have a right and wrong answer; but also when, for any questions, respondents make an effort to be agreeable and polite with the interviewer (Sudman and Bradburn, 1982). To avoid such distortion to the extent possible, interviewers must not only formulate their questions in a certain way but also ask them in a non-judgemental way, conveying neither approval nor disapproval to the respondent.

Interrogators, too, oddly enough, must ask questions in a non-judgemental manner. As the manuals repeatedly point out, what the interrogator needs is truthful information; others, later, will make the judgements. 'The interrogator is never the judge,' says Buckwalter (1983, p. 196). 'You do not interrogate to gain the victory over a person. You interrogate to obtain and verify information' (p. 194). Far from being judgemental, here are the attitudes and qualities to be exhibited by the interrogator: understanding, considerate, sympathetic, empathic, concerned, gentle, kind, courteous, tactful, reasonable, fair, honest, warm, respectful, friendly (pp. 190–197). One manual is even entitled 'the gentle art of interrogation' (Royal and Schutt, 1976).

It is this manner of questioning, rather than the Hollywoodish opposite, that more likely induces a person who is fraughtfully implicated in a bad situation to tell the truth. The pragmatics of this question–answer situation are likely to be that the suspect or otherwise involved person comes to believe something like, 'The truth is the best solution to my predicament; I can trust him, he will understand, I can explain.' By contrast, a judgemental, superior, threatening or intimidating style of questioning seems to confirm the person's initial reluctance to disclose what he knows. If people in an opinion poll have trouble averring that they do not hold a library card or that they prefer this opinion over that, one can imagine the difficulty of confessing to murder, rapine and mayhem.

The case of teachers is all the more complicated because they, too, need to know what the students truly think (for instance, in a discussion) and know (for instance, in a recitation), at the same time that they are required to be judgemental. In classroom question–answer situations, whether for questions of fact or opinion, it is obligatory that the teacher follow the answer with a judgement as to its quality (for example, accept/reject and/or modify). In not a single observed case did teachers fail to provide such 'follow-up' (Johnson, 1979, p. 45). Even without empirical verification, it is known that the role of teaching, by definition, entails judgement and correction of pupils' thought processes.

Finally, as noted, the case of counsellors and therapists — as well as of others, such as personnel interviewers — is not only complicated but variegated. According to therapeutic purpose and process as variously and divergently conceived, one form of question and one manner of questioning, as well as their contraries, might serve to purpose and either be required or prohibited in practice. It is odd to think that some counsellors can appear to be inquisitors, whereas interrogators adopt the attitude of counsellors.

To summarise, there is no one form of question and no one manner of asking questions that is reliably known to have one given effect, even in given situations. In a field where the most extensive research has been carried on for half a century, Schuman and Presser (1981), having themselves performed over 200 experiments, state that 'knowledge of questioning effects of all kinds is likely to be a slow and uphill struggle' (p. 77).

What, then, are the types of questions that should be used? What strategies of questioning should be pursued? These are pressing questions in practice and they are perplexing ones for theoretical and empirical understanding of questions. To both questions, the fairest answer is, 'No one but you knows'. That is, the answer is to be found by the practitioner in his or her particular circumstance. One of the best ways to look for this answer is to attend not so much to questions and questioning as to answers and answering.

Answers

Of the three elements of questioning, this last is equally as complex, more interesting and the most important both conceptually and practically. Understanding what answers are is a good way to understand what questions are; a theoretical knowledge of answers is the best practical guide to formulating and asking questions — and then seeing what the answer is and whether it is an answer at all.

Like the other elements of questioning, this one consists of a sentence and an act, or answer and answering. This is better thought of as response and responding, for it turns out that, of all the things that people may say and do when asked a question, the very least is to give an answer. Types of responses and styles of responding will now be examined.

Types of Responses. It may help to appreciate at the outset that most responses are not answers and that the defining characteristic of an answer is not 'something said in response to a question'. For, although answers are indeed responses to a question, so also are all manner of other things.

In conceptual terms, it can be said that 'answer' is not a thing but a *notion* and, in large part, a pragmatic one. It describes a certain character that is attributed to a given sentence such that the sentence is conceived as being of the kind 'answer', when following upon a given question, and that same sentence as 'non-answer' when following upon some other question or no question at all.

What, then, makes a sentence an answer? That is not an easy question, and so far there is not a good answer to it. This question can be approached by considering the variety of responses that can be given to a question.

Unfortunately, the available terminology is unclear and the typologies are ill-founded. It will have to be accepted for the moment that there are multiple terms used in divergent senses for the variety of things that have to be described and distinguished. Some of the terms will refer to the response-sentence, others to the act of responding and yet others to the respondent; still other terms will confound these three. Attention will be paid to the notions. First, there are things that follow a question but are non-responses, next there are responses that are non-answers and last, there are answer-responses.

1. Non-responses. Nothing at all may follow upon a question, or nothing remotely connected with it, or nothing appropriately connected. For an instance of each: silence, wild talk, change of topic (although any of these could also represent a deliberate mode of responding).

Speech wildly unrelated to the preceding question is a non-response. Speech that is somehow related is a response. (Behaviour may also be considered a response.) There are multiplicitous relations that a piece of speech can have with a preceding question. For example, Strenstroem (1984) views response as an utterance coherently related to a preceding question by grammatical and lexical cohesion (for example, reference, substitution, ellipsis) and/or by prosodic, semantic and pragmatic agreement.

There are also delayed responses such as requests for repetition and clarification (Stenstroem, 1984) or other procedural problems (Churchill, 1978). 'Huh?'

2. Non-answer responses. The questioner may fancy that the other person is required to give an answer, and he may expect, want or intend an answer of some particular type, but all that seems to be required in most question–answer situations is that the person give a response. All manner of non-answer responses can be given, most of which must be politely treated as acceptable in address to the question (or to the act of asking it).

'Procedural problem, completion of invitation, ellipsis, interruption, emotion, and clarification' are among the types of non-answer responses that Churchill (1978) found in conversations of a married couple; only half of the responses were answers. Not only were the non-answers given by the respondent, they were also accepted or tolerated by the questioner. The questioner apparently applies two tests to what follows upon the question (p. 150):

1. Is it recognisable as a response?
2. If not, can the noncompliance be explained away?

Some types of response supply or constitute explanations. 'Excuses' are any responses that explicitly indicate either inability or unwillingness to answer (Johnson, 1979, p. 33). 'I don't know' indicates inability, as also does a denial of the question's presupposition — 'the best possible excuse for not answering' (p. 31). But respondents rarely indicate, in a serious way, an unwillingness to answer. For example, students will camouflage unwillingness as inability (for instance, 'I don't know'), while teachers choose to infer inability rather than face what both parties suspect is an unwillingness to answer (pp. 86, 89).

'Evade' and 'disclaim', in Stenstroem's (1984) analysis, are appropriate responses (though not answers) because they relate coherently to the questioning act (though not to the question sentence). As the terms suggest, these are inter-actional moves rather than sentences. A respondent may evade with 'You know that' or 'What a stupid question'; disclaim by 'I don't know' or 'I don't want to tell you'; and do either by saying 'How should I know?'

These examples are taken from everyday conversations, and are probably rare in professional question–answer situations. Yet even in the everyday case studied by Stenstroem (1984), evade and disclaim together accounted for only 4 per cent of all responses. People seem to manage to give acceptable responses without having to admit their inability or reveal their unwillingness to respond with an answer.

3. Answer-responses. There remains the class of responses that are answers. A variety of definitions have been proposed and a variety of types distinguished. All of these exhibit a degree of confusion among three criterial aspects: the cognition of the questioner; the form of the question; and the act of questioning. To which one, and in which respect, is the character of answer being attributed?

Sociolinguists, for example, have defined 'answer' as those responses that fulfill the logical or substantive expectations of the question (Johnson, 1979). Logicians, on the other hand, have viewed answers as those responses that are appropriate from the questioner's point of view (Harrah, 1985). Sociolinguists have distinguished 'direct answer' as a response that gives exactly the information required, and an indirect answer as giving information from which a direct answer may be deduced (Stenstroem, 1984). Logicians distinguish a direct answer as giving exactly what the question calls for, while an indirect gives some of that (Harrah, 1985).

Who and what is requiring, expecting, calling for? It has to be borne in mind that answers are imperfectly understood as relating now to the questioner, now to the question, and now to the questioning.

As expected, most manuals of practice give confused and useless typologies of answers, as they do of questions. And, as expected, logicians provide helpful ones.

To the question, 'Is glass a liquid at 70°F?' Belnap and Steel (1976, pp. 126–7) say that:

1. A *just-complete* (or direct) answer is, 'Glass is a liquid at 70°F';
2. A *complete* answer (implies direct answer) is 'Glass is a liquid at 70°F, and China is populous'.

To the question, 'Was she wearing the green dress, the emerald bracelet, or both?', a *partial* answer (implied by a direct answer) is, 'She was wearing green' or 'emerald'; an *eliminative* answer (negation of partial answer, implies denial of some direct answer) is, 'She wasn't wearing green' or 'emeralds'; and a *corrective* answer (implies denial of every direct answer) is, 'She was naked'.

More generally, Harrah (1985) distinguishes replies that are *sufficient*, comprised of the set of indicated replies plus wanted replies (a subset of indicated), plus corrective replies (negate the presupposition or core assertion of the question); and replies that are *relevant*, comprised of full replies (imply the sufficient) and partial replies (implied by the sufficient).

With these lists in hand, a practitioner can ask himself, 'what are the kinds of answers that I am after, and what kinds am I actually getting?'

When does a reply to a question constitute a *conclusive answer* to it? asks Hintikka (1983) — if and only if it brings about the truth of the desideratum in question, making it the case that the questioner conclusively knows the X in question and answer. 'Who killed Julius Caesar?' The answer is 'Cassius' and it is a direct and true answer. But it is a conclusive answer only if the questioner can say not only, 'I know that Cassius killed Julius Caesar' but also essentially, 'I know who Cassius is' (p. 180). The conclusiveness criterion describes answers in relation to the knowledge-state of the questioner.

Both the purposes and the knowledge of the questioner are described in Grewendorf's (1983) concept of a *pragmatically significant answer*. An answer that is pragmatically significant is informative with respect to the questioner's state of knowledge and it is useful with respect to his purpose or project, both of these relative to the situation in which the question is asked.

For a simple example, one knows how informative and useful 'Paris' is as an answer to the question 'Where is the Eiffel Tower?' asked on the streets of Paris. Grewendorf gives a sophisticated example, illustrating five different answers to the same question asked in five different situations. All five answers are correct, all five may be informative, but only one is in addition valuable and useful, and that one is different in each of the five cases. Furthermore, the *range* of significant answers differs in each situation, to the point that in no case does the given answer in any one situation belong to the range of alternative answers available for any of the other situations.

The respondent therefore makes estimates about the questioner's knowledge and purposes in this situation; assesses the value to the questioner of the various answers possible in this situation; and then gives an answer according to this pragmatic postulate: 'Choose among the answers which you think are true that one for which the assumed/expected pragmatic significance is greatest'. (pp. 79, 80).

Here is seen a demonstration that answerhood is a pragmatic notion. Answer is a character attributed to a response that exhibits certain qualities in relation to the question that is asked, the knowledge and the purposes of the questioner, and the situation wherein question and answer transpire.

Necessarily, *answer* also entails the knowledge and purposes of the respondent in that situation. What are the different ways that people may use to respond to questions?

Styles of Responding

From the questioner's point of view, the most desirable way to respond is described by Grewendorf's (1983) concept of a pragmatically significant answer. But, just as was the case with responses and answers, so too there are many ways of responding without answering the question. Practitioners have to know these responding strategies in theory in order to spot and outmanoeuvre them in practice.

Evading and Lying. In 'How to not answer a question', Weiser (1975) identifies seven purposive devices used to evade or otherwise not to answer the question, 'How old are you?' One device is to be pointedly non-responsive: 'Nice weather we're having'. Another is a masquerade over something unconnected with the question. The respondent has a sudden thought 'Oh, no! I think I left my headlights on.' Something is happening: 'Look at the sunset — quick — before it changes.' The respondent does not hear the question so responds with: 'What are you writing your dissertation on?' A third device is to respond with a question that is semantically connected with the question asked. 'Why do you ask?' or 'How old do you think I am?'

The respondent might also maintain silence or give a direct refusal to answer: 'I'd rather not answer that.' But two other devices seem more useful, especially as they are not evasive.

Selective ambiguity is used in a pretence of co-operativeness, answering as if the questioner wants to know that one term of the ambiguity in question rather than the other. The question is taken in another way: 'Don't worry, they'll let me into that bar.'

Lying is the most satisfying strategy for the respondent. It is not an evasive strategy, for it directly answers the question. 'Lying is the only way of "not answering" a question that will work when the questioner is absolutely determined to get an answer' (p. 653).

Given that these strategies are used in everyday exchanges between peers, their use can be appreciated in other situations where people are asked questions by those of superior authority or social status. Reisman and Benny (1956) nicely explain: 'People in power have the "right" to ask questions; people of less power feel they have the right to lie or to evade in answering.'

Stonewalling. Far from evading or lying, stonewalling is giving direct, correct answers to questions when and as asked. But the answers may be meaningless. A witness, for example, might answer just exactly as required but, if not asked or if not asked rightly, he will not answer with the crucial knowledge that he has.

The problem for the questioner is to ask *all* the right questions, each in *just* the right way. Yet he might not know enough to ask and what he does know might be mistaken. Thus the questions may be based on false presuppositions and mistaken presumptions which the stonewalling witness affirms to be true in the course of giving a perfectly direct and correct answer that only confounds or misleads the questioner. If the questioner is lucky enough to catch on, he must press against the stone wall with a series of little, corrective questions pointed this way and that. Each will yield just one more tiny bit of information.

For example, suppose an administrative official is called to a hearing about racial discrimination in his department's employment practices, and suppose that no employment tests happened to be given during October:

'How many minority candidates failed the test in October?'
'None.'
'They all passed?'
'No.'
'Well, how many passed, then?'
'Zero.'
'Did any minorities even take the test?'
'No.'
'Why not? How many candidates were there in all?'
'Zero.'
'You mean, nobody even took the test?'
'Right.'
'What — you do have a test, don't you?'
'Yes.'
'And you give it regularly?'
'Yes.'
'Did you give it in October?'
'No.'
'All right, how about November?' (and so on)

By contrast, a co-operative witness would have answered to the very first question, 'There wasn't any test in October.' *Co-operative responding* consists of giving a corrective, indirect response rather than a correct, direct one; it corrects the false presuppositions and mistaken presumptions entailed in the questioning, and goes on to provide the supportive and/or suggestive information at issue. Joshi

(1983) defines it as 'both giving a truthful and informative response and "squaring away" the discrepancies in mutual beliefs discerned during the interaction' (p. 237). The conversational principle here runs that not only must the respondent not give a false answer, but also he must not permit the questioner to infer from the true answer something that the respondent knows to be false (Joshi, 1982).

Natural-language query systems like CO-OP (Kaplan, 1981) have been designed to give 'co-operative responses' and are being used in practice to give 'communicatively adequate answers' to government officials (Berry-Rogghe, Kolvenbach and Lutz, 1981). Unlike machines, respondents cannot be so programmed. Some respondents know the presuppositions and presumptions better than the questioner does, and use them to better advantage.

Withholding and Concealing. Some respondents do not disclose what they know, either intentionally concealing it or unknowingly withholding it. In various types of investigations (criminal, insurance, industrial), both the innocent as well as the guilty may withhold or conceal information intentionally and unintentionally.

Investigators have to question not only the classically hardened and tight-lipped criminal but also other suspects, informants, witnesses, victims, litigants and complainants, as well as other people who may be accomplices or accessories of the suspects, or friends and relatives of suspects or victims or witnesses, and various parties who, for one reason or another, are hostile, reluctant, unco-operative or just have their own prejudiced view of events (Buckwalter, 1983). *Any* of these respondents may withhold or conceal information. Why?

Even friendly and co-operative witnesses still may not give information, for any of 15 reasons cited by Royal and Schutt (1976, p. 97), or a dozen by Buckwalter (1983, p. 100). For example: protection of self or of others or of something (for instance, a business); fear of becoming involved; personal inconvenience; nature of the subject (too unpleasant, taboo); faulty perception or memory.

The respondent may not even be aware of withholding information, by reason of ignorance of the legalities or other failure to recognise that what he knows is relevant. Finally, one good reason is that respondents often are *not asked* for that information.

There are a dozen signals of speech, body and circumstance that permit the practitioner to perceive the withholding, and a variety of direct questions that he can ask to overcome it, first by asking about the withholding itself, then about information withheld (Buckwalter, 1983).

Distorting. To respond without answering, people need not be caught in the dramatic situation of suspects or witnesses to a crime. Respondents in market surveys and opinion polls commonly respond with distorted information about simple everyday matters.

The matters in question are those that can be seen as socially desirable or undesirable, and the questions are those that can be felt to have a right or wrong answer. The distortion is a matter of over- and under-reporting the behaviours in question. The common categories are identified by Sudman and Bradburn (1982).

Behaviours that are over-reported relate to being a good citizen (for instance, voting, knowing the issues), being an informed and cultured person (reading books, going to plays, education), fulfilling moral and social responsibilities (being employed, giving to charity). Under-reported events include illness and disabilities, financial status and illegal behaviour, including traffic violations. The proportion of distorted responses increases from least to most as the questions ask about voter registration, library card, bankruptcy, voting and drunken driving (Bradburn and Sudman, 1980).

Why would people respond to such questions that way? By now it should be clear that, used wilfully or not, non-answering strategies need not signify malicious or negative motives. They present a problem to the questioner, but they solve a problem for the respondent. Indeed, in the case of survey research, the respondent's problem is precisely that of *being a good respondent* (Sudman and Bradburn, 1974). For the respondent and the way he responds, that may mean, for example, choosing to: tell the truth, or appear to be socially undesirable; be embarrassed for not knowing the answer, or be a good respondent and answer the question (by guessing or haphazardly choosing); get into conflict over controversial questions, or be polite and agree with the interviewer's statements.

By now it should also be clear that the choice of responding strategy depends not just on the question but on the situation in which it is asked. A recent book on questioning (Hogarth, 1982) proclaims in its very first sentence: 'It is well known that people often respond inconsistently to the same question asked at different times and that different forms of semantically identical questions can induce systematically different responses' (p. 1).

A good example was provided long ago by Getzels (1954): suppose that strangers make a certain individual feel nervous and inferior; this person is asked, in three different situations, the question 'How do you like meeting strangers?' In the job interview he answers, 'Strangers are all right. I enjoy meeting them.' To the opinion pollster who has just walked up to him, obviously having no difficulty meeting strangers, he responds, 'Depends on the stranger.' During a therapy session he avers, 'Strangers make me feel nervous and inferior' (pp. 84–5).

Surprisingly enough, the general implication for practice does not deal with some kind of questioning strategy. Rather, it is to *listen to answers*. A basic communication problem in question–answer situations is to get the respondent to give an answer and to get the questioner to listen to it.

The practical importance of listening to answers should be obvious, yet practitioners seem to be preoccupied with asking their questions and thinking up the next one to ask. Manuals have to stress repeatedly that they should carefully listen to the answers that come (for instance, Kestler, 1982). A manual for private investigators (Buckwalter, 1983) states that communication in that field is the practice of two arts — questioning and listening, and it further states: 'For the private investigator, listening is the most important part of the communication in the investigative interview' (p. 46).

The practical importance can also be stressed of attending to theoretical aspects of answers and answering. Understanding what answers are is a good way to understand what questions are. Knowing the answers that may come to questions is an excellent practical guide to formulating and asking them. Here is a specific recommendation.

As part of preparing the questions beforehand, one should construct a dummy answer modelled after the question and showing all the possible answers to it (Dillon, 1984b). Then one can look at the model and see if that is the kind of thing one wants to know in answer. If not, the question is re-formed and the dummy answer re-moulded. Dummy answers are clever: they can tell us what we want to know and also how to ask for it. So: make a dummy of the answer before the answer makes a dummy out of you.

Conclusion

As a communication skill, questioning is far harder to study and describe than to acquire and practice. It is not a simple matter in practice, yet there is nothing mysterious about it — the skill is well within the reach of interested practitioners.

The better thing to reach for is understanding, not technique. Two things have to be understood — the purposes of practice and the elements of questioning. 'What am I asking questions *for?*' Then the elements of questioning are turned to purpose. 'What happens as a result?' It may help to tape-record the questions and answers, to identify the elements as they appear, to trace their turnings and to reconnect them to purpose.

The practitioner may discover that no manner of questioning seems to achieve the purpose. In that case the use of questioning itself is a communicative blunder. Many other devices can be used to get people to respond in the desired way (for example, Dillon, 1979, 1981). Communicative skill may turn on the choice to question as well as on the choice of questions.

References

Arbuckle, D.S. (1975) *Counseling and Psychotherapy: An Existential-Humanistic View*, Allyn & Bacon, Boston

Belnap, N.D. and Steel, T.B. (1976) *The Logic of Questions and Answers*, Yale University Press, New Haven, CT

Benjamin, A. (1977) *The Helping Interview*, 2nd edn., Houghton Mifflin, Boston

Berliner, D.C. (1983) 'Developing Conceptions of Classroom Environments', *Educational Psychologist*, *18*, 1–13

Berry-Rogghe, G.L., Kolvenbach, M. and Lutz, H.D. (1980) 'Interacting with PLIDIS, A Deductive Question Answering System for German' in L. Bolc (ed.), *Natural Language Question*

Answering Systems, Hanser, Munich

Blankenship, A.B. (1940) 'The Influence of the Question Form upon the Response in a Public Opinion Poll', *Psychological Record, 3,* 345–422

Bolc, L. (ed.) (1980) *Natural Language Question Answering Systems,* Hanser, Munich

Bradburn, N.M. (1982) 'Question-wording Effects in Surveys' in R.M. Hogarth (ed.), *Question Framing and Response Consistency,* Jossey-Bass, San Francisco

───── and Sudman, S. (1980) *Improving Interview Method and Questionnaire Design: Response Effects to Threatening Questions in Survey Research,* Aldine, Chicago

Buckwalter, A. (1983) *Interviews and Interrogations,* Butterworth, Stoneham, MA

Carlson, L. (1983) *Dialogue Games: An Approach to Discourse Analysis,* Reidel, Dordecht, Holland

Chester, D. and Bowring, N. (1962) *Questions in Parliament,* Clarendon, Oxford

Chisholm, W. (ed.) (1984) *Interrogativity,* Benjamins, Amsterdam

Churchill, L. (1978) *Questioning Strategies in Sociolinguistics.* Newbury, Rowley, Massachusetts

Clark, M. (1972) *Perplexity and Knowledge: An Inquiry into the Structures of Questioning,* Nijhoff, The Hague

Curran, C.A. (1952) *Counseling in Catholic Life and Education,* Macmillan, New York

Dillon, J.T. (1978) 'Using Questions to Depress Student Thought', *School Review, 87,* 50–63

───── (1979) 'Alternatives to Questioning', *High School Journal, 62,* 217–22

───── (1981) 'To Question and Not to Question during Discussion II: Non-questioning Techniques', *Journal of Teacher Education, 32* (6), 15–20

───── (1982a) 'The Multidisciplinary Study of Questioning', *Journal of Educational Psychology, 74,* 147–65

───── (1982b) 'The Effect of Questions in Education and Other Enterprises', *Journal of Curriculum Studies, 14,* 127–52

───── (1983) *Teaching and the Art of Questioning,* Bloomington, IN, Phi Delta Kappa (Fastback No. 194)

───── (1984a) 'Research on Questioning and Discussion', *Educational Leadership, 42*(3), 50–6

───── (1984b) 'Finding the Question for Evaluation Research', paper presented at the annual meeting of the American Educational Research Association, New Orleans

Drake, J.D. (1972) *Interviewing for Managers,* American Management Association, New York

Ellis, A. (1977) 'The Rational-emotive Facilitation of Psychotherapeutic Goals', in A. Ellis and R. Grieger (eds), *Handbook of Rational-Emotive Therapy,* Springer, New York

Fisher, S. and Todd, A. (eds) (1983) *The Social Organization of Doctor — Patient Communication,* Center for Applied Linguistics, Washington

Getzels, J.W. (1954) 'The Question-Answer Process', *Public Opinion Quarterly, 18,* 80–91

Goody, E.N. (ed.) (1978) *Questions and Politeness: Strategies in Social Interaction,* Cambridge University Press, Cambridge

Graesser, A. and Black, J. (eds) (1985) *The Psychology of Questions,* Erlbaum, Hillsdale, New Jersey

Grewendorf, G. (1983) 'What Answers Can Be Given?' in F. Kiefer (ed.), *Questions and Answers,* Reidel, Dordrecht, Holland, pp. 45–84

Harrah, D. (1985) 'The Logic of Questions' in F. Guenthner and D. Gabbay (eds), *Handbook of Philosophical Logic,* Reidel, Dordrecht, Holland

Hintikka, J. (ed.) (1981) *Scientific Method as a Problem-solving and Question-Answering Technique,* Reidel, Dordrecht, Holland, special issue of *Synthese, 47,* no. 1.

───── (1983) 'New Foundations for a Theory of Questions and Answers', in F. Kiefer (ed.), *Questions and Answers,* Reidel, Dordrecht, Holland

Hogarth, R.M. (ed.) (1982) *Question Framing and Response Consistency,* Jossey-Bass, San Francisco

Hunkins, F.P. (ed.) (1972) *Questioning Strategies and Techniques,* Allyn & Bacon, Boston

Hyman, R.T. (1979) *Strategic Questioning,* Prentice-Hall, Englewood Cliffs, New Jersey

Inbau, F.E. and Reid, J.E. (1967) *Criminal Interrogation and Confession,* Williams & Wilkins, Baltimore

Johnson, M. (1979) *Discussion Dynamics,* Newbury, Rowley, MA

Joshi, A.K. (1982) 'Mutual Beliefs in Question-answer Systems' in N.V. Smith (ed.), *Mutual Knowledge,* Academic Press, London

───── (1983) 'Varieties of Co-operative Responses in Question-answer Systems' in F. Kiefer (ed.), *Questions and Answers,* Reidel, Dordrecht, Holland

Kaiser, A. (1979) *Questioning Techniques,* Hunter, Pomona, CA

Kaplan, S.J. (1981) 'Appropriate Responses to Inappropriate Questions' in A.K. Joshi, B.L. Webber, and I.A. Sag, (eds), *Elements of Discourse Understanding,* Cambridge University Press, Cambridge

Kearsley, G.P. (1976) 'Questions and Question-Asking in Verbal Discourse', *Journal of Psycholinguistic Research, 5,* 355–75

Kestler, J.L. (1982) *Questioning Techniques and Tactics,* Shepard/McGraw-Hill, Springs, CO

Kiefer, F. (ed.) (1983) *Questions and Answers,* Reidel, Dordrecht, Holland

Lehnert, W.G. (1978) *The Process of Question Answering: A Computer Simulation of Cognition,* Erlbaum, Hillsdale, New Jersey

Loftus, E.F. (1979) *Eyewitness Testimony,* Harvard University Press, Cambridge, Massachusetts
——— (1982) 'Interrogating Eyewitnesses — Good Questions and Bad', in R.M. Hogarth (ed.), *Question Framing and Response Consistency,* Jossey-Bass, San Francisco

Long, L., Paradise, L. and Long, T. (1981) *Questioning: Skills for the Helping Process,* Brooks/Cole, Monterey, CA

Metzler, K. (1977) *Creative Interviewing: The Writer's Guide to Gathering Information by Asking Questions,* Prentice-Hall, Englewood Cliffs, New Jersey

Meyer, M. (1983) *Meaning and Reading,* Benjamins, Amsterdam

Mishler, E.G. (1975) 'Studies in Dialogue and Discourse II, Types of Discourse Initiated by and Sustained through Questioning', *Journal of Psycholinguistic Research, 4,* 99–121

Muscio, B. (1916), 'The Influence of the Form of a Question', *British Journal of Educational Psychology, 8,* 351–89

Olinick, S.L. (1954) 'Some Considerations of the Use of Questioning as a Psychoanalytic Technique', *Journal of the American Psychoanalytic Association, 2,* 57–66

Payne, S.L. (1951) *The Art of Asking Questions,* Princeton University Press, Princeton, NJ

Philips, S.U. (1984) 'The Social Organization of Questions and Answers in Courtroom Discourse', *Text, 4,* 225–48
——— (in press) 'Wh-Questions in Courtroom Language Use', in L. Kedar, (ed.), *Power Through Discourse,* Ablex, Norwood

Reisman, D. and Benney, M. (1956) 'Asking and Answering', *Journal of Business, 29,* 225–36

Richardson, S.A., Dohrenwend, B.S. and Klein, D. (1965) *Interviewing: Its Form and Functions,* Basic Books, New York

Robinson, W. (1980) *Questions Are the Answer: Believing Today,* Pilgrim Press, New York

Roby, T.W. (1985) 'Commonplaces and Models of Discussion', Paper presented at the annual meeting of the American Educational Research Association, Chicago

Rogers, C.R. (1942), *Counseling and Psychotherapy,* Houghton Mifflin, Boston
——— (1951) *Client-Centered Therapy,* Houghton Mifflin, Boston

Rowe, M.B. (1974) 'Wait-time and Rewards as Instructional Variables', *Journal of Research in Science Teaching, 11,* 81–94

Royal, R.F. and Schutt, S. (1976) *The Gentle Art of Interviewing and Interrogation,* Prentice-Hall, Englewood Cliffs, NJ

Schuman, H., and Presser, S. (1981) *Questions and Answers in Attitude Surveys,* Academic Press, New York

Slavens, T.P. (ed.) (1978) *Informational Interviews and Questions,* Scarecrow Press, Metuchen, New Jersey

Stenstroem, A. -B. (1984) *Questions and Responses, in English Conversation,* Gleerup, Malmoe, Sweden

Stevens, R. (1912) 'The Question as a Measure of Efficiency in Instruction', *Teachers College Contributions to Education, No. 48,* Teachers College Press, New York

Stodolsky, S.S., Ferguson, T.L. and Wimpelberg, K. (1981) 'The Recitation Persists, but What Does it Look Like?' *Journal of Curriculum Studies, 13,* 121–30

Sudman, S. and Bradburn, N.M. (1974) *Response Effects in Surveys,* Aldine, Chicago
——— (1982) *Asking Questions,* Jossey-Bass, San Francisco

Swift, J.N. and Gooding, C.T. (1983) 'Interaction of Wait Time Feedback and Questioning Instruction on Middle School Science Teaching', *Journal of Research in Science Teaching, 20,* 721–30

Weiser, A. (1975) 'How Not to Answer a Question' in R.E. Grossman, L.J. San and T.J. Vance (eds), *Papers From the 11th Regional Meeting of the Chicago Linguistic Society,* Chicago Linguistic Society, Chicago, pp. 649–60

Wellman, F.L. (1903) *The Art of Cross-Examination,* (4th edn, 1936, reprinted 1974), Macmillan, New York

Wessler, R.A. and Wessler, R.L. (1980) *The Principles and Practices of Rational-Emotive Therapy,*

Jossey-Bass, San Francisco

West, C. (1983) ' ''Ask me no questions'': An Analysis of Queries and Replies in Physician-Patient Dialogues' in S. Fisher and A.D. Todd (eds), *The Social Organization of Doctor-Patient Communication,* Center for Applied Linguistics, Washington

Woodbury, H. (1984) 'The Strategic Use of Questions in Court', *Semiotica, 48,* 197–228

Xerox Corporation (1976) *Professional Selling Skills II,* Xerox Learning Systems, Greenwich, Connecticut

Yamada, S. (1913), 'A Study of Questioning', *Pedagogical Seminary, 20,* 129–86.

5 REINFORCEMENT

Len Cairns

In most people's everyday activities and communication with others, considerable use is made of the skill of reinforcement. Parents, at 2am, feeding their newborn baby smile and attentively murmur 'That's a good girl' as the infant finishes her bottle of milk. At work, the foreman calls the apprentice welder aside and congratulates him on the important part he played in yesterday's big job at the plant. At school, young Lisa is awarded a gold star and verbal praise for the improvement she has shown in her daily spelling work. Each of these brief examples could be said to illustrate the daily use, in natural communication settings, of the skill of reinforcement.

The concept of reinforcement is a keystone of the behaviourist psychology area and, more particularly, it is associated with what is known as operant psychology as espoused by Skinner (1953). Simply put, reinforcement, in this mode of thinking, can be described as *a stimulus that follows a response made by a person that increases the likelihood of the response being repeated.*

This chapter presents the skill of reinforcement as a basic and important skill in interpersonal communication and shows, briefly, some of the many areas of application of this skill in current thinking and practice. As a first step, reinforcement is clarified and discussed in relation to the traditional concept of feedback in communication theory and models. Next, reinforcement is defined and elaborated on within the framework of the operant psychology approach. Finally, the research and application of ideas about reinforcement in some of the applied professions are discussed.

Clarifying the Concept

The term reinforcement was introduced to psychology by Pavlov (1927), whose famous salivating dogs have led to much academic research and writing — as well as having a substantial and pervasive influence on modern society where many popular jokes, cartoons and even a pop music group's name have made reference to his work. In the current theory and research, however, Pavlov's work is described as 'classical' conditioning, whereas the modern view of reinforcement theory is more closely associated with the ideas of Skinner, who pointed out the difference in the following manner: 'Pavlov himself called all events which strengthened behaviour "reinforcement" and all resulting changes "conditioning". In the Pavlovian experiment, however, a reinforcer is paired with a *stimulus;* whereas in operant behavior it is contingent upon a *response*' (1953, p. 65).

In the past there has been some debate as to the definition and usage of the term reinforcement (Berlyne, 1967), and the general area of psychology that has become known as 'learning theory' has seen a number of publications focused on the meaning and interpretation of reinforcement and related topics (Honig, 1966; Ferster and Perrott, 1968; Glaser, 1971). What has emerged is a clearer understanding that, in most modern views, the concept of reinforcement is concerned with the *after-effects* of a person's response and how consistently *related* (that is, contingent) *after-effects* can lead to the likely repetition of the original type of response. Once this basic point is clear, the significance of reinforcement in everyday life becomes obvious.

Feedback and Reinforcement

In the field of communication theory, one of the basic and most quoted models is that based on the work of Berlo (1960), which has been characterised as the 'S-M-C-R' model (Rogers and Agarwala-Rogers, 1976). In this model, S stands for source of the communication, M for the message sent, C for the channel of communication and R for the receiver. An important element of the model is that once a message has been received by the receiver there is *feedback* to the sender. The concept of feedback in these models of the communication process is an important aspect for the present discussion, as it is argued here that the feedback concept described in most communication theory is equivalent to the reinforcement concept of operant psychology, but it is often not so attributed by authors in the field. Rogers and Agarwala-Rogers (1976), define *feedback* in the following way: '*Feedback* is a response by the receiver to the source's message. The source may take account of feedback in modifying subsequent messages: thus feedback makes communication a dynamic, two-way process. Feedback may be thought of as messages to the source conveying knowledge of the effectiveness of a previous communication. *Positive feedback* informs the source that the intended effect of a message was achieved; *negative feedback* informs the source that the intended effect of a message was *not* achieved' (p. 13).

Recent publications on communication have continued with the same basic model with stress on feedback as an integral component of communication that has a 'regulatory effect upon the speaker' (Brooks, 1981, p. 12) and without which 'it is difficult to judge with any degree of accuracy how effective any communication transaction is' (Ruffner and Burgoon, 1981, p. 6). In addition to the assertion that the basic components of the concept of feedback can be seen as being a consequential *after-effect* of a communication message (Gardiner, 1971), there has been research and discussion on the place and effects of feedback on the communication process.

Verplanck (1955), in an early study, examined the effects of positive and negative feedback (in the forms of agreement or disagreement) applied according to a pre-arranged schedule by a receiver to the person who is the source of communication in two-way personal conversations. The findings indicated that a higher rate of personal opinion statements were made by the source participants under the positive feedback conditions than negative feedback conditions. Similar findings and discussions were presented by Stolz and Tannenbaum (1963), though their feedback situation made use of a laboratory apparatus response rather than anything approaching natural conversational situations. The parallels, in studies such as the above, with the operant psychology theory and definitions of reinforcement are both close and evident.

Perhaps the strongest evidence for the 'bridging' of the argument that the feedback tradition of communication was really a 'soft' definition and application of early operant thinking without the specific labels of that area, comes from the study conducted by Minkin, Braukmann, Minkin, *et al.* (1976). In a three-part study, Minkin *et al.* set out first to behaviourally define and observe components of conversation, then to attempt to train some young female delinquents in these behaviours, and finally, to examine whether the trained increases in the conversation behaviours in the girls were seen by observers to be beneficial, socially validated behaviours.

The two 'socially validated' conversation behaviours identified in the study were: (1) 'conversational questions', and (2) 'positive conversational feedback'. The latter element of conversation was defined in behavioural terms in the tradition of behavioural psychology and in a manner that clearly showed the link with 'reinforcement'. The study was very successful in demonstrating, in the context of a training centre, that the two components (or skills) of conversation could be behaviourally defined, observed and trained. In addition, the girls trained in the skills were evaluated by a community panel of judges to be better conversationalists than they had been before the training. While research in this tradition also has shown that reinforcement in communication can be manipulated as a behavioural change procedure (O'Leary and O'Leary, 1972, 1977), many of the early procedures described and reported on studies that used special laboratory or classroom situations and reinforcements that were far from 'natural contingencies' (Stokes and Baer, 1977).

One recent attempt to deal with this problem and the related one of the generalisation of findings across situations other than the 'special' experimental setting, has been the study of Kleitsch, Whitman and Santos (1983). In this piece of research, the authors attempted to improve the conversational interaction of four socially isolated, elderly, retarded men. The procedures used involved quite natural social praise and conversation in language learning groups; the results suggested that these procedures were not only effective in increasing the overall rate of the men's verbalisations, but generalised to other situations (Kleitsch *et al.*, 1983).

Studies such as those mentioned above have added to the strength of the assertion that reinforcement is an important and basic skill in communication and that there has been a gradual recognition by many researchers that what has traditionally been identified as 'feedback' in many communication models is similar in definition to operant theory's concept of reinforcement.

Another model of social interaction that makes use of a similar conceptualisation of feedback is the social skills model of behaviour (Argyle and Kendon, 1967). This model argues that in pursuing social and other goals in life, people act according to rules and constantly modify their behaviour on the basis of 'feedback' from the environment.

This model was based on a motor skill model and specifies how a person who is pursuing a goal at first perceives another actor (perception), then considers how to take action to meet the goal (translation). Next, the person puts into action the behaviour that appears to be required (response) and then receives feedback from the other person. This feedback may lead to changes in the perception the originator had and so starts the model's cyclical loop again. The feedback element was seen as a major point in the social skills model. (See Chapter 2 for a more detailed discussion of the model.)

In a later elaboration and extension of the model, Trower, Bryant and Argyle (1978), acknowledged a relationship between the social skills model and behavioural psychology principles, and maintained that 'feedback' in their model was an 'optional' term for reinforcement (p.71), while at the same time discussing the importance of 'rewardingness and control' elements (p.22). It is argued here that there is a need to be more specific and careful in the matter of the definition of reinforcement when using the term in such explanatory ways.

The straightforward definition of reinforcement offered at the beginning of this chapter provides a simple and clinical approach, but avoids the issues that usually surround discussion of the concept and its application. In interpersonal communication situations, an event may be described and its characteristics defined quite differently according to the theoretical perspective of the observer. For some, the use of supportive nonverbal and verbal responses to others in interview, therapy or other contexts could be described as 'empathic listening' (Rogers, 1980), 'encouragement in "good listening"' (Wallis, 1973), or 'influencing' (Ivey and Gluckstern, 1976; Munro, Manthei and Small, 1979).

For others, such communications could be a form of reinforcement that facilitates further communication and encourages the interviewee to continue in a similar vein as she was before the supportive response from the interviewer. Perhaps the most important elements of any such reinforcement analysis of communication events are whether the consequences of a response by one individual to another are perceived by the receiver as having some social approval, reward or value effect, and whether the consequences are clearly linked to the response (that is, contingent upon it).

For a comment or gesture to have a reinforcing effect (that is to increase the likelihood of a re-occurrence), it should be a positively valued and contingently linked consequence. The possibility of certain stimuli acting as reinforcers for some individuals and not for others is an important point to recognise at this stage. This element has been discussed in detail within the educational context of teachers using reinforcement in the classroom as a deliberate manipulation to improve pupil attention and performance. In this discussion, MacMillan (1973), argued for the concept of a continuum of reinforcers from more 'primary' reinforcers such as food and water, through to more sophisticated (or mature) reinforcers such as social approval and 'sense of mastery'. The list of six types of reinforcers presented by MacMillan in his continuum was as follows:

1. Primary rewards — food and water;
2. Toys or trinkets;
3. Tokens or checks — with backup reinforcers (toys, food and so on);
4. Visual evidence of progress — graphs, letter grades;
5. Social approval;
6. Sense of mastery — 'learning for the love of it'.

Such lists of possible reinforcement hierarchies, or continua, are not statements of universals since individuals may vary in response to such consequences. Variations are due to such aspects as previous experiences, age factors, frequency of past exposure and, often, the context in which a potential reinforcer is applied. What is evident, however, is that to describe all such levels as 'feedback' is to over-simplify the description and ignore the important elements of difference between the categories, as well as reduce the evaluative or reward component that is inherent in reinforcement components.

Another element of the reinforcement concept in need of clarification before further discussion is the common confusion among the terms 'positive reinforcement', 'negative reinforcement' and 'punishment'. Such confusion has frequently arisen in education literature where negative reinforcement has been equated with punishment, and the term is used in this manner by Trower *et al.* (1978) in a social skills model discussion. A clear and simple presentation (Table 5.1) shows the distinctive characteristics as outlined within the operant theory.

The term positive reinforcement can be seen to be the element that was defined at the outset of this chapter — the contingent application of a positively valued stimulus (such as money, praise or other tokens).

Table 5.1: Characteristics of Positive and Negative Reinforcement

	Positively valued stimulus	Negatively valued stimulus
Contingent application	Positive reinforcement	Punishment
Contingent removal	Reponse cost	Negative reinforcement

Negative reinforcement, on the other hand, is defined as the contingent removal of a negatively valued stimulus. An example of this might be the removal of a shoe that is ill-fitting and causing some pain (Skinner, 1976). Punishment, as shown in Table 5.1, refers to the contingent application of a negatively valued stimulus, and could cover such events as receiving criticism for the performance of a task or acts of physical violence as a consequence of some act toward another person.

Finally, Table 5.1 shows response cost, which describes the way a positively valued stimulus can be removed following some response. An everyday example of this is the police speeding or parking fine system where the positively valued stimulus of money is removed following an infringement. It is possible to argue that most people use these various components of reinforcement in our daily dealings with others. Some people opt for strategies where the application or withholding of positive reinforcement is the major influencing behaviour, while others actually employ response cost or punishment techniques. The latter are usually seen as more 'severe' and often less socially acceptable in many societies.

A final area in need of some clarification is the matter of contingency or the sequential and connected nature of reinforcement and the response it is meant to reinforce. As already mentioned, for an action to be positively reinforcing it must not only be valued but it should also be contingent upon the behaviour it is aimed to reinforce. Trower *et al.* (1978) borrowed four kinds of contingencies in social relationship communications from the analysis of Jones and Gerard (1967) for their discussion, and they are useful categorisations for this discussion as well. These four patterns offer a useful adjunct to the basic concept of simple contingent reinforcement in that they show how the reciprocity of communication is an important element in the social skills model analysis. The four kinds of contingency are:

1. Reactive contingency, which refers to the way each person responds to the last action of the other participant;

2. Asymmetrical contingency, which describes a pattern where one person reacts to the other but the reaction is not reciprocated by the second person, who is following a plan of his own;

3. Mutual contingency, which occurs when each person reacts to the other but also each pursues a plan of his own;

4. Pseudo-contingency, where each person is not actually responding to the other but seems to be (as in acting in a play).

While the reinforcement-based theoretical model of the way humans learn and behave has led to an enormous body of research data and writing, there have been many critics who have voiced strong, and at times controversial, attacks on the Skinnerian behaviourist interpretation of learning and communication. Among Skinner's most vocal and skilful critics have been the influential American writers and theorists, Noam Chomsky and Carl Rogers.

Chomsky, a linguistics scholar, has been particularly critical of the Skinnerian analysis of the way language develops, as well as being philosophically opposed to the behaviourist approach to the explanation of how humans develop and learn (Chomsky, 1959). Rogers, whose approaches to counselling and psychotherapy have led to a sub-field of psychology known as Rogerian humanistic psychology, has claimed that his 'struggle with behaviourist psychology' has been one of the major concerns in his professional life (1980, p. 55). Rogers acknowledged that Skinner's work in establishing behaviourism had been a 'creative achievement' of significance, but, nevertheless, he could not accept the theory at a philosphical level and found the whole area repugnant. Some writers in the field of counselling, however, have argued that reinforcement is an important skill for counsellor–client communication (Munro, Manthei and Small, 1979). Ivey and Gluckstern (1976) even claimed that Roger's technique of attempting to find something positive to emphasise in his sessions with clients shows that he 'is reinforcing positive verbal statements about the self' (p. i).

Another approach to formulating a model of the learning process that incorporates some of the reinforcement theory and adds some new dimensions is the field that has become known as social learning theory. Arising out of the writing and research of Bandura (1971), social learning theory argued that man learnt not only by external reinforcement but that imitation, cognitive mediation of reinforcement and self-regulation all played parts in what was described as a 'continuous reciprocal interaction between behaviour and its controlling conditions' (1971, p. 39). The importance of such reciprocity and imitation in the application of reinforcement concepts to communication considerations is a feature of the analysis of the relevant theory and research that follows.

With these considerations in mind, the role of reinforcement in communication considerations becomes one of closely examining the manner in which consequential behaviours are presented to other individuals in interaction situations, and how the behaviours are perceived as reinforcers by the parties involved. A number of areas of social psychology, education and management have developed theoretical and applied works which have specifically examined the usefulness and effectiveness of such reinforcement analyses of communication.

Reinforcement and Interpersonal Communication

The extent and nature of interpersonal communication is carefully analysed in Chapter 2 where the reciprocal nature of the process is discussed within a social skills model framework. In Chapter 3 a detailed discussion of nonverbal communication as one important core communication skill shows how parties act and react to each other using nonverbal responses in the process of communicating thoughts and feelings. In Chapter 4 the skill of questioning is presented as another core element of effective communication, this time in the verbal mode. Reinforcement is a core skill that influences the initiation, continuation and the reactions to the messages of others in both nonverbal and verbal modes of communication.

Reinforcement and Nonverbal Communication

In the nonverbal mode of communication, reinforcement can be provided in a number of ways and involve elements of positive reinforcement, negative reinforcement and even punishment in a mild form. Such reactions to communications as making and maintaining eye contact and pleasant facial expressions are usually positive indications of openness to communication and act as simple, subtle reinforcers for the continuance of the interaction (Argyle, 1967). Similarly, avoidance of eye contact and facial or body movements that indicate rejection of communication overtures can be described as mild punishments in the terms of the definitions in Table 5.1. The significance of gaze and its role as a learned response in communication that results from and is, in turn, influential in terms of reinforcement for further learning, has been discussed in some detail by Argyle and Cook (1976) and Cook (1977). The argument in their interpretation was, however, that these types of feedback behaviours were largely low in level of consciousness and regulatory in their contribution to the start and end of communication encounters; the implication being that the higher levels of feedback (perceptions of moods, emotions and the refinement of first impressions) were more conscious reactions.

Research reviewed in this area (Cook, 1977; Schneider, Hastorf and Ellsworth, 1979) offers some support for this interpretation and highlights the simple fact that different people perceive and react to similar responses in different ways. An additional point in this work was also to show that not only are the nonverbal reinforcers differential in effect between people, but that the learning about the meanings of such nonverbals varies between people. The whole area of facial expression, posture and gesture as forms of body language that make use of behavioural ideas and demonstrate the attempts of one person to deliberately manipulate others has been extensively explored by writers in the field of kinesics (Scheflen, 1972).

Reinforcement and Verbal Communication

It is no coincidence that the nonverbal communication area is often referred to as a form of language, nor that the reinforcement skill analysis can usefully contribute to the explanation of these learned responses. The fact that in language situations, one speaker reacts to another and encourages communication to begin, to continue or to terminate according to the way the speaker uses both language cues and nonverbals, is an important initial concept. When the verbal mode of communication is added to the nonverbal and language, in its usual sense, becomes the major part of communication, additional evidence for the efficacy of the reinforcement analysis becomes available.

In addition to the studies discussed previously with reference to conversation, another early study in the field of language in interpersonal attraction that firmly supports the reinforcement interpretation was conducted by Clore and McGuire (1974). In this study, which Clore later reported was originally aimed at examining the view that attractiveness was a function of the characteristics of the stimulus person (Clore, 1977), 40 women had six conversations with each other and were interviewed after the taping of the sessions.

The interesting findings for the present discussion were that when the conversations were rated by observers, the results showed that 'the only stimulus person behaviour that consistently led to higher attraction was that coded as "positive responses" '(p. 28). In addition, the only behaviours that led to dislike were those coded as 'negative response' and 'dissimilarity statements'. Clore used this evidence to argue strongly for a reinforcement interpretation of attraction in interpersonal relationship theory. Clore (1977) summarised a number of his previous studies, and extended some, to conclude that attraction was influenced by reinforcement, and that gains and losses in attraction may depend on the way the perceiver is affectively involved. He also argued that the perceiver's behaviour was as important as the stimulus person's, and that rewards and punishment can influence attraction even when not supported by consistent beliefs within the participants. Such studies within the field of interpersonal attraction have examined the way attraction is influenced by mutual reinforcements and how expectations of reinforcements can also be a powerful element in attraction. Much of the research drawn together in publications such as Duck's 1977 collection have added significantly to this interpretation (Huston, 1974; Duck, 1977) and highlighted some of the advocacy of reinforcement theories of person perception (Byrne, 1971; Byrne and Clore, 1967; Lott and Lott, 1974).

Within the general social psychological area of interpersonal relationships, other fields of study have applied and, in some cases, adapted the reinforcement analysis, particularly in the discussion and testing of reciprocity in interaction. Reciprocity has been described as a form of mutual reinforcement between two persons (Patterson and Reid, 1970), and has been studied in marriage relationships (Burgess, 1981), sexual relationships between same sex and opposite sex partners (Przybyla and Byrne, 1981) and in children's friendships (La Gaipa, 1981). The common thread of argument in these areas and their interpretations of the reinforcement concept is that interpersonal skills are learned, and that in the process of learning, the way one person responds and reinforces another is a significant aspect of the communication between the people that leads to attraction, friendships or even more intimate relationships.

As previously mentioned, language is an important element in this analysis. The operant model has been applied to attempt to explain early language development (Skinner, 1957), and other extensions of the theory have influenced the study of language and education. The study of how verbal social reinforcement (praise, supportive comments) influences the development of learning in a number of areas, including communication, has become a stable foundation discipline in some educational thinking (Sulzer and Mayer, 1972; Bijou, 1976; Bijou and Baer, 1978). Studies of the language of the classroom and the way teachers communicate with pupils has been at the heart of much research and development in teaching (Flanders, 1970; Dunkin and Biddle, 1974); many of the thousands of studies in this genre have focused on elements of teachers' use of reinforcement or closely related concepts and skills.

Reinforcement in Classroom Communication

Reinforcement as a basic communication skill in the classroom has been one of the most commonly studied and discussed elements of all classroom teaching skills (Allen and Ryan, 1969; Cairns, 1973; Turney, Eltis, Hatton *et al.,* 1983). In early research within the field of education, the examination of the effects of teacher praise and blame on pupil achievement was conducted at the general level of correlation; it led to conclusions such as the following from Kennedy and Willcutt (1964): 'Praise has been found generally to have a facilitating effect on the performance of school children while blame has been found generally to have a debilitating effect on the performance of school children' (p. 331).

Studies since the Kennedy and Willcutt time have been focused on reinforcement more as a contingent and evaluative component of the teacher's communication with pupils, rather than the more general concepts of non-contingent praise and blame. The studies in this area of research have examined the use of teacher's attention and verbal reinforcement comments of praise and encouragement, linked contingently to specific pupil behaviours in an endeavour to change those behaviours by increasing some or modifying others (O'Leary and O'Leary, 1972; 1977).

Among the studies in this tradition have been those of Birnbrauer, Bijou and Wolf (1965), in which the attending behaviour to a reading task by eight retarded children was significantly increased by reinforcement procedures, and Broden, Cruce, Mitchell, *et al.* (1970), in which the teacher's attention was used to increase a pupil's attending behaviour. Other studies in this tradition have examined the way reinforcement has been successfully utilised and manipulated to increase such pupil behaviours as passing arithmetic tests (Rosenfeld, 1972), verbal responses (Reynolds and Risley, 1968), and class participation (Cormier and Wahler, 1971). In addition to the studies of the effects of reinforcement on pupil attending and work completion behaviours, it has been shown that the effective communication of contingent reinforcement to pupils has had measurable effects on pupil motivation (Spear, 1970; Allen, Spear and Lucke, 1971) and classroom misbehaviour (Madsen, Becker and Thomas, 1968; Thomas, Becker and Armstrong, 1968). In many of the studies reported in this latter tradition, with specific reference to what has become known as behaviour modification, the components of the classroom teaching skill of reinforcement used range from token reinforcement, acitivity reinforcement (acitivities preferred by the children), to the more usual social reinforcement, which is praise and teacher approval. In a related manner, other research on teaching (Dunkin and Biddle, 1974) has also shown that teacher criticism and punishment have negative effects on pupil attitudes, learning and self-concepts (Parke, 1969; Walker and Buckley, 1972).

While the advocacy of the importance of these research findings for classroom communication, teaching effectiveness and management issues has been prominent in the last two decades and, in particular, in teacher education materials (Allen and Ryan, 1969; Turney, Cairns, Williams, *et al.,* 1973; Turney, Eltis, Hatton *et al.,* 1983), there have been some points of concern raised in the literature on the topic. In his review and critical examination of the way teachers use praise in the classroom, Brophy (1981) argued that much of the praise teachers use is non-contingent and therefore not reinforcing. Further, he pointed out that pupils are often more attuned to the reinforcement variable than many teachers have given them credit for in the past. He even suggested that 'students also tended to reward teachers for their praise by responding very positively to it — smiling, beaming proudly and the like' (p. 13).

An additional major point in Brophy's discussion was that teacher praise should meet four criteria if it is to be reinforcing: first, it should be specific in reference to the behavioural element that it is to reinforce; second, it should be clearly contingent upon the behaviour; third, it should be credible to the pupils involved; and, fourth, it should be varied according to the teacher's understanding and knowledge of the individual pupils. Brophy's discussion does provide a note of caution against the all-too-ready acceptance of the notion that all supportive and praise comments made by teachers (and others in similar social situations) are clear examples of reinforcement in the sense defined at the outset of this chapter. This further stresses the point that loose usage of terms that have specific and carefully documented meaning and applications is a danger in the areas under consideration.

Reinforcement and Social Skills Training

There have been many other applications of the theory and practice of reinforcement as a communication skill in other fields of social and professional endeavour in addition to education. One such area has been that of social skills training (Trower *et al.*, 1978). This approach, developed at the Department of Experimental Psychology at the University of Oxford, has become a widespread tool during therapy for patients in hospitals and other institutions who have social inadequacy problems (Spence and Shepherd, 1983). This method uses the model mentioned earlier which was based on motor skills training and in which demonstration, guidance, practice and feedback are used to develop and train social skills.

Trower *et al.* (1978) clearly set their approach to this model within a behaviour change context and make use of many of the same types of components defined more rigorously as reinforcement in other works, such as the educational approaches already outlined. The social skills authors acknowledge that they are using different terminology for basically the same concepts (Trower *et al.*, 1978), but they apparently feel more comfortable with less overtly recognisable behaviourist terms — though they do, at the end of their presentation, deal with the strategies of rewarding and controlling others using these direct and less 'optional' terms. There is also considerable use of reinforcement elements in the many training sections in the 1978 manual and recommendations for the therapists to use plenty of praise and positive feedback focused on the tasks completed in the training procedures. This approach emphasises both non-verbal and verbal communication in social skills training. Within those divisions the importance of feedback and response for the initiation, facilitation and reciprocation of social communication is stressed and demonstrated.

In his 1982 publication, Kelly, writing for the United States market, presented a social skills analysis of intervention procedures for dealing with many interpersonal interaction problems. The approach advocated in this volume is more direct in acknowledging the centrality of reinforcement than the Trower *et al.* (1978) British approach. Kelly puts his position in the following terms: 'All of the interpersonal skills that facilitate the building of relationships have in common with one another the fact that they increase the social attractiveness or reinforcement value of the person exhibiting them. Because others respond positively to individuals who are skilful in conversation, date-initiation, commendatory behaviour or, in the case of children, prosocial-play skills, these competencies serve not only as avenues by which a person can initiate reinforcing relationships, but they also increase the likelihood that others will seek out further opportunities to interact with the individual' (p. 5).

Kelly offers training suggestions in the areas of conversational skills, date-initiation and other heterosocial skills, assertiveness training and job interview skills, as well as a section on social skills training for children. Within each of these sub-areas Kelly includes some reinforcement components. In conversational skills he describes 'reinforcing or complimentary components' (p. 141), which includes 'verbalisations' that demonstrate that the person approves, concurs or understands what the other has said. In the dating initiation section, Kelly describes the nonverbal component of eye contact and another reinforcement concept, 'complimentary comments' (p. 157). In the section on assertiveness training, Kelly presents a concept he calls 'commendatory-assertion', which he clearly indicates includes such components as 'praise and appreciation statements', 'personal feeling statements' and 'reciprocal positive behaviour' (p. 182). In the job interview section of his handbook, Kelly details the skills training components of 'eye contact, appropriate affect, and statements conveying job interest and enthusiasm', each of which has elements of the previously mentioned reinforcement interpretation that he has based the work on. Finally, in his presentation of social skills training with children, Kelly is even more specific as he describes the component of 'praise' in the following way: '. . . the child who develops the ability of praising his or her peers will be an effective dispenser of reinforcement to them' (p. 219).

Kelly's book is an example of the further development of the social skills training methodology beyond the original model devloped by Argyle and his Oxford colleagues in that Kelly has taken more of the social learning model of behaviour into his approach and less of the Oxford motor-skills analogy.

The importance of communication training, as different and of older roots than social skills training, is shown in such 'course' materials as presented in Heun and Heun (1975), which includes explanations, examples and worksheet materials to learn about and use different forms of 'communicating'. Similar books aimed at the market of training communicators have been produced by Brooks (1981) (the fourth edition of this popular work), and Ruffner and Burgoon (1981), who claim their's as an introductory text in the field. Each of these publications includes sections on the importance of feedback (defined and discussed in a reinforcement mode), as one of the central components of communication.

Reinforcement in Counselling Communication

An additional area of professional work within a communication model that directly applies the theory of reinforcement is the microcounselling approach to the training of clinical counsellors and other 'helping' professionals (Ivey, 1971). This approach is described by Ivey and Gluscksternn (1974) as a technique that 'is especially effective in the early stages of training as its emphasis on observable specific behaviours of the effective helper provides a framework for later more in-depth understanding of the helping process' (p.1). In line with this description, Ivey and Gluckstern have organised training materials in two skill clusters which they called basic attending skills (1974) and basic influencing skills (1976). One of the main thrusts in both these manuals was that the 'helper' should always 'accentuate the positive', and this element is openly related to behaviourist reinforcement theory.

An interesting point was made by Ivey and Gluckstern (1976) in the basic influencing skills manual where they argued that the microtraining workshops try to avoid commitment to any single theoretical model. This point is of interest in the context of this chapter because the materials under discussion so evidently draw on the obvious reinforcement concepts in the presentation and when it is considered that the whole microskills analysis concept (in microteaching and derivatives such as microcounselling) was a behavioural-psychology-dependent idea. Ivey and his colleagues have stimulated others to apply their concepts and analyses of the counsellor's behaviours with some significant reported success (Kasdorf and Gustafson, 1978) (also see Chapter 19).

The concepts of attending (interpreted as an important communication element that involves the juxtaposing of some of Roger's ideas interpreted via a behaviourist theory that emphasises the role of response in communication) and influencing (which provided an even stronger basis for the behaviourist involvement of reinforcement elements) have been taken up in other extensions and developments in the area of nurse–patient communication (Jessop, 1979) and general interviewing training for doctors, nurses, teachers, ministers, psychologists and other helping professionals (Evans, Hearn, Uhlemann, *et al.*, 1979).

Within the field of counselling there have been additional applications of the reinforcement model of communication that have gone beyond the subskills approach and the Ivey microtraining idea. These have included the concepts of using reinforcement as communication to systematically and deliberately change clients' behaviour and to teach them new or modified communication techniques (Munro, Manthei and Small, 1979). One example of this is neatly summarised by Munro *et al.* in the following manner: '. . . a client lacking in conversational ability might be coached by the counsellor in basic attending skills. Used in social situations, these skills act as rewards to speakers who are thus encouraged to respond to the client by conversing with her. A client should be encouraged to practise such skills in her own time and to report on their effects. Responding skills would likewise be valuable as general social skills' (p. 64).

What is apparent from the writing and the training materials developed in the counselling (or in the general area of helping) field is that many of the communication skill analyses are based heavily on the reinforcement concepts and interpretations of the interpersonal interaction situation. For some of the writers, no doubt, there would be little or no communication process without the reinforcement contingencies of the nonverbal and verbal types discussed above.

Reinforcement in Management Communication

There have been a number of other fields of endeavour where the reinforcement model of communication has been applied and developed as a useful analysis. One such area has been the field of business management and supervision. Here, it has been commonplace for communication to be stressed as a key variable in the successful supervision and management of staff and business organisations (Wofford, Gerloff and Cummins, 1977) with frequent references to the importance of feedback to effective communication. As Crane (1979) succinctly put the point: 'The single most important aspect of communication is feedback. It is the reaction from those receiving a message that can be used by the sender to evaluate the message' (p. 77).

Even a cursory reading of management and personnel practices handbook publications shows that communication is viewed as singularly important to supervision and management, and that within the topic of communication, the concepts earlier outlined as components of reinforcement are evident; they are advocated as useful procedures for enhancing the communication skill of those charged with supervisory or management responsibilities.

More specifically, however, the systematic application of reinforcement techniques to manipulate management practices has been advocated very strongly in some management procedures (Luthans and Kreetner, 1975; Beecroft, 1976). In these approaches the use of reinforcement in communication and in other forms such as promotion and granting favours has been advocated under the general rubric of an organisational approach to behaviour modification. In these contexts, it is argued, the procedures have helped to improve attendance, output quantity and quality and, more importantly, the harmonious relationships of workers and their communications (Crane, 1979). In his study of supervisory communication in two urban hospitals, Jain (1973) argued that the reinforcing nature of a supervisor's communications to subordinates (as perceived by them) will facilitate the sharing of information and the receptiveness of the subordinates to information from the administration that the supervisor passes on (1973).

Following on from the use of reinforcement ideas in the management field, the wheel of chance has turned full circle and more recently, educators have argued that the models developed in management should be applicable to teaching and classroom management (Berliner, 1983). One aspect of this movement is that the effective communication work (which includes the concept of reinforcement as a core communication skill), that had been researched, developed and advocated originally in teacher education and then taken up by management, has now been re-emphasised and applied to education as an adaptation from management with renewed vigour.

Not only is the general assertion that teachers and teacher educators can learn from the management analogy gaining some credence, but specific concepts from the supervision area such as the 'personalisation and specificity' of praise and recognition have being directly moved from management (George, Collins and Gill, 1979) to the supervision of pre-service and in-service teachers (Turney *et al.*, 1982). The version presented in this work and the supervision model advocated by Turney *et al.* (1982) has also drawn together aspects of Ivey's microcounselling skills in the communication areas of attending, responding and helping (Turney *et al.*, 1982).

The significance of reinforcement as a communication skill in management and education has been well demonstrated by such recent developments. The manner in which many fields of endeavour have adopted and, in some cases adapted, the basic skill of reinforcement as a core communication aspect is extensive, pervasive and, it appears, effective as a development and application of theory into practice in the professions.

Overview

What has emerged from this brief examination of some of the trends and applications of reinforcement as a core communication skill in the applied professions, is that there is a consistent and inter-related fabric of theory, assertions and research that communication as an interpersonal interaction skill that affects friendships, attraction and affection, involves the consistent and contingent positive responses of one person to another. When positive feelings are communicated then reinforcement is taking place. When the receiver of such communication responds by changing or adapting behaviour, he/she has been reinforced. The resultant interaction between the parties is a reciprocal process of reinforcement.

This chapter began by discussing the way in which the term 'feedback' was closely synonymous with reinforcement in most of the ways it was used in communication writings. It also examined how, over time and through many studies, writers and researchers moved to acknowledge more directly the reality of this assertion. Perhaps here, too, the wheel of chance (or change?) has rolled around, as recently Knapp, Hopper and Bell (1984), have presented an analysis of the positive verbal reinforcers people offer each other in conversations under the heading of 'compliments'. Knapp *et al.* present a detailed discussion and descriptive taxonomy of compliments 'that people recalled as having been recently given or received' (p. 12). Researchers of the behaviourist persuasion may be justified in claiming that reinforcement, by any other name, is still reinforcement.

References

Allen, D.W. and Ryan, K. (1969) *Microteaching*, Addison-Wesley, Reading, Massachussetts

Allen, S.A., Spear, P.S. and Lucke, J.R. (1971) 'Effects of Social Reinforcement on Learning and Retention in Children', *Developmental Psychology, 5(1)*, 73–80

Argyle, M. (1967) *The Psychology of Interpersonal Behaviour*, Penguin Books, Harmondsworth
——— and Cook, M. (1976) *Gaze and Mutual Gaze in Social Interaction*, Cambridge University Press, London

Argyle, M. and Kendon, A. (1967) 'The Experimental Analysis of Social Performance' in L. Berkowitz (ed.), *Advances in Experimental Social Psychology*, vol. 3, Academic Press, New York

Bandura, A. (1971) *Social Learning Theory*, General Learning Press, Morristown, New Jersey

Beecroft, J.L. (1976) 'How Behavior Modification Improves Productivity at 3–M', *Training HRD*, October, 83–65

Berliner, D.C. (1983) 'The Executive Who Manages Classrooms' in B.L. Fraser, (ed.), *Classroom Management*, WAIT, Perth

Berlo, D.K. (1960) *The Process of Communication*, Rinehart and Winston, New York

Berlyne, D.E. (1967) 'Arousal and Reinforcement' in D. Levine (ed.), *Nebraska Symposium on Motivation*, Loncoln, University of Nebraska

Bijou, S.W. (1976) *Child Development*, Prentice-Hall, New Jersey

Bijou, S.W. and Baer, D.M. (1978) *Behavior Analysis of Child Development*, Prentice-Hall, New Jersey

Birnbrauer, J.S., Bijou, S.W. and Wolf, M. (1965) 'Programmed Instruction in the Classroom' in L.P. Ullmann and L. Krasner (eds), *Case Studies in Behavior Modification*, Holt, Rinehart and Winston, New York

Broden, M., Cruce, C., Mitchell, *et al.* (1970) 'Effects of Teacher Attention on Attending Behavior of Two Boys at Adjacent Desks', *Journal of Applied Behavior Analysis, 3*, 205–11

Brooks, W.D. (1981) *Speech Communication*, Wm. C. Brown, Dubuque, Iowa

Brophy, J.E. (1981) 'Teacher Praise: A Functional Analysis', *Review of Educational Research, 51(1)*, 5–32

Burgess, R.L. (1981) 'Relationships in Marriage and the Family' in S. Duck and R. Gilmour (eds), *Personal Relationships, 1*, Academic Press, London

Byrne, D. (1971) *The Attraction Paradigm*, Academic Press, New York
——— and Clore, G.L. (1967) 'Effectance Arousal and Attraction', *Journal of Personality and Social Psychology, 28*, 313–20

Cairns, L.G. (1973) 'The Skill of Reinforcement' in C. Turney, L.G. Cairns, G. Williams, *et al.* (eds), *Sydney Micro Skills. Series 1 Handbook*, Sydney University Press, Sydney

Chomsky, N. (1959) 'A Review of B.F. Skinner's *Verbal Behavior*', *Language, 35(1)*, 26–58

Clore, G.L. (1977) 'Reinforcement and Affect in Attraction' in S. Duck (ed.), *Theory and Practice in Interpersonal Attraction*, Academic Press, London
——— and McGuire, H. (1974) 'Attraction and Conversational Style', paper presented at the Society of Experimental Social Psychology, Urbana, Illinois

Cook, M. (1977) 'The Social Skill Model and Interpersonal Attraction' in S. Duck (ed.), *Theory and Practice in Interpersonal Attraction*, Academic Press, London

Cormier, W.H. and Wahler, R.G. (1971) 'The Application of Social Reinforcement in Six Junior High School Classrooms', ERIC ED 051 109

Crane, D.P. (1979) *Personnel: The Management of Human Resources*, Wadsworth, Belmont, California

Duck, S. (ed.) (1977) *Theory and Practice in Interpersonal Attraction*, Academic Press, London

Dunkin, M.J. and Biddle, B.J. (1974) *The Study of Teaching*, Holt, Rinehart and Winston, New York

Evans, D.R., Hearn, M.T., Uhlemann, M.R. *et al.* (1979) *Essential Interviewing*, Brooks/Cole, Monterey

Ferster, C.B. and Perrott, M.C. (1968) *Behavior Principles*, Appleton-Century-Crofts, New York

Flanders, N.A. (1970) *Analyzing Classroom Behaviour*, Addison Wesley, New York

Gardiner, J.C. (1971) 'A Synthesis of Experimental Studies of Speech Communication Feedback', *Journal of Communication, 21,* 17–25

George, C.S. Jr, Collins, D. and Gill, B. (1979) *Supervision in Action. The Art of Managing Others,* Prentice-Hall of Australia, Sydney

Glaser, R. (ed.) (1971) *The Nature of Reinforcement,* Academic Press, New York

Heun, L.R. and Heun, R.E. (1975) *Developing Skills for Human Interaction,* Charles E. Merrill, Columbus, Ohio

Honig, W.K. (ed.) (1966) *Operant Behavior: Areas of Research and Application,* Appleton-Century-Crofts, New York

Huston, T.L. (ed.) (1974) *Foundations of Interpersonal Attraction,* Academic Press, New York

Ivey, A.E. (1971) *Microcounseling: Innovations in Interviewing Training,* Charles C. Thomas, Springfield, Illinois

——— and Gluckstern, N.B. (1974) *Basic Attending Skills,* Microtraining Associates, North Amherst, Mass.

——— (1976) *Basic Influencing Skills* Microtraining Associates, North Amherst, Mass.

Jain, H.C. (1973) 'Supervisory Communication and Performance in Urban Hospitals', *The Journal of Communication, 23,* 103–17

Jessop, A.L. (1979) *Nurse-Patient Communication: A Skills Approach,* Microtraining Associates, North Amherst, Mass.

Jones, E.E. and Gerard, H.B. (1967) *Foundations of Social Psychology,* Wiley, New York

Kasdorf, J. and Gustafson, K. (1978) 'Research related to Microcounseling' in A.E. Ivey and J. Authier (eds), *Microcounseling: Innovations in Interviewing, Counseling, Psychotherapy and Psychoeducation,* Charles C. Thomas, Springfield, Illinois

Kelly, J.A. (1982) *Social-Skills Training,* Springer Publishing, New York

Kennedy, W.A. and Willcutt, H.S. (1964) 'Praise and Blame as Incentives', *Psychological Bulletin, 62,* 323–32

Kleitsch, E.C., Whitman, T.L. and Santos, J. (1983) 'Increasing Verbal Interaction Among Elderly Socially Isolated Mentally Retarded Adults: A Group Language Training Procedure', *Journal of Applied Behavior Analysis, 16(2),* 217–33

Knapp, M.L., Hopper, R. and Bell, R.A. (1984) 'Compliments: A Descriptive Taxonomy', *Journal of Communication,* 12–31

La Gaipa, J.L. (1981) 'Children's Friendships' in S. Duck and R. Gilmour (eds) *Personal Relationships, 2,* Academic Press, London

Lott, A.J. and Lott, B.E. (1974) 'The Role of Reward in the Formation of Positive Interpersonal Attitudes' in T.L. Huston (ed.), *Foundations of Interpersonal Attraction,* Academic Press, New York

Luthans, F. and Kreetner, R. (1975) *Organizational Behavior Modification,* Scott, Foresman, Glenview, Illinois

MacMillan, D.L. (1973) *Behavior Modification in Education,* Macmillan, New York

Madsen, C.H., Becker, W.C. and Thomas, D.R. (1968) 'Rules, Praise and Ignoring: Elements of Elementary Classroom Control', *Journal of Applied Behavior Analysis, 1,* 139–50

Minkin, N., Braukmann, C.J., Minkin, B.L., *et al.* (1976) 'The Social Validation and Training of Conversation Skills', *Journal of Applied Behavior Analysis, 9(2),* 127–39

Munro, E.A., Manthei, R.J. and Small, J.J. (1979) *Counselling: A Skills Approach,* Methuen, Wellington

O'Leary, K.D. and O'Leary, S.G. (1972) *Classroom Management,* Pergamon, New York

——— (1977) *Classroom Management,* 2nd edn, Pergamon, New York

Parke, R.D. (1969) 'Some Effects of Punishment on Children's Behavior', *Young Children,*

Patterson, G.R. and Reid, J.B. (1970) 'Reciprocity and Coercion: Two Facets of Social Systems' in R.B. Cairns (ed.), *Social Interaction Methods, Analysis and Evaluation,* Lawrence Erlbaum, New Jersey

Pavlov, I.P. (1927) *Conditioned Reflexes,* Dover Reprint, New York

Przybyla, D.P.J. and Byrne, D. (1981) 'Sexual Relationships' in S. Duck and R. Gilmour (eds) *Personal Relationships, 1,* Academic Press, London

Reynolds, M.J. and Risley, T.R. (1968) 'The Role of Social and Material Reinforcers in Increasing Talking of a Disadvantaged Pre-School Child', *Journal of Applied Behaviour Analysis, 1,* 253–62

Rogers, E.M. and Agarwala-Rogers, R. (1976) *Communication in Organizations,* The Free Press, New York

Rogers, C.R. (1980) *A Way of Being*, Houghton Mifflin, Boston

Rosenfeld, G.W. (1972) 'Some Effects of Reinforcement on Achievement and Behavior in a Regular Classroom' *Journal of Educational Psychology, 63(3)*, 189–93

Ruffner, M. and Burgoon, M. (1981) *Interpersonal Communication*, Holt, Rinehart and Winston, New York

Scheflen, A.E. (1972) *Body Language and Social Order*, Prentice-Hall, New Jersey

Schneider, D.J., Hastorf, A.H. and Ellsworth, P.C. (1979) *Person Perception*, Addison-Wesley, Reading, Mass

Skinner, B.F. (1953) *Science and Human Behavior*, Macmillan, New York

——— (1957) *Verbal Behavior*, Appleton-Century-Crofts, New York

——— (1976) *About Behaviorism*, Vintage Books, New York

Spear, P.S. (1970) 'Motivational Effects of Praise and Criticism on Children's Learning', *Developmental Psychology, 3(1)*, 124–32

Spence, S. and Shepherd, G. (1983) *Developments in Social Skills Training*, Academic Press, London

Stokes, T.F. and Baer, D.M. (1977) 'An Implicit Technology of Generalization', *Journal of Applied Behavior Analysis, 10*, 349–67

Stolz, W.S. and Tannenbaum, P.H. (1963) 'Effects of Feedback on Oral Encoding Behavior', *Language and Speech, 6*, 218–28

Sulzer, B. and Mayer, G.R. (1972) *Behavior Modification Procedures*, The Dryden Press, Hinsdale, Illinois

Thomas, D.R., Becker, W.C. and Armstrong, M. (1968) 'Production and Elimination of Disruptive Classroom Behavior by Systematically Varying Teacher's Behavior', *Journal of Applied Behavior Analysis, 1*, 35–45

Trower, P., Bryant, B. and Argyle, M. (1978) *Social Skills and Mental Health*, Methuen, London

Turney, C., Cairns, L.G., Williams, G., *et al.* (1973) *Sydney Micro Skills Handbook 1*, Sydney University Press, Sydney

——— Cairns, L.G., Eltis, K.J. *et al.* (1982), *Supervisor Development Programmes*, Sydney University Press, Sydney

Turney, C., Eltis, K.J., Hatton, N., *et al.* (1983), *Sydney Micro Skills Redeveloped Series 1 Handbook*, Sydney University Press, Sydney

Verplanck, W.S. (1955) 'The Control of the Content of Conversations: Reinforcement of Statements of Opinions', *Journal of Abnormal Social Psychology, 61*, 668

Wallis, J.H. (1973) *Personal Counselling*, Allen and Unwin, London

Walker, H.M. and Buckley, N.K. (1972) 'Effects of Reinforcement Punishment and Feedback upon Academic Response Rate', *Psychology in the Schools, 9(2)*, 186–93

Wofford, J.C., Gerloff, E.A. and Cummins, R.C. (1977) *Organizational Communication: The Keystone to Managerial Effectiveness*, McGraw-Hill, New York

6 REFLECTING

David Dickson

In this chapter 'the interview' is used as a generic term encompassing a range of largely dyadic interpersonal encounters. It should be interpreted broadly to refer to a conversation engaged in for a particular purpose. The interviewer is the participant who has the major responsibility for conducting the transaction and, from a professional perspective, may be a doctor, teacher, lawyer, social worker, policeman or therapist, to name but a few. 'Interviewee' refers to the person interviewed. The role relationship is typically characterised, in part, by an imbalance of power and, as far as the content is concerned, the extent and nature of revelation. The interviewee is much more likely to reveal information to the interviewer, and especially personal information, than *vice versa.*

A pervasive stylistic feature of interaction would seem to be that of directness, and approaches which differ in this respect have been commented upon in the contexts of teaching (Flanders, 1970), social work (Baldock and Prior, 1981), counselling (Stewart and Cash, 1974) and psychotherapy (Corsini, 1968). Style can be thought of as *how* what is done is done; with the characteristic manner in which, for instance, an interviewer carries out an interview. (For a more detailed account of the construct, see Norton, 1983.) Directness has to do with the degree of constraint placed upon the interviewee and his or her responses by the interviewer at each stage of the interview. Theoretically, it can be conceived of in accordance with the views of Jones and Gerard (1967), on patterns of dyadic interaction. They proposed that the response of each participant during interaction is a consequence of two potential sources of influence. The first has to do with subjective needs and motives, the second with external considerations in the form of the preceding contribution of the other interactor.

Imbalances can occur between these two contributory factors for each individual. A particular pattern labelled asymmetrical contingency occurs when the responses of one member are largely determined by that person's desires and goals, with the second person's behaviour being essentially determined by the responses of the first. When the first person is given the role of interviewer this pattern is the archetype of the direct style of interviewing. At this end of the continuum of directness, the interviewer dictates, uncompromisingly, the form, content and pace of the interview. The nature and content of the interviewee's involvement is determined overwhelmingly by this consideration. At the other extreme, the interviewer who favours an indirect style will act essentially in response to the contributions of the interviewee, with the subjective concerns of the latter having the major influence on events during the encounter.

The types of specific utterance commonly associated with interviewing styles which differ in this respect have been discussed by Benjamin (1974). Interviewers who follow a direct approach typically employ 'leads', it is proposed, while those whose style is less direct make greater use of 'responses'. Although both terms are difficult to define unambiguously, responding has to do with reacting to the thoughts and feelings of the interviewee, with exploring his world and keeping him at the centre of things. On the other hand, the interviewer who leads tends to replace the interviewee on centre stage and become the dominant feature in the interaction. Reflections are a type of response in this sense. They involve the interviewer mirroring back to the interviewee what he or she has just said, as understood by the interviewer. Reflections can be contrasted with questions, which are a method of leading.

The utility of reflecting as an interviewing technique has frequently been over-shadowed by the ubiquity of the question. It would seem that this pervasion has led on occasion to the assumption that the process of interviewing is synonymous with the asking and answering of questions. The limitations of this approach in many circumstances have often been overlooked as a result. Boy and Pine (1963) stated that a reliance upon questioning in the counselling-type interview is inappropriate. This assertion has also been supported by others including Mucchielli (1983), who wrote that questions serve to induce client responses; that is, to effect responses that are more dependent upon the cognitions, values and attitudes of the person asking the question than the respondent. Questions can produce feelings of threat and evoke reactions of resentment, hostility and defensiveness. Consequently the kind of warm, understanding relationship conducive to the disclosure of important but possibly embarrassing information can be jeopardised. Questions may also cause the interviewee to produce a reply in keeping with conceptions of social desirability and in fulfilment of an acceptable projection of self. In addition, their tendency to divert emphasis from the expressive needs of the interviewee to the informational requirements of the interviewer should be appreciated.

The effectiveness of questions as a means of promoting pupil discussion in the classroom has been challenged by Dillon (1981). Instead of producing the intended outcome, a question–answer regime tends to become established, with pupils socialised into the role of respondents. This role is characterised by 'dependency, passivity and reactivity' (Dillon, 1981, p. 53). Initiative is suppressed and contributions are proffered only in response to further questions. Responsibility for the progress and direction of the interaction is placed firmly on the shoulders of the inquisitor.

Reflecting has been recommended in such situations as a more satisfactory alternative to questioning and as a means of obviating these undesirable contingencies. It is with both functional and structural aspects of this activity that the present chapter is concerned. The various functions of the skill are outlined in a subsequent section, and contrasting theoretical perspectives brought to bear upon it. A review of research into reflecting is also presented and conclusions drawn as to the effects of this procedure on different aspects of interviewee performance.

However, the chapter continues with a conceptual analysis of reflecting from a more structural perspective in an attempt to clarify issues to do with definition.

Issues of Definition

Reflecting, as a topic for deliberation and area of inquiry, is bedevilled by conceptual confusion, terminological inconsistency and definitional imprecision. An attempt is made here to disentangle the central issues and provide, hopefully, some measure of elucidation. At a broad level, reflecting is operationally concerned in some way with presenting to the interviewee all or part of the message which has just been received from him. Commenting from a more profoundly functional point of view, Rogers (1951), who is commonly credited with coining the term, regarded it as a method of communicating an understanding of the interviewee and his concerns, from the interviewee's point of view, and of 'being with' that person. Attempts to introduce greater precision and, in particular, to specify how these effects can be achieved by the interviewer have, however, led to some of the difficulties mentioned above. (Causes of these incongruencies, traceable to the evolving theorisations of Rogers and colleagues are discussed in the following section.) These can be illustrated by considering the following definitions of the term: 'Reflecting is the activity of merely repeating a word, group of words or sentence exactly as it was said' (French, 1983, p. 176); and 'Reflection techniques are implemented by rephrasing the core of the client's attitude' (Shertzer and Stone, 1968, p. 365).

According to the first definition, reflecting comprises mere repetition of the exact words used by the interviewee in the preceding exchange. The second definition disagrees on two important accounts concerning both form and content of the expression: Shertzer and Stone (1968), stipulated that the reflection is a rephrasing (rather than a simple repetition) of the essential (rather than the total) message received.

Some have regarded reflecting as a unitary phenomenon (Benjamin, 1974) while others have conceived of it as a rubric subsuming a varying number of related processes (Brammer, 1973). Among the latter, only limited consistency is evident in the discriminatory level achieved and the nomenclature employed. While the most common distinction would appear to be between reflection of feelings and paraphrasing (Hargie, Saunders and Dickson, 1981; Ivey and Authier, 1978), reference can also be found to reflection of content (Nelson-Jones, 1983); reflecting experience (Brammer, 1973), content responses and affect responses (Danish and Hauer, 1973), restatement (Auerswald, 1974), echoic and paraphrasic responses (Hoffnung, 1969) and primary level empathic responses (Egan, 1975). In some cases, ostensibly different titles have essentially the same behavioural referent (for instance, paraphrasing, reflection of content and content responses), while in others the same label is used to denote processes which differ in important respects. (Compare, for example, the definitions of restatement provided by

Benjamin, 1974, and Auerswald, 1974.) In order to fully appreciate the issues involved and locate the sources of these confusions and inconsistencies, it is necessary to begin with communication and what it entails.

A widely accepted distinction is that between verbal and nonverbal communication. Laver and Hutcheson (1972) further differentiated between vocal and non-vocal aspects of the process. The latter relates to those methods of giving information which do not depend upon the vocal apparatus and includes, for example, facial expressions, posture, gestures and other body movements. Vocal communication incorporates all of the components of speech; not only the actual words used (verbal communication) but features of their delivery (the vocal element of nonverbal communication). These features encompass, for example, speech rate, volume, pitch and voice quality, and have been collectively referred to as extralinguistic or paralinguistic communication (Siegman, 1978). In the face-to-face situation, therefore, people make themselves known by three potential methods: first, and most obviously, by words used; second, via the paralinguistic accompaniment of language; and third, by means of various other bodily movements and states. (In the interests of clarity and convenience, 'nonverbal communication' will be restricted to the latter.)

Another common distinction with respect to content rather than mode of communication is that between the cognitive and the affective (Hargie *et al.*, 1981). The former has to do with the domain of the logical and rational, with facts and ideas which are mostly predicated on external reality, although they can be subjective; but in either case lack emotional infusion. On the other hand, affect relates to emotional concerns, to feeling states and expressions of mood. In actual practice, of course, both types of communication coalesce. In addition, both can be carried by each of the three channels previously outlined if the definition of paralanguage is extended to cover whistles and comparable utterances which could not be described as verbal. Ekman and Friesen (1969) identified a category of nonverbal act which they called emblems. These include such gestures as the 'V-for-victory' sign and have the distinction of having precise and commonly accepted verbal translations. But the particular forte of the nonverbal and paralinguistic channels is in conveying information which is more affective in nature. Bull (1983), among others, has written extensively on the important role played by such procedures in the communication of emotions and attitudes and in the organisation of relationships. Hargie *et al.* (1981) used the term 'inferred' to refer to affective information conveyed by these means; it has been suggested that reflecting these frequently more nebulous feeling states can be not only more difficult, but potentially more beneficial (Pietrofesa, Hoffman, Splete, *et al.*, 1978; Egan, 1975).

The emotional aspect of a message can also be expressed in two additional ways. It can be stated explicitly, as is the case when someone says, 'I am disappointed'. It can also be contained implicitly within the verbal utterance, for example, 'I worked really hard for that examination. It was really important for me to pass it and after it was over I thought I had done reasonably well. But when the results came out my name was not on the pass-list'. Here the speaker does not directly say that he was disappointed but this emotion can be implied from what is said.

It may be useful to recap briefly at this point. The proposal is that interviewee communications may contain cognitive/factual material, affective/feeling information or, indeed, as is more commonly the case, elements of both. Such content can be conveyed verbally (both explicitly and implicitly), paralinguistically or nonverbally.

The cognitive–affective dimension would appear to be highly salient to this issue of reflecting, and is one factor at the centre of much of the inconsistency and confusion. A second concerns the extent of homomorphic correspondence between the reflection and the original message. This is, does the interviewer merely repeat verbatim what has been said, or does he reformulate it in his own words while retaining semantic integrity? (This dimension has more to do with the verbal than paralinguistic or nonverbal modes of delivery. It is possible, however, for the interviewer when repeating to echo, more or less accurately, the original para-linguistic accompaniment. Similarly, the interviewer can mirror a nonverbal gesture. While such paralinguistic and nonverbal features have been regarded as being an essential part of empathic communication, this has not usually been in the context of a simple verbal repetition and so will not be discussed further at this point.) Since the question of repetition–reformulation has been alluded to and since this issue is less convoluted than that of cognition–effect, it is dealt with first.

Returning to the term 'reflecting', it is recalled that one example of a defini-tion which suggests that reflections are essentially repetitions has already been provided (that is, French, 1983). In a similar vein, Nicholson and Bayne (1984) wrote that, when using this technique, 'The interviewer repeats a word or phrase which the client has used . . .' (p. 36). They contrasted reflections with paraphrases in this respect. For others, as shown shortly, the cognitive–affective dimension is of greater relevance in conceptualising paraphrases. Simple repeti-tions have alternatively been referred to as verbatim playbacks (Gilmore, 1973), reflections of content (Porter, 1950), but perhaps more frequently as restatements (Hackney and Nye, 1973). In its most extreme form, according to Benjamin (1974), the restatement is an exact duplication of the original statement including the pronoun used, although more frequently this is changed and, indeed, the restatement may repeat in a more selective fashion.

Those who talk about restatements set them apart from reflections on the basis not only of form but also function. It is generally felt that restatements are of limited utility and have more to do with indicating attempts at rudimentary hearing than with understanding. Indeed, depending upon circumstances, they may convey incredulity, disapproval or sarcasm. Brammer and Shostrom (1977) commented that, 'perhaps the most glaring reflection error of the novice counsellor is to express his reflection in words already used by the client' (p. 182). Therefore, restraint has been recommended in their use and there is some empirical evidence in substantiation (Hoffnung, 1969).

Reflections are more commonly located at the reformulation end of the repetition–reformulation continuum and the process has been typically described as that 'of mirroring back, in the interviewer's own words, the essence of the interviewee's previous statement' (Hargie *et al.,* 1981, p. 96). Comparable definitions, in this respect, have been provided by, among others, Nelson-Jones (1983), Cormier and Cormier (1979), and Shertzer and Stone (1968).

Switching attention to matters of content, it has most commonly been regarded that reflections contain the essential core of the interviewee's previous communication. Thus, they can include both cognitive and affective material. This is evident in, for example, the definition provided by Hill and Gormally (1977), who stipulated that a reflection comprised 'a statement with a subject, verb, feeling word and subordinate clause . . . The feeling word reflected the subjects overt feelings, and the subordinate clause restated the content . . .' (p. 94). It will be recalled that some who have conceived of reflections in this general way have made distinctions between reflective statements which are restricted to feeling issues and those which are concerned with what is frequently called 'content', although it is generally accepted that the difference is more one of relative emphasis than mutual exclusion.

The former are known largely as reflections of feeling and the latter as paraphrases. Reflecting feeling has been defined by Hargie *et al.* (1981) as 'the process of feeding-back to the interviewee, in the interviewer's own words, the essence of the interviewee's previous statement, the emphasis being upon feelings expressed rather than cognitive content' (p. 104). Paraphrasing is defined similarly, although in this case the emphasis is placed 'upon factual material (e.g. thoughts, ideas, descriptions, etc.) rather than upon affect' (p. 99).

In spite of this criterion, definitions of paraphrasing can be found which include both affect and cognition. According to French (1983), for example, paraphrasing 'involves the activity of putting the client's statement, apparent thoughts and feelings into one's own words' (p. 177). Similar definitions have been offered by Gilmore (1973), among others. In some of these cases, as previously mentioned, the repetition–reformulation dimension, rather than the cognitive–affective, would appear to be the major consideration, with paraphrases being contrasted with simple repetitions. In other cases it would seem that a somewhat different and more subtle distinction is being exploited, although one which emerges only vaguely due to frequent lack of detail and clarity in the definitions provided. It would appear to involve primarily neither cognitive–affective content of interviewee message nor the extent of repetition–reformulation by the interviewer, but rather the mode of expression of the information divulged by the interviewee. It will be recalled that three modes of expression have already been outlined, the verbal, paralinguistic and nonverbal. Paraphrasing, according to those who have favoured this view, could be said to focus essentially upon the verbal statement and, since feelings can be related in this manner, encompass by implication, cognition and affect.

It would seem, in this case, that it is very much the literal meaning of the term which is being operationalised. Thus researchers, including Citkowitz (1975) and Haase and DiMattia (1976), employed paraphrases to promote affective self-referenced statements among subjects. Paraphrases regarded in this manner are presumably contrasted with reflections as defined by Benjamin (1974), for example, in the following way: 'Reflection consists of bringing to the surface and expressing in words those feelings and attitudes that lie behind the interviewee's words' (p. 117).

While paraphrases are restricted to what is actually said, reflections concentrate upon less obvious information frequently revealed in more subtle ways. This confusion can, in large part, be traced back to the word 'content' which features in many definitions of paraphrasing and sets it apart from reflection of feeling. Ivey and Authier (1978), for instance, proposed that paraphrasing 'could be considered an attempt to feedback to the client the content of what he has just said, but in a restated form' (p. 83). However, 'content' has been used in slightly different ways, which have largely gone unnoticed, to refer to somewhat different aspects of the other's message, namely, mode of communication (that is, verbal) and type of information conveyed in this manner (that is, cognitive). Note that the term is not used in a more global manner to describe all of the information communicated. The issue stated as unambiguously as possible would seem to be this: is by 'content' meant the verbal facet or, on the other hand, the non-affective component of the message? It is, of course, possible for the verbal to be affective. Since the word 'content' is commonly used in the literature as the antonym of 'feeling', one would suspect the latter.

Following this line of argument, paraphrases defined as involving content would emphasise the non-affective or factual (see above definition by Hargie *et al.*, 1981) while reflections of feeling would deal with the feelings expressed both verbally and nonverbally. This is the stance taken by such as Cormier and Cormier (1979), when they wrote: 'The portion of the message that expressed information or describes a situation or event is referred to as the content, or the cognitive part, of the message . . . Another portion of the message may reveal how the client feels about the content; expression of feeling or an emotional tone is referred to as the affective part of the message' (p. 65). The fact that 'content' concerns factual components and that reflections of feeling can draw upon affect, verbally stated, is underlined: 'You can identify the affect part of the message by finding the affect words . . . Sometimes a client may not express feelings directly by using an affect word, but will express feelings indirectly or subtly' (pp. 67–8).

Similar sentiments are manifested by Barnabei, Cormier and Nye (1974), who defined a reflection of feeling as 'a restatement of what the client was saying in the counsellor's own words . . . used to reflect the feeling(s) the client was expressing, whether or not the feeling was directly expressed or only implied' (p. 356).

By contrast, others would appear to equate 'content' with the verbal mode of communication. It is therefore permissible when paraphrasing to include both aspects of fact and feeling, as has already been mentioned. However, the position is less straightforward than this. Some seemingly straddle this particular divide. Ivey and Authier (1978), for example, wrote that , 'responding to the feeling being expressed rather than attending solely to the content and decision issues is what is important in (reflection of feeling). What the client is saying is the content portion of the message. One must also listen to how the client gives a message . . . It is this feeling portion of the communication to which you are to pay attention' (p. 539). Here, 'content' obviously refers to the verbal message, while the paralinguistic and nonverbal components are emphasised in relation to the communication of feeling states. Reflections of feeling utilise the latter, while paraphrases tap content. Thus it could be assumed (and in accordance with the views of those already mentioned, for instance, Citkowitz, 1975; Haase and DiMattia, 1976) that mode of expression was the defining characteristic and that paraphrases could mirror back facts and feelings verbally expressed. But in actual fact Ivey and Authier (1978) stressed that paraphrases address the non-affective and by so doing, invoke the cognitive–affective dimension as being of prime importance.

In concluding this section, it may be useful to represent the three dimensions which seem to be conceptually central to the structural aspects of reflecting. Much of the inconsistency and ambiguity which exists in the literature stems from a lack of appreciation of, or confusion between, them. First, the cognitive–affective issue is concerned with the content of communication and the extent to which the reflective statement focuses upon facts, feelings or, indeed, both. The repetition–reformulation continuum addresses the extent to which the reflection departs from the original interviewee expression. The mode of communication of this message is the basis of the third dimension. (In actual practice this dimension is not entirely independent of the second, that is, opportunities for repetition decrease in conjunction with decreases in explicit verbal presentation.) Was the material transmitted verbally or by other and often less conspicuous means? Allied to this is the implication that information gleaned from paralinguistic and nonverbal features is typically less obvious and explicit than that which is verbally stated. (This, of course, is not invariably so.) The importance of the latter dimension should not be overlooked, however, especially in situations where the interviewee is striving to come to grips with a personal difficulty. Under these circumstances, a reflection which encapsulates an aspect of the problem of which the interviewee was but vaguely aware can be extremely beneficial. Such considerations are fundamental to the distinction by Egan (1975), between primary-level and advanced-accurate empathy. In the case of the former 'the helper merely tries to let the client know that he understands what the client has explicitly expressed . . . He does not try to dig down into what the client is only half-saying, or implying, or stating implicitly' (p. 77).

The difficulty of producing categorically an operational definition of reflecting in keeping with the popular use of the term, and meeting with total acceptance, should be obvious from the foregoing. Nevertheless, the following claims, although tentatively made, would appear warrantable and, in combination, serve to establish meaning and delineate behavioural referents. Reflections are statements which re-present the essence of the interviewee's previous message. They can incorporate cognitive and affective components and are expressed in the interviewer's own words. Reflections which concentrate more single-mindedly upon affective issues, whether or not these were explicitly shared by the interviewee in the original communication, have more frequently been labelled reflections of feeling. On the other hand, those which address the non-affective content of the utterance have been called, for the most part, reflections of content or paraphrases. In this latter respect, however, there is but limited commonality.

The issues perused in this section have concerned structure rather than function. Of course, one must not become so embroiled in these aspects that one loses sight of proposed outcomes attendant upon appropriate skill deployment. These are discussed subsequently. The following section considers the process of reflecting from contrasting theoretical perspectives.

Theoretical Perspectives on Reflecting

At the theoretical level, the process of reflecting can be interpreted from at least three fundamentally different positions; humanistic psychology, behaviouristic psychology and linguistics. In keeping with the former it is, in part, the communication of those attitudes and conditions which promote psychological growth and maturity. To the behaviourist it is a means of influencing and modifying behaviour and verbal behaviour in particular. Finally, reflecting can be thought of as part of the elaborate business of organising conversation.

The Humanistic Approach

Carl Rogers is commonly credited with being one of the central figures of the humanistic movement in psychology and, in the helping context, the founder of non-directive counselling. (Also known as client-centred or person-centred counselling.) A detailed consideration of his theoretical position lies far beyond the scope of this chapter. (For fuller details see Rogers, 1951, 1961, 1980; Stefflre and Grant, 1972.) At a rudimentary level, however, an outline of his theory of human functioning can be provided, based upon several inter-related key concepts. These include the organism, actualising tendency, phenomenological field, self, positive regard and incongruence.

The organism, psychologically speaking, is at the centre of all experience and is a totally organised system comprising physical, cognitive, affective and behavioural facets of the individual. It is energised by a single and immensely powerful motivating force, the actualising tendency. This is a positive influence towards growth and development. Rogers (1951) wrote that, 'The organism has one basic tendency and striving — to actualize, maintain, and enhance the experiencing organism' (p. 487).

Were this natural and constructive force permitted to operate unimpaired, the outcome would be the fully functioning person. Such individuals would be max-imising their potential and living fulfilled, harmonious and integrated lives. They would be completely open and receptive to all experiences, have a complete and honest appreciation of themselves and their relationships with others, and be more accepting and understanding of other individuals. They would not, however, be dependent upon others as a source of evaluation but would be confidently self-reliant in this respect. They would experience a sense of freedom to live as they determined and an ability to relate to themselves and the world in an undefensive, realistic, flexible and creative fashion: 'It involves the stretching and growing of becoming more and more of one's potentialities. It involves the courage to be. It means launching oneself into the stream of life' (Rogers, 1961, p. 196).

Few, unfortunately, achieve this state of being. The reason, according to Rogers, isn't due to a labile actualising tendency, but rather to the frustrating and distorting of this force by environmental circumstances. In order to fully appreciate this point, it should be realised that, in keeping with this theory, the world which has an impact upon the person and which is responded to is an essen-tially private, subjective one which may more or less accurately correspond to the outside world of objective reality. This personally experienced world is sometimes called the phenomenological field and consists of everything which is, at least potentially, available to awareness. Part of this totality relates to the self; the individual develops a particular self-concept. This can be thought of as a view of self together with an evaluation of it. Significant others, such as parents, have a key role to play in this process due to the individual's need for positive regard. This need to gain the love, respect and esteem of others important to the individual is deeply felt.

Such positive regard is generally not provided unconditionally, however. Instead, certain conditions of worth are attached — the child knows that behaviour of a certain type must be displayed in order to win the approval of mother. Therefore, it becomes imperative for the child to behave not only in keeping with the actualising tendency but to ensure that conditions of worth are not violated. Such dual standards invariably lead to conflicts and attempted compromises. Experiences which are dependent upon the values of others rather than those of the organism may be introjected to become part of a self-concept which gradually becomes detached from the 'real self' as a result. Similarly, self-experiences which fail to promote positive regard, while they may be organismically valid, tend to become dissociated from conceptions of self. The outcome is incongruence; the self-concept becomes divorced from the actual experiences of the organism.

Incongruence is associated with feelings of threat and anxiety and, consequently, the falsification or indeed denial of experiences and the distortion of the self-concept. This state is the antithesis of that of the fully functioning person previously described. Apart from inconsistencies involving the self-concept and experiences of self, incongruence can result from disparities involving the ideal self, the real world and the phenomenal field. In the extreme, the effects go beyond the prevention of self-actualisation to produce neurotic or psychotic disturbances.

It will be realised from Roger's theory of personality that the source of such problems is, to a great extent, the conditional nature of positive regard. This imposes a value system upon the individual which is at variance with that of the actualising tendency. In order to prevent this, conditions of worth should be removed from positive regard. The individual already subjected to incongruence can be encouraged to further growth and psychological maturity in this way within the context of a particular relationship with another. This other should manifest congruence and provide unconditional positive regard. Since he or she does not attempt to impose values or be judgemental, but responds in a warm and totally accepting manner, threat is reduced, thus enabling the individual to explore feelings previously denied or distorted, and to assimilate them into the self-concept. Reflecting is one method of responding which, since it is centred within the interviewee's frame of reference, satisfies these requirements.

Reflecting is, however, more commonly associated with the third characteristic of the effective relationship — accurate empathic understanding. In his earlier writings Rogers (1951) proposed that the empathic counsellor assumes, 'in so far as he is able, the internal frame of reference of the client, to perceive the world as the client sees it, to perceive the client himself as he is seen by himself, to lay aside all perceptions from the external frame of reference while doing so and to communicate something of this empathic understanding to the client' (p. 29). This state, as it was originally conceived, involves suspending one's own world perspective and unjudgementally striving to become familiar with that of the interviewee (or as he is more commonly termed in this context, the client). In addition, it is imperative that the client be made aware of the existence of this deep level of understanding if moves towards greater exploration, awareness and change are to take place. It was considered that accurate reflecting was the most effective means of making this happen although, as will be outlined, more recent views on this issue have changed somewhat.

Developments which have taken place in the client-centred movement as a whole have been charted by Hart (1970). Three distinct phases in the ongoing evolutionary process labelled, chronologically, non-directive, reflective and experiential, were identified, each characterised by a particular outlook on counsellor function and style. The non-directive counsellor strove to create a permissive, nonjudgemental climate by unintrusively displaying acceptance. Clarification of client contributions in order to gradually promote increased insights was also provided. With the advent of the reflective era, greater stress was placed upon effecting a more integrated self-concept and putting the client more completely in touch with his phenomenological world. As far as technique is concerned, reflecting was employed extensively during both of these phases, but particularly in the latter. However, it would seem that subtle differences in use are detectable, which go some way to shedding light on the reasons for the various nuances of definition disentangled in the previous section. Thus, a gradual switch in emphasis took place from reflecting, largely at a fairly superficial level, the factual content of the client's verbalised message (and frequently doing so by simply repeating what was said) to dealing with the affective dimension through mirroring back, in fresh words, feelings expressed. Reflection of feeling became the most widely used technique.

More recently, Rogers (1975) utilised the concept of experiencing, a term introduced by Gendlin (1961), to account for what takes place during counselling and to provide an updated statement on the nature of empathy. (Experiencing means, according to Hart (1970) 'the apperceptive mass of the individual's subjective life, the implicitly felt and directly known inner sense that is the source of personal meaning', p. 10.) Empathy is now conceived as a process rather than a state and 'involves being sensitive, moment to moment, to the changing felt meanings which flow in this other person, to the fear, or rage . . . or whatever, that he/she is experiencing' (Rogers, 1975, p. 4). It requires a moving closer to the client by gaining a greater awareness of his or her presently experienced inner world of perceptions, thoughts and feelings and the personal meanings attached to these. It is this process and the corresponding attitude of the counsellor which is important, rather than the particular technique performed.

A corollary of this view, and a notable development from the reflective phase, is that the same outcome can be achieved by a variety of responses including, for example, interpretation and self-disclosure. In marked contrast to earlier attitudes, the supremacy of reflecting feeling as a means of interaction with the client has now been removed. However, reflecting is still a legitimate activity, but its effectiveness is dependent upon relating directly to the client's current experiencing and encouraging him or her to focus more intensely upon and become more fully aware of it. It should also assist in the process of converting implicit (or unverbalised) meaning into a communicable form without misrepresentation. The effect is to promote the individual's experiential process and consequently produce change towards greater congruence.

Since such responses must be directed at the felt meanings experienced by the client, there is no longer the stipulation that reflections must deal with only affective issues. Content in this sense becomes less important. The reflective statement may be cognitive, affective or perhaps more usefully both. A further development is a greater move away from the explicitly stated and obvious in the client's utterance to inchoate and vaguely expressed concerns. Egan (1975) proposed that at more advanced levels of empathic understanding the reflection should move beyond the familiar to point tentatively towards experiences only faintly hinted at and less clearly grasped by the client. Although possibilities of inaccuracy are increased, such reflections have the potential to move the client forward in his experiencing and attain a greater level of realisation. Here again can be identified a further source of the conceptual confusion discussed previously.

While the process of empathising may theoretically be manifested by a range of specific responses, in practice the centrality of reflecting has been espoused (Van der Veen, 1970). Links between this skill and empathy as a construct have been established empirically by researchers including Zimmer and Anderson

(1968) and Uhlemann, Lea and Stone (1976). Indeed, in a recent investigation which involved the analysis of one of Roger's videotaped counselling sessions it emerged that the most frequently occurring counsellor response, as coded, took the form of reflective statements (Lee and Uhlemann, 1984).

Although reflecting is still an acceptable method of responding to the client, in terms of this theoretical outlook on counselling, the past 40 years have witnessed changing attitudes, as outlined above, concerning both the structure and function of this skill.

The Behaviourist Approach

Reflecting has also been interpreted and investigated in keeping with behaviourist principles. This theoretical outlook is in marked contrast to the tenets promulgated by Rogers and his fellow humanists. Beginning with Watson (1913), behaviourists have traditionally regarded psychological inquiry as an extension of the natural sciences. As such, the stipulation has been that the only legitimate considerations acceptable to a truly scientific enterprise are those which are observable, verifiable and measurable. This eliminates, at a stroke, the whole domain of mentalistic states and constructs including consciousness, experiencing, self-concept, thoughts, desires and so on. Since these, it is argued, are at best available to only a single person because of their fundamentally subjective nature, they are ineligible as bona fide scientific concepts.

What organisms actually do, and how they respond and behave is quite a different matter. Being objective and potentially open to the scrutiny of as many as may be present, events of this type are amenable to proper scientific exploration. Man is viewed from an external rather than internal frame of reference. The fact that the psychologist is a fellow human is of no consequence and any preconceptions which, as a result, may be entertained as to what may be happening 'in the mind' of the person observed, have no part to play. Man is treated as just another object of inquiry, in this respect, similar to any other organism.

Behaviourists, therefore, have historically restricted psychological inquiry to behaviour, environmental happenings associated with it, and the relationships between these two types of phenomena. (More recently, however, the rigid exclusion of all things mentalistic has been less rigorously enforced.) But events in the individual's environment are seen as belonging to the real world of external reality rather than a private phenomenal one. They are of paramount importance in motivating and shaping what the individual does and determining what he or she becomes. The goal of the psychologist, it was held, is to describe, explain, predict and control behaviour by identifying the regularities which exist between it and features of the surroundings in which it is manifested. The early theorists, including Pavlov and Watson, placed emphasis upon certain environmental stimuli serving to elicit particular responses from the organism in a characteristically stereotypical fashion. While some of these stimulus–response connections are basic and evident from birth or shortly afterwards (for instance, pupillary contraction in response to a bright light) others are learned (for instance, fear of spiders). In either case, however, the individual was regarded as being essentially passive and having specific responses triggered off by events taking place within and around him (such as bright lights or spiders).

Thorndike (1911) drew attention to the fact that the influence of the environment on behaviour is not only restricted to those features which precede and elicit action. The consequences for the organism of those actions which are carried out have a considerable bearing upon further responding. These ideas, embodied in the Law of Effect, were developed more fully by Skinner (1938) in his work on operant conditioning. Skinner stressed the 'operant' rather than the 'respondent' nature of behaviour. Instead of merely responding to happenings, the organism was seen as spontaneously emitting behaviour which operated on the environment to bring about consequences which, in some cases, were experienced positively by the organism. These consequences were termed 'positive reinforcers' or 'positive reinforcing stimuli' and 'operant conditioning', the process whereby they served to increase the frequency of occurrence of behaviour by sytematically being made contingent upon it. Reflecting has been conceived of and researched in terms of operant conditioning procedures (Dickson, 1981).

Positive reinforcing stimuli can take a variety of different forms. Primary or unconditioned reinforcers include such things as food, drink, air, sex and so on, upon which people are biologically dependent. The power of reinforcers of this type to change behaviour resides in their ability to satisfy such fundamental needs. Inspite of their considerable potency, only a small percentage of everyday operation is devoted to these ends. Instead, most of what people do is determined by immediate outcomes which are less basic. Secondary or conditioned reinforcers refer to stimuli which have become valued through association with primary reinforcers, money being an obvious example in contemporary society. Skinner (1953) also identified a group of conditioned reinforcers which are typically paired with several other reinforcing stimuli in a broad range of circumstances. These were labelled generalised reinforcers. A less tangible example noted was the giving of one's attention to another: 'The attention of people is reinforcing because it is a necessary condition for other reinforcements from them. In general, only people who are attending to us reinforce our behaviour. The attention of someone who is particularly likely to supply reinforcement — a parent, a teacher, or a loved one — is an especially good generalized reinforcer . . .' (Skinner, 1953, p. 78).

This observation suggested the possibility of a variety of verbal and nonverbal behaviours having reinforcing potential. Such stimuli have become known as social reinforcers. Using a rather broad definition, Raben, Wood, Klimoski, *et al.* (1974) considered 'a reinforcing stimulus to be social if its reward value is related to another individual or group interacting with the reinforced subject' (p. 39). For some, reflecting acts as a social reinforcer due to the fact that it connotes attention, interest and acceptance, and serves to increase verbal output of the type reflected. Powell (1968), for example, conducted an experiment which examined the effects of reinforcing subjects' self-referent statements (statements about themselves) by means of reflections. Subjects took part, individually, in a 20-minute interview.

The first ten-minute period was used in order to obtain a baseline measurement of the dependent variable. During the second half of the interview, the experimenter responded to self-referenced statements by reflecting them. The results revealed a significant increase in the occurrence of this type of utterance.

Other research, which is reviewed more fully in a later section of this chapter, has produced comparable findings. However, some of these researchers, while remaining within an operant conditioning framework, have proffered a slightly different explanation to account for these effects. Reflections are thought to function more as discriminative than reinforcing stimuli. Discriminative stimuli are part of the environmental context within which the organism responds and, as such, have more to do with what happens before rather than after responding (and differ from reinforcing stimuli in this respect). Few responses produce the same reinforcing consequences in all settings. Discrimination occurs when the individual learns to distinguish between instances when reward for a particular response is available and when it is not. The cues which form the basis of such judgements can be thought of as discriminative stimuli. The proposal, therefore, by such as Merbaum (1963) and Kennedy, Timmons and Noblin (1971), is that by, for example, reflecting feeling the interviewer signals to the interviewee that further affective responses are desirable and, presumably, the occasion for subsequent reinforcement.

In the ongoing sequential stream of interaction, the task of locating sources of influence is fraught with difficulty. While no attempt will be made to establish categorically the modus operandi of reflective statements in terms of either discriminative or reinforcing stimuli, some evidence tentatively favouring the latter explanation is briefly outlined. It could be hypothesised that if interviewer responses such as reflections act primarily as discriminative stimuli, then degree of intrusion would be positively related to effectiveness. Indeed, findings along these lines were detailed by Merbaum (1963) in support of this view. He revealed that reflecting feeling was associated with greater levels of affective self-referenced statements than either noncommittal interviewer expressions (for instance, 'Mmm-hmm', 'Uh-huh') or mild positive utterances ('Good', 'Fine', 'I see'). The former, it was pointed out, are more intrusive when compared with the two contrasting interventions, being much more difficult to ignore. However, Powell (1968) discovered a difference in reinforcing potential among interviewer responses, including reflections, which were ostensibly equally intrusive and consequently equally effective as discriminative stimuli. Further doubt was cast upon the acceptability of this explanation by Hoffnung (1969), who noted a marked difference in affective self-referencing depending upon whether these interviewee responses were rephrased or merely repeated back by the interviewer. In spite of the fact that both interjections would appear to be of comparable discriminative value, the latter were much less effective in the production of the dependent variable. This technique was also actively disliked by the interviewees.

Pursuing a different line of argument, it could be reasoned that the noncontingent application of reflections would have a more detrimental effect on the modification of verbal behaviour if such interventions served as reinforcing rather than discriminative stimuli. Although the available evidence is meagre, partly due to lack of specificity by researchers in outlining experimental procedures, there would seem to be a trend confirming this proposition. It is of interest that in one of the few pieces of research which have failed to report a conditioning capability, interviewer reflective statements were administered on a noncontingent or random basis (Barnabei *et al.*, 1974).

To summarise, reflecting on the part of the interviewer is a method of influencing interviewee verbal behaviour by affecting the frequency of occurrence of particular types of response. This can be accounted for in terms of the behaviouristic principles of operant conditioning. While the evidence is far from definitive, it would seem that such statements act as reinforcing stimuli and, by implication, are valued positively by interviewees.

The Linguistic Approach

A reflection, whatever else it may be, is a component of language and as such is subject to the sphere of influence of linguistics. The final theoretical perspective presented, unlike the preceding two, owes more to this discipline, and to that of sociology, than to psychology. From this background, reflections can be regarded as forming part of the complex and often subtle operation of organising and orchestrating conversation. More specifically, they would appear to be a means of formulating talk. This process of formulating can be thought of as providing comment upon what has been said or what is taking place in the interaction. It has been outlined as follows: 'A member may treat some part of the conversation as an occasion to describe that conversation, to explain it, or characterize it, or explicate, or translate, or summarize, or furnish the gist of it, or take note of its accordance with rules, or remark on its departure from rules. That is to say, a member may use some part of the conversation as an occasion to formulate the conversation' (Garfinkel and Sacks, 1970, p. 350).

Formulations, as discussed by McLaughlin (1984), serve to promote, transform, delete or indeed terminate talk. They may relate to something the person providing the formulation has contributed (A–issues or events), something the other participant has mentioned (B–issues or events) or, less frequently, both (AB–issues or events). A further distinction is that between formulations of 'gist' and 'upshot' (Heritage and Watson, 1979). The former involves extracting and highlighting the central events and issues featured in the immediately preceding conversation. Formulations of upshot go beyond this to frequently draw conclusions based upon assumptions which may or may not meet with the agreement of the other partner. It would seem that from this standpoint reflections are essentially B–event or issue formulations of gist.

It has been noted that formulations of this type are often tentative proposals and require a decision from the other interactor as to their acceptability. If the other is unwilling to agree to a particular representation of his or her position, one or more modifications are likely to be presented and worked through until agreement is forthcoming. The frequent association between a formulation of this type and confirmation by the other led Heritage and Watson (1979) to characterise them as adjacency pairs. It is of interest that those, such as Ivey and Authier (1978), who have discussed reflecting solely from the counselling/interviewing frame of reference, have stressed the necessity to be frequently tentative, and to give the interviewee the opportunity to agree or disagree with the reflection; they have also commented upon the tendency of the interviewee to express acceptance if it is, in fact, accurate.

According to the two theoretical interpretations previously considered, reflections promote more intense experiencing or reinforce continued discussion of a particular topic. However, one of the functions of formulations would seem to be to engineer a change of topic or even the termination of conversation. It has been reported that conversational lapses are often immediately preceded by an utterance of this sort (McLaughlin and Cody, 1982). A related point was also made by Albert and Kessler (1976), to the effect that summary statements commonly signal the end of an encounter.

How can these seemingly contradictory findings be reconciled? First, differences in the type of interaction and the level of intimacy of relationship shared by the participants may be significant. The findings by, for example, McLaughlin and Cody (1976) would appear to be drawn from normal conversations between relative strangers. It is of interest that Scott (1983), focusing upon conversations involving married couples, discovered that formulations frequently lead to more prolonged discussion. Second, it must be borne in mind that reflections are only a sub-set of formulations. Some types of formulation may be more effective than others in the process of ending discussion. A third reason for these disparate outcomes could be due to paralinguistic accompaniments of the verbal content of the reformulation. Variations in intonation can act to make a statement either interrogative or declarative. Based upon the linguistic analysis of naturally occurring interactions, Schegloff and Sacks (1973) reported that words spoken with a downward intonation served to terminate topic discussion.

Weiner and Goodenough (1977) conceived of reflections as repetition passes (that is, speech acts which serve to forego the opportunity of making a substantive contribution to the continued exploration of the topic), which can be used in order to bring about a conversational change. However, it was emphasised that in order for reflections to function in this fashion, they had to be delivered with a downward rather than a sustained or rising vocal intonation. The corollary of this, it could be argued, is that when reflections are used to facilitate interviewee exploration, they should be spoken with a sustained or rising intonation pattern. Additional features of contemporaneous non-verbal behaviour may also be influential (see Nelson-Jones, 1983). If reflecting is truly a skilled behaviour, its effectiveness must also be determined in part by its location within the context of the temporal structure of interaction. Such matters have received only limited comment and need to be more fully investigated.

Three radically different views of reflecting have been outlined in this section. According to the person-centred humanist, reflections are a means of accepting the other without condition; of empathising with him or her and enabling that person to become more fully aware of significant components of their phenomenal being. To the behaviourist, reflections act as social reinforcers to influence the verbal performance of the other by increasing the amount of pre-ordained talk. Lastly, reflections have been depicted as techniques which are used in the organisation and management of conversation to not only maintain or change it, but also bring it to an end.

A Functional Analysis of Reflecting

Functional aspects of reflecting have already been mentioned in this chapter, and particularly in the last section. Some of these have been elaborated upon to a greater extent than others. The present section, however, will concentrate more single-mindedly and in a pan-theoretical fashion upon the various potential effects attendant upon the proper use of this skill. Many are equally applicable to reflections generally, and more specifically to paraphrases and reflections of feeling. Those which are more specialised are identified as such.

One of the more basic functions of reflecting is to indicate to the interviewee that he or she is being fully attended to by the interviewer. Unless this were so it would obviously be impossible for the interviewer to reproduce the core element of the interviewee's previous communication (Cormier and Cormier, 1979). The implication is that the interviewee is sufficiently valued and accepted for the interviewer to be interested in, and prepared to become involved with, him or her. It is therefore suggested that this technique forms the basis for the creation of a positive, facilitative relationship typified by openness, trust, respect and empathy.

It is widely accepted that reflections are also frequently used in order to clarify (Brammer, 1973). Since problems and concerns, especially of a personal nature, are things which are experienced, for the most part, at a 'gut' level rather than being intellectualised or even verbalised, it often proves difficult for interviewees to find the words and indeed thoughts to unambiguously express them. By encapsulating and unobtrusively presenting to the interviewee the most salient facts of his previous attempt, he can be helped to become more completely aware of the exigencies of his predicament. This is accomplished while maintaining the interviewee and his frame of reference at the centre of things. Other clarifying techniques such as questioning tend to place the emphasis upon the interviewer.

In addition to acting as a means of enabling the interviewee to appreciate more clearly his concerns, reflecting assists the interviewer in obtaining a clearer realisation of the actualities of the case. As a continuation of this train of thought, the skill has been associated with the promotion of understanding. By reflecting, not only does the interviewer convey a desire to get to know, but when he or she is accurate, demonstrates to the interviewee the level of understanding accomplished, despite the fact that the original message may have been inchoate and vague. Supported in this way, the latter is motivated to continue to explore particular themes more deeply (Pietrofesa *et al.*, 1978), concentrating upon facts, feelings or both depending upon the content of the reflective statement (Ivey and Authier, 1978). From the interviewer's point of view, a confirmatory response serves as feedback indicating that he is in fact closely in touch with the other. In this sense, reflections can prove useful as a form of perception-check.

Commenting more particularly upon reflecting feeling states, Brammer (1973) pointed out that interviewees are influenced to devote greater attention to phenomena of this type, as a result. Furthermore, they can be assisted in becoming more completely aware of their feelings by being encouraged to explore and express them in this way. This can be difficult to accomplish and requires tact but is very worthwhile. Egan (1977) notes that while some feelings are quite laudable and easily accepted, many others prompt defensive reactions and, consequently, are either consciously or subconsciously repressed and denied. As a result, people become estranged from these affective facets of their being. Through the reflection of feeling such individuals can be put more fully in touch with these realities. By using this technique the interviewer acknowledges the interviewee's right to feel this way and indicates that it is permissible for those feelings to be expressed and discussed. This frequently does not happen in everyday conversations, which typically dwell upon factual matters. Here, affective shifts can cause stress and embarrassment and tend to be actively avoided. This is especially so if the emotions disclosed are negative, currently experienced and about someone in the present company.

The importance of helping interviewees' to 'own' their feelings has been mentioned by Pietrofesa *et al.* (1978), among others. Having acknowledged the existence of the feeling, the interviewee must be brought to realise that ultimately he or she is the source of it and has responsibility for. Passons (1975) identified various ploys which are adopted such as the impersonal use of 'one' rather than 'I', in order to disown affective states (for instance, 'One tends to be rather angry . . .'). By constantly using the pronoun 'you' when reflecting feeling, Brammer and Shostrom (1977), suggested that this depersonalisation can gradually be overcome and the interviewee brought to appreciate the difference between what is felt, which is his and over which he can have control, and those events in the environment which have acted as a catalyst for these feelings but which may be beyond his sphere of influence.

The frequent benefits to be derived from including affective and factual aspects of the interviewee's message in a single reflective statement have already been stated. Carkhuff (1973) proposed the use of a format such as 'You feel . . . because . . .', although this structure should not be permitted to become inflexible and habitual. However, by locating emotions in the context of associated thoughts, behaviours, ideas and happenings, an added dimension of meaning can be provided. The interviewee can begin to grasp the often complex relationships which exist between these phenomena, gaining insights into the reasons and motives which underpin emotions and how these in turn can have significant causal ramifications for behaviour (Brammer and Shostrom, 1977).

Finally, the possibility of reflective statements being employed in order to regulate conversation by perhaps serving to engineer the termination of discussion, should not be overlooked.

The various propositions outlined in this section differ considerably in terms of their epistemological basis. While many are, for the most part, theoretically derived or experientially grounded, others have emerged from systematic empirical inquiry. The final section of this chapter selectively reviews some of the research which has been conducted into reflecting.

A Select Review of Research on Reflecting

The lack of consistency in the operational definition of reflections and related terms has already been discussed at length. The work of categorising individual investigations and trying to abstract broad and consistent relationships between variables is consequently made that much more difficult. It may be useful to remind the reader at this point of the general definitions of reflecting, paraphrasing and reflection of feeling proposed earlier, since the present review is structured on this basis. Thus, reflections are considered as statements, in the interviewer's own words, which mirror-back the essence of the interviewee's previous communication and may contain both affective and factual content. Utterances of this type, which concentrate upon affective issues, are called reflections of feeling; paraphrases, on the other hand, deal largely with the non-affective element of what is said. The reader is alerted to marked deviations from this convention.

Further disparities in the research conducted relate to the theoretical basis of the inquiry; research design and procedures; number and type of subjects; and dependent variables chosen for investigation. As far as the latter is concerned, a broad distinction can be drawn between measures of behaviour (for example, Powell, 1968; Beharry, 1976; Mills, 1983) and of attitude (for example, Zimmer and Anderson, 1968; Silver, 1970; Ehrlich, D'Augelli and Danish, 1979). In some cases, the interviewee's attitudes towards the interviewer were examined (for example, Silver, 1970; Highlen and Baccus, 1977), while in others those of external judges were sought (for example, Zimmer and Anderson, 1968; Turkat and Alpher, 1984).

Reflections

The attitudinal effects of a reflective style of interaction have been variously compared with those of an intrusive style (Ellison and Firestone, 1974), an evaluative style (Silver, 1970), and with both interrogative and predictive approaches (Turkat and Alpher, 1984).

The contrasting evaluative style investigated by Silver (1970) was one in which the interviewer reacted judgementally to interviewee contributions and, unlike the reflective condition, was conceived as a powerful technique for enhancing interviewer status. The status of the interviewees' was also manipulated prior to each taking part in a 30-minute unstructured interview in which they were requested to talk about themselves. The relative status of half the group was enhanced by being informed that they could help the interviewer, who was described as being deficient, in his training. For the low status subjects, interviewers were presented as widely acclaimed experts in their field. It was assumed that a status differential would be created as a result. Following the interviews, subjects' level of personal comfort was obtained by means of a questionnaire. A significant interaction was found between interviewee status and interviewer style of interaction such that low status interviewees felt much more comfortable with interviewers who responded reflectively.

Interviewer–interviewee status differential was also varied by Ellison and Firestone (1974) in a manner similar to that employed by the previous researcher. In addition, the effects of subject self-esteem were investigated. Subjects were not actually involved in interaction, however, but rather listened to part of an interview featuring the interviewer, in anticipation of a subsequent interviewing encounter. Apart from status differences, interviewer style was also manipulated. Interviewers displayed either a reflective or an intrusive style. The latter was characterised by the interviewer controlling the direction and pace of the interaction and being active, assertive and interpretive. A control group of subjects completed the post-experimental questionnaire without listening to any of the taped material. It emerged that subjects who observed the reflective interviewer indicated a greater willingness to reveal highly intimate details to such a person who was perceived as being passive, easy-going and non-assertive. A tendency also emerged for low self-esteem subjects to reveal a greater potential for self-disclosure towards a high-status reflective interviewer. Such subjects regarded high-status interviewers as more competent, trustworthy, concerned, accepting, genuine and positive. These findings would seem consistent with those of Silver (1970), accepting the comparability of the interviewer high-status condition in this investigation with that of interviewee low-status in the previous.

Turkat and Alpher (1984) compared judges' reactions to a reflective style of interacting with an interrogative approach in which further information was requested, and a predictive style which required the interviewer to accurately predict interviewee's reactions in situations yet to be discussed. Impressions were based upon written transcripts of actual interviews which were tailored to meet the needs of the experiment. Those interviewers who used reflections were perceived as understanding their interviewees, although no signficant differences between treatments were found on this variable. The predictive style, however, was regarded as a more effective method of actually demonstrating understanding. The generalisability of these results are, nevertheless, limited by the fact that the subjects were introductory psychology students and, more importantly, that judgements were based exclusively upon written transcripts. It should be realised that reflections of more subtle paralinguistically or non-verbally conveyed information would not have been appreciated as a result. A videotaped counselling interview was used instead by Zimmer and Anderson (1968), who discovered a positive relationship between reflecting and not only empathic understanding but also positive regard. Measures of these variables were again provided by trained judges.

A number of researchers have tried to establish the effects of reflecting upon the actual behaviour of the interviewee subjected to this procedure. They have largely adopted, as a dependent variable, some measure of interviewee self-disclosure. This has sometimes been labelled as such but has also been referred to as self-referenced statements. Powell (1968), for example, examined the effects of reflections on subjects' positive and negative self-referent statements. Reflections (which, from the definition provided, would appear to mirror back the verbal content of contributions) were compared with approval–supportive and open–disclosure conditions. The former included interviewer statements supporting subjects' self-referent statements, while the latter referred to the provision of self-referent statements by the interviewer. Subjects within each treatment were encouraged to disclose either positive or negative self-revelations. Each was interviewed for 20 minutes, although the various treatments were only administered during the final ten, with the initial stage being used to obtain a base-line measure of the dependent variable. Reflections were found to produce a significant increase in the number of negative but not positive self-references. While omitting the distinction between positive and negative instances, Kennedy *et al.* (1971), based upon a similar experimental procedure, reported that reflections successfully increased the frequency of personal pronouns mentioned by subjects. These, of course, are also an estimation of extent of self-referencing.

A number of researchers have distinguished between the amount of self-disclosure entered into by subjects and the level of intimacy of such information. Vondracek (1969) employed an experimental design similar to that of Powell (1968), as outlined above. Reflecting was contrasted with a revealing (interviewer self-disclosure) and a probing treatment. The latter proved to be more successful at increasing the extent but not the level of intimacy of self-disclosure. Following the initiation of reflections, the degree of intimacy provided increased significantly. This, however, also held for both comparison conditions. Beharry (1976), also measured the extent and intimacy of self-disclosure and found that reflecting resulted in both being increased significantly. However, the comparison treatments of self-disclosure, probes and supportive statements were equally successful in this respect. Relying solely upon a between-treatments design, Mills (1983), again reported that reflecting produced significantly higher rates of self-disclosure than a no-treatment control, but not when compared with the alternative conditions of probing and self-disclosure. Nevertheless, none of the treatment groups were significantly superior to the control in terms of what was called quality of self-disclosure. Due to the procedure employed in the measurement of this dependent variable, it may be inappropriate to equate it with intimacy of self-disclosure as featured in the previous studies.

Feigenbaum (1977) also investigated the quantity (measured in terms of number of self-referent words spoken) and intimacy of subjects' self-disclosures. In addition, however, he included sex of subject as an independent variable. No main effect for treatments was found. It did emerge, however, that while females disclosed more, and at more intimate levels, in response to reflections, male subjects scored significantly higher on both counts under the interviewer self-disclosure treatment. Although further confirmation is required, it should be noted that the subjects in Mill's experiment were largely male and, in the case of Vondracek (1969), exclusively so.

In an investigation with perhaps greater external validity than any of the others previously mentioned, a complex relationship was revealed involving not only sex but also social status of subject. The study by Cline, Merjia, Coles *et al.* (1984) featured male marital therapists and couples actually receiving marital therapy. One of the categories of therapist behaviour was labelled therapist reflectiveness. Although the reliability of measurement was low, this variable was found to correlate positively with subsequent changes in positive social interaction for middle-class husbands, but with negative changes for both lower-class husbands and wives. It also related positively to changes in expression of personal feeling for middle-class husbands and wives. When assessed three months after the termination of therapy, a positive relationship emerged between therapist reflectiveness and outcomes of marital satisfaction, but for lower class husbands only. While this finding would seem to be consistent with the effects of status mentioned earlier, the evidence does not support the increased effectiveness of reflective procedures for female subjects. It must also be realised, of course, that the dependent variables in this piece of research differ from those of simple measures of self-disclosure. (See Chapter 9 for more detail on self-disclosure.)

Not all research has attested to the efficacy of the technique of reflecting. According to Hill and Gormally (1977), this procedure was largely ineffective in increasing the use of affective self-referents by experimental subjects. However, not only was a non-contingent procedure of application employed in this study, but the rate of administration was low, thus militating against potential reinforcing influences.

To summarise, it would seem that attitudes towards interviewers who make use of reflections are largely positive and that this may be particularly so in the case of low-status subjects. At a more behavioural level, this technique would also seem capable of producing increases in both the amount and intimacy of information which interviewees reveal about themselves, although it would not appear to be significantly more effective than alternative procedures in these respects. In the actual therapeutic context, there is some evidence linking reflecting with positive outcome measures for certain clients.

Reflections of Feeling.

Again, studies which have focused specifically upon reflections of feeling have, by and large, examined their effects upon impressions of (or attitudes towards) the interviewer and impact on interviewee behaviour. In many instances, both types of dependent variable have featured in the same investigation.

Uhlemann *et al.* (1976), examined the relationship between reflections of feeling and judgements, by trained external raters, of the degree of empathic understanding revealed by the interviewers. These assessments were based upon both written responses as well as an audio-recording of an actual interview for each participant. A significant relationship emerged between extent of reflection of feeling and the dependent measure. Nevertheless, reflecting feeling accounted for a much smaller proportion of the verbal expression of empathy. This would support the view of, for example, Nelson-Jones (1983) that paralinguistic and nonverbal accompaniments of verbal content are important dimensions of the meaningful use of this skill.

Techniques which, while differently labelled, would appear to equate with reflection of feelings, have also been reported to contribute to positive interviewer evaluations. Ehrlich *et al.* (1979), for instance, found that interviewers who made use of affective responses (defined as statements reflecting feelings not yet named by the interviewee) were regarded by the interviewees as being more expert and trustworthy. A similar device this time called 'sensing unstated feelings' emerged as a significant predictor of counsellor effectiveness when assessed by surrogate clients following a counselling-type interview (Nagata, Nay and Seidman, 1983).

This type of interaction also featured in an inquiry conducted by Greenberg and Clarke (1979), which contrasted the outcomes of two counselling approaches — one reflection of feeling, the other a Gestalt procedure. Following their encounters, subjects who experienced the reflection of feeling regime reported feeling involved and understood. They experienced the counsellor as empathic and expressed satisfaction with the interview. However, the two treatments were not distinguishable in these respects. Similarly, Highlen and Baccus (1977) reported that when clients allocated to a reflection of feeling condition were compared with those who experienced a probe treatment, no substantial differences emerged in perception of counselling climate, counsellor comfort or client satisfaction.

A number of researchers including Merbaum (1965), Barnabei *et al.* (1974), Highlen and Baccus (1977) and Highlen and Nicholas (1978) adopted affective self-referents as a dependent variable in their investigations of how reflections of feeling influence interviewee performance. With the exception of Barnabei *et al.* (1974), this interviewing technique was found to produce significant increases in the incidence of affective self-talk by subjects. In the case of Highlen and Nicholas (1978), however, reflections of feeling were combined with interviewer self-referenced affect statements, thus confounding the effects attributable to them. Although Highlen and Baccus (1977) failed to find a differential effect for reflections of feeling and probes, Merbaum (1963) discovered that this condition (defined as paraphrasing or restating explicitly expressed feelings) was significantly more successful than the use of noncommittal interviewer vocalisations or mild positive statements in promoting both positive and negative self-references of an affective nature. Ehrlich *et al.* (1979) revealed that interviewer affective responses were effective in generating higher percentages of affect words and also self-referent pronouns during interviewee responding.

It is of interest that, in the case of the study which failed to establish a significant relationship between reflections of feeling and various interviewee behavioural measures, including affect words, self-referent pronouns and use of present tense verbs (Barnabei *et al.*, 1974), the experimental treatment was administered on a non-contingent basis. Of further interest, in view of the comments made in the previous section concerning the possible effects of sex of subject, is the fact that the investigations by Ehrlich *et al.* (1979), Highlen and Baccus (1977) and Highlen and Nicholas (1978), all featured females in this capacity and produced positive outcomes. However, the subjects taking part in the Barnabei *et al.* (1974) study were also female, although any potential effects which may have been due to this factor were likely to be overshadowed by the nature of the experimental manipulation.

It would appear that the outcome of the research on reflection of feeling is largely consistent with that of reflections in general. There is substantial evidence to suggest that this technique contributes to positive interviewee perceptions and attitudes towards the interviewer, and is capable of influencing the extent to which interviewees reveal affective detail about themselves. Whether it is more effective in this respect than alternative procedures still has to be shown, however.

Paraphrases

The few studies which have focused upon the subjective impressions created by the use of paraphrases have reported favourable outcomes consistent with those already mentioned relating to reflections and reflections of feeling. Thus, Dickson (1981) detailed a significant positive relationship between the proportion of paraphrases to questions asked by a group of employment advisory personnel and ratings of interviewer competency provided by independent judges. Similarly, an interviewing behaviour which would seem to be comparable to paraphrasing was found by Nagata *et al.* (1983) to be an accurate predictor of client perceptions of interviewer effectiveness.

The majority who have researched the effects of paraphrasing have selected behavioural characteristics as dependent variables. In some cases, however, paraphrases are defined to include both factual and affective material (for example, Hoffnung, 1969), while in others affective content is not explicitly excluded (for example, Kennedy and Zimmer, 1968; Haase and DiMattia, 1976). Conceived of as such, paraphrases have been associated with increases in self-referenced statements (Kennedy and Zimmer, 1968), and self-referenced affective statements (Hoffnung, 1969; Haase and DiMattia, 1976), although in the case of Citkowitz (1975), this effect was limited.

A number of researchers have made the distinction between the affective and non-affective content of these interviewer responses much more pronounced. Waskow (1962), for example, investigated the function of selective interviewer responding on the factual and feeling aspects of subjects' communication in a psychotherapy-like interview. Subjects were matched for initial levels of factual and affective verbal expression and assigned to one of three experimental treatments. In the first, the interviewer reflected feelings; in the second, factual content was paraphrased; while in the third, a combination of feelings and content conveyed by the subject was reflected back. Subjects' responses were assessed as being factual, feeling or both. It emerged that the group which had received the paraphrasing treatment emitted a significantly higher percentage of factual responses. The findings which emerged from the investigations by Auerswald (1974) and Hill and Gormally (1977) were less positive. In both cases, however, affective responses by subjects were selected as the dependent variable and the experimental treatment was administered on a non-contingent basis.

Conclusion

This chapter is concerned, at practical, empirical and theoretical levels, with reflecting as an interviewing technique. Having identified and attempted to disentangle a number of conceptual confusions, three contrasting theoretical perspectives on the process deriving from humanistic psychology, behavioural psychology and linguistic are presented. The various functional claims for the skill, based upon theoretical and experiential, as well as empirical considerations, are discussed.

From the research reviewed it would seem that reflections, whether of fact, feeling or both, are perceived positively by both interviewees and external observers. There is also evidence that they can promote interviewee self-disclosure but that such disclosure may be dependent upon the type of reflective utterance employed. This is important, suggesting, as it does, that structural nuances can be functionally significant.

However, the primacy of reflecting as a means of promoting disclosure has yet to be established empirically. Further research should concentrate upon more naturalistic settings rather than the psychology laboratory. The possible effects of such interviewer and interviewee variables as sex, status, socio-economic class and ethnic background deserve further inquiry, as do situational factors including the nature of the encounter. The impact of the location of the reflection in the sequence of exchanges and the effects which paralinguistic and nonverbal accompaniments may have on the interviewee merit closer examination.

More fundamental is the need for those writing and researching in this area to devote increased attention to the sorts of issues raised at the beginning of this chapter so that the present semantic inconsistencies and definitional imprecisions may be superseded by a greater conceptual stringency and a more commonly accepted nomenclature.

References

Albert, S. and Kessler, S. (1976) 'Processes for Ending Social Encounters: The Conceptual Archaelogy of a Temporal Place', *Journal for the Theory of Social Behaviour, 6,* 147–70

Auerswald, M.C. (1974) 'Differential Reinforcing Power of Restatement and Interpretation on Client Production of Affect', *Journal of Counselling Psychology, 21,* 9–14

Baldock, J. and Prior, D. (1981) 'Social Workers Talking to Clients: A Study of Verbal Behaviour', *British Journal of Social Work, 11,* 19–38

Barnabei, F., Cormier, W.H. and Nye, L.S. (1974) 'Determining the Effects of Three Counselling Verbal Responses on Client Verbal Behaviour', *Jounal of Counselling Psychology, 21,* 355–9

Beharry, E.A. (1976) 'The Effect of Interviewing Style upon Self-disclosure in a Dyadic Interaction', *Dissertation Abstracts International, 36,* 4677B

Benjamin, A. (1974) *The Helping Interview,* Houghton Mifflin, Boston

Boy, A.V. and Pine, G.J. (1963) *Client-Centred Counselling in the Secondary School,* Houghton Mifflin, Boston

Brammer, L.M. (1973) *The Helping Relationship: Process and Skills,* Prentice Hall, Englewood Cliffs, New Jersey

Brammer, L.M. and Shostrom, E.L. (1977) *Therapeutic Psychology: Fundamentals of Counselling and Psychotherapy,* Prentice-Hall, Englewood Cliffs, New Jersey

Bull, P. (1983) *Body Movement and Interpersonal Communication,* Wiley, Chichester

Carkhuff, R.R. (1973) *The Art of Helping: An Introduction to Life Skills,* Human Resource Development Press, Amherst, Massachussetts

Citkowitz, R.D. (1975) 'The Effects of Three Interview Techniques — Paraphrasing, Modelling, and Cues — in Facilitating Self-Referent Affect Statements in Chronic Schizophrenics', *Dissertation Abstracts International, 36,* 2462B

Cline, V.B., Merjia, J., Coles, J., *et al.* (1984) 'The Relationship Between Therapist Behaviours and Outcome for Middle and Lower Class Couples in Marital Therapy', *Journal of Clinical Psychology, 40,* 691–704

Cormier, W.H. and Cormier, L.S. (1979) *Interviewing Strategies for Helpers: A Guide to Assessment, Treatment and Evaluation,* Brooks/Cole, Monterey

Corsini, R.J. (1968) 'Counselling and Psychotherapy' in E.F. Borgatta and W.W. Lambert (eds), *Handbook of Personality Theory and Research,* Rand McNally, Chicago

Danish, S.J. and Hauer, A.L. (1973) *Helping Skills: A Basic Training Program,* Behavioral Publications, New York

Dickson, D.A. (1981) *Microcounselling: An Evaluative Study of a Programme,* unpublished PhD Thesis, Ulster Polytechnic

Dillon, J.T. (1981) 'To Question and Not to Question During Discussion: 1. Questioning and Discussion', *Journal of Teacher Education, 32,* 51–5

Egan, G. (1975) *The Skilled Helper,* Wadsworth, Belmont, CA

—— (1977) *You and Me: The Skills of Communicating and Relating to Others,* Brooks/Cole, Monterey, CA

Ehrlich, R.P., D'Augelli, A.R. and Danish, S.J. (1979) 'Comparative Effectiveness of Six Counsellor Verbal Responses', *Journal of Counselling Psychology, 26,* 390–8

Ekman, P. and Friesen, W.V. (1969) 'The Repertoire of Non-verbal Behaviour: Categories, Origins, Usage and Coding', *Semiotica, 1,* 49–98

Ellison, C.W. and Firestone, I.J. (1974) 'Development of Interpersonal Trust as a Function of Self-Esteem, Target Status, and Target Style', *Journal of Personality and Social Psychology, 29,* 655–63

Feigenbaum, W.M. (1977) 'Reciprocity in Self-Disclosure Within the Psychological Interview', *Psychological Reports, 40,* 15–26

Flanders, N.A. (1970) *Analyzing Teaching Behaviour,* Addison-Wesley, Reading, MA

French, P. (1983) *Social Skills for Nursing Practice,* Croom Helm, Beckenham

Garfinkel, H. and Sacks, H. (1970) 'On Formal Structures of Practical Actions', in J.C. Mckinney and E.A. Tirayakian (eds), *Theoretical Sociology,* Appleton-Century Crofts, New York

Gendlin, E.T. (1961) 'Experiencing: A Variable in the Process of Therapeutic Change', *Psychiatric Quarterly, 35,* 134–9

Gilmore, S.K. (1973) *The Counsellor-in-Training,* Prentice-Hall, Englewood Cliffs, New Jersey

Greenberg, L.S. and Clarke, K.M. (1979) 'Differential Effects of the Two-Chair Experiment and Empathic Reflections at a Conflict Marker', *Journal of Counselling Psychology, 26,* 1–8

Haase, R.F. and DiMattia, D.J. (1976) 'Spatial Environment and Verbal Conditioning in a Quasi-Counselling Interview', *Journal of Counselling Psychology, 23*, 414–21

Hackney, H. and Nye, S. (1973) *Counselling Strategies and Objectives*, Prentice-Hall, Englewood Cliffs, New Jersey

Hargie, O., Saunders, C. and Dickson, D. (1981) *Social Skills in Interpersonal Communication*, Croom Helm, Beckenham

Hart, J. (1970) 'The Development of Client-Centred Therapy' in J.T. Hart and T.M. Tomlinson (eds), *New Directions in Client-Centred Therapy*, Houghton Mifflin, Boston

Heritage, J.C. and Watson, D.R. (1979) 'Formulations as Conversational Objectives' in G. Psathas (ed.) *Everyday Language: Studies in Ethnomethodology*, Irvington, New York

Highlen, P.S. and Baccus, G.K. (1977) 'Effects of Reflection of Feeling and Probe on Client Self-referenced Affect', *Journal of Counselling Psychology, 24*, 440–3

——— and Nicholas, R.P. (1978) 'Effects of Locus of Control, Instructions, and Verbal Conditioning on Self-referenced Affect in a Counselling Interview', *Journal of Counselling Psychology, 25*, 177–83

Hill, C.E. and Gormally, J. (1977) 'Effects of Reflection, Restatement, Probe and Non-verbal Behaviours on Client Affect', *Journal of Counselling Psychology, 24*, 92–7

Hoffnung, R.J. (1969) 'Conditioning and Transfer of Affective Self-References in a Role-played Counselling Interview', *Journal of Consulting and Clinical Psychology. 33*, 527–31

Ivey, A.E. and Authier, J. (1978) 'Microcounselling', *Innovations in Interviewing, Counselling, Psychotherapy, and Psychoeducation*, C.C. Thomas, Springfield, Illinois

Jones, E.E. and Gerard, H.B. (1967) *Foundations of Social Psychology*, Wiley, New York

Kennedy, T.D., Timmons, E.O. and Noblin, C.D. (1971) 'Non-verbal Maintenance of Conditioned Verbal Behaviour Following Interpretations, Reflections and Social Reinforcers', *Journal of Personality and Social Psychology, 20*, 112–17

——— and Zimmer, J.M. (1968) 'Reinforcing Value of Five Stimulus Conditions in a Quasi-counseling Situation', *Journal of Counselling Psychology, 15*, 357–62

Laver, J. and Hutcheson, S. (eds) (1972) *Communication in Face-to-Face Interaction*, Penguin, Harmondsworth

Lee, D.Y. and Uhlemann, M.R. (1984) 'Comparison of Verbal Responses of Rogers, Shostrom, and Lazarus', *Journal of Counselling Psychology, 31*, 91–4

Merbaum, M. (1963) 'The Conditioning of Affective Self-reference by Three Classes of Generalized Reinforcers', *Journal of Personality, 31*, 179–91

McLaughlin, M.L. (1984) *Conversation: How Talk is Organised*, Sage, Beverly Hills

——— and Cody, M.J. (1982) 'Awkward Silences: Behavioural Antecedents and Consequences of the Conversational Lapse', *Human Communication Research, 8*, 299–316

Mills, M.C. (1983) 'Adolescents' Self-Disclosure in Individual and Group Theme-Centred Modelling, Reflecting, and Probing Interviews', *Psychological Reports, 53*, 691–701

Mucchielli, R. (1983) *Face-to-Face in the Counselling Interview*, MacMillan, London

Nagata, D.K., Nay, W.R. and Seidman, E. (1983) 'Nonverbal and Verbal Content Behaviours in the Prediction of Interviewer Effectiveness', *Journal of Counselling Psychology, 30*, 85–6

Nelson-Jones, R. (1983) *Practical Counselling Skills*, Holt, Rinehart and Winston, London

Nicholson, P. and Bayne, R. (1984) *Applied Psychology for Social Workers*, MacMillan, London

Norton, R. (1983) *Communicator Style: Theory, Applications, and Measures*, Sage, Beverly Hills

Passons, W.R. (1975) *Gestalt Approaches in Counselling*, Holt, Rinehart and Winston, New York

Pietrofesa, J.J., Hoffman, A., Splete, H.H., *et al.* (1978) *Counselling: Theory, Research and Practice*, Rand McNally, Chicago

Porter, E.H. (1950) *An Introduction to Therapeutic Counselling*, Houghton Mifflin, Boston

Powell, W.J. (1968) 'Differential Effectiveness of Interviewer Interventions in an Experimental Interview', *Journal of Consulting and Clinical Psychology, 32*, 210–15

Raben, C.S., Wood, M.T., Klimoski, R.J. *et al.* (1974) 'Social Reinforcement: A Review of the Literature', *US AFHRL Technical Report*, no. 7, 4–9(1)

Rogers, C.R. (1951) *Client-centred Therapy*, Houghton Mifflin, Boston

——— (1961) *On Becoming a Person: A Therapist's View of Psychotherapy*, Houghton Mifflin, Boston

——— (1975) 'Empathic: An Unappreciated Way of Being', *The Counselling Psychologist, 5*, 2–10

——— (1980) *A Way of Being*, Houghton Mifflin, Boston

Schegloff, E.A. and Sacks, H. (1973) 'Opening Up Closings', *Semiotica, 8*, 289–327

Scott, M. (1983) 'Formulation Sequences in Marital Conversation: Strategies for Interactive Interpretive

Alignment', paper presented at the meeting of the International Communication Association, Dallas

Shertzer, B. and Stone, S.C. (1968) *Fundamentals of Counselling,* Houghton Mifflin, Boston

Siegman, A.W. (1978) 'The Telltale Voice: Nonverbal Messages of Vocal Communication' in A.W. Siegman and S. Feldstein (eds), *Nonverbal Behaviour and Communication,* Lawrence Erlbaum Associates, Hillsdale, New Jersey

Silver, R.J. (1970) 'Effects of Subject Status and Interviewer Response Program on Subject Self-Disclosure in Standardized Interviews', *Proceedings of the 78th Annual Convention, APA, 5,* 539–40

Skinner, B.F. (1938) *The Behaviour of Organisms,* Appleton-Century-Crofts, New York

———— (1953) *Science and Behaviour,* Collier MacMillan, London

Stefflre, B. and Grant, W.H. (1972) *Theories of Counselling,* McGraw-Hill, New York

Stewart, C.J. and Cash, W.B. (1974) *Interviewing: Principles and Practices,* W.C. Brown, Dubuque, Iowa

Thorndike, E.L. (1911) *Animal Intelligence,* MacMillan, New York

Turkat, I.D. and Alpher, V.S. (1984) 'Prediction Versus Reflection in Therapist Demonstrations of Understanding: Three Analogue Experiments', *British Journal of Medical Psychology, 57,* 235–40

Uhlemann, M.R., Lea, G.W. and Stone, G.L. (1976) 'Effect of Instructions and Modeling on Trainees Low in Interpersonal Communication Skills', *Journal of Counselling Psychology, 23,* 509–13

Van der Veen, F. (1970) 'Recent Trends in the Client-Centred Framework' in J.T. Hart and T.M. Tomlinson (eds), *New Directions in Client-Centred Therapy,* Houghton Mifflin, Boston

Vondracek, F.W. (1969) 'The Study of Self-Disclosure in Experimental Interviews', *The Journal of Psychology, 72,* 55–9

Waskow, I.E. (1962) 'Reinforcement in a Therapy-like Situation Through Selective Responding to Feelings or Content', *Journal of Consulting Psychology, 26,* 11–19

Watson, J.B. (1913) 'Psychology as the Behaviourist Views It', *Psychological Review, 20,* 158–77

Weiner, S.L. and Goodenough, D.R. (1977) 'A Move Toward a Psychology of Conversation', in R.O. Freedle (ed.), *Discourse Production and Comprehension,* Ablex Publishing, Norwood, New Jersey

Zimmer, J.M. and Anderson, S. (1968) 'Dimensions of Positive Regard and Empathy', *Journal of Counselling Psychology, 15,* 417–26

7 OPENING AND CLOSING

Christine Saunders

First encounters in all human relationships are crucially important. If handled well, they can begin the process of strengthening social relationships between interactors and, at the same time, lay the foundation for future productive and mutually beneficial transactions. Equally important is the business of leave-taking or closing an encounter. The termination of social relationships, even if only temporary, can evoke strong emotions since participants have usually revealed some of their most important feelings and thoughts and perhaps given and taken help and advice from each other. Goffman (1972), commenting on the relationship between greetings and farewells, suggests that they are 'heightened periods of access', in that they are structured, formalised sequences during which interactors have a greater opportunity to make important points or create an effective impact upon others.

Despite both the importance and universality of openings and closings, systematic investigations of how people begin and end their human transactions have largely been neglected (Knapp, Hart, Friedrich, *et al.*, 1973). Unfortunately, this state of affairs still persists today, despite some more recent investigations by authors such as Schegloff and Sacks (1973) and Bakken (1977).

Perhaps one of the major reasons for this lack of research is that greetings and partings are seen as taken-for-granted, common-place and ordinary events usually occurring beneath one's awareness, simply because they fail to cause trouble or anxiety. They appear to be orderly, highly regularised and ritualised sequences, with conventional formats and predictable outcomes. However, while research has turned its back on investigating more closely the nature of these so-called rule-following sequences, most interactors fail to perform these so-called automatic sequences at some stage in their everyday encounters. For instance, at a social level, most people have wondered 'how to begin' when meeting a person for the first time; and at a professional level, policemen, for example, must surely ponder over 'how to approach' a family with news of a tragic accident to one of the family members. Similarly, busy executives sometimes instruct their secretaries to buzz them on the telephone when they are finding it difficult to extricate themselves from a talkative client. In this case, the telephone call becomes a convenient closure marker.

While most people can recall the difficult openings and closings they have experienced, few can clearly and systematically analyse how the difficulties have been overcome, if indeed they have. At best, one is usually offered a few hints and tips from others who have experienced similar problematic sequences; at worst, one has 'muddled' through, perhaps injuring or destroying any chance of further meaningful exchanges. This chapter attempts to illuminate the nature of openings and closings, by identifying those behaviours which are associated with them, across a wide variety of social situations in order to help both the social and professional interactor to achieve appropriate exchanges.

Openings

The term 'opening' has been used in preference to at least two other terms commonly found in the literature, namely, greetings and set induction. Kendon and Ferber (1973) define the term 'greeting' as 'that unit of social interaction often observed when people come into one another's presence, which includes a distinctive exchange of gestures or utterances in which each person appears to signal to the other, directly and explicitly, that he has been seen' (p. 592).

In this definition the authors have confined their analyses to the verbal and nonverbal behaviours of the interactors with reference solely to the management of good social relationships between the interacting persons.

Set induction, on the other hand, is the term used by psychologists to describe that which occurs when 'an organism is usually prepared at any moment for the stimuli it is going to receive and the responses it is going to make' (Woodworth and Marquis, 1949, p. 298). In other words, set induction establishes in the individual a state of readiness, involves gaining attention and arousing motivation, as well as providing guidelines about that which is to follow. In relation to social interaction, it is more all-embracing than the term 'greeting' in that it involves establishing rapport, arousing motivation, establishing expectations and evaluating these in terms of their realism to the nature and purpose of the ensuing interaction. However, the term 'set induction' has become more associated with the education profession which has focused particularly on the gaining and maintaining of pupils' interest and establishing sound educational goals for pupil achievement rather than the establishing of rapport, which is more associated with the social goals of interaction (Turney, Owens, Hatton, *et al.,* 1976; Hargie, 1980).

The term 'opening' is more general in nature and commonly found across a wider range of contexts, including counselling (Ivey, 1978), interviewing (Pope, 1979), selling (Poppleton, 1981), negotiating (Scott, 1981), public speaking (Knapper, 1981) and teaching (Wragg, 1984), to name but a few. In this chapter, openings are defined as the interactor's initial strategy at both personal and environmental level, utilised to achieve good social relationships, and at the same time establish a frame of reference deliberately designed to facilitate the development of a communicative link between the expectations of the participants and the realities of the situation.

There are a number of purposes for employing the skill of opening depending upon the duration and nature of the interaction. For instance, openings may be brief affairs as when one stranger is introduced to another stranger in a line of many at a large formal function. On the other hand, it may involve a complex range of skills designed to allow participants to mutually benefit from an interactive sequence of a more protracted duration, as, for example, a salesman might employ when attempting to persuade sceptical potential customers to purchase his product. Alternatively, helpers, wishing to establish a more non-directive approach during a first session with a client, will adopt different techniques from those of a teacher attempting to arouse and maintain the interest of 30 disinterested pupils at the start of a lesson.

From these few examples it is apparent that the skill of opening involves a whole range of different activities depending upon the context in which the participants are engaged. In addition, other factors which will influence the choice of opening are the nature of the subject matter to be discussed, the duration of the interaction, the location of the encounter, the social status, personality and sex of the participants and their degree of familiarity with each other. These factors need to be taken into account when selecting the main techniques for an effective opening sequence.

The remainder of this first section of the chapter focuses upon five main types of opening which can gainfully be employed across a wide range of situations; they are social, perceptual, motivational, factual and client-initiated. While this typology is useful in helping to analyse and evaluate appropriate opening techniques, inevitably there are points of overlap between the categories, depending upon the function of the skill. These are noted where they occur throughout the text.

Social Opening

In order to establish and maintain a good rapport with another person before proceeding with the main business of the interaction, it is usually desirable to employ a number of social techniques. Such techniques serve to introduce a human element into the encounter which, in turn, facilitate the attainment of the main goals of the interaction. It is possible to identify three main types of social opening commonly employed: social reinforcers, establishing rapport and setting a receptive atmosphere.

Social Reinforcers. In order for any interaction to take place, the attention of the person one wishes to interact with must first be gained. Receiving the attention of those one likes and respects is something most people positively value and, therefore, something which can be used to influence behaviour. Eye contact is a preparatory step to initiating interpersonal interaction and, as such, it will be examined initially.

The importance of this element has been noted by Trower, Bryant and Argyle (1978) in their work with mental patients. They found that some patients had a problem when attempting to engage others in conversation; that is, they approached the other with their heads bowed and avoided eye contact. In the introductory skills training programme provided for such patients, Trower encouraged them to look and give an eyebrow flash of recognition before they uttered a verbal greeting. While such work points to the crucial nature of eye contact as a precursor to verbal greeting, it is fair to say that most people engage in the skill of initiating eye contact with others as a basic social norm. Nevertheless, there are occasions when difficulty is experienced with this aspect of behaviour, usually when under some kind of emotional stress. Argyle and Cook (1976) describe how being the subject of visual scrutiny can cause high levels of anxiety in some speakers, especially when they are novices. For instance, job interviewees often find it anxiety-provoking to maintain eye contact when being introduced to the selection interviewing panel. Novice teachers, too, often deliver whole lessons to the clock on the back of the classroom wall and so fail to see the responses of their students.

Other accompanying non-verbal social reinforcers such as touch, usually in the form of handshake or a kiss, smiling and tone of voice also serve to make others feel more at ease in most situations. Unlike these movements which tend to be of a short duration and on a limited scale, there are proximity reinforcers which include movements of the body or substantial parts of it. Briefly, proximity reinforcement refers to the potential reinforcing effects which can come about when one person alters the distance between that of another. A reduction in interpersonal distance usually accompanies a desire for increased intimacy and involvement (Hall, 1966). The optimal distance will depend upon a number of factors, including the nature of the relationship, the sex of the participants and the topic of conversation.

As well as nonverbal reinforcers, those who are opening the interaction can also employ accompanying verbal ones. The actual wording of the initial remark will depend upon the respective social status of the participants, their degree of familiarity with each other and the purpose of the interaction. Out-of-place openers such as making a formal remark in a casual situation and *vice versa* often indicates 'staidness' on the one hand and 'flippancy' on the other (Kendon and Feber, 1973).

One other verbal reinforcer, crucial in any effective social opening, is that of using the names of the other interactors. Rackham and Morgan (1977), in their study of BOAC telephone sales agents, found a significant correlation between calling a passenger by name and degree of expressed satisfaction from the passenger. Plato was one of the first of the ancient philosophers to write that using a man's name makes him more attentive to the speaker's argument. Nothing has changed in the intervening years to denigrate his wisdom.

Thus the initial approach of an individual using social reinforcement skills including eye contact, smiling, tone of voice, touch, proximity and the other's name to accompany the verbal greeting will undoubtedly make the other interactor feel more at ease in any given interactive situation.

Establishing Rapport. Following the initial greeting, establishing rapport is also an effective technique which can be used to 'soften' or 'break the ice' in social situations. This process of 'ice-breaking' usually precedes the main purpose of the interaction. Statements relating to the weather, topical events or non-controversial current affairs are fairly typical general opening remarks. However, as Goffman (1972) points out, the comments employed to establish rapport will depend upon the context of the interaction. So, for example, salesmen are usually trained to use non-task comments, and to relate these to some feature of the client or his environment (for example, 'This is a lovely place you have here, Mrs Smith') before proceeding towards the sales pitch. Sullivan (1954), on the other hand, draws attention to the dangers of engaging in too much of what he calls 'social hokum' at the start of a therapist/patient interview, since he feels the therapist's attitude should be one of 'respectful seriousness'. This implies that within the psychotherapy context there should be an avoidance of any forced or excessive non-task comments at the beginning of the interview. In the end, the interviewer must make the final selection and assess if there is need for small talk at the outset to help the interviewee to get started. Benjamin (1974) makes this point when he says, 'we should attempt this only when we truly feel that it will be helpful. Brief statements such as the following may break the ice: "With traffic the way it is around here, you must have found it hard to get a parking place" ' (p. 13).

There is a role for the use of non-task comments in all social situations and, indeed, when social conversations are analysed, the range of remarks made are varied and inventive. This is best illustrated by noting the 'chatting up' process indulged in by most young males when attempting to date an attractive female. However, in a professional context, establishing rapport by the use of non-task comments needs to be carefully considered and genuinely delivered.

Setting a Receptive Atmosphere. An atmosphere in which interaction can flourish is another vital aspect in establishing an effective social opening. Hargie, Saunders and Dickson (1981) employed the phrase 'the provision of creature comforts' to refer to those items which can be utilised in order to make others feel welcome and at ease in any given situation. This would include a lounge rather than upright chair to sit on; the offer of a beverage if the time is available, or the offer of a cigar or cigarette, if the individual smokes. Haines (1975) refers to this essential element when identifying crucial communication skills for social workers. He states that 'courtesy, kind words and gestures and attempts to ensure that clients are seated comfortably in an atmosphere that is warm both physically and psychologically are all aspects of reception that go far to create a sound basis for the development of effective communication' (p. 171). In many professional situations this role is often carried out by the skilled behaviour of experienced reception staff who can do much to allay the anxieties of clients seeking assistance or advice from a professional for the first time (for instance, dentists, consultants, social workers, lawyers). However, this aspect of opening is examined more fully in the section which deals with perceptual openings.

These are the principal means by which effective social openings are achieved, thereby establishing a sound, amicable working relationship on which subsequent encounters can be based. They include the ritualised nonverbal social reinforcers such as eye contact, raised eyebrows, smile, touch, appropriate proximity and friendly facial expressions, plus the accompanying conventional verbal greetings, followed by the use of the other person's name. In addition, rapport can often be established by the use of non-task comments creating the impression of personal interest as opposed to more formal interest in the subsequent part of the interactive sequence. Ensuring that the atmosphere is conducive to the development of rapport also helps to underline the 'human' factor in any meaningful professional exchange.

Perceptual Opening

The expectations of the interacting participants can be influenced by the initial perceptions which are received in any social situation. In other words, people are surrounded by smells, sounds, sights, touches and pressures in various combinations, which provide a constant source of feedback regarding their surroundings. As Oscar Wilde once said, 'only superficial people ignore first impressions', and although it is often true that first impressions can be deceiving, nevertheless, it is necessary to be aware of their effects upon the ensuing social encounter. Therefore, in professional encounters, the practising professional must be aware of the factors which create those 'first impressions' since they will strongly influence the expectations of clients. The factors which influence perceptual openings can be examined within two broad areas, namely environmental and personal.

Environmental Format. When a person enters a room for the first time he will receive perceptions concerning the furniture, architectural style, interior decor, lighting conditions, colours, temperatures and so on. Variations in the arrangements of these environmental factors can be extremely influential on the outcome of interpersonal communication (Canter and Wools, 1970; Knapp, 1972; Smith, 1974). Korda (1976), who has carried out research into the arrangement of furniture, particularly within offices, differentiates between two distinct areas; the zone around the desk he calls the 'pressure area'; the semi-social area is the area away from the desk in which there are armchairs and a coffee table. According to Korda, the effective businessman will select that area of his office more appropriate to the task he wishes to carry out with his particular client or colleague.

Situations which are largely unpalatable to most people are visits to NHS hospitals either as a patient or visitor. Such visits are not made any more comforting by the nature of the environment which tends to be sparsely furnished with uncomfortable chairs if any, brightly lit, decorated with cold colours such as white, pale green or pale blue, unnaturally warm and with a distinctly overpowering smell of chemicals. Yet a very different perceptual set is apparent in private clinics, which usually provide easy chairs laid out in small groups around a coffee table to encourage social interaction, and appropriate lighting, muted colours in walls and furnishings, pictures and accompanying light music. While these conditions may not directly eliminate patient fears and anxieties, they do go some way to reducing the 'de-humanising' process often felt in such circumstances. Although many more examples of effective and ineffective environmental influences abound in everyday situations, this example helps to illustrate the principle that interactions are affected by the environmental context in which they are set.

Personal Characteristics. The personal characteristics of the interactor will also have an influence on how each is expected to behave in the forthcoming interactive sequence. Factors such as age, sex, facial characteristics, hair, physique, voice, dress and attractiveness, will all affect the initial perceptions of the participants. Cook (1977), in reviewing a number of aspects of interpersonal attraction, particularly during initial social encounters, and in emphasising the importance of first impressions, notes that the majority of people search for someone who is attracted to them. This usually takes the form of making some preliminary judgement about the person's personality type, life-style, social background or outlook on life in general. In other words, 'an attempt to "place" the other will be made' (Cook, 1977, p. 323). Thus it would seem that someone regarded as attractive, popular and friendly will seek out a suitable friend or marital partner, while a relatively unattractive and unpopular person who attempts to befriend or date someone considered much more attractive and friendly than themselves is likely to be rejected.

Murstein (1972), in a study of physical attractiveness and marital choice, demonstrated that married couples matched each other closely in physical attractiveness. Attractiveness, however, is usually based on more than mere physical characteristics and includes factors such as dress, perceived neatness and cleanliness, knowledge state, level of competence and personality. First impressions are normally based on the first three variables since information on these factors is obviously more accessible to evaluation. However, people do not usually make a single judgement or form a single impression when assessing personality, while judgements regarding knowledge level and competency are made in specific situations (Rosenblatt, 1977).

While first impressions are crucially important in establishing an interactive framework, it is also important to be aware of being affected by stereotypes based upon the abilities and other characteristics of people from certain social, racial, religious or educational backgrounds. Such stereotypes are often incorrect and in any case imply that all members of a particular category are more similar than they actually are. Some stereotypes are based on appearance. McKeachie (1952), for instance, found that girls who wore a lot of lipstick were seen as frivolous and flirtatious. More recently, Gibbins (1969) showed that people were prepared to make specific predictions about women according to the type and style of clothing they wore. However, Knapper (1970), in investigating the relationship between personality and style of dress, came to the conclusion that there was no systematic relationship between perceived clothing style and the personality of the wearer and that when judgements are made, they tend to be of an irrational nature.

Nevertheless, professional people are frequently evaluated on the basis of their mode of dress. The reason for this is that the style of dress which one adopts is often a sign of the group with which one identifies. Thus, certain professions have become associated with a particular style of dress, with the deliberate intention of carrying a distinct public image. For example, doctors, nurses, soldiers, priests and policemen, by adoption of specific uniforms, immediately induce certain expectations in the observer. At a less restricted level, business executives, civil servants, salesmen, solicitors and managers still adopt a type of 'uniform', namely the executive suit, shirt and tie for a man and the business suit and blouse for the women. When these modes of dress are flouted by the professional, it can have an effect upon the client's expectations. Thus, for example, a bank manager dressed in pullover and old slacks might give the impression that his bank is rather casual about financial matters and 'sloppy' in its transactions when in fact he should be attempting to convey the opposite impression in order to create new business.

There is, however, some evidence to suggest that the initial effects of appearance upon stereotyping may only be transitory. Argyle and McHenry (1971) found that while a person wearing spectacles is judged to have an IQ of 13–15 points higher than when he is not wearing spectacles, observing that person talking for approximately five minutes is enough to eliminate the effects of wearing spectacles on judgements regarding intelligence. This would suggest that the follow-up behaviour is a crucial factor in establishing a lasting impression which will endure for the period of the interaction.

Thus, the two main elements subsumed under perceptual openings are the nature of the immediate environment and the personal attributes of the people with whom interaction is taking place. This is really encapsulated in MacKinnon and Michels' (1971) comment on the formation of first impressions: 'Important clues to the conduct of the interview can often be obtained during these few moments of introduction. The patient's spontaneity and warmth may be revealed in his handshake or greeting . . . Suspicious patients might carefully glance around the office searching for clues about the physician' (p. 52).

Motivational Opening

Whereas there will always be some form of perceptual opening in evidence, contrived or otherwise, and there should always be a social opening of varying duration, it is not always appropriate to execute a motivational type of opening. It must be left to the discretion of the initiator of the interaction to decide whether or not it is necessary to employ motivational techniques at the start.

The function of a motivational opening is to gain attention and arouse motivation at the start of an interactive sequence. It cannot always be assumed that all participants come willingly prepared to interact. In many situations such as learning environments, medical treatments and committee meetings it is important to be aware that perhaps some pupils, patients and group members are less than enthusiastic about taking part in the ensuing experience. Therefore, it is vitally important at the outset to both stimulate and enthuse participants so that the particular task involved may proceed as smoothly as possible thereafter. Otherwise the main objectives of the interaction may be difficult to achieve.

There are a number of techniques which can be adopted to induce a motivational opening; the appropriate one to use will depend upon the context in which the interaction is located. It should also be borne in mind that on some occasions it can be difficult to distinguish certain types of motivational openings from perceptual and social ones since there is some overlap between the categories. Where this does occur, it will be pointed out at the appropriate place in the text.

Psychologists have long since recognised that people can begin to communicate effectively only if they pay attention to some kind of input or stimulus. Stone and Nielson (1982) claim that 'a stimulus is a point of sensory focus' (p. 88). There are a number of mechanisms or techniques which can provide the primary focus for gaining the attention of individuals. The next section focuses upon four such types common across a range of social situations.

Initial Behaviour. The initial behaviour of the speaker will influence the perceptions of the listener or listeners. The adoption of unexpected or unusual behaviour on the part of the speaker can be a powerful method for gaining attention initially. This technique for arousing motivation is most successfully achieved where the 'initial behaviour' referred to previously departs from the normal pattern. As Berlyne (1960) comments, all humans have a basic cognitive structure, which will attempt to accommodate new information of an unexpected nature. It is this element of 'behavioural surprise' which is an essential precursor to the process of the development and assimilation of thoughts and ideas.

In addition to selecting an effective stimulus, the intensity of the stimulus must also be considered, particularly when there are many distractions and asides present. The stimulus must be 'above the threshold' of hearing or vision to provide adequate impetus. Thus a loud noise, a bright light or a large object will usually stimulate attention much more quickly than a faint noise, a weak light or a small object.

The main elements of behaviour which the speaker has at his disposal to motivate his listeners' attention are the use of voice and gestures. Public speakers have long since been aware that the use of the voice is a potent source with which to arouse the attention of their audience. In speeches which are intended to persuade as opposed to merely inform, there is some evidence to suggest that attitudes are more likely to change under conditions of high emotional arousal and, therefore, effective propagandists try to establish a strong emotional tone at the start of their speech (Sargant, 1957).

The old adage 'actions often speak louder than words' becomes a truism in the opening context. Thus a supervisor or manager who has gathered his workforce together with the intention of giving them a 'pep talk' to boost flagging morale will display what Ausubel (1964) calls 'enthusiasm, energy and surgency' in order to communicate a sense of excitement about the company's future. However, Ausubel does not cite actual behaviours which convey this feeling of enthusiasm. French (1983), on the other hand, notes that a crucial aspect of gaining the patient's attention is for the nurse to be aware of proximity, posture and orientation.

Although the main function in this situation is not to excite the patient as such, he feels that 'the nurse must be close enough to the patient so as to demonstrate the "being with the other" attitude. The nurse's goal in this stage is to establish rapport' (pp. 173–4).

The speaker's general appearance can also have a dramatic effect upon encouraging audience interest and motivation, although there is some overlap here with the category related to perceptual opening. For example, Bligh (1972) notes the case of a psychology lecturer in a North American university who is well known for occasionally appearing in the guise of one of the great men whose work is being discussed. However, at a more modest level, a coach who is dressed in a track suit, or a physiotherapist dressed in a keep-fit leotard or teaching pants is more likely to establish a favourable opening at the start of a practical or work out session than if he or she is dressed in everyday clothes.

Introduction of Novel Stimuli. This is a method which can be effectively employed to arouse curiosity and hence the interest and attention of participants. While most of the research evidence relating the use of novel stimuli to effective interest arousal has been carried out in educational contexts (Aubertine, 1968; Gage, 1972; Brown, 1975) the findings have implications for other professionals engaged in stimulating clients' interest. For instance, there are a large number of visual aids which can be used in order to stimulate audience response. These may be diagrammatic (such as flow chart, picture or drawing), real objects (such as a piece of equipment or an ornament), or audiovisual recordings (such as films, tape slides or audio- or videotapes). By introducing these aids at the outset, the ensuing interactive sequence can be enriched accordingly.

Thus, Busch and Wilson (1976) found that when a salesperson had a product which was either unique or clearly superior to other products in short supply, it was made easier for the salesperson to procure a sale, so minimising interaction time and negotiating.

Nurses, health visitors, occupational therapists, speech therapists and physiotherapists, too, often introduce a technical aid to assist treatment. However, a word of caution is needed here. Romiszowski (1974), in researching into the relationship between appropriate media selection and task effectiveness, found that careful consideration must be given to situational factors such as characteristics of participants, practical constraints, knowledge state and so on before deciding upon appropriate media and materials.

A second cautionary note is issued by Turney *et al.* (1976) who point out that 'Gimmickry is to be avoided, for unconnected novelty may secure short-term attending . . . but fail to establish an appropriate set enduring for the task' (p. 92).

Posing of an Intriguing Problem. The posing of such a problem at the beginning of an interactive sequence can capture the listener's attention and hold it for a long time in order eventually to make a decision or solve a problem. Studies by Allen (1970) and Peeck (1970) have shown that the use of thought-provoking problems at the beginning of lessons is related to increased pupil achievement. More recently, Brown (1975) advocates the use of problem-setting as an effective opening device to classroom lessons. Thus teachers, public speakers or lecturers can begin their discourse by setting an intriguing problem designed to establish involvement and participation at either covert or overt level.

The use of case histories, too, can be particularly relevant to begin a discussion, providing the case outlined is applicable to the target audience. Thus, for example, a tutor of trainee counsellors may relate the problems presented to him by a difficult client, and ask the trainees how they would have handled the situation described. Alternatively, a nursing tutor can begin a lecture on 'Care for the Elderly' by describing a typical geriatric problem and asking the students how they would handle the situation. While it is not advisable to begin all lecture/discussion sessions in this way, it is a method which, when used with discretion, can have a marked impact on the involvement of most listeners. However, Feather (1969), researching student attitudes to lecture styles, noted that some students resist this type of approach and prefer lectures which are more predictable and straightforward.

This technique is also applicable in a one-to-one interview when the topic or the problem being discussed has reached a stalemate position. Here the interviewer can inject into the discussion a thought-provoking idea, perhaps beginning with the words, 'What would happen if . . .' This could have the effect of stimulating the interactors to consider information which previously had not been mentioned.

Making a Controversial or Provocative Statement. This can also have the impact of stimulating or encouraging involvement. The situation in which this method is effectively employed is that of the political interview. Journalists and television interviewers ask or make provocative statements in order to test the intensity of the interviewee's views or opinions. Their objective being mainly to make 'good copy' or 'good viewing'.

However, this technique is also applicable in other contexts. For example, French (1983) notes that it can be an apt technique for a nurse to use with patients and cites statements which are 'emotive or value-ridden and which are difficult to conclude by acceptable responses or identifying single correct answers' (p. 81) as being particularly useful. However, he warns that this should only be done without being offensive to the other person. Brown (1975) advocates the use of the provocative question or statement, particularly as an introduction to a group discussion session. Thus, for example, the teacher of 'A' level English, draws attention to the debate surrounding the authenticity of the works of Shakespeare by starting off the discussion with, 'Who wrote Shakespeare's plays?'

In addition, it is a useful device for a chairperson to use at committee meetings, staff meetings or more general group discussions when perhaps interest in the issue or problem under review has begun to wane prematurely. If one of the main aims of a chairperson is to get the group to come to a well-informed, clear decision on a problem, he or she must ensure that all possible arguments or statements have been aired coherently. Alternatively, controversial or provocative statements could also be used by the group leader when he is aware that there is only one view being expressed by the group members because of ignorance of any other prevailing opinions. In this case, the leader can challenge the group's existing views by clearly stating the opposing case. However, this method of motivational opening must be carefully thought out, since the object of the exercise is to provoke comment, not aggression on the part of the listener. Great caution should be exercised when using this particular technique with very sensitive topics or volatile audiences.

Factual Opening

The main purpose of many social encounters is concerned with substantive issues such as fact-finding, knowledge sharing, problem-solving, decision-making and the assessment of opinions or views. Before proceeding to these issues, however, it is important to ensure that a common frame of reference is established at the outset. In order to achieve this objective, it is necessary to draw up a kind of 'social contract' with the person or persons involved so that all are in clear agreement as to the nature and objectives of the ensuing interaction. In essence, therefore, it is important to use an appropriate factual opening so that participants are mentally prepared for the main business of the encounter. This can be achieved in four main ways.

Establishing a Common Frame of Reference. This is a necessary technique to employ at the beginning of all new relationships between the professional and the client (Schulman, 1979). Each is approaching the first encounter from a different standpoint: the professional is asking the question, 'What is the problem here? How will I be able to help this person?' The client is asking, 'What kind of help can I get?' Am I going to appear stupid or helpless?' These questions will persist and remain unanswered until a framework is established in which participants can share and understand the role of the other.

Stating One's Role. This is an important function at the beginning in order to point out to clients what can and, sometimes more importantly, what cannot be done within the limitations of professional functions. Pope (1979) points to this necessity of stating the role expectations in the beginning segment of the interview before communication proceeds and warns that, 'Unless these role expectations complement each other, the dyad lacks stability, and communication remains uninhibited' (p. 515).

Benjamin (1974), on the other hand, issues a cautionary note when explaining one's role to a client or patient. He feels that it is best, 'not to involve the interviewee in the intricacies of our role, profession or professional background' (p. 15). By and large, the client need only understand the professional's role within the agency in order that he or she can ascertain whether the 'right person' has been approached.

Thus the social worker can state her role simply by saying: 'I'm your social worker, Miss Davidson. You can discuss with me the possibilities of residential care for your mother.' Alternatively, if the role of the professional is incongruent with the needs of the client, the professional can state that this is not her role, but will arrange for the client to be seen by someone else. Thus the role expectations of the client, patient or customer should be related to the problems and needs of the client. Once this has been established, the interaction should proceed more smoothly, with conflicts being kept to a minimum. As a result, client and customer satisfaction should be enhanced accordingly.

Goal-setting. This is an essential element at the beginning of an encounter if the purpose of the interviewer is to structure, albeit loosely, the forthcoming interactive sequence. Ryan and Gizyuski (1971) demonstrated this in a study of clients' retrospective views of their experience in behaviour therapy. They found that good working relationships were established between therapist and client when the therapist explained his function, presented a credible rationale for the treatment he was proposing and clearly specified treatment techniques he hoped to adopt. Goldfried and Davison (1976) endorsed these findings and, in addition, suggested that when the behaviour therapist adopted these goal-setting techniques, the client's motivation and willingness to co-operate increased. It should be noted, however, that client-centred therapists prefer to encourage the interviewee to structure events, particularly when the interview is client-initiated (Rogers, 1977).

As early as 1934, Lewis was advocating that in a psychiatrist/patient situation, 'The student physician who approaches the case without a definite plan in mind is certain to overlook important facts or permit the patient to lead too much in the examination, often with the result that the time is not spent to the best advantage or that he is misled into drawing false conclusions' (p. 11). More recently, Pope (1979) emphasises this approach, particularly when the behaviour therapist is conducting an assessment interview. For instance, the therapist, intent on finding out more about the problems presented by the client on the previous occasion, might begin the interview: 'Last time you told me some of the things that were troubling you at home. Today, I'd like to go into a little more detail about some of the things you were saying about your relationship with your eldest son.'

Benjamin (1974), on the other hand, warns that there is a great danger when setting goals in these interviewer-initiating sessions that they will turn out to be 'monologues or lectures or a combination of both' (p. 15). One way of overcoming this danger, he suspects, is for the interviewer to stop talking and listen after he has indicated the purpose of the interview and furnished information, if any, which allows the interview to proceed smoothly. This warning is reiterated by McHenry (1981), who was particularly concerned with the selection interviewer's attempts to 'establish rapport' at the start of a job selection interview. He suggests that, 'the best thing an interviewer can do is to tell the candidate briefly how long the interview is likely to last, that he will do most of the questioning, and that there will be plenty of time left at the end of the interview should the interviewee have anything he would like to raise. All this can be achieved in a couple of sentences' (p. 9).

This technique of providing guidelines about the probable nature and content of a forthcoming sequence allows participants to prepare themselves fully. They will, therefore, be mentally set for the topics discussed and in addition, will be thinking about possible contributions they may be able to make. It also means that the person is more likely to feel secure in the situation, knowing in advance what the purpose of the interaction is, what the main themes are likely to be, how the sequence of discussion should proceed and how long the interaction is likely to last.

Summarising. A summary is also a useful way to begin a discussion, particularly when decisions were made and commitments undertaken at the previous encounter. Aubertine (1968), for example, showed that teachers who introduced new material by linking it with knowledge already familiar to pupils were rated by pupils as being more effective. This process of linking that which is known with the unknown material to follow has also been shown to be an effective teaching procedure in facilitating the understanding and retention by pupils of new information (Novak, Ring and Tanir, 1971).

A summary is also a useful device for an interviewer to use at the beginninng of subsequent interviews in order to allow the client the chance to clear up any disagreements or points of confusion that might emerge as a result of the interviewer's observations. It is important to establish that both parties are in agreement as to the main points arising from prior interactions, so that the present discussion can proceed unhindered.

Client-initiated Openings

While the four previously described categories are more suitable to use in interviewer-initiated situations, it is more appropriate to use a client-centred opening when the interviewee has requested a meeting. Benjamin (1974) distinguishes between these two types of first interviews and suggests that if a person has requested an interview it is better to let him state in his own words just what prompted him to make this request and what in particular is on his mind. While it is still important for the interviewer to initiate some form of social opening, once the greeting and seating are over, it is advisable to adopt an active listening response. However, Benjamin observes that there are occasions when the interviewer may need to help the interviewee to verbalise his problem. When this does occur, the interviewer ought to be as brief as possible by using phrases such as, 'I understand you wished to speak to me', 'How can I be of help to you?' or 'Would you like to tell me what's on your mind?' To accompany these phrases the interviewer should adopt an active listening pose, such as proximity to client, a forward trunk lean, steady eye gaze and relaxed posture to establish to the client at the outset that he is ready to listen to whatever it is that the client wishes to talk about. Seay and Altekruse (1979) examined the amounts of verbal and nonverbal behaviours used by behavioural therapists and concluded that the therapist conveyed mainly interest and attentiveness when he increased the amount of nonverbal behaviour and was less verbally active. While this approach to client-initiated openings has its roots in client-centred therapy (Rogers, 1957) in which the therapist rarely directs the therapeutic process, preferring instead to respond to clients rather than teaching them, it can be a useful opening technique in other contexts.

Closing

Closing is in many ways complementary to the skill of opening in that while there are social norms for opening an interaction sequence, there are also common interaction rituals for closing an encounter. However, there are some differences between the two social skills. First, at a social level, while a person may contemplate and plan the best way to greet someone, particularly when that person is a stranger or a comparative stranger, he will seldom think about the appropriate way to say goodbye to that person. In general social terms, therefore, closing can be seen more as an impromptu action than a planned one. However, it is argued in this chapter that unplanned closures are the least effective way to achieve formal closure since, as Bakken (1977) observes, goodbyes or parting rituals may serve to regulate and maintain relationships. In other words, how one takes leave of another person will to a great extent determine one's motivation for meeting that person again.

A second major difference, suggested by Goffman (1972), is that 'greetings mark a transition to increased access and farewells to a state of decreased access' (p. 79). Perhaps this anticipation of lack of access is one of the factors that contributes to some of the difficulties that many people have experienced in leave-taking. For instance, many people prolong an interactive sequence simply to avoid being the first to indicate closure markers for fear of seeming to end a relationship. These periods of 'decreased access' signal a change in the amount of access interactants will have with one another. If the probability of future access is very high then phrases such as 'See you soon', 'Bye for now', may well be employed. On the other hand, if the departure is of a more permanent duration, something more dramatic is likely to be used, namely 'Goodbye' or 'Bon voyage'. The parting terms appropriate in the former situation would be totally inappropriate in the latter, and *vice versa*.

Simply to stop talking is not always an effective method of closing an interpersonal encounter and, in fact, any attempt to close in this way could often be interpreted as 'anger', 'brusqueness' or 'pique'. Instead, closure can be defined more appropriately as the ability 'to organize the simultaneous arrival of the conversationalist at a point where one speaker's completion will not occasion another speaker's talk, and that will not be heard as some speaker's silence' (Schegloff and Sacks, 1973, p. 295). In other words, closure can be seen as drawing attention to the satisfactory completion of an interaction sequence.

At a simple, conversational level, short terminal exchanges such as 'Cheerio',

'All the best' or 'So long' will suffice. At a more complex level, where a great deal of information and ideas have been exchanged, it is usually necessary to provide a more structured closure, perhaps in the form of a summary immediately preceding the final social exchange.

Alternatively, leave-taking can have an important supportiveness function, often taking the form of an expressed desire to continue the interaction at a later date. After all, say Knapp *et al.* (1973), 'What could be more supportive than doing it all again?' (p. 185).

Drawing upon these findings, closing, in relation to social interaction, can be defined as directing attention to the termination of social exchange by summarising the main issues which have been discussed, drawing attention to what will happen in the future and, finally, breaking interpersonal contact without making participants feel rejected or shunned.

Although these are the main general functions of the skill of closing, they are not all appropriate on every occasion. Some are more important than others depending upon the social context in which the skill of closing is employed. For instance, those employed in the 'helping' professions (such as nurses, doctors, therapists, counsellors, social workers, probation officers and so on) may lay more stress on establishing a conducive relationship in their closure than in consolidating facts and information, which are sometimes at a minimum in this type of encounter. On the other hand, where the participants are concerned with transmitting or exchanging ideas and information (such as teachers, judges, salesmen, public speakers, interviewers), there may be greater emphasis placed on summarising and consolidating information for the benefit of less well informed clients.

In addition, the skill of closing, as with opening, can manifest itself in a number of ways depending upon the number of participants involved, the purpose of the encounter, location and time of day, as well as the personal characteristics of participants such as personality, intellect, experience and socioeconomic background. Therefore, when assessing the effectiveness of the skill of closing it is crucial to consider these factors which directly influence any evaluation thereof.

The remainder of the chapter focuses upon four main types of closing which can be commonly executed, namely, factual, motivational, social and perceptual. The following section sets out in more detail the different types of closure which can be applied and illustrates how each type may be more appropriate in one social context than another.

Factual Closing

From our knowledge of memory processes, it is apparent that both the passage of time and the learning of new material facilitate forgetting (Hilgard, Atkinson and Atkinson, 1971). In essence, individuals tend to remember best what they hear first and what they hear last, the in-between parts being more easily forgotten. This is one of the reasons why it is important to pay careful attention to both the introduction and conclusion in contexts where information-giving is at a premium. For example, it would be unthinkable for a judge not to 'sum up' the evidence provided by all witnesses towards the end of a trial in order to help the jury arrive at a valid, majority verdict.

Factual closure can be achieved in a variety of ways using three main techniques; summary, initiating or inviting questions and developing future links.

Summary. Writing about some of the main functions of speech conclusions many centuries ago, Aristotle claimed that recapitulation of the main points of an argument or speech helped to dramatise or draw attention to the speaker's case; modern-day thinking does not appear to be radically different.

Reynolds and Glaser (1964), for instance, in research into biology teaching found that regular summaries, or 'spaced reviews' as they called them, increased pupils' knowledge of the subject area. The implication is that regular and progressive summing up at various intervals facilitates the retention of knowledge. Wright and Nuthall (1970) confirmed this finding when they found from their research that concluding remarks by the teachers were positively correlated with pupil achievement.

Although teachers find this a worthwhile skill to achieve in the classroom, other professional interactors should attempt to incorporate it into their repertoire of skills, particularly when a range of ideas and information is being discussed. Testimony to this is the study carried out by Rackham and Morgan (1977) to assess the skills of chairpersons. They noted that group members felt that meetings lacked clarity and structure when the chairperson did not summarise at the end. Also, careers officers, who may be giving pupils information on a range of job opportunities, can usefully employ a summary. Similarly, nurses and health visitors when advising patients about the most suitable way to dress a wound, feed a baby, administer an injection and so on, can quickly and effectively recap the main points of the process to ensure the patient's understanding. However, it must be stressed that brevity is the order of the day. Repeating in a more concise form the elements involved helps to cement them in the listener's memory.

Ivey, Normington, Miller *et al.* (1968) identified the skill of summarisation in a counselling context and found that the skill contained both affective and cognitive dimensions. In other words, it was sometimes helpful for the interviewer to distinguish between summarising feelings which the client had expressed on the one hand and demographic information which he had disclosed on the other, in order to bring a greater understanding to bear on the client's needs or problems. Ten years later, Ivey and Authier (1978) confirm that summarisation in a counselling setting 'involves attending to the client, accurately sensing the feelings and content being expressed, and meaningfully integrating the various responses of the client . . . in such a way that the client may say, "That's right, I never looked at it that way before", and continue on with the discussion of the issue' (p. 87).

An additional function of making an explicit summation either at the end of an interview or at the termination of a particular topic, is put forward by Benjamin

(1974) who feels that it gives both the interviewer and interviewee the chance to check if each has understood the other. Thus, for example, a social worker could end with the words, 'Before you go, I just want to make sure I understand your position . . . Have I left anything out or does that appear to be the right position?' Munro, Manthei and Small (1983) agree that this is useful technique for counsellors to use but, as an alternative, claim that it is also effective to have the client summarise what has taken place or been discussed in order that the counsellor gets a better understanding of the client's view of things as well as helping the client to assess what progress has been made.

In conclusion, it would appear that the summary is a useful technique to employ when achieving closure, although Knapp *et al.* (1973) warn that it can be overlooked in practice. In a study designed to identify functions and elements of leave-taking in an information-seeking interview, they found the act of summarising was not evident. However, they speculate that this could have been the limited time available to the subjects in the experimental interviews. It would appear, therefore, that sufficient time ought to be left available for a concise summary to be made where the interviewer considers it to be an important part of the interview process.

Initiating or Inviting Questions. Drawing again from research into teaching, it has been found that the use of oral feedback questions to assess understanding of material previously presented is positively related to pupil learning (Wright and Nuthall, 1970; Rothkopf, 1972; and McKeown, 1977). This could be termed the evaluating aspect of factual closure. Evaluating is an essential part of closure where the focus is on what has been learned. Specific questions can be asked which are designed to check for accuracy of facts or understanding, to assimilate the logical sequence of ideas or evaluate the comprehensiveness of a range of arguments. The responses can then serve as a basis for future courses of action, such as to supply accurate information, consolidate ideas or provide omissions where they occur.

While initiated questions are useful check-aids for teachers, lecturers, job trainers, coaches and demonstrators, they can be used at various times throughout a dyadic interview-type situation as an alternative to the summary. Nelson-Jones (1983) notes this alternative strategy in a counselling context and feels that this process helps the client to consolidate learning. For instance, when the client says that the sessions with the helper have been invaluable in helping to solve a set of problems, the helper should on occasions respond, 'What exactly have you learned that will help you to sort out your problems?' This conveys to the helper exactly what the client has gained from the interactive sessions.

Future Links. Along with summarising and checking for accuracy of mutual understanding, closure may also draw attention to the work which will continue after the termination of the interview. At a simple level this may include making future organisational arrangements such as where and when to meet. At another level, it may involve mapping out, albeit loosely, the agenda for a future meeting. In other words, the summary states the position arrived at while the future link focuses on prospective tasks or decisions to be made. For instance, the chairperson of a committee meeting will usually recap the main points of the day's discussion but will also finish with a brief statement of what still has to be discussed at a future meeting. This has the express function of bringing together into a meaningful whole what may seem diverse elements simply because they have occurred over a period of time.

Identifying areas of future concern is considered by Schulman (1979) to be an important function of the counsellor's role. He states that the helper's task is 'to create an agenda for future work, and to use their experience together to determine how the client can continue to work on these concerns' (p. 100). Knapp *et al.* (1973) refer to this aspect of leave-taking as a strategy of 'futurism', that is, an expressed desire on the part of the interviewer to continue the interaction at a later date. The authors claim this element has a strong supportive function and as such it is dealt with more fully in the next section of this chapter.

Motivational Closure

Although it is stated in this chapter that one of the main functions of the skill of closure is to focus on both the completion and consolidation of the main facets covered during interaction, there are times when to do so would be inappropriate. Instead, it would be more useful to motivate people to explore and consider further some of the issues which have been revealed as a result of the interactive process. Not all transactions can be accomplished in any one session and, indeed, it may be more expedient to employ a motivational type of closure when a series of sessions is required. By employing this type of closure, individuals can be directed to reflect more carefully, consider in greater depth and relate any new insights gained from the present encounter to more general issues in a wider context. Schulman (1979) notes the need for a motivational closure in some counselling situations when he states, 'The worker's task is to help the client to inventory these (concerns), to create an agenda for future work, and to use their experience together to determine how the client can continue to work on these concerns' (p. 100). In essence, three principal methods can be employed effectively to bring about a motivational closure, the choice of any one being heavily dependent upon the social situation in which it is to be used.

Explicitly Motivating Statements. These are perhaps the most basic and obvious means of encouraging people to relate experiences and insights gained to some future event. For instance, final statements such as, 'Give it everything you've got' 'Let's show them what we can do', 'Go get 'em' . . . are frequently used by sales promotion managers, sports coaches and entertainment promoters, to name but a few, in order to encourage greater effort following the 'pep' talk.

However, this type of statement is not only confined to the business of selling, the sports field or the entertainment business; it can also be used successfully by those in the helping professions, whereby clients can be motivated to put into practice some of the decisions that have been reached during the interview. Concluding statements such as 'You must try these out for yourself . . .', 'It's up to you to come to some agreement . . .' 'Only you can make the final decision . . .' and so on are employed explicitly to facilitate future action.

Use of Thought-provoking Comments. As well as being an effective method of encouraging participation at the start of encounters, these comments can be equally effectively used at the conclusion, with the express function of leaving a person or group of people with more questions than answers. It is a technique used commonly by specific groups such as teachers, lecturers, public speakers and television presenters to encourage their audience to reflect further, in their own time, on complex or controversial matters revealed during the presentation. By providing an audience with a problematic situation to finish, the speaker can encourage further exploration of the topic, thus creating a link between present and future experiences. This is a particularly apt device to use in an episodal type of situation such as the follow-on lesson, or lecture, or a six-part drama series.

Use of Future Orientation Statements. These also allow people to further consider some issues long after the interaction sequence has ended. The main function of these statements is to give individuals the opportunity to relate any new experience they have gained from the immediate encounter to a similar one in a wider environment, or else to relate knowledge gained in one context to another outside the present encounter.

Teachers often use this type of closure by setting the class homework at the end of the lesson, specificially designed to consider an issue more deeply. For example, after a lesson which has concentrated on posing questions designed to illuminate racial prejudice, pupils can be directed to ask the same question of their parents, grandparents, brothers, sisters and friends 'to give them added knowledge on attitude formation and attitudinal change.

These future orientation statements or questions are not the sole prerogative of those involved in the teaching profession. Trower *et al.* (1978) stress the need for patients in a clinical context to be given 'between-session homework assignments' in social situations they have found difficult to master during practical skills training sessions. In addition, Ellis and Whittington (1981) suggest that the trainee, engaged in a variety of social skills training (SST) programmes, should be 'asked to obtain feedback from real-life "others" for discussion when he returns to the (training) unit' (p. 74).

Apart from training situations, other professionals can use future orientation comments or questions. For instance, a nurse can motivate her patient to try new and more up-to-date techniques, even when she is not present, with a concluding statement such as, 'The next time you need to inject you can use the method I've shown you this morning, can't you?' Similarly, counsellors can encourage their clients to examine their problems with new insights gained during the interview session.

In essence, therefore, in a situation where it is neither apt nor fitting to leave a person with a sense of finality or completion, it is more appropriate to use a type of motivational closure; which particular one to employ will depend upon the interactive situation, the nature of the task and the relationship between the interactors.

Social Closing

In order to ensure that not only has an interaction been a fruitful one (in the sense that problems have been partly or wholly resolved or decisions reached in part or in total), but also that it has been a pleasurable experience for all parties, it is appropriate to apply a type of social closure. The main function of this type of closure, therefore, is to establish a conducive relationship so that participants look forward with pleasure and enthusiasm to a future encounter. Goffman (1972) notes this when he states, 'The Goodbye brings the encounter to an unambiguous close, sums up the consequences of the encounter for the relationship, and bolsters the relationship for the anticipated period of no contact' (p. 79). Support for the importance of this final leave-taking stage of the encounter also comes from Benjamin (1974) when he says, 'Closing is especially important because what occurs during this last stage is likely to determine the interviewee's impression of the interview as a whole' (p. 34). There are specific verbal behaviours associated with the termination of communicative exchanges and these are examined in the next section.

Concluding Task-related Statements. When these are supportive in nature and uttered immediately following the cognitive closure, they provide participants with a sense of satisfaction by drawing attention to that which has been achieved as a result of the interaction. Statements such as 'That's good. We're really beginning to get somewhere now' and 'Well Eric, it's been great talking to you', convey to someone that the speaker has appreciated the opportunity to meet with and talk to them in order to bring about a greater understanding of their problems and needs. Bales (1950) in his interesting studies of group behaviour noted that group leaders are more effective if they administer concluding rewarding comments either to particular individuals or to the group as a whole when the meeting has been a particularly fruitful one.

Non-task-related Statements. These are also frequently used when the main business of the interaction has been concluded satisfactorily. Knapp *et al.* (1973) refer to these statements as personal or welfare aspects of leave-taking. In other words, when decisions have been reached, solutions to the probelms found or the general business has been concluded, participants recognise the 'human' aspect of leave-taking and invariably proceed to make statements or ask questions designed to show a warm and friendly disposition. Phrases such as, 'When are you going on holiday?' 'Now take it easy' and 'I hope the weather stays fine until the weekend', can be used by a range of professionals depending upon both the social situation and the relationship between the interactors.

Acknowledgement Statements. These will often follow both task- and non-task-related supportive comments, and are principally employed to indicate appreciation of the opportunity to meet. Irrespective of the context, most professionals have the opportunity in a face-to-face situation to say to their clients, 'It's been nice talking to you. I hope we'll meet again'. Alternatively, at the end of a telephone conversation, it is appropriate to conclude with the words, 'Thank you for talking to me. I look forward to our meeting next Tuesday'. All of these statements help to 'round off' the conversation and signal to the client that his presence has been appreciated.

Perceptual Closure

In order to effectively terminate a discussion, conversation, talk or interview, it is important to use specific closure markers, and so avoid embarrassing people who are not quite sure whether to carry on talking or rise and take leave. Goffman (1961) recognises the significance of 'terminal exchanges' by pinpointing a series of physical manoeuvres and positionings related to leave-taking. Schegloff and Sacks (1973) note that what is perceived as the final closing acts can be achieved by verbal means alone (such as 'Bye', 'See you' and so on) but that they are usually accompanied by specific non-verbal behaviours (such as posture shifts, extended eye-gaze, an increase in interpersonal distance, edging towards an exit). However, whichever strategy is used to terminate interaction, it is important that closure be accomplished between participants as sensitively and effectively as possible. The two main techniques available to achieve perceptual closure are verbal closure markers and non-verbal closure markers, sometimes occurring separately but more often in tandem.

Final Verbal Closure Markers. 'Goodbye', 'So long', 'Cheerio', 'All the best' and 'Bye' are words or phrases commonly used and point to the normative function of leave-taking. Berne (1964) notes this when he says, 'an informal ritual, such as leave-taking, may be subject to considerable local variations in details, but the basic form remains the same' (p. 36). However, the appropriate use of these final closure markers is heavily dependent upon the situation, whether formal, semi-formal or informal, in which the interaction is taking place, the relationship between the interactors, that is, friends of long-standing or recent acquaintances, and whether the actual termination of the interaction is of a long-term or short-term nature. It is important to bear these aspects in mind when selecting the appropriate closure word or phrase, since failure to do so could result in altering, albeit implicitly, the relationship previously set up in the encounter. Knapp *et al.* (1973) neatly encapsulate this when they state, 'Though minute and seemingly irrelevant on the surface, leave-taking behaviors do appear to be powerful interpersonal forces . . . (and) . . . the intitiation and reception of leave-taking cues provides an offhand view of general interpersonal sensitivity' (p. 198).

Non-verbal Closure Markers. Those which can be used to complement the verbal message are of two main types. First, the kinds that have almost universal meaning include a handshake, a wave or a kiss, which signify the departure of one person from another. Second, more subtle cues signify that the interaction is drawing to a close, for example, a major change in body posture, hand leveraging (on the knees, legs or on the chair itself), breaking eye contact, explosive hand contacts (either on a part of the body such as the thighs, or an object such as a desk, files or books), movement towards an exit or looking at a watch or clock. These more subtle nonverbal cues have the distinct advantage of communicating closure to another person, thus avoiding the use of explicit, less sensitive verbal markers such as 'You may go now' or 'I've finished with you now'.

Bearing in mind that people are mostly concerned with terminating interactions on the 'right note', that is, on a note of mutual regard, it is important to combine these nonverbal behaviours with supportive verbal ones. According to Zaidel and Mehrabian (1969), verbal and nonverbal behaviours can be at variance with each other, in which case more credence is apt to be placed on what one sees rather than what one hears, although they point out that this varies with age; children and young adolescents pay more attention to visual components than older adolescents and adults (Bugental, Kaswan, Love, *et al.,* 1970).

Since the support function is such a critical element in leave-taking, it is important to control the use of these nonverbal elements of leave-taking so that misinterpretations do not arise. For example, it is often difficult to break eye contact in situations where one wants to communicate support, but also wants to leave. The use of appropriate supportive verbal statements can help to reduce any potential ambiguity which may arise as to the nature of the relationship. Busy professionals, such as doctors, social workers, college tutors and business executives who all work to a heavily burdened time schedule should be aware of the importance of verbal and nonverbal leave-taking behaviours in bringing social encounters to a congenial and satisfactory conclusion.

Conclusion

At the outset, this chapter attempts to signify the important functions which the skills of opening and closing have in the management of relations between individuals. By reasoning that the concepts of opening and closing are more all-embracing than those of greeting and final leave-taking, it is adduced that these skills are more complex in nature than might initially be thought. In addition, by providing an albeit eclectic collection of both theoretical and empirical research findings, main features of the skills of opening and closing are explored and identified. Finally, these main elements contained in each of the skills are analysed and evaluated using a range of professional and social contexts to exemplify their effective use.

While no claim is made to suggest that this is an exhaustive analysis of the two skills of opening and closing, it is an attempt to add to the range of techniques currently available from which to choose. If knowledge of these skills is to increase at all, more research is needed into the normative and specialised functions and strategies of these communicative acts. To gain insights into those relatively unexplored aspects of opening and closing, those little-noticed, seemingly irrelevant verbal and nonverbal opening and closing behaviours, is to discover crucial information about the nature of social interaction itself.

References

Allen, D.I. (1970) 'Some Effects of Advance Organizers and Level of Questions on the Learning Retention of Written Social Studies Material', *Journal of Educational Psychology, 61*, 533–9

Argyle, M. and Cook, M. (1976) *Gaze and Mutual Gaze*, Cambridge University Press, England

Argyle, M. and McHenry, R. (1971) 'Do Spectacles Really Increase Judgements of Intelligence?' *British Journal of Social and Clinical Psychology, 10*, 27–9

Aubertine, H.E. (1968) 'The Set Induction Process and its Application to Teaching', *Journal of Educational Research, 61*, 363–7

Ausubel, D.P. (1964) 'How Reversible are the Cognitive and Motivational Effects of Cultural Deprivation? Implications for Teaching the Culturally Deprived Child', *Urban Education, 1* (19), 214–9

Bakken, D. (1977) 'Saying Goodbye: An Observational Study of Parting Rituals', *Man-Environment Systems, 7*, 95–100

Bales, R.F. (1950) *Interaction Process Analysis*, Addison-Wesley, Cambridge, Massachussetts

Benjamin, A. (1974) *The Helping Interview*, Houghton Mifflin Co., Boston

Berlyne, D.E. (1960) *Conflict, Arousal and Curiosity*, McGraw-Hill, New York

Berne, E. (1964) *Games People Play*, Grove Press, New York

Bligh, D. (1972) *What's the Use of Lectures?*, Penguin, Harmondsworth

Brown, G.A. (1975) *Microteaching: A Programme of Teaching Skills*, Methuen, London

Bugental, D., Kaswan, J.W., Love, L.R. *et al.* (1970) 'Child versus Adult Perception of Evaluative Messages in Verbal, Vocal and Visual Channels', *Developmental Psychology, 2*, 267–375

Busch, P. and Wilson, D.T. (1976) 'An Experimental Analysis of a Salesman's Expert and Referent Bases of Social Power in the Buyer-seller Dyad', *Journal of Market Research, 13*, 3–11

Canter, D. and Wools, R. (1970) 'A Technique For the Subjective Appraisal of Buildings', *Building Science, 5*, 187–98

Cook, M. (1977) 'The Social Skill Model and Interpersonal Attraction' in S. Duck (ed.), *Theory and Practice in Interpersonal Attraction*, Academic Press, London

Ellis, R. and Whittington, D. (1981) *A Guide to Social Skill Training*, Croom Helm, London

Feather, N.T. (1969) 'Preference for Information in Relation to Consistency, Novelty, Intolerance of Ambiguity and Dogmatism', *Australian Journal of Psychology, 21*, 235–50

French, P. (1983) *Social Skills for Nursing Practice*, Croom Helm, London

Gage, N.L. (1972) 'An Analytical Approach to Research on Instructional Methods' in A. Morrison and D. McIntyre (eds), *The Social Psychology of Teaching*, Penguin, Harmondsworth

Gibbins, K. (1969) 'Communication Aspects of Women's Clothes and Their Relation to Fashionability', *British Journal of Clinical Psychology, 8*, 301–12

Goffman, E. (1961) *Encounters*, Bobbs-Merrill, Indianapolis

——— (1972) *Relations in Public; Micro-studies of the Public Order*, Penguin, Harmondsworth

Goldfried, M.R. and Davison, G.C. (1976) *Clinical Behaviour Therapy*, Holt, Rinehart and Winston, New York

Haines, J. (1975) *Skills and Methods in Social Work*, Constable, London

Hall, E.T. (1966) *The Hidden Dimension*, Doubleday, New York

Hargie, O.D.W. (1980) 'An Evaluation of a Microteaching Programme', PhD thesis, University of Ulster, Jordanstown, Northern Ireland

Hargie, O., Saunders, C. and Dickson, D. (1981) *Social Skills in Interpersonal Communication*, Croom Helm, London

Hilgard, E., Atkinson, R.C. and Atkinson, R.L. (1971) *Introduction to Psychology*, 5th edn, Harcourt Brace Jovanovich, New York

Ivey, A.E. Normington, C.J., Miller, C.D., *et al.* (1968) 'Microcounselling and Attending Behavior: An Approach to Prepracticum Counselor Training', *Journal of Counseling Psychology, 15*, 1–12

—— and Authier, J. (1978) *Microcounseling: Innovations in Interviewing, Counseling, Psychotherapy, and Psychoeducation*, Charles C. Thomas, Illinois

Kendon, A. and Ferber, A. (1973) 'A Description of Some Human Greetings' in R. Michael and J. Crook (eds), *Comparative Ecology and Behaviour of Primates*, Academic Press, London

Knapp, M. (1972) *Nonverbal Communication in Human Interaction*, Holt, Rinehart and Winston, New York

—— Hart, R., Friedrich, G. *et al.* (1973) 'The Rhetoric of Goodbye: Verbal and Nonverbal Correlates of Human Leave-Taking', *Speech Monographs, 40*, 182–98

Knapper, C.K. (1970) 'The Relationship Between Personality and Style of Dress', *Bulletin of British Psychological Society, 23*, 155–6

Korda, M. (1976) *Power in the Office*, Weidenfeld and Nicolson, London

Lewis, N.D.C. (1934) *Outlines for Psychiatric Examinations*, The New York State Department of Mental Hygiene, Albany

McHenry, R. (1981) 'The Selection Interview' in M. Argyle (ed.), *Social Skills and Work*, Methuen, London

McKeachie, W.J. (1952) 'Lipstick as a Determiner of First Impressions', *Journal of Social Psychology, 36*, 241–4

McKeown, R. (1977) 'Accountability in Responding to Classroom Questions: Impact on Student Achievement', *Journal of Experimental Education, 45*, 24–30

MacKinnon, R.A. and Michels, R. (1971) *The Psychiatric Interview in Clinical Practice*, Saunders, Philadelphia

Munro, E.A., Manthei, R.J. and Small, J.J. (1983) *Counselling: A Skills Approach*, Methuen, New Zealand

Murstein, B.I. (1972) *Love, Sex and Marriage Through the Ages*, Springer, New York

Nelson-Jones, R. (1983) *Practical Counselling Skills*, Holt, Rinehart and Winston, New York

Novak, J.D., Ring, D.G. and Tanir, P. (1971) 'Interpretation of Research Findings in Terms of Ausubel's Theory, and Implications for Science Education', *Science Education, 55*, 483–526

Peeck, J. (1970) 'Effects of Prequestions on Delayed Retention of Prose Material', *Journal of Educational Psychology, 61*, 241–6

Pope, B. (1979) *The Mental Health Interview: Research and Application*, Pergamon Press, Oxford

Poppleton, S.E. (1981) 'The Social Skills of Selling' in M. Argyle (ed.), *Social Skills and Work*, Methuen, London

Rackham, N. and Morgan, T. (1977) *Behaviour Analysis in Training*, McGraw-Hill, Maidenhead

Reynolds, J.H. and Glaser, R. (1964) 'Effects of Repetition and Spaced Review upon Retention of a Complex Learning Task', *Journal of Educational Psychology, 5*, 297–308

Rogers, C. (1957) 'The Necessary and Sufficient Conditions of Therapeutic Personality Change', *Journal of Consulting and Clinical Psychology, 21*, 95–103

—— (1977) *On Personal Power: Inner Strength and its Revolutionary Impact*, Delacarte Press, New York

Romiszowski, A.J. (1974) *The Selection and Use of Instructional Media*, Kogan Page, London

Rosenblatt, P.C. (1977) 'Cross-cultural Perspective on Attraction' in T.L. Huston (ed.), *Foundations of Interpersonal Attraction*, Academic Press, London

Rothkopf, E.Z. (1972) 'Variable Adjunct Question Schedules, Interpersonal Interaction and Incidental Learning from Written Material', *Journal of Educational Psychology, 63*, 87–92

Ryan, V.L. and Gizynski M.N. (1971) 'Behavior Therapy in Retrospect: Patients' Feelings About their Behavior Therapists', *Journal of Consulting and Clinical Psychology, 37*, 1–9

Sargant, W. (1957) *Battle for the Mind*, Heinemann, London

Schegloff, E.A. and Sacks, H. (1973) 'Opening-up Closings', *Semiotica, 8*, 289–327

Schulman, L. (1979) *The Skills of Helping*, Peacock Publishers, Illinois

Scott, W.P. (1981) *The Skills of Negotiating*, General Publishing Co., Hampshire

Seay, T.A. and Altekruse, M.K. (1979) 'Verbal and Non-verbal Behavior in Judgements of Facilitative Conditions', *Journal of Counseling Psychology, 26,* 108–19

Smith, P. (1974) 'Aspects of the Playgroup Environment' in D. Canter and T. Lee (eds), *Psychology and the Built Environment,* Architectural Press, London

Stone, D.R. and Nielson, E.C. (1982) *The Development of Teaching Skills,* Harper and Row, New York

Sullivan, H.S. (1954) *The Psychiatric Interview,* Norton, New York

Trower, P., Bryant, B. and Argyle, M. (1978) *Social Skills and Mental Health,* Methuen, London

Turney, C., Owens, L.C., Hatton, N., *et al.* (1976) *Sydney Micro Skills: Series 2 Handbook,* Sydney University Press, Sydney, Australia

Woodworth, R.S. and Marquis, D.G. (1949) *Psychology: A Study of Mental Life,* Methuen, London

Wragg, E.C. (ed.) (1984) *Classroom Teaching Skills,* Croom Helm, London/Nichols, New York

Wright, C. and Nuthall, G. (1970) 'Relationships between Teacher Behaviours and Pupil Achievement in Three Experimental Elementary Science Lessons', *American Educational Research Journal, 7,* 477–93

Zaidel, S.F. and Mehrabian, A. (1969) 'The Ability to Communicate and Infer Positive and Negative Attitudes Facially and Vocally', *Journal of Experimental Research in Personality, 3,* 233–41

8 EXPLAINING

George Brown

Explaining is a core skill in communicating. Yet, paradoxically, it is probably the most neglected area of research in communication studies. There are perhaps two reasons for this neglect. First, explaining is a taken-for-granted activity; a great deal of time is spent explaining in everyday life and in various professional contexts, so it is assumed that everyone knows how to explain. Second, for some professional groups such as counsellors, therapists and social workers, explaining has associations with authority-centred approaches, with telling, instructing and didactics; hence the study of explaining is shunned. Yet in reality the skills of explaining are necessarily and frequently used by all health professionals, as well as by managers, teachers and lecturers. Indeed, it could be argued that all professional groups who work with people should know *how* to explain effectively and *when* to explain.

In this chapter a framework is provided for understanding the processes of explaining and the nature of explanations. The chapter provides an outline of the nature of explaining and then reviews research on explaining in classrooms, in higher education, in the doctor–patient consultation and explaining in other contexts. However, it is not a litany of research findings on explaining, but rather a guide to the essential features of explaining and to the problems and issues to be resolved in the study of explaining.

The Nature of Explaining

The term explaining is derived from *explanare*, to make plain. At its lowest level, explaining involves presenting sets of facts or simple instructions. Higher levels of explaining go beyond facts to consider relationships between facts and to consider reasons, motives and causes. Smith and Meux (1970), in their perceptive study of transcripts of explanatory lessons, state that 'to explain is to set forth an antecedent condition of which the particular event or process to be explained is taken as the process'. This definition of explaining is rather narrow. It is certainly not a helpful description of the process of explaining. As Martin (1970) points out, the process of explaining involves an explainer, a problem to be explained and a set of explainees. The explainer has to take account of the problem and of the existing knowledge, attitudes and skills of the explainees. The goal of explaining is to provide understanding to others.

Martin's view stresses the importance of intentions. For her, explaining is essentially a *task* verb, like shooting or fishing (see Ryle, 1963). For Thyne (1966), one of the few British authors to discuss explanatory teaching, explaining is an achievement verb:

'If the teacher really has explained something to his class, they will understand it, and if they do not understand it, despite his efforts, what purported to be an explanation was not an explanation after all.'

Martin's work is part of a tradition concerned primarily with analysing intentions and processes of explaining (Bellack, Hyman, Smith *et al.*, 1966; Ennis, 1969; Smith and Meux, 1970; Hyman, 1974), whereas Thyne (1966) is almost a forerunner of the process-product researchers who explore relationships between the processes of teaching or communication and some external outcome such as student learning (Dunkin and Biddle, 1974) or patient compliance (Pendleton, *et al.*, 1984).

A full account of explaining as a process of communicating has to take account of the intentions of the explainer, the actual processes of explaining adopted and the subsequent changes in understanding of the explainee. Hence a useful working definition of explaining is: 'Explaining is an attempt to provide understanding of a problem to others.'

It follows from this definition that explaining involves taking account of a problem in relation to a set of explainees. In other words, the explainer has to attempt to see the problem through the eyes of the explainees. Indeed, it could be argued that explaining is a supreme example of hermeneutics in action (Ricoeur, 1981). A identifies certain ideas which he/she thinks will assist B. A articulates the ideas; B receives the articulations and constructs meanings from them which either fit B's existing framework of understanding, change that framework or are rejected.

The task of the explainer is threefold: the problem, the process, the outcome. First, he or she has to identify the problem that requires explanation. The problem may be posed initially by the explainer or by the explainee. It may require clarification and refinement. The problem might be expressed in the form of a central question and that question may be subdivided into a series of implicit questions or hidden variables. Thus the question 'How do local anaesthetics work?' contains the implicit questions 'What is a local anaesthetic?' and 'How are nerve impulses transmitted?'

Second, the explainer has to present or elicit a series of linked statements, each of which is understood by the explainees and which together lead to a solution of the problem for that particular set of explainees. These linked statements may be labelled 'keys' since they unlock understanding. Each of these keys will contain a key statement. This may be a generalisation, principle or even an appeal to an ideology or a set of personal values (Nettler, 1970). The key may also contain examples, illustrations and perhaps qualifications to the main principle. When the problem to be explained is complex there might also be a summary of key statements during the explanation as well as a final summary.

The keys are the nub of explaining. But, as emphasised earlier, for an explanation to be understood, it follows that the explainer has not only to consider the problem to be explained but also the knowledge and characteristics of the explainees. What is appropriate as an explanation of the structure of DNA to postgraduate biochemists is unlikely to be appropriate as an explanation to first-year English literature students! There is no such thing as the good explanation. What is 'good' for one group may not be good for another. Its quality is contingent upon the degree of understanding it generates in the explainees. For different groups of explainees, the keys of the explanation and the explanation itself will be different — although the *use* of keys and other strategies may not be.

Similarly, one uses keys when trying to explain a problem, such as the disjunctive relationship between truth and meaning. The problem for the explainer is *explaining the problem*. The problem itself may not have any solutions or perhaps several unsatisfactory solutions, but at least the problem may be understood. (To say that the problem cannot be understood unless it has been solved implies a very narrow definition of understanding.) This point is emphasised since much of high level teaching and much of counselling is concerned not with explaining the solutions of problems but with explaining the nature of problems.

Third, the explainer has to check that the explanation is understood. This task is akin to feedback (see Chapter 2) and it is sometimes neglected by teachers, counsellors and others.

Understanding may be checked on by a variety of methods. The most primitive method is to ask 'Do you understand?'. The answer one usually gets is 'Yes'. The response is more a measure of superficial compliance than of understanding. Other methods are to invite the explainee to recall or recite the explanation, to apply the explanation to another situation or related problem, to provide other examples of where the explanation might hold or to identify similar sorts of explanations.

To sum up, explaining is an attempt to give understanding to another. It involves identifying the problem to be explained, a process of explaining which uses key statements and a check on understanding.

However, it would be wrong to leave the nature of explaining without pointing out that explaining is only *usually* an intentional activity. One may intend to explain a particular problem but one may explain points that one did not intend to explain and alas, may sometimes not explain what one intended to explain.

Types of Explanation

The literature on explaining abounds with typologies of explanations (Swift, 1961; Bellack *et al.*, 1966; Ennis, 1969; Smith and Meux, 1970; Hyman, 1974). For the author's studies of explaining at the University of Nottingham (Brown, 1978; Brown and Hatton, 1982; Brown, 1982; Brown and Armstrong, 1984), it was decided to design a simple, robust typology which would be relatively easy to use but which was related to the work of earlier researchers (Table 8.1).

The typology consists of three main types of explanation: the interpretive, the descriptive and the reason-giving. They approximate to the questions, What? How?

Table 8.1: A Typology of Explanations

After Hyman, 1974	After Smith and Meux, 1970	After Brown, 1978
Type I: Generalisation –specific instance		*Reason-giving,* answering the question 'Why?' Why does the volume of a gas decrease as
Empirical The effects of pressure on the volume of gas	*Empirical-substantive* Seasonal changes on mammals	pressure increases? Why do certain mammals hibernate in winter?
Probabilistic Relation between lung cancer and smoking	*Judgemental* Causes of higher crime rate in urban areas	Why do heavy smokers have a greater risk of contracting cancer? Why is there more crime in inner city areas?
Non-empirical A verb agrees with its subject	*Normative* The proper use of knives and forks	Why do we say, 'he runs', but 'they run'? Why do we put a fork in the left hand?
Type II: Functional *Purpose* The motives behind Lord Jim's actions	*Teleological* Birds of prey as efficient hunters	*Interpretive,* answering the question, 'What?' What led Lord Jim to become the strange character he was? What uses do talons and curved beaks serve in birds of prey?
Function Unions and their members	*Consequence* Inflation and our money	What can unions do in an industrial dispute? What are the effects of a high inflation rate on currency?
Type III: Serial *Sequential* Making a sponge cake	*Sequential* Constructing a perpendicular to a given line	*Descriptive,* answering the question, 'How?' How do you make a light sponge cake? How can a perpendicular be constructed using compass and ruler?
Genetic Differences between cats and dogs	*Mechanical* The operation of a car engine	As animals, how do cats differ from dogs? How does the internal-combustion engine work?
Chronological Events leading to the war in Vietnam	*Procedural* Conducting a formal meeting	How did colonial history lead to the Vietnamese war? How does the chairman lead a meeting?

and Why? Intepretive explanations interpret or clarify an issue or specify the central meaning of a term or statement. Examples are answers to the questions: What is a biome?; What is enantriopy?; What is a novel? Descriptive explanations describe processes, structure and procedures such as: How does a bicycle pump work?; How is a sentence used in logic?; How is sulphuric acid made? Reason-giving explanations involve giving reasons based on principles or generalisations, motives, obligations or values. Included in reason-giving explanations are those based on causes, although some philosophers prefer to distinguish causes and reasons. Examples of reason-giving explanations are answers to the questions:

Why are some people cleverer than others?; Why am I reading this book?; Why do people pay income tax?; Why is Shakespeare a greater writer than Harold Robbins?; Why did this fuse blow?

Of course, a particular explanation may involve all three types of explanation. Thus, in explaining how a bill becomes a law one may want to describe the process, give reasons for it and perhaps define certain key terms.

Research on Explaining

Most research on explaining has been conducted in classrooms or lecture rooms. It is only recently that studies of explaining in other professional contexts are beginning to emerge. Hence this section is concerned primarily with explaining in formal learning settings, although a review of findings and issues in other settings is provided.

Explaining in the Classroom

Given that most teachers talk for two-thirds of the time in classrooms (Flanders, 1970) and two-thirds of their talk is lecturing, then explaining is clearly a common activity in the classroom. Estimates of the proportion of time spent on explaining by teachers vary from 10 to 30 per cent, according to the definition of explaining adopted (Dunkin and Biddle, 1974).

Time spent on a task is but a crude measure of its importance. More important is the quality: the way the time is spent. As Gage, Belgard, Dell, *et al.* (1968) wryly observe: 'Some people explain aptly, getting to the heart of the matter with just the right terminology, examples, and organisation of ideas. Other explainers, on the contrary, get us and themselves all mixed up, use terms beyond our level of comprehension, draw inept analogies, and even employ concepts and principles that cannot be understood without an understanding of the very thing being explained.'

Reviews of the literature (Gage and Berliner, 1979; Turney, Ellis, Hatton, *et al.* (1983) reveal that good explanations are not only clearly structured, they are also interesting. However, clarity and interest are complex notions which involve, amongst other things, the use of structuring moves such as framing statements which delineate sections of the explanation, focal statements which highlight its essential features and the use of carefully chosen examples. While it is easy to offer the advice 'Be clear and interesting', it is less easy to provide detailed hints and guidelines which will help someone to provide clear, interesting explanations when teaching.

The main characteristics of explaining, which are summarised in Table 8.2, were identified in the literature, in discussions with teachers and from the studies of explaining which the author and colleagues undertook at Nottingham (for instance, Brown and Hatton, 1982; Brown and Armstrong, 1984).

Table 8.2: Planning Strategies and Performance Skills in Explaining

Planning strategies
Analyse topics into main parts, or 'keys'
Establish links between parts
Determine rules (if any) involved
Specify kind(s) of explanation required
Adapt plan according to learner characteristics

Basic skills

Clarity and fluency:	through defining new terms through use of explicit language through avoiding vagueness
Emphasis and interest:	by variations in gestures by use of media and materials by use of voice and pauses by repetition, paraphrasing or verbal cueing
Using examples:	clear, appropriate and concrete in sufficient quantity positive and negative where applicable
Organisation:	logical and clear sequence pattern appropriate to task use of link words and phrases
Feedback:	opportunities for questions provided understanding of main ideas assessed expressions of attitudes and values sought

Views on Explaining. Pupils' views on explaining appear to have been consistent over a period of at least 50 years. Hart (1934) and Hollis (1935) found that the foremost reason for liking a teacher were helpfulness with school work and clear explanations of lessons, assignments and difficulties. Kennedy, Cruickshank, Bush, *et al.* (1978) and Bush, Kennedy and Cruickshank (1977) also show that pupils favour teachers who are clear explainers and who provide help when necessary.

Planning and Preparation. The maxim, 'Know your subject, know your students', appear to be borne out by the evidence on planning and preparation. Hiller (1971) showed that a teacher's prior level of knowledge is linked to clarity of explaining. In general, the teachers who were more knowledgeable made fewer vague statements and provided clearer explanations. However, knowledge of subject is a necessary but not sufficient condition of effective explaining. Some people are knowledgeable but remain poor explainers. What also may be required is training in preparation and planning.

Miltz (1972), in an intensive training course based on analysing the concepts to be explained, demonstrated that the trained group provided clearer explanations which had a logical structure and contained apt, interesting examples. In a study of explaining in biology, Brown and Armstrong (1984) showed that student teachers trained in methods of preparing, analysing and presenting explanations were significantly better than a comparable untrained group. The criteria were independent observers' ratings of the videotaped lessons and measures of pupil achievement and interest in the lesson.

The Features of Explaining. Structure and presentation are the essential features of explaining. Of these, presentation techniques have been the subject of most studies and these have focused upon clarity, fluency, emphasis, interest, the use of examples and of summaries.

Rosenshine and Furst (1973) point to the consistent findings that clarity yields greater pupil or student achievement. This finding holds at primary level (Good and Grouws, 1977), secondary level (Gage *et al.*, 1968) and tertiary level (Land, 1985). Explicit definitions are a component of clarity and these are correlated with pupil achievement (Borg, 1975; Armento, 1977). Fluency, including the notions of emphasis, clear transitions, absence of vagueness, assurance, absence of false starts and of verbal tangles, have all been shown to be associated with effective presentation (Land, 1979).

Studies of expressiveness (Rosenshine, 1972) show that purposeful variations in voice, gesture, manner and use of teaching aids all contribute to the interest of an explanation. So, too, does the use of examples. Indeed, examples may promote both clarity and interest (Armento, 1977). However, examples *per se* are not sufficient. The number of examples provided is not a discrimination between effective and ineffective explanatory lessons (Gage, 1972). What may be more important is the pattern of examples and principles enunciated and elicited. Rosenshine (1972) claimed that the pattern of 'rule-example-rule' was more effective than rule-example or example-rule. This finding has not been borne out by other research (Shutes, 1969; Brown and Armstrong, 1984). The Brown and Armstrong study suggests that the pattern of examples should be associated with both the type of explanation and the pupils' prior knowledge of the topic. Thus, in providing an interpretive explanation on an unfamiliar topic, examples should take primacy. In restructuring pupils' ideas, then principles and generalisations should take primacy.

The use of summaries appears to be related to both ratings of clarity (Bush *et al.*, 1977) and to achievement (Wright and Nuthall, 1970; Armento, 1977). As Turney *et al.* (1983) note: 'There is no doubt that teachers who pause to review prior material, who repeat main points in summary form and who repeat instructions slowly so that all can comprehend are favoured as clear teachers, and therefore competent explainers, by secondary pupils' (p. 3).

In the recent study of explaining (Brown and Armstrong, 1984), both presentational variables and structural features were explored. Quantitative and qualitative methods were used in this task. Pupil achievement scores, pupil ratings of interest and independent observer ratings were obtained for 120 lessons collected in two experiments. The lessons were videorecorded and transcribed. Analyses of the lesson based on the system known as SAID (system for analysing instructional discourse), were used to obtain the number of types and keys, framing moves, focusing statements and other structural features (Brown and Armstrong, 1978). The transcript lessons were also analysed quantitatively to search for patterns, sequences and critical incidents.

The study revealed that better explanatory lessons had more keys and more types of keys. In other words, they varied the cognitive demands on the pupils and they used higher levels of cognitive demands. Better lessons also contained more framing statements, which delineate the beginning and ending of sub-topics, more focusing statements, which emphasise the key points, more relevant examples and better use of audiovisual aids and fewer unfinished summaries. However, the better lessons did contain more rhetorical questions. These were usually used as attention-gaining devices in the early stages of a new key.

The qualitative analysis of the lessons showed that better lessons had a more meaningful structure to the pupils. For example, ten short lessons were taught by ten teachers on the topic: What is an ecological succession? This required an interpretive explanation of a topic which was completely new to the pupils. Thus, the teachers were faced with the problem of deciding how much it was necessary for the children to know in order to understand the process of ecological succession. The teachers of the low-scoring lessons assumed they had to explain differences between taxonomies and ecology, or between consumers and producers. The high-scoring lessons were the simple ones which described the process in words with which the children were familiar and to which they could relate. The low-scoring lessons introduced so many new ideas that the children became confused. This is illustrated in the examples given in the comparison of high- and low-scoring lessons.

Orientations.
1. High-scoring:

Teacher —	'Well, first of all I wonder if you could tell me what this is.'
Pupil —	'A piece of concrete.'
Teacher —	'Yes, it's a piece of concrete, a slab of concrete, out of my garden. Now, if I wanted to plant a tree or a shrub on here what would you say was missing?'
Pupil —	'Soil'
Teacher —	'Yes, the soil. And today I want to start by talking about some plants that can grow straight on to a rock.'

2. Low-scoring

Teacher —	'I'm going to talk to you about ecological succession. It's not as difficult as it sounds.'

Keys.
High-scoring:
1. Which plants can grow straight on to rock?
2. How do mosses replace lichens?
3. Which plants replace mosses?
4. What is this process called?
5. What other examples of ecological succession are there?

Low scoring:
1. In what two ways can we group organisms?
2. Which organisms are consumers?
3. Which organisms are producers?
4. What is it called when we group organisms that depend on each other together?
5. What do we call it when one community takes over from another?
6. How does ecological succession take place on bare rock?

Feedback and Checking Understanding. The studies cited above of explaining in the classroom have all been based upon measures of pupil achievement or reaction. They contained built-in checks on understanding and thereby provided measures of effective explaining.

In the hurly burly of normal classroom life it is not always possible to conduct detailed evalutions of one's teaching or explanatory skills. Nonetheless, it is worth noting that feedback and checks on understanding are important features of explaining. Without feedback, one is left only with one's intentions and hunches and these may not always be correct. For example, in a recent study of pupil learning in the primary school (Bennett, Desforge and Wilkinson, 1984), it was shown that a group of infant teachers was not able to readily identify pupils' learning difficulties. Bright pupils' abilities were frequently underestimated whereas those of less able pupils were frequently overestimated. Most of the teachers focused upon assessing the final product of the children's work rather than checking the processes which the children used to arrive at their answer. Other studies showed that inviting questions and the use of recall questions at the close of a lesson leads to high achievement (Shutes, 1969; Tisher, 1970). Tisher also showed that teachers tend not to correct wrong responses or explore reasons underlying answers. This evidence suggests that feedback and checks on understanding are necessary and that further studies of ways that teachers analyse and use responses from children to develop understanding are required.

Summary. Studies of explaining in the classroom indicate that clarity and interest are crucial but complex variables. These variables are valued by pupils and lead to better achievement. Preparation and planning are important aspects of training and using feedback to check understanding is an important, but relatively neglected, feature of explaining in the classroom.

Explaining in Higher Education

In higher education explaining occurs in lectures, small group teaching and laboratory work. There appears to be no direct studies of explaining in seminars or tutorials and virtually none in laboratories. Luker (1985) is currently analysing transcripts of explaining and questioning in seminars. Davies (1978) has developed a training programme for assisting postgraduate demonstrators, and Ogborn and Bliss (1977) discuss students' views of laboratory demonstrations as well as of lectures in physics. Daines and Brown (1985) report that 'explaining clearly' is a much valued characteristic of demonstrators.

Most studies of explaining in higher education have been concerned with explaining in lectures or with brief, uninterrupted explanations. Indeed, lectures may be conceived as a set of linked explanations (Brown, 1978) and brief uninterrupted explanations as microlectures which contain opening moves, a structure based on key points and a summary. A microlecture also provides a sample of verbal, extra-verbal and nonverbal behaviour of the presenter.

The studies of explaining in higher education parallel those in classrooms. The same sets of variables are manifested and similar results obtained.

Views on Explaining. Clarity of presentation and logical presentation are the most important features for students and the most frequently mentioned (Flood-Page, 1974; French-Lazovik, 1974). Students' main dissatisfaction with lecturers appear to be inaudibility, incoherence, failure to pitch at an appropriate level, failure to emphasise main points, difficult to take notes from, poor blackboard work and reading aloud from notes (Schonell, Rae and Middleton, 1962; Brown, 1979, 1980).

Lecturers' views on explaining are not dissimilar. In one study (Brown and Daines, 1981), lecturers were invited to rate a set of 40 items for their value in explaining and their 'learnability' (whether lecturers could learn them). The most valued characteristics were clarity, interest, logical organisation and selection of appropriate content. The most learnable were use of diagrams, use of variety of materials, examples and selection of appropriate content. There were significant differences between the arts and science lecturers' on 17 of the items. Science lecturers valued logical and structural characteristics more highly than arts lecturers; science lecturers also considered more features of explaining were learnable than the arts lecturers did.

In a study of styles of lecturing (Brown and Bakhtar, 1983), the five most common weaknesses reported by lecturers were 'saying too much too quickly; assuming too much knowledge; forgetting to provide summaries; not indicating when making an aside (rather than a major point); difficulty in timing length of lectures'. Similar views to those described in this section are reported in earlier studies (Hildebrand, 1973; Kozma, Belle and Williams, 1978).

Planning and Preparation. The planning and preparation of explanations and lectures are neglected research topics in higher education. While Beard and Hartley (1984), Brown (1978) and Bligh (1972) all suggest guidelines for preparing lectures, there are no studies extant of how lecturers actually prepare their lectures. However, in the following section an experiment is described in which lecturers were trained in preparing, planning and presenting brief lectures.

Processes of Explaining. The process of explaining, as indicated earlier, has structural and presentational features. These types of feature fuse into one another; thus logical organisation — a structural feature — may also be considered as part of clarity. Enthusiasm, which is clearly a presentational variable, may be considered as a structural variable, if it includes the use of examples.

The sequence and organisation of explanations in lectures have not been studied in detail. Lecturers report that their most common method of organising lectures is the classical approach of subdividing topics and then subdividing subtopics (Brown and Bakhtar, 1983). There are no studies of the transcripts of lectures to identify pattern and sequence, although two unpublished studies describe attempts to apply linguistic analyses to transcripts of lectures (Montgomery, 1976; Pirianen-Marsh, 1985). Brown (1980) analysed the structural moves in a series of transcripts of explanations and related these to ratings of clarity and interest.

Expressiveness, which includes enthusiasm, friendliness, humour, dynamism and even charisma, have long been regarded as essential ingredients of lecturing and explaining. The meta analysis of twelve experimental studies of expressiveness conducted by Abrami, Leventhal and Perry (1982) suggest that expressiveness is more likely to influence students' response to the lecturer and their attitude towards the subject than to produce marked changes in achievement. However, the studies reviewed were rather extreme in their use of expressiveness and variation in content. Furthermore, favourable changes in attitude to the subject may be important, long-term motivating characteristics.

Land (1985) has summarised the main studies of clarity of explanations which have been conducted in the United States during the past decade. Essentially, the results spanning a decade show that higher student achievement scores were obtained when explanations had fewer verbal mazes (false starts, redundant phrases, tangles of words) and greater use of specific emphasis and clear transitions from one subtopic to another.

The combination of the results described so far suggest that the ideal strategy for improving learning and generating interest is a blend of clarity and expressiveness.

This conclusion led to the development of a training programme for lecturers (Brown, 1982) which contained a series of activities concerned with preparation, planning and presentation. The training programme was evaluated using independent observers' ratings and analyses of transcripts of the pre-test and post-test microlectures.

Four structuring moves identified in the transcript analysis were closely associated with ratings of clarity. These were:

1. *Signposts.*   These are statements which indicate the structure and direction of an explanation:
(a) 'I want to deal briefly with lactation. First, I want to outline the composition of milk; second, its synthesis; third, to examine normal lactation curves.
(b) 'Most of you have heard the old wive's tale that eating carrots helps you to see in the dark. Is it true? Let's have a look at the basic biochemical

	processes involved.'
2. *Frames.*	These are statements which indicate the beginning and end of the subtopic: (a) 'So that ends my discussion of adrenalin. Let's look now at the role of glycogen.' Framing statements are particularly important in complex explanations which may involve topics, subtopics and even subtopics of subtopics.
3. *Foci.*	These are statements and emphases which highlight the key points of an explanation: (a) 'So the main point is . . .' (b) 'Now this is very important . . .' (c) 'But be careful. This interaction with penicillin occurs only while the cell walls are growing.'
4. *Links.*	These are words, phrases or statements which link one part of an explanation to another part: (a) 'So you can see that reduction in blood sugar levels is detected indirectly in the adrenalin gland and directly in the pancreas. This leads to the release of two different hormones . . .'

The independent observer ratings revealed that the openings of the explanations, and the structure, interest and use of audiovisual aids were significantly better at the end of the course. The transcript analyses revealed significant increases in the use of signposts, frames and links and fewer hesitations, stumbles and incomplete statements. The ratings and comments of the lecturers at the end of the course and six months later indicated it was highly valued, in particular the activities on preparing, presenting and analysing explanations.

Feedback and Checks on Understanding. Studies of explaining in higher education have been largely concerned with explaining as a lecture method. This mode of teaching has the disadvantage of not usually providing any checks on understanding during or soon after the lecture. Hence, some writers advocate the use of activities during lectures which require students to demonstrate their understanding (Brown, 1985).

However, feedback signals may be used by lecturers to appraise the attending behaviour of students (Brown, 1978), and feedback signals from students may influence a lecturer's behaviour even though he or she is unaware of it. In one set of studies (Klein, 1971), the behaviour of the lecturer was manipulated by the simultaneous use of smiling, head nods, frowning and other signals by groups of students.

Summary. Studies of explaining in higher education have been confined largely to the lecture method. Students value clear, well structured explanations and, to a lesser extent, interesting explanations. Training in explaining can improve the clarity, structure and interest of explanations. Explanations with these characteristics also yield higher measures of recall and understanding.

Explaining in the Consultation

Most studies of the doctor–patient consultation do not isolate the skill of explaining from the other skills involved in the consultation. However, it is possible to identify features of the research on doctor–patient interactions which are relevant, if not crucial, to the processes of explaining to patients.

Patients' Views and Beliefs. Patients value in medical practitioners the characteristics of warmth, interest, concern and the ability to explain things in terms that they understand (Pendleton, 1983). For the doctor to explain things clearly it may be necessary for him or her to understand the patient's perspective — their anxieties, knowledge and beliefs about health. This suggestion is of particular importance when a doctor is working with patients from relatively unfamiliar cultures and subcultures. Bain (1976, 1977) has shown that some doctors explain less to patients from lower social classes. Cooper and Metcalfe (1974) show that knowledge about health co-varies with social class, yet Pendleton and Bochner (1980) state that doctors offer fewer explanations to patients of social classes IV and V.

Tuckett, Boulton, Olson, *et al.* (1985) showed that this sample of general practitioners rarely discovered patients' beliefs about their problems and even more rarely presented explanations which took account of patients' beliefs.

In the light of these findings it is not surprising to discover that patients express more dissatisfaction with the information that they receive from doctors than with any other aspect of medical care (Cartwright and Anderson, 1981).

There does not appear to be, as yet, any British studies of the beliefs and views of patients from different cultures, although this is clearly an important area for research and practice. Rodin's (1978) review of the evidence on patients' explanations points out the implications for management and compliance.

Preparation and Planning. Wakeford's survey of communication skills training in undergraduate medical schools in the United Kingdom (Wakeford, 1983) showed that one-third of them did not offer any training in communication skills. Of those that did offer training, most only provided a few hours' videotaped or role-play work in psychiatry or general practice.

In contrast, about 95 per cent of medical schools in the United States provide courses on communication and interpersonal skills. Kahn, Cohen and Jason (1979) and Carroll and Munroe (1979), in their review of American programmes, show that instruction in clinical interviewing has produced significant gains as measured by various cognitive tests, effective instruments and direct observations. In Britain, Maguire (1981) has reviewed various studies of consultations and shown how training can be used to improve doctors' communciation skills. Ley (1983), in his studies and reviews of patient compliance, has offered suggestions on how doctors might improve the quality of their explanations to patients. These include taking account of the patients' existing knowledge, using simple direct speech, categorising clearly the different parts of the explanations and repeating the important points. No training programme based on this advice has been devised but Skinner, Wilkinson and Brown (in press) have devised a simple game-simulation which is designed to improve the quality of doctors' explanations and which achieves its objectives within the game setting.

Processes and Outcomes. Explanations by doctors occur, typically, towards the end of a consultation, whereas patients' explanations occur towards the beginning of a consultation (Byrne and Long, 1976). The quality of the doctor's explanation is therefore, in part, dependent upon the quality of the patient's explanation as well as the doctor's diagnostic skills. Despite this well known finding and those of Rodin (1978), there are few reported successful attempts, known to this author, which train patients to provide better explanations (Roter, 1977).

Studies of processes have been tackled from the perspective of sociolinguistics (Skopek, 1979; Cassell, Skopek and Fraser, 1977) and of interaction analysis (Stiles, 1978). The sociolinguistic studies have identified explaining as one of the eight major types of utterances. Furthermore, aspects of explaining lie behind complex communication problems. Among these are the problems of shared meanings, intentionality, credibility, and the belief systems of the doctor and patient. So far, the interactive analysis studies, like the sociolinguistic studies, have been more concerned to develop fine-grained analytical systems than to collect data (Sanson-Fisher and Poole, 1980; Stiles, *et al.* 1979). However, a relatively robust system is being developed for general practitioners to analyse the topics and strategies of consulting in their own consultations (Pringle, Robins and Brown, in press).

Studies of processes *per se* yield normative data — which is sadly lacking — but they do not reveal which strategies or methods of consulting are more likely to yield desired outcomes. Hence the importance of process–outcome studies. These are admirably reviewed by Pendleton (1983). Outcomes may be measured using such variables as patients' recall, understanding, changes in attitudes, beliefs, compliance and improvements in patient health. Each of these variables has been measured using a variety of methods; measures of outcome have been taken immediately after a consultation, soon afterwards and up to a year after a course of treatment. However, most of these studies have been concerned with immediate and short-term outcomes. This is largely because of the difficulty of attributing long-term outcomes solely to the consultation.

Ley (1979, 1983), in a wide range of studies, has shown that patients recall less than half of the doctor's explanations. Although Pendleton (1981) has demonstrated that patients probably remember the important points, the evidence of Tuckett *et al.* (1985) shows that they may not understand what they recall. Ley has shown that forgetting is related to the patient's age, level of anxiety and medical knowledge and, as indicated earlier, that increases in recall and understanding are related to simplification of information by the doctor, his or her use of explicit categorisation and repetition.

Locker and Dunt (1978) point out that methods of determining and defining satisfaction vary widely between studies. Hence one should be wary of over-generalising about patient satisfaction.

Nonetheless, clear explanations are an important determinant of patient satisfaction with the consultation (Ley, 1983). Stiles *et al.* (1979) also show that the patient's emotional satisfaction is related to the patient being given an opportunity to explain his/her condition, while patients' cognitive satisfaction is related to the clear explanation of the illness and its treatment by the doctor. Nonverbal expressions of care and concern (Friedman, 1979) and mode of presentation (Ben-Sira, 1980) are also related to patient satisfaction with the consultation.

For many medical practitioners the most powerful test of a consultation is the compliance of the patients. Podell (1975) suggests a 'one-third rule' derived from his studies of hypertension. One-third of patients comply, one-third comply partially and one-third ignore advice and medication. An Office of Health Economics report (OHE, 1983) suggests only half of all patients continue to take long-term medication, and a quarter of patients do not take short-term medication. Such wastage puts an added burden on the National Health Service budget. The report suggests various ways of overcoming non-compliance, such as providing better explanations and prescribing fewer pills. Given the wastage of drugs, it might also be useful to teach patients about health care and management without drugs. But, as Kafka's country doctor observed, 'To write prescriptions is easy, but to come to an understanding with people is hard' (quoted by Balint, 1970).

Ley (1979) argues that compliance is a product of satisfaction, which in its turn is a product of understanding and recall. However, the evidence he reviews shows well defined links between recall, understanding and satisfaction but more tenuous links between satisfaction and compliance. In addition to the variables in his model, one may have to take account of patients' 'locus of control' and their private theories of the problems that they present. Patients with an 'external' locus of control tend to be fatalistic and feel helpless; those with an internal locus believe events are controllable to some extent through their own actions. 'Externals' tend to be poorer compliers than 'internals' (Strickland, 1978). Modifying patients' private theories through discussion and explanation, as well as treating their physical condition, is being applied successfully to pain (Meichenbaum, 1977); headache (Holroyde, Andraski and Westbrook, 1977); and coronary prone behaviour (Suinn, 1977).

However, modifying a patient's incorrect theory may not always be good for compliance. For example, a person might 'explain' that he must exercise to avoid getting cancer (his explanation might be based on the facts that his father never exercised and died of cancer). If the doctor corrected this belief by explaining successfully the probable cause of cancer, it could lead to the patient not complying to the regime of exercise.

Feedback and Checks on Understanding. The process–outcome measures reviewed in the previous section show the importance of feedback and checks on understanding. There appears to be no direct study of feedback from patients or of checks on understanding *during* the consultation. However, it is clear that doctors interpret patients' nonverbal signals as well as their verbal behaviour (Friedman, 1979). But there is a tendency to reject or ignore information once a diagnosis has been reached (Maguire and Rutter, 1976).

Summary. Studies of the consultation indicate that patients value warmth, care, concern and the ability to explain clearly. Patient recall and understanding is enhanced when doctors provide simple, clear and well structured explanations. Improved recall and understanding lead to higher patient satisfaction and probably to higher patient compliance.

Explaining in Other Contexts

Explaining is ubiquitous. It occurs in everyday life and in every professional context. Yet despite its ubiquity there appears to be little research on explaining or on training people to explain other than that reviewed so far in this chapter. However, there is a wealth of folklore and practice wisdom, within every profession which is transmitted from one generation to another and which becomes the working system of values and beliefs of that profession.

Unfortunately, it is beyond the scope of this chapter to analyse the practice wisdom of every professional group. Texts and articles which provide some practice wisdom are Roper (1973) and Sheahan (1976) in nursing; Wagstaff (1982) and Caney (1983) in physiotherapy; Cross (1974) and Sutton (1979) in social work; and Nelson-Jones (1983) in counselling. While such writings are useful they are not, in the author's view, as helpful as they could be. They are not sufficiently specific and concrete for an initiate nor are they rooted sufficiently firmly in empirical or analytical studies for an experienced member of the profession. An exception to this rule is Hargie, Saunders and Dickson (1981) on interpersonal professions. However, the basic message to be culled from practice wisdom is: 'Know your subject, know your client and know your goal.' Difficulties, as usual, arise in translating these maxims into action.

Towards an Elementary Task Analysis

One way is to begin by analysing the tasks of explaining which are required by a particular professional group. In general, there are two types of explanatory task: explaining to a single client and explaining to a group. The research outlined in this chapter on doctor–patient consultations and on teaching provide extended models for these tasks. Most of the professions use client-based explanations and many of them are also required to explain to groups. For example, social workers, occupational therapists, physiotherapists, speech therapists and counsellors may explain procedures and so on to clients. They present cases at case conferences and they may also have to outline their approaches to other interested (or hostile) groups. Barristers and solicitors explain procedures and possible outcomes to their clients and they try to present their cases persuasively to a court. Architects and town planners have to present their projects to individual clients and to planning boards.

It should be noted that the professional context influences the task. Sometimes the influences are explicit and formalised, as in the rules of evidence for barristers. More often they are implicit — but no less potent.

Towards Studies of Reality

A second approach to the practice of explaining in various contexts is to investigate what professionals actually do. Preferably, this should be reported in terms which are intelligible to the professional group. This approach involves direct observation and discussions with professionals and clients (Singleton, Spurgeon and Stammers, 1980). It was used by Hoffman (1959) who discovered that explaining is a frequent sub-role of counsellors, yet one which many texts on counselling and social work still neglect (for instance, Ivey and Authier, 1978; Bessel, 1979). Clear (and friendly) explaining also appears to be related to client satisfaction in vocational counselling (Newton and Caple, 1974) and in social work (Sainsbury, 1975; Aldgate, 1977).

More recently, the approach of direct observation and discussion has been adapted by Saunders and Caves (1984) in their detailed study of speech therapists working with adults and children. Instructing/explaining was one of the most common social skills used by the therapists.

Towards Training Programmes for Professionals

Specific training programmes on explaining for professionals other than teachers and medical staff are, as yet, an undeveloped field. In the United Kingdom, the work of the Social Skills Unit at Ulster University is probably the most advanced. Ellis and Whittington (1981) have provided a conceptual guide to social skills training. Hargie, Saunders and Dickson (1981) have outlined the generic skills, including explaining, which are relevant to interpersonal work. Hargie and Morrow (1984) have described a training programme for pharmacists; Dickson and Maxwell (1984) for physiotherapists; Dickson, Hargie and Tittmar (1977) for employment advisory officers; and Hargie, Tittmar and Dickson (1978) for social workers. Caves and Saunders (1985) have also written a text which could be the basis of a training programme for speech therapists.

Other training programmes based on social skills approaches are reviewed by Trower (1981) on psychotherapy, Hudson (1981) on social work interviewing and by Davis (1981) on nursing. The Bar Association provides some training materials on advocacy and working with clients; the Architectural Association and the Institute of Town Planning supply some suggestions on training for consultancy. The British Dental Association is currently developing materials for trainee general practitioners which includes suggestions for talking with patients.

Many of the training programmes which are being developed have, of course, not yet been evaluated. Perhaps the second edition of this handbook will be able to report on the evaluations of these new developments.

Summary

This chapter explores the nature of explaining and outlines the research on explaining in various professional contexts. Explaining is essentially concerned with providing understanding to others. Explaining may occur in groups, as in teaching or lecturing, or in one-to-one situations such as the doctor–patient consultation. Most research has centred on teaching and the medical consultation but most other professions are also involved in explaining to groups and to singletons.

The research on explaining indicates strongly that clear, relevant explanations are valued highly by pupils, students and clients, that interest is an important variable in pedagogic explanations and friendliness in consultative explanations. Clear explaining is related to improvements in understanding in all contexts and, less strongly, to patient compliance. The evidence on training in explaining indicates that teachers, lecturers and medical practitioners can be trained to be better explainers. As yet, evidence on other professional groups is scant but it is very likely that specific training on explaining will also yield good results.

However, it would be wrong to end this chapter with the impression that all the problems of explaining have been solved. There are several issues which require deep exploration. Notable among these are: the precise nature of understanding, the meanings of such terms as clarity, interest, expressiveness and structure, the relative strengths and weaknesses of various methods of studying explaining, the effects of value and belief systems on the processes of explaining and, perhaps most important of all, the criteria of successful explaining and of effective training in giving explanations.

It is hoped that this chapter not only provides its readers with an illuminating survey of explaining but also that it encourages them to explore the fascinating subtleties of explaining in their own professional contexts.

Acknowledgements

To Dr Madeleine Atkins for her perceptive comments on this chapter and Mrs Diana Simons for her good humour and patience, as well as for her typing.

References

Abrami, P.C., Leventhal, L. and Perry, R.P. (1982) 'Educational Seduction', *Review of Educational Research, 52,* 446–64

Aldgate, J. (1977) 'Identification of Factors Influencing Children's Length of Stay in Care', unpublished PhD thesis, University of Edinburgh

Armento, B.J. (1977) 'Teacher Behaviour Related to Student Achievement on a Social Science Concept Test', *Journal of Teacher Education, 28,* 46–52

Bain, D.J. (1976) 'Doctor-patient Communications in General Practice Consultations', *Med. Education, 10,* 125–31

———— (1977) 'Patient Knowledge and the Content of the Consultation in General Practice', *Med. Education, 11,* 347–50

Balint, M. (1970) *Treatment or Diagnosis,* Tavistock Publications, London

Beard, R. and Hartley, J. (1984) *Teaching and Learning in Higher Education,* Harper Row, London

Bellack, A.A., Hyman, R.T., Smith, F.L. *et al.* (1966) *The Language of the Classroom,* Teacher College Press, New York

Bennett, N., Desforge, S. and Wilkinson, A. (1984) *The Quality of Pupil Learning,* Lawrence Erlbaum Associates, London

Ben-Sira, Z. (1980) 'Affective and Instrumental Components in the Physician-patient Relationships', *J. Health Soc. Beh., 21,* 170–80

Bessel, R. (1979) *Interviewing and Counselling,* Batsford, London

Bligh, D.A. (1972) *What's the Use of Lectures?* Penguin Books, Harmondsworth

Borg, W.R. (1975) 'Protocol Materials as Related to Teacher Performance and Pupil Achievement', *J. of Educational Research 69,* 21–30

Brown, G.A. (1978) *Lecturing and Explaining,* Methuen, London

———— (1979) *Learning from Lectures,* University of Nottingham, Nottingham

———— (1980) 'Explaining: Studies from the Higher Education Context', Final Report to SSRC, University of Nottingham, Nottingham

———— (1982) 'Two Days on Explaining and Lecturing', *Studies in Higher Education, 2,* 93–104

———— (1985) *Lecturing,* Higher Education Research and Development Society of Australia, Green Guide No. 4 (in press).

Brown, G.A. and Armstrong, S. (1978) 'SAID: A System for Analysing Instructional Discourse', in R.W. McAleese and D.R. Hamilton (eds), *Understanding Classroom Life,* NFER, Slough

———— (1984) 'On Explaining' in E.C. Wragg (ed.), *Classroom Teaching Skills,* Croom Helm, London

———— and Daines, J. (1981) 'Can Explaining be Learnt? Some Lecturers' Views', *Higher Education, 10,* 575–80

———— and Hatton, N. (1982) *Explaining and Explanations,* Macmillan, London

———— and Bakhtar, M. (eds) (1983) *Styles of Lecturing,* Loughborough University Press, Loughborough

Bush, A.J., Kennedy, J.J. and Cruickshank, D.R. (1977) 'An Empirical Investigation of Teacher Clarity', *J. of Teacher Education, 28,* 53–8

Byrne, P.S. and Long, B.E. (1976) *Doctors Talking to Patients,* HMSO, London

Caney, D. (1983) 'The Physiotherapist' in W.T. Singleton (ed.), *The Study of Real Skills,* MTP Press, Lancaster

Carroll, J.G. and Munroe, J. (1979) 'Teaching Medical Interviewing: A Critique of Educational Research and Practise', *J. of Med. Education, 54,* 478–500

Cartwright A. and Anderson, R. (1981) *General Practice Revisited,* Tavistock Publication, London

Cassell, E.J., Skopek, L. and Fraser, B. (1977) 'A Preliminary Model for the Examination of Doctor-Patient Communication', *Language Science, 43,* 10–13

Caves, R.D. and Saunders, C.Y.M. (1985) 'Communication Skills in Speech Therapy' (in press)

Cooper, J. and Metcalfe, D. (1979) 'How Much Do Patients Know?' *J. Royal College of Gen. Practitioners, 29,* 482–88

Cross, C.P. (ed.) (1974) *Interviewing and Communication in Social Work,* Routledge and Kegan Paul, London

Daines, J. and Brown, G.A. (1985) 'Demonstrators and Demonstrating in a Vocationally Oriented Course' (in press)

Davies, R.R. (1978) 'Helping Postgraduate Demonstrators in the Laboratory', *Studies in Higher Education, 3,* 81–9

Davis, B. (1981) 'Social Skills in Nursing' in M. Argyle (ed.), *Social Skills and Health*, Methuen, London

Dickson, D.A., Hargie, O. and Tittmar, H. (1977) 'The Use of Microcounselling in the Training of Employment Advisory Officers', *Vocational Aspects of Education, 29*, 45–7

—— and Maxwell, M. (1984) 'The Interpersonal Dimension of Physiotherapy: Implications for Training', Social Skills Centre, University of Ulster

Dunkin, M.J. and Biddle, B.J. (1974) *The Study of Teaching*, Rinehart, New York

Ellis, R. and Whittington, D. (1981) *A Guide to Social Skills Training*, Croom Helm, London

Ennis, R.H. (1969) *Logic in Teaching*, Prentice Hall, New York

Flanders, N.A. (1970) *Analysing Teaching Behaviour*, Addison-Wesley, New York

Flood-Page, C. (1974) *Student Evaluation of Teaching - The American Experience*, Society for Research into Higher Education at the University of Surrey, Guildford

French-Lazovik, G. (1974) 'Predictability of Students' Evaluations of College Teachers from Component Ratings', *J. of Educ. Psychology, 66*, 373–85

Friedman, H.S. (1979) 'Non-verbal Communications Between Patients and Medical Practitioners', *J. Soc. Issues, 35*, 82–99

Gage, N.L. (1972) in I. Westbury and A. Bellack (eds), *Research into Classroom Processes*, Teachers College Press, New York, Chapter 9

Gage, N.L., Belgard, M., Dell, D., *et al.* (1968) *Explanations of the Teacher's Effectiveness in Explaining*, Technical Report No. 4, Stanford University Center for R and D in Teaching, Stanford, CA

Gage, N.L. and Berliner, D.C. (1979) *Educational Psychology*, 2nd edn, Rand McNally, Chicago

Good, T.L. and Grouws, D.A. (1977) 'Teaching Effects: A Process–product Study in Fourth Grade Mathematics Classrooms', *J. of Teacher Education, 28*, 49–54

Hargie, O., Saunder, C. and Dickson, D.A. (1981) *Social Skills in Interpersonal Communication*, Croom Helm, London

Hargie, O. and Morrow, N. (1984) 'Communication Skills Training for Pharmacists', paper presented at the conference of the Society for Research in Higher Education, London

Hargie, O., Tittmar, H. and Dickson, D. (1978) 'Microtraining: A Systematic Approach to Social Work Practice', *Social Work Today, 9*, 14–16

Hart, W. (1934) *Teachers and Teaching*, MacMillan, New York

Hildebrand, M. (1973) 'The Character and Skills of the Effective Professor', *Journal of Higher Education, 44*, 41–50

Hiller, J. (1971) 'Verbal Response Indicators of Conceptual Vagueness', *American Educ. Research Journal, 6*, 661–75

Hoffman, A.E. (1959) 'An Analysis of Counselor Sub-roles', *Journal of Counseling Psychology, 6*, 61–7

Hollis, J. (1935) referred to in P. Taylor (1962) 'Children' Evaluations of the Characteristics of a Good Teacher', *British Journal of Educational Psychology 32*, 258–66

Holroyde, K., Andraski, F. and Westbrook, T. (1977) 'Cognitive Control of Headache Tension', *Cognitive Therapy Research, 1*, 121–33

Hudson, B.L. (1981) 'The Social Casework Interview' in M. Argyle (ed.), *Social Skills and Health*, Methuen, London

Hyman, R.T. (1974) *Teaching: Vantage Points for Study*, Lippincott Press, New York

Ivey, A. and Authier, J. (1978) *Microcounselling*, C.C. Thomas, Illinois

Kahn, G.S., Cohen, B. and Jason, H. (1979) 'The Teaching of Interpersonal Skills in US Medical Schools', *J. Med. Education, 54*, 29–35

Kennedy, J.J. *et al.* (1978) 'Additional Investigations into the Nature of Teacher Clarity', *J. of Educational Research, 71*, 795–9

Klein, S.S. (1971) 'Student Influence on Teacher Behaviour', *American Educational Research Journal, 8*, 403–21

Kozma, R.B., Belle, L.W. and Williams, G.W. (1978) *Instructional Techniques in Higher Education*, Educational Technology Publications, Englewood Cliffs, New Jersey

Land, M.L. (1979) 'Low Inference Variables of Teacher Clarity: Effects on Student Concept Learning', *J. of Educational Psychology, 30*, 55–7

—— (1985) 'Vagueness and Clarity in the Classroom' in T. Husen and T.N. Postlethwaite (eds), *International Encyclopaedia of Education: Research Studies*, Pergamon Press, Oxford

Ley, P. (1979) 'The Psychology of Compliance' in D.J. Oborne, M. Gruneberg and J.R. Elser (eds),

Research in Psychology and Medicine, 12, Academic Press, London

——— (1983) 'Patients' Understanding and Recall in Clinical Communication Failure' in D. Pendleton and J. Hasler (eds), *Doctor-Patient Communication,* Academic Press, London

Locker, D. and Dunt, D. (1978) 'Theoretical and Methodological Issues in Sociologica! Studies of Consumer Care', *Soc. Sci. Medicine, 12,* 283–92

Luker, P.M. (1985) 'Some Case Studies of Small Group Teaching in Higher Education', Mimeo. University of Nottingham, Nottingham

Maguire, P. (1981) 'Doctor-Patient Skills' in M. Argyle (ed.), *Social Skills and Health,* Methuen, London

——— and Rutter, D.R. (1976) 'History-taking for Medical Students 1 — Deficiencies in Performance', *Lancet, 2,* 556–8

Martin, J.R. (1970) *Explaining, Understanding and Teaching,* McGraw-Hill, New York

Meichenbaum, D. (1977) *Cognitive-behaviour Modification,* Plenum Press, New York

Miltz, R. (1972) 'Development and Evaluation: A Manual for Improving Teachers' Explanations', Technical Report No. 26, Stanford University Center for R and P on Teaching, Stanford, CA

Montgomery, J. (1976) 'The Lecture as Discourse', unpublished M.Phil thesis, University of Aston, Birmingham

Nelson-Jones, R. (1983) *Practical Counselling Skills,* Holt, Rinehart and Winston, London

Nettler, G. (1970) *Explanations,* McGraw Hill, New York

Newton, F.B. and Caple, R.B. (1974) 'Client and Counselor Preferences for Counselor Behavior in the Interview', *Journal of College Student Personnel, 15,* 220–4

Office of Health Economics (1983) *Keep on Taking the Tablets,* OHE Briefing No. 21, London

Ogborn, J. and Bliss, N. (eds) (1977) *Small Group Teaching in Undergraduate Science,* Heinemann, London

Pendleton, D. (1981) 'A Situational Analysis of General Practice Consultations' in M. Argyle *et al.* (eds), *Social Situations,* Cambridge University Press, Cambridge

——— (1983) in D. Pendleton and J. Hasler (eds), *Doctor Patient Communication,* Academic Press, London

Pendleton, D. *et al.* (1984) *The Consultation: An Approach to Teaching and Learning,* Oxford University Press, Oxford

——— and Bochner, S. (1980) 'The Communication of Medical Information in General Practice Consultations as a Function of Patients' Social Class', *Soc. Sci. Medicine, 14,* 669–73

Pirianen-Marsh, A. (1985) 'The Lecture as Discourse. Studies in Philology', unpublished thesis, University of Oulu, Finland

Podell, R.N. (1975) *Physician's Guide to Compliance in Hypertension,* Merck, Pennsylvania

Pringle, M., Robins, S. and Brown, G. 'A Method of Analysing Consultations', *British Medical Journal,* (in press)

Ricoeur, P. (1981) *Hermeneutics and the Human Sciences,* Cambridge University Press, Cambridge

Rodin, J. (1978) 'Somatophysics and Attribution', *Pers. Soc. Psychol. Bulletin, 4,* 531–8

Roper, N. (1973) *Principles of Nursing,* Churchill-Livingstone, Edinburgh

Rosenshine, B. (1972) 'Teaching Behaviours and Student Achievement', IEA Studies No. 1, National Foundation of Education Research

——— and Furst, N. (1973) *The Use of Direct Observation to Study Teaching'* in R.W. Travers (ed.), *Second Handbook of Research on Teaching 122–183,* Rand McNally

Roter, D.L. (1977) 'Patient Participation in the Patient Provider Interactions', *Health Ed. Monographs, 5,* 281–315

Ryle, G. (1963) *The Concept of Mind,* Penguin (reprint), Harmondsworth

Sainsbury, E. (1975) *Social Work with Families,* Routledge and Kegan Paul, London

Sanson-Fisher, R.W. and Poole, D.A. (1980) 'Simulated Patients and the Assessment of Medical Students' Interpersonal Skills', *Medical Education, 14,* 249–85

Saunders, C.Y.M. and Caves, R.D. (1984) 'The Identification and Analysis of Communication Skills with Reference to Speech Therapists', paper given at Conference of Society for Research in Higher Education, London

Schonell, F.J., Roe, E. and Middleton, I.G. (1962) *Promise and Performance,* University of Queensland Press, Brisbane

Sheahan, J. (1976) 'Education 7: Communication Skills and Assessment Learning', *Nursing Times, 72,* 1570–2

Shutes, R. (1969) 'Verbal Behaviours and Instructional Effectiveness', *Dissertation Abstractions*

International, 30, (1970)

Singleton, W.T., Spurgeon, P. and Stammers, R.B. (1980) *The Analysis of Social Skill,* Plenum, New York

Skopek, L. (1979) 'Doctor-patient Conversations: A Way of Analysing Its Linguistic Problems', *Semiotica,* 301–11

Smith, B.O. and Meux, M.O. (1970) *A Study of the Logic of Teaching,* University of Illinois Press, Illinois

Stiles, W.B. (1978) 'Verbal Response Modes and Dimensions of Interpersonal Roles', *J. Pers. Soc. Psychol. 36,* 693–7

Stiles, W.B. *et al.* (1979) 'Verbal Response Mode Profiles of Patients and Physicians in Medical Screening Interviews', *J. Med. Education, 54,* 81–9

Strickland, B. (1978) 'Internal-external Expectancies and Health-related Behaviour', *Consult. Clin. Psychol. 46,* 1192–211

Suinn, R. (1977) 'Type A Behaviour Pattern' in R.B. Williams and W.D. Gentry (eds), *Behavioural Approaches to Medical Treatment,* Ballinger, Cambridge

Sutton, C. (1979) *Psychology for Social Workers and Counsellors* Routledge and Kegan Paul, London

Swift, L.F. (1961) 'Explanation' in R.H. Ennis and B.O. Smith (eds), *Language and Concepts in Education,* Rand McNally, Chicago

Thyne, J.M. (1966) *The Psychology of Learning and Techniques of Teaching,* University of London Press, 2nd edn, London

Tisher, R.P. (1970) 'The Nature of Verbal Discourse in Classrooms and Association Between Verbal Discourse and Pupil Understanding in Science', in W.J. Campbell (ed.), *Scholars in Context,* Wiley, Sydney

Trower, P. (1981) 'Psychotherapy' in M. Argyle (ed.), *Social Skills and Health,* Methuen, London

Tuckett, D.A., Boulton, M.G., Olson, C.S. *et al.* (1985) *Meetings Between Experts: A Study of Medical Consultations,* Tavistock, London

Turney, C. et al (1983) *Sydney Microskills Redeveloped,* University of Sydney, Sydney

Turney, C., Ellis, K.J., Hatton, W. *et al.* (1975) *Sydney Microskill Series, Vol. 1.,* University of Sydney Press, Sydney

Wagstaff, G.F. (1982) 'A Small Dose of Common-sense Communication, Persuasion and Psychotherapy', *Phsyiotherapy, 68,* 327–9

Wakeford, R. (1983) 'Communication Skills Training in United Kingdom Medical Schools' in D. Pendleton and J. Hasler, *Doctor-Patient Communication,* Academic Press, London

Wright, C.J. and Nuttall, G. (1970) 'The Relationships Between Teacher Behaviours and Pupil Achievement in the Experimental Elementary Science Lessons', *Amer. Educ. Res. J. 7, 477–491,* reprinted in Morrison and McIntyre (1972) *Social Psychology of Teaching,* Penguin Books, Harmondsworth

This chapter is divided into two main sections. The first part deals with the skill of self-disclosure in general terms. It provides a definition of the skill, outlines the main functions thereof and considers a number of factors which govern the appropriate usage of self-disclosure in various contexts. As such, it provides an overview of this particular aspect of communication. It also provides a necessary backdrop for the second part of the chapter, in which a different perspective is presented on the relevance of this skill in therapeutic settings. In particular, the use of self-disclosure is related to a number of other skills pertinent to the helping process. In this way, a useful analysis is provided of the types of disclosures which can be made, and at what stages of the helping interview.

A The Skill of Self-Disclosure

Owen Hargie

A great deal of social interaction is concerned with participants giving opinions, relating feelings and making statements about a wide variety of topics; in other words making disclosures. Such disclosures can be about objective matters ('It is six o-clock') or they can involve a subjective dimension regarding the speaker ('I am tired'). This latter type of disclosure is referred to as self-disclosure, which can be defined as: 'The act of verbally and nonverbally sharing with another some aspects of what makes you a person, aspects the other individual would not be likely to recognize or understand without your help' (Stewart, 1977).

Self-disclosure, therefore, involves both verbal and nonverbal communication, since both channels will convey information of a personal nature. Verbal self-disclosures are statements in which the individual reveals personal information about himself. Nonverbal self-disclosures are behaviours displayed by an individual which convey to others an impression of his or her attitudes or feelings. As discussed in Chapter 3, facial expressions, posture, gaze, paralanguage and all the other features of nonverbal communication are the main means whereby information is provided about emotional state. Thus we can 'say' nonverbally, 'I am very happy' by smiling, having an upright posture and looking at the other person. An important difference between verbal and nonverbal self-disclosure is that we tend to have much greater control over the former than the latter.

The importance of self-disclosure, as a social skill, is usually associated with the work of Jourard (1964, 1971) who emphasises the value of this skill in the helping situation. Jourard stresses the need for a high degree of openness between individuals in many contexts, and illustrates the potency of self-disclosure as a technique for encouraging deep levels of interpersonal sharing. The appropriate use of self-disclosure can be a useful indicator of listening and attention, wherein the listener follows up a self-disclosure made by the speaker with a related self-disclosure. As Jourard points out, this in turn will encourage the other person to make further self-disclosures. In this respect, one way to encourage another person to talk about himself is for the interviewer to use self-disclosure initially. Thus, for example, a health visitor visiting a young mother who has just had her first child may say 'I know the problems associated with motherhood, since I have three children myself', and in this way lead to a discussion of the particular problems faced by this mother.

For many professionals, getting clients to talk freely about themselves and their personal affairs is a major objective. Therefore, it is necessary for such professionals to be aware of the nuances of self-disclosure, in order to encourage disclosures from clients. However, while some self-disclosure from the professional can be very appropriate, in most contexts clients will neither expect nor welcome prolonged disclosures from professionals (Archer, 1979). Patients do not want to have to sit and listen to a doctor detailing a litany of illnesses from which he suffers, just as students do not want to listen to prolonged versions of the problems faced by a lecturer within a university department. Brief, pertinent disclosures from professionals are usually sufficient and most effective.

Features of Self-Disclosure

As Ivey and Authier (1978) point out, there are four main features of self-disclosure:

1. The use of the personal pronoun 'I' or some other personal self-reference pronoun such as 'my' or 'mine'. While these words may be implied from the context of the speaker's utterances, their presence serves to remove any ambiguity about whether or not the statement being made is a self-disclosure. For this reason, the basic reference point for all self-disclosures should be a personal pronoun. Compare, for example the statements: (a) Selection interviews can create a great amount of stress; (b) I find selection interviews very stressful. In (a) it is not immediately clear whether the speaker is making a general statement, or referring to his own feelings about attending selection interviews. The use of the personal pronoun 'I' in (b), however, serves to clarify the nature of the statement as a self-disclosure.

2. Self-disclosures can be about either facts or feelings. When two people meet

for the first time, it is more likely that they will focus upon factual disclosures (name, occupation, place of residence), while keeping any feeling disclosures at a fairly superficial level ('I hate crowded parties': 'I like rock music'). This is largely because the expression of personal feeling involves more risk and places the discloser in a more vulnerable position. At the same time, however, deep levels of disclosure may be made to a complete stranger providing we feel sure that we will never meet the person again (Chaikin and Derlega, 1974). Thus two strangers sitting beside one another on a long-haul plane journey who discover that their encounter is likely to be 'one-off' may reveal personal information and feelings, which they would not do if they were planning to meet one another on a regular basis.

Generally speaking, the expression of deep feeling or of high levels of factual disclosure (for instance 'I was in prison for five years') will increase as a relationship develops. For this reason, professionals should expect clients to experience difficulties in self-disclosing at the early stage of an encounter. Even if the client has a deep-rooted need to 'tell someone', such an experience will inevitably be embarrassing, or at least awkward, where the disclosures relate to very personal details. The skilled helper will be aware of this and employ techniques which help the client to overcome such initial feelings of embarrassment.

Factual and feeling disclosures at a deeper level can be regarded as a sign of commitment to a relationship (Newcomb, 1961). Two people who are in love will usually expect to give and receive disclosures about their feelings — especially towards one another. They will also want to know everything about one another. There will be a high level of trust in such a relationship, just as there will be in the confession box, a doctor's surgery or a counsellor's office (areas where disclosures will also be high).

3. The third aspect of self-disclosure relates to the object of the statement. A self-disclosure can be about one's own personal experience, or it can be about one's personal reaction to the experiences being related by another person. Ivey and Authier (1978) contend that the latter type of self-disclosure is at a deeper level than the former, and that it can therefore serve to enhance the development of interpersonal relationships. Consider the following:

Joan: 'Our marriage is going through a really bad patch just now. We seem to argue about even the smallest things. Every time we talk it seems to end up with a fight. I'm beginning to wonder if we're really meant for each other.'

Carol: 'It seems to me that this is obviously a difficult time for you. I can see that you are really worried about the way things are going . . .'

This is an example of a self-disclosure as a personal reaction to the experiences of another person, in which one individual is expressing concern and giving an opinion about the statements made by the other. In the example given, Carol could have chosen to give a self-disclosure about her *own* personal experience by saying something like: 'I know exactly what you are going through. At one point our marriage was going through an identical stage with row after row developing.

In the end I decided to confront the situation by making Jim sit down and discuss our relationship . . .' In this case, while Carol is reciprocating by self-disclosing she is taking the focus away from Joan and on to herself. Both types of self-disclosure are appropriate in different contexts, depending upon the nature of the interaction which is taking place, and the goals of the interactors. If it is desirable to give concerted attention to an individual and encourage her to disclose fully, then the type of self-disclosure which concentrates upon reactions to the feelings or thoughts of the other person would probably be most successful. If, however, the intention is to demonstrate to someone that they are not alone in feeling as they do, then the use of a parallel self-disclosure relating to one's own experiences may be more effective.

4. Self-disclosure can be about the past ('I was born in Ireland': 'I was really grief-stricken when my father died'), the present ('I am divorced': 'I am very happy'), or the future ('I hope to get promotion': 'I want to get married and have a family'). One situation in which people are expected to self-disclose in terms of facts and feelings about the past, present and future, is in the selection interview. Candidates will be asked to talk about their previous experience or education, to say why they have applied for the job and to outline their aspirations. Not only will candidates be expected to give factual details about themselves, they will more often than not be expected to relate their attitudes and feelings towards these factual experiences. The depth of self-disclosure required will, of course, vary from one interview to another. In selection interviews at an executive level, for example, the candidate may even be asked to answer the question 'What type of person would you say you are?'.

Functions of Self-Disclosures

The skill of self-disclosure serves a number of purposes in social interaction, depending upon the nature of the interaction which is taking place. Hargie, Saunders and Dickson (1981) have identified the main functions as follows.

To Open Conversations

When two people meet for the first time they will give and receive self-disclosures. Chaikin and Derlega (1976) identify three main stages or levels of relationship development. The first of these is *awareness,* when two people have not actually interacted but are becoming aware of the presence of one another. At this stage, for example, a female may stand close to, or walk slowly past, a male whom she is interested in. The second stage is that of *surface contact,* when individuals give superficial information about themselves, and make judgements about whether or not to pursue the relationship. The final stage is *mutuality* where the two people begin to disclose personal feelings and engage in more intimate self-disclosures. Many professionals will use self-disclosure to open interactions and establish surface contact. Thus, a social worker visiting a family for the first time will usually begin by saying something like 'Hello. My name is John Whiteside. I'm a social worker from the . . .' Such disclosures will be directly related to the job role.

To Encourage Reciprocation

In everyday interaction, reciprocation of self-disclosures will usually occur in that if one person is prepared to reveal personal details about herself, this usually results in the listener also revealing personal details (Tubbs and Baird, 1976). In professional situations, clients can often be encouraged to 'open up' by receiving a self-disclosure from the professional. Such a disclosure can have a very potent effect on the client, who will then be more likely to begin to self-disclose more freely. O'Neill and O'Neill (1977) point out that where reciprocation of self-disclosure does not occur, one of three types of situations will usually prevail:

1. The person making the disclosures is not really interested in the listener. This type of person's need is so great that he or she wants to tell all, without worrying about the effect this may have upon the listener. The speaker is simply using the listener as a receptacle into which he pours his disclosures. This is quite common when someone is undergoing some form of inner turmoil, and needs a friendly ear to encourage the ventilation of fears and emotions. To use another analogy, the listener becomes a 'wailing wall' for the speaker. In professional contexts this is often acceptable, as in counselling and therapy.

2. The person who is receiving the disclosures does not care about the speaker. In this case the speaker is foolish to continue disclosing, since it is possible that the listener may use the disclosures against the speaker, either at the time of the disclosure or later.

3. Neither one cares about the disclosures of the other. In this case there is no real relationship. If one person discloses, it is a monologue; if both disclose, it is a dialogue in which exchanges are superficial. A great deal of everyday, fleeting conversation falls into the latter category.

To Overcome Fear

Many people have a fear of disclosing too much about their thoughts and feelings, since they feel they may not be understood or will be subjected to ridicule. Indeed, self-disclosure will be actively discouraged in many subcultures, with the child being told to 'keep himself to himself' or 'tell people only what they need to know'.

This attitude then persists into later life where respect is often given to the person who 'plays his cards close to his chest'. While in a game of poker it is wise not to disclose too much, either verbally or nonverbally, the attitude of avoiding self-disclosure can cause problems for people. However, the initial dangers of self-disclosure are such that an equal commitment to this process is expected from people with whom one may wish to develop a relationship. For this reason, reciprocation is expected in the early stages of everyday interaction.

In relation to the poker analogy, it is a case of the individual wanting to see all of the cards on the table! The fear of self-disclosure can sometimes be overcome partially by a self-disclosure from the professional to the effect that he has often dealt with this type of problem, or that he feels it is quite acceptable for the client to have the problem. This form of 'reassuring' self-disclosure will usually be appreciated by clients.

To Facilitate Self-expression

It can become a burden not being able to tell others about personal matters, and having to keep things 'bottled up'. Self-disclosure can have a therapeutic effect, by enabling people to 'get it off their chest', which is why counselling, the confessional or discussing something with a close friend can all make people feel better. Indeed, it is interesting to note that, when people may not be able to utilise one of these channels, they often use substitutes such as keeping a personal diary, talking to a pet or conversing with God. Thus, most people have a strong need to express themselves to others, and professionals should be aware both of the existence of this need, and of ways to allow clients to satisfy it.

To Heighten Person Knowledge

This is exemplified by the saying 'How do I know what I think until I hear what I say?' The value of the 'talking cure' in therapy is a good example of how the process of allowing someone to freely express their thoughts, ideas, fears, problems and so on actually facilitates the individual's awareness of the type of person they are (Levin, 1977). It can also help people to understand their feelings and the reasons for them; in other words, it encourages them to know themselves more fully. People who do not have access to a good listener may not only be denied the opportunity to heighten their self-awareness, they are also denied valuable feedback as to the validity and acceptability of their inner thoughts and feelings. By discussing such inner thoughts and feelings with others, we receive feedback as to whether these are experiences which others have as well, or whether they may be less common. As a result, we learn what it is acceptable and unacceptable to disclose.

To Gain Knowledge of Others

Impressions of other people can be totally wrong in many cases since we do not know what is 'going on inside them'. As Jourard (1964) points out, 'Man, perhaps alone of all living forms, is capable of *being* one thing and *seeming* from his actions and talk to be something else'. The only method of attempting to overcome this problem, of finding out what people are 'really like', is to encourage them to talk about themselves openly and honestly. If we cannot facilitate others to self-disclose freely, then we will never really get to know them.

To Search for Commonalities

At the surface contact stage of a relationship, people give self-disclosures in the hope that the other person may be able to identify with them. At this stage they search for shared interests or experiences in order to identify some common ground on which to build a conversation. Consider the following conversation:

J: 'Hello, my name is John. Excuse me if I look somewhat tired, but I was running in the marathon today . . .'

R: 'Oh, really! Actually I've just taken up jogging recently but I couldn't run six miles let alone 26. By the way, my name is Rose.'

J: 'Sorry about my manners, but I already know your name. You see I asked Tom Robson. I saw him talking to you.'

R: 'Oh, so you know Tom. Him and I work together in the computer department.'

J: 'Well, you're not going to believe this, but I sell computers!'

In this excerpt, a number of commonalities have already been identified and these can be used to keep the conversation going. It is also obvious that both individuals are listening to one another, since each new self-disclosure is linked to the preceding statement. There is also reciprocation of self-disclosures, and this is vital in the development of new relationships. As Hargie, Saunders and Dickson (1981) point out, the egocentric individual who continually wants to talk about himself without listening to others will be viewed as a conversational bore by others and avoided by them accordingly.

These functions of self-disclosure can be illustrated with reference to the Johari window developed by two psychologists, Joseph Luft and Harry Ingram (and named after the initial letters of both forenames). As Figure 9.1 illustrates, there are four aspects of the self. There are aspects which are known both by the self and by others (A); aspects unknown by the self but known to others (B) including personal mannerisms, annoying habits and so on; aspects known by the self but not revealed to others (C) such as embarrassing personal details, thoughts or feelings; and aspects which are unknown both to the self and others (D). One of the effects of self-disclosing is that the size of segment A is increased and the size of the segments B, C and D reduced. In other words, by encouraging clients to self-disclose, not only will they find out more about themselves, but the professional will also gain valuable knowledge about them, and thereby perhaps understand them more fully.

Figure 9.1: The Johari Window

	Known to Self	Unknown to Self
Known to others	A	B
Unknown to others	C	D

Other Aspects of Self-Disclosure

A number of important facets of self-disclosure have been identified by Derlega and Grzelak (1979), and these need to be taken into consideration in any evaluation of the effectiveness of self-disclosure in social interaction.

Informativeness

This relates to the amount of information being provided by the discloser. Self-disclosures can be assessed along two dimensions, namely breadth and depth. The relationship between these two dimensions is such that as the depth (or intimacy) of disclosures increases, the breadth (or total number) decreases. Derlega and Chaikin (1975) give an example of a questionnaire designed to measure both breadth and depth of disclosures. Examples of shallow levels of disclosure given in this questionnaire include: 'Laws that I would like to see put into effect'; 'Whether I would rather live in an apartment or a house after getting married'; and deeper levels such as: 'How frequently I like to engage in sexual activity'; 'The kinds of things I do that I don't want people to watch.' In everyday interaction, deeper disclosures are more appropriate once relationships have been built up.

Appropriateness

This is perhaps the most crucial aspect of self-disclosure. Each disclosure needs to be evaluated in the light of the context in which it occurs. While there are no hard and fast rules about the exact appropriateness of self-disclosure in every situation, there are some general indicators. Self-disclosures are more appropriate:

1. From low status to high status individuals but not vice versa. Thus, workers may disclose personal problems to their supervisors, but the reverse does not usually happen. This is because for a supervisor to disclose personal information to a subordinate would cause a 'loss of face' which would affect the status relationship. However, research findings tend to suggest that self-disclosures are more often employed between people of equal status (Slobin, Miller and Porter, 1968).

2. When the listener is not flooded with them. There is a relationship between psychological adjustment and self-disclosure in that individuals who are extremely high or low disclosers will have low adjustment.

3. Depending upon the roles of the interactors. For example, someone may disclose information to their spouse which would not be disclosed to their children. Similarly, clients will often discuss a problem with a 'neutral' counsellor, that they would not wish to discuss with their spouses or with close friends. Indeed, most professionals will be reluctant to counsel close friends as part of their professional role, since to do so may well pose difficulties for both parties.

4. Depending upon the setting. Thus, bowel problems are not usually discussed during meal-time conversations.

5. At deeper levels later in a relationship. Exceptions to this include interacting with a stranger who will never be seen again, or in a crisis situation (for

instance, counselling, the confessional).

Truthfulness

Self-disclosures can be true or false. In some instances an individual may disclose false information in order to impress. This type of disclosure can place the person under a lot of stress. In effect, the greater the discrepancy between the real self and the image of the self as portrayed to others, then the greater will be the pressures and tensions within the individual, since the person has constantly to maintain the facade which has been presented. This can lead to breakdown in extreme cases. One example of this is where someone gives the impression of being confident and in control, when underneath the surface they are full of self-doubt and uncertainty; yet they feel unable to admit this since they feel that to do so would irrevocably damage their image. Eventually, such mismatch can no longer be maintained, and the person ends up being unable to cope. Some professionals (for example, detectives, judges) will have to make judgements about the truthfulness of self-disclosures made by individuals, and here an awareness of some of the nonverbal indicators of deception (Ekman and Friesen, 1974; Ekman, Friesen and Scherer, 1976) should form an important part of their training (see Chapter 3).

Accessibility

This refers to the ease with which the person discloses information. Some individuals will be more reluctant, for whatever reason, to talk about themselves. This may be due to personality (introverts will talk less generally and will tend to self-disclose less than extroverts), upbringing (parents may have taught the child to be more closed than open) or lack of learning about how and what to disclose in social interaction. An awareness of such self-disclosure difficulties is crucial to many professions. Quite often clients will come along with a 'presenting' problem and only after they have been eased into an interaction will they reveal the real problem. An excellent case example of this from the medical sphere is given by Maguire (1984): 'A 53-year-old woman noticed that she had a small lump in her left breast, and feared that it might be cancer, but told herself that it was probably nothing and would soon go away. Not wishing to waste her general practitioner's time she waited until it was clear that the lump was not going to disappear. She thought it might be easier if she first mentioned that she had suffered 'bad headaches' for three months following a change to a busy and stressful job, since this would be an acceptable reason for seeking help. She therefore rang the receptionist and asked for an appointment to discuss her 'headaches'. When she arrived the surgery was full and on entering the consulting room her doctor appeared harrassed. He clarified rapidly the nature of her headaches and their relation to tension. Before she could add anything about her lump he wrote a prescription for a tranquilliser and said he would like to see her again in a month's time. She felt flustered and left without mentioning her lump, which was later found to be cancer.'

Rewardingness

This aspect concerns the outcome of the disclosure for both the discloser and the listener. The outcome may be positive or negative for either or both. Some individuals disclose negative information about themselves too often ('I am depressed': 'I have piles'). Equally, some individuals make negative disclosures about the listener ('You have a lot of spots': 'I see you have a problem with dandruff'). In both instances, this type of person will have difficulties in interpersonal relationships, since the outcome of their disclosures is negative and unrewarding for the listener. Such people need to learn to be more positive and rewarding in the information which they disclose.

Effectiveness

Finally, the effectiveness of the disclosure is of crucial importance. Does the disclosure help the individual to obtain his or her goals? If an individual's disclosures are ineffective in so doing, then it is necessary to examine the nature and pattern of such disclosures.

Encouraging Others to Self-Disclose

Self-disclosures are used in many different situations in social interaction. Differences in personality mean that some people will employ self-disclosures frequently, while others will be more reluctant to talk about themselves. Similarly, there are some individuals who will receive more self-disclosures than others. In particular, individuals who do not reveal self-disclosures made by others will tend to be confided in, since they will be seen as less likely to betray the trust given to them. For this reason, deep levels of self-disclosure are rarely given to complete strangers, although, as already mentioned, this may occur where there is a professional bond of confidentiality prevalent (for instance, a confession to a priest; consultation with a doctor), or where the person feels confident that he, or his friends, are not likely to meet the listener again. In addition, the reactions of the listener are important, in that if the listener seems disinterested or rejects initial self-disclosures, the chances are that the speaker will stop disclosing. On the other hand, if the listener appears interested or reciprocates with self-disclosures, the likelihood is that the speaker will continue to disclose personal information.

A 'warm' environment has also been found to encourage more self-disclosures; if there are soft seats, gentle lighting, pleasant decor and potted plants in an office, then a client will be more likely to 'open up' (Chaikin, Derlega and Miller, 1976). This finding is interesting, since interrogation sessions normally take place in 'cold' environments (bare walls, bright lights). Presumably, the willingness of the person to self-disclose will be an important factor in determining the type of environment for the interaction.

The attractiveness of the listener is another important element in encouraging self-disclosures. Brundage, Derlega and Cash (1977) and Cash and Soloway (1975) report findings which suggest that individuals will disclose more to a physically attractive, as opposed to an unattractive, recipient, irrespective of the sex of discloser and recipient. Similarly, there is evidence to indicate that more disclosures are made to individuals who are liked by the discloser. Interestingly, it has also been found that people tend to like those who disclose more to them. As Taylor (1979) puts it, 'self-disclosure leads to liking and liking leads to self-disclosure'. Not surprisingly, therefore, more self-disclosures tend to be made to individuals who are perceived as being similar (in attitudes, values, status etc.) to the discloser, since such individuals will usually be better liked.

As previously indicated, an awareness of the 'one-off' nature of an interaction can encourage self-disclosure in certain situations. This is referred to by Thibaut and Kelly (1959) as the 'stranger-on-the-train phenomenon'. However, this phenomenon can apply to some professional situations. For example, a client may be reluctant to return to a counsellor following an initial session in which deep self-disclosures may have been made to the counsellor who is usually a complete stranger. Therefore counsellors should employ appropriate closure skills in order to help overcome this problem (see Chapter 7).

Finally, people are more likely to self-disclose in situations where they are undergoing some form of stress, especially if this stress is shared by both participants. Thus, patients in a hospital ward who are awaiting operations will generally disclose quite a lot to one another. The author has often noted how professionals involved in social skills training will likewise self-disclose freely to one another, especially during the most stressful part of training, namely practicals involving CCTV and video feedback; indeed, for this reason, such training is a useful method for encouraging group familiarisation.

Overview

From this analysis of self-disclosure, it will be clear that this is an important skill for professionals to be aware of, from two perspectives. First, many professionals operate in contexts wherein it is vital that they are able to encourage clients to self-disclose freely; thus a knowledge of some of the factors which facilitate self-disclosure is very useful. Second, professionals need to be aware of the likely effects, upon the clients with whom they come into contact, of any self-disclosures they may make.

Self-disclosure serves a number of useful functions in that it can be used by the professional to begin an interaction, to encourage client reciprocation and to help overcome any fear the client may have. Through self-disclosure, clients can gain more personal insight into their own thoughts and feelings, and can talk through their problems in such a way that they will often feel better having done so. When giving and receiving self-disclosures the professional needs to take into account:

1. The total number of disclosures made;
2. The depth of these disclosures;

3. The nonverbal, as well as verbal, disclosures;
4. The physical environment;
5. The status and role relationships between the interactors;
6. The timing of the disclosures;
7. The effectiveness of the disclosures.

The general importance of self-disclosure in everyday interaction reflects the fundamental value of this skill in many professional contexts. Therefore it is useful to conclude with a quote from Chaikin and Derlega (1976) which neatly encapsulates the central role which this aspect has to play: 'The nature of the decisions concerning self-disclosure that a person makes will have great bearing on his life. They will help determine the number of friends he has and what they are like: they will influence whether he is regarded as emotionally stable or mal-adjusted by others: they will affect his happiness and the satisfaction he gets out of life. To a large extent, a person's decisions regarding the amount, the type, and the timing of his self-disclosures to others will even affect the degree of his own self-knowledge and awareness.'

References

Archer, R. (1979) 'Role of Personality and the Social Situation' in G. Chelune (ed.) *Self-Disclosure,* Jossey-Bass, San Francisco

Brundage, L., Derlega, V. and Cash, T. (1977) 'The Effects of Physical Attractiveness and Need for Approval on Self-disclosure', *Personality and Social Psychology Bulletin, 3,* 63–6

Cash, T. and Soloway, D. (1975) 'Self-disclosure Correlates of Physical Attractiveness: An Exploratory Study', *Psychological Reports, 36,* 579–86

Chaikin, A. and Derlega, V. (1974) *Self Disclosure,* General Learning Press, New Jersey

——— (1976) 'Self-Disclosure' in J. Thibaut, J. Spence and R. Carson (eds), *Contemporary Topics in Social Psychology,* General Learning Press, New Jersey

Chaikin, A., Derlega, V. and Miller, S. (1976) 'Effects of Room Environment on Self-disclosure in a Counseling Analogue', *Journal of Counseling Psychology, 23,* 479–81

Derlega, V. and Chaikin, A. (1975) *Sharing Intimacy: What We Reveal to Others and Why,* Prentice-Hall, Englewood-Cliffs, New Jersey

——— and Grzelak, J. (1979) 'Appropriateness of Self-Disclosure' in G. Chelune (ed.), *Self-Disclosure,* Jossey-Bass, London

Ekman, P. and Friesen, W. (1974) 'Detecting Deception From the Body or Face', *Journal of Personality and Social Psychology, 29,* 288–98

——— Friesen, W. and Scherer, K. (1976) 'Body Movement and Voice Pitch in Deceptive Interaction', *Semiotica, 16,* 23–7

Hargie, O., Saunders, C. and Dickson, D. (1981) *Social Skills in Interpersonal Communication,* Croom Helm, Beckenham

Ivey, A. and Authier, J. (1978) *Microcounseling: Innovations in Interviewing, Counseling, Psychotherapy and Psychoeducation,* C.C. Thomas, Springfield, Illinois

Jourard, S. (1964) *The Transparent Self,* Van Nostrand Reinhold, New York

——— (1971) *Self-Disclosure,* Wiley, New York

Levin, M. (1977) 'Self-Knowledge and the Talking Cure', *Review of Existential Psychology and Psychiatry, 15,* 95–111

Maguire, P. (1984) 'Communication Skills and Patient Care' in A. Steptoe and A. Mathews (eds), *Health Care and Human Behaviour,* Academic Press, London

Newcomb, T. (1961) *The Acquaintance Process,* Holt, Rinehart and Winston, New York

O'Neill, N. and O'Neill G. (1977) 'Relationships' in B. Patton and K. Giffin (eds), *Interpersonal Communication in Action,* Harper and Row, New York

Slobin, D., Miller, S. and Porter, L. (1968) 'Forms of Address and Social Relations in a Business Organization', *Journal of Personality and Social Psychology, 8*, 289–93

Stewart, J. (ed.) (1977) *Bridges Not Walls*, Addison Wesley, Reading, Massachussetts

Taylor, D. (1979) 'Motivational Bases' in G. Chelune (ed.), *Self-Disclosure*, Jossey-Bass, San Francisco

Thibaut, J. and Kelley, H. (1959) *The Social Psychology of Groups*, Wiley, New York

Tubbs, S. and Baird, J. (1976) *The Open Person . . . Self-Disclosure and Personal Growth*, Merrill, Columbus, Ohio

B Self-Dislosure in Therapy

Maryanne Galvin and Allen Ivey

This chapter focuses primarily on the specific skills utilised in teaching professionals the art and science of *self-disclosure*. Other authors in this book address the means by which therapists need to develop areas of effectiveness as helpers. The focus here is multi-faceted; that is, interest lies in the roles of self-disclosure, interpretation, feedback and cognitive reframing in the interview process, pertaining to both client and helper.

So it begins at the beginning or, as Tweedledee said to Alice in *Through the Looking Glass,* 'If it were so, it would be; but as it isn't it ain't. That is logic.'

Truly effective counsellors, it can be suggested, are those who are equipped with more than one method of helping, thus enabling them to reach different clients. Ivey and Matthews (1984) propose the importance of ascertaining both the client's and the therapist's world view in the primary phases of the interview. The major thrust of their work suggests 'not only does the counselor influence the client, but the client also influences the counselor'. The authors' quest to operationalise the skill of self-disclosure will encapsulate the concept of mutual influence as their definition unfolds.

Self-disclosure is based on the constructs of expression of content, expression of feelings and summarisation. Microtraining (Ivey, 1982) defines self-disclosure in terms of four key dimensions: use of the pronoun 'I'; inclusion of an expression of content or expression of feeling statement; the object of the sentence; and the tense of the statement. (See Chapter 19 for information on Microtraining.)

In the 'classic' definition of self-disclosure by a therapist in an interview (Jourard, 1971a), not all professional helpers would use this skill. With the duality of focus on *'world views'* and *'alternative perspectives'* in problem-solving, to which heed is paid in current literature (Ivey and Matthews, 1984; Galvin, 1983), self-disclosure represents much more than the four dimensions above on the part of the helper in all helping sessions.

The key dimensions that will embellish the idea of self-disclosure as the authors see it are: developing alternative perspectives on problems; interpretation and meaning; directives; and feedback.

The Skill of Intepretation

'To sum up, psychological interpretation viewed as a behaviour consists of bringing an ultimate frame of reference, or language system, to bear upon a set of observations or behaviors, with the end in view of making them more amenable to manipulation' (Levy, 1963).

During the initial stages of rapport-building and problem-definition with a client, the counsellor is apt to call upon the client's 'view' of the world for structure of his or her language and response (Ivey and Matthews, 1984). However, in interpretation, the interviewer provides the client with a new, potentially more functional frame of reference. Thus, self-disclosure becomes imminent for therapist and client alike. A compilation of variables about the counsellor's values, philosophy, definition of the problem and subsequent outcome, assessment of the client's resources and vulnerabilities, and reflection of himself as a potential helper all come into being once he has achieved self-disclosure through interpretation.

In the business of meaning–making in the evolution of the client–counsellor relationship, Rogers (1959) describes a basic platform for interpretation and a basic movement in psychotherapy 'from living only to satisfy the expectations of others, and living only in their eyes and in their opinions, toward being a person in his/her own right, with feelings, aims, ideas of his own; from being driven and compelled, he moves toward the making of responsible choices'.

Thus, choices are made on both the client's and therapist's parts regarding how the interview itself evolves. Following the classic definition of interpretation already elucidated, the operationalisation of this specific skill is required in true self-disclosure.

More on Meaning and Interpretation

Eliciting and reflecting meaning helps clients to explore values and beliefs. The importance of elucidating one's own attitudes and views regarding the use of self-disclosure in the interview is stated above. One format for examing attitudes and beliefs before offering them in the context of self-disclosure exists in 'reflecting meaning' in one's statements. Knowledge and skill in reflection of meaning results in:

1. Facilitating clients' and counsellors' interpretation of their own experience. Reflection of feeling and the shell of interpretation are closely related. However, clients can use reflection of meaning to interpret themselves what their experience means;
2. Assisting clients (and counsellors) to explore their values and goals in life;
3. Understanding deeper aspects of client experiences.

For instance, consider the following statement: 'My daughter has just gone off to kindergarten. Now I have plenty of time.' What does this statement mean? The words are clear and explicit, but to different people the same words may have vastly different meanings. For example, client A may mean that she feels guilty and has a need to restructure her life through psychotherapy; client B attaches anger and abandonment to the feelings she's experiencing; therapist C deems it necessary to explore the clients' unfinished statement: 'Time for what?'

The same words may mean different things to different people. The task in this chapter on self-disclosure is to assist both counsellors and clients in identifying the underlying structure of this skill through examination of one's feelings, thoughts and actions.

Before delving into the intricacies of self-disclosure/interpretation one assumes that explicit observable levels of information have been worked with first. Listening, questioning, reinforcing, reflecting and summarising all focused on reacting specifically to what a client says or does. Thus previous authors in this edition pinpoint *basic attending skills* vital to this process. In reflection of feeling, the concept that was introduced promoted exploration of explicit and implicit feelings. One knows cognitively that one's feelings may sometimes be deeper than one's awareness of them. As deep as, and sometimes deeper than, feelings are meanings, which provide basic organising constructs for a person's life. The skill of noting and reflecting meaning often operates at an implicit level. Interrelationships among specific skills already highlighted is the key at this phase of development. That is, ascertaining an understanding for the following points is important in relating the concepts to one's practice:

1. The four dimensions of 'meaning' are operating simultaneously and constantly in any individual or group. As one operates in 'systems', change in any one part of the system affects the total (Frankl, 1959);

2. As a rough rule, paraphrases speak to thoughts, reflections of feelings to feelings, attending behaviours and client observation to behaviours, and reflection of meaning to meaning. Different helping methods view different areas of the model as most important (see Figure 9.2).

3. In the usage of attending skills, the complex behaviour of the client is broken down into component parts. It is possible that attacking only one dimension will lead to a change in client behaviour which, in turn, affects change in feelings and meanings. A change in any one part of the system may result in a change in other parts as well. Even though, for practical purposes, the client and the counselling interview are broken into component parts, interaction of the parts cannot be escaped.

4. For many clients and counsellors, meaning is the central issue, and it is here that the most profound changes may occur. For other clients, however, change in thoughts (rational–emotive therapy, cognitive behavioural, reality therapy) all work on feelings (Rogerian, encounter therapy). Meaning-oriented therapies include psychoanalysis, logotherapy and certain cognitive-behavioural modalities;

5. A multimodal approach (Lazarus, 1976) may involve using all the skills and concepts in an effort to maximise change and personal growth.

To practice and attain a sense of how meaning may differ among people, consider the concept of the child/parent relationship as the youngster begins school.

Figure 9.2: Examples of Microskill Leads used by Interviewers of Differing Theoretical Orientations

	Microskill lead	Nondirective	Modern Rogerian encounter	Behavioural	Psychodynamic	Gestalt	Trait and factor	Tavistock group	Vocational group (such as life planning)	Business problem-solving	Medical diagnostic interview	Correlational interrogation	Traditional teaching	Student-centred teaching	Eclectic
Attending skills	Open question	○	○	◑	◑	●	●	○	◑	◑	◑	●	◑	●	◑
	Closed question	○	○	●	○	◑	◑	○	◑	◑	◑	●	●	◑	◑
	Encourage	◑	◑	◑	○	◑	◑	◑	◑	◑	◑	◑	○	◑	◑
	Paraphrase	●	●	◑	◑	○	◑	○	◑	◑	◑	◑	○	●	◑
	Reflection of feeling	●	●	○	◑	○	◑	○	○	◑	◑	◑	○	●	◑
	Reflection of meaning	◑	◑	○	◑	○	○	○	◑	◑	◑	◑	○	●	◑
	Summarisation	◑	◑	◑	○	○	◑	○	◑	◑	◑	◑	○	●	◑
Influencing skills	Feedback	○	●	○	○	◑	○	○	○	◑	○	◑	○	○	◑
	Advice/information/ and others	○	○	◑	○	○	●	○	●	◑	◑	◑	●	●	◑
	Self-disclosure	○	●	○	○	○	○	○	◑	◑	○	○	○	◑	◑
	Interpretation	○	○	○	●	●	○	●	◑	◑	◑	◑	○	◑	◑
	Logical consequences	○	○	◑	○	◑	◑	○	◑	◑	◑	●	●	◑	◑
	Directive	○	○	●	○	●	◑	○	◑	◑	◑	●	●	◑	◑
	Influ. summary	○	○	◑	○	○	○	○	●	●	◑	◑	◑	◑	◑
	CONFRONTATION (combined skill)	◑	◑	◑	◑	◑	◑	●	◑	◑	◑	◑	●	◑	◑
Focus	Client	●	●	●	●	●	●	○	◑	◑	◑	●	◑	●	◑
	Counsellor, interviewer	○	◑	○	○	○	○	○	◑	○	○	○	○	◑	◑
	Mutual/group/'We'	○	◑	○	○	○	○	●	◑	○	○	○	○	◑	◑
	Other people	○	○	◑	◑	◑	◑	◑	◑	○	○	◑	○	◑	◑
	Topic or problem	○	○	◑	○	○	●	○	●	●	●	◑	●	●	◑
	Cultural/ environmental context	○	○	◑	○	○	◑	○	◑	◑	○	○	○	◑	◑
	ISSUE OF MEANING (Topics, key words likely to be attended to and reinforced)	Feelings	Relationship	Behaviour problem-solving	Unconscious motivation	Here and now behaviour	Problem-solving	Authority, responsibility	Future plans	Problem-solving	Diagnosis of illness	Information about crime	Information/ facts	Student ideas/ info./facts	Varies
	Amount of interviewer talk-time	Low	Medium	High	Low	High	High	Low	High	High	High	Medium	High	Medium	Varies

Key:
● Frequent use of skill
◑ Common use of skill
○ May use skill occasionally

Source: Ivey and Matthews, 1984

Write below what this transition means to you.

Now compare your personally felt and stated meanings with those of others. How are you similar and how are you different?

In the process of inter-relating self-disclosure and meaning in the interview, one must turn attention to the structures by which one organises our world. The data of the world are processed through one's auditory, visual and kinesthetic senses and organised into meaningful patterns (for example, what does 'the empty nest' mean?) Some of those patterns of organisation come from society and culture, others from parents and close friends, and some are totally unique to the individual. Some suggest that people use a form of inner speech in which they metaphorically talk to themselves and make sense of things. Everyone seems to have some system of meaning, concepts and judgements, but with varying levels of clarity.

Psychotherapy can help individuals clarify underlying meanings. Thoughts and feelings are not usually worked through until they are organised into some meaningful value pattern, which often provides reasons for what happened: 'Separation, I guess, is part of life'; 'Leaving and then coming together creates seeds for growth'; 'I guess rejection is implicit in going away.' These are just three responses, representing organised meaning systems in the client's life or in the therapist's construction of the world that may be facilitated by attending and eventually self-disclosing.

Self-disclosing and reflecting meaning may at times be a difficult skill. Yet, used discreetly and with effectiveness, it can help clients and counsellors to call their values and directions more clearly.

In practice, the skill of reflection of meaning (and hence self-disclosure) looks and sounds like reflection of feeling or paraphrasing. However, it is distinctly different in tone and purpose. You will often find the reflection of meaning following a 'meaning probe' or question (that is, 'What does that mean to you?') or an encouraged focusing on an important single key word ('separation'). The reflection of meaning is structured like the reflection of feeling with the exception that 'you feel' becomes 'you mean'. The reflection of meaning then paraphrases the important ideas of meaning expressed by the client.

The skill is particularly important in cognitive behaviour modification, existential approaches to counselling, and logotherapy. Reference again to Figure 9.2 and careful assessment of your particular approach to interview style with varying clients will provide an index for your abilities with self-disclosure through reflection of meaning. More information dealing specifically with reflection of meaning can be found in Frankl (1959), Lukas (1980), Rogers (1961), Gendlin (1979), Beck (1976), Meichenbaum (1977).

Influencing Skills and the Combination Skill of Confrontation

With the backdrop of the self-disclosure scenario being therapist awareness of one's own values and meanings and interpretations well defined, this chapter continues to expand usage of the skill. In so doing, the influencing skills of feedback, confrontation and summarisation are encompassed to embellish the picture.

Feedback and Self-disclosure

> To see ourselves as others see us,
> To hear how others hear us,
> And to be touched as we touch others:
> These are the goals of effective feedback.

Feedback provides clients with a more precise database on their performance and/or how others may view them. Once a therapist has established rapport (as mentioned earlier) with his clients, feedback about impressions of them is one of the most powerful influencing tools. This type of feedback should probably be reserved until later stages of the interview or until the clinician has had ample experience and practice. Effective feedback may involve self-disclosure. Guidelines exemplified to this point concerning preliminary thoughts on self-disclosure now can be embellished with the following elements:

1. The client receiving the feedback should be in charge. Feedback tends to be most successful if a client solicits it. However, at times the interviewer may need to determine if the client is ready and able to hear accurate feedback. Proportion feedback to the client accordingly. Only give as much as you deem the client can use now;

2. Ideally, feedback should focus on strengths and/or something the client can do something about. Little good is done in telling a client to change the many things that are wrong. Supplying feedback on positive dimensions aids the client in building strengths. In addressing negatives, it is suggested that they be in areas the client can do something to change or adapt to;

3. The more concrete and specific the feedback, the better. Little good is accomplished in offering vague directives in feedback;

4. Remaining nonjudgemental is essential in giving feedback — paired with utilising an accepting vocal tone and body language. Feedback need not be evaluation: 'You did that exercise very well' versus 'I saw you relax and heard your joys as you went through that exercise'. Adhere to the facts and specifics. Facts can be friendly; judgements may or may not be.

5. Most people have many areas worthy of change. However, keeping feedback lean and precise affords opportunities to approach and select one's challenge. Save subsequent bits of information for later. Seek not to overwhelm;

6. Check out the reception of your feedback. 'How do you react to that?';

'Does that sound close?'; 'What does that mean to you?' are three examples that involve the client in feedback and will indicate the accuracy and usefulness of your message.

Reiteration of a basic 1-2-3 pattern is noteworthy. That is: (1) attend to the client; (2) use the influencing skills and perhaps self-disclosure; and (3) check to determine how well the skill is received and how useful it is.

Feedback in systems

Joining the realm of family therapy and system theory, *morphogenesis* (structure changing) is currently appreciated. This concept had been introduced to cybernetics by Maruyama (1963), who described morphogenesis in this way: 'Once a system is kicked in a right direction and with sufficient initial push, the deviation-amplifying mutual positive feedbacks take over the process, and the resulting development will be disproportionately large as compared with the initial kick.'

The need for a concept of morphogenesis was described by Buckley (1967): 'In dealing with the sociocultural system . . . we jump to a new system level and need yet a new term to express not only the structure-maintaining feature, but the strucure-elaborating and changing feature of the inherently unstable system, i.e., a concept of morphogenesis.' (The full description of an epistemology for family therapy is beyond the scope of this chapter, which is primarily clinical and skills-oriented in focus.)

Bateson (1978) notes 'that information is the difference which makes a difference'. In this, he is referring to that use of distinction, within any given set of variables, which makes further and continued transformation of differences possible.

Bateson describes one of the sources for an idea as developing from having two descriptions of the same process or sequence that are differently coded or differently collected. That is, in the sense of providing feedback, the relationship between the two descriptions is a bonus or the news of a difference.

The first step is to recognise that the unit of survival is the message-in-circuit in the *ecosystem*, whether the ecosystem in question be methodologically defined at the biological, the sociocultural, the psychological or at some other level. Unlike energy, information (messages, feedback) can be both created and destroyed, primarily because the very possibility of information depends upon a code that is shared by both sender and receiver. (By 'sender' and 'receiver' is meant the heuristic device that enables one to talk about the message-in-circuit.) In fact, the code as Bateson (1978) points out, is the relationship. Without the reciprocity of the code, the message is received as 'noise'. When the possibility of information is destroyed by the breakdown of the sender–receiver relationship, the ecosystem perishes.

Thus, the 'sender' (therapist) of the therapeutic message (or feedback/self-disclosure) needs to share a code or a relationship with the 'receiver' (family subsystem) of the message, otherwise the message will not get from one component of the ecosystem to the other and the therapeutic ecosystem will perish. But that message within the 'code' needs to contain information that is about a difference that makes a difference, otherwise there will be no change. And change is, after all, the business of therapy.

The Skill of Summarisation

It becomes timely as this chapter on self-disclosure concludes that the skill of summarisation is identified and operationalised. This needs only brief mention. The intentional therapist summarises the interview from his/her point of view. Special attention is often given to what the interviewer has suggested and commented on during the session. An influencing summary integrates the several strands of thought involved in an interviewer's intervention and provides an opportunity to obtain client feedback (for further discussion see Chapter 7).

Self-Disclosure in Past, Present and Future

As stated previously, self-disclosure is based on the constructs of expression of content, expression of feelings and summarisation. It is considered a broadly based skill that is appropriate for advanced helpers, primarily in existential–humanistic schools. Jourard (1971a; 1971b) has been the primary exponent of self-disclosure in the helping interview. His theoretical discussion of the need for and importance of interpersonal openness between helper and helpee is basic to the developing of extensive literature in professional journals. Laing (1967), more recent statements by Rogers (1975) and the clearly stated work on self-disclosure of Carkhuff (1969) are some other important theoretical statements on the value of self-disclosure in the helping session.

The sharing of personal experience in the encounter group is in the tradition of self-disclosure, but group leaders within the encounter group movement vary in their opinions as to the wisdom of leader self-disclosure. The more radical psychiatry movement (for instance, Steiner, 1975) does not give the term self-disclosure important play but does lay stress on the helper and the helpee moving toward a more natural relationship.

The ultimate use of self-disclosure may be found in *re-evaluation counselling* (RC) (Jackins, 1965). Although the RC movement contains a leadership hierarchy, the actual counselling enacted within its framework is done by two clients, each helping the other. The partners face each other, holding hands, and one serves as the helper for one-half hour. A systematic, eclectic set of helping leads are prescribed by RC; the result is extensive catharsis and re-enactment of past personal traumas. At the end of the 30 minute period, the partners switch roles, and the former helper becomes the new helpee. The mutual self-disclosure of RC, coupled with very specific techniques of questioning, directions, and interpretation, can result in powerful and meaningful changes for both participants. Unfortunately, no research data are known to be available on the effectiveness of this increasingly popular method of helping.

Haase, Forsyth, Julius *et al.* (1971) used microtraining as a format to pretrain counsellors before they initiated counselling sessions in a university counselling service. They found client expression of feeling facilitated by such training. Extremely troubled patients or clients begin therapy frequently with difficulties making 'I' statements, expressing emotions and speaking in the present tense. Training the skills of self-disclosure through counsellor modelling is an effective tool.

In summary, it must again be stressed that self-disclosure in the interview — particularly 'here and now' immediate self-disclosure of the helper's personal experience of the helpee — remains a controversial issue in the professional helping field. Clearly, further research on the impact and value of such helping leads is needed. One advantage of the microtraining paradigm is that the relatively vague construct of self-disclosure is made more precise, thus enabling research on alternative types of self-disclosure. For example, Authier and Gustafson (1976) in a study included self-disclosure as one of the skills they researched. They defined self-disclosure as containing the above components and trained raters to code trainee utterances as self-disclosures if they contained these criteria. Unfortunately, a problem in researching the influencing skills is that criterion segments are often relatively brief. Skills such as self-disclosure should not be expected to appear frequently in microsessions evaluating real interviews. This is generally true of all the *influencing skills*. For example, it seems inappropriate for the helper to offer five or six interpretations, directions or self-disclosures in a brief ten-minute segment of the interview. This is especially so as one effective influencing skill lead can sometimes take a helper through an entire interview.

Nevertheless, the study did demonstrate the viability of researching self-disclosure training and its use with clients in a microcounselling paradigm. Perhaps this is possible since although self-disclosure contains many dimensions and types, microtraining allows breaking down self-disclosure so that it can be defined more precisely and the effectiveness of different types of self-disclosure can be studied. Unfortunately, however, most research in self-disclosure simply uses the term without adequate definition. An examination of these pages suggests that practically any helper statement beginning with an 'I' statement could be rated as a self-disclosure. As alluded to, the nature of the self-disclosure can be delineated far more precisely using the several dimensions suggested here, thus making for more meaningful research.

Conclusion

Many things are not what they sound like: a seedless orange is (according to the citrus industry) an orange with five seeds or fewer; there is no lead in a lead pencil; plum pudding contains no plums; minorities, according to the United States Department of Health, Education and Welfare, include only Blacks, American Indians, Orientals and the Hispanic-surnamed. Asked to define a word, most people want to take advantage of St Augustine's ingenious evasion: 'I know what it is when you don't ask me.' Or they sound like Polonius talking about Hamlet (II: 1; pp. 92–4): 'Your noble son is mad. Mad call I it, for, to define true madness, what is't but to be nothing else but mad?'

Clearly, a word's origin or etymology may be found in any good dictionary. It may be interesting and relevant and therefore worth mentioning — but, of course a word's present meaning may be far from its original meaning, or those of its origins. 'Doctor', for instance, is from a medieval Latin word meaning 'teacher'. Although this etymology is relevant if one is talking about the classroom skills of PhDs, it is probably irrelevant if you are talking about the word in its commonest sense today, 'physician'.

Returning to the premises established as this chapter began, self-disclosure is highly entwined with definition. A formal definition is a kind of analysis, in reference to words. It normally takes a term (for instance, 'professor') and places it within a class or family ('a teacher'), and then goes on to differentiate it from other members of the class ('in a college or university'). Such a definition is sometimes called inclusive/exclusive because it includes the word in a relevant category and then excludes other members of that category. Plato is said to have defined 'man' as 'a featherless biped' but a companion pointed out that this definition was not sufficiently exclusive: a plucked chicken also fits the definition. Plato therefore amended it satisfactorily by adding 'with flat toenails'.

Another example: in Hitchcock's *Stagefright*, Marlene Dietrich suggests that 'detectives are merely policemen with smaller feet'. If this definition is inaccurate, it is not so because of its structure.

What use can be made of formal definition? Suppose one wants to define 'shark'. A desk dictionary will give something like this: 'a cartilaginous (as opposed to bony) fish with a body tapered toward each end'. Such a definition puts sharks within the family of a type of fish and then goes on to exclude from this type (which happens also to include rays as well as sharks) other members by calling attention to the distinctive shape of the shark's body. But if one is not writing a strictly formal definition (instead, working within the context of psychotherapy), one may expand it into something like this: 'Although the shark and the ray are closely related, being cartilaginous rather than bony fish, the two could scarcely be more different in appearance. The ray, a floppy pancake-like creature, is grotesque but not terrifying; the shark, its tapering body gliding through the water, is perhaps the most beautiful and at the same time most terrifying sight the sea can offer.' Similarly, difficulties exist in defining precisely what the term self-disclosure actually means in therapy.

In short, in the therapist's definition and subsequent disclosures in psychotherapy, one will probably want to talk not only about sharks as remote objects (like marriage, mortgage, inflation), but about one's sense of them, one's response to them. Good luck fishing the waters of self-disclosure in psychotherapy.

References

Authier, J. and Gustafson, K. (1976) 'The Application of Supervised and Nonsupervised Microcounseling Paradigms in the Training of Registered and Licensed Practical Nurses', *Journal of Consulting and Clinical Psychology, 44,* 704–9

Bateson, G. (1978) 'The Birth of a Matrix or Double Bind and Epistemology', in M. Berger (ed.), *Beyond the Double Bind,* Dutton, New York

Beck, A. (1976) *Cognitive Therapy and Emotional Disorders,* International Universities Press, New York

Buckley, W. (1967) *Sociology and Modern System Theory,* Prentice Hall, Englewood Cliffs, New Jersey

Carkhuff, R. (1969) *Helping and Human Relations,* vol. 2, Holt Rinehart and Winston, New York

Frankl, V. (1959) *Man's Search for Meaning,* Simon and Schuster, New York

Galvin, M. (1983) 'Making Systematic Problem-solving Work with Children', *The School Counselor, 31* (2), 130–6

Gendlin, E. (1979) 'Experimental Psychotherapy' in R. Corsini (ed.) *Current Psychotherapies,* Peacock, Itasca, Illinois

Haase, R., Forsyth, D., Julius, M. *et al.* (1971) 'Client Training Prior to Counseling: An Extension of the Microcounseling Paradigm', *Canadian Counsellor, 5,* 9–15

Ivey, A. (1982) *Intentional Interviewing and Counseling,* Brooks/Cole Co., Monterey, CA

——— and Matthews, W. (1984) 'A Meta-model for Structuring the Clinical Interview', *Journal of Counseling and Development, 63,* 237–43

Jackins, H. (1965) *The Human Side of Human Beings: The Theory of Re-evaluation Counseling,* Rational, Seattle

Jourard, S. (1971a) *Self-Disclosure,* Wiley, New York

——— (1971b) *The Transparent Self,* Van Nostrand, New York

Laing, R. (1967) *The Politics of Experience,* Ballantine, New York

Lazarus, A. (1976) *Multimodal Behavior Therapy,* Springer-Verlag, New York

Levy, L. (1963) *Psychological Interpretation,* Holt, Rinehart and Winston, New York

Lukas, E. (1980) 'Modification of Attitudes', *International Forum for Logotherapy, 3,* 24–5

Maruyama, M. (1963) 'The Second Cybernetics: Deviation, Amplifying Mutual Casual Processes', *American Scientist, 5,* 169–79

Meichenbaum, D. (1977) *Cognitive Behavior Modification,* Plenum, New York

Rogers, C. (1959) *Client-Centered Therapy,* Houghton-Mifflin, Boston

——— (1961) *On Becoming a Person,* Houghton-Mifflin, Boston

——— (1975) 'Empathic: An Unappreciated Way of Being', *The Counselling Psychologist, 5,* 2–10

Steiner, C. (ed.) (1975) *Readings in Radical Psychiatry,* Grove, New York

10 LISTENING

Voncile Smith

A university professor *en route* to a professional meeting awaited a connecting flight in the passenger area at the Atlanta airport. To pass the time she conversed with one of the other passengers. When asked her destination she replied that she was travelling to Orlando, Florida, to attend the sixth annual convention of the International Listening Association.[1]

'Oh,' the other passenger gasped. 'Are you reading my lips now?'

The professor smiled as she answered. The other passenger obviously felt that she was either a teacher of the hearing handicapped or had a hearing problem herself.

'No, the members of the organisation holding the meeting I am attending do not work with people who are deaf or who have hearing problems,' she explained. 'We are concerned with trying to develop a better understanding of others by interpreting more carefully what they say. We do this by trying to learn just what listening is. We are primarily interested in helping people who have normal hearing to communicate more effectively.'

The professor's experience illustrates a common misconception about listening. *Hearing* is a purely physical response to sound waves stimulating the sensory receptors of the ear. Many people mistakenly believe that listening occurs when one hears another speaking. But the reception of sound waves should not be confused with conscious perception. Hearing is generally regarded as a passive activity, while listening requires active participation. Listening is more than the mere reception of sound. Listening is the basis for human interaction. It is deliberate, active behaviour. Some of the reasons why misconceptions about listening may occur are now examined.

The Slow Emergence of Listening as a Teachable Skill

Teachers and writers in the field have divided communication into four categories — reading, writing, speaking and listening. That order of listing is commonly used and is representative of the attitudes many people hold toward the divisions. Listening is usually identified and defined as the fourth communication skill. Unfortunately, its assignment to that fourth place has tended to minimise its importance. Many people view it as a substantially lesser skill than reading and writing, at least in terms of its importance as a subject for specific instructional effort.

Perhaps contemporary society emphasises reading and writing because, historically, they have been subjects schools have been expected to teach. Literacy has been equated to one's ability to use written forms. As students advance through the educational systems, instruction for these forms has, typically, been designed to provide for progressively more difficult learning situations to enhance the students' proficiency in both written composition and in reading. In short, much time and effort has been spent to develop instructional methodologies for reading and writing, and they have been discussed and applied for years. Much of the literature on education has indicated that the primary purpose of the schools is to teach the students reading, writing and 'rithmetic. Society has viewed the teaching of the 'three r's' as the teaching of the educational essentials.

In the process of simplifying scholastic expectations in this way, any consideration of speaking and listening as parts of the subject matter has usually been ignored. However, speech has had some legitimacy from the time of Aristotle to the present, and at many institutions speaking has been accorded some consideration as a skill worthy of instructional effort. Despite the widely held belief that as a part of the human developmental process, 'everyone learns to speak', most people recognise that one's speech skill can be enhanced through appropriate training.

The recognition of the value of specialised instruction in listening is another matter. Listening is perhaps the least developed of one's comprehensive skills. In the past, few teachers or educational institutions have paid heed to instructional techniques for listening, and until recently little has been published about its characteristics. Teachers and researchers have made slight effort to investigate it in depth. Within the last five or six years, however, scholars and educators have begun to take a new look at listening. The number of books and articles on the subject has increased remarkably, and people are beginning to ask what they can do to improve performance in this most used of communication skills.

Yes, *most used*. Each person typically spends 70–80 per cent of his waking hours in verbal communication activities. Of this, nearly half, or 45 per cent or more, is spent listening. People speak only about 30 per cent of the time; read 16 per cent of the time; and write only about 9 per cent of the time.

Objectives of the Listening Chapter

If one asks oneself, 'How do we use listening?', most people would answer immediately, 'Why, to learn about things' or 'To get information'. Certainly, listening is important for acquiring information vital to education and to the development of general knowledge. However, on the surface one might not immediately identify the importance of listening as a creative activity essential to establishing relationships with others, to establishing within everyone a sense of self, or to simply enhancing pleasure through awareness about the surrounding world.

All these uses go beyond merely 'getting information'. They imply a commitment to giving of oneself and to recognising one's feelings that make behaviour regarding what is available more uniquely human than the simple 'receptor' impression that the collection of information suggests.

The purposes in the discussion which follows are:

1. To develop a general definition of listening;
2. To identify factors affecting the listening environment;
3. To describe techniques one may employ to enhance skill in listening;
4. To identify possible difficulties;
5. To examine current trends in the study and research of listening.

Representative Definitions

The development of a definition for listening has been a problem. In proposing definitions, writers and researchers have generally agreed about the need to separate the complex process of listening from the simpler physiological process of 'hearing', but there has been little agreement on whether listening itself involves (1) selected auditory stimuli of any type; (2) only spoken language, (3) spoken language and other selected cues, or (4) 'ideas'. The following are some representative definitions that have been proposed under each of these four divisions. They are listed chronologically under each division to illustrate the consistent views that have been maintained for so many years.

Selected Auditory Stimuli

All the following definitions in some way emphasise aural stimulation. Accordingly, listening is:

1. '. . . a selective process by which sounds communicated by some source are received, critically interpreted, and acted upon by a purposeful listener' (Jones, 1956); '
2. '. . . the active process involved in attaching meaning to sounds' (Spearitt, 1962);
3. '. . . the selective process of attending, hearing, understanding and remembering aural symbols' (Barker, 1971);
4. '. . . a process that takes place when a human organism receives data aurally' (Weaver, 1972);
5. '. . . the process whereby the human ear receives sound stimuli from other people and through a series of steps interprets the sound stimuli in the brain and remembers it' (Hirsch, 1979);
6. '. . . the act of selectively discriminating among the available aural inputs within any given environment' (Colburn and Weinburg, 1981);
7. '. . . the process of receiving, attending to, and assigning meaning to aural stimuli' (Wolvin and Coakley, 1982).

Spoken Language

Other writers emphasise the use of oral verbal symbols. For them listening is:

1. '. . . the ability to understand spoken language' (Rankin, 1926);
2. '. . . the ability to understand and respond effectively to oral communication' (Johnson, 1951);
3. '. . . the act of giving attention to the spoken word, not only in hearing symbols, but in the reacting with understanding' (Hampleman, 1958);
4. '. . . the composite process by which oral language communicated by some source is received, critically and purposefully attended to, recognized, and interpreted (or comprehended) in terms of past experiences and future expectancies' (Petrie, 1971);
5. '. . . the process by which spoken language is converted to meaning in the mind' (Lundsteen, 1971);
6. '. . . hearing, attending to, understanding, evaluating, and responding to spoken messages' (Floyd, 1985).

Spoken Language and Other Cues

Other writers feel, however, that listening involves not only verbal but other environmental cues. For them listening is:

1. '. . . the aural assimilation of spoken symbols in a face-to-face speaker–audience situation, with both oral and visual cues present' (Brown and Carlsen, 1955);
2. '. . . the perceptual process by which verbal and nonverbal communication (including mechanical sounds) from some source or sources are selectively received, recognized, and interpreted by a receiver or receivers in relation to the perceptual fields of the parties to the process' (Anderson, Nichols and Booth, 1974);
3. '. . . attention to both verbal and nonverbal speech stimuli' (McBurney and Wrage, 1975);
4. '. . . a unitary receptive communication process of hearing and selecting, assimilating and organizing, and retaining and covertly responding to aural and nonverbal stimuli' (Wolff, Marsnik, Tacey, *et al.*, 1983).

'Ideas'

For some writers, the concepts that the listener derives and may store and act upon after exposing himself to information or to an empathic relationship constitutes the basis for a definition. From their view, listening is:

1. '. . . an analysis of the impressions resulting from concentration where an effort of will is required' (Tucker, 1925);

2. '. . . the total process of receiving, interpreting, analyzing and retaining data' (Zimmerman, 1979);

3. '. . . getting inside the other person and seeing things from his or her point of view' (Montgomery, 1981);

4. '. . . the whole interpretative process whereby you make sense out of communicative stimuli' (Ehninger, Gronbeck, McKerrow *et al.*, 1982);

5. '. . . absorbing ideas in the mind, where they can be stored, interpreted, recalled, and acted upon' (Cohen, 1983).

All the definitions listed under this subheading are very general and include the type of stimuli — visual, tactile, olfactory, or other — that the 'listener' might select.

A Competency Based Definition

The Speech Communication Association (SCA) at its annual meeting in 1984 adopted for the first time a definition of listening competency. The definition stresses the concept of comprehending and assimilating ideas through the use of spoken language. Although the emphasis is on speech, nonverbal messages are mentioned within the essential skills of one of the sub-competencies.

To the Speech Communication Association: listening is the process of receiving and assimilating ideas and information from verbal messages. Effective listening includes both literal and critical comprehension of ideas and information transmitted in oral language.

The SCA adoption includes two 'sub-competencies' and the essential skills one should be expected to demonstrate for each:

1. Sub-competency A: The effective listener comprehends *literally* the ideas and information transmitted by oral language. The listener should have the following essential skills:
(a) Recognise main ideas;
(b) Identify supporting details;
(c) Recognise explicit relationships among ideas;
(d) Recall basic ideas and details.

2. Sub-competency B: The effective listener comprehends *critically* ideas and information transmitted by oral language. The listener should have the following essential skills:
(a) Attend with an open mind;
(b) Perceive the speaker's purpose and organisation of ideas and information;
(c) Discriminate between statements of fact and statements of opinion;
(d) Distinguish between emotional and logical arguments;
(e) Detect bias and prejudice;
(f) Recognise the speaker's attitude;
(g) Synthesise and evaluate by drawing logical inferences and conclusions;
(h) Recall the implications and arguments;

(i) Recognise discrepancies between the speaker's verbal/nonverbal messages;
(j) Employ *active* listening techniques when appropriate.

The membership of SCA is comprised primarily of educators and the orientation of these definitions reflects their concern about defining listening from the point of view of teaching and assessment. They have also been concerned about developing a generalised definition which can be applied to various types of communication situations.

Defining Listening as an Active Process

All of the definitions listed above suggest the importance of understanding or interpretation. This emphasis contrasts with a common view held by many people who think of listening as a passive process in which the listener is a receiver or a mere receptacle who blandly stands by waiting for some message to float through the air and impinge upon the sensory mechanisms of the ear and the mind.

This view tends to place a heavy burden of responsibility upon the source by suggesting that the speaker is the one who controls or determines the communication. It tends to accord the listener no more than a minor role. But as noted at the beginning of this chapter, listening is more than a simple process of hearing. Listening is an *active* process that each person chooses to make happen. Certain occurrences around individuals are selected upon which to focus attention, then process and use, and perhaps retain and integrate with whatever other information has been previously chosen to store in the memory (see Chapter 2).

Research indicates many people are poor listeners. Although virtually everyone listens, only a few do it well. Skill in listening is not a 'natural ability', but one that everyone must work to develop. Active listening demands concentration. The listener searches for meaning and understanding. It requires energy and effort and is thus potentially tiring because it can be hard work.

For the purposes here, the information that the person acquires through listening is not limited to oral language — words, phrases and sentences. It includes all sounds produced by the communication participants that the individual will interpret or assign meaning. In addition to verbal forms, those sounds that are intentional as well as those that are unintentional are included — moans, groans, cries, sighs and music, because the listener interprets and evaluates all of these and acts accordingly. It must be kept in mind that people base their interpretations on various non-auditory factors, too — the appearances and mannerisms of the other participants, the context and the situation and their individual expectations. This is a rather complex definition, but listening is a complex process and all these factors should be taken into account in attempting to determine what it encompasses.

The Listening Environment

What happens when one listens? The physical process called hearing has already been mentioned, during which sound waves strike the structures within the ears and cause a physiological reaction. The sound waves are physical phenomena within the environment that surrounds everyone, and they compete with one another and with other stimuli for one's attention. Everyone chooses certain of these various noises or happenings around him to focus attention upon. These choices are sometimes known as 'selective attention', because there are so many potential stimuli available at any time that one cannot possibly act upon *all* of them. Meaning is assigned to this chosen information, or 'selectively perceived' or interpreted, based upon associations one may relate to it and the contexts in which the information occurs. The interpretation and subsequent evaluation of it is acted upon. A portion of action will be to determine what to retain in one's mental storehouse, and what to disregard and thus discard.

Why People Listen

Listening is used in multiple ways, usually employing a number of purposes at the same time. The following are not meant to imply that one listens exclusively at any one time with only one purpose in mind. As social beings, humans derive a sense of participation with others or acknowledgement of themselves whether they are seeking information or an aesthetic appreciation. The acquisition of information in some form permeates each situation. In short, purposes are frequently interwoven when listening occurs. Only the needs generated within a particular context determine which may be paramount.

To Acquire Information. Complex modern societies demand that one understands and retains a tremendous amount of information. In the business and professional world, the ability to understand the spoken word is essential to success. This is important in virtually every job. An employee must be able to understand the instructions and advice of superiors and colleagues; a supervisor must be able to listen for the needs and reactions of subordinates; and each professional must be able to discover the concerns of clients and other members of the public. All need more information about people. Listening helps reduce pressure in dealing with people, since many problems are the result, in part, of someone's failure to listen.

Improved skill in listening can provide one with more and better information on which to base decisions. People must also depend upon being able to gather information through listening to function effectively in their personal lives. The ability to move around; to acquire goods and services; to maintain one's home, automobile, and other effects; and to otherwise care for oneself and for those for whom one may be responsible all require listening skill. A person also acquires a better informational background for speaking and writing.

Each person's social life is dependent upon the ability to acquire and remember information about others with whom he wishes to establish and continue to maintain relationships.

To Empathise. In addition to acquiring information about other people, the individual needs to understand and 'feel' with the emotions and thoughts of the other. The ability to empathise is an important element in effective communication for many social roles. Empathy affects every listening situation whether one is a business supervisor, a teacher, a member of a health care team, a counsellor or a friend. Listening empathically is a valuable way to help someone with a problem.

Two of the more obvious values to the listener are the pleasure to be derived from having helped solve another person's problem, and the insight one gains for dealing with issues in his own life. The listener can broaden his understanding by learning from the other person's experiences what to think and what to do under similar circumstances.

Rogers and Farson (1973) note the risks taken by one who practises active listening in order to empathise with the speaker. In achieving understanding of a situation from the speaker's point of view, one risks being changed by the experience to coming to see within oneself the world as that other person does. One will sense deeply the feelings of someone else so that one understands the meaning that person's experiences have for him. When one achieves this, one risks a shift in thinking to the terms of another. One may come to see the world as this person sees it; to find it threatening to set aside, even for a short time, one's own beliefs to try to interpret and evaluate from another's viewpoint. The willingness to do this requires a strong sense of one's self. It requires confidence in one's own feelings and values.

For example, if you are a manager, are you willing to attempt to take the point of view of one of your employees? Are you willing to examine yourself as the employee sees you? Can you set aside your tendency to listen to and examine only that which you would ordinarily select, and risk looking at the world (and yourself) from that other's frame of reference? You may hear hostile or negative comments about yourself. It is not easy to maintain the strength to listen to such attacks without deciding that you must defend yourself or retaliate in some way. If you are able to undertake risks such as this, you are capable of truly empathic listening, and you gain a better view of yourself and the way you affect others.

To Discriminate. Discriminative listening enables one to select from among the many auditory stimuli around. It is the basis for selective attention and perception. It is the means by which one learns very early in one's life to identify the differences in the voices and mannerisms of the important others who care for and share with us. It enables the particular sounds of the language of one's social group to be distinguished and subsequently to develop within oneself the ability to match the sounds so that one can use them symbolically.

Discriminative listening enables one to determine whether someone's voice is happy, angry, sad, annoyed, indifferent, bored, tired, excited, soft or loud. Through it, one defines the sense or nonsense of vocalisations, whether they are speech, coos or screams. One identifies the noises around — a bird chirping, a dog barking, a tyre leaking air, a car arriving or leaving, a visitor knocking or a thunderstorm approaching. Throughout one's lifetime, one adds to the store of sounds that can be identified and used.

To Evaluate. The evaluative listener is able to listen to the speaker's words and to understand the ideas without necessarily accepting them totally. He will accept or reject a message on the basis of valid criteria. Every day one encounters those who want to persuade a change in one's behaviour. Sales people urge others to buy their products. Political candidates urge people to vote for them or their programmes. Religious leaders urge others to attend their churches, accept their faith or support their causes. Friends or family urge their kin to redecorate their houses, take a holiday or go on a diet. Some speakers will be concerned about one's welfare and seek to change one because they honestly believe there will be a benefit. Others are concerned with their own gain and may adopt whatever tactic they think will prompt others to yield to their suggestions.

Listening skill in critical evaluation must be developed to maintain control over oneself rather than allowing someone else to have control. The evaluative listener can weigh alternatives and choose an appropriate course of action. He can help individuals and societies understand themselves and recognise the accuracy or inaccuracy of their ideas. He is able to observe a society to note its obsessions, fears, strengths and weaknesses.

To Be Acknowledged. Everyone has a basic human need to be recognised and acknowledged by others. Listening is one of the most fundamental means by which this is achieved. When someone engages in the act of listening, having chosen to listen to a particular person, that person's existence is affirmed, as is his importance as a speaker. By nonverbal actions alone, the listener tells that person he has importance in the listener's frame of reference. The degree to which this occurs will vary, of course, based upon the situation and the role the speaker fills at a particular time in that other person's life. For example, one would not expect more than a few minutes' exchange with an acquaintance one happened to encounter while out shopping, but a friend might spend hours listening to one talk over a personal problem. Although this second situation also requires empathic listening, both occurrences serve as recognition and acknowledgement of the person as a member of human society.

Another result of acknowledging the speaker will be that there will be better speakers to listen to: if one listens better, most speakers may be stimulated to speak more effectively.

To Appreciate. Maslow (1970) defined one of the human needs that form the basis of one's motivations as an aesthetic need. He felt that to have a happy, healthy life, an individual must seek and experience, in addition to other things, beauty, order and symmetry. This need can be met in part through some of one's opportunities to listen appreciatively. One experiences appreciative listening for pleasure. It can enable one to enjoy and realise value and excellence in a multitude of situations. One may attend planned performances with gatherings of other people to listen to speakers, plays, cinematic productions and concerts; one may play recordings, radios or the television; converse with friends or family members, talk with children or listen to them at play; or listen to the sounds of nature on a walk through the woods or along the seashore. Each of these has the potential to enrich one's life by enlarging one's experiences.

To Derive Other Benefits. Other types of benefits derived from improved listening skill include the better use of time. In conversing or giving instructions, a speaker will not need to repeat so often, and both speaker and listener will benefit. Meetings in which one participates can do more than simply take up time. Their proceedings can become shorter, more productive and more satisfying.

Listening skill can also facilitate the development of self-control, which becomes easier because of improved communication. As one's interactions become more pleasant because of fewer misunderstandings, one feels less frustration. This can lead to smoother operation of one's home, business and other relationships.

Developing Skill as a Listener

The listening patterns most people have established can be improved. Memory and the knowledge available to relate to the listening situation are important. One should also be aware of the types of actions the effective listener performs.

Memory and Knowledge

Most people recognise that skill in listening requires that certain other types of information and skill at their command can be combined with the listening techniques. One begins to build breadth or proficiency in these very early in one's life and continues to develop them as one grows older. Memory is a skill that relates directly to quality in listening performance. One's knowledge of certain specific subjects, such as paralanguage and dialectal differences, is also a factor.

Memory. To be able to recall what one has listened to requires that one processes information effectively. Memory refers to the storage of data for anything from a few seconds to an indefinite period, perhaps a lifetime. In listening, processing requires that one organises what the speaker says in such a way that one can relate it to other information previously stored, and recall it when one wants it. Among the procedures one can use to aid memory are: (1) organising material into categories; (2) noting sequencing; (3) using mnemonic devices; and (4) visualisation.

1. For organising material into categories, the listener groups information according to the main ideas and their supporting details. This requires ranking the material into a mental outline so that the relationships become apparent. Nichols and Stevens (1957) noted a speech rate-thought rate differential which they advised using to advantage to categorise material. The average speaker utters about 125 to 140 words per minute, but the brain is capable of comprehending words and thoughts much more rapidly — it is not known just how much so, but to say that it is five to ten times faster is probably a conservative estimate.

One can learn to use this thinking time efficiently while the speaker is talking. This requires that one anticipates what the speaker will say, weighs the evidence to determine its value for supporting the speaker's points, periodically reviews what the speaker has said so far, and listens for the 'unspoken' meaning that may not necessarily be in the words.

2. Noting the sequence of items is another aid to memory. A listener may arrange material according to space, time, position or some similar relationship. One often finds the sequences the speaker provides useful too. Commonly used sequences include addresses, telephone numbers, scheduled events, directions, grocery lists and other similar data.

3. Mnemonic devices, sometimes called memory aids, use association techniques. Remembering names may be easier if the listener can relate the name to some characteristics of its owner. For purposes of illustration, consider a fictional young dancer named Tom Streeter, who walks very erect with wonderful posture, a light step and his head lifted. A listener might think, 'Streeter walks straighter', to remember Tom's name.

Creating little rhymes also may be used to recall names — 'Susan Wise has big blue eyes.'

Acronyms represent another type of memory aid commonly used in listening — NATO (North Atlantic Treaty Organization); MADD (Mothers Against Drunk Driving).

4. Visualisation is a technique one uses to translate the speaker's words into some type of sensory impression. Besides relating an impression to sight where one actually creates a mental 'picture' of what the words describe, one may 'visualise' through association with any of the other senses. Sometimes, through listening, one 'tastes' in one's mind the tangy lemon custard the nextdoor neighbour talks about baking, or 'smells' the pungent odours of an Indian restaurant when a friend describes her evening meal of the night before. Creating such mental images of what we hear helps us to recall sometime later what the speaker has said.

Knowledge. Knowledge can give insight into cultural and individual differences among the people encountered in one's highly mobile world. Understanding about others is the key to effective relationships. One can always add to one's store of knowledge and, indeed, the curious, conscientious person will be involved in a lifelong quest to do just that. Two categories about which one should seek additional information which relate to sound and thus to listening, are paralanguage and dialects.

1. Paralanguage pertains to vocal characteristics — rhythm, rate, pitch, volume and intonation — and to nonverbal vocalisation such as 'uh'. These nonverbal vocal cues may carry messages quite apart from the words they accompany. They may reinforce or contradict a verbal message. Mehrabian (1971) noted that if a contradiction occurs between verbal and nonverbal communication, one tends to be more influenced by the nonverbal aspects. Awareness of vocal cues and how one interprets them is important for the listener. The ability to distinguish both obvious and subtle differences in paralanguage will affect one's ability to understand the messages of others.

2. Dialect differences may be paralinguistic. Such cues as rate, intonation and even pitch and volume may be tied to regional patterns, but dialects also use varying verbal forms. Sound and word choice, arrangement, and semantic factors often distinguish dialects between geographic regions that are close in proximity. These differences often make it necessary for a listener to readjust her thinking when she anticipates one word and then hears the speaker use a different one. On other occasions, she will have to refer back to reinterpret a word misheard or misinterpreted because the context following it clarifies the meaning. Sometimes, however, the content will suggest to the listener words and ideas the speaker does not state. The listener should attend to the ideas being expressed, but for the sake of accuracy, she must still interpret the words actually being used.

One difficulty speakers encounter is the tendency of some listeners to stereotype a person whose dialect differs from their own. Rather than focusing on the ideas of the speaker, and extending their efforts to facilitate understanding, these listeners tend to let their misconceptions about the social or educational level they associate with the dialect affect their perceptions of the speaker and his message. Becoming aware of regional dialect differences and the general characteristics of pronunciation can help one develop an appreciation of the richness of language variations. It should help reduce the frequency with which one misunderstands words others pronounce differently from one's own pronunciations.

Listening Actions

Being Receptive. Anyone who wishes to improve skill in listening must be willing to expend the time and effort to permit others to express their feelings and ideas. To do this, one must be willing to give something of oneself. This requires that the person must, first of all, *be receptive*. Receptiveness is a deliberate action, consciously performed with the intention of relating in some way to the other.

A receptive person enhances the self-image of others by creating a climate that is supportive, not one that is defensive. The listener seeks to help the speaker convey meaning. For example, one may read another's need and provide encouragement by such comments as 'Perhaps you'd like to talk?'; 'Something seems to be troubling you'; or 'Tell me about it.' One's nonverbal actions may also help. Often, by looking into the face of the person who is talking to him, one may find it easier to attend to what the words say as they issue forth, than if one permits one's eyes to wander within the environment to other cues that may tend to distract.

As the person talks, he can be encouraged to continue if the listener acknowledges him verbally. Frequent comments such as 'I see', 'Yes', 'Really', 'That's interesting', and 'Hmm' may add to one's receptiveness. If one feels that something has been missed or misunderstood, he should ask the speaker to repeat it. To try to reinforce for the speaker that one has been listening, he should choose carefully the phrasing of the request. One can indicate, perhaps by paraphrasing a portion of the speech that one listened to, that one has understood. One can then indicate that he has missed another portion: this may help encourage the speaker, too, since the listener is indicating his interest in developing a mutual understanding.

If one is listening to someone who is presenting material that is too complicated to understand, the speaker should be told. Perhaps he or she will provide additional information or examples to help the listener gain a clearer insight into the meaning. If, however, the material is too simple or too basic, one may want to encourage the speaker to provide more depth. In effect, both these suggestions encourage one to try to communicate one's level to a speaker so that one can derive more from the interaction.

Paying Attention. To become a good listener requires that a conscious effort is made to pay attention. To do this, one should exhibit active signs of attentiveness: attention is tied to one's ability to concentrate and requires that one directs physical and mental energies toward listening. One should seek to avoid disrupting concentration. Remember that oral communication is not repeatable: if one lets attention wander, one has no way to replay the missed episode. Even if one asks a speaker to repeat what he has said, his movements, paralinguistic and other nonverbal cues, and the situational conditions tied to the verbal information, cannot be duplicated. Attempts at repetition become original messages themselves. The communicants should recognise that this is irretrievable loss because a person's words, even if repeated in full, will fail to produce the same affect as the original. The result may be new insight, but it may just as likely be tension, irritation or boredom.

One should avoid interrupting the other person when possible. One can demonstrate interest, alertness and caring through one's nonverbal behaviours.

Using Silence. Sometimes one can communicate interest and concern through silence accompanied by appropriate nonverbal behaviour. Nodding, eye contact and erect posture can contribute to the other's feeling that the listener cares. One may encourage the other person to speak simply by remaining silent, which helps to assure the speaker that one is waiting, interested and concerned about what may be said.

Seeking Agreement. One should seek areas of agreement by recognising values or experiences shared with a speaker. One should search to find the broader meaning rather than focusing on specific words. One may miss the intent if one listens to small, isolated facts rather than trying to determine the main ideas or the general purpose of a speaker. Some people jump from fact to fact rather than trying to connect them with major points to develop an integrated whole. If one does not exercise care, one may react to a word or phrase in an unusual manner. One may find a particular concept distasteful or inappropriate or may not understand the meaning of a term. This may result from the lack of familiarity with a regional pronunciation or the speaker's use of an unfamiliar word.

Avoiding Ambiguity. One's actions as a listener should be clear and unambiguous so that one does not mislead the other participant. One should be willing to ask questions when one does not understand something. One should withhold evaluation until confident that a speaker has finished and one is sure that one has understood what he intended. To do this, one should: (1) direct one's attention to the main ideas the speaker is presenting; (2) keep in mind the arbitrary nature of words and other symbols; and (3) focus on the intent as well as the content. One must endeavour to keep an open mind in order to evaluate what is said rather than what is 'wanted' or 'expected'.

Removing Distractions. When someone talks to another person, that person should attempt to remove any distractions so that he can provide his full interest to the speaker. The conscious removal or the ignoring of various types of distractions is important. The problems resulting from focusing on isolated facts and unfamiliar or variant words and phrases have been mentioned previously. Sometimes, listeners take what amount to 'mental holidays' while another is speaking to them. These might be classified as daydreaming, formulating counterarguments, reminiscing or planning for the future. However they are labelled, they distract from what the speaker is saying and tend to interfere with the potential for full interpretation of whatever is going on.

If one plans to discuss a topic over lunch or dinner with a client or associates, it is better to wait until after the waiter has taken the order to move into the topic, or until after the meal is served so that there will not be any interruptions. Many organisations that hold dinner meetings have long recognised the importance of waiting until members have finished eating before conducting their business. The programme approach to scheduling an 'after-dinner' speaker also reflects cognisance of the importance of a relatively distraction-free time for optimal listening.

In other situations such as being in the office when a colleague or other employee enters to talk, it is best to move from behind one's desk so that one is not tempted to rearrange its contents or to continue working. The speaker may feel that one's attention is divided between the conversation and concern with whatever one has on the desk. If one moves out, one may also be enhancing the openness of the situation nonverbally, since a desk may provide a psychological and a physical barrier between communicants.

One should listen for the major ideas of the speaker, but one should also try to understand the emotional state which may be underlying them to help assess how those emotions may be affecting the ideas. If a friend asks one to join him for a game of tennis, is it for the exercise, the challenge of the game or primarily to prevent loneliness? If a person one supervises requests a meeting, is it to express discontent, to share an idea or to affirm self?

The listener who is truly concerned about providing full attention to the efforts of the speaker will also seek to overcome being distracted by physical stimuli such as sounds, sights and smells which may constitute a part of the immediate environment. Generally, in deference to the speaker, one should attempt to disregard such things as the buzz from fluorescent lights; a lisp or other speech articulation variation of the speaker; noise from nearby machinery such as fans, air-conditioning units or other building or lawn equipment; bright lights; unusual clothing styles or colours; the aroma of food being cooked; medicinal odours; or whatever else is irrelevant to the speaker's ideas.

Being Patient. Sometimes it is vital for one to demonstrate patience. Listening probably requires more patience than perhaps any other human activity. In interpersonal situations, one sometimes has things one wants to say or to contribute to a discussion or a conversation, but other participants also have comments they wish to make or to continue. Patience requires that one lets people finish what they have to say. One must not become so engrossed with what he himself has to say that he ignores the responsibility to listen to others. The others may be more willing to listen, if one has listened to them. If a person has had an opportunity to complete a comment, he will find it easier to relax and listen attentively. Patience can aid understanding and may help prevent what began as a friendly conversation from turning into an argument.

Delaying Evaluation. Evaluation is an important part of listening but one should delay until one is sure one understands the other person's position. A speaker should be allowed to finish, and then, whenever possible, the remarks should be paraphrased by means of statements such as, 'Let me see if I can put into my own words what I think you said,' or 'Are you saying . . .?' One can ask questions to clarify meaning, but should avoid commenting evaluatively on the speaker's ideas. One should try to derive as fully as possible what the speaker has to offer by keeping the speaker's meaning clear of the listener's influence. This does not mean that one cannot offer evaluation, but one should do so after the speaker has fully presented his ideas so that the evaluation will not distort them.

Although the primary concern in this discussion is the role of the listener in the direct interpersonal relationship, other communication settings sometimes place responsibilities upon the listener that are extensions of the interpersonal situation. If one is listening to a public speaker, one should permit the speaker to develop completely his theme before evaluating his effort. Of course, this should be one's practice for a direct interpersonal situation, too, Whatever the setting, a good listener should 'hear the speaker out' before making judgements.

One should mentally review what the speaker has said to try to rephrase the main theme in one's own words. Can the speaker's reasons for the main theme be identified? Can the principal bits of evidence the speaker presented to establish his point be recalled? Is the evidence consistent, relative, valid, timely? One should establish that one knows what the speaker is talking about, and then evaluate what he or she said in light of one's own knowledge.

The improvement of listening requires capacity, willingness and effort. Each person must work to eliminate faulty habits. One must constantly make personal evaluations of one's own strengths and weaknesses and look for competencies that can be added or strengthened.

Listening Difficulties

Sometimes people indicate they have listened when their behaviour in relation to what the speaker has said suggests otherwise. They may act in a manner that inhibits their understanding. For example, several types of behaviours people create in situations in which they may describe themselves as listeners involve: (1) not actually listening at all but only pretending to; (2) practising a type of partial listening where the listener consciously determines that he will attend to only certain portions of the speaker's remarks; and (3) viewing oneself as the centre of any exchange or activity.

Pretend Listeners

To someone observing them, good pretenders appear to be attentive. They have learned to establish eye contact and to nod, smile or frown at the appropriate times. Occasionally, they even answer, but their thoughts and attention are not directed toward the speaker. Pretenders practise inattention because:

1. They are preoccupied with something that is more important to them than what the speaker is saying;
2. They think they have heard previously what the speaker is saying;
3. They are bored;
4. They feel the topic is difficult to understand;
5. They feel the topic is irrelevant;
6. They feel the topic is inconsistent with their beliefs.

Limiting Listeners

People who are 'limiting listeners' engage in a type of self-indulgent listening behaviour in which they do some actual listening, but they choose to perceive only part of what the speaker has to say. They practise giving limited attention because:

1. Only parts of what the speaker is saying interest them, and they seek those parts;
2. They choose to interpret what the speaker intends as innocent remarks as personal attacks and to become defensive toward the speaker because of their own personal insecurities;
3. They take an offensive position by collecting information to attack the speaker later in hopes of inciting him to behave defensively;
4. They practise insensitivity to subtle cues that may alter the meanings of the words the speaker chooses by actually failing to acknowledge part of the situational elements that contribute to the meaning.

Self-centred Listeners

Self-centred listeners are concerned only with themselves and pay little or no attention to others. They may dismiss anything anyone else has to say as irrelevant and view their own remarks as the only ones with merit. When they appear to be listening, self-centred listeners seek speakers who echo or reinforce their own views because:

1. They find it comforting to listen to others say things they believe in, and the stronger these beliefs the more comforting it is to hear them said;
2. They find it unpleasant to hear others speak favourably about concepts, viewpoints and other people about whom they have strong negative feelings.

Assessing Listener Competence

The publicly financed educational systems in a number of states in the United States have attempted to establish some means for assessing listener competence. To try to provide reliable data the developers of most assessment instruments have used standard passages which the examiner presents to the examinee by playing an audio or video cassette recording followed by the administration of some type of paper and pencil test. The acceptance of the use of such assessment procedures has been mixed. Nevertheless, researchers in both education and industry continue to develop new instruments based upon this format.

In 1972 Clark discussed the reviews to date of the Brown-Carlsen listening comprehension test and the STEP listening tests published by the Educational Testing Service in 1956.

Taylor (1984) has reviewed several of the tests — the Dow listening test which was developed in the 1950s, the Brown-Carlsen listening comprehension test which was also developed in the 1950s, and the communication competency assessment instrument (CCAI) that has recently been developed under the auspices of the Speech Communication Association (1982). He has also included a brief description of the Sperry Corporation's *Your Personal Listening Profile* which is a self-perception instrument intended to improve the listening performance of Sperry employees. Rubin (1982) developed the CCAI which assesses both speaking and listening skills without requiring paper and pencil responses. Bostrom (1983) has compiled extensive normative data on the Kentucky comprehensive listening test, and Watson and Barker (1984) have quantitative studies underway on the Watson-Barker listening test.

Generally, the major criticisms of such tests have centred on the administration costs, the quality of their normative data, the difficulty of finding and training qualified evaluators and the question of whether such tests measure listening or the same things measured by tests of thinking, memory, inference, intelligence or by other written tests.

Another difficulty with the currently published tests is that of correlation. They all purport to measure 'listening', but the different tests are divided into subsections that have made correlation of results difficult and sometimes questionable.

A Look Ahead

With the expanding interest in research into listening mentioned at the beginning of this chapter, one would hope that better descriptions of the listening process and better means of assessing it will be forthcoming in the near future. The data now available demonstrate that listening ability, however one defines it, can be improved substantially when specific instruction is undertaken. There is much, too, that a motivated individual can do to become aware of his or her current skills and what needs to be improved. One who persists in increasing personal sensitivity and concern for others will accord them the courtesy of understanding through listening.

Summary

The recognition of the value of defining listening as a skill which can be taught and improved has developed slowly but has received increased focus recently. Listening researchers have disagreed about what listening encompasses. Some feel it involves the perception of any sounds; others feel it includes only speech sounds; some feel it is the perception of speech coupled with other stimuli; and still others emphasise the perceptual processing of data. This chapter defines listening as an active process that involves all sounds the communication participants produce, intentional or unintentional, that they perceive and which may be influenced by various nonauditory factors associated with the context.

Some major reasons people listen are to acquire information, to empathise, to discriminate, to evaluate, to be acknowledged and to appreciate. Other benefits from listening may include better use of time and improved self-control.

The person who wishes to become an effective listener should be concerned about improving memory and general knowledge. Specific knowledge about paralanguage and dialect can help increase the listener's understanding of others.

Actions the effective listener can develop include: being receptive; paying attention; using silence; seeking agreement; avoiding ambiguity; removing distractions; being patient; delaying evaluation.

Some people behave in ways which interfere with effective listening. They only pretend to listen, attend to a limited portion of the speaker's remarks or are self-centred.

Attempts to develop some standardised means for assessing listening performance have met with limited success. The awakening of interest in listening as a skill that can be learned and improved with instruction should lead to new research and, subsequently, to the development of new techniques and improved assessment procedures.

Notes

1. The International Listening Association (ILA) was founded in 1980 to bring together from throughout the world professional individuals representing various fields to promote research, education and skill enhancement in listening. For information contact Dr Richard L. Quianthy, Executive Director, International Listening Association, c/o Broward Community College, North Campus, Pompano Beach, Florida 33066, USA.

References

Anderson, M.P., Nichols, E.R., Jr and Booth, H.W. (1974) *The Speaker and His Audience*, Harper and Row, New York

Barker, L.L. (1971) *Listening Behavior*, Prentice-Hall, Englewood Cliffs, New Jersey

Bostrom, R. (1983) *The Kentucky Comprehensive Listening Test*, Kentucky Listening Research Center, Lexington

Brown, J.I. and Carlsen, R.G. (1955) *Brown-Carlsen Listening Comprehension Test*, Harcourt, Brace and World, New York

Clark, M.L. (1972) *Hierarchical Structure of Comprehension Skills*, vol. 1, Australian Council for Educational Research, Hawthorn, Victoria

Cohen, E. (1983) *Speaking the Speech*, Holt, Rinehart and Winston, New York

Colburn, C.W. and Weinberg, S.B. (1981) *Listening and Audience Analysis*, Science Research Associates, Chicago

Educational Testing Service (1956) *Sequential Tests of Educational Progress: Listening*, Cooperative Test Division, Educational Testing Service, Princeton, New Jersey

Ehninger, D., Gronbeck, B.E., McKerrow, R.E. *et al.* (1982) *Principles and Types of Speech Communication: Theory and Practice*, Scott, Foresman and Company, Glenview, Illinois

Floyd, J.J. (1985) *Listening: A Practical Approach*, Scott, Foresman and Company, Glenview, Illinois

Hampleman, R. (1958) 'Comparison of Listening and Reading Comprehension Ability of Fourth and Sixth Grade Pupils', *Elementary English*, *35*, 49

Hirsch, R.O. (1979) *Listening: A Way to Process Information Aurally*, Gorsuch Scarisbrick, Publishers, Dubuque, Iowa

Johnson, K.O. (1951) 'The Effect of Classroom Training upon Listening Comprehension', *J. Communication*, *1*, 58

Jones, M.S. (1956) 'A Critical Review of Literature on Listening with Special Emphasis on Theoretical Bases for Further Research in Listening', unpublished MA thesis, North Carolina State College, p. 12, in A.W. Wolvin and C.G. Coakley (eds), *Listening*, Wm. C. Brown Company, Dubuque, Iowa

Lundsteen, S.W. (1971) *Listening: Its Impact on Reading and Other Language Arts*, National Council of Teachers of English, New York

Maslow, A.H. (1970) *Motivation and Personality*, second edn, Harper and Row, New York

McBurney, J.H. and Wrage, E.J. (1975) *Guide to Good Speech*, Prentice-Hall, Englewood Cliffs, New Jersey

Mehrabian, A. (1971) *Silent Messages*, Wadsworth Publishing Company, Belmont, CA

Montgomery, R.L. (1981) *Listening Made Easy*, AMA COM, New York

Nichols, R.G. and Stevens, L.A. (1957) *Are You Listening?*, McGraw-Hill, New York

Petrie, C.R., Jr. (1971) 'What is Listening?' in S. Duker (ed.), *Listening: Readings*, Scarecrow Press, New York

Rankin, P.T. (1926) 'The Measurement of the Ability to Understand Spoken Language', unpublished PhD dissertation, University of Michigan in *Dissertation Abstracts*, *12*, 6, 847

Rogers, C.B. and Farson, R.E. (1973) 'Active Listening' in R. Huseman, C.M. Logue and D.I. Freshley (eds), *Readings in Interpersonal and Organizational Communication*, second edn, Holbrooks Publishing Company, p. 541

Rubin, R.B. (1982) 'Assessing Speaking and Listening Competence at the College Level: The Communication Competency Assessment Instrument', *Communication Education, 31* (1), 19–32

Spearitt, D. (1962) *Listening Comprehension: A Factoral Analysis*, Australian Council for Educational Research, Melbourne

Speech Communication Association (1982) *Communication Competency Assessment Instrument*, Speech Communication Association, Annandale, VA

Taylor, K.P. (1984) 'The Florida Speaking and Listening Test: The Promise and the Reality', *FL. Speech Comm. J., 12* (2), 31–7

Tucker, W. (1925) 'Science of Listening', *19th Century, 97*, p. 548, cited in A.D. Wolvin and C.G. Coakley (1982) *Listening*, Wm. C. Brown Company, Dubuque, Iowa

Watson, K. and Barker, L. (1984) *Watson-Barker Listening Test*, Spectra Inc., New Orleans

Weaver, C.H. (1972) *Human Listening: Processes and Behavior*, Bobbs-Merrill Company, Indianapolis, Indiana

Wolff, F.I., Marsnik, N.C., Tacey, W.S. *et al.* (1983) *Perceptive Listening*, Holt, Rinehart and Winston, New York

Wolvin, A.D. and Coakley, C.G. (1982) *Listening*, Wm. C. Brown Company, Dubuque, Iowa

Zimmerman, G.L. (1979) *Public Speaking Today*, West Publishing Company, St Paul, Minnesota

Part 3:
GROUP SKILLS

11 INTERACTING IN GROUPS

Herbert H. Blumberg, Martin F. Davis and Valerie Kent

Findings from small-groups research can help people to interact more effectively with others. This chapter looks at some possible implications of a variety of major contemporary studies. Reports of most of the original studies may be found in Volume One of *Small Groups and Social Interaction* (Blumberg, Hare, Kent *et al.*, 1983). Material on negotiation is largely excluded here, as it is covered in Chapter 13.

The overall organisation — of both the small groups work and this chapter — follows the simple rationale of progressively bringing more things 'on stage'. The topics in this chapter begin with the physical space, then the backgrounds and personalities that parties bring with them to a site, and members' impressions of the group and of being part of it. The second part of this chapter deals with social influence — the mere presence of other people, the effects of interacting with them and the formation of friendship. Social interaction itself is covered in the third part: broad differences among groups; specialisation into 'roles', and particularly into 'leadership' roles.

The Situation and Things that People Bring with Them

Physical Space

Sommer (1983) describes the different distances between people that are appropriate for various kinds of encounter — intimate distance, personal, social and (furthest apart) public distance. The optimal distance varies with a diversity of factors, including the familiarity and liking between people, their social distance, sex/culture/age/noise and eye contact. It is as if one walks around surrounded by a bubble of space. If anybody invades this — comes too close physically or metaphorically — one shows symptoms of anxiety. Sommer describes two goals, both of which have implications for social skills training: one is the design and layout of public spaces to minimise or eliminate uncomfortable intrusions. While people do not always have control over the architecture of the spaces which they occupy, some limited control is usually available. Often rooms can be selected, and furniture arranged, in a way conducive to harmonious interaction for a particular kind of group. Even in the absence of furniture, people can note the effects of standing too close or too far from others in a particular setting. The other goal Sommer mentions is the mapping of signs of difficulty; for instance, if the first five rows are vacant at a lecture, one might wonder why.

The boundaries between people, both physical and metaphorical, can of course vary in strength or permeability. Various kinds of evidence have been integrated by Taylor and Altman (1983) to the effect that: '. . . while some relationships generally proceed toward greater openness, they also probably have cycles or phases of closedness. People not only make themselves accessible to one another, they (also) shut themselves off to greater or lesser degrees, break off contact, and engage in more distant styles of interaction' (p. 29). (This is similar perhaps to some of the findings and proposals of Bales (1983), Shambaugh (see Hare, 1982), and Randall and Southgate (1983).)

One implication for social skills is the apparent need for all parties to accept and perhaps 'tune' themselves to different optimal 'distances' (metaphorically speaking) between people in different situations. At times there may be a need for extreme patience, and for a willingness to take up (broken-off) communication again when necessary. However, the work reported by Taylor and Altman (1983) does also go beyond the passive acceptance of cycles. They describe a proposal by Patterson that 'in a dyadic interaction, sufficient changes in the intimacy behaviours of one person will produce arousal changes in the other person' (p. 33). In other words, people are continually sampling other parties' outputs, and when a change in intimacy is sensed, this will be coded either positively (and reciprocated) or negatively (and elicit some compensation). On the one hand, the work implies a question of 'pump priming': how to facilitate positive cues and (by a stretch of the imagination) the other steps which might lead to a combination of shared identity. On the other hand, there nevertheless remains a need for leaving intact others' identity and 'privacy'.

Taylor and Altman also point out laboratory studies showing that parties sharing an isolated accommodation stay together longer if they begin with communication for demarking territories — and gradually ease boundaries — rather than the other way around. It is not yet clear how generally this might apply, what the causal linkages are, nor how best to proceed from a situation with existing boundaries (or lack thereof) which are unpopular to some parties.

Certainly, parties sometimes show a need for feeling 'in control' of their situation. In one experiment Rodin, Solomon, and Metcalf (1983) found that, in essence: if one is in a lift, it *feels* less crowded (but is not) if one is near the control panel. Work in other settings confirms that 'control' decreases feelings of crowdedness; some kinds of control — for instance, having the power to terminate interaction — were more important in a small room; and being a 'co-ordinator' was more important in a larger room. One problem, of course, is that control can be a scarce resource. How can it be distributed or delegated in a way which is equitable and *seen* to be equitable? Perhaps the 'answers' are setting–specific: for instance, different kinds of control may be appropriate for households, casual meetings among friends and workplace committee meetings. But the 'sharing and delegating of control' is a common element, which people may wish to discuss and demonstrate in a social skills context.

Those are some of the major issues related to physical space: can one 'map' signs of difficulty; learn to accept (and perhaps to change) natural cycles of how 'close' or 'distant' various relationships are; and allocate 'control' in a just way?

Personality and Social Characteristics

Webster and Driskell (1983) offer a theory about the effects of status on how people behave and what others think of them. The theory is somewhat complex, but one main view is as follows. Many other differences among people — age, sex, obviously social class — often reduce to status differences.

One frequent property of lower status is talking less. For women, this can be counteracted by (1) a certain amount of experience in all-women groups and (2) being seen, in mixed groups, to be competent. It should be noticed that change apparently need not await a drastic modification in everyone's lifelong socialisation process (which will typically have included various kinds of sex discrimination).

Nemeth's (1983) work on sex differences and decision-making in juries could be seen as being aligned with the Webster–Driskell viewpoint. Indeed, in 1976 — unlike the 1960s — in a set of simulated jury deliberations, women did show similar contributions to men, even though they were still perceived differently by the other mock jurors.

In predicting outcomes, one does of course need to consider not only status characteristics but also motivation, including comparisons with the level and nature of motivation of those with whom one is working.

According to Aronoff, Messé and Wilson (1983), groups composed of people with different motivations will prefer different structures. For example, in one study, safety-oriented (security-conscious) groups established a more hierarchical task structure than did esteem-oriented groups. Group productivity was found to be greater when personality/motivation and structure were thus aligned. One question for training in social skills — and related research — is: what structure is appropriate when different parties have different needs? This problem would appear to require more empirical work. Some possibly obvious things to try would be (1) compromise structures or (2) teaching people to function effectively in non-preferred structures.

Lastly in this section, Shaw (1983) offers a set of hypotheses about high-cohesive groups. For instance, they have more communication, are more positive, more influential over members, more successful and more satisfied. Similar hypotheses are offered for highly *compatible* groups, as estimated by Schutz's six interpersonal need scales (that is, better outcomes are likely from groups having an array of necessary skills, both sexes represented, and so forth) (see Shaw, 1983). These hypotheses might be of use, in the present context, if one were advising on how to compose a compatible group for any particular purpose.

Thus some of the material on personality and social characteristics suggests: (1) that inequitable socialisation is reversible; (2) that it is helpful if group structure is aligned with personality — for instance, a non-hierarchical structure when needs for esteem are high (but then, what do you do when there is a mixture of needs?); and (3) that there have been various advances in research on how to compose compatible productive groups.

Members' Impressions of the Group and of Being Part of It

Compatibility may require a degree of common identity, according to Katz (1983), who writes of different models of stigmatisation. One possible cause of stigmatisation is simply the attribute of 'being different'. Katz cites an experiment by Tajfel (1983) to the effect that simply knowing that one is supposedly part of one group (the yellow group, say) means that one is likely to divide rewards so that other people will get more if they are listed as being part of the same group than if they are part of, say, the green group. The mere *attribution* of being part of a *different group* is sufficient to generate discrimination.

Other paths to stigmatisation, according to Katz, are: a *scapegoat* model, in which a minority group is stigmatised, to take the blame for various bad events which in fact it has not caused; and a *labelling* model. A group having a bad 'label', a bad reputation (whether justified or not), can be party to a self-fulfilling prophecy. People's perceptions of the group are likely to be negatively biased, and possibly the group will even come to act as expected.

What are the implications for social skills — on the part of 'victims', of 'accusers' and of third-parties? In general, when confronted with a false accusation, one might do best to try at least briefly to assert 'the truth' in a 'mildly friendly, mildly dominant' way. Third parties who are present might usefully publicise accurate information — or alternative interpretations or values for information — in order: (1) to separate truth from myth; (2) to diminish over-reaction to partially valid fears; and (3) to promote consciousness of the *processes* of negative (and positive) stereotyping. In the absence of suggestions for specific instances of stigmatisation, it would be worth role-playing various ways of responding, and comparing the results.

An information-processing paradigm might emphasise the varying extent of (information's) impact on the recipient of the information. In the case of stigma, the information might be a response, to an 'accuser', from a 'stigmatised person' or a third party. Typically, several steps could be measured. In order for myths and rumours to be countered successfully, it is necessary, for the recipient, not only to be *exposed* to information, but also to *receive* it, *attend* it, *react* to it; and for any resultant attitudinal and behavioural change to persist.

One advance merits special attention — the work of Aronson and Yates (1983). The potential impact of 'the jigsaw classroom' on stigmatisation is becoming more widely appreciated. If a classroom of school children is divided into small groups, and if a body of material to be learned is split into several essential component parts and distributed among the members of each small group (to learn, discuss, and present to the group), it has typically been found that both quality of learning and satisfaction are higher than for control classrooms using more traditional methods. Moreover, within the small groups, there is characteristically an increase not in competitiveness but in cohesiveness — even when the group is multicultural or includes members who might, in a programme of different format, be stigmatised. It would be worth exploring the possibility that in many 'real world' problems, 'pieces of the solution' really are, already, distributed among the parties. Shared goals plus specialisation in skills and information — even if assigned on a rota — may help in finding solutions or resolutions. The jigsaw classroom work can be viewed in part as a refinement of what Sherif (1958) has called 'super-ordinate goals' — leading eventually to a shared identity. Principles of the jigsaw classroom can help overcome stigmatisation, as has been demonstrated at an in-terpersonal level and, by extension, to teams of mixed culture.

Influence of Others

By now, one has 'on stage' a physical environment, with various people of par-ticular background and personality, who hold specific impressions of the immediate group. The 'influence of other people' is now turned to, including: (1) the mere presence of others; (2) the effects of interacting with them, and, especially (3) positive and negative interaction — helping and hurting.

Presence of Others

Social facilitation, as dealt with by Geen and Gange (1983) and by Sanders (1983), is of course the effect whereby a person will carry out a current task with more zest (which may be better or worse than otherwise) if there is even the *mere presence* of another person or group. Mere 'presence' can mean either that the other person (or group) is *watching* (like an audience) or otherwise evaluating what one is doing, for positive or negative or neutral reasons; or possibly the other party is *co-acting* — doing the same thing as the target person or group, or possibly doing something different but in visible presence. As regards social skills, perhaps the main value of this research is to help make people aware of the effects that others' presence may have on performance and feelings.

Sanders compares three different recent theories of social facilitation. In fact, to anticipate his conclusion, they are not competing theories, but rather they act as a series of filters or hurdles, each of which may give rise to a certain amount of social–facilitation–effect. The first is Zajonc's *mere presence* position: that the mere presence of other parties will increase drive or motivation, due to heightened alertness (Sanders, 1983). The second, Cottrell's *learned drive* theory, suggests that the presence of others can be part of a conditioning process, usually linked to the other party's triggering off feelings of having competition or of being evaluated, so there is little or no social facilitation effect, unless the other party is manifestly competing with one or evaluating one's work (Sanders, 1983). The third paradigm or filter is Thibaut and Kelley's *distraction/conflict* position, which traces facilitation to the distracting influence of others' presence (Sanders, 1983).

The foregoing has dealt with *facilitation*: increased drive and motivation, with either positive or negative effects. Social *inhibition*, on the other hand, is described by Petty, Cacioppo and Harkins (1983). They are part of a group, including Latané and others, whose best known work no doubt includes the 'cheeseburger' study (Petty, Williams, Harkins, *et al.*, 1977). In this study unknowing subjects find themselves in a lift: this time there is a coupon on the wall entitling one to a free sandwich. If, as a subject in this study, one were alone in the lift, one would have been much more likely to take the coupon than if someone else were in the lift as well. And this was true even when there were enough coupons to go around.

Other perhaps less colourful but more systematic studies by these and other authors have made similar points. One general view is that group responsibility for a cognitive task *can lead* to diminished effort. There is also work dealing explicitly with 'social loafing'. For instance, in a 'tug of war' — two groups of people pulling on opposite ends of a rope — the second or third person has been found to add a larger increment of pull than, say, the tenth person. That is, each person in smaller groups pulls harder.

How can increased contributions be encouraged? At least one finding hints at one possible answer. It deals with the effort people put into evaluating a communication. For instance, when a position paper or a proposed solution to a problem is being circulated, readers seem to put more effort into processing the arguments if they feel *individually responsible* for evaluating the message.

So the presence of other parties can have a facilitating or inhibitory effect on information-processing or on behaviour or on both, and in all of these cases the results might be potentially either positive or negative. The various findings might be applicable in very diverse settings.

Social Influence

Milgram and Sabini (1983) recount their study in which people on underground trains ask a seated person, 'May I have your seat please?' Not surprisingly, perhaps, younger target persons were more likely to accede; and both sexes were more likely to agree if the requester were a woman — and also if the requester offered *no* justification rather than a non-urgent reason. The requesters themselves, who were postgraduate students, often felt a bit upset at the moment of making the request, and this feeling would continue until they left the train — when they would feel all right again, once they were no longer in the presence of witnesses. The authors conclude that, 'Knowledge of the objective social order controls behaviour not only cognitively, but also . . . [emotionally — an inhibitory] emotion restricts individual action to the routine patterns that constitute the stable background of everyday life' (Milgram and Sabini, 1983, p. 192).

As if to complement the emotionally based perpetuation of viewpoints, Langer's (1983) work on mindlessness describes a primarily *cognitive* problem in people's customs — the problem of *mindlessness*, which is especially likely to occur in anything which a party does frequently or which *appears* similar to previous events. Readers may be familiar with some of the studies — for instance, the 'photocopier experiment'. Imagine that, carrying a few papers in hand, one approaches the first person in a queue to use a self-service photocopier, and says,

'May I go ahead of you, as I would like to make some copies?' One would typically be much more likely to be let in, than if one offered no reason at all. This was found to be so, even though the reason is merely a reason *in form*. (Why else would anyone use a photocopier, if not to make copies?) Langer describes one form of mindlessness as acceding to requests without really processing their content. Where there is a greater cost, however — if, say, one wished to make 80 photocopies — then the person at the front of the queue would be quite likely to process your request mindfully, and the hollow reason would afford no benefit or might even be counterproductive.

The obvious advice, related to social skills, might be to encourage people to act *mindfully* as well as responsibly. This is advice which, if it were not offered explicitly, one might otherwise take for granted but not bother to follow. Another bit of advice might be to give at least a small reason when requesting a minor favour!

As one possible way to encourage mindfulness, small groups can intentionally be composed of parties from different 'sides' of a dispute plus one or more impartial facilitators. Fisher (1983) has reviewed the relevant literature and also has stressed the importance of further research.

Turning to social influence within existing groups: Newcomb (1983) describes (and quantifies) coercion and resentment in juvenile correctional institutions in America. 'The coercive conditions of group membership', especially in *larger* institutions, 'do not favour cohesiveness and unity.' Here, the shared expectations and characteristics of membership are negative — resentment of incarceration, offence histories, eagerness to 'get out', uncertainty about the future (including the possibilities of stigmatisation and lack of job opportunities). Retaliation — offences within the institution — are, in a sense, *normal* and understandable.

Newcomb's research may in part simply provide more evidence of the need for people who are concerned about social skills to devote at least some energy toward institutional reform: for instance, possibly, community service in lieu of incarceration; as much 'participatory democracy' as possible, when incarceration is unavoidable; programmes to test and implement such apparently needed reforms.

Finally, it is not enough to dwell only on the dominant norms of the majority (be they emotional or cognitive, positive or negative, laboratory or real-world). Moscovici and Paicheler (1983) speak of minority influence: basically, that a persistent, clear dissenting voice, if it generally contains truth, *will* come to be attended to. This view is in contrast to that of the potentially variable effects on a coercive minority (see, for instance, Leites and Wolf, 1970, Chapter 8). It is also in contrast to the view — put forward, for example, years ago in Merei's (1949) studies of children's play — that by closely *following* the customs and values of the group, people build up what have more recently been called 'idiosyncracy credits' which enable trusted members to exert *some* influence toward change. Effort seems to be needed, not so much in deciding *between* these paradigms, but in deciding when and where each of them comes into effect.

So, at least in these samples of research on social influence, a few things to understand and at times 'overcome' may be: emotional maintenance of customs; mindlessness (for instance, in processing requests from others); shared negative characteristics in the processes of some groups; and majority dominance.

Helping and Hurting

Kent (1983) has provided a review of *prosocial behaviour*: altruism and some relevant personal and situational characteristics. Rather than review this work here, it seems sufficient just to mention that there *is* a growing literature on 'helping', with obvious relevance to social skills and interpersonal communication. (For a review of social skills training, see Argyle, 1984.)

Are there examples of specific strategies which help to develop prosocial behaviour? In a study described by Zahn-Waxler (1983), 'mothers were trained to observe and report . . . behaviours [of their young children] in incidents of emotion'. As a sample finding: 'Children of mothers who frequently explained [— with emotional embellishment —] the consequences of their [that is, the children's] hurtful behaviour for the victim had reparation scores that were significantly higher than those of children whose mothers rarely used this technique.' *Socialisation* is also of interest in terms of how a harmonious society might be built and perpetuated. Moreover, the principles of socialisation might also be of use in explaining post-childhood learning. One might imagine a kind of 'social skills training' — to the parties of some disputes, for instance, or possibly *before* hurtful behaviours give rise to disputes. This is a large task, but perhaps one which is worth strong efforts.

Tedeschi and Melburg (1983) emphasise that *aggression* is usually perceived as the *illegitimate* use of coercive power. Whether force is 'aggressive' depends on how one sees and attributes it. There is also a caution against generalising too confidently from (1) legitimately sanctioned aggression in the laboratory to (2) offensive and illegitimate coercion outside.

In summary, there is a growing literature on altruism and helping, directly relevant to inter-party harmony. As one example of a strategy promoting the early learning of prosocial behaviour, it seems important actually to communicate, with some emotional embellishment, the consequences of a party's hurtful behaviour.

Friendship

Nahemow and Lawton (1983) systematically interviewed people in various blocks of flats. They concluded that 'people will travel greater distances and generally put themselves out to see those who are like themselves' with respect to age, ethnicity and so on. 'However, social contacts with different kinds of people, which is one aspect of an enriched lifestyle, did occur in the presence of environmental supports.' One of the blocks of flats appeared 'to have some of those supports; there is a good age, race, and sex mix, and there are enough [flats] . . . in close propinquity so that each person has the possibility of running into at least 11 others on the way to the' lift (p. 290).

Reviewing friendship in a different context, Rubin (1983) has recently been contributing observation-based knowledge of friendship — among children, for example. The main inference of relevance here is simply that there may be specific 'rules' or strategies which are effective in *particular* situations. Parties can learn the skills of becoming friendly with a group of others without sparking off major rebuffs. Perhaps a similar conclusion, about rules, and also content, being specific to settings, follows from Argyle's (1983) descriptions of different kinds of groups.

Broderick (1983) reminds one that different parties may have totally different assumptions as to what consitutes a proper relationship — and indeed different breadths of openness to accepting other parties' assumptions. One needs, too, to look 'under the carpet' of similarity. *Why* does one travel a distance to be with similar/congenial others? Is it having more things to talk about, a feeling of common values (is it just a feeling?), shared motivational forces?

Structure and Function

Social Interaction and Task

The focus here shifts to the structure and function of groups themselves, beginning with social interaction in different kinds of groups. Perhaps one use of Argyle's (1983) discussion of the differences among groups is as a cautionary note against assuming that the principles from one type of group (for example, say a typical laboratory problem-solving group) would necessarily apply to other groups or levels, such as to committees which mediate conflicts. Argyle's work does demonstrate the value of preparing almost ethological accounts of the interaction processes in different kinds of groups.

Careful study of negotiation groups might suggest specific ways in which output could be improved. It appears from the work of Hackman and Morris (1983) that particular effort could be directed toward fostering the positive potential shown in Table 11.1 (the three entries in the third column).

To take just one hint which might be applied or advised in various contexts, it was found in a study by Shure and others (cited by Hackman and Morris, 1983, p. 336) that: ' "planning" activities tended to be generally lower in priority than actual task performance — even when group members were aware that it was to their advantage to engage in planning before starting actual work on the task, and when it was possible for them to do so without difficulty. A closely related phenomenon is the tendency for group members to begin immediately to generate and evaluate solutions when they are presented with a task, rather than to take time to study and analyse the task itself . . . one function of strategy discussion is to "unfreeze" individuals from traditional, well-learned approaches to the task, and thereby open the possibility of discovering a more task-effective way of proceeding.'

For yet another of social interaction, Krokoff and Gottman (1983) looked mainly at the interaction within married couples who were either distressed

Table 11.1: Summary of the Proposed Functions of Group Interaction

Summary variables postulated as important in affecting performance outcomes	Impact of interaction process on the summary variables	
	(A) Inevitable process losses	(B) Potential for process gains
Member effort brought to bear on the task	Interaction serves as the less-than-perfect means by which member efforts are co-ordinated and applied to the task	Interaction can serve to enhance the level of effort members choose to expend on task work
Performance strategies used in carrying out ':e task	Interaction serves as a less-than-perfect 'vehicle' for implementing pre-existing strategies brought to the group by members and (often) shared by them	Interaction can serve as the site for developing or reformulating strategic plans to increase their task-appropriateness
Member knowledge and skills used by the group for task work	Interaction serves as a less-than-perfect means for assessing, weighting, and applying member talents to the task	Interaction can serve as a means for increasing the total pool of knowledge and/or skill available to the group (i.e., when the group is the site for generation of new knowledge or skill by members)

Source: Hackman and Morris (1983). © John Wiley & Sons Ltd. Reprinted by permission of John Wiley & Sons Ltd

or nondistressed (as indexed by the seeking, or not, of marriage guidance counselling, and by scores on a relationship inventory). Sequences of interaction were rated on various dimensions which included separate verbal and nonverbal tallies of positive and negative communication. Distress was particularly associated with nonverbal and with negative behaviours, that is, more negative behaviour and, moreover, positive things being said in a negative way. Whether the negative manner is mainly a symptom or cause of distress, or both at once, is not clear — and should be further evaluated. Perhaps positive manners are positively reciprocated (for example, see Hare, Kritzer and Blumberg, 1979), but in tone only; or maybe the reciprocation even of positive *tone* can help keep a situation from going out of control.

Another interesting finding from Krokoff and Gottman's work is that distressed couples had the same rates of positive reciprocation (in interaction sequences) as did nondistressed couples, but showed *higher* rates of reciprocating *negative* behaviour (than did nondistressed couples). Again, it might be worth trying to determine the *cause(s)* of the association — though a 'negative spiral' does have face validity as a source of distress in itself.

Among other findings were: less 'counter-complaining' among non-clinic couples; more readiness to agree to an accusation (if a complaint is legitimate); briefer comments on the process of the communication itself; a tendency in conflict situations for the more dominant party to be responsive to the other party's momentary shifts in mood. The authors feel it is worth analysing *sequences* of interaction, as distinct from simple tallies. They also describe experimental interventions which suggest that 'correcting' the interaction pattern can in fact improve outcomes.

Roles and Relationships

It is not enough to look just at interaction, as if all parties had similar jobs and equivalent expectations. One needs to consider *roles* as well. Hinde (1983) provides, among other things, a commentary on areas important for describing and understanding relationships between parties — applicable within small groups. His approach might also be useful for raising questions about the relationships *between groups*, even if some of the answers are still to be provided.

Hinde lists eight categories of criteria that he has found valuable for describing relationships, which, for the present context, have been both shortened and liberally embellished. These help to consolidate some of the discussion so far:

1. Contents. What do the participants usually do together? How has this changed over time? How does it compare with the *other* relationships which each party maintains?
2. Diversity of interactions — uniplex (*primarily* just one or two areas) or multiplex?
3. Qualities of interaction — frequency, underlying tone, degree of co-ordination/harmony/mutual benefit.
4. Relative frequency. Is an apparent characteristic manifest in a *variety* of ways? How do the frequencies of interaction compare with what each party would want them to be? Are there particular patterns or sequences of interaction?
5. Reciprocity versus complementarity of behaviour.
6. Intimacy — degree of mutual revelation.
7. Interparty reception. 'This concerns the extent to which the participants in a relationship see each other as they really are', and as the others see themselves (that is, understand the others), and perceive themselves as being seen accurately (that is, feel understood), construe the world in similar ways, and so forth.
8. Commitment — the consistency and/or continuity of the relationship.

Four dynamic principles are then described: (1) Does each party bring the same 'standards' to the relationship (cultural values); (2) What qualities does each attribute to the other? (3) Are 'exchanges' fair and are they seen as fair? and (4) What are the extent and effect of positive and negative feedback between the parties? These four areas might be seen as corresponding respectively to the 'LIAG' sectors in functional theory (see Hare, 1983).

The above list might well be useful, for example, in any situation where one might wish to compare interaction in different social settings for either didactic or research purposes.

To turn from general criteria and principles to a specific phenomenon, it seems to follow from the writing of Cicourel (1983), among others, that the socialisation of children includes their learning the general rules or norms of expected behaviour and thought, that these are maintained by agreement, often tacit, among people, and may change according to the interpretations made by new generations. Groups may maintain conditions, even arbitrary ones, which can outlast their suitability, or can moreover form incremental social traps, unsuited to the common good (to take just one possible example: the accumulation of 'verbal ammunition' which some parties 'store' to use against one another in rows).

As Cicourel points out, '. . . roles are learned in everyday life. We must clarify the way that such learned roles are represented in memory, the extent to which their enactment is contingent on information emanating from the interactional setting and institutional constraints perceived by the actor, and the way that beliefs and reasoning strategies assign significance to the different sources of information' (pp. 373–4).

Although much has been written about social change (see, for instance, Moore, 1974; Blumberg *et al.*, 1983, volume 2, part II), it is not yet clear how change can most effectively be promoted with respect to the ways that people relate to each other.

It might help if one knew more about the effects of specific roles in particular settings. Sometimes role differences can emerge at an early age. Jacklin and Maccoby (1983), who have been working on the West Coast of the United States, found that even at 33 months of age, previously unacquainted boys and girls showed more frequent social behaviour when paired with another of the *same* sex; also, both boys and girls (especially girls) showed more 'withdrawal' when paired with boys. It was also found that, when paired with girls, girls showed less passive behaviour than boys did; but when paired with boys, girls showed much more passive behaviour than boys did. The study does confirm the view that role-based behaviour can emerge at an early age and can follow different patterns for different specific behaviours. Sometimes it is the absolute attribute of the other party that matters (for instance, male v. female), sometimes the 'relative attribute' (for instance, same as self v. different, with regard to some attribute, such as sex), and sometimes neither, or an interaction. Thus for different purposes there might be different preferred configurations of people. Moreover, having a variety of configurations for different purposes can help prevent gross cleavages, such as along lines of sex, age, race or status (see Etzioni *et al.*, in Smith, 1972).

Zimbardo's (1983) prisoner–guard study shows a potentially immediate relevance of roles to social harmony. This is the study in which people were randomly assigned to roles of prisoner or guard in a 'mock prison'. The subjects soon conformed to some of the stereotyped behaviours of such roles. The study may reinforce the view that one cannot depend on 'normal rational' people acting in thoughtful rational ways if role constraints (or perceived or expected role constraints) should dictate otherwise, especially, for instance, in periods of emergencies or when constituencies dictate particular behaviours. Can excessive role constraints be eased? Concerned about the need for international disarmament and other issues, Rogers (1982) and Burton (1979), among others, have suggested general procedures for informal secluded meetings — *not* role-dictated — and with some people assigned to facilitate discussion. These suggestions, related to fostering skills for resolving conflict, surely deserve even more widespread trials and further development.

Leadership

Leadership roles merit special attention. Stein and Heller's (1983) work does not have extensive obvious application to social skills, though one might infer a general suggestion that in a small conflict-resolving group, high participation rates might sometimes mistakenly be taken as an indication of the best, 'leading' solutions. However, when some parties have relatively little to say, the group should nonetheless try to ensure that everyone's views and suggestions are taken into account. Janis (1983) makes a similar suggestion in describing 'groupthink'.

Fiedler and Potter (1983) discuss accumulated evidence about the varying effectiveness of relationship-motivated and task-motivated leaders in different situations. Relationship-motivated leaders are defined as those with high LPC scores, and task-motivated leaders are those with low LPC scores. The LPC (least-preferred co-worker) scale is a personality-type measure 'on which the individual rates the characteristics of the one person with whom he or she has been able to work least well'. Particularly 'negative' ratings represent low LPC. The main finding is that relationship-motivated leaders are most effective when there is moderate situational control, and task-motivated leaders are most effective when there is either low or high situational control. ('The leader's situational control, or favourableness, indicates the degree to which the leader feels secure and confident that the task will be accomplished . . .' (Fiedler and Potter, 1983, p. 407), and is defined as the group being supportive, the task and goals being clear, and the leader having power to reward and punish.)

The paper by Fiedler and Potter describes a six-hour programmed training procedure which enables leaders to adjust the favourableness of the situation (for instance, how the task is structured) to their LPC level. Various experimental results confirmed that leaders thus trained in good 'leader match' were subsequently evaluated as being particularly effective. It would be worth confirming, in other contexts, that the productivity and satisfaction of other group members is also thereby increased. Also it would be worth measuring the effects if such training were provided for non-hierarchical groups or teams.

With regard to non-hierarchical groups, Schneier and Goktepe (1983) do confirm predictions from the contingency (LPC) model in emergent leadership: where emergent leaders had low LPC scores (under situational favourableness), *group performance* was significantly better. Moreover, in contrast with a previous finding, both men and women were equally likely to emerge as leaders in mixed-sex task groups. Gender differences, or other clear relationships, may vary with time, place and situation. Likewise, the *principles* which seem to provide for effective mediation or conflict resolution might also vary (for instance, preference for clear directives v. nondirective 'facilitation'). Even clear findings (such as some of those concerned with leadership) must be periodically verified.

Hollander (1983) notes, among other things, that one determinant of whether gender differences appear in particular studies of leadership is, in fact, whether leadership is assigned (for instance, from random pools of women and men) or emergent (for instance, carried out by people who 'want to lead' and are wanted for the role, possibly in a pre-existing group). Gender differences are particularly likely in the 'assigned' situation, presumably because women are disproportionately put into roles that many would not choose. The analysis reminds one of the advice, sometimes given, that people (and perhaps nations) should fill the roles that they *desire*, as far as possible (see Blumberg and DeSoto, 1968). For a further discussion of 'leading group discussions', see Chapter 12.

Application

There is a need: (1) to sharpen just how the small-group findings relate to social skills; (2) to see what suggestions seem useful to a fairly wide variety of relevant parties (or particularly useful even to a narrow sector of people); and (3) to try out and develop the suggestions.

A discussion of how to expand a potential base of enquiry, and then to contract it to manageable proportions is provided by Cronbach (1982), who deals especially with the problems of developing and extending a body of findings (in programme evaluation) from particular sampling units, experimental treatments and observing-operations (or instruments). He emphasises the value of having at least some samples with a 'natural mix' of parties, as distinguished from controlling or holding constant too many variables, and the value of 'going behind' gross quantitative findings, to provide clearly understandable explanatory examples of what is going on — and generally to see who is reacting in what ways and for what reasons. (To paraphrase one of Cronbach's examples, take an initially strange numerical finding, that advanced children did better if they were in *mixed*-ability groups, and expand it as follows: 'Advanced children learned at least as much when they were in mixed-ability groups, because they spent time re-wording difficult concepts in a way that would be clear even to less comprehending classmates.') Then, when one needs to advise in, say, setting up a finance sub-committee for a work co-operative, one can make an educated guess about applying a body of findings, even with a new population mix, without having the impossible burden of having newly to replicate an entire body of research. Of course, at least some ongoing local verification of findings is invariably advisable.

One 'shortcut' in dealing with a large number of variables, clearly, is to concentrate effort on those variables, or those aspects of particular variables, that 'make a substantial difference' in preliminary work; or to concentrate on a few variables at a time. However, assessment of variables can still require very substantial effort — and sometimes a fairly large number of variables can all matter at least a little (for an example in a different context, see Blumberg, Fuller and Hare, 1974). One possible compromise in programmatic research related to social skills training is to collect much information about key or global variables and at least a little information about a large number of additional variables and their potential interactions (perhaps by asking different but overlapping rotas of subjects — every *n*th person, say — about some matters).

Some economy can be effected by using a *variety* of methods (again see Cronbach, 1982); for example, ranging from largely *field-based* studies to observe the 'natural' range of phenomena, through *laboratory/experimental* work for a small number of comparisons investigating causal linkages, to computer *simulation* (plus empirical data) to estimate *which* of a variety of parameters may have large impacts (see, for example, Penrod, 1983; Tindale and Davis, 1983).

A Moderately Dominant-Positive Approach

If one wished to offer simple advice on how to minimise negative outcomes from conflict, 'acting in a moderately-positive moderately-dominant way' might capture a good bit of the variance in a number of more complex findings.

The present chapter provides some possible examples in line with an earlier empirical finding. In 1972 the author joined in collecting accounts in which people (who had received training in nonviolent direct action — see Blumberg, Hare, Fuller *et al.*, 1974) had responded to actual or threatened violence. Although one cannot be sure about the causal linkages, the joint outcome did seem to be most favourable when the response to the violence was moderately positive (that is, friendly but not so much so as to seem sarcastic) and moderately assertive (taking some initiative to express one's views but leaving room for the violent party to do the same).

For the work considered in the present paper, one can make tentative inferences related to dominant–positive behaviour in interpersonal and possibly international contexts. For example: architectural–environmental engineering might be able to 'prop up' the likelihood of (moderately dominant–positive) friendly interaction between 'different' kinds of people (or of groups/cultures?) (see Nahemow and Lawton, 1983). Accounts of different kinds of situations are still required, in part to describe the differences among situations, with which the 'meaning' of dominant and positive — and the optimal dominant-positive level — may vary (see the discussion of friendship, above). Negative reciprocated chains of responses are to be avoided, as are mixed-modes (saying something positive in a negative way) (Hackman and Morris, 1983). In order to describe differences systematically (a need just mentioned above), it is useful to have a list of dimensions important in describing and classifying relationships (as provided by Hinde, 1983).

How norms govern behaviour in *practice* depends on consensus in particular contexts (Cicourel, 1983); moreover, role-specific behaviour may emerge at an early age (Jacklin and Maccoby, 1983). Such views and findings can be used normatively, to suggest the absolute dominant-positive levels at which parties might feel most comfortable. Or they can be used didactically, to suggest that people might benefit from escaping from role-dictated behaviours. An experimental example of this is, arguably, provided by the mock prison study (Zimbardo, 1983), where the (randomly assigned) guards were too dominant, the prisoners too submissive and both groups too negative. Murton (1983) gives a concrete example of prison reform in this regard.

Other dimensions, such as parties' task seriousness and conformity, may affect outcomes but do not appear to account for as much variance as do dominance and positivity.

It would be helpful if the applications presented in the various sections of the present paper could be integrated into a unified approach. For now, one can at least specify a number of areas — all of which require attention. A degree of systematicness is achieved by the heuristic device of 'bringing on stage', one at a time, a progression of topics — starting with the 'physical space' for a group and proceeding in stages to complex social interaction.

Notes

This chapter has been developed, in part, from material presented in two papers (Blumberg, 1982, 1983). In these papers it was argued that many of the findings might, as hypotheses, be applicable not only in small groups but also among representatives and mediators of large groups and even of nations. The second half of this chapter, beginning with the section on friendship, consists largely of extracts from Blumberg (1983) and should be regarded as quotations from the *Proceedings*, used with the permission of the conference organisers. Valerie Kent and Martin Davies did the primary editing of those sections of the *Small Groups* work (these constitute volume one) described in this chapter.

Acknowledgements

To Paul Hare, C.R. Mitchell and others for helpful comments on an earlier draft of this chapter.

References

Argyle, M. (1983) 'Five Kinds of Small Social Group' in H.H. Blumberg, A.P. Hare, V. Kent *et al.* (eds), *Small Groups and Social Interaction*, volume 1, John Wiley and Sons, Chichester and New York (extracted from M. Argyle (1969) *Social Interaction*, Methuen, London, pp. 240–63)
——— (1984) 'Some New Developments in Social Skills Training', *Bulletin of the British Psychological Society, 37*, 405–10
Aronoff, J., Messé, L.A. and Wilson, J.P. (1983) 'Personality Factors in Small Group Functioning'

in H.H. Blumberg, A.P. Hare, V. Kent *et al.* (eds), *Small Groups and Social Interaction*, volume 1, John Wiley and Sons, Chichester and New York

Aronson, E. and Yates, S. (1983) 'Cooperation in the Classroom: The Impact of the Jigsaw Method on Inter-ethnic Relations, Classroom Performance, and Self-esteem' in H.H. Blumberg, A.P. Hare, V. Kent *et al.* (eds), *Small Groups and Social Interaction*, volume 1, John Wiley and Sons, Chichester and New York

Bales, R.F. (1983) 'SYMLOG: A Practical Approach to the Study of Groups' in H.H. Blumberg, A.P. Hare, V. Kent *et al.* (eds), *Small Groups and Social Interaction*, volume 2, John Wiley and Sons, Chichester and New York

Blumberg, H.H. (1982) 'Group Processes, Conflict Resolution and Disarmament; 1: Background Situation, and 2: Influence of Others', paper presented at the joint meetings of the Conflict Research Society and the Peace Science Society, Reading

—— (1983) 'Group Processes, Conflict Resolution and Disarmament; 3: Structure and Function of the Group', paper presented at the International Symposium on Research on Social Conflict and Harmony, Erasmus University, Rotterdam (*Proceedings*, in press)

—— and DeSoto, C.B. (1968) 'Avoiding Distortions in Sociometric Choices', *International Journal of Sociometry and Sociatry, 5* (3–4), 90–5

——, Fuller, C. and Hare, A.P. (1974) 'Response Rates in Postal Surveys', *Public Opinion Quarterly, 38,* 113–23

——, Hare, A.P., Fuller, C. *et al.* (1974) 'Evaluation of Training for Nonviolent Direct Action', *Mental Health and Society, 1,* 364–75

——, Hare, A.P., Kent, V. *et al.* (eds) (1983) *Small Groups and Social Interaction* (two volumes), John Wiley and Sons, Chichester and New York

Broderick, C.B. (1983) 'Men and Women' in H.H. Blumberg, A.P. Hare, V. Kent *et al.* (eds), *Small Groups and Social Interaction*, volume 1, John Wiley and Sons, Chichester and New York

Burton, J. (1979) *Deviance, Terrorism, and War: The Process of Solving Unsolved Social and Political Problems*, Robertson, Oxford

Cicourel, A.V. (1983) 'Interpreting Normative Rules in the Negotiation of Status and Role' in H.H. Blumberg, A.P. Hare, V. Kent *et al.* (eds), *Small Groups and Social Interaction*, volume 1, John Wiley and Sons, Chichester and New York

Cronbach, L.J. (1982) *Designing Evaluations of Educational and Social Programs*, Jossey-Bass, San Francisco, Washington and London

Fiedler, F.E. and Potter, E.H. (1983) 'Dynamics of Leadership Effectiveness' in H.H. Blumberg, A.P. Hare, V. Kent *et al.* (eds), *Small Groups and Social Interaction*, volume 1, John Wiley and Sons, Chichester and New York

Fisher, R.J. (1983) 'Third Party Consultation as a Method of Intergroup Conflict Resolution: A Review of Studies', *Journal of Conflict Resolution, 27,* 301–34

Geen, R.G. and Gange, J.J. (1983) 'Social Facilitation: Drive Theory and Beyond' in H.H. Blumberg, A.P. Hare, V. Kent *et al.* (eds), *Small Groups and Social Interaction*, volume 1, John Wiley and Sons, Chichester and New York

Hackman, J.R. and Morris, C.G. (1983) 'Group Tasks, Group Interaction Process, and Group Performance Effectiveness' in H.H. Blumberg, A.P. Hare, V. Kent *et al.* (eds), *Small Groups and Social Interaction*, volume 1, John Wiley and Sons, Chichester and New York

Hare, A.P. (1982) *Creativity in Small Groups*, Sage, Beverly Hills

—— (1983) 'A Functional Interpretation of Interaction' in H.H. Blumberg, A.P. Hare, V. Kent *et al.* (eds), *Small Groups and Social Interaction*, volume 2, John Wiley and Sons, Chichester and New York

——, Kritzer, H.M. and Blumberg, H.H. (1979) 'Functional Analysis of Persuasive Interaction in a Role-playing Experiment', *Journal of Social Psychology, 107,* 77–88

Hinde, R.A. (1983) 'Dyadic Relationships' in H.H. Blumberg, A.P. Hare, V. Kent *et al.* (eds), *Small Groups and Social Interaction*, volume 1, John Wiley and Sons, Chichester and New York

Hollander, E.P. (1983) 'Women and Leadership' in H.H. Blumberg, A.P. Hare, V. Kent *et al.* (eds), *Small Groups and Social Interaction*, volume 1, John Wiley and Sons, Chichester and New York

Jacklin, C.N. and Maccoby, E.E. (1983) 'Social Behavior at 33 Months in Same-sex and Mixed-sex Dyads' in H.H. Blumberg, A.P. Hare, V. Kent *et al.* (eds), *Small Groups and Social Interaction*, volume 1, John Wiley and Sons, Chichester and New York (extracted from *Child Development*, 1978, *49,* 557–69)

Janis, I.L. (1983) 'Groupthink' in H.H. Blumberg, A.P. Hare, V. Kent *et al.* (eds), *Small Groups* and Social Interaction, volume 2, John Wiley and Sons, Chichester and New York

Katz, I. (1983) 'The Process of Stigmatization' in H.H. Blumberg, A.P. Hare, V. Kent *et al.* (eds), *Small Groups and Social Interaction*, volume 1, John Wiley and Sons, Chichester and New York

Kent, V. (1983) 'Prosocial Behaviour and Small Group Processes' in H.H. Blumberg, A.P. Hare, V. Kent *et al.* (eds), *Small Groups and Social Interaction*, volume 1, John Wiley and Sons, Chichester and New York

Krokoff, L.J. and Gottman, J.M. (1983) 'The Structural Model of Marital Interaction' in H.H. Blumberg, A.P. Hare, V. Kent *et al.* (eds), *Small Groups and Social Interaction*, volume 1, John Wiley and Sons, Chichester and New York

Langer, E.J. (1983) 'The Mindlessness/Mindfulness of Social Cognition' in H.H. Blumberg, A.P. Hare, V. Kent *et al.* (eds), *Small Groups and Social Interaction*, volume 1, John Wiley and Sons, Chichester and New York

Leites, N. and Wolf, C. (1970) *Rebellion and Authority: An Analytic Essay on Insurgent Conflicts*, Markham, Chicago

Merei, F. (1949) 'Group Leadership and Institutionalization', *Human Relations, 2*, 23–39. (Reprinted in E.E. Maccoby, T.M. Newcomb and E.L. Hartley (eds) (1958) *Readings in Social Psychology*, 3rd edn, Holt, Rinehart and Winston, New York)

Milgram, S. and Sabini, J. (1983) 'On Maintaining Social Norms: A Field Experiment in the Subway' in H.H. Blumberg, A.P. Hare, V. Kent *et al.* (eds), *Small Groups and Social Interaction*, volume 1, John Wiley and Sons, Chichester and New York

Moore, W.E. (1974) *Social Change*, second edn, Prentice-Hall, Englewood Cliffs, New Jersey

Moscovici, S. and Paicheler, G. (1983) 'Minority or Majority Influences: Social Change, Compliance, and Conversion' in H.H. Blumberg, A.P. Hare, V. Kent *et al.* (eds), *Small Groups and Social Interaction*, volume 1, John Wiley and Sons, Chichester and New York

Murton, T. (1983) 'One Year of Prison Reform' in H.H. Blumberg, A.P. Hare, V. Kent *et al.* (eds), *Small Groups and Social Interaction*, volume 2, John Wiley and Sons, Chichester and New York

Nahemow, L. and Lawton, M.P. (1983) 'Similarity and Propinquity: Making Friends with "Different" People' in H.H. Blumberg, A.P. Hare, V. Kent *et al.* (eds), *Small Groups and Social Interaction*, volume 1, John Wiley and Sons, Chichester and New York

Nemeth, C. (1983) 'Sex Differences and Decision Making in Juries' in H.H. Blumberg, A.P. Hare, V. Kent *et al.* (eds), *Small Groups and Social Interaction*, volume 1, John Wiley and Sons, Chichester and New York

Newcomb, T.M. (1983) 'Coercion and Resentment in Juvenile Correctional Institutions' in H.H. Blumberg, A.P. Hare, V. Kent *et al.* (eds), *Small Groups and Social Interaction*, volume 1, John Wiley and Sons, Chichester and New York

Penrod, S. (1983) 'Mathematical and Computer Models of Jury Decision Making' in H.H. Blumberg, A.P. Hare, V. Kent *et al.* (eds), *Small Groups and Social Interaction*, volume 2, John Wiley and Sons, Chichester and New York

Petty, R.E., Williams, K.D., Harkins, S.G. *et al.* (1977) 'Social Inhibition of Helping Yourself: Bystander Response to a Cheeseburger', *Personality and Social Psychology Bulletin, 3*, 575–8
———, Cacioppo, J.T. and Harkins, S.G. (1983) 'Group Size Effects on Cognitive Effort and Attitude Change' in H.H. Blumberg, A.P. Hare, V. Kent *et al.* (eds), *Small Groups and Social Interaction*, volume 1, John Wiley and Sons, Chichester and New York

Randall, R. and Southgate, J. (1983) 'Creativity in Self-managed Groups' in H.H. Blumberg, A.P. Hare, V. Kent *et al.* (eds), *Small Groups and Social Interaction*, volume 2, John Wiley and Sons, Chichester and New York

Rodin, J., Solomon, S.K. and Metcalf, J. (1983) 'Role of Control in Mediating Perceptions of Density' in H.H. Blumberg, A.P. Hare, V. Kent *et al.* (eds), *Small Groups and Social Interaction*, volume 1, John Wiley and Sons, Chichester and New York (abridged from *Journal of Personality and Social Psychology*, 1978, *36*, 988–99)

Rogers, C.R. (1982) 'Nuclear War: A Personal Response', *Monitor* (American Psychological Association), *13*, (8), 6–7

Rubin, Z. (1983) 'The Skills of Friendship' in H.H. Blumberg, A.P. Hare, V. Kent *et al.* (eds), *Small Groups and Social Interaction*, volume 1, John Wiley and Sons, Chichester and New York (extracted from Z. Rubin (1980), *Children's Friendships*, Harvard University Press, Cambridge)

Sanders, G.S. (1983) 'Attentional Processes and Social Facilitation: How Much, How Often, and How Lasting?' in H.H. Blumberg, A.P. Hare, V. Kent *et al.* (eds), *Small Groups and Social Interaction*, volume 1, John Wiley and Sons, Chichester and New York

Schneier, C.E. and Goktepe, J.R. (1983) 'Issues in Emergent Leadership: The Contingency Model of Leadership, Leader Sex, and Leader Behavior' in H.H. Blumberg, A.P. Hare, V. Kent *et al.* (eds), *Small Groups and Social Interaction*, volume 1, John Wiley and Sons, Chichester and New York

Shaw, M.E. (1983) 'Group Composition' in H.H. Blumberg, A.P. Hare, V. Kent *et al.* (eds), *Small Groups and Social Interaction*, volume 1, John Wiley and Sons, Chichester and New York

Sherif, M. (1958) 'Superordinate Goals in the Reduction of Intergroup Conflict', *Am. J. Soc., 63*, 349–56. (Reprinted in H. Proshansky and B. Seidenberg (eds) (1965) *Basic Studies in Social Psychology*, Holt, Rinehart and Winston, New York)

Smith, C.G. (ed.) (1972) *Conflict Resolution: Contributions of the Behavioral Sciences*, University of Notre Dame Press, Notre Dame (Indiana) and London

Sommer, R. (1983) 'Spatial Behavior' in H.H. Blumberg, A.P. Hare, V. Kent *et al.* (eds), *Small Groups and Social Interaction*, volume 1, John Wiley and Sons, Chichester and New York

Stein, R.T. and Heller, T. (1983) 'The Relationship of Participation Rates to Leadership Status: A Meta-analysis' in H.H. Blumberg, A.P. Hare, V. Kent *et al.* (eds), *Small Groups and Social Interaction*, volume 1, John Wiley and Sons, Chichester and New York

Tajfel, H. (1983) 'Experiments in Intergroup Discrimination' in H.H. Blumberg, A.P. Hare, V. Kent *et al.* (eds), *Small Groups and Social Interaction*, volume 1, John Wiley and Sons, Chichester and New York

Taylor, D.A. and Altman, I. (1983) 'Environment and Interpersonal Relationships: Privacy, Crowding, and Intimacy' in H.H. Blumberg, A.P. Hare, V. Kent *et al.* (eds), *Small Groups and Social Interaction*, volume 1, John Wiley and Sons, Chichester and New York

Tedeschi, J.T. and Melburg, V. (1983) 'Aggression as the Illegitimate Use of Coercive Power' in H.H. Blumberg, A.P. Hare, V. Kent *et al.* (eds), *Small Groups and Social Interaction*, volume 1, John Wiley and Sons, Chichester and New York

Tindale, R.S. and Davis, J.H. (1983) 'Group Decision Making and Jury Verdicts' in H.H. Blumberg, A.P. Hare, V. Kent *et al.* (eds), *Small Groups and Social Interaction*, volume 2, John Wiley and Sons, Chichester and New York

Webster, M. and Driskell, J.E. (1983) 'Processes of Status Generalization' in H.H. Blumberg, A.P. Hare, V. Kent *et al.* (eds), *Small Groups and Social Interaction*, volume 1, John Wiley and Sons, Chichester and New York

Zahn-Waxler, C. (1983) 'Maternal Child Rearing Practices in Relation to Children's Altruism and Conscience Development' in H.H. Blumberg, A.P. Hare, V. Kent *et al.* (eds), *Small Groups and Social Interaction*, volume 1, John Wiley and Sons, Chichester and New York

Zimbardo, P.G. (1983) 'Transforming Experimental Research into Advocacy for Social Change' in H.H. Blumberg, A.P. Hare, V. Kent *et al.* (eds), *Small Groups and Social Interaction*, volume 1, John Wiley and Sons, Chichester and New York (abridged from *Applications of Social Psychology*, M. Deutsch and H.A. Hornstein (eds), Erlbaum, Hillsdale, New Jersey)

12 CHAIRMANSHIP

Dorothy Whittington

From parliament to pigeon club, the chaired committee meeting is the setting for some of the most significant social performances in society. It could even be suggested that it is precisely when the most difficult or far-reaching problems are confronted that committees, working parties, discussion groups and so on are set up.

Chairing such groups is clearly an important task — and a likely target for social skill analysis. Surprisingly little literature seems to exist, however, and few if any social skill training programmes get beyond the relatively simple skills of dyadic interaction (see Ellis and Whittington, 1981, for a compendium of skills pervasive in such programmes).

With the notable exception of Rackham and Morgan (1977), detailed empirical analysis of chairmanship seems not to have been undertaken. Exhortatory handbooks of advice to novices do exist (Doyle and Strauss, 1976; Marshall, 1957; Maude, 1975) but they are uneven in quality, make little reference to relevant social psychological literature and are largely based on the intuitions of experienced chairmen. Such intuitions systematically explored and tested for their predictive value might, of course, provide useful insight into the 'expert system' of effective chairmanship, but without such validation they are an unsteady basis for advice and training.

Any aspirant designer of social skill training for chairmen could thus be caught between the relevant but empirically unsound handbooks and the sound but largely irrelevant social psychological literature on the generalities of group process and interaction.

This chapter will try to steer a course between these dangers and will address the following questions:

1. What is a chairman?
2. What tasks do chaired groups undertake?
3. Are there chairmanship skills specific to such tasks?
4. Are there generic chairmanship skills?
5. What further research is needed?

What is a Chairman?

The *Oxford English Dictionary* gives chairman as 'the occupier of a chair of authority, specifically the person who is chosen to preside over a meeting, to

288

conduct its proceedings and to occupy the chair or seat provided for the exercise of that function'. Chairmanship skills are, therefore, behaviours relevant to the conduct of those group interactions usually referred to as 'meetings'.

But what are 'meetings' and how can such group interactions best be described? The size of chaired meetings can vary considerably, from the political meeting or business conference attended by some hundreds to the small working party of three or four. There are upper and lower limits, however. If the group is so large that contribution to the discussion is not possible for each member, then the group is being addressed rather than chaired. Conversely, groups of two are so small that participation is easily managed without the formality of chairmanship.

The term 'chairman' is most commonly applied to the leader of formally constituted committees but it can also be used of leaders of less formal groups in educational or therapeutic settings. Even so, such groups are clearly at the 'formal' end of the formal–informal continuum. (No one thinks of chairing a party or a bus queue!) They are likely to have a fixed membership and to meet on predetermined occasions. The frequency of their meetings may be specified and they may have explicit 'terms of reference'. Their proceedings may also be constrained by mutually agreed 'rules of procedure', whether these are explicated as 'standing orders' or merely a rough consensus about such matters as addressing the chair and avoiding all talking at once.

Committees and formal discussion groups are thus among the most highly ritualised of group interactions, and chairmanship skill can be conceived as the management of such ceremonial. For individual group members, however, (and, indeed, for the chairman himself) the group may also be interpreted as a setting for the achievement of informal goals such as the establishment of friendship bonds, the settling of old scores, the buttressing of self-esteem and so on. Interaction thus has 'hidden agendas' and group members 'presumably engage in differential perception of their "statuses" thus creating the possibility of ambiguity and misinterpretation' (Cicourel, 1983).

However such ambiguities are managed the chairman, as the OED puts it, occupies a chair 'of authority' — he is in a position of leadership and to be effective he must exercise his authority judiciously. Study of leadership styles has a long history in social psychology (Stogdill, 1974) and many early lists existed of desirable leadership characteristics. These, however, were generally lacking in either specificity or empirical validation.

Other studies (Bales, 1958; Bales and Slater, 1955; Gibb, 1969) have noted the emergence in groups studied of two types of leader — the 'task' leader who is oriented towards achievement of the group's formal goals, and the 'maintenance' leader whose orientation is towards the support of group cohesiveness and members' personal well-being and morale. Fiedler (1967) develops the idea further by suggesting that effective leadership (and by implication, chairmanship) depends upon matching leadership style to the characteristics of the group concerned and of the task it is undertaking. He has also developed leadership training programmes based on these principles in which trainees are taught to analyse situations and tasks to determine their suitability for leadership in their own accustomed style. Interestingly, Fiedler does not suggest that styles can be changed or improved upon.

More recent work has criticised Fiedler for undue separation of task and maintenance roles and several studies (Borgatta, Couch and Bales, 1954; Rees and Segal, 1984) have described so-called 'great men' who manage to integrate task and maintenance roles and to alter their behaviour flexibly as tasks and situations demand. Increasingly, leadership studies stress the importance of fine-grained analysis of leadership behaviour (as opposed to 'style') (Davis and Luthans, 1984; Schneier and Goktepe, 1983) and emphasise communication variables as predictors of effective leadership (Schultz, 1984; Reynolds, 1984). Such an emphasis is, of course, close to the communication skills approach adopted in the present volume.

Chairmanship for the present author, is an area of socially skilled behaviour. As such it is learned and can be improved upon however expert or inexpert the performer is. Further, its execution can be analysed as suggested by models originating in the analysis and development of motor skills (Argyle, 1967; Holding, 1965; Welford, 1968) and discussed at length in Ellis and Whittington (1981) and in Chapter 2 of this volume.

Thus the component processes of skilled performance can be categorised as perception, translation, response and use of feedback in pursuit of a specified goal. The chairman might, for example, decide to move the meeting along more quickly as part of his strategy for completing the business before lunch. To do this he would first size up the situation: Who is speaking? What about? How are the others responding (verbally and nonverbally)? He would then consider various possible tactics and, translating one into a plan for action, might select and execute the response 'Well, we seem to have covered most of that. Could Fred and Charlie maybe get together afterwards on the detail?' and, depending on feedback from Fred and Charlie, will or will not move on to the next business.

Clearly, such action–feedback–action loops operate at many levels and over varying timespans. Contrast, for example, deciding precisely when to nod the head indicating attention to the current speaker and deciding that in future, discussion of matters arising from the minutes will be kept as short as possible. Both are strategies for skilled chairmanship involving perception, translation, response and feedback and both will be significant for the effective management of the meeting. The first, however, will normally be automatised and unremarked by either party, while the second is likely to be a conscious decision and may be so noticeable it has to be approved by the members of the meeting before implementation.

The chairman, then, is one who is formally recognised as leader of a group (often called a committee). He is in consequence required to execute socially skilled behaviour appropriate to the group's conception of the chairmanship role and to the tasks confronting it.

What Tasks do Chaired Groups Undertake?

Many committees and other chaired groups have stated terms of reference and their formal tasks are thus explicit. What they actually do in any given period will vary, however, according to the interpretations made of the terms of reference and the various ambiguities and informal pressures referred to above. Some formally allotted tasks may be virtually ignored and others hammered into the ground.

No empirically derived categorisation of the tasks undertaken by chaired groups seems to be available but they might be classified as follows:

1. Discussion: sharing and clarifying information.
2. Problem-solving: putting information in new configurations relevant to the solution of a specified problem.
3. Negotiation: resolving conflict and effecting acceptable compromise.
4. Decision-making: reaching group consensus.

These categories are not mutually exclusive, nor do they afford a neat way of categorising groups since many groups will engage in several or even all of these activities in the course of one meeting. Indeed, much of the social psychological literature on group interaction has been criticised on the grounds of artificiality precisely because researchers set up laboratory groups said to be exclusively negotiation groups, problem-solving groups and so on.

Nonetheless, the classification may be a useful bridge between one's intuitions about the tasks confronting chaired groups and aspects of the psychological literature which may be of relevance to those who would improve their own or others' chairmanship skills.

Are There Chairmanship Skills Specific to Such Tasks?

Discussion

All groups spend a fair amount of time finding out each others' ideas and opinions. Discussion groups are set up for that sole purpose and membership of working committees is often determined by the range of ideas, opinions and past experience likely to be contributed by each member. Whatever the group the chairman, therefore, spends some of his time facilitating discussion.

Most of the literature on leadership of group discussion comes either from group psychotherapy (Foulkes and Anthony, 1957) or from teacher education (Turney, 1976; Kozma, Belle and Williams, 1978; Beard and Hartley, 1984). Effectiveness in group leadership tends therefore to be assessed in terms of participant satisfaction (Foulkes and Anthony, 1957; Abercrombie, 1974), amount learned (Costin, Greenough and Menges, 1972; McLeish, 1976) or enthusiasm for the subject taught (Elliott, 1950; Beach, 1970). None of these are necessarily objectives of discussion in other types of chaired group, yet it seems sensible to suggest that a problem-solving or negotiating group may proceed more smoothly towards achievement of its goals if participants learn something from each other and have relatively positive attitudes towards the process.

Assuming then that the chairman wishes to facilitate full discussion of a topic how should he proceed? Most sources suggest that he should begin before the meeting. Newton and Seville (1977) and Collier (1983) report that undergraduate seminars are much improved if students are given specific tasks to complete before the seminars begin; Trosky (1973) describes a series of 'pre-discussion discussions' used to improve interaction in school discussion groups. Therefore, it seems likely that papers circulated before a meeting will improve discussion once it takes place. Such papers are themselves subject to the rules of good communication, however, and a chairman who circulates a three-inch pile of papers 24 hours before his meeting is unlikely to stimulate lively discussion. Similarly, a chairman might do well to talk separately to key individuals before his meeting. He will thus have some feel for issues likely to provoke lengthy debate and those more likely to be dealt with quickly. It may even be possible to allocate tasks to committee members (to raise a particular issue or to research a particular aspect of the topic to be discussed) before the meeting.

Once discussion of the topic has begun, the chairman has an important role in introducing and clarifying the issues for discussion. Turney *et al.* (1976) term this 'focusing' and divide it into introducing the aims of the discussion and stating the specific issue to be discussed. He also proposes a controlling role for the chairman in restating the issue as necessary when the meeting digresses. Schmuck and Schmuck (1971) also stress the importance of the chairman's initiating and topic control functions.

Once the discussion is underway, discussion leaders often clarify or refine what has been said. Scheidel and Crowell (1964) reported that group leaders spent 25 per cent of their time doing so and most teacher interaction analyses (Flanders, 1970; Wragg, 1984) include some such category. Turney *et al.* (1976) suggest that this global skill comprises subskills of paraphrasing, summarising, using probing questions and elaborating on contributions (see Hargie, Saunders and Dickson, 1981, and the earlier chapters of this book for discussion of these skills). It seems clear that this is an important aspect of the chairman's role in keeping discussion full and to the point.

The promotion of an appropriate amount of discussion and ensuring that each group member has a reasonable opportunity to contribute also gets considerable attention in the literature. The silent group seems intuitively less of a problem in committees than in instructional groups but the first few meetings may be fairly hesitant and certainly the author has encountered committee monopolists whose tactics needed very firm handling from the chair.

Turney *et al.* (1976) give a very full account of techniques for promoting and distributing discussion. They suggest, for example, that the use of 'key questions' at predetermined points in the discussion helps to ensure that each aspect of the topic is adequately discussed and also serves to stimulate new ideas and further discussion. They also place great emphasis on the discussion leader's response to members' contributions, identifying 'reinforcement' (see Chapter 5) and 'attentive listening' (see Chapter 10) as important components of effective response. More recently, Beattie (1982), studying undergraduate tutorial groups, found that discussion leaders spoke for a disproportionate amount of time and that the probability of their speaking immediately after a student contribution was approximately 0.8, while that of a student following up a student contribution was 0.4. Tutors also tended to interrupt students as they were ending their contributions and made little use of silence. Foulkes and Anthony (1957), Abercrombie (1974) and Turney *et al.* (1976), each working in rather different contexts, all emphasise the importance of the group leader simply being quiet while group members talk to each other, think over what has been said or pluck up courage to initiate a new theme in the discussion. Indeed, psychotherapists (Luft, 1984) often recommend not only silence but diminution in nonverbal behaviour and withdrawal of eye contact as potent forces in encouraging group autonomy and maximum participation.

There is also a good deal of evidence to suggest that the physical layout of the room can foster or hinder free discussion (Hawkins *et al.*, 1981; Sommer, 1969, 1983; Steinzor, 1950; and see Chapter 14, this volume). Certainly, the chairman should ensure that all participants can see both him and each other so that nonverbal as well as verbal behaviour can make its impact.

Ensuring that all group or committee members have an opportunity to participate demands slightly different chairman behaviour, although the skills discussed above should go some way to making members feel they could contribute if they wanted to. Turney *et al.* (1976) suggest seeking views from or sensitively questioning silent members. They are clear that those who talk too much should be ignored when next they try to catch the attention or, if necessary, should be explicitly asked to keep quiet. They also suggest that the chairman should try to prevent overtalk and should ensure smooth turn-taking procedures between himself and members, and between the members themselves.

Finally, having seen the discussion through to something like a conclusion (or merely having run out of time), it is the chairman's task to close the discussion. All sources suggest that summarisation of points discussed, decisions reached and an indication of 'the way ahead' are useful at this stage. Turney *et al.* (1976) also suggest that some measure of critical but generally positive evaluation of the discussion which has just taken place improves future sessions.

Problem-solving

While most chaired groups may look like discussion groups to the untrained eye — 'doing their work by talk' as Argyle (1969) puts it — it has already been noted that some groups have distinguishably different aims from those of simple discussion groups. Most committees at some time have to solve problems and, while most of the literature on the topic is derived from work in the artificiality of the psychology laboratory, it may still be relevant to real groups.

In classic problem-solving studies (Davis and Restle, 1963; Shaw, 1932) groups are given simple problems to solve collectively; their performance is observed and variables which are thought to predict effectiveness (accurate and rapid solution of the 'problem') are determined. Early studies (Lewin, 1947) were said to show that democratic approaches to group work produced solutions as good as, or even better than, those produced in a more autocratic ambience or by individuals working in isolation.

However, subsequent studies have been less sanguine about the beneficial effects of group interaction upon problem-solving performance. Hackman and Morris (1983) conclude that 'the few general findings that have emerged from the literature do not encourage the use of groups to perform important tasks'. They stress, however, that existing studies may not have done enough to help groups to maximise the potential benefits of being a group, such as the increased amount of available information or number of proposed solutions. They particularly emphasise the importance of developing and improving systems for the description and analysis of effective group interaction, thus demonstrating yet again the increasing interest in communication variables in the study of groups and group leadership.

A number of specific techniques have been developed in the study of group problem-solving which could be of interest to chairmen. Best known of these may be 'brainstorming' (Osborn, 1953) in which group members are encouraged to produce as many thoughts and ideas as they can in a set time, without criticising or commenting upon their own or other members' contributions. This technique has been popular in both industrial and educational settings and participants generally rate the experience favourably. However, systematic studies of performance (Dunnette, Campbell and Jaastad, 1963) do not show any particular advantage for brainstorming over other techniques.

More recently, the 'Delphi method' and 'syndicate method' (Collier, 1983) have received attention. These methods involve separating people and letting them work on the problem (or aspects of it) in isolation before bringing them back together to compare and collate solutions in the group. In theory this should capitalise on both individual superiority in the solution of difficult or abstract problems (Davis and Restle, 1963) and group superiority in noticing errors, planning problem-solving in the widest context of previous experience and, if appropriate, producing alternative solutions.

Negotiation

Negotiation groups are, by definition, groups set up when more than one solution to a problem is available and when these solutions conflict. In these groups, the chairman is generally (but not necessarily) selected for his neutrality and capacity to mediate the conflict. Not all chaired groups are set up for the specific purpose of negotiation but almost all such groups will spend some of their time involved in the negotiation process — even if only over the way to hand round the coffee! The process has been defined (Susskind and Rubin, 1983) as 'the settlement of differences and the waging of conflict through verbal exchange', or as (Morley, 1981) 'letting the other side have your own way'. What can the chairman learn from the literature about such a complex process?

Thompson (1985) suggests that negotiations tend to follow a common sequence. Before they begin, each party tends to meet to discuss their position and strategy and generally to prepare their case. These meetings enhance commitment and possibly entrenchment and, therefore, may not assist the achievement of a negotiated solution. However, Morley (1981) suggests that these preparatory phases can influence 'the ways in which negotiators formulate and define the problems they are likely to have'. The second phase according to Thompson (1985) is usually 'negotiations about negotiations': who will attend, how they will be seated, what the agenda will be and so on. These initial exchanges also afford an opportunity to size up the opposition's negotiating style and skill and, indeed, the firmness or otherwise of the chairman.

Once true negotiation is underway, Douglas (1957) suggests three phases. In the first of these — 'reconnoitring' — positions are established, cases made and strength of feeling (on both sides) is tested. Subsequently, the 'range is explored' as alternatives are produced and the opposition's reactions ascertained. Finally, negotiating teams may have to return to their 'constituencies' before agreement can be confirmed.

Rubin (1983) gives six prescriptions for negotiators. First, they (and no doubt their chairman) should be aware that both parties walk tightropes between frankness and machiavellian deceipt, between co-operation and competition for maximum gain, and between short-term and long-term outcomes. Second, they should recognise that both sides need to save face when compromising — the neutral third-party chairman has a particular role here in taking the blame for a solution not to the liking of one of the negotiating parties. Third, they should be interpersonally sensitive. Fourth, they should induce a feeling of competence in their opponents by being seen to react differentially to their initiatives. Neither total flexibility nor total intransigence has this effect since the opponent's actions have no effect on the strategy being employed. Fifth, negotiators should avoid commitments to intransigence with no back-up position for face-saving purposes. Lastly, they should be aware that the intensity of conflict between the parties may influence the strategies available.

Somewhat more explicitly, Fisher and Ury (1981), reporting on the work of the Harvard Negotiation Project, advocate a move towards principled negotiation. This they describe as 'negotiation on the merits'. It will, they suggest, produce easier solutions than either hard adversarial postures or soft concessionary strategies. They give four major rules for principled negotiation which are as much rules for chairmen of negotiations as they are rules for members of either 'side'. They can be paraphrased as follows:

1. People should be separated from the problem thus reducing psychological identification with it. Only in an atmosphere of mutual co-operation on attacking

the problem can hostility be reduced. (Note that the chairman has a particular role here in clarifying issues, selecting apparently trivial but easily resolved parts of the problem for first attention or even encouraging opposing parties to try to solve each others problems — 'What would you do if you were Fred?');

2. Focus on interests not position. Bargaining positions are often adopted for effect and may even conceal the real motivations of their proponents. (Again, the chairman's probing questions and test clarifications — 'What Fred seems to be saying is . . .' are important);

3. Generate a variety of options before deciding what to do. Set aside time away from the adversary for generating solutions. (Again, the chairman has a role to play either in the full meeting where he may engage with each party in trying to produce alternatives or in splitting the meeting up into 'buzz' groups or Delphi groups, as discussed in the previous section).

4. Insist that the result be based on some objective criteria. It may be possible to draw the sting from the dispute by establishing what a solution should look like before actually trying to find one. (And again the chairman can help by proposing exemplar criteria.)

Decision-making

Groups solving problems or negotiating are, of course, in some sense making decisions. They are deciding what the answer is or where the acceptable area of compromise lies. However, groups can often be faced with problems where there is no immediately available right answer and where there are no particular vested interests to be satisfied. In these circumstances the group as a whole is being asked to make a judgement. Such judgements can be value judgements about what 'ought' to be but perhaps more frequently they are judgements based on inadequate data or untestable assumptions about future events. Management planning meetings are often of this kind. The best possible data have been amassed on past performance and available resources, the experts have been consulted about future trends in markets, government policy and so on — but in the end, a judgement must be made.

How do such decisions emerge and how can the chairman facilitate the emergence of the right ones? There is a very substantial literature on decision-making, and models of group variables related to outcomes proliferate. Early findings by Stoner (1968) and others suggested that groups were more likely to take 'risky' decisions than were individuals alone. This 'risky shift' phenomenon seemed to have alarming significance for important decision-making groups like governments, local councils and so on, and the idea attracted considerable attention. However, it soon became clear (Stoner, 1968) that individual-group shift could be obtained from 'neutral' or even 'cautious' choices, and indeed Moscovici and Zavalloni (1969) have suggested that groups have the effect of pushing individuals into more extreme versions of the position they already held. Thus, risky groups become more risky, cautious groups more cautious and so on.

Regrettably, few of these studies have focused on the detail of the interpersonal processes and skills evinced by participants in decision-making although several authors (Davis and Hinsz, 1982) call for such an emphasis. It is difficult, therefore, to make behavioural prescriptions for chairmen or, indeed, members of such groups beyond those which have already been suggested for general problem-solving and negotiation.

Some negative exemplars of 'how not to do it' might, however, be derived from Janis' (1972) studies of group think. Janis studied policy-planning groups whose deliberations had led to historic fiascos including Chamberlain's appeasement decision, Kennedy's Bay of Pigs decision and Lyndon Johnson's decision to escalate the war in Vietnam. From these studies and subsequent laboratory validations (Janis and Mann, 1977), Janis identifies what he terms as the 'adverse effects of concurrence seeking' — going for agreement at any price. These adverse effects include the following: incomplete survey of alternatives; failure to examine the risks of a preferred choice; failure to reappraise initially rejected alternatives; poor information search; selective bias in processing information at hand; and failure to work out contingency plans (Janis and Mann, 1977, p. 132).

Janis (1982) calls for much more research on the area but does put forward prescriptive hypotheses to be tested, many of which make specific reference to the chairman's function. These hypotheses can be paraphrased as follows:

1. Knowing about group-think will have a beneficial deferring effect;
2. The chairman should initially be impartial;
3. The chairman should encourage group members to express doubts;
4. Members should act as devil's advocate;
5. Groups should occasionally break into subgroups;
6. Rival or opponent groups should be closely observed and a range of alternative interpretations of their actions should be derived;
7. After preliminary agreement has been reached the group should have an opportunity to rethink;
8. Outsiders should be brought in occasionally to challenge established views;
9. Group members should discuss proceedings with colleagues who are not members;
10. For any given policy area there should be more than one group involved.

Chairmen clearly have a pivotal role in ensuring that such strategies are adopted.

The chairmanship skills thus addressed from the literatures on discussion leadership, problem-solving, negotiation and decision-making vary considerably in their behavioural specificity (from arranging the chairs so that everyone can see the chairman to fostering an atmosphere of co-operation) and in level of analysis (from allowing pauses at the end of member contributions to giving the group an opportunity to rethink). In each of the literature areas reviewed, however, there can be discerned an increasing awareness of the importance of communication variables in the characterisation of effective group and chairmanship performance. There is an obvious need for closer and more specific analysis of chairmanship behaviour.

Are There Generic Chairmanship Skills?

The only empirical study of chairmanship *per se* to be found in the literature was carried out by Rackham and Morgan in 1977. They identified 31 chairmen as 'effective' on criteria of: committee members' perceptions of fairness and efficiency; track record of chairmanship experience and 'expert' judges' observations. Each chairman was then observed conducting a meeting and his behaviour (and that of other members) was categorised under the following headings: content proposals; procedural proposals; building; supporting; disagreeing; defending/attacking; testing understanding; summarising; seeking information; giving information; bringing in; shutting out.

Chairman behaviour was then compared with the behaviour of other members of the group for frequency of each of the above categories.

Rackham and Morgan found that effective chairmen:

1. Made more procedural proposals than other members;
2. Used less supporting behaviour;
3. Used a very high level of testing understanding and summarising;
4. Used less disagreeing behaviour;
5. Were high in their use of information-seeking and relatively low on information-giving.

They also found that their chairmen varied in their use of bringing-in and shutting-out behaviour and conducted a further study which showed that this was closely related to bias and attempts to influence meetings. They had recorded the meetings on videotape and were able to show that where the chairman was neutral on an issue he looked at the speaker for over 70 per cent of the time and exerted little control (through bringing-in and shutting-out) over who spoke next. Where the issue was one in which he had a clear opinion or where it was in some other way 'loaded', Rackham and Morgan's chairmen looked at the speaker for less than 50 per cent of the time and tended to invite a specific person to speak immediately after the 'loaded' contribution. Interestingly, these behaviours were not perceived by group members as an increase in manipulativeness.

In the absence of other empirical data on effective chairmanship, recourse is now taken to two typical sources of guidance for designers of social skill training programmes: the general social psychological literature (as reviewed above) and the author's own judgement and intuition as an experienced chairperson. The author in no way suggests that her notes for guidance are exhaustive, uniformly important or even internally discrete. The hope is, however, that they are sufficiently specific to allow social skill trainers and trainees to address themselves to the development of chairmanship skills. An existing group has been assumed, so membership and terms of reference are already determined.

Before the Meeting

Agenda. Consider existing agenda items, add new ones and make sure all members have an opportunity to contribute items. Order the agenda logically and place important items early.

Strategy. Consider the main task of the meeting — is it a problem-solving or negotiating meeting? Would it benefit by splitting into smaller groups? Should members have tasks to do before coming to the meeting? Should working parties be set up? Should outsiders be invited? (It may be helpful at this stage to run through an imaginary meeting in one's head — bearing in mind what is known about members' past views and performance styles and about the formality with which standing orders are observed.) What do you expect the meeting to achieve?

Location and Geography. Make sure appropriate room(s) are available for a long enough time and that furnishing can be organised to facilitate suitable communication flow. Be sure that lighting and ventilation are adequate and that chairs are neither uncomfortable nor so comfortable as to induce sleep.

Sustenance. If the meeting is to go on beyond an hour or so, plan for a break for coffee — or at least for a walk round. Make it clear in the agenda that there will be a break.

Papers. Circulate papers well in advance. Encourage contributors of agenda items to produce brief papers giving background information when necessary, but always including a brief summary and list of points for debate.

Canvassing and Delegation. Talk to significant members of the group to solicit views and determine whether they will introduce particular items or propose or oppose particular outcomes.

At the Meeting

Initiation. At the beginning of the meeting establish what it is for and, if members have not met before, introduce them to each other. Clarify the objectives of the meeting, deal with any minor procedural matters and introduce the main business. As each item is addressed, again state the purpose of including it on the agenda and give an indication of the main points for discussion.

Observation. As the meeting proceeds, be sensitive to nonverbal as well as verbal communication. Keep a check on who are and are not participating, who interrupts or is interrupted, who speaks most and so on.

Attentive Listening. Use questions, reinforcers and nonverbal signals such as eye contact, direction of gaze, orientation, head nods and facial expression matching, to indicate attention to speakers (or, negatively, to close off someone's contribution).

Bringing-in and Shutting-out. Bring in non-participants and shut-out monopolisers. Bring in participants who you know have relevant contributions to make or who, as in Rackham and Morgan's study, can be relied upon to support your own position. If the group is in danger of easy group-think concurrence, bring in known criticisers.

Directional Control. Repeat or paraphrase statements which seem significant. Use probing questions to establish new themes in discussion. Make procedural proposals for closing or opening topics.

Summary and Clarification. Use summary and clarification after each item or if discussion seems confused. Tell speakers what you think they mean (they may not know themselves!). At the end of the meeting state what has been discussed, what conclusions have been reached and give an indication of the way ahead.

After the Meeting

Read. Read minutes or other records soon and prepare an appropriate version for the next meeting.

Propose. Prepare an action sheet for yourself and for other members.

Consult. Consult with other members on the way ahead, ask for feedback on the handling of the meeting, help to resolve any remaining difficulties, salve interaction wounds and so on.

The author hopes this unashamedly exhortatory list will be helpful but is more than conscious that she has assumed that the novice chairman is already an expert in everyday interaction, in possession of a repertoire of microskills of verbal and nonverbal communication and able to integrate them at the molar level of this list.

What Further Research is Needed?

As is clear from much of the preceding discussion, there is little or no research on the specifics of chairmanship. Likewise, research on group process is often at a very global level and lacks any real emphasis on communication variables.

There is a great need for detailed empirical analysis of real life committees and problem-solving groups in action. Video and computer technology has advanced considerably in the last ten years and should now be able to handle the sequential analysis of interactional data which has with some honourable exceptions (Duncan and Fiske, 1977; Beattie, 1982) so far eluded researchers. Greater emphasis on cognitive variables like Burnstein's (1978) 'persuasive communication' and on aspects of linguistic and paralinguistic phenomena could also be recommended. Meanwhile, the author returns to her committees amazed that anything is ever done, decided or agreed!

References

Abercrombie, M.L.J. (1974) 'Aims and Techniques of Group Teaching', Society for Research in Higher Education, London

Argyle, M. (1967) *The Psychology of Interpersonal Behaviour*, Penguin, Harmondsworth
———— (1969) *Social Interaction*, Methuen, London

Bales, R. (1958) 'Task Roles and Social Roles in Problem Solving Groups' in E. Maccoby, T. Newcomb and F. Hartley (eds), *Readings in Social Psychology* (3rd edn), Holt, Rinehart and Winston, New York
———— and Slater, P. (1955) 'Role Differentiation' in T. Parsons (ed.), *The Family, Socialisation and Interaction*, Macmillan, New York

Beach, L. (1970) *Learning and Student Interaction in Small Self-Directed College Groups*, Department of Health, Education and Welfare, Washington

Beard, R. and Hartley, J. (1984) *Teaching and Learning in Higher Education*, 4th edn, Harper and Row, London

Beattie, G. (1982) *Talk*, Open University Press, Milton Keynes

Borgatta, E., Couch, A. and Bales, R. (1954) 'Some Findings Relevant to the Great-man Theory of Leadership', *Amer. Soc. Review, 19*, 755–9

Burnstein, E. (1978) 'Persuasion as Argument Processing', paper presented to the International Symposium on Group Decision Making, Schloss Reisenburg, W. Germany

Cicourel, A. (1983) 'Interpreting Normative Rules in the Negotiation of Status and Role' in H.H. Blumberg, A.P. Hare, V. Kent *et al.* (eds), *Small Groups and Social Interaction*, Wiley, London

Collier, A. (1983) *The Management of Peer Group Learning: Syndicate Methods in Higher Education*, SRHE, Guildford

Costin, F., Greenough, W. and Menges, R. (1971) 'Student Ratings of College Teaching: Reliability, Validity and Usefulness', *Rev. Ed. Research, 41* (5), 511–35

Davis, J. and Hinsz, V. (1982) 'Current Research Problems in Group Performance and Group Dynamics' in H. Brandstetter, J. Davis and H. Stocker-Kreichgauer (eds), *Group Decision Making*, Academic Press, London

Davis, J. and Restle, F. (1963) 'The Analysis of Problems and Prediction of Group Problem Solving', *J. Abnormal and Soc. Psychology, 66*, 103–16

Davis, T. and Luthans, F. (1984) 'Defining and Researching Leadership as a Behavioural Construct', *J. App. Behavioural Science, 20* (3), 237–51

Douglas, A. (1957) *Industrial Peacemaking*, Columbia University Press, New York

Doyle, M. and Strauss, D. (1976) *How to Make Meetings Work*, Wyden Books, San Francisco

Duncan, S. and Fiske, D. (1977) *Face to Face Interaction*, Wiley, New York

Dunnette, M., Campbell, J. and Jaastad, K. (1963) 'The Effect of Group Participation on Brainstorming Effectiveness for Two Industrial Samples', *J. App. Psychology, 47*, 30–7

Elliott, P. (1950) 'Characteristics and Relationships of Various Criteria of College and University Teaching', *Purdue University Studies of Higher Education, 70*, 5–61

Ellis, R. and Whittington, D. (1981) *A Guide to Social Skill Training*, Croom Helm, Beckenham

Fiedler, F. (1967) *A Theory of Leadership Effectiveness*, McGraw-Hill, New York

Fisher, R. and Ury, W. (1981) *Getting to YES*, Houghton-Mifflin, Boston

Flanders, N. (1970) *Analysing Teaching Behaviour*, Addison-Wesley, Boston, Massachussetts

Foulkes, S. and Anthony, E. (1957) *Group Psychotherapy: The Psychoanalytic Approach*, Penguin, London

Gibb, C.A. (1969) 'Leadership' in A. Lindzey and E. Aronson (eds), *The Handbook of Social Psychology, vol. IV*, Addison-Wesley, Reading, Massachussetts

Hackman, J.R. and Morris, C. (1983) 'Group Tasks, Group Interaction and Group Performance Effectiveness' in H.H. Blumberg, A.P. Hare, V. Kent *et al.* (eds), *Small Groups and Social Interaction*, Wiley, London

Hargie, O., Saunders, C. and Dickson, D. (1981) *Social Skills in Interpersonal Communication*, Croom Helm, Beckenham

Hawkins, S., Davies, I., Majer, K. *et al.* (1981) *Getting Started: Guides for Beginning Teachers*, 2nd edn, Blackwell, Oxford

Holding, D. (1965) *Principles of Training*, Pergamon, Oxford

Janis, I. (1972) *Victims of Groupthink*, Houghton-Mifflin, Boston

——— (1982) 'Counteracting the Adverse Effects of Concurrence-seeking in Policy-planning Groups: Theory and Research Perspectives' in H. Brandstatter, J. Davis and A. Stocker-Kreichgouer (eds), *Group Decision Making*, Academic Press, London

——— and Mann, L. (1977) *Decision-making: A Psychological Analysis of Conflict, Choice and Commitment*, Free Press, New York

Kozma, R., Belle, L. and Williams, G. (1978) *Instructional Techniques in Higher Education*, Educational Technology Publications, Englewood Cliffs

Lewin, K. (1947) 'Group Decision and Social Change' in T. Newcomb and E. Hartley (eds), *Readings in Social Psychology*, Holt, Rinehart and Winston, New York

Luft, J. (1984) *Group Processes*, 3rd edn, Mayfield, Palo Alto

McLeish, J. (1976) 'The Lecture Method' in N. Gage (ed.), *The Psychology of Teaching Methods*, University of Chicago Press, Chicago

Marshall, J. (1957) *Chairmanship and Meeting Procedure*, Arnold, London

Maude, B. (1975) *Managing Meetings*, Ivory Head Press, London

Morley, I. (1981) 'Negotiation and Bargaining' in M. Argyle (ed.), *Social Skills and Work*, Methuen, London

Moscovici, S. and Zavalloni, M. (1969) 'The Group as a Polariser of Attitudes', *J. Pers. and Soc. Psychology, 12*, 125–35

Newton, J. and Seville, A. (1977) 'Syndicate Studies for the Systems and Management Degree', *Physics Education, 12* (4), 217–20

Osborn, A. (1953) *Applied Imagination*, Scribner, New York

Rackham, N. and Morgan, T. (1977) *Behaviour Analysis in Training*, McGraw-Hill, Maidenhead

Rees, C.R. and Segal, M.W. (1984) 'Role Differentiation in Groups', *Small Group Behaviour, 15* (1), 109–23

Reynolds, P. (1984) 'Leaders Never Quit', *Small Group Behaviour, 15* (3), 404–13

Rubin, J. (1983) 'Negotiation: Some Issues and Themes', *American Behavioural Scientist, 27* (2), 135–47

Scheidel, T. and Crowell, L. (1964) 'Idea Development in Small Discussion Groups', *Quarterly Journal of Speech, 50*, 140–5

Schmuck, R. and Schmuck, P. (1971) *Group Processes in the Classroom*, W.C. Brown, Dubque, Iowa

Schneier, C. and Goktepe, J. (1983) 'Issues in Emergent Leadership' in H.H. Blumberg, A.P. Hare, V. Kent *et al.* (eds), *Small Groups and Social Interaction*, Wiley, Chichester

Shaw, M. (1932) 'A Comparison of Individuals and Small Groups in the Rational Solution of Complex Problems', *American J. of Psychology, 44*, 491–504

Sommer, R. (1969) *Personal Space: The Behavioural Basis of Design*, Prentice-Hall, Englewood Cliffs

Steinzor, B. (1950) 'The Spatial Factor in Face to Face Discussion Groups', *J. Abnormal and Soc. Psychology, 45* (3), 552–5

Stogdill, R. (1974) *Handbook of Leadership*, Free Press, New York

Stoner, J. (1968) 'Risky and Cautious Shifts in Group Decisions: The Influence of Widely Held Values', *J. Exp. Soc. Psychology, 4*, 442–59

Susskind, L. and Rubin, J. (1983) 'Introduction to the Special Issue on Negotiation', *American Behavioural Scientist, 27* (2), 134–5

Thompson, J. (1985) *Psychological Aspects of Nuclear War*, British Psychological Society and Wiley, London

Trosky, O. (1973) 'Discussion — Intuitive or Learned?' *Elementary School Journal, 6*, 328–32

Turney, C., Thew, D., Owens, L., Hatton, N. and Cairns, L. (1976) *Sydney Micro Skills: Series 4 Handbook*, Sydney University Press, Sydney

Welford, A. (1968) *Fundamentals of Skill*, Methuen, London

Wragg, E. (1984) *Classroom Teaching Skills*, Croom Helm, Beckenham

13 NEGOTIATING AND BARGAINING

Ian Morley

Introduction

Negotiation is a process of joint decision-making used to handle *issues* as they arise in particular social contexts. It is a mechanism for deciding what can be achieved politically, and at what cost. It is used to manage change. It functions to define the terms on which persons or parties will do future business. The end point of the process is a set of *rules*. There may also be an agreed *story* about what has happened, and why. For these reasons, social order is often considered as negotiated order.

Negotiation may have many objectives. Reaching an agreement is only one (Jensen, 1963). The author is concerned primarily with negotiation as it occurs in the context of large-scale organisations. He is also concerned primarily with those kinds of negotiation in which the parties have decided to search for agreement. There are two main objectives: the first is to review what has been learned about the skills of negotiation from empirical research, integrating findings from a wide variety of contexts; the second is to provide a systematic theoretical treatment of the nature of the skills of negotiation. This will show how skilled performers are able to select tactics and sequence their behaviour in organised and coherent ways.

Empirical Research

The account of negotiating skills to be presented is grounded empirically, in the following kinds of research.

Studies Which Use the Behaviour Analysis Approach Outlined by Morgan (1980)

In some cases the focus is on negotiators, comparing the behaviour of those with and without a track record of success in industrial relations or contract negotiation. Relevant work includes that of the Huthwaite Research Group, particularly of Rackham and Carlisle (Rackham and Carlisle, 1978a, 1978b; Carlisle and Leary, 1981). In other cases the focus is on successful negotiations, comparing behaviours which lead to successful outcomes and those which do not (Morley and Stephenson, 1977; Stephenson, Kniveton and Morley, 1977; Webb, 1985a, 1985b). The analysis has been confined to negotiations between union and management, sometimes with third parties, sometimes not. There are a small number of other studies of this kind, such as Landsberger (1955).

303

The first step in the method is to establish criteria which define successful outcomes. This has been accomplished, in practice, by variations on the following themes. First, avoid partisan criteria which reflect the views of only one of the sides. Instead, use multi-partisan criteria which reflect the fact that negotiation is an exercise in joint decision-making. Consider, for example, the product criterion used by McGrath and his associates (McGrath, 1966). They measure overall effectiveness in negotiation in terms of the product of ratings of agreements, obtained from officials of each of the parties. (They even include judges representing the position of the community at large.) Second, examine what happens when agreements are implemented. Ultimately, successful negotiations are those which the parties regard as viable. To quote Davey (1972): 'The mutual purpose of negotiation should be achievement of a collective agreement that will work' (p. 128).

Ideally, an agreement should satisfy *both* kinds of criteria. Agreements which are regarded as mutually acceptable are, no doubt, more likely to work than those which are not. However, negotiators make mistakes, like everyone else. For example, negotiations regarded as mutually acceptable at the time may conceal, or put a gloss on, differences in intent (Morley, 1981a; Davey, 1972). Such agreements are unlikely to work in the long run.

The second step in the method is to give a detailed description of what is said during the process of negotiation. This is accomplished using category systems of various kinds. In some cases researchers design special purpose sets of categories to apply specifically to negotiation groups. Morley and Stephenson's (1977) conference process analysis is one example. In other cases, however, researchers use general purpose systems which would apply to any kind of decision-making group. The best known examples are the interaction process analysis categories of Bales (Landsberger, 1955) and the behaviour analysis categories developed by Rackham and Morgan (Rackham and Morgan, 1977; Rackham and Carlisle, 1978a, 1978b).

Case Studies of Negotiation

Most describe collective bargaining in industry or diplomacy in international relations. In general, they say more about institutional procedures than the psychology of negotiation. However, it is also suggested that different relationship patterns, sometimes called bargaining structures, emerge in response to different social contexts (Harbison and Coleman, 1951; Walton and McKersie, 1965; Clegg, 1979). This is a very important conclusion. It shows that bargaining cannot be understood apart from the social context in which it occurs. However, the treatment of context is much too mechanistic for the author's taste. It falls squarely within what has been called the structural–functionalist perspective (Zey-Ferrell and Aiken, 1981). It focuses on the 'condition of being organised' rather than the 'act of organising' (Hosking and Morley, 1985b). As such, it ignores just those cognitive, discretionary and politically problematic aspects of organising which are central to the study of social skill (Hosking and Morley, 1985a). A much more promising line of research has been initiated by Strauss (1978), from within the perspective of symbolic interactionism. He is more concerned, however, with the sociological fact that there are different varieties of negotiation than with the psychological analysis of the nature of negotiation skill.

The account given here relies heavily on Snyder and Diesing's (1977) comprehensive studies of bargaining during international crises (see Lockhart, 1979; Morley, 1981a). It also relies on Morley's (1982) analysis of the psychological problems faced by the negotiator's at the Paris Peace Conference of 1919 (which led to the Treaty of Versailles).

Studies which Focus on the Behaviour of Managers and Officials of Trade Unions

Much of this work is concerned with differences between effective and ineffective performers (Kotter and Lawrence, 1974; Stewart, 1976; Batstone, Boraston and Frenkel, 1977; Sayles, 1979; Kotter, 1981; Kanter, 1984). The literature has little to say directly about negotiation, although it has much to say about the nature of social power, and 'power skills in use' (Kanter, 1984). Its major contribution, therefore, has been to identify some of the components required by a general model of social skill (Hosking and Morley, 1985a).

Surveys of Wage Determination in Various Industries

Like the studies cited under the above heading, these surveys (Brown, 1973; Daniel, 1976) also show that different patterns of bargaining occur in different social contexts. However, they are most useful, perhaps, because of the information they provide about who does the bargaining, and under what circumstances. For example, Daniel (1976) reported that, in his study, full-time trade union officers were involved in bargaining too little and too late. They were not, typically, involved from the start, but brought in to solve problems when negotiations looked like breaking down. When they were involved from the start there was a dramatic drop in the incidence of strikes, and other withdrawals of labour.

Studies of the Rhetoric of Conflict

Rhetorics show the importance of ideology in conflict (including negotiated conflict) because they are what Breakwell (1983) calls 'ideology in action' (p. 197). That is, they are context specific arguments which 'encapsulate beliefs and objectives and actively seek to inculcate them in others' (Breakwell, 1983, p. 197).

Descriptions of Practical Methods of Negotiation, Devised by Consultants

Some of these have considerable merit (for instance, Miron and Goldstein, 1979; Fisher and Ury, 1983). The author has found the work of Fisher and Ury (1983), based on negotiation workshops at the Harvard Law School, to be particularly useful.

Laboratory-based Studies of the Process of Negotiation

These have to be treated with care. Nevertheless, some of those which fit what

Morley and Stephenson (1977) call the substitute debate paradigm provide useful information. Here, the essence of the procedure is to get practising negotiators to do, in the laboratory, the kinds of thing they might otherwise do elsewhere. The author has personally found Winham's reports of laboratory simulations of complex trade negotiations very instructive (for instance, Winham, 1977; Morley, 1982).

To complete this section, the author adds a few words of caution. There is a large literature dealing with negotiation. However, very little of it is concerned *explicitly* with the nature of negotiators' skills. (It is no accident that the term 'skill' rarely appears in the subject index in basic texts.) The author has not attempted to review this literature in detail, but simply has indicated the kinds of research found to be useful. It is this research the author shall try to integrate into a general account of the nature of social skill in negotiation.

Bargaining Process and Bargaining Theory

Social psychological research on negotiation has been conducted, usually, within the paradigm established by Sawyer and Guetzkow (1965). It has attempted to characterise the process of negotiation in general terms, and to show how that process is affected by systemic, situational and population variables (Walton and McKersie, 1965; Druckman, 1973, 1977; Snyder and Diesing, 1977). Typically, negotiation is seen as a problem in *bargaining* (Bacharach and Lawter, 1981), to be described in terms of an exchange of concessions (Pruitt, 1981). It is assumed that concession behaviour is determined by bargaining strength, and that agreement is reached at the point where concessions converge. Strategies and tactics are described as competitive or collaborative. The former are designed to get the other to make unilateral concessions (that is, accept one's current offer, or demand). The latter are designed to co-ordinate the process of convergence or to promote a search for other ways of handling the issues (integrative bargaining). Strategies and tactics of this kind have been described in great detail, and related to various theories of individual choice (Walton and McKersie, 1965; Snyder and Diesing, 1977; Bacharach and Lawler, 1981; Pruitt, 1981).

The author takes the view that an adequate social psychological theory of bargaining requires three main components: a model of the *bargainers*; a model of the *bargaining process*; and a (macro-) model of the larger *social context* (Strauss, 1978; Morley, 1981b). He supposes, also, that such components need to be brought together in mutually supportive ways. If this is correct, it is evident that traditional theories contain some important defects.

First, they have not been informed by psychologically realistic models of the bargainers. It is not enough to identify population variables and treat them simply as dimensions of individual difference. What is needed is an account which allows one dynamically to explore the ways in which negotiators formulate and define the problems they are likely to face (Morley, 1982). It should allow one to explore the role of ideology, broadly defined. It should recognise that negotiators have theories of negotiation which 'enter and affect the negotiations themselves' (Strauss, 1978). It should allow one sensibly to consider the problems of information processing which arise as negotiations become increasingly complex (Winham, 1977).

Second, negotiation is not adequately described as a process of concession–convergence (Morley and Stephenson, 1977; Zartman, 1977; Webb, 1985b); particularly when there are many parties (Midgaard and Underdal, 1977) and issues are complex (Winham, 1977). If concessions are to be exchanged there must, after all, be agreement about the rate of exchange. Traditionally, the rate of exchange is determined by measures of bargaining strength, based on the utility functions of the participants (Coddington, 1968; Bacharach and Lawler, 1981). The author is inclined to extend the arguments of Midgaard and Underdal (1977) and say that it is impossible to find measures of this kind which are feasible, precise and compelling. There are, of course, some who would say that it is also unnecessary. To quote Davey (1972): 'Knowledgeable practitioners do not experience a burning need or desire to measure or weigh . . . bargaining power in precise fashion' (p. 97). This does not mean that bargaining power is unimportant. It means rather that it must be conceptualised in ways which link it to the operational knowledge of the participants (Bacharach and Lawler, 1981). It means also that one should adopt a different view of the process of negotiation.

The author's view of the matter is like that of Zartman (1977) and Webb (1985b). Concession-making is frequently not the most prominent feature of formal negotiations, such as those between union and management (Morley and Stephenson, 1977). Rather, negotiation proceeds through two stages. The first allows negotiators to find a *formula*, a set of principles linking what is happening now to what has happened in the past, and to what will happen in the future. The second allows the formula to be applied. Once negotiators know the general form agreement will take, and why, they can work out the details; what this means in the particular case.

Third, inadequate attention has been paid to aspects of continuity in the relationship between the sides (Pruitt, 1981; Webb, 1985b; Morley and Stephenson, 1977). There are many economic models of the single bargaining process, but none which develop theories of the long-term relationship between the parties (Coddington, 1968). More generally, there has been a failure to describe the social context in ways which make it clear what is of historical significance and what is not.

What this means is that current theories lack a concept of social skill, broadly defined. There is, instead, a focus on *dilemmas* which arise because competitive and collaborative tactics act in opposite ways, psychologically or in practice (Snyder and Diesing, 1977; Pruitt, 1981). The author's view is that dilemmas are one crucial component in the analysis of social skills because they represent fundamental choices inherent in the social processes by which decisions are made.

Two related dilemmas have been described in detail by Snyder and Diesing

(1977). They apply to negotiation in which the *major goal* is to reach a settlement. The settlement is *constrained*, however, by the desire to minimise certain kinds of cost. The dilemmas are dilemmas in decision-making (literally, choice dilemmas). They arise because there are antinomies between (collaborative) tactics aimed at achieving the major goal and (competitive) tactics aimed at satisfying the constraint. To achieve the major goal it is assumed that each party will, at some stage, have to indicate a change in position. The first dilemma (the first choice) is whether to make the change clear and explicit, or to leave it ambiguous. The second dilemma (the second choice) is when to indicate the change, early or late? Each is now considered in turn.

To begin with it may be supposed that a clear and explicit statement of a change in position is likely to facilitate the process of accommodation (Snyder and Diesing, 1977). However, it may also lead to what Pruitt (1971) has called *position loss* and *image loss*. One solution is to communicate the change tacitly, implying the change in position without stating it explicitly. This may be taken to mean that the message sent has to be ambiguous (Jervis, 1970). Thus, the negotiator is protected from position loss and from image loss because others cannot be sure what the message is. The risk is that the message is not received at all. Further discussion is given in Walton and McKersie (1965) and Pruitt (1981).

Negotiators who make an early move sacrifice a position and jeopardise their reputations for resolve. Their opponents may assume that there is more to come, if only they persist. On the other hand, negotiators who stand firm for too long risk being seen as totally intransigent. They may also risk becoming committed to positions they cannot defend. The available empirical evidence suggests that while there may be various ways of handling the first dilemma (Morley, 1981a; Pruitt, 1981) there is, realistically, only one way to handle the second (Snyder and Diesing, 1977). To quote Snyder and Diesing (1977): 'The only good way to meet the loss-avoidance constraint on accommodation is *first* to establish a convincing image of firmness' (p. 248). If moves are made before then they 'will be considered signs of general weakness, to be exploited' (Snyder and Diesing, 1977, p. 248).

Dilemmas of this kind are important in the analysis of the skills of negotiation (or other kinds of social skill). They show an underlying *logic* to the process which participants cannot afford to ignore.

Two Approaches to Negotiation Skill

This section relates to a certain kind of skilled performance. This implies talk about control and talk about organisation (Reason, 1978). In this case the control is control over values and interests. The organisation comes from understanding what the process of negotiation is all about. The view taken here is that the skilful negotiator is someone who is able to create and maintain a social order based on systems of power and systems of value. What makes this possible, broadly speaking, is an understanding of the threats and opportunities, and of the resources which can be mobilised, within a given social context.

It shall be assumed, also, that negotiation is a matter primarily of macro rather than micro skills. It is assumed that negotiators have a basic competence in those aspects of communication outlined by Argyle (1969; 1978). The author is far more concerned with whether, in some sense, they know their way around the social system (or context) in which negotiation takes place. Thus, Argyle's recent work is more germane to this position. The author agrees with him that: 'In order to function effectively one needs a good map, showing how the system works' (Argyle, 1984, p. 97). The author believes that what he has to say will provide the information to draw just such a map.

To make the same point in a different way: at one level the skills of negotiation may be described in terms of different processes of information interpretation, information search, influence and choice (Snyder and Diesing, 1977; Lockhart, 1979). These shall be called *core processes*. What is important is that more and less skilled performers *structure* these processes in different ways (Morley and Stephenson, 1977).

There are two models of social skill which are directly concerned with structure in the process of interaction. One is a general model which would apply to any kind of social skill (Welford, 1980). The other is directly geared to the study of negotiation (Morley, 1981a; 1981b; 1982; 1983). A general model of the skills of negotiation is proposed which includes elements from each of these models. Accordingly, it may be helpful to consider each of them in turn.

Welford's Model

Welford's model is essentially an information-processing model, grounded in cognitive psychology. It helps to explain why negotiation is frequently described (correctly) as the dialogue of the deaf. Part of the reason is that people have a limited capacity to process information about the social environment. They can only handle limited amounts of mental work (because they run out of mental resources). If one task takes a lot of mental effort, negotiators may not be able to do another at the same time. All of this is very familiar. The crucial point is that skilled negotiators may be expected to recognise this and help others to work through the core processes outlined above. From this point of view, skill may be seen as the use of efficient strategies linking the capacities of performers to the demands of the task.

It is important to note that the phrase 'help others' may refer to members of the other side in the negotiation. Help of this kind is an essential element in hostage negotiations (Miron and Goldstein, 1979), and crisis bargaining (Snyder and Diesing, 1977), but is also of more general significance.

It may be helpful to consider the work of Snyder and Diesing (1977) in rather more detail. It may also be helpful to say a little more about the role of ambiguity in negotiation. There are sub-processes in bargaining. Different people define them in different ways. Some function to establish *exactly* what is implied by a given position. Others function to co-ordinate shifts in position, and signal a willingness to shift from a competitive to a collaborative mode. Clarity and precision is the *sine qua non* of the former: ambiguity is the *sine qua non* of the latter.

Consider now Synder and Diesing's (1977) model of the bargaining process in more detail. So far it has been treated simply as an example of a traditional approach to the construction of a social psychological theory of negotiation. This is not entirely fair.

Although Snyder and Diesing operate with an economic model of bargaining, that of Coddington (1969), it is one in which psychological elements are of obvious importance. The model contains three parts: a theory of individual decision making (simple utility maximisation); a theory of expectations (that, in general, expectations will not be fulfilled); and a theory of the adjustment to expectations (based on a comparison of actual concession rate and expected concession rate). Essentially, Snyder and Diesing retain Coddington's emphasis on concession–convergence, but add a great deal of psychological plausibility to the theory of expectations, and to the theory of the adjustment of expectations.

To begin with, they assume that bargainers learn from the process of bargaining by interpreting messages in terms of existing systems of beliefs. Beliefs are divided into *theories* and *images*. The former are beliefs about cause and effect which define certain *general* threats and opportunities in international affairs. The latter are beliefs about the nature and characteristics of *specific* actors. Taken together, they allow negotiators to deduce how opponents are likely to respond to changes in the *status quo*.

What happens next depends on the type of bargainer. There are those who are *rational*, and those who are *irrational*, in an information-processing sense. In terms of Coddington's model, the former are able 'to interpret disconfirming evidence correctly and to adjust mistaken expectations and strategy accordingly' (Snyder and Diesing, 1977, p. 333). The latter are committed to abstract and extensive patterns of belief which render expectations and strategy virtually immune to change. Incoming information which does not fulfil expectations is denied, distorted or ignored. There are also those whose bargaining behaviour falls between the two extremes.

From the point of view of bargaining skill it is important to note:

1. The rational bargainer has low confidence in his initial diagnosis of what has happened, and why. The process of bargaining allows him or her to test hypotheses; to root out ideas which are plausible, but false or incomplete;

2. The rational bargainer assumes that opponents are also finding it difficult to work out what is going on, and why. Thus 'he tries to send a message several different ways, always through a different channel, *and keeps repeating the same theme*. The purpose is to break through the resistance set up by the opponent's mistaken expectations and also *to give him time to test, retest, and adjust his expectations*' (Snyder and Diesing, 1977, p. 334: emphasis added).

There may be a number of special features associated with crisis bargaining between nations. However, there is evidence from other contexts that skilled negotiators are rational bargainers in Snyder and Diesing's sense (Rackham and Carlisle, 1978a; 1978b; Fisher and Ury, 1983). More precisely, it seems that effective negotiators use a variety of techniques designed to *reduce ambiguity, clarify communications and generally slow down negotiations.* In this way they help others to work through the core processes of information interpretation, influence and choice. Some examples may help to show the point;

3. Skilled negotiators *label* behaviour. They recognise that social behaviour is inherently ambiguous. Unless special care is taken, it is all too easy for people to see what they want to see. Effective negotiators take pains to label behaviour, making frequent use of verbal forms such as, 'May I ask you a *question?*', 'If I could make a *suggestion* . . .' and so on;

4. The skills of listening are described in Chapter 10 of this volume. They are important because it has been said (correctly) that *the cheapest concession one can make is to show that one is listening actively to what is being said.* There are actually two sides to this. First, it is important to be able to see the negotiation as others see it. Quite simply, if you want to influence them it is important to understand the appeal *for them* of their point of view. Second, it is important to communicate that understanding to members of the other side. Otherwise, when you try to say something they will not be listening. They will, instead, be considering how to rephrase their argument so that this time you will understand it (Fisher and Ury, 1983). This is unlikely to build an atmosphere in which problems can be solved constructively.

It is not surprising, therefore, that skilled negotiators are significantly more likely than average negotiators to *test understanding* and *summarise* what had been said (Rackham and Carlisle, 1978a). Nor is it surprising that the New York State Police have trained hostage negotiators to *restate content* and *reflect feelings* (Miron and Goldstein, 1979) (see Chapter 6).

5. A good rule seems to be: 'Present proposals as solutions to problems. State the problem before you give your answer.' If one begins by stating the problem, one will find that the other side will soon stop paying attention. They will not be listening to what one has to say. Instead, they will devote their mental resources to the task of working out their own response (Fisher and Ury, 1983).

Morley's Model

The skilful negotiator is defined as one who 'through an understanding of the risks and opportunities associated with negotiation, and of the resources he can bring to bear, is able to take active and effective measures to protect or pursue the values and interests he has at stake' (Morley, 1981a, p. 112). This sort of emphasis follows fairly naturally from a consideration of the differences between successful and unsuccessful negotiations, as revealed by the behaviour analysis approach. Research within this tradition suggests the following conclusions:

1. Negotiation may be described as a joint exercise in decision-making of a complex kind. It has within-group and between-group elements. Some regard the former as different in kind to the latter. It may, for example, involve intra-organisational bargaining rather than distributive bargaining (which is competitive) or integrative bargaining (which is collaborative) (Walton and McKersie, 1965). The author prefers, however, to emphasise certain similarities in the negotiations which occur within and between groups. Anthony (1977) is surely correct when he argues that the process of intra-organisational bargaining raises no new strategic or tactical concerns. It is, as he puts it, an 'environmental characteristic of the total field within which bargaining takes place' (Anthony, 1977). It is assumed that, in each case, negotiators must handle the core problems of identification (of issues), development (of solutions) and selection (of policies). These terms are taken from Burnstein and Berbaum (1981). In plain language, negotiators have to work out what is going on, and why and what to do about it;

2. Negotiations cycle and recycle through stages in which negotiators emphasise, respectively, what Douglas (1962) calls the interpersonal and inter-party climates. The interparty climate exists because negotiators act as representatives of groups. The interpersonal climate exists because negotiators build up relationships with opponents (sometimes long-term ones). The party relationship is the superordinate or dominant one. It is defined by the substantive issues. The personal relationship is the subordinate or diplomatic one. It has been described as the people problem in negotiation (Fisher and Ury, 1983). It may function to tidy up the 'battle', or it may aggravate the contest of will. What is important here, however, is the idea that negotiations cycle and recycle through what might be called competitive (interparty) and collaborative (interpersonal) stages. There is some evidence that the difference in emphasis between the stages is more marked in negotiations which end in success (Douglas, 1962; Stephenson, 1981);

3. It would be very difficult to underestimate the importance of the long-term relationship between the parties. It may frequently be more important than the outcome of any particular negotiation (Walton and McKersie, 1965; Batstone, Boraston and Frenkel, 1977; Morley, 1979; Fisher and Ury, 1983). This is why it is in negotiators' long-term interests to lose some cases. As Anthony and Crichton (1969) say: 'Judgement comes in selecting the cases to be lost' (p. 110);

4. The process of negotiation includes much more than the negotiations at the 'bargaining table'. Negotiators build networks within the organisation which help them collect information, disseminate information and generate support for party positions (Kotter and Lawrence, 1974; Batstone, Boraston and Frenkel, 1977; Kanter, 1984). The relevant unit of analysis for the study of negotiation is thus what Dachler (1984) calls the *issue group*;

5. The networking skills of the negotiator help control the agenda of the negotiation (Ikle, 1964; Walton and McKersie, 1965; Batstone, Boraston and Frenkel, 1977);

6. The form taken by negotiation is determined partly by the *dilemmas* negotiators face. The dilemmas occur because negotiation is *complex* in the sense

of Steinbruner (1974). A given settlement will satisfy some values, but not others. Consequently, difficult choices may have to be made. It may even be difficult to 'frame' issues in ways which allow 'one alternative to be viewed as having a significant edge over other alternatives' (Huff, 1984). Steinbruner (1974) calls this the problem of structural uncertainty. Under such circumstances negotiators may feel that they have important decisions to make, and that whatever they do is likely to be wrong. Decisional conflicts of this kind may produce intense stress, leading negotiators defensively to avoid warning signs that things are going wrong (Janis and Mann, 1977; Morley, 1981b). This is one of the reasons why negotiators sometimes fail to agree, even when they have compatible minimum goals;

7. Successful negotiations contain periods in which contenders seek 'to intrench their seeming disparity', as Douglas (1957, p. 73) puts it. This is one way of handling the loss avoidance constraint on bargaining outlined above. It also seems to increase the chances of 'a good and stable settlement in the end' (Douglas, 1957, p. 73), despite the risk that disagreement between the parties will be interpreted as dislike between the persons (Morley, 1981a; Fisher and Ury, 1983). There is evidence that skilled negotiators learn not to treat attacks on party positions as if they were attacks on people (Fisher and Ury, 1983). They do this, partly, by separating the interpersonal and interparty aspects of their bargaining in time, and possibly space. Skilled negotiators are also able rapidly to *switch* between competitive and collaborative styles; between roles as 'intergroup antagonists' and 'group problem-solvers' (Stephenson, 1981).

A General Model of Negotiation Skill

Figure 13.1 sets out the most important elements in a general model of negotiating skill. Many of them have been mentioned already. They now need to be brought together in a more systematic way.

Information interpretation, information search, influence and choice have been described as *core processes* in negotiation. These are identified in the centre of the triangle in Figure 13.1. It has also been argued that more and less skilled negotiators *structure* these processes in different ways. A general model of the skills in negotiation would show how this is possible. It would also explain why one kind of structure is more effective than another.

Such a model requires three further elements, set out along the sides of the triangle. The first deals with the kinds of *knowledge* negotiators need. The second deals with the activities of *networking*. The third locates the core processes within the context of a decision-making task. It deals with what the author calls the *decision problems* in negotiation.

The Knowledge Base

Many writers have attempted to list the qualities of the 'ideal' negotiator (for instance, Margerison and Leary, 1975; Pedler, 1977). The author agrees with Davey (1972) that the ability to see a problem whole comes high in the list, perhaps

Figure 13.1: A General Model of Negotiating Skill

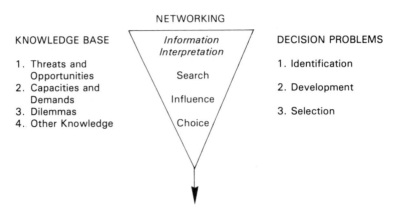

PROTECT AND PURSUE VALUES AND INTERESTS THROUGH UNDERSTANDING

highest of all. As he says: 'An understanding of the compulsions and pressures operating on practitioners on the other side of the bargaining table is an indispensable requisite to intelligent bargaining' (p. 22). The key word is *intelligent*. Any intelligent performance has to be guided by an appropriate knowledge base, as recent work in cognitive science has shown (Dehn and Schank, 1982).

The Perception of Threats and Opportunities. It has been argued that negotiation is an exercise in joint decision-making. It is political activity because participants will attempt to exploit asymmetries in the situation, generated by unequal resources and unequal stakes in the issues. It can now be added that issues arise when decision-makers recognise and respond to change, or the possibility of change, in the existing social order.

Changes of this kind are inherently ambiguous. They are given meaning when they are seen as changes of a certain kind. What is important is that negotiators see the change as an element in a *script* (Morley, 1981a; Hosking and Morley, 1985a). The script has a dual role (Gioia and Poole, 1984). It exemplifies threats and opportunities, and indicates how they are to be handled.

The perceptions of threats and opportunities are generated because negotiators have organised systems of attitudes, values and beliefs. The nature of the organisation is captured in constructs such as operational codes (George, 1969; Holsti, 1970); images (Jervis, 1970, 1976; Snyder and Diesing, 1977); and ideologies (Marengo, 1979). What is important is that the skilled negotiator has available more or less systematically organised knowledge of the environment, and how to work in it. This gives him or her the ability to detect in the environment features which others have missed, or perhaps simply ignored. This means that *the skilled negotiator is a skilled perceiver*.

The belief systems of negotiators have been studied in some detail in the context of international relations. Some provide paradigm cases for Steinbruner's (1974) 'syndrome of theoretical thinking'. Holsti (1970), for example, has classified the belief system of John Foster Dulles as 'teleological, conflict-oriented, enemy-centred, universal in scope, internally quite consistent, and generally impervious to evidence which might call basic premises into question' (p. 154). When scripts about the Soviet Union were derived from this system of beliefs, Dulles could always find evidence to confirm the script. In other words, he saw what he expected to see.

Risks of this kind are endemic to all kinds of perception (Neisser, 1976). What Neisser calls ordinary seeing is veridical simply because expectations are adjusted as people *move around* in the world. Social perceptions are less easy to correct, as the example of John Foster Dulles shows. But the analogy with ordinary seeing is important. Somehow the negotiator must move around his environment. Given appropriate feedback from enough of the right people he, or she, may be forced to adjust their ideas of what is going on, and why. There may be serious consequences if groups of people remain insulated from corrective forces of this kind, as Janis' (1972) studies of groupthink have shown.

One of the ways in which negotiators move around their environment is by building and using networks. The work of Batstone, Boraston and Frenkel (1977) shows, for example, that certain shop stewards, those who acted as leaders rather than delegates, were particularly likely to develop close relationships with certain management negotiators. Information was exchanged about the internal politics of the two sides, much of it preventing opponents from 'getting into difficulty' or 'being conned'.

Capacities of Performers and Demands of Tasks. Many negotiations are extremely complex (Davey, 1972; Midgaard and Underdal, 1977; Morley, 1982; Webb, 1985b). The range, diversity and complexity of issues create problems of information overload. Imperfect information, ambiguity and discretionary content create structural uncertainty, in Steinbruner's (1974) sense. One coping strategy has been described by Snyder and Diesing (1977). Apparently, skilful negotiators structure the intellectual activity in negotiation so that participants deal with one thing at a time (Rackham and Carlisle, 1978a; Fisher and Ury, 1983). In addition, they control the pace of negotiations so that participants *have time* to work out what is going on, and why.

In cases where there is a mismatch in skills, they may have to provide skills their opponents lack. This is particularly important in hostage negotiations. Miron and Goldstein (1979) report that they are 'constantly struck by the inadequacy of the hostage taker' (p. 18). In such cases they recommend that police negotiators focus on interests, not on positions (Fisher and Ury, 1983); slow down the pace of events; and provide rationalisations which help the hostage-taker to save face.

Dilemmas. There are four kinds of dilemma, according to Brown and Hosking (in press). Dilemmas of type 1 are those which derive from problems such as 'being demanding with superiors without being perceived as unco-operative' (or incompetent) (Kotter, 1982, p. 16); 'being hard on the problem but being soft on the people' (Fisher and Ury, 1983, p. 55). That is, they are dilemmas in managing relationships. Dilemmas of type 2 are dilemmas in managing resources: balancing long-run and short-run concerns (for example). Dilemmas of type 3 are concerned with activities: working out what to do, when, how, and for how long. Dilemmas of type 4 are concerned with the relationship between ends and means: between what one wants to achieve and how one wants to achieve it.

Dilemmas of type 1 arise in the environment of intra-organisational bargaining. They may occur because negotiators receive too much guidance and advice (Winkler, 1974); or because they receive too little (Morley, 1982). For example, the American delegation at the Paris Peace Conference found President Wilson 'shockingly ignorant of the European situation' (Elcock, 1972). It was almost impossible, for them, therefore, to work out a coherent point of view.

Dilemmas of type 3 arise with particular force when there are complex issues and many parties to a negotiation. In such cases it may be advisable to delay framing a position until the various threats and opportunities have been clearly defined. However, it is costly to delay too long. For one thing, it may give someone else the opportunity to provide a frame. They may then begin to define the issues (Mitchell, 1981; Huff, 1984) and locate them within a 'framework of broad objectives and principles' (Ikle, 1964, p. 215).

This is exactly what happened to the Americans at Versailles. They were unable to get appropriate guidance from President Wilson. In general, therefore, negotiations proceeded from positions defined by a British or French draft. The President was forced to adopt 'a persistent attitude of obstruction, criticism, and negation if the draft was to become at all in line with his own ideas and purpose' (Keynes, 1961, p. 24). Such an attitude could not realistically be maintained in the long term.

Other Knowledge. Kanter (1984) has analysed the power skills in use of those responsible for corporate innovation. One theme which runs through her work is that power is 'the capacity to mobilise people and resources to get things done' (p. 213). A second theme is that effective innovators are effective negotiators. Like other effective negotiators, they believe that what happens is a function of their own actions and skills (Miron and Goldstein, 1979). A third theme is that power comes when *information, resources and support are invested in action.* It is information which is of concern here. Following Kanter (1984), it is divided into *technical information, political information and expertise.* Each is considered in turn.

The importance of a technical knowledge base is hardly ever discussed in texts dealing with psychological aspects of negotiation. The obvious exception is Marsh (1974), who treats the topic at some length in his discussion of the negotiation team (in contract negotiations). In his view, a team leader should not be selected simply because he or she is *the* technical expert on a product. Other kinds of knowledge are *also* important. Nevertheless, the team leader needs 'sufficient knowledge of all the problems involved in the negotiation; commercial, technical and contractual to enable him to make an intelligent contribution to each item discussed and to direct and co-ordinate the activities of the functional specialists' (Marsh, 1974, p. 213). In other words, the team leader should have suitable professional expertise.

Marsh argues strongly that professional expertise is not enough. In his view it is of prime importance that negotiators are *suitable* for the negotiation in question. This is taken to mean that negotiators must understand the process of negotiation in general. They must also understand the dynamics of power in use in a particular social system (or social order). There are at least two kinds of political information which they need to obtain. The first is information about existing stakes in the issues. The second is information about the needs of others who may be affected by the current negotiation, but are not directly engaged in it. Without such information any attempt at change is unlikely to succeed (Kanter, 1984).

Kanter (1984) regards expertise as knowing more about a project than anyone else. Expertise of this kind may be particularly important when negotiation occurs *within* a party. Those who are doing the negotiation frequently develop rather different ideas about what is feasible, and what is desirable, from those who are not (Walton and McKersie, 1965; Mitchell, 1981). At some stage they will have to *sell* their ideas to principals or constituents. Here it is important that the position of the chief negotiator 'allows him to be persuasive', to quote Walton and McKersie (1965). As they say, the chief negotiator 'attempts to discuss issues on their merits or to cast new light on the question of feasibility . . . He has the advantage of specific information and general expertise' (Walton and McKersie, 1965).

Networking

Networking is described as activity in which negotiators *move around* their environment. The author believes that negotiators are effective because they are able to shape networks. That is, they are able to build relationships with other people based on the exchange of information, resources and support (Batsone, Boraston and Frenkel, 1977; Hosking and Morley, 1985a). These are what Kanter (1984) calls the 'basic commodities' of organisational power.

One important aspect of negotiators' activity in networking is that they may sometimes develop close bargaining relationships with opponents (Brown, 1973; Batstone, Boraston and Frenkel, 1977; Batstone, 1979; Morley and Hosking, 1985). According to Batstone (1979) what is important about such relationships is that 'each recognises the extent to which the other is important for his own success in concluding agreements and maintaining them' (pp. 65–6). There is an exchange of information which gives participants increased understanding of what is happening, what is likely to happen and why. It is this understanding which makes them credible as negotiators. It means that agreements reached are more likely to stick because they are politically realistic, or otherwise make sense.

There may also be an exchange of support in the sense that each helps the other to work out how goals can be achieved, and made to seem legitimate in terms of previous agreements, or rules of custom and practice.

The Decision Problems: Identification, Development and Selection

Negotiation is an exercise in joint decision-making. It may occur within or between parties. What is negotiated is the identification of issues, the development of solutions and the selection of policies (Hosking and Morley, 1985a). This is a much wider view of negotiation than is usual. It is to be contrasted with that, say, of Burnstein and Berbaum (1981) who treat negotiation as only one element (or 'routine') in the selection stage.

Burnstein and Berbaum's (1981) analysis reminds one that the first problem in negotiation is *recognition*, that is, what to count as an issue. Groups will be very tolerant of changes in the *status quo* when they are already engaged with pressing matters. At other times they may actively monitor the environment, looking for opportunities to exploit. This is particularly likely when a group that has been successful in the past gains significant new information, resources or support (Janis, 1972; Burnstein and Berbaum, 1981).

Recognition is followed by *diagnosis* (sometimes called the 'amplification' of beliefs). Diagnostic routines function to define threats and opportunities by locating them within a script. It is a collective process in which different people may use different scripts. What happens depends on *who* has the scripts (Morley and Hosking, 1985); whether other people share the scripts (Janis and Mann, 1977); and whether the scripts represent all the revelant contingencies (Burnstein and Berbaum, 1981). The outcome is the outcome of a negotiation in which people establish which views they are willing to support, and at what cost.

The idea that the obvious interpretation is not the correct interpretation is at the heart of Walton and McKersie's (1965) account of integrative bargaining. For example, a demand by a union for a guaranteed annual wage may really reflect concern about the inadequacy of unemployment compensation. If this is so, payment of supplementary employment benefits may turn out to be one way of handling the issue, satisfactory to both sides (Walton and McKersie, 1965; Morley, 1981a).

Development. Development is development of possible solutions (typically only one or two). What is crucial is that negotiators recognise that each option will have some advantages *and* some disadvantages (Steinbruner, 1974; Jervis, 1976). If Marsh (1974) is correct, there are three critical elements to do with strength of negotiating position, competing objectives and requirements for resources. In his view 'these three factors have a single total value so that an increase in the value of one can be secured only at the expense of a decrease in the value of one or both of the others' (Marsh, 1974, p. 47).

Selection. It is selection of a policy which most obviously involves elements of struggle, or pressure bargaining. The political aspects of the process have been described in detail by Walton and McKersie (1965); Marsh (1974); Mitchell (1981); and Pruitt (1981). The author's own contribution has been to emphasise that not to disagree means not to solve the problem (Morley, 1981a; 1981b; 1983; Morley and Stephenson, 1977). Two themes were in mind: the first was that agreement too early might mean that things were going wrong, because the issues had not been properly understood (Drucker, 1970; Janis, 1972). The second was that a long period of conflict (competition) may be necessary before people look beyond ready-made solutions and find those which maximise joint gain (Douglas, 1957; 1962; Morley and Stephenson, 1977; Pruitt, 1981).

What is evident in all of this is a contrast between two kinds of bargaining process (Pruitt, 1981). Processes which are *cognitive*, primarily help negotiators to organise their intellectual activity, and think clearly about the issues. The skilful negotiator *removes unnecessary obstacles to agreement and thus makes negotiation no harder than it need be*. In some cases the solution is to slow things down. In others it is explicitly to locate events in the context of what has gone before. This may be particularly important in the context of intra-organisational bargaining, as Winham and Bovis (1978) have shown. Processes which are *political*, primarily, function to manage differences between the parties. These may be generated by conflicting goals or by basic differences in outlook. The skilful negotiator is not afraid to disagree and makes negotiation *as hard as he or she must*.

Frequently, negotiations which end in success go through something like the following stages. First, negotiators begin by emphasising their representative roles. Speakers set up apparently entrenched positions and get on record a 'turgid account' of what they have to say (Douglas, 1962). Second, negotiators engage in various kinds of problem-solving activity, designed to seek out where agreements may realistically be obtained. Finally, negotiators return to their representative roles. Typically, they engage in internal bargaining with clients or principals as they seek authorisation to agree specific terms.

There is a compelling internal logic to progression of this kind. First, the (relatively) clear separation of stages in this kind of way makes it (relatively) easy to separate conflict between parties from conflict between persons. Second, a long period of conflict is often necessary if people are to look beyond the obvious options in search of those which provide mutual gain. Third, negotiations begin with the expectation of a fight, so to speak. Finally, agreements are validated by struggle. Representatives may allow their problem-solving activity to come to the fore only when they have been seen to do justice to the position of the party they represent.

It is important that cognitive and political tactics are integrated, so that tactics are seen to follow naturally from the bargaining process as it unfolds (Brandt, 1972). It is possible, for example, to slow negotiation down to the point where one is not seen to be negotiating at all. In one case, described by Warr (1973), union negotiators were presented with a management draft, outlining a possible pay and productivity agreement. Management recognised that the proposals were both complex and controversial. Initially, their strategy was to note what had been said. This was combined with assertions that the documents had not been understood. To quote Warr: 'This soon irritated the stewards who had entered the meeting with an expectation of settling several of the items and then reporting back to the shop stewards' committee. There was also a strong feeling of impatience of the union side . . . and the stewards were quite thirsting for a fight. *How infuriating then that management would not even leave their corner*' (Warr, 1973, p. 97: emphasis added). This led to a hardening of attitude, and negotiation had to be adjourned.

Skilled negotiators are able to organise disagreement, using a variety of situational and attitudinal tactics, as described by Marsh (1974). The organisation is important in two ways. First, it helps to establish the strength of case of the parties concerned (Morley and Stephenson, 1977; Marsh, 1974). It provides an indication of the resolve of each of the participants (Snyder and Diesing, 1977). Second, it ensures that disagreement between the parties is not seen as antagonism between the persons (Fisher and Ury, 1983).

The skilful negotiator knows when to compromise (making negotiation no harder than it need be) and when to stand firm (making negotiation as hard as it needs to be). He or she recognises that some kinds of compromise are worse than useless in the long run. Agreements reached must be compatible with each side's power in use. They will not be viable, otherwise, and do little except generate misunderstanding and ill will (Morris, 1973).

Negotiation and Social Order

The various elements in this model of social skill are displayed in Figure 13.1. They are arranged around a central triangle which contains within it the core processes of information interpretation, information search, influence and choice. The intention here is to indicate that the three components outside the triangle are intimately related.

For example, making things no harder than they need be involves complex inter-relationships between a negotiator's knowledge base, use of networks and attempts to handle the decision problems in negotiation. It is presumed that skilful negotiators will use cognitive strategies which facilitate the effective exchange of information. They will engage in an active, and sometimes aggressive, search for information, especially from those with whom they have close relationships (Morley and Hosking, 1985; Hosking and Morley, 1985a). Accordingly, they will be better able to structure the core processes as they are engaged in the decision problems outlined. Many of the details of these inter-relationships remain to be worked, but the author is optimistic that progress can be made.

Deliberately, very little is said in this chapter about what Hargie calls the core communication skills. This is not because the author thinks them to be unimportant. It is first because they are treated in Chapters 3 to 10 by others more qualified.

It is also because their role in negotiation can only be appreciated fully when one has an understanding of what the process of negotiation is all about.

Talk about skill implies talk about control. The control comes because negotiation functions to manage change. Negotiators view that change in ways which reflect the values and interests of those they represent. They manage the change by working out rules, regulating the activity of those affected by the change. There is thus a clear sense in which negotiators are writing organisational history. Further outcomes of any negotiation are, therefore, reports about the past designed 'to elicit the present actions required for the future' (Kanter, 1984, p. 288). For these reasons, the author believes that the skills of the negotiator are the skills of the leader. Many failures of management are failures successfully to negotiate the terms on which people will do business (Strauss, 1978). For an analysis of the skills of leadership, using the present model, the reader is referred to Hosking and Morley (1985a). If they are correct, there may be a very large range of political skills which can be understood in this general kind of way.

Talk about skill also implies talk about organisation. The author is interested in explaining how negotiators are able to select strategies and tactics and sequence their behaviour in a coherent and orderly way. That is, in showing how more and less skilled negotiators structure the core processes of negotiation in different ways. Broadly speaking, the structure comes from the elements outlined in Figure 13.1, and from an understanding of the relationships between them.

The author has chosen deliberately to emphasise certain similarities between negotiations as they occur in different contexts. This is partly a reflection of the current state of knowledge. It is simply easier to assume that the processes are similar, rather than to work out the important differences. It is also a reflection of the kind of account the author wishes to present. The kinds of concepts needed to understand the skills of negotiation in any organisational context have therefore been introduced. To the extent that different kinds of negotiation occur in different domains, the same concepts will need to be instantiated in different ways. Indeed, a social situation would be recognised as *being different* to the extent that it requires changes in the *content* of the elements in Figure 13.1 (Hosking and Morley, 1985a).

Finally, the elements in Figure 13.1 go a long way towards doing three jobs. They provide a realistic psychological model of negotiators, showing what they can and can not do, and why; they provide a model of the process of negotiation, considered as political decision-making of a complex kind; and they provide a description of the social context, showing what is of historical significance, and what is not. For these reasons the author believes that a broadly based analysis of social skill is a prerequisite in the development of an adequate social psychological theory of negotiation.

References

Anthony, P. and Crichton, A. (1969) *Industrial Relations and the Personnel Specialists*, Batsford, London

—— (1977) *The Conduct of Industrial Relations*, Institute of Personnel Management, London

Argyle, M. (1969) *Social Interaction*, Tavistock Publications, London

—— (1978) *The Psychology of Interpersonal Behaviour*, 3rd edn, Penguin, Harmondsworth

—— (1984) 'Chapter 4 Commentary: A Look at Functionalism as an Alternative Approach to Studying Leadership' in J.G. Hunt, D.M. Hosking, C.A. Schreisheim *et al.* (eds), *Leaders and Managers: International Perspectives on Managerial Behaviour and Leadership*, Pergamon Press, Oxford, pp. 95–9

Bacharach, S.P. and Lawler, E.J. (1981) *Bargaining: Power, Tactics, and Outcomes*, Jossey-Bass, San Francisco

Batstone, E. (1979) 'The Organization of Conflict' in G.M. Stephenson and C.J. Brotherton (eds), *Industrial Relations: A Social Psychological Approach*, Wiley, Chichester, pp. 55–74

——, Boraston, I. and Frenkel, S. (1977) *Shop Stewards in Action*, Blackwell, Oxford

Brandt, F.S. (1972) *The Process of Negotiation: Strategy and Tactics in Industrial Relations*, Industrial and Commercial Techniques, London

Breakwell, G.M. (1983) 'Identities and Conflicts' in G.M. Breakwell (ed.), *Threatened Identities*, Wiley, Chichester

Brown, H. and Hosking, D.M. (in press) 'Distributed Leadership and Skilled Performance as Successful Organisation in Social Movements', *Human Relations*,

Brown, W. (1973) *Piecework Bargaining*, Heinemann Educational, London

Burnstein, B. and Berbaum, M. (1981) 'Stages in Group Decision-making: The Decomposition of Historical Narratives', paper presented at Fourth Annual Scientific Meeting, International Society of Political Psychology, Mannheim, W. Germany, June 24–27

Carlisle, J. and Leary, M. (1981) 'Negotiating Groups' in R. Payne and C.L. Cooper (eds), *Groups at Work*, Wiley, Chichester, pp. 165–88

Clegg, H.A. (1979) *The Changing System of Industrial Relations in Great Britain*, Blackwell, Oxford

Coddington, A. (1968) *Theories of the Bargaining Process*, George Allen & Unwin, London

Dachler, H.P. (1984) 'Chapter 5 Commentary: On Refocusing Leadership from Social Systems Perspective of Management' in J.G. Hunt, D.M. Hosking, C.A. Schriesheim *et al.* (eds), *Leaders and Managers: International Perspectives on Managerial Behavior and Leadership*, Pergamon, Oxford, pp. 100–8

Daniel, W.W. (1976) *Wage Determination in Industry*, PEP, London

Davey, H.W. (1972) *Contemporary Collective Bargaining*, 3rd edn, Prentice Hall, Englewood Cliffs, New Jersey

Dehn, N. and Schank, R. (1982) 'Artificial and Human Intelligence' in R.J. Sternberg (ed.), *Handbook of Human Intelligence*, Cambridge University Press, Cambridge, pp. 352–91

Douglas, A. (1957) 'The Peaceful Settlement of Industrial and Inter-group Disputes', *Journal of Conflict Resolution, 1*, 69–81

—— (1962) *Industrial Peacemaking*, Columbia University Press, New York

Drucker, P. (1970) *The Effective Executive*, Pan Business Management, London

Druckman, D. (1973) 'Human Factors in International Negotiations: Social-psychological Aspects of International Conflict', *Sage Professional Papers in International Studies, 02–020*, Sage, Beverly Hills

—— (1977) 'Social Psychological Approaches to the Study of Negotiation' in D. Druckman (ed.), *Negotiations: Social-Psychological Perspectives*, Sage, Beverly Hills, pp. 15–44

Elcock, H. (1972) *Portrait of a Decision: The Council of Four and the Treaty of Versailles*, Eyre Methuen, London

Fisher, F. and Ury, W. (1983) *Getting to Yes*, Hutchinson, London

George, A.L. (1969) 'The Operational Code: A Neglected Approach to the Study of Political Leaders and Decision-making', *International Studies Quarterly, 13*, 190–222

Gioia, D. and Poole, P.P. (1984) 'Scripts in Organisational Behaviour', *Academy of Management Review, 2*, 449–59

Harbison, F.H. and Coleman, J.R. (1951) *Goals and Strategy in Collective Bargaining*, Harper and Row, New York

Holsti, O. (1970) 'The "Operational Code" Approach to the Study of Political Leaders. John Foster Dulles: Philosophical and Instrumental Beliefs', *Canadian Journal of Political Science, 3*, 123-57

Hosking, D.M. and Morley, I.E. (1985a) 'The Skills of Leadership', paper presented to the Eighth Biennial Leadership Symposium, Texas Tech University, Lubbock, Texas, USA

———— (1985b) 'Leadership and Organisation: Processes of Influence, Negotiation and Exchange', working paper, Department of Psychology, University of Warwick

Huff, A.S. (1984) 'Situation Interpretation, Leader Behavior, and Effectiveness' in J.G. Hunt, D.M. Hosking, C.A. Schriesheim *et al.* (eds), *Leaders and Managers: International Perspectives on Managerial Behavior and Leadership*, Pergamon, Oxford, pp. 253-62

Ikle, F.C (1964) *How Nations Negotiate*, Praeger, New York

Janis, I.L. (1972) *Victims of Groupthink: A Psychological Study of Foreign Policy Decisions and Fiascoes*, Houghton-Mifflin, Boston, Mass.

———— and Mann, L. (1977) *Decision Making: A Psychological Analysis of Conflict, Choice and Commitment*, Collier Macmillan, London

Jensen, L. (1963) 'Soviet-American Bargaining Behavior in the Postwar Disarmament Negotiations', *Journal of Conflict Resolution, 7*, 522-41

Jervis, R. (1970) *The Logic of Images in International Relations*, Princeton University Press, Princeton

———— (1976) *Perception and Misperception in International Politics*, Princeton University Press, Princeton

Kanter, R.M. (1984) *The Change Masters: Corporate Entrepreneurs at Work*, George Allen & Unwin, London

Keynes, J.M. (1961) *Essays in Biography*, Mercury, London

Kotter, J.P. (1982) *The General Managers*, Free Press, New York

———— and Lawrence, P. (1974) *Mayors in Action: Five Studies in Urban Governance*, Wiley, New York

Landsberger, H.A. (1955) 'Interaction Process Analysis of Professional Behavior: A Study of Labor Negotiators in Twelve Labor-management Disputes', *American Sociological Review, 20*, 552-8

Lockhart, C. (1979) *Bargaining in International Conflicts*, Columbia University Press, New York

Marengo, F.D. (1979) *The Code of British Trade Union Behaviour*, Saxon House, London

Margerison, C. and Leary, M. (1975) *Managing Industrial Conflicts: The Mediator's Role*, MCB Books, Bradford

Marsh, P.D.V. (1974) *Contract Negotiation Handbook*, Gower Press, Epping

McGrath, J.E. (1966) 'A Social Psychological Approach to the Study of Negotiation' in R. Bowers (ed.), *Studies on Behavior in Organizations: A Research Symposium*, University of Georgia Press, Georgia, pp. 101-34

Midgaard, K. and Underdal, A. (1977) 'Multiparty Conferences' in D. Druckman (ed.), *Negotiations: Social Psychological Approaches*, Sage, Beverly Hills, pp. 329-45

Miron, M.S. and Goldstein, A.P. (1979) *Hostage*, Pergamon Press, Oxford

Mitchell, C.R. (1981) *The Structure of International Conflict*, Macmillan, London

Morgan, R.G.T. (1980) 'Analysis of Social Skills: The Behaviour Analysis Approach' in W.T. Singleton, P. Spurgeon and R.B. Stammers (eds), *The Analysis of Social Skill*, Plenum Press, New York, pp. 103-30

Morley, I.E. (1979) 'Behavioural Studies of Industrial Bargaining' in G.M. Stephenson and C.J. Brotherton (eds), *Industrial Relations: A Social Psychological Approach*, Wiley, Chichester, pp. 211-36

———— (1981a) 'Negotiation and Bargaining' in M. Argyle (ed.), *Social Skills and Work*, Methuen, London, pp. 84-115

———— (1981b) 'Bargaining and Negotiation' in C.L. Cooper (ed.), *Psychology and Management: A Text for Managers and Trade Unionists*, Macmillan/The British Psychological Society, London, pp. 95-130

———— (1982) 'Preparation for Negotiation: Conflict, Commitment and Choice' in H. Brandstätter, J.H. Davis and G. Stocker-Kreichgauer (eds), *Group Decision Making*, Academic Press, New York, pp. 387-419

———— (1983) 'What Skilled Negotiators Do', paper presented to Sixth Annual Scientific Meeting of the International Society of Political Psychology, St Catherine's College, Oxford

———— and Stephenson, G.M. (1977) *The Social Psychology of Bargaining*, George Allen & Unwin, London

———— and Hosking, D.M. (1985) 'Decision-making and Negotiation: Leadership and Social Skills' in M. Gruneberg and T.D. Wall (eds), *Social Psychology and Organisational Behaviour*, Wiley, Chichester, pp. 71–92

Morris, E. (1973) *Blockade: Berlin and the Cold War*, Hamish Hamilton, London

Neisser, U. (1976) *Cognition and Reality*, W.H. Freeman & Co., San Francisco

Pedler, M. (1977) 'Negotiation Skills Training — Part 4', *Journal of European Industiral Training*, 2, 20–5

Pruitt, D.G. (1971) 'Indirect Communication and the Search for Agreement in Negotiation', *Journal of Applied Social Psychology*, 1, 205–39

——— (1981) *Negotiation Behavior*, Academic Press, New York

Rackham, N. and Carlisle, J. (1978a) 'The Effective Negotiator — Part 1. The Behaviour of Successful Negotiators', *Journal of European Industrial Training*, 2, 6–10

——— (1978b) 'The Effective Negotiator — Part 2. Planning for Negotiations', *Journal of European Industrial Training* 2, 7, 2–5

——— and Morgan, T. (1977) *Behaviour Analysis in Training*, McGraw-Hill, Maidenhead

Reason, J. (1978) 'The Passenger' in W.I. Singleton (ed.), *The Study of Real Skills*, MTP Press, Lancaster

Sawyer, J. and Guetzkow, H. (1965) 'Bargaining and Negotiation in International Relations' in H.C. Kelman (ed.), *International Behavior and Social Psychological Analysis*, Holt, Rinehart & Winston, New York, pp. 466–520

Sayles, L. (1979) *Leadership: What Effective Managers Really Do . . . and How They Do It*, McGraw-Hill, New York

Snyder, G.H. and Diesing, P. (1977) *Conflict Among Nations: Bargaining, Decision-Making and System Structure in International Crises*, Princeton University Press, Princeton, New Jersey

Steinbruner, J. (1974) *The Cybernetic Theory of Decision*, Princeton University Press, Princeton, New Jersey

Stephenson, G.M. (1981) 'Intergroup Bargaining and Negotiation' in J.C. Turner and H. Giles (eds), *Intergroup Behaviour*, Blackwell, Oxford, pp. 168–78

———, Kniveton, B.K. and Morley, I.E. (1977) 'Interaction Analysis of an Industrial Wage Negotiation', *Journal of Occupational Psychology*, 50, 231–41

Stewart, R. (1976) *Contrasts in Management: A Study of the Different Types of Managers' Jobs, Their Demands and Choices*, McGraw-Hill, London

Strauss, A. (1978) *Negotiations: Varieties, Contexts, Processes and Social Order*, Jossey-Bass, San Francisco

Walton, R.E. and McKersie, R.B. (1965) *A Behavioral Theory of Labor Negotiations: An Analysis of a Social Interaction System*, McGraw-Hill, New York

Warr, P.B. (1973) *Psychology and Collective Bargaining*, Hutchinson, London

Webb, J. (1985a) 'Interaction Analysis of Industrial Arbitration and the Relationship Between Arbitration, Negotiation and Problem-solving Processes', unpublished research paper, Organisational Sociology/Psychology Group, Management Centre, University of Aston

——— (1985b) 'The Effects of the Relative Simplicity or Complexity of Dispute on the Process of Arbitration in the Public Sector', unpublished research paper, Organisational Sociology/Psychology Group, Management Centre, University of Aston

Welford, A.T. (1980) 'The Concept of Social Skill and its Application to Social Performance' in W.T. Singleton, P. Spurgeon and R. Stammers (eds), *The Analysis of Social Skill*, Plenum Press, London, pp. 11–22

Winham, G.R. (1977) 'Complexity in International Negotiation' in D. Druckman (ed.), *Negotiations: Social Psychological Perspectives*, Sage, Beverly Hills, pp. 347–66

Winham, G.R. and Bovis, H.E. (1978) 'Agreement and Breakdown in Negotiation: Report on a State Department Training Simulation', *J. Peace Research*, 15, 285–303

Winkler, J.T. (1974) 'The Ghost at the Bargaining Table: Directors and Industrial Relations', *British Journal of Industrial Relations*, 12, 191–212

Zartman, I.W. (1977) 'Negotiation as a Joint Decision-making Process' in I.W. Zartman (ed.), *The Negotiation Process: Theories and Applications*, Sage, Beverly Hills

Zey-Ferrell, M. and Aiken, M. (1981) (eds) *Complex Organisations: Critical Perspectives*, Scott Foresman, Glenview, Illinois

14 CASE CONFERENCE PRESENTATION

John McMaster

The case conference would seem to be a necessary feature common to most professional groups involved in social, physical, emotional and educational care, but research and literature remains sparse. Indeed, a computerised 'key word' search and a manual search of British journals and periodicals from 1978 to 1985 were both unproductive on case conferences. This is puzzling since it can be argued that the case conference should epitomise professional practice at the highest level leading to effective decision-making in the interests of the client. (Throughout this chapter 'client' will be used to represent the subject at the centre of the case conference discussion.) Here, an attempt will be made to describe and analyse the elements which constitute the case conference with a view to substantiating this approach.

Definition and Characteristics

The salient features of the chapter title 'Case Conference Presentation' need to be clear. *Case*, here, means a set of circumstances or conditions, or series of developments normally constituting a problem and where reference is usually to one person, although other people will often be involved. *Conference* is the act of consulting, usually in a formal manner in which an interchange of views, discussions and deliberations take place with a view to making a decision or decisions about an individual. *Presentation* is the *act* of presenting and this is normally undertaken in a formal manner. It will almost always include verbal and written contributions.

Although there is a strong emphasis upon 'formality', this often applies to the structure and the standardisation of format and frequently within the parameters of the 'conference' there will be informality. Other important features are: the number involved is usually between four and 15; there is a chairman, often a minuting secretary and an acknowledged procedure. There is a marked resemblance to established committee practices.

The formalisation surrounding the group process distinguishes the case conference from a seminar or an informal group discussion, and it is this formalisation which helps to determine the kind of interaction which takes place within the meeting. It is considered by many that the degree of formality is an aid to making the conference more 'professional', and this is usually true in that it assists the effectiveness and efficiency of a meeting (Table 14.1).

The participants in the case conference should come with detailed knowledge of the case from their respective professional stances.

Table 14.1: Case Conference: Main Characteristics

Number:	4–15 persons
Participants:	Professional — from a variety of disciplines Client Non-professional } occasionally
Purpose:	Information } Written exchange } Verbal } Nonverbal
Structure:	Formal: — chairman — secretary — members
Function:	To examine, describe, co-ordinate, monitor, analyse and evaluate
Outcome:	Effective decision(s) in the interest of the client; assisting client to make his own effective decisions

The distillation resulting from this knowledge should mean a better decision in line with the best interests of the client. However, there is also a considerable danger in the formal process. The conference can be reduced to an administratively convenient action in which the major outcome is solely one of monitoring, and where effective decision-making in the interests of the client is minimal. The formal nature of the case conference should not inhibit a full, detailed discussion and presentation by all parties to the conference. Not least in this respect is the part which the client may play.

Unfortunately, this latter point is neglected in many case conferences. Examples from medicine, education and social work abound where the client is excluded from the very situation which can shape his future in a significant way. Recently, great concern has been expressed at the frequency with which children in the care of the local authority are excluded from case reviews, a classic example of the type of case conference in which the outcome affects, intimately, the life of the client. Similar concern exists where case conferences are held in hospitals, and where the patient is excluded from the proceedings.

Although there may be extremely sound reasons why the client should not attend the whole conference, there is no doubt that most case conferences would be enriched by the presence of the client at some stage. If there was no client, there would be no case. Even where the client does not attend the conference, it is imperative that accurate information supplied by the client is brought to the conference. In almost all cases the client has the right to have the findings of the conference reported to him fully and accurately. This should go beyond mere communication of any decision reached and at least one member of the conference should be designated for this purpose.

A Skills Approach

The rationale behind this approach is that the professional carer's performance may be examined and analysed in order to identify skills appropriate to that performance. A repertoire of basic skills, allied to a knowledge and understanding of the elements which constitute social interaction in a professional setting, leads to increased professional competence and credibility. This is in accord with basic social skills approaches to interaction and socialisation developed by a number of writers (Argyle and Kendon, 1967; Argyle, 1975; McMaster, 1982).

It is important to make the distinction between knowledge, method and skill and to understand their complementary nature. When knowledge, method and skill come together in appropriate amounts, then one has the true *professional* carer (Figure 14.1).

Figure 14.1: The True Professional Carer

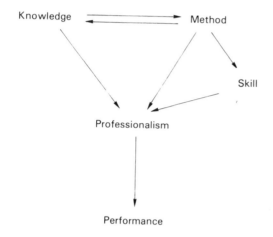

Unfortunately, these terms are frequently used as synonyms which results in generalisation and diffuseness. 'Knowledge' is more easily dealt with than 'method' or 'skill'. If it is considered that 'knowledge' in this context means the substantive body of information appropriate to the professional carer's specialism, then this would seem clear and easily understood. Thus, for the psychiatrist specialising in manic depressive states, one would realistically expect him to *know* the condition; the characteristics, the different therapies, how it differs from other psychological disorders and so on. For the teacher of electronics, *knowing* about microcomputers would be an essential prerequisite to doing the job. For the social worker dealing with the elderly, a *knowledge* of the ageing process and the effects of senility would be a realistic expectation.

Method differs from skill in a number of ways. Method in itself is inert and does not become active until harnessed to appropriate skill. Good method will be systematic, effective and efficient, but it will only achieve this when put into *operation*. Skill becomes personified by the execution of some activity or other. Skill therefore, becomes equated with practice — in short, skill is doing. It is the 'doing' aspect with regard to people that links the caring professions. All are practitioners and their ultimate value lies in how effective they are in the operational sense. A common factor is that all interact with people and make relationships as an integral part of doing their job. This interaction should be essentially a highly skilled activity which reflects expertise and proficiency. Yet the skills of the caring professions related to practice have been sadly lacking in identification, definition and articulation. This does not mean to say that they are not talked and written about at considerable length, but unfortunately vagueness and generality often prevail.

The following is a typical example of a list of skills appropriate to the caring profession:

1. The ability to observe, collect and record information;
2. The ability to understand and evaluate professional language;
3. The ability to distinguish between comment, opinion and fact;
4. The ability to locate sources of information;
5. The ability to use time constructively in relation to data;
6. The ability to listen;
7. The ability to hear what is said and note what is left unsaid;
8. The ability to pick up emotionally significant cues;
9. The ability to note significant factors relating to the environment;
10. The ability to note nonverbal signals.

At first sight the list may appear helpful with regard to the identification of skills, but close scrutiny highlights a problem. The identification, articulation and definition of the actual *skills* involved remains hidden within the phrase, 'the ability to'. What one does not know in this respect is *how* to do it and to what degree.

Thus, *how* does one observe, collect and record information? *How* does one distinguish between comment, opinion and fact? *How* does one pick up emotionally significant cues? And so on.

This is a difficult and complex exercise which has bedevilled the caring professions for many years; a number of critics have made this clear, especially with regard to social work, education, psychology and psychiatry (Brewer and Lait, 1980; Morrison and McIntyre, 1973; Eysenck, 1960; Szasz, 1970). Since the view adopted in this chapter is that practice in the case conference is an integral part of professional performance, then issues such as the above become central to an examination and analysis of the case conference.

Function of Case Conference

Although the specific objectives of different case conferences will be many and varied, all will include the salient features associated with effective decision-making. There is a collective professional responsibility to ensure that the ultimate objective of the case conference is achieved, namely effective decision-making which is in the best interests of the client or which allow the client to make decisions in his own best interest. However, members of the case conference frequently lose sight of the criteria for effective decision-making — the processes of examining, describing, co-ordinating, monitoring, analysing and evaluating. The terms are often misunderstood and used as synonyms, yet may refer to processes which, although occasionally related, can be clearly distinguished.

Examining

Examining is the act of looking over and inspecting information. This is done in two main ways, that is, reading and discussion. The case conference will always have a number of written reports and documentation and careful reading becomes extremely important. Since there are the reports of professionals from different disciplines, then this inspecting and scrutinising function is a salient feature of most case conferences. Much of this scrutiny is an attempt to determine the accuracy of information in the light of other information. Discussion and questioning often arise directly from scrutiny and this is used for clarification purposes. Examining is the seeking and searching process which is a necessary prerequisite for the individual participants to be thoroughly appraised of the case.

A more subtle and less well acknowledged part of the examination process is the scrutiny which individual members receive, both in their report and in their behaviour, from each other during the case conference.

Describing

The real purpose of the case conference is *information* and the members of the conference are both dependent upon and responsible for sound description. This is given by either a written report or a verbal report. The information which is supplied sets the scene for the other processes and the quality of the description, therefore, becomes central to good and effective decision-making. Some of the characteristics of good description are clarity, conciseness, accuracy and fluency, and the conference will benefit enormously where these are in evidence. When they are not, then it is difficult or impossible for the conference to achieve its objectives.

Co-ordinating

One clear function which the good case conference should exhibit is that of co-ordinating. This means that the various aspects of the case are brought together in order that harmonious action will ensue. It is an especially important function of the case conference, since the information will often come from a wide variety of sources. This function of combining 'pieces' and 'units' of information to produce a cohesive picture when effectively practised, reduces or eliminates confusion and clears the way for sound evaluation.

Monitoring

A function of the case conference, often included within the processes of analysing and evaluation, is that of monitoring. This is especially so where a number of conferences are about the same client held over a relatively long period of time. Two aspects of monitoring are checking and adjusting.

Concern is often, rightly, expressed that many case conferences *only* monitor. When this happens then the major objective of the case conference, namely effective and appropriate decision-making, is never achieved.

Analysing

Analysing is a process which is frequently confused with examining. Many people will consider that the terms are synonyms but this is not so. Examining is certainly an integral part of the process of analysis, but to analyse one must go further. Bloom (1956) indicates the position of analysis in his hierarchical structure of cognitive functioning, that is, knowledge, comprehension, application, analysis, synthesis and evaluation. Analysis includes knowledge, comprehension and application, but goes beyond these states.

Analysis is the breaking up of information into component parts. It means separating and comparing units of information and seeing the relationships which exist between these units. In the context of the case conference this process is most important in considering the verbal and written reports from diverse sources.

Evaluating

Evaluating is essentially concerned with judging, but it depends upon a number of other activities before the judging can be accomplished. True evaluation will always include examination, analysis and assessment. Evaluation and assessment are sometimes used as synonyms, but there is a clear distinction between them. Assessment is concerned mainly with measurement but where valuing or judging need not be part of the course of action. Effective case conferences should always involve evaluation, but frequently this does not happen.

A number of writers have indicated that evaluation is the process of obtaining information and using this information to make judgements. However, although such a definition is helpful, it is perhaps important to add that in the context of the case conference the judgement or judgements should lead to an effective decision. Thus, when evaluation has been made it will be used to influence the outcome of decisions. Often in the case conference the evaluations which are made will be helpful in allowing the client or others in the client's family to make decisions.

These processes are applied to the main object of the case conference — the information — which is presented in three ways; written, verbal and nonverbal. In this context, nonverbal information refers to that subtle, influential and important area concerning the interaction of the group as a group and of the individuals within the group, and the nonverbal cues which emanate from those interactions.

Interaction Elements

In most case conferences the participants have little detailed knowledge and awareness of each other, and the fact that the conference is already formalised makes it difficult to know what other people are 'really like'. This has implications for the encoding and decoding in the ensuing interaction. The highly complex nature of the inter- and intrapersonal interaction is significant in the case conference, but it is rarely considered. Krasner and Ullmann (1973) highlight the problem: 'So many behaviours are occurring at any given time that we cannot process and respond to all of our own and others' acts. Rather, we are forced by realistic limitations to select a relatively small sample, and may well miss important behaviour. This is indeed one way in which interpersonal problems arise. We may not hear or ignore subtle nuances or not so subtle ones.'

Any individual in the case conference will influence the other members by the interpersonal signals which they send either knowingly or unwittingly. The amount of influence exercised will be far from equally distributed among the members. A discussion of some of the elements which contribute to the interaction in a case conference may demonstrate how influence (or lack of it) occurs. Elements such as appearance (physiognomy, clothes and facial expression), posture, gesture, gaze and eye contact must be included and considerable attention has been given to this approach within the framework of social psychology (Argyle, 1975; Cook, 1971). However, the literature predominantly describes dyadic situations and the informal group or unstructured setting, but the elements are just as important in the formal or structured setting. Indeed, it is probable that they are more important since professional decisions affecting the lives of individuals are being made.

Appearance

Appearance can be divided into physiognomy, clothes and facial expression. Physiognomy refers to the topography of the individual and inference of the type or kind of person is often made from this information. Thus, the general 'set' or 'cast' of the face, the skeletal frame and estimates of height and weight are perceived and the information reduced to an impression of what he or she is like. Clothes, in this context, are much more than functional items and give cues which are assimilated into an overall impression by the receiver. This overall visual impression is vitally important since it seems to take place at both conscious and subconscious levels. It is also a potent factor in establishing whether the individual is 'accepted' or 'rejected' by the receiver (see Chapter 2).

Even when this initial impression is found to be incorrect as a result of a much better acquaintance and more information, it is surprising how lasting it can be. This has serious implications when professional judgement may be influenced by what are, apparently, non-professional elements. This combination of physiognomy and clothing produces powerful cues, but it is seldom *explicitly* recognised as an important aspect of the professional carers' 'equipment' when engaged in the case conference. Everyone appreciates the significance of this when extreme examples are cited, and although little can be done to change one's physiognomy, what one wears is very much under one's control.

An *appropriate* appearance in context is helpful in achieving professional objectives. It is here that the formality and structure of the case conference are indicators of what perhaps should be mirrored in the appearance of the members. Perceptual cues which, when decoded, give impressions of being 'smart', 'clean', 'businesslike', 'efficient', 'effective', will enable the person to be much more influential than cues which produce impressions of being 'casual', 'scruffy', or 'disorganised'.

It is not being suggested that appearance at case conferences should be epitomis-ed by 'formal dress' as expected at the traditional wedding or funeral — but the underlying principle is important. The point is often well illustrated in the job interview where, usually, considerable efforts are made by the interviewee to produce the most effective and professional impression to the panel. Certainly, there are many other factors involved but 'appearance' does become critically important. Another way of making the same point is to say that the cues which emanate should be compatible and congruent for maximum effect. Much of the work on 'status' positions and influence support this point (Krasner and Ullmann, 1973; Temerlin, 1968).

Facial Expression

Facial expression, unlike physiognomy, is inordinately flexible and changeable. It is to the face that one pays most attention in one's interactions with other people. When it is considered that the case conference will, on average, last for an hour and that individuals are in close proximity to each other, then, clearly, facial expression is a vital and important influential element which can be used to professional advantage. Unfortunately, there is often lack of congruence between facial expression cues as received and as sent out. A disconcerting condition is where a face is considered 'expressionless' for any length of time, because there is no feedback by which to monitor further actions or responses. Frequently, visual cues are either insufficient or misleading, with the result that one is either unsure of how the other person is reacting, or one misjudges. Indeed, if the visual signals are inadequate, wrongly interpreted or wrongly received, then this leads to erratic interaction, unevenness or breakdown of the verbal interaction. This encoding–decoding discrepancy is a factor which often affects professional decision-making to the disadvantage of the client in the case.

Although the detail within the study of facial expression is complex, there are two major expressions which tend to convey the general states of broadly accept-ing and agreeing, or rejecting and disagreeing. These are smiling and frowning. The smile usually means 'I like you', 'I approve of you', 'I agree with what you are saying', 'I am on your side'; whereas the frown usually suggests 'I find you perplexing', 'I do not approve', 'I do not accept'. At least this tends to be the *reaction* of people to the smile or frown, but the author believes that often in a professional interaction what is intended by the sender is not matched by appropriate facial expressions. It must also be remembered that facial expression does not occur in isolation and is often accompanied by many other features such as head-nodding or shaking, posture and gesture. But, if one *understands* the significance of the individual elements then one should be in a much better position to control and co-ordinate them in a professional manner.

Posture

Posture can have a number of definitions, but here it is used simply to mean the way a person sits or stands. This will often convey a general state such as boredom, tiredness or keen interest. There is some evidence to show that certain postures can be associated with states indicating stress. It is unlikely that there will be excessive stress generated within the case conference, but there is no doubt that posture becomes a significant element in the encoding and decoding which is constantly taking place in the conference. Not least in this respect is the realisation that posture becomes one of the vehicles for conveying interpersonal attitudes.

A postural style indicating relaxation is often conveyed by an asymmetrical arm or leg position, a sideways lean, a backward lean and hand and arm relaxation. This style is often used towards people considered to have lower status. It is also used more to individuals of the opposite sex, and it seems to be generally agreed that the more 'important' people in gatherings adopt the most relaxed postures (Mehrabian, 1972). Argyle (1975) suggests that there are postural components of dominance and submission which are additional to this relaxation dimension. For example, a dominant posture tends to be erect with the head tilted back, whereas the submissive posture is much less erect and with the head lowered. Clearly, posture is an important aspect of how information is conveyed between people, and this is no less significant in the case conference setting where, frequently, dominant and submissive roles are evident and where the status element looms large.

Gesture and Body Movement

Gesture and body movement normally indicate some form of 'language' and the more global aspects have importance for knowledge, comprehension and application in the interaction of the case conference.

Gestures in isolation can be difficult, or even impossible, to understand and may only take on real significance when considered alongside other elements in the interaction process. This is especially so when gesture is linked with speech. Argyle (1975) lists ways in which bodily movement and gesture support verbal communication and these are pertinent to the case conference. For example, in punctuating and displaying the structure of utterances, emphasising, framing (providing further information about utterances), illustrating, providing feedback from listeners, signalling continued attention and controlling synchronisation. Gesture alone can give considerable feedback and can also be of great assistance in illustrating actions which are difficult to describe verbally. In case conferences gesture will obviously accompany speech a great deal, and there is evidence to suggest that people with greater verbal facility use more gestures rather than less (Baxter, Winter and Hammer, 1968). This means that gestures are often supplements to speech rather than substitutes for speech. There are a number of gestures which have an almost categorically agreed meaning; for example, the head nod signifying agreement, head-shaking signifying disagreement, yawning usually indicating boredom and clapping indicating approval. These gestures are signals to other people but there is also an area within gestures and bodily movements which is related to the 'self' and where the gestures indicate a type of interpersonal interaction which has significance for the self-image being presented.

Much of the gestural behaviour displayed at case conferences is learned but idiosyncratic. Frequently, this indicates a self-protection device when under threat or feeling apprehensive. Detailed knowledge of an individual is often necessary to appreciate this, since similar gestures by others may have different meanings. For example, pulling at one's ear lobe may indicate anxiety for one person but indicate deep thought for another.

Gaze and Eye Contact

Sighted people use 'looking' to gain and collect information rather than to send information, but individuals react to gaze patterns and so looking becomes a channel for much communication. Although gaze has been studied at some depth in social psychology, it has been almost totally neglected in professional interaction. Table 14.2 shows the average percentage figures for gaze for two people in conversation at a distance of six feet when discussing an emotionally neutral topic.

Table 14.2: Average Percentage Figures for Gaze

	Per cent
Individual gaze	70
while listening	75
while talking	40
length of glance	3 seconds
Eye-contact (mutual gaze)	30
length of mutual glance	1.5 seconds

Obviously, these figures for the analysis of gaze patterns would have considerable differences in a case conference setting. Thus, there will be considerable variation in the amounts of 'mutual gazing' since there will be a group of four or more people and, of course, this will not mean that 'mutual gaze' periods will be equal for all participants. The important point is that this analysis can be undertaken in analysing the patterns of gaze between more than two people. There is no doubt that patterns of gaze play an influential part in the relationship which exists between people during the case conference.

There is an important division which operates within gaze and that is direction of gaze as against eye contact. When looking at someone, but where this is not reciprocated, then there is no eye contact. This gives the opportunity to study the other closely. There is little threat or tension in this situation, until the person looked at makes eye contact when one or other of the parties looks away, usually the one who was looking first.

Individuals tend to look more at people they like and less at people they do not like and it would seem to be the case that when one is looked at then this is interpreted as a signal of being liked, provided the length and intensity of the gaze conform with socially accepted norms.

When there is verbal interaction in the conference the members tend to look at each other, at relevant papers or documents concerned in the discussion, into the 'middle distance' or at the general background and surroundings. There is a greater degree of direction of gaze at a speaker when the remainder of the group are listeners and this is often increased if the speaker is looking at notes periodically.

Written reports circulated prior to or during the conference often fulfil the dual purpose of providing information and enabling members to spend less time in eye contact — an activity which can involve a substantial degree of apprehension or threat, especially when members are not well known to each other.

Although there are few established findings in professional interaction settings such as the case conference, there is little reason to doubt that what is known is applicable to that setting with regard to direction of gaze and eye contact. In this connection the importance of the direction of gaze and eye contact become potent factors in both the amount and the quality of the interaction. This is especially so when the role of chairman is considered (see Chapter 12).

Physical Factors

The physical environment in which any social interaction takes place is significant, but it is not always realised how powerful it can be in determining the kind and quality of interaction which takes place. When extreme examples are used the point becomes clearer. Thus, St Paul's Cathedral would hardly be the most suitable location for an intimate dinner party — especially in winter with the heating turned off. Equally unsuitable would be the waiting room at Crewe Railway Station as a venue for a board meeting of ICI. It must be emphasised that our surroundings affect us — often to a very considerable and substantial degree. It therefore becomes important to consider this in any setting for professional interaction, and the case conference is no exception.

There are a number of more obvious physical factors which can be dispensed with briefly such as size of room, temperature and furnishings. Provided the room is big enough to comfortably accommodate the members of the case conference, its size does not usually create a problem. Only when participants feel that there is a lack of space is the functioning of the meeting seriously impaired. The temperature should be between 65–70°F. Whenever members feel cold attention to business is diluted and if the room is too warm sleepiness and lethargy begin to intrude. Neither state is helpful in promoting sound discussion.

With regard to furnishings, it is helpful to have a carpetted and curtained room with uniform chairs and tables. Chairs should be comfortable with reasonable support and of such a height that papers and reports can be perused easily and notes made without difficulty. Pencils and paper should be provided which will fulfil the dual purpose of being functional and aiding the professional image.

All this helps to set the tone of the meeting and assists in creating a businesslike, efficient and professional atmosphere. Visual and auditory distraction should be kept to a minimum.

A less obvious factor is the positioning of chairs and the effects of position on the participants. Most case conferences take place around a rectangular table or a number of tables which create a rectangular well.

Figure 14.2: Rectangular Structure of Case Conference

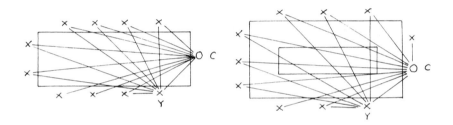

C: Chairman
Y: Conference member

Although the rectangular structure is the most common (Figure 14.2), it is not the most effective in a case conference if social skill elements such as gaze, eye contact and orientation are to be used to advantage. Gaze and eye contact have already been mentioned, but orientation merits a word of explanation. Orientation is the angle at which one person sits (in the case conference) facing another and is usually defined as 'the angle between a line joining him to another and a line perpendicular to the plane of his shoulders, so that directly facing is 0 degrees. It refers to the orientation of the body, not the head or eyes' (Argyle, 1975).

Figure 14.2 illustrates the orientation of people from the chairman and one other member. Here it is shown that while the chairman is able to interact with all the members, it is not possible for any other person to do so when there are three or more places along one side. This is a great disadvantage when discussion is taking place and it causes many interaction signals to be missed.

In contrast to this it should be possible to arrange the seating to the advantage

of the meeting. From Figure 14.3 it can be seen that orientation can be established for each 'person' and the chairman, and each person with every other, even
when the members at the conference number as high as 14.

Figure 14.3: Establishing Orientation for Everyone

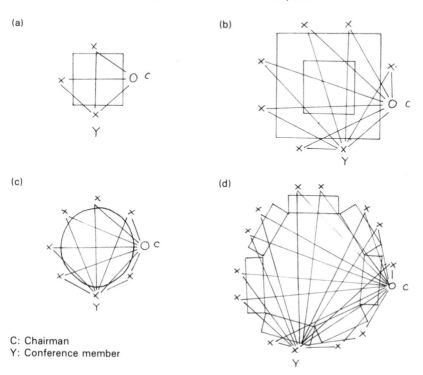

(a)

(b)

(c)

(d)

C: Chairman
Y: Conference member

Some orientations have acquired standard significance, for example, face-to-
face or head-on signifying hostility, dispute or confrontation; side-by-side signifying co-operation, friendliness and acceptance. In the case conference, although
positions are sometimes totally pre-determined, for instance, the chairman is placed
at the 'head' of the table and individuals allocated places by name tags, it is more
common for members, apart from the chairman, to be free to select their position. An analysis of these positions can often yield interesting information regarding the relationships between the members.

An additional factor which, allied to orientation may influence the nature of
the interpersonal interaction, is proximity. The distance between people is not
usually arbitrarily determined and follows certain cultural and social laws as well
as individual preference. An influential study by Hall (1959) categorised distance
into four major areas; intimate — up to 18 inches; personal — 18 inches to four
feet; social–consultative — nine to 12 feet; and public — 12 feet and above. In
the case conference the areas which are most operative are the social–consultative

and personal, although there are sometimes interactions between members sitting side by side which would come into the intimate category, as in whispering in someone's ear. It is not unknown for case conference tables to be longer than 12 feet and this alone is sufficient to inhibit communication, consultations and interaction of the type which leads to effective decision-making.

The Chairman

The chairman of the conference is usually the most influential and powerful member of the group. A large part of this is due to the powers invested in the office of chairman and there is an expectancy in most professional groups, and indeed many lay groups, regarding the more obvious aspects of what this office entails. There is also, however, considerable complexity and subtlety surrounding this role.

The chairman should have a global perception of the totality of the case which is denied any other member of the group. This perception should include factors surrounding the case which are outside the conference as well as the dynamics of the conference itself. A thorough knowledge of the case before the conference takes place is desirable. This applies especially to the written reports and documents which will be discussed. Since these will come from different professional personnel, then a considerable amount of time is required for this purpose. Adequate attention to the written reports will often enable the chairman to foresee areas of difficulty, complexity or dispute which will enable him to gauge time and tactics. As far as possible the chairman should have knowledge of the various members constituting the conference. This enables him to anticipate to some extent the kind and level of interaction which will take place.

A detailed knowledge and awareness of the client is most desirable (indeed, one could say essential), but this is an area which is frequently neglected by chairmen. In recent years this criticism has been voiced more strongly, especially in the spheres of medicine, education and the social services. Where the client feels uninvolved or excluded then there is always real cause for concern about the effectiveness of the conference; the chairman then has a clear responsibility to ensure that this does not happen. Rather, he should take special care to speak with the client before the conference to reassure him that the proceedings are being held with his best interest in mind, and to emphasise that should he wish to contribute to the meeting there will be an opportunity for him to do so.

Frequently, there is the need for nonprofessional people who are intimately involved to attend the conference. For example, in the case of a child it may be one or both parents or other significant adults in the child's life. Attendance at the conference for the lay person can be a threatening and anxious experience which should be recognised by the chairman. Here there is the need to assist in reassuring and helping that person to feel valued and able to contribute when appropriate. The chairman has a responsibility to see that this has happened, even though he may not have personally counselled the client.

A good chairman must attempt total objectivity with regard to the case. This is probably impossible in the absolute sense since the chairman will almost always be involved in some professional capacity. However, it should manifest itself in an attempt to be objective so that the final evaluation and subsequent decisions made are not obscured by facts which are not central to the case. Experience suggests that on many occasions decisions *are* influenced by the way in which the chairman has reacted as a result of his perception of members rather than on the salient factors relating to the case under scrutiny.

In conducting the case conference the chairman is faced with the complex interaction process surrounding written, verbal and nonverbal information and he must use his skills in these areas to ensure the smooth and purposeful running of the meeting.

The opening few minutes are vital in setting the scene and indicating how members are to be treated. Within the formality of the conference the chairman should convey that the members of the conference are welcome and that their presence is valued. This initial interaction is especially important where all the members have not met previously together. How the members perceive the chairman influences the quality of the contribution which each will make, even though this perception is often registered at a less than conscious level.

The chairman should introduce the case concisely, succinctly and in a businesslike manner. A common failing is to spend too much time on this introduction at the expense of detail and discussion which can be supplied by members much more adequately and expertly later in the conference. The responsibility for the effective use of time needs emphasising since one objective in bringing together different personnel is to maximise resources with a view to an appropriate outcome.

As the conference progresses the chairman should keep the discussion orderly, systematic and balanced. Implicit in this order and balance is the need for control and at all times the chairman should be very much in command of the situation. This control should be achieved without antagonising any of the members and without appearing to impose undue pressure. It is very important that the chairman avoids confrontation with any member of the conference. This is so, even when faced with awkward participants.

Individuals should feel that they have been given full opportunity to express their views and that their contribution has been significant in making the decisions. Equally, individuals should soon recognise that the chairman is not prepared to accept woolly or lengthy expositions where it is clear that little of substance is being achieved. The use of social interaction skills, especially social reinforcers, becomes a desirable prerequisite if the chairman is to be effective and succesful in encouraging contributions. The chairman should also be aware of the relative status of members within the conference and should be sensitive to a status hierarchy which can result in domination by one or two members because of their position. He must ensure that the contributions are judged on information and not because of the office a participant holds.

An interesting area which is not often considered in the discussion of skills in a professional context is the inhibition of performance due to an acute consciousness of self. This may be reflected in a superficial perception on the part of the chairman where cues and information are being attended to but only partially. When this happens much of the intellectual and perceptual attention is devoted to wondering what other people are thinking of the performance. Of course such 'poor execution' or over-concern with one's performance may be inaccurate in that the perception of the other members may be quite different. This discrepancy between encoding and decoding is extremely common but it is a facet which is not given sufficient prominence in the study of behaviour where professional carers are involved.

Still on the theme of 'self' but in a different dimension, is the problem of being seduced by the power and status of the office of chairman. This may be reflected in an exaggeration of the aspects of the role which portray influence and authority. When this happens the 'genuineness' of the chairman with *regard* to the client is no longer credible and the case conference becomes a vehicle for self-aggrandisement.

Perhaps the most important function of the chairman is enabling and assisting the group to make appropriate and effective decisions which are in the best interests of the client. Although not a mandatory requirement, the decisions arrived at should, as far as possible, be unanimous. In attempting to achieve this objective the chairman should be able to call on a considerable range of skills which include the following: ordering; leading; directing; controlling; initiating; identifying; exploring; clarifying; co-ordinating; classifying; condensing; analysing; synthesising; summarising; evaluating.

Participation by Members

In the case conference members usually participate by speaking about a particular point of the case, but they also converse informally with each other. During the formal proceedings the order of speaking is controlled by the chairman and does not usually present a problem. However, within the formal boundaries of the conference there is much flexibility and variability. If a member wishes to contribute he may go through the prescribed channels which means he will make signals to the chairman, such as raising a finger or hand in conjunction with a facial expression in which both eyebrows are raised plus a leaning forward of the upper half of the body. All of this 'says' 'I want to contribute', is typical of established and appropriate signals and gives the chairman an opportunity to allow for another speaker.

It is often the case that some members contribute much more than others, and although this may be directly related to the relative amount of appropriate information, it is occasionally related more to personal influence and the utilisation, consciously or subconsciously, of subtle and not so subtle devices or signals. Many of these signals are visual and play an important part in how the sequence of verbal exchanges develop. They include speaking to the middle distance so that no eye contact is made, and failing to respond to other indicators that someone wishes to make a point. When a contributor wishes to keep speaking he will often raise his voice if he perceives another member wishing to speak, especially if there is actual verbal interruption. This may be accompanied by a gesture of emphasis by raising the arm, especially towards the end of phrases, and there may be a faster rate of speech without any pauses.

There are less polite devices. For example, an interruption by cutting across the speaker. The success of this manoeuvre is usually directly related to volume (in extreme cases being shouted down), and the 'overlap' of speaking is extremely short — in short clashes of this type it will be less than a second. (Of course, if the chairman is effective and efficient this will not be a common feature of the meeting.) Another device is the use of a series of nonverbal signals indicating considerable impatience, such as the shuffling of feet or papers, or leaning alternately forwards, backwards and sideways, often in conjunction with a series of muttered verbal grunts. The noisier strategies are common in interactions where there is a certain amount of dispute, although there may be some in evidence in animated discussions even where the various members are in general agreement with each other.

The indicators that a contributor has finished or wishes someone else to take over are: dropping of the voice at the end of the contribution, pausing, or tailing off and leaving a phrase or sentence unfinished, sometimes filling the silence with 'err' or 'mm'. Other signs are hand gestures for coming to an end, and the speaker looking directly at someone else, usually the chairman.

Occasionally, members will indicate that they have no wish to contribute by looking down or avoiding eye contact by shading the eyes as if in deep thought. Even when given the opportunity this can be declined by giving indicators such as a slow and deliberate nodding to the previous speaker's comments which seems to signify that that contribution was significant and that he is thinking about it seriously. Often, completing the trailed off statement of the prior speaker serves this purpose, as does requesting further clarification from him.

It is likely that there will be informal conversation before and after the formal discussions at the case conference. This provides a useful barometer about the way the proceedings may develop, or how they have been received. Informal conversation during the meeting is not likely to enhance the deliberations, and where it becomes more than a sentence, may indicate that the perpetrator considers his status and therefore conversation, superior to that of the speaker. The recipient is also in a difficult position since he is aware of where his thoughts should lie but may also be unable to send sufficiently strong signals to inhibit his neighbour, or they may be interpreted as encouragement. The chairman must be vigilant and direct the member's attention to the case if he perceives informal conversation during the meeting.

While it has been indicated that the responsibility for a smooth and effective meeting lies ultimately with the chairman, it must also be emphasised that it is incumbent upon the professional carers involved in the case conference to examine their own performance and make it as efficient as possible with the interests of the client foremost.

Written Reports

Case records and written reports for case conferences are undeniably important documents. It is far from axiomatic, however, that because they are written mainly by professionals, they will be of a high calibre. Serious concern has been voiced by a number of writers on this point, for example, Brewer and Lait (1980). Major criticisms are that case records and reports for case conferences are often lengthy, rambling and anecdotal. Sometimes the defence for this is that they give detailed insight into how the carer 'sees' and 'feels' about the client. Whatever view is taken about the length and detail, it is obvious that written reports should be clear, concise and concentrate upon the salient features of the case.

Hunt and Young (1984) give an interesting, if somewhat extreme, example in which a report, some 600 words in length (Figure 14.4) is reduced to 28 words (Figure 14.5) and in their view, improved substantially. They point out that the dense block of unbroken type is daunting for the reader to tackle. A common reaction is to skip the page, searching for the significant items. They argue that sub-headings, short paragraphs, using colours or symbols, putting key information in the margin and underlining are ways in which the reader is helped in understanding the information quickly and accurately.

Although the first report has been reduced by 95 per cent, Hunt and Young argue that the second report in summary form gives the vital and significant information more effectively and efficiently.

A telling point made by Hunt and Young is that in starting to seriously question *how* something is written, it is a short step to examining *what* is written.

It is not being suggested that all written reports should be reduced to a chronicle of events or that they must be unduly brief. It would appear, however, that most written reports would benefit from heavy pruning and real consideration of the salient features to be presented.

The examples which follow are from a case conference held at an assessment centre and attended by a consultant psychiatrist, educational psychologist, teacher, senior social worker, social worker, principal and three senior members of staff from the centre. Lack of space prohibits reproduction of the reports in full.

Extract from Social Worker's Report

Mr Grant reports that whilst he would be firm with Jack, Mrs Grant has always tended to give in. There has been concern about the sort of punishment Jack received at home, although Mr Grant has always maintained he never hits Jack. This is because he received many beatings as a boy and it 'never did him any good'.

Figure 14.4: 600-word Case Report

SMITH, Susan

Susan's GP phoned in the afternoon to say that she hadn't seen Susan for four weeks since the birth of baby Simon but that during the routine post-natal check-up Susan had become very upset for no apparent reason and had become violent during what had seemed to be a perfectly ordinary examination, and had left in tears, damaging some of the waiting room fittings as she went. I called on Susan early evening. The door was answered by Susan's youngest sister, Janine, who is an attractive, intelligent girl of 14. Her mother was out late-night shopping with her father. Janine obviously wasn't expecting me. The house is a council house and is in very good condition, very neat. Janine took me into the kitchen and made me a cup of tea and biscuits while I waited for Susan to finish her bath. She came downstairs into the kitchen. She looks very young for 18 and her face is very pale with wispy blonde hair which looks as though it used to be a punk cut, and she has large blue eyes. She is average height, and although she seems to be very concerned with her weight, quite well proportioned. We discussed her problems for 45 minutes and she paced around and fiddled nervously with things, and very rarely looked at me. Most of the conversation was taken up by describing the difficulties that she has had with the putative father and then her obsessions which seem to be very important in her life. She is desperately worried about them and her efforts not to indulge them make her ill with worry. She desperately wants to be cured so that she can lead an ordinary life. I spent some time explaining what treatment the hospital can offer for her kind of illness and how much the doctors and specialists now know about it and how it can be treated. She very tentatively agreed that if the baby can be looked after she might consider coming in for treatment, and I detected a suggestion that it would be the last resort and an admission that this really is an illness, and that she is perhaps afraid that the treatment will not succeed. She said she liked the fact that I had come to see her at home and we agreed that I would continue to visit her at home. On my way out I met Mrs Smith (Mother) in the front garden. She was not very pleased to see me, and said, when I mentioned it, that she supposed they would be able to manage the baby if Susan decided to go into hospital and when I said I'd be coming back again in a couple of weeks she said if I must I must, but thought that Susan would grow out of it especially now that she had the responsibility of a baby. Mrs Smith seems likely to be an important figure in this situation.

Figure 14.5: Shortened 28-word Case Report

SMITH, Susan   Summary

INCIDENT at Dr Forrest's (GP): Susan violent and upset.
HOME VISIT: S worried about weight, obsessions. Tentatively agreed to admission. Mother not v. supportive. Home visits to continue.

In the past there has been mention that Jack's grandfather favoured Mary to the extent that he would give Mary money and not Jack. The Grants were aware of this at the time and attempted to tackle it by ensuring that Mary shared whatever she was given with Jack. Jack still knew, however, that he was not loved. I have discussed this with the Grants recently and they say the grandfather favoured Mary only because she was born in their home. Things have been much better for many years now and the grandparents are equally, if not more, fond of Jack now as they see more of him.

The Grants report that Jack is generally well liked and that people will do anything for him. Before his court appearance Jack has a Saturday job with a local electrical shop where he helped with deliveries. He enjoyed this and worked hard. At school Jack seems to have got on well with some teachers and not others. He had a particularly poor relationship with the headmaster. Jack was extremely unco-operative towards the head, and was openly defiant at times. However, Jack does speak with some respect for him, and admits that he was usually right. Jack is also very unco-operative and defiant with the police. In this connection there is an interesting incident which the Grants have told me of. On a recent visit to Six Hills, Jack broke down in tears with them after he had lost his temper with a member of staff he felt had been on at him all day. The Grants said this is the first time Jack has ever cried like that.

Both Mr and Mrs Grant have also reported to me that Jack likes a great deal of affection. It is only recently, however, that this has been mentioned and one wonders how much of this was lacking in the past.

This is certainly excessively wordy and much could be dismissed as irrelevant. There is a great deal of anecdotal information which is not helpful.

Extract from Teacher's Report

Jack has quite a healthy attitude towards school. Although he is very immature at times and needs firm directives and instructions he appears quite keen to learn and is prepared to conform to rules. He enjoys producing good end results and will endeavour to improve himself.

Although Jack can settle in the classroom and has the ability to concentrate, he is easily distracted by other members of the group. He becomes involved in silly behaviour, particularly when he finds the work difficult or uninteresting. He is prepared to join in any anti-social or anti-authority behaviour, seldom becoming loud or abusive but preferring to interfere with other children in the class who are trying to concentrate.

Jack relates well with both girls and boys in the group. He is not a 'leader' figure and prefers to be led in his dealings with other children. He is willing to work with other children as a group or in a team and contributes to the success of any venture. He does, however, gain satisfaction from disrupting the children less able than himself, thus creating a conflict situation. In so doing he shows less regard for these children and does not relate as freely with them.

Jack is a pleasant boy who presents no particular behaviour problems in school, and has applied himself to school work when he is able to receive personal attention and supervision. However, Jack's immaturity and level of attainment academically lead one to believe that Jack would find it difficult to adjust to a normal secondary school. Unless provision can be made to ensure that he received the level of education compatible with his attainment in a setting that would enable him to receive enough personal attention to hold his interest, Jack would choose to opt out of education and receive no benefit from his last year at school.

This is a better report in that it provides more information which is helpful to the conference members, although it is contradictory at times and repetitious. The salient information is: works well — needs direction — keen — easily distracted — joins in anti-social behaviour — relates well to peers — immature.

Extract from Psychologist's Report

Jack looked very anxious when introduced to me although, when told who I was and having the situation explained to him, he was able to relax. He was not, however, at all communicative about himself. I felt that he was probably very depressed and apathetic — he was listless in his attitude and did not express interest in anything. He was very cagey in talking about his delinquency and kept the details of this very vague. He would obviously like to return home but I felt was doubtful in his own mind whether this would be allowed.

He told me that he had truanted from school, giving as the reason that he did not like some of the teachers. He seemed very worried that he will have difficulty in gaining employment because he has been in trouble. He said that he would like to become a motor mechanic although, again, he did not seem to express much pleasure in this either. He co-operated in the tests as well as he was able to. He performed at a level well below average in picture arrangement where he was asked to put pictures in order to tell a story, while in a test where he was asked to assemble pieces to make an object he performed at a good average level. The reason for this discrepancy was not immediately apparent.

This is hardly precise and one wonders how valuable the content would be to the conference. The psychologist's main message is — Jack co-operated in the testing situation. There was discrepancy in ability levels. He appeared apathetic, depressed and was largely uncommunicative about himself. He does not like school, and wishes to become a motor mechanic.

Extract from Psychiatrist's Report

Jack admits to feel that all the painful feelings which have been exacerbated over the past four years at an age when he is entering puberty and adolescence have led him into behaviour which has made all his court appearances necessary and is defensive against underlying deprivation.

I do not consider that he is a seriously disturbed boy. His present rather macabre pre-occupation with death can also be understood in terms of his present underlying conflicts. However, I feel it is quite likely that he would respond to therapeutic help particularly if this was supported by therapeutic help for the family. I would therefore respectfully suggest that the court make a supervision order so that this may be facilitated.

I consider that removal from home at this stage would probably be destructive, although I am making this comment without having had the opportunity so far of meeting the rest of his family.

Again, this could certainly be presented more effectively in a shortened version. One wonders how much of the sentiment in the first paragraph is an accurate reflection of what Jack really feels.

The second paragraph only says that Jack and his family need help. There is no indication what might comprise this help or therapy, and one is told later that the psychiatrist has not seen the family. This would seem to be the main message: Jack is a mixed-up adolescent, blaming his background for being before the court. He needs help. Supervision Order recommended.

Extract from the Principal's Report

He is introverted, self-centred and shows no remorse for his offences. He describes these with bravado one moment and dismisses them lightly the next. There are no behaviour problems, and he is not grossly disturbed. Jack wants to go home . . . I believe he may repeat the type of offence if he is allowed to, but there is no strong case for a further removal from home.

This short paragraph leaves the reader in no doubt of the writer's intentions, and is to be welcomed for its directness, although it clearly does not solve the problem.

Finally, an extract from his previous school report which, although short, is singularly unhelpful.

Bad attendance record for no particular reason other than a dislike for attending anywhere that requires effort. He has no interest in mathematics, physical education or games. History, geography and metalwork all record the same melancholy story. He is of low ability and his attainment is puerile. He was admitted for a fresh start. He has yet to start. I think his parents are concerned about him.

Most professional carers spend some 20 per cent of their time writing reports and records. This is a vital aspect of the job and needs to be recognised as such. It would seem, however, that it is often viewed as a chore rather than an integral part of the professional task, and part of the reason for this may be that report writing is almost totally neglected in most training courses.

Training

Traditional approaches to the training of professional carers such as social workers, teachers, doctors and psychologists, have undergone changes in content in recent years, but there is still a major emphasis upon substantive knowledge appropriate to each profession. Although this substantive knowledge is vital and essential, the essence of professional caring should manifest itself in practical activities. The 'practice' has, in all cases, the common feature of interaction with other people and it is in the professional performance that one should expect to see highly developed skills. The basis for the acquisition of these skills should be an integral part of the professional training process, but although there has been a recognition that the 'practice' component needs attention, skills training still remains a neglected area in most courses.

While the question of skills is usually considered to be appropriate only to the carer/client relationship, it is suggested here that 'performance' in the case conference should be equally 'professional' and there is a need for this to be reflected in the training programme. There are a number of methods by which this can be achieved, but brief reference to four will indicate the scope available: (1) microtraining; (2) role play; (3) critical incident recording; and (4) modelling.

Microtraining

Microtraining is a development from microteaching which originated at Stanford University in the early 1960s. The principle upon which microtraining was based is applicable to all professional caring situations. It is that the interaction process in the professional setting is so complex that separate skills have been identified. A typical microtraining session reduces teaching time (three to 15 minutes), the pupils (four to seven children) and incorporates videotape recording where replay is immediately available. The student teaches concentrating on one skill, the lesson is played back on the videotape recorder — there is discussion and analysis of the performance — the student teaches again with amendments and can see the improved performance without delay. Microtraining is an extension of microteaching principles and is applicable to the identification and analysis of skills in a wide variety of professional settings.

A microtraining session would include: identification of the skill to be used, use of skill in controlled circumstances (time, person and videotape recording), playback of recording, discussion of performance with tutor or colleague, recording of amended performance, replay and discussion. There are variations on this format. (See Chapter 19 for further information on microtraining.)

The application of microtraining to the case conference can result in a detailed knowledge and awareness of the importance of the social skill elements which are constantly operative in the conference. The method then personalises this knowledge in a practical setting. The students are supplied with detailed fictitious documents concerning the case. They study the information and one is selected as chairman. The ensuing shortened conference is videotaped and replayed immediately. Analysis and discussion of individual members' performance, including the chairman, focuses on good points and those which might be changed.

Role Play

In traditional role play there is an artificially created situation which stands for the real thing. There are usually four main stages: (1) a talk or discussion about the role to be played and any specific aspects of that role; (2) a specific problem situation is outlined and there is a general scene setting. This stage can range from extremely simple problems to those in which complex series of skills is expected from the role player; (3) the role is played; (4) there is some feedback and discussion with a view to improvement and development.

Role play can operate at different levels of difficulty and there can be a number of different roles within a group setting.

The case conference lends itself to role play exercises where specific skills may be concentrated upon. For example, the student group become the members and respective roles are allocated. Real and imaginary case material is introduced which, if carefully structured, can highlight the problems which arise. An advantage of role play is that the role can be scripted to emphasise skill deficiencies and strengths which become obvious and which merit detailed discussion.

Critical Incident Recording

In critical incident recording, problem situations are designed which highlight the major difficulties which confront the professional in some aspect of his practice. These may be real or imaginary and may be presented in a number of ways, including videotape and live demonstration. An essential characteristic is confronting the students with the need for immediate action. Two brief examples illustrate the method.

Students on a course in dental surgery view a 'live' demonstration in which the patient in the dentist's chair will not open her mouth sufficiently wide for the dentist to make an examination. She is also complaining that he is hurting her. The tutor stops the demonstration and discussion ensues on possible solutions to the problem. Some of these are then role-played with further discussion.

Twenty-five students on an education course view a 'critical incident' role played by professional actors on videotape. This depicts a female teacher in the classroom confronted by an adolescent boy hurling verbal abuse at her and threatening her with physical assault. The incident lasts for one minute and immediately after it each student writes down how he or she would react if confronted with a similar problem. The students divide into groups of five and discuss the incident and the suggested solutions. The total group then come together for a full discussion.

Modelling

In modelling, the emphasis is upon increasing skills as a result of observing people and demonstrating the skills in either a real or imaginary setting. Two main ways of achieving this are through model film or videotape, or by actual demonstration. Frequently, there is a combination of the two, whereby students view a tape showing good practice and the tutor then elaborates by demonstrating further aspects of the skill. The students are then, usually, given the opportunity to practice the skill in small groups.

Modelling also lends itself to the examination and analysis of 'bad practice' where common faults can be demonstrated and discussed. It would seem obvious from other spheres, where performance or 'doing' is the key factor, that modelling or teaching by demonstration is invaluable in achieving a degree of competence quickly. This is especially easily seen in perceptual–motor activities such as piano-playing, golfing, skiing and fly-fishing. It would be unthinkable to attempt to become proficient in these pursuits without practising the skills appropriate to the activity, and it is this writer's view that performance in the case conference is no different in principle.

Interaction Analysis Systems

A meeting of professional carers may *appear* to be automatically beneficial with regard to effective decision making for the client. This needs more than impressionistic evidence but, as mentioned in the opening paragraph of this chapter, there is little research available on the effectiveness of the case conference. It should be made clear that this is not because of any fundamental difficulty in research design or techniques — more a lack of application of existing resources.

Lack of space prohibits a detailed description and examination of such procedures, but reference to one — interaction analysis — should indicate the possibilities and potential which exists. Although there are more than 80 established interaction analysis systems, all have the common principle of attempting to record and categorise the behavioural flow and interaction in a manner which allows for subsequent analysis and interpretation. This concern for establishing encoding and decoding procedures in some overt manner is critical to all interaction analysis systems.

Since one of the real difficulties confronting individual members of any case conference with regard to a personal evaluation concerns the accuracy of recall, any procedure which enables a subsequent systematic assessment to be undertaken should be beneficial. Not least in this respect is that a reasonably accurate *record* can be obtained which allows for a more objective appraisal of the behavioural interactions. The simple quantifying of verbal utterances on a frequency and duration basis, together with the sequential patterns of these utterances, can provide an insight which may be contradictory with the impressionistic picture and, of course, be much more realistic and accurate.

Bales interaction process analysis system has been influential in this direction and, although used predominantly for less formal meetings than the case conference, could be profitably applied to it. This is especially relevant to a social skills model approach since the term 'process-analysis' distinguishes the method from other methods which concentrate upon 'content-analysis'. Thus, the categories do not classify *what* is said but *how* it is said. As Bales puts it, 'who does what to whom in the process (time and order) of their interaction' (Bales, 1970). The twelve categories (Figure 14.6) indicate the emphasis upon the mode of interpersonal communication. There is a form which is used for scoring the interaction and which may be used to display individual profiles.

In looking to the future, an interaction analysis system incorporating videotape

Figure 14.6: Categories for Interaction Process Analysis

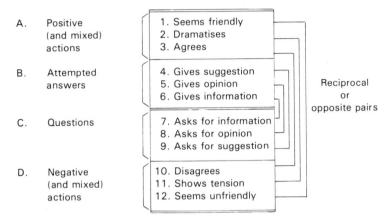

recording and based on the core communication skills in Part 2 of this book would enable the kind of objective appraisal of case conferences to be made and also establish a sound basis for professional development.

Experience would suggest that few professional carers welcome exposure where their practice is subjected to the kind of objective analysis outlined above. One reason is that of threat and apprehension occasioned by the categorical illumination of weaknesses. But this would seem to indicate a typically negative approach to performance. Objective analysis can highlight strengths as well as weaknesses. It enables the individual to understand the elements involved in a complex interaction setting and also quantify self-perception. Above all, it can lead to dramatic improvement in professional performance.

Research and training issues should become closely related when looking to the development of the caring professions. There is no doubt that the knowledge, ability and enthusiasm which clearly exists is beginning to be harnessed to a more scientific approach to analysis and development. The case conference must be included in this approach if it is to epitomise professional practice at the highest level, leading to effective decision-making in the interests of the client.

References

Argyle, M. and Kendon, A. (1967) 'The Experimental Analysis of Social Performance' in L. Berkowitz (ed.), *Advances in Experimental Social Psychology*, vol. 3, Academic Press, New York

Argyle, M. (1975) *Bodily Communication*, Methuen and Co. Ltd., London

Bales, R.F. (1970) *Personality and Interpersonal Behaviour*, Holt, Rinehart and Winston, New York

Baxter, V.C., Winter, E.P. and Hammer, R.E. (1968) 'Gestural Behaviour during a Brief Interview as a Function of Cognitive Variables', *Journal of Personality and Social Psychology*, 8, 303–7

Bloom, B.S. (ed.) (1956) *Taxonomy of Educational Objectives: 1, Cognitive Domain*, David McKay, New York

Brewer, C. and Lait, R. (1980) *Can Social Work Survive?* Temple Smith, London

Cook, M. (1971) *Interpersonal Perception*, Penguin Education, Middlesex
Eysenck, H.J. (ed.) (1960) *Behaviour Therapy and the Neuroses*, Pergamon, London
Hall, E.T. (1959) *The Silent Language*, Doubleday, Garden City, New York
Hunt, P. and Young, A. (1984) 'Plainly Put', *Social Work Today*
Krasner, L. and Ullmann, L.P. (1973) *Behaviour Influence and Personality*, Holt Rinehart and Winston, New York
Mehrabian, A. (1972) *Non-verbal Communication*, Aldine Atherton, Chicago
McMaster, J. McG. (ed.) (1982) *Skills in Social and Educational Caring*, Gower Publishing Company, Aldershot
Morrison, A. and McIntyre, D. (1973) *Teachers and Teaching*, Penguin, Harmondsworth
Szasz, T.S. (1970) *The Manufacture of Madness*, Delta, New York
Temerlin, M.K. (1968) 'Suggestion Effects in Psychiatric Diagnosis', *Journal of Nervous and Mental Disease, 147*, 349–53

Part 4:

DIMENSIONS OF COMMUNICATION

HUMOUR AND LAUGHTER

Hugh Foot

To consider humour as a social skill is a somewhat unusual perspective to place upon it. Most of us take it for granted that we have a sense of humour without feeling in any need of having to nurture and cultivate it. And, of course, we would defend ourselves bitterly against any accusation of our lacking a sense of humour. Grotjahn (1957) aptly sums up the cultural value that is implicitly ascribed to humour when he wrote:

> Humour implies strength, maturity, superiority in the face of danger and calamity; it symbolizes victory and triumph over defeat. The humorist is a hero, and he is human, too. He recognises reality, usually as bad, but then behaves as if it does not matter, as if it does not concern him (p. 51).

Not to have a sense of humour is, therefore, a distinct handicap and few would own up to it.

Much of the research on humour has occupied itself with explaining why we find jokes funny and why we are amused by certain eposides in real life. So the focus of attention has been primarily on the features or ingredients of the joke or episode which render it humorous. Rather less attention has been paid to the creation or production of humour, either in terms of the task facing the professional comedian in consciously constructing new jokes for a comedy show, or in terms of the ordinary man or woman deciding when or how to initiate humour in a social situation. Sometimes, we might argue, such a 'decision' to initiate humour is not under our conscious control; an amusing event occurs and quite spontaneously an apt comment or witticism 'pops out' which neatly captures the feeling of the moment. This is probably a naive view; with few exceptions we are in control of what we say and we do 'initiate' humour in order to achieve some interpersonal goal.

Essentially, the distinction we are drawing here is that between the 'decoding' of humour — understanding the meaning of a joke that we have just read or heard — and the 'encoding' of humour — understanding how and when we use humour to convey a message to others. To consider humour and laughter as social skills, therefore, is to be concerned with encoding characteristics, the reasons why we initiate humour. The bulk of this chapter is devoted to the social uses to which we put humour and laughter in our everyday interactions with other people.

Before embarking upon this analysis, some of the main humour theories are briefly summarised.

Theories of Humour and Laughter

As LaFrance (1983) adroitly says, it is customary for humour researchers to begin a treatise on humour with an admission that although the 'problem' has been with us for centuries, the 'solution' remains as elusive as ever. In other words, humour somehow foils any attempt to capture its essence. There has even been a reluctance to define humour and laughter among humour theorists, most choosing to emphasise some particular elements, like incongruity or surprise, as necessary prerequisites for a stimulus to appear humorous.

One of the problems is that humour is so multifaceted that it is simply not possible (and probably never will be) to develop a single broad theory that adequately accounts for all the main qualities of humour simultaneously. So one has to be content with a variety of different explanations which separately account for different aspects of humour.

As far as definitions are concerned, humour can be viewed as a stimulus, a response and a disposition. According to Chapman and Foot (1976):

> *The Penguin English Dictionary* allows all three possibilities: humour may refer to that which causes 'good tempered laughter' (stimulus); or 'cheerful and good-tempered amusement' (response); or 'the capacity for seeing the funny side of things' (disposition). While no-one would dispute that laughter is generally a response, it is just as much a response to non-humorous stimuli as it is to humorous stimuli. In fact, though not a humorous stimulus itself, laughter can act as a stimulus in inducing or augmenting laughter in other persons (p. 3).

Historical conceptions of humour and laughter and problems of definition are outlined in more detail in Goldstein and McGhee (1972), Chapman and Foot (1976) and McGhee (1979).

Incongruity and Developmental Theories of Humour

These theories stress the absurd, the unexpected, the inappropriate or out-of-context events as the basis for humour. While these incongruities are necessary, they are not sufficient prerequisites for humour (McGhee, 1979). After all, incongruous events or statements can lead to curiosity or anxiety rather than to humour; so the perception of humour is dependent upon how the incongruity is understood in the context in which it occurs. Suls (1972) suggests that not only does an incongruity have to be perceived for humour to be experienced but it has to be resolved or explained. Rothbart (1976), on the other hand, proposes that the incongruity itself is sufficient to evoke humour as long as it is perceived in a joking or playful context.

McGhee (1979) has proposed a developmental-stage approach to incongruity theory which maps out the types of incongruities understood by children across the stages of their increasing cognitive development. For example, the child first recognises incongruity when he or she makes pretend actions with an absent object, based upon an internal image of that object. Then the child learns the fun of deliberately giving incongruous labels to objects; 'girls' may be called 'boys', 'cats' may be called 'dogs'. Later come more subtle forms of incongruity like endowing animals with human characteristics ('the dog is talking to me') and learning that words and phrases may have multiple meaning (puns and riddles).

Superiority Theories of Humour

These theories have a long tradition going back at least three centuries to the work of the philosopher, Thomas Hobbes. They are based upon the notion that humour stems from the observations of others' infirmities or failures. Hobbes spoke of 'sudden glory' as the passion which induces laughter at the afflictions of other people and it results from favourable comparison of ourselves with these others. So, at one level for example, we find it amusing when our companion slips on a banana skin; at another level we take delight in the downfall of our enemies. Zillmann (1983) and Zillmann and Cantor (1976) take a 'dispositional' view that humour appreciation varies inversely with the favourableness of the disposition towards the person or object being disparaged. In other words, the less friendly disposed we are towards someone, the more humorous we find jokes or stories in which that person is the butt or victim. The source of the disparagement is also important; we are highly amused when our friends humiliate our enemies but much less amused when our enemies get the upper hand over our friends. These ideas relate very much to jokes and humour involving social, national, ethnic and religious groupings, with which we personally identify. Scotsmen may find jokes about the English very amusing but not the same jokes in which Scotsmen are the butt.

These theories are, of course, limited to humour which is characterised by disparagement, and Suls (1977) has argued that they can be conceptualised in terms of incongruity and resolution.

Arousal Theories of Humour

A number of theories have been proposed which suggest that the most important qualities of humour operate at a physiological level. These theories assume that the initiation of humour brings about measurable arousal changes which directly influence the experience of amusement. Berlyne (1972) has linked humour with fluctuations in arousal in two ways: first, humour is associated with the reduction of high arousal and, second, it is associated with moderate increases in arousal followed by a sudden drop. This 'arousal boost-jag', as he terms it, accounts for the pleasure derived from many jokes. The build-up to the joke is moderately arousing in that it attracts attention (for example, the audience latches onto the fact that a joke is being told and becomes attentive). The joke may be additionally stimulating by virtue of having a sexual, aggressive or anxiety-arousing theme, or it may be intellectually arousing. The punch-line comes when the audience is suitably aroused and seeking a resolution to the joke; the resolution produces a rapid dissipation of arousal frequently associated with laughter. The build-up and subsequent dissipation of arousal are rewarding and pleasurable, and produce the experience of amusement. An important aspect of Berlyne's position is his belief that there is a curvilinear relationship between arousal level and amount of pleasure experienced: that is, moderate levels of arousal are more enjoyable than either very low or very high levels.

This and similar arousal theories which concern the construction and analysis of humour are intuitively convincing, but problems have arisen in connection with exactly how and when to measure arousal in the context of particular jokes.

Psycho-analytic Theories of Humour

Freud's (1905, 1928) view of the function of humour is akin to his view of dreaming, namely that they both serve to regulate sexual and aggressive desires. Humour is the outcome of repressed sexual and aggressives wishes which have been pushed into the unconscious due to society's prohibition of their expression. Wit and humour are not forbidden; indeed, they may be socially valued and therefore present an acceptable outlet for such repressed feelings. The process of repression, according to Freud, involves the use of 'psychic energy' which is saved once the joke has been emitted; thus repression is no longer necessary. The experience of humour and laughter flows directly from the saving of psychic energy whose repressive function is (momentarily) relaxed.

Freud's theory shares with arousal theory the basic view that humour serves a physiological as well as a psychological function by manipulating arousal or the level of felt tension. The well-known criticism that psychoanalytic theory is rarely amenable to scientific investigation does not debase the insights and ideas which the theory has generated.

These main theories of humour have only briefly been outlined here. Their disparate nature emphasises the point made earlier that there is no single theory which adequately accounts for all humour phenomena. The other main theoretical focus of attention has been on the social functions of humour and it is to this area that the remainder of the chapter is devoted.

The Social Functions of Humour

Functionally, there are few more useful social skills than humour. Indeed, there are scarcely any social situations in which it is not appropriate even in the direst of plights. Throughout history the most frequently remembered and oft-quoted last remarks of men waiting to be led to the gallows are their rueful witticisms about their fate, society, mankind, or life after death. The most formidable and powerful feature of humour as a source of social influence is its inherent ambiguity, as Kane, Suls and Tedeschi (1977) acknowledge. We can use humour to communicate a message that we mean; we can use it to communicate the opposite of what we mean. Because humour is playful and can be interpreted in several different ways at the same time, we can retract our message at any time, if it so suits us. According to the reaction of our audience and the impression we wish to create, we can choose, through the use of humour, whether to claim or disclaim responsibility for our message or action.

The idea that humour can be interpreted in several different ways accords with common sense; it has also been empirically supported. In a study by Suls and Miller (1976), a male speaker's joke about women-libbers was interpreted entirely from the reaction of his audience. If the audience consisted of a group of liberated women who laughed at his joke, then the speaker was attributed with liberated views and as one who did not agree with the content of the joke. If the same group glared at him, he was seen as chauvinistic. Thus the response of the audience is taken as evidence of whether the speaker is merely teasing or in deadly earnest.

It goes without saying, therefore, that any hostile reaction to humour can readily be countered by the source with the reply, 'Can't you take a joke?' or 'It was only a joke'. Not only does the aggrieved party suffer from the affront to his or her own attitudes or self-image provoked by the original joke, but has salt rubbed into the wound by virtue of appearing a humourless individual. The only satisfactory way of parrying humour of which one is the target may be to turn the humour back on the perpetrator, always easier said than done.

The mechanics of encoding humour are poorly understood. Timing and pausing may be crucial. But, generally, when we are considering the skill of using humour in our everyday lives, we are not talking about cracking jokes or how the jokes are constructed; we are talking about making decisions to encode humour from the particular circumstances we are in at that moment in time. It is important, therefore, that we try to identify what the reasons and occasions are for encoding humour.

Humour as a Search for Information

Social Probing. A common objective in social interaction, especially when striking up conversations with comparative strangers, is to discover what attitudes, motives and values the other individuals possess. Standards of propriety may prohibit us from directly asking their views on certain issues, and in any case we may not initially want to engage in a detailed conversation about politics, religion or anything else, which direct questioning may commit us to. The injection of humour helps to probe indirectly the other interactant's general attitudes and values about an issue and we can take our cue in pursuing or changing the topic of conversation from the other person's response. Whether or not the humour is reciprocated may determine whether the discussion becomes more personal and intimate and whether the relationship moves forward.

Social Acceptance. In addition to probing for information about others, we may also be interested in finding out how others respond to us. Telling jokes is a way not only of drawing attention to ourselves but of gauging others' acceptance of us and disposition towards us. It is their response to our humour which provides the social barometer by which we assess our popularity or lack of it. This constitutes a reason for encoding humour and is not to be confused with social laughter whose primary function, to be discussed later, is to win social approval.

Humour as a Means of Giving Information

Self-disclosure. Humour may often be used as a vehicle for conveying to others our motives and intentions and it is especially useful when we wish to intimate feelings that we might not normally wish to reveal publicly: for example, fears about imminent hazards and anxieties about forthcoming ordeals. Humour may also convey sexual interest in our companion in a lighthearted and socially acceptable way which is easily revoked or shrugged off if the message is not reciprocated. Of course such 'humour' can become excessive and may reach the proportions of sexual harrassment if carried too far.

Humour used as a tactic to disclose sexual interest was demonstrated in a study by Davis and Farina (1970). Male subjects were asked to rate the funniness of a series of sexual and aggressive jokes in front of either a rather plain female experimenter or in front of the same experimenter made up to be sexually attractive and provocative. The ratings were made privately on paper and pencil scales by half the subjects but reported orally to the experimenter by the other half. The sex jokes were rated as funniest by those subjects who made their ratings orally to the sexually attractive experimenter. Davis and Farina took this to indicate that the male subjects wanted the experimenter to know that they enjoyed sex and were sexually attracted to her. It could be argued further that self-disclosure is not an end in itself but a means of trying to elicit reciprocated feelings or interest by others, so it serves to obtain information as well as give it.

Denial of Serious Intent. Kane *et al.* (1977) refer to this function of humour as 'decommitment':

> When a person faces failure, a false identity is about to be unmasked, an inappropriate behaviour is discovered or a lie uncovered, he may attempt to save the situation by indicating that the proposed or past action was not serious, but was instead meant as a joke (p. 14).

Recourse to humour, then, is a way of backing down without injury in the event of having our credibility or motives challenged. A serious confrontation or one in which our actions or intentions are likely to be maligned can be converted into jocular repartee by which we admit we were jesting all the time. Timing may be crucial here: the longer the delay between the initial action and the subsequent attempts to 'decommit' the source, the greater the suspicion that the action did have a serious intention behind it.

Unmasking Hypocrisy. Another information-giving function of humour is when we use ridicule or sarcasm to show that we do not believe the ostensible motivation for someone's behaviour. Political cartoons are rife with examples of satirists' attempts to highlight what they believe to be the essential motivation for the actions or pronouncements of a prestigious political figure or the absurdity of professional pretensions, privileges of class or institutional rules. At an interpersonal level, our jest at the expense of other people may serve as a gentle hint that we do not accept the image of themselves that they are projecting; for example, the eager young trainee doctor presenting an identity as an experienced and competent expert on a medical symptom.

Humour in Interpersonal Control

Expression of Liking and Friendship. Humour is valued as a social asset and, exercised judiciously, confers upon its encoder the animated interest and welcoming approval of others. Sharing humour fosters rapport and intimacy and promotes friendship by showing common sentiment and reducing tensions. As a basis for developing friendship and attraction, therefore, humour signals three affective ingredients about its encoder: first, as a jovial person who is rewarding and fun to be with; second, as a sensitive person who has a friendly interest and willingness to enter relationships with others; and third, as one who seeks, and probably wins, the social approval of others (or likes to be liked). Mettee, Hrelec and Wilkens (1971) found that a job candidate giving a short lecture was rated as more likeable by an audience when he used humour.

Humour is also seen as an expression of character when used in times of adversity. If disaster has befallen us or threatens to do so, we may encode humour in a 'grin-and-bear-it' fashion, putting on a brave face for the world to show others that we can bear it and that perhaps we can see the irony of our predicament.

Expression of Dislike and Hostility. We have already seen under the heading 'Unmasking Hypocrisy' that humour can be used to inform others that we do not accept the image of themselves that they are trying to project. In a more general manner, humour is one way, possibly the only socially acceptable way, of expressing personal antagonism. We are inclined to enjoy cruel forms of humour, obtaining amusement from incompetence and deformity and from the oddities and incongruities of others' behaviour. On the one hand, we may not be able, on occasion, to conceal our amusement at the *faux pas* of our friends; our suppressed aggression leads us to savour their little defeats with gentle relish. On the other hand, against those we do not like, our ridicule and amusement at their undoing may be out of proportion to their defeat; we revel in their downfall out of the feeling of superiority that it gives.

Among social equals and friends, the use of reciprocal sarcasm and derision may constitute a normal and regular feature of their interactive style. Indeed, what may appear to an outsider as a hostile slanging match may be seen as playful bantering to the participants. Those with power and authority may avoid being cast as figures of fun to their face but may frequently be the butt of ribald laughter and ridicule behind their backs.

Controlling Social Interaction. Humour, like laughter, helps maintain the flow of interaction in daily encounters, 'filling in pauses in our conversations and maintaining the interest and attention of our conversational partner' (Foot and Chapman, 1976, p. 188). In terms of sheer social expediency, therefore, the motive in encoding humour may be little more than to create and sustain a congenial atmosphere, as when breaking the ice at a party. Humour helps regulate interactions and serves as a social mechanism to facilitate or inhibit the flow of conversation (LaGaipa, 1977). Hostile wit within a group, for example, may dampen the social interaction or the tempo of conversation because it threatens the cohesiveness of the group.

Humour also provides a smooth and acceptable means of changing the level or direction of a conversation. It provides spontaneous comic relief in the context of a turgid or boring conversation and draws attention away from a topic of conversation which one of the interactants does not wish to pursue. It also helps to indicate to others that they are taking things too seriously and need to look at their problems from a more detached or balanced perspective. As will be illustrated later, this is a particularly useful tactic in psychotherapy when the patient is over-anxious and completely bound up with his or her own problems.

Ingratiation. While humour can be used to win from others approval that is genuinely sought and valued for no other motive than friendship, it can also be employed to capture the approval of others from whom favours are sought or who happen to be in powerful positions. The humour may be self-or-other-enhancing or it may be self-disparaging as a tactic to express a submissive, dependent posture (Wilson, 1979). The risk with ingratiation humour is always that its insincerity will be revealed.

Anxiety Management

Saving Face. Humour offers a path to control and restraint in more tense interpersonal encounters. An individual encodes humour, for example, to defuse a tense or hostile situation prevailing between two other interactants, thus enabling the contesting parties to back off from the confrontation without loss of face. At the very least such humour may make it difficult for the parties to continue their altercation without incurring the wrath or scorn of other bystanders. The humour serves not only as a corrective to restore the normal boundaries of social etiquette, but as an admonition that the argument has gone quite far enough.

Coping with Embarrassment. Humour is invoked as a control to restore composure and self-presentation on occasions when they are undermined by some sudden and perhaps unexpected event, for example, being caught out in a lie. More commonly, we are embarrassed by some little accident which spoils the image we wish to convey at that particular moment in time: the elegantly dressed lady at a formal dinner party tripping on the carpet as she is about to be presented to her fellow guests; the spilling of a drink down someone else's clothes; some clumsy or unscripted act by a well-known politician or television personality which becomes typical subject matter for satirical television programmes. Joking is about the only way to save the situation, treating the event as a trivial one, merely an accident that could have happened to anyone.

Safety-Valve for Excessive Arousal. Humour has already been suggested as a mechanism of social control in as much as it brings comic relief to a boring conversation or relieves the tedium of an uneventful activity like waiting for a bus or queueing for an exhibition. On the other side of the coin humour can help reduce unwanted and unpleasantly high levels of anxiety and stress. Laughter, according to Berlyne's (1969) arousal theory of humour, results from the tension–release that follows heightened arousal, albeit pleasant arousal, such as that created by the build up of a joke before the punch-line. It may be that the impetus for encoding humour in times of anxiety stems from anticipation of the release of tension which dissipates pleasurably through laughter. Perhaps doctors and dentists could help to alleviate their patients' anxieties before the consultation by the liberal provision of humorous literature and cartoons in their waiting rooms!

But solitary amusement may not be the answer here. In stressful situations, sharing humour with a fellow sufferer may be a more potent way of dissipating unwanted anxiety. The pleasurable experience of mutually appreciating a joke may establish rapport and reduce concern over one's own plight.

Humour may be experienced as a direct consequence of realising that one is safe after a threatening stimulus has been removed (Rothbart, 1973, 1976). Shurcliff (1968) varied the level of anxiety in three groups of college students. In the low anxiety group the students were told they would be asked to pick up a docile white rat and hold it for five seconds. In the moderate and high anxiety groups students were asked to take a blood sample from a white rat. In the moderate anxiety condition a small sample only was requested and the students were told it would be an easy task. In the high anxiety condition the students were asked to remove two cubic centimetres of blood from a rat that might be expected to bite through their glove. Having then discovered that the rat they were given was only a toy, the students were asked to rate how funny this trick was upon them. Of the three groups, students in the high anxiety condition found the trick most amusing. Shurcliff attributes this to their greater sense of sudden relief at realising that they were completely safe from a potentially harmful situation.

Humour as a Means of Changing and Sustaining the Status Quo

Freedom from Conventional Thought. Writers and social commentators have waxed lyrical about the emancipating power of humour. Mindess' book, *Laughter and Liberation* (1971), outlines and illustrates all the many ways in which humour frees us from the shackles of our mundane daily lives. Humour is an escape; as Mindess puts it: 'In the most fundamental sense, it (humour) offers us release from our stabilizing systems, escape from our self-imposed prisons. Every instance of laughter is an instance of liberation from our controls' (p. 23).

It is also a frame of mind which transcends both reality and fantasy. It frees us from moral inhibitions, from the constraints of language, from rationality, from a sense of inferiority and feelings of inadequacy. It is a guilt-free release from frustration and aggression.

This perspective accords with Freud's (1905) view that humour and laughter occur when repressing energy, which normally keeps one's thoughts channelled in socially prescribed and rational directions, is momentarily freed from its static function of keeping something forbidden away from consciousness. A witticism starts with an aggressive tendency or intent which is repressed. The aggressive intentions are manipulated and disguised in the unconscious mind with 'playful pleasure repressed since childhood and waiting for a chance to be satisfied' (Grotjahn, 1957, p. 256). The thoughts emerge into consciousness when they are socially acceptable and the energy originally activated to keep the hostility under repression is freed. By this time the repressed energy is no longer needed and the shock of this freedom from repression spills out in pleasure and laughter.

Joking, therefore, may be seen as a revolt against the structure of society. It may not, in practical terms, bring about much change in the world, but it is enjoyable for its own sake in making the unthinkable thinkable.

The Reinforcement of Stereotypes. While this freedom of thought may be characteristic of the way humour is used to perceive and experience life, it is paradoxical but also true that, in its overt expression, humour serves to sustain and reinforce narrow-minded attitudes and blinkered vision within society. Wilson (1979) put his finger on the same point when he wrote that 'Joking is a powerful conservative. Its effects reinforce existing ideology, power, status, morality and values within a society' (p. 230). So much of the content of our humour concerns human weakness and foolishness that if we were freed from ignorance, inhibitions, fear and prejudice, there would be little room left for humour:

> Though jokes feed on subversive thought, on deviations from the normal and expected, they reinforce established views of the world. Though their content appears to undermine norms, mores, established power and authority, jokes are potent in preserving that *status quo* (Wilson, 1979, p. 228).

In the present author's view the power of humour in perpetuating myths and reinforcing stereotyped and traditional attitudes is greatly underestimated. How else, except through humour, do we derive our stereotyped views about the Irish, the Scots, the Welsh, the Latin-American temperament, protestants, Jews and Catholics? Because the joke is a socially acceptable form, the message it conveys is extremely powerful and the recipient or target, however much offended, can scarcely denounce it without standing accused of the greatest crime of all — lacking a sense of humour. While real institutional changes have been taking place in the outside world through legal and social reform in relation to, say, homosexuality, equal pay, sex and race discrimination, the old attitudes about 'poofs' and 'women libbers' still remain enshrined in jokes which span the generations and are as popular as ever.

We are undoubtedly caught in a cleft-stick. In an ironic way, as Husband (1977) points out in relation to racial humour in the mass media, such humour reinforces existing prejudice and yet its mere usage sustains the mythology of our national tolerance, since racial jokes are supposed to be characteristic of a tolerant society.

Humour as a Device for Group Control

Intra-Group Control. One of the most enduring techniques for describing and categorising the processes that are involved in group discussion and group decision making is 'interaction process analysis', devised by Bales in the late 1940s (see Bales, 1950, 1958). From his observations of many different kinds of groups in many different situations he identified two types of function which need to be operative if a group is to be effective in its task. Sometimes these functions are channelled through one 'leader' within the group, sometimes through two or more group members. One function, fairly predictably, relates to task-relevant variables, for example, ensuring that the group gathers relevant information, examines appropriate views and directs the group towards a solution. This goal-orientated function is complemented by a socio-emotional task function which relates to the maintenance of the cohesion and well-being of the group. Basically, then, the group needs safe outlets by which to express its feelings, sustain its morale and deal with internal conflicts if it is to remain intact, and humour has an important role to play in these processes.

Building on the earlier work of Middleton and Moland (1959), Martineau (1972) has provided a model of the intragroup processes that humour serves, based upon how the humour is judged by the members of the group. It is, of course, within such a group context that in-group jokes can thrive, often barely understood by others outside the group. As La Gaipa (1977) says:

> Jocular gripes require some common experiences. Teasing requires knowledge about the butt of the joke and an acceptance and accurate perception of intent. Hostile wit is often not expressed unless the group has achieved a level of cohesiveness able to tolerate it . . . Situational jokes are likely to reflect the dynamics underlying the social interactions at any given point in time (p. 421).

According to Martineau, when the humour is judged as esteeming the in-group, it functions to solidify the group. When it is judged as disparaging the in-group, it may still serve positively to solidify the group (for example, the football coach using sarcasm to motivate his players against imminent defeat) or to control group members who step out of line. But disparagement may also provoke demoralisation, conflict within the group and ultimately the disintegration of the group.

Intergroup Control. Martineau's model also addresses itself to the effects of humour upon the in-group when that humour emanates from a member or members of an out-group. Zillmann and Cantor (1976) have stressed that hostile or derogatory jokes are least appreciated when they attack ourselves or group members whom we like or with whom we identify. And one reason for humorous disparagement in the first place is to bring about dissention in the out-group. An ethnic in-group, for example, will use anti-out-group humour not only to express hostility against that out-group, and in an attempt to undermine the morale of its members, but also to strengthen the morale and solidarity of its own members (Bourhis, Gadfield, Giles *et al.*, 1977).

Anti-out-group humour can, therefore, be a creative and effective way of asserting in-group pride and distinctiveness from a dominant out-group. But it cuts both ways because hostile humour directed at the in-group from an out-group may also tend to produce greater consensus and cohesion on the part of the in-group members as they close ranks to meet and challenge the implied threat to their position. Intergroup disparagement and hostile wit, therefore, serve only to increase the tension and conflict between the groups, and they are tactics used the world over in parliamentary wrangling, professional disputes, industrial strife and international gamesmanship.

The Social Functions of Laughter

The reasons for laughing may have nothing to do with humour, and this is why one needs to consider laughter separately from humour. The encoding and decoding of humour may take place in circumstances where the emission of laughter could be singularly inappropriate. Conversely, laughter may frequently occur when nothing humorous has happened. This is not to deny that on many occasions they may function as displays of the same social purpose. After all, we may well be laughing while we are in the process of encoding humour.

To understand laughter, therefore, one must enquire into the situational context from which it emerges. In her book, *Laughter: A Socio-Scientific Analysis*, Hertzler (1970) makes the useful point about the function of laughter in society that it is an economical aid ('almost a gift') in getting things done. It is a quick, spontaneous reaction to the immediate situation which, often because it is not subject to the normal controls of deliberate speech, gives away directly the perpetrator's thoughts, feelings or desires:

> A good laugh may contribute more than vocal or written admonitions or commands; it may be easier, cheaper, and more successful than laws and ordinances, police and supervisors, hierarchical chain of command, or other regulative and operative personnel and organisational machinery (Hertzler, 1970, p. 86).

This is not to signify that laughter is not regulated by conscious control. There would be little point considering it as a social skill if it were entirely outside one's control. As in the case of most other habitual behaviours, we have each developed our own particular style of expressing ourselves: for some individuals laughter is free-flowing and virtually automatic, for others it is a scarcer commodity, reserved for a more limited range of social occasions.

Attempts to distinguish between different functions of laughter based upon the physical characteristics of laughs (for example, their intensity or amplitude) have generally failed, although small effects from measures of laughter duration have sometimes been reported. For example, La Gaipa (1977) found that hostile wit directed towards an out-group generated longer laughter than either teasing or 'jocular gripes', whereas laughter lasted longer when teasing an in-group member than when teasing an out-group member.

Within everyday language, one talks about laughs as being 'hollow', 'forced', 'mocking', 'bubbling' and so on, as if they possessed characteristic attributes which were uniquely disparate. There is also a rich vocabulary by which to denote types of laughter: giggle, titter, chortle, chuckle, guffaw, cackle, roar, crow, snigger, jeer, which also give substance to the view that there are many types of laughter which qualitatively differ from each other. No one would deny this. What humour researchers have failed to show is any systematic correlation between particular types of social situations and particular types of laughter. So when an individual displays his incompetence in front of others, audience reaction is just as likely to consist of raucous guffaws as a quiet chuckle or restrained snigger.

The interpretation of what the laugh means, therefore, comes from the participants' understanding of the social situation they are in and not from any inherent characteristics of the laugh itself.

The functions and purposes of laughter have been reviewed at length by Gruner (1978) and by Hertzler (1970). Giles and Oxford (1970) and Foot and Chapman (1976) have summarised these functions. For the purposes of this social skills analysis it is important to recognise that laughter is wholly a social phenomenon. As Hertzler (1970) points out, it is 'social in its origin, in its processual occurrence, in its functions, and in its effects' (p. 28).

Humorous Laughter

Following Giles and Oxford's (1970) analysis, humorous laughter may be regarded as an overt expression of rebellion to social pressures, codes and institutions:

Individuals in probably all civilized cultures are continually active social conformers to an almost infinite system of legal codes, occupational constraints, marital-familial ties and moral-ethical restrictions — all of which appear drastically to limit individual freedom, sometimes to an almost insufferable degree. It would not seem implausible that a constant accumulation of frustration in this manner needs to be effectively displaced among some socially harmless channel or channels if society as a whole is to maintain any reasonably adequate level of sanity. Humorous laughter would seem to function perfectly in this respect, and so it would not be surprising to discover that the vast majority of ludicrous experiences, jokes, wit, etc, all involve some occurrence of the socially unacceptable as the crux of their humour (p. 99).

Interestingly, laughter that is *purely* generated by one's amusement at a humorous story, cartoon or joke is comparatively uncommon. It is not often in a solitary situation that one bursts out laughing at something amusing on television or in a book. Normally, it is the presence of others with whom one is able to share the humour that elicits a vocal response, as distinct from merely a smile (Chapman, 1976). Humorous laughter is very responsive to social facilitation effects, and the frequency and amplitude of its emission is governed by the responsiveness of those around us (Chapman, 1973, 1974, 1975a; Chapman and Chapman, 1974; Chapman and Wright, 1976). The more responsive they are, the more we reciprocate.

So our primary purpose in engaging in humorous laughter may typically be to convey the message to others that we also find social conventions funny and that we also are continually frustrated by social pressures and social niceties by which our lives are largely controlled.

Social Laughter

Social laughter may serve very much the same purpose as encoding humour in a group situation as a means of expressing friendship and liking, of gaining social approval and of bolstering group cohesiveness. This function of laughter for integrating ourselves within a particular group does not depend upon the individual having experienced anything amusing, and far from expressing rebellion against social pressures, it can be viewed as an act of social conformity, fulfilling normative group expectations. It is more intended to convey an image of good natured 'sociability'. Possibly as much as humour, social laughter is used for controlling conversations and oiling the wheels of social interaction.

An obvious form that social laughter takes is polite laughter when we laugh at what others have said not because we find it funny but out of consideration for them or in order to make them feel that we are attentive to them or appreciate them. We laugh at our boss's feeble jokes because it might be undiplomatic not to do so.

Ignorance Laughter

A third type of laughter is ignorance laughter which implies both the presence of humour stimuli and the presence of others. Typically, we recognise that a joke has been told but wish to conceal our ignorance or inability to comprehend it. So we laugh along with everyone else in the group in order not to be left out or not to look stupid.

Evasion Laughter

In an important way, laughter, like humour, may serve as an emotional mask behind which to hide our true feelings. If a friend or acquaintance of ours is being attacked or ridiculed by others behind his or her back, we have a choice to defend our friend or, out of expediency, go through the motions of joining in the ridicule in order not to appear different. Laughter gives the impression of sharing in the prevailing feeling of the group. Embarrassment laughter is another example of masking our feelings and stalling for time. We laugh because we are not quite sure what the other person's comments to us mean, or whether his or her intentions towards us are amicable or hostile.

We use laughter, therefore, in ambiguous encounters as a means of deflecting potential animosity directed at us and to earn a little more time to decide how we are going to respond to the other person. The very act of laughing may cause us to tilt our head back, avert our gaze and thereby relieve our embarrassment by momentarily detaching ourselves from the interaction. Chapman (1975a) has argued that children break off interactions in this way to draw attention away from themselves when the interaction is too intense.

Apologetic Laughter

Related to embarrassment laughter and laughter designed to mask our feelings, is apologetic or defensive laughter. This may precede an action on our part, the outcome of which we are uncertain about. We sometimes say, 'I've never done this before . . .' or 'I can't guarantee what's going to happen . . .' when we embark upon a novel task. Laughter may either accompany or substitute for the oral statement and its meaning is clear. We are paving the way for possible failure or for making ourselves look foolish and thereby preparing the audience to believe that we are not taking the situation too seriously ourselves. We may also preface the telling of bad news with laughter, perhaps partly in an attempt to soften the blow and partly by way of apologising for being the one to announce it. Defensive laughter also occurs retrospectively, as when we wish to excuse our lack of action or indecision with respect to some earlier event.

Anxiety Laughter

Tension in social encounters stems from anxiety as well as from embarrassment, and anxiety laughter is a manifestation of tension–release to a specific anxiety-provoking situation. Such laughter may be provoked directly by the feeling of relief when a period of acute tension comes to an end. To cite an extreme example, the hostages from a hijacked aircraft may, when suddenly freed, break down in laughter (or weeping, of course) bordering on the hysterical at the sheer relief that they are safe and the crisis has passed. Rothbart (1976), as mentioned earlier, has noted the close relation between laughter and fear in young children and has argued that laughter comes as a consequence of the child realising that he or she is safe again, the moment his or her fear or distress is over.

Various theories of laughter have taken the view that laughter serves as a 'safety-valve' against excessive social arousal (see Berlyne, 1969; Chapman, 1975a; Godkewitsch, 1976) and that it is a way of dissipating unwanted high arousal. The author's own research on children's social sensitivity conducted jointly with

Chapman and Smith has explored ways in which laughter is used by children to dissipate tension in social situations. We have suggested that boys and girls react differentially to the perceived intimacy of the situation they are in (Foot, Chapman and Smith, 1977; Smith, Foot and Chapman, 1977). Boys are more likely to use laughter as a means of breaking attention away from an interacting companion and girls use it as a means of establishing or restoring their companion's attention towards them.

It appears that boys are less able to tolerate close, intimate interaction with their friends than are girls. For the boys, laughter serves to release tension and momentarily break off the encounter when intimacy becomes too intense. Girls, on the other hand, laugh more in situations with their friends when they are not receiving sufficient attention and wish to increase the intimacy of the encounter. Far from averting their gaze and 'disengaging' while they laugh, they are more likely to gaze directly at their companion in an attempt to attract and sustain her attention.

Laughter, therefore, reflects 'felt tension' in an encounter or a relationship and assists in the regulation of intimacy development.

Derision Laughter

Derision or sinister laughter is another category of laughter which is obviously an alternative, or an additive, to the encoding of hostile humour in situations where one wishes to express superiority over another individual. It is particularly prevalent among children whose laughter may be quite cruel or mocking, for example, in the face of another child's physical or mental deformity. But as McGhee (1979) says, children under the age of seven have great difficulty in taking the perspective of another person and therefore they are largely unaware of other children's feelings. Consequently, their laughter cannot be evaluated as hostile in intent as it may appear to adults. As children grow older, they can begin to understand what the victim must feel, so they begin to inhibit this kind of laughter, especially if the victim is present. Adults use derision laughter as a weapon in more subtle, psychological ways and less for deriding the physical abnormalities of their victims (for which they cannot be blamed) and more for ridiculing the odd behaviours, mannerisms, attitudes or incompetence of their victims (for which they can more readily be blamed).

Derision laughter is also used as a form of refusal or exclusion, particularly when aimed at an individual by the members of a group and at that individual's expense. Such laughter may draw attention to some characteristics of the individual (voice, accent, manner of dress, age, size) which sets him or her apart from the rest of the group and it may be based upon the group's desire to exclude that person from joining in their activities.

Joyous Laughter

One final category of laughter might be described as joyous laughter which is a pure expression of excitement or *joie de vivre* (Foot and Chapman, 1976). This is a spontaneous reaction to pleasurable and exhilarating activities and particularly characteristic of children at play. Joyous laughter is of less interest in the present context because it is largely non-functional, at least as far as its impact upon others is concerned.

Humour, Laughter and Nonverbal Behaviours

It has already been argued that many of the functions of laughter overlap with the functions served by encoding humour; others clearly do not. But while humour is something that one subjectively appreciates, laughter is an overtly observable behaviour which occurs in the context of other behaviours. At face value, laughter may appear to be little more than high-intensity smiling where the teeth are bared more widely and the lips extended more broadly than in smiling, and where expelled breath is sufficiently rapid and massive to precipitate an articulated sound. We are often aware that our laughs grow out of increasingly broad smiles, as when we hear the punch-line of a joke following the build-up to it. Similarly, a full-bodied laugh tends not to switch off suddenly but to taper off into a diminishing smile. Yet there are situations where laughter and smiling are not altogether interchangeable responses and where one would be hardly likely to substitute for the other.

Van Hooff (1972) argues that these behaviours have quite different phylogenetic origins, but this is not an argument that needs to be pursued here. Whatever their origin, they are both archaic adaptive mechanisms which have merged over time and involve manipulation of similar muscles around the mouth and eyes. Certainly, and by definition, if we are laughing then we cannot be smiling at the same time because they are mutually exclusive activities, but we may be engaging in a wide range of other characteristic activities which complement our laughter and help convey the meaning we intend it to have. When telling a joke, therefore, we may modulate our tone of voice, move closer to our audience, lean towards them, raise our hands and make emphatic manual gestures, look straight into their eyes and so on, all signals designed to command their attention and positive interest in us. When engaging in apologetic or embarrassment laughter, we may take a step back, orientate our bodies away from the others and avert our gaze. The other verbal and nonverbal cues in the social situation, therefore, greatly assist the decoder (possibly the butt of the laughter) in determining what the motives and intentions of the encoder are.

Regrettably, very little research has been conducted to study the interplay of humour and laughter with other simultaneously occurring social behaviours. Foot, Chapman and Smith (1980) have attempted to examine the patterning of laughter, smiling and other nonverbal behaviours in encounters between children who are friends or strangers. In developing Patterson's (1976) model of interpersonal intimacy, Foot *et al.* have argued that smiling reflects the congeniality or degree of felt comfort of a social situation, while laughter occurs more frequently and for longer durations in non-preferred intimacy conditions, that is, where children do not find the level of intimacy to their liking. The congeniality of the situation, however, is crucial to promoting other nonverbal behaviours and in pleasurable, desired encounters, increasing amounts of smiling and sociable laughter normally tend to go hand in hand with increases in physical proximity and eye contact.

As already noted, these effects have only been explored with children and in nondemanding situations. They do not necessarily apply to adults and, if all the many kinds of social encounters where laughter may occur are considered, the range and variety of accompanying verbal and nonverbal responses will be immense.

Applications of Humour to Professional Contexts

Humour so evidently is a skill by which people control their relationships and social encounters that it is surprising its use in professional and commercial settings has not received more widespread attention than it so far has. It tends to be accepted as an incidental rather than as a necessary ingredient to life's rich pattern and one rarely stops to think about putting humour to use more deliberately. The very notion of cultivating it as a skill may be anathema to many people who see it as intrinsically unpremeditated and spontaneous, arising fortuitously from the situation of the moment. Yet we all remember certain influential people through our lives who have injected humour consistently into their work as part of their interactive style and no doubt as part of their own coping strategy: the doctor who tells funny stories or jokes to put us at our ease, the teacher who uses sarcasm and hostile wit to put down precocious pupils.

In terms of what has been written about the applications of humour within particular professions, two main themes have been pursued: first, that humour is *persuasive* and, second, that it is *healthy*. If the addition of humour to a message enhances the persuasiveness of that message, then humour has obvious application to teaching, advertising, public speaking and political propaganda. If humour promotes good mental health, then it has obvious applications for the health care professions.

The Persuasive Power of Humour

As Gruner (1976) argues, there are several theoretical reasons why the addition of humour to a message might be expected to enhance the persuasiveness of that message. These may be summed up as follows:

1. Appropriate humour may make the audience more favourably disposed towards the source of the message, for example, the teacher, the advertiser, the public speaker. If the source is more favourably perceived, then the credibility and the persuasiveness of that source is likely to be increased;

2. Appropriate humour is entertaining and liked and may make the message

more interesting and therefore more actively attended to by its audience. If the message is attended to more closely its persuasive power should be increased;

3. Appropriate humour may serve as additional supporting material for a position or idea which the source wishes the audience to accept, and may therefore boost the persuasiveness of the message;

4. Appropriate humour may make a persuasive message more memorable and therefore render it more effective over a longer period of time;

5. Appropriate humour may distract the audience from concocting counter-arguments to the message and therefore increase the persuasiveness of the message.

There is another argument, too, that humour relaxes the audience which might make it more receptive to the message (Hegarty, 1976).

Empirical research which has addressed these questions has generally found little evidence to support the idea that humour enhances the persuasiveness of a message. In probably the earliest controlled study on the effect of humour in persuasive messages, Lull (1940) used serious and humorous versions of the same speeches either in favour or against 'state medicine'. The speeches were presented live to audiences whose previous attitudes towards the issue had been tapped. After hearing one of the speeches the audience's attitudes were retested, and ratings were obtained of the perceived 'interestingness', 'humour' and 'convincingness' of the speaker. The amount of audience laughter was also measured during the speech presentations. Clearly, the funniness of the humorous speeches was perceived; audience members laughed considerably during the presentation of these speeches and they rated them as humorous. The serious speeches elicited no laughter at all and were not rated as humorous. However, there were no differences whatsoever between the humorous and serious speeches in their rated interestingness and convincingness, nor in the amount of actual attitude change they elicited.

Later studies by Kilpela (1961), Youngman (1966), Brandes (1970), Gruner and Lampton (1972) and Kennedy (1972) confirmed that humour added to a speech or sermon has no effect upon the persuasiveness of the message. However much the humour may be appreciated and anticipated by the audience, it does not seem to matter whether the humour is appropriate or inappropriate to the content of the speech nor what form the humour takes: jokes, puns or sarcasm.

The effect of satire as distinct from humour has also been investigated on the basis that it is actually intended as a form of propaganda by the satirist. Gruner (1976, 1978) has reviewed the evidence testing satire and concluded tentatively that 'satire may be an effective persuasive force but only if the receivers of the satire can perceive the persuasive intent' (Gruner, 1976, p. 301). Gruner claims, however, that many people miss the serious point of satirical messages and this may detract from the satire's value as a vehicle for attitude change. Those already favouring the satire's main serious point may be reinforced in their attitude and those strongly opposed to its message may distort the satirist's intention and react against it. Probably most affected are those who are neutral or mildly opposed towards the message.

Whatever the effect of the use of humour and satire upon the persuasiveness of a message, there is no doubt that they enhance the image of the source. People still flock to hear entertaining speakers or preachers who pepper their speeches and sermons with jokes and witticisms. So, not only do people enjoy humour but they react more favourably towards the speaker who provides it. Nevertheless, the kind of humour used is important to judgements of the speaker. Goodchilds (1959) has suggested that 'sarcastic wits' are seen as influential but not popular, while 'clowning wits' are seen as popular but not influential. It has also been suggested that speakers who use too much humour make a poor impression by virtue of being judged as 'frustrated comedians' (Taylor, 1974). So the judicious use of the right kind of humour is inevitably related to the speaker's credibility.

One would also imagine that liking would be closely associated with perceived credibility or authoritativeness: the more popular a speaker is, the more his or her message would be likely to be evaluated as authoritative. This appears to be the case for dull, uninteresting speeches. Gruner (1970) found that dull but humorous speakers were evaluated as more authoritative than dull and non-humorous speakers. However, interesting speakers were judged as equally authoritative whether they were humorous or non-humorous: the intrinsic interest of the speech presumably made the use of humour redundant.

Turning from these general considerations, humour is now briefly considered in some specific applied contexts.

Humour and Public Speaking. Hegarty's book, *Humour and Eloquence in Public Speaking* (1976), provides a persuasive account of the benefits that accrue from the use of humour in public life. Based upon a life-time's experience as a public speaker, Hegarty enumerates anecdotally the many reasons why humour helps people to become successful speakers whether they have to make after-dinner addresses or speak at meetings with their business associates. One of his main points is that humour makes friends and projects an image of a friendly, warm person; it also promises shared enjoyment between the speaker and audience. Listeners like humour; often they expect it; they are relaxed by it and it captures their attention. Above all, the exploitation of humour is a skill which, like learning to ride a bicycle, can be acquired by almost anyone.

Humour and Teaching. Humour in the classroom can clearly make lessons more enjoyable. *Sesame Street* is an obvious example of an educational television programme designed to present teaching in an atmosphere of fun by use of the 'Muppets' as well as to inject humour into specific lessons to be taught. The question is, does humour actually help children learn? Unfortunately, the evidence is equivocal; studies showing that humour does not aid memory outnumber the studies that show a positive or negative effect.

Clearly, humour may distract from the lesson in the sense that it draws the child's attention towards the joke and away from the message, but if the humour is related to and integrated directly with the items to be learned, it may assist the learning of those items (Chapman and Crompton, 1978). Davies and Apter (1980) argue that the type of humour, length of the joke, temporal position of the insertion of the humour and the method of presentation may all contribute to the humour's effectiveness, and the type of lesson or material to be learned may also be crucial. So there are no easy answers. The case for humour as a means of aiding subsequent recall is not yet proven, but this is no reason why teachers should abandon it as a means of maintaining their pupils' attention (see also Brown and Bryant, 1983). There is very little evidence that it actually could be detrimental.

It is also worth noting, first, that much of the research has involved students rather than children, and second, that the materials which have typically been used in research are relatively novel or of high intrinsic interest value. As has already been seen, the use of humour with less interesting material serves to increase the perceived authoritativeness of the source and it may, therefore, be a relatively useful adjunct to a boring lesson or with uninteresting material to be memorised.

Humour, Advertising and Political Propaganda. Surprisingly few formal studies have been conducted on the persuasive power of humour in political debate and in advertising. Welford (1971) simulated a radio debate between two (anonymous) political candidates in which one candidate was heard to refute the speech of the other, either in completely serious vein or in a humorous vein, where each issue addressed was accompanied by a joke. When the audience's attitudes towards the content of the serious and humorous refutational speeches were compared, there were virtually no differences except on two of the issues; in both cases the serious version of the speeches led to more favourable attitudes on the part of the audience members.

Memorability for humorous and non-humorous printed advertising was tested by Perreault (1972) who found no difference between them as far as audience recall was concerned. This is perhaps not surprising; one might expect humour to work more effectively through radio or television than through the medium of print, where it is difficult to do justice to everyone's tastes. There is no doubt that humour is remarkably popular in television advertising and there is no doubt that it can be successful in selling products.

According to Gruner (1974), significant increases in sales of cigarettes, soft drinks, food, cosmetics, airlines and other 'products' have been found in the USA when advertisers have turned from straight to humorous advertising. However, it appears that very little field research has been conducted to demonstrate the power of humour in influencing potential customers' choice of one product over another. The laboratory research has tended to test the influence of humour with more sophisticated social messages and, in consequence, has failed to find an effect.

Advertisers and political actors may at least derive some satisfaction from knowing that no research has shown that humour detracts from the persuasiveness of a message, that is, as long as the humour is appropriate to the audience and does not make the source of the message appear too clownish.

The Health-giving Power of Humour

Implicit and explicit in much of what has been said is the notion that humour and laughter are desirable, if not essential, for satisfactory mental health. They act as a tonic in adversity, a dissipator of unwanted tension and as a means of coping with failure, tyranny, inferiority and life's many other trials and tribulations. We seek out comedy as a form of escape in the knowledge that it can elevate us from the depths of depression and dispel our fears and anxieties. Cousins (1979) describes how his own sense of humour helped rescue him from a painful and debilitating illness; he sees laughter as 'internal jogging', oxygenating the blood, massaging vital organs and facilitating digestion. Moody (1978), drawing upon his experience as a medical practitioner, relates a variety of case studies and anecdotes revealing the positive health benefits derived from humour.

Millions of dollars are spent each year by the mass media in the provision of comedy shows and on the assumption that their value lies in their therapeutic potential (McGhee, 1979). Few would dispute that humour provides an acceptable outlet for sexual and aggressive energy; without some such form of substitute expression, sexual and aggressive impulses would either be bottled up or spill over in (sexually) aggressive behaviour. This cathartic function, therefore, pleads the case that humour promotes healthy adjustment, and that those possessing a rich sense of humour will enjoy good mental health.

What evidence is there, though, that a sense of humour is associated with good mental health? Little research has been undertaken on this question, but there are a few studies which support the view that humour does reflect good adjustment. O'Connell (1960) found appreciation of humour to be a relatively stable personality trait and positively associated with maturity. O'Connell (1968a, 1968b) also found that individuals who appreciate humour have a more constructive and creative orientation to life, with little preoccupation or anxiety about death and dying. Greenwald (1977) echoes the view that humour is one of the few ways by which we can deal with the knowledge that we all have to die sometime, which is why there are so many jokes about death. Conversely, individuals who lead a more repressed life style tend to be more limited in their reactions to humour (O'Connell and Cowgill, 1970). Teenage children who are judged by their teachers to be more poorly adjusted tend to show a predilection for aggressive and non-social forms of humour (Nicholson, 1973).

While the positive connection between sense of humour and good adjustment has been demonstrated, there is little evidence to link lack of humour appreciation with poor adjustment or mental ill-health. Ecker, Levine and Zigler (1973) have found that patients from clinical populations fail to see the humour in jokes that are closely related to their area of conflict, but this is not to say that they fail to appreciate other kinds of humour. Derks, Leichtman and Carroll (1975) were unable to pinpoint any particular differences in the kinds of humour appreciated by samples of neurotic, schizophrenic and normal individuals. Thus, as a diagnostic tool for aiding in the discrimination of different types of mental disorders, humour may not be very helpful, with the possible exception of acute depression. McGhee (1979) argues that depth of depression is reliably mirrored by the absence of laughter and joking, and that an increasing level of humour by the patient is a good index of his or her day-to-day progress towards recovery.

Given that humour is, then, an index of healthy adjustment, it is perhaps surprising that its potential use by those in the caring professions is largely, if not completely, ignored. No doubt this reflects attitudes about the ephemeral nature of humour and the purely incidental and spontaneous role that humour is seen to play in professional activities. The notion that we might make deliberate use of humour in order to manipulate the attitudes or perspectives of those with whom we share a professional relationship is rarely seriously entertained. Humour is just not considered among the repertoire of interpersonal skills which respectable doctors, nurses or social workers should bring to their casework. Textbooks on the bedside manner, on establishing rapport with patients or clients, on counselling strategies and on social skills training studiously avoid any reference to the potential value which humour might serve.

The one area where discussion on the use of humour with clients has been going on for years is in psychotherapy; many therapists are agreed on its potential value, although Kubie (1971) has warned that humour introduced by the therapist too soon can be destructive if the therapist is assumed to be laughing at the patient rather than with him or her.

It is important that we establish what kind of humour we are talking about in relation to therapy. Clearly, it is not the intrusion of jokes nor any direct attempt to make the patient laugh. Mindess (1971) endeavours to define it as conveying an 'inner condition, a stance, a point of view, or in the largest sense an attitude to life' (p. 214). As a therapeutic tool it must be flexible, unconventional and playful, the kind of humour which erupts as a spontaneous reaction to the patient's account of his tale of sorrow or state of mind. Killinger (1977) sees therapeutic humour as the spontaneous creation of a situation–specific amusing event.

The key to it is to train the patient to adopt a wider perspective of him or herself, to articulate a view from which his or her troubles seem less calamitous. Highly depressed or over-anxious patients may be so bound up with their problems and their state of mind that they have lost the ability to step outside of themselves and see themselves in a wider context and in a more self-detached way. Humour helps in this process. When patients begin to see the irony or the absurdity of their own predicament, when they begin to switch off and distance themselves from their own problems, they are on the road to recovery. Mindess (1976) recounts the story of one of his own patients (a former student of his) which is beautifully illustrative of the use of humour in widening a patient's perspective. The patient's marriage was falling apart; she had just discovered that, after 15 years of marriage, her husband had frequently been unfaithful. In a distraught state she rang up the therapist and made an appointment to see him the following day. That evening, however, the therapist had a call from the patient's husband who reported that his wife had just attempted to commit suicide by taking a bottle of pills. The therapist told him to contact the emergency hospital as quickly as possible and, assuming his wife was all right, to ensure that she kept the appointment next day. The patient duly arrived and recounted what had happened the previous night. After explaining the reasons for her taking the pills, she told how her husband had rung the hospital and how they had suggested that, to make her sick, she should be given the whites of eggs liberally salted. He had gone to the kitchen to prepare this emetic while she had lain waiting on the bed. Eventually, near to passing out, she had staggered into the kitchen only to find that her husband was still there trying to work out how to separate the egg whites from the yolks. She had to help him so that he could save her life!

Apparently, the full tragi–comedy of the situation was not lost on the patient, and confused and shocked as she was, by the end of the account, she was laughing with the therapist, not just at the events of the previous night but at the idealised conception she had held of her marriage over many years.

It is, of course, most satisfactory, as in this case, if the patient generates and initiates the humour himself or herself. Then the therapist's role is merely one of reinforcing the humour by appreciating it. However, the therapist may have to activate the humour in indirect ways, as by setting an example. The main consideration is that the humour used by the therapist should not overwhelm or threaten the patient, but should make the patient aware of the therapist's understanding of his or her feelings (Grossman, 1977). This view of the psychological fragility of patients has, however, been questioned. Salameh (1983) describes the technique of 'provocative therapy' (see Farrelly and Matthews, 1981) in which humour is explicitly used as a means of challenging the patients' pathology and provoking them reactively into relinquishing their self-defeating behaviours.

Other therapists have talked about the value of humour to help patients tolerate ambiguity in their lives (Hershkowitz, 1977) or to enable them to accept paradoxes, for example, that one moment they can feel totally isolated and worthless and, the next moment, their life has both worth and meaning (O'Connell, 1977).

Conclusion

The versatility of humour in sharing thoughts and feelings and in conveying intentions and reactions cannot be matched by any other kind of social signal. In this chapter the variety of uses of humour and laughter in different kinds of social situations has been outlined. Patently, humour is a subtle and complex skill and some individuals are more proficient in its use than others. The origins and development of the skill are poorly understood and little is known about why some adults and children become particularly versed and adept at using it to express themselves. As a social skill, however, humour is both an ability and an integrated set of verbal and nonverbal behaviours; it is cultivated through regular use in specific social settings; it is goal-directed and subject to influence through processes of reinforcement and imitation.

There is a view that, unlike other skills we try to master, humour slips from our grasp or somehow evaporates if we endeavour to make it the object of scientific scrutiny. Similar attacks have been levelled at attempts to study the appreciation of good art, literature or music. But rarely does close analysis remove fascination for a phenomenon. Humorists, reviewers and art critics remain passionate devotees of their subject long after their detailed inquisition on particular acts of creativity. There seems little danger that the intrinsic pleasure of humour will be destroyed by our serious attempts to comprehend and exploit it.

References

Bales, R.F. (1950) *Interaction Process Analysis: A Method for the Study of Small Groups*, Addison-Wesley, Reading, Massachussetts
――― (1958) 'Task Roles and Social Roles in Problem-solving Groups' in E. Maccoby, T. Newcomb and E. Hartley (eds), *Readings in Social Psychology*, 3rd edn, Holt, Rinehart & Winston, New York
Berlyne, D.E. (1969) 'Laughter, Humor and Play' in G. Lindzey and E. Aronson (eds), *Handbook of Social Psychology*, 2nd edn, vol. 3, Addison-Wesley, Reading, Mass.
――― (1972) 'Humor and Its Kin' in J.H. Goldstein and P.E. McGhee (eds), *The Psychology of Humor*, Academic Press, New York
Bourhis, R.Y., Gadfield, N.J., Giles, H. *et al.* (1977) 'Context and Ethnic Humour in Intergroup Relations' in A.J. Chapman and H.C. Foot (eds), *It's a Funny Thing, Humour*, Pergamon Press, Oxford
Brandes, P.D. (1970) 'The Persuasiveness of Varying Types of Humor', paper presented at the Speech Communication Association Convention, New Orleans in *SCA Abstracts*, pp. 12–13
Brown, D. and Bryant, J. (1983) 'Humor in the Mass Media' in P.E. McGhee and J.H. Goldstein (eds), *Handbook of Humor Research, Volume 2: Applied Studies*, Springer-Verlag, New York
Chapman, A.J. (1973) 'Social Facilitation of Laughter in Children', *Journal of Experimental Social Psychology*, 9, 528–41
――― (1974) 'An Experimental Study of Socially Facilitated "humorous laughter" ', *Psychological Reports*, 35, 727–34
――― (1975a) 'Humorous Laughter in Children', *Journal of Personality and Social Psychology*, 31, 42–9
――― (1975b) 'Eye-contact, Physical Proximity and Laughter: A Re-examination of the Equilibrium Model of Social Intimacy', *Social Behavior and Personality*, 3, 143–56
――― (1976) 'Social Aspects of Humorous Laughter' in A.J. Chapman and H.C. Foot (eds), *Humour and Laughter: Theory, Research and Applications*, Wiley, Chichester
――― and Chapman, W.A. (1974) 'Responsiveness to Humour: Its Dependency Upon a Companion's Humorous Smiling and Laughter', *Journal of Psychology*, 88, 245–52
――― and Crompton, P. (1978) 'Humorous Presentations of Material and Presentations of Humorous Material: A Review of the Humour and Memory Literature and Two Experimental Studies' in M.M. Gruneberg, P.E. Morris and R.N. Sykes (eds), *Practical Aspects of Memory*, Academic Press, London
Chapman, A.J. and Foot, H.C. (eds) (1976) *Humour and Laughter: Theory, Research and Applications*, Wiley, Chichester
――― and Wright, D.S. (1976) 'Social Enhancement of Laughter: An Experimental Analysis of Some Companion Variables', *Journal of Experimental Child Psychology*, 21, 201–18
Cousins, N. (1979) *Anatomy of an Illness as Perceived by the Patient*, Norton, New York
Davies, A.P. and Apter, M.J. (1980) 'Humour and its Effects on Learning in Children' in P.E. McGhee and A.J. Chapman (eds) *Children's Humour*, Wiley, Chichester
Davis, J.M. and Farina, A. (1970) 'Humor Appreciation as Social Communication', *Journal of Personality and Social Psychology*, 15, 175–8

Derks, P.L., Leichtman, H.M. and Carroll, P.J. (1975) 'Production and Judgement of ''Humor'',
    by Schizophrenics and College Students', *Bulletin of the Psychonomic Society, 6,* 300–2
Ecker, J., Levine, J. and Zigler, E. (1973) 'Impaired Sex-role Identification in Schizophrenia Ex-
    pressed in the Comprehension of Humor Stimuli', *Journal of Personality, 83,* 67–77
Farrelly, F. and Matthews, S. (1981) 'Provocative Therapy' in R. Corsini (ed.), *Handbook of In-
    novative Psychotherapies,* Wiley, New York
Foot, H.C. and Chapman, A.J. (1976) 'The Social Responsiveness of Young Children in Humorous
    Situations' in A.J. Chapman and H.C. Foot (eds), *Humour and Laughter: Theory, Research and
    Applications,* Wiley, Chichester
────── Chapman, A.J. and Smith, J.R. (1977) 'Friendship and Social Responsiveness in Boys and
    Girls', *Journal of Personality and Social Psychology, 35,* 401–11
────── Chapman, A.J. and Smith, J.R. (1980) 'Patterns of Interaction in Children's Friendships'
    in H.C. Foot, A.J. Chapman and J.R. Smith (eds), *Friendship and Social Relations in Children,*
    Wiley, Chichester
Freud, S. (1905) 'Wit and its Relationship to the Unconscious' in A. Brill (ed), *Basic Writings of
    Sigmund Freud,* Modern Library, New York, pp. 633–803
────── (1928) 'Humour' in *Collected Papers,* vol. V, Hogarth, London, pp. 215–21
Giles, H. and Oxford, G.S. (1970) 'Towards a Multi-dimensional Theory of Laughter Causation and
    its Social Implications', *Bulletin of the British Psychological Society, 23,* 97–105
Godkewitsch, M. (1976) 'Physiological and Verbal Indices of Arousal in Rated Humour' in A.J.
    Chapman and H.C. Foot (eds), *Humour and Laughter: Theory, Research and Applications,* Wiley,
    Chichester
Goldstein, J.H. and McGhee, P.E. (eds) (1972) *The Psychology of Humor,* Academic Press, New York
Goodchilds, J.D. (1959) 'Effects of Being Witty on Position in the Social Structure of a Small Group',
    Sociometry, 22, 261–72
Greenwald, H. (1977) 'Humour in Psychotherapy' in A.J. Chapman and H.C. Foot (eds), *It's A
    Funny Thing, Humour,* Pergamon Press, Oxford
Grossman, S.A. (1977) 'The Use of Jokes in Psychotherapy' in A.J. Chapman and H.C. Foot (eds),
    It's a Funny Thing, Humour, Wiley, Chichester
Grotjahn, M. (1957) *Beyond Laughter: Humor and the Subconscious,* McGraw-Hill, New York
Gruner, C.R. (1970) 'The Effect on Speaker Ethos and Audience Information Gain of Humor in
    Dull and Interesting Speeches', *Central States Speech Journal, 21,* 160–6
────── (1974) 'Dogmatism: A Factor in the Understanding and Appreciation of Editorial Satire?'
    paper presented at the SCA Convention, Chicago
────── (1976) 'Wit and Humour in Mass Communication' in A.J. Chapman and H.C. Foot (eds),
    Humour and Laughter: Theory, Research and Applications, Wiley, Chichester
────── (1978) *Understanding Laughter: the Workings of Wit and Humour,* Nelson-Hall, Chicago
────── and Lampton, W.E. (1972) 'Effects of Including Humorous Material in a Persuasive Ser-
    mon', *Southern Speech Communication Journal, 38,* 188–96
Hegarty, E.J. (1976) *Humour and Eloquence in Public Speaking,* Parker, West Nyack, New York
Hershkowitz, A. (1977) 'The Essential Ambiguity Of, and In, Humour' in A.J. Chapman and H.C.
    Foot (eds), *It's A Funny Thing, Humour,* Pergamon, Oxford
Hertzler, J.O. (1970) *Laughter: A Socio-scientific Analysis,* Exposition, New York
Hooff, J.A.R.A.M. Van (1972) 'A Comparative Approach to the Phylogeny of Laughter and Smil-
    ing' in R. Hind (ed.), *Nonverbal Communication,* Cambridge University Press, Cambridge
Husband, C. (1977) 'The Mass Media and the Functions of Ethnic Humour in a Racist Society' in
    A.J. Chapman and H.C. Foot (eds), *It's a Funny Thing, Humour,* Pergamon, Oxford
Kane, T.R., Suls, J.M. and Tedeschi, J. (1977) 'Humour as a Tool of Social Interaction' in A.J.
    Chapman and H.C. Foot (eds), *It's a Funny Thing, Humour,* Pergamon, Oxford
Kennedy, A.J. (1972) 'An Experimental Study of the Effect of Humorous Message Content upon
    Ethos and Persuasiveness', *Doctoral Dissertation,* University of Michigan
Killinger, B. (1977) 'The Place of Humour in Adult Psychotherapy' in A.J. Chapman and H.C. Foot
    (eds), *It's a Funny Thing, Humour,* Pergamon, Oxford
Kilpela, D.E. (1961) 'An Experimental Study of the Effect of Humor on Persuasion', *Masters Thesis,*
    Wayne State University, Detroit, Michigan
Kubie, L.S. (1971) 'The Destructive Potential of Humor in Psychotherapy', *American Journal of
    Psychiatry, 127,* 861–86
LaFrance, M. (1983) 'Felt Versus Feigned Funniness: Issues in Coding Smiling and Laughing' in

P.E. McGhee and J.H. Goldstein (eds), *Handbook of Humor Research*, volume I, Basic Issues, Springer-Verlag, New York

LaGaipa, J.J. (1977) 'The Effects of Humour on the Flow of Social Conversation' in A.J. Chapman and H.C. Foot (eds), *It's a Funny Thing, Humour*, Pergamon, Oxford

Lull, P.E. (1940) 'The Effects of Humor in Persuasive Speeches', *Speech Monographs*, 7, 26–40

McGhee, P.E. (1979) *Humor: its Origin and Development*, Freeman, San Francisco

Martineau, W.H. (1972) 'A Model of the Social Functions of Humor' in J.H. Goldstein and P.E. McGhee (eds), *The Psychology of Humor*, Academic Press, New York

Mettee, D.R., Hrelec, E.S. and Wilkens, P.C. (1971) 'Humor as an Interpersonal Asset and Liability', *Journal of Social Psychology*, 85, 51–64

Middleton, R. and Moland, J. (1959) 'Humor in Negro and White Subcultures: A Study of Jokes Among University Students', *American Sociological Review*, 24, 61–9

Mindess, H. (1971) *Laughter and Liberation*, Nash, Los Angeles

———— (1976) 'The Use and Abuse of Humour in Psychotherapy' in A.J. Chapman and H.C. Foot (eds), *Humour and Laughter: Theory, Research and Application*, Wiley, Chichester

Moody, R. (1978) *Laugh after Laugh: The Healing Power of Humor*, Headwaters Press, Jacksonville, Fla.

Nicholson, W.S. (1973) 'Relation Between Measures of Mental Health and a Cartoon Measure of Humor in Fifth Grade Children', *Doctoral Dissertation*, University of Maryland

O'Connell, W.E. (1960) 'The Adaptive Functions of Wit and Humor', *Journal of Abnormal and Social Psychology*, 61, 263–70

———— (1968a) 'Organic and Schizophrenic Differences in Wit and Humor Appreciation', *Diseases of the Nervous System*, 29, 276–81

———— (1968b) 'Humor and Death', *Psychological Reports*, 22, 391–402

———— (1977) 'The Sense of Humour: Actualizers of Persons and Theories' in A.J. Chapman and H.C. Foot (eds), *It's a Funny Thing, Humour*, Pergamon, Oxford

———— and Cowgill, S. (1970) 'Wit, Humor and Defensiveness', *Newsletter for Research in Psychology*, 12, 32–3

Patterson, M.L. (1976) 'An Arousal Model of Interpersonal Intimacy', *Psychological Review*, 83, 235–45

Perreault, R.M. (1972) 'A Study of the Effects of Humor in Advertising As Can Be Measured By Product Recall Tests', *Masters Thesis*, University of Georgia, Georgia

Rothbart, M.K. (1973) 'Laughter in Young Children', *Psychological Bulletin*, 80, 247–56

———— (1976) 'Incongruity, Problem-solving and Laughter' in A.J. Chapman and H.C. Foot (eds), *Humour and Laughter: Theory, Research and Applications*, Wiley, Chichester

Salameh, W.A. (1983) 'Humor in Psychotherapy' in P.E. McGhee and J.H. Goldstein (eds), *Handbook of Humor Research, Vol. 2: Applied Studies*, Springer-Verlag, New York

Shurcliff, A. (1968) 'Judged Humor, Arousal, and the Relief Theory', *Journal of Personality and Social Psychology*, 8, 360–3

Smith, J.R., Foot, H.C. and Chapman, A.J. (1977) 'What Makes Us Laugh?', *Psychology Today (UK)*, 3, 18–23

Suls, J.M. (1972) 'A Two-stage Model for the Appreciation of Jokes and Cartoons: An Information-processing Analysis' in J.H. Goldstein and P.E. McGhee (eds), *The Psychology of Humor*, Academic Press, New York

———— (1977) 'Cognitive and Disparagement Theories of Humour: A Theoretical and Empirical Synthesis' in A.J. Chapman and H.C. Foot (eds), *It's A Funny Thing, Humour*, Pergamon, Oxford

———— and Miller, R.L. (1976) 'Humor as an Attributional Index' cited by Kane, T.R., Suls, J. and Tedeschi, J. in A.J. Chapman and H.C. Foot (eds), *It's A Funny Thing, Humour*, Pergamon, Oxford

Taylor, PH. (1974) 'An Experimental Study of Humor and Ethos', *Southern Speech Communication Journal*, 39, 359–66

Welford, T.W. (1971) 'An Experimental Study of the Effectiveness of Humor Used as a Refutational Device', *Doctoral Dissertation*, Louisiana State University, Louisiana

Wilson, C.P. (1979) *Jokes: Form, Content, Use and Function*, Academic Press, London

Youngman, R.C. (1966) 'An Experimental Investigation of the Effect of Germane Humor Versus Non-germane Humor in an Informative Communication', *Masters Thesis*, Ohio University, Ohio

Zillman, D. (1983) 'Disparagement Humor' in P.E. McGhee and J.H. Goldstein (eds), *Handbook of Humor Research, Volume I: Basic Issues*, Springer-Verlag, New York

——— and Cantor, J.R. (1976) 'A Disposition Theory of Humour and Mirth' in A.J. Chapman and H.C. Foot (eds), *Humour and Laughter: Theory, Research and Applications*, Wiley, Chichester

16 HANDLING STRONG EMOTIONS

R. Glynn Owens

Even those who show considerable skill in their everyday social interactions may experience difficulty in situations where strong emotions are involved. Yet it is often in such situations that effective communication is most critical. When an interaction involves love, hate, panic, despair or anger the person experiencing such emotions may be likely to show patterns of behaviour which are, for them, far from typical. The person who panics in a university finals examination may sit petrified, or run from the room, or show some other inappropriate response which ruins a future career. Despair may drive a person to suicide; anger to their striking, injuring or even killing a loved one. In all cases the effect may be to give rise to behaviour which the individual later regrets.

The problem is not only one for the individual experiencing the emotions. Because such emotions are associated with atypical behaviour patterns, the effect is to make that individual's behaviour less predictable to others. Those who have to deal with the angry, panicky or otherwise highly emotional individual thus have the problem of not knowing what the person may do next. Yet if such a person is to be helped, it is necessary that the communication skills employed be appropriate, to help avoid action which is later regretted.

The problem is further compounded by the fact that the unpredictability of one person's behaviour may itself produce strong emotions in another. Thus an inexperienced professional confronted with an angry client may panic. The result is that both individuals are then having to handle strong emotions, the client having to handle the panic of the professional, the professional the anger of the client. Yet each is in the worst possible position to do so, since the judgement and skills of each may be impaired by the emotions being experienced.

Strong emotions, then, present a number of problems. The person experiencing such emotion may do something which is later regretted. The unpredictability in behaviour associated with the strong emotion may make it difficult for others to handle. This difficulty may itself produce similar or other strong emotions in the other people concerned. Thus even with only two people involved the situation can soon become highly complex. Each individual has to deal with the strong emotions being experienced and in addition has to handle the other person's strong emotions. Yet the potentially serious consequences of strong emotions implies that those situations in which appropriate interaction is most difficult may also be those in which it is most critical, since if handled badly the consequences may be of lasting significance.

Inevitably, a detailed consideration of the skills necessary in handling all strong emotions would require considerably more space than is available in a single chapter of this nature. For present purposes, therefore, it is useful to consider in detail a single example of the types of strong emotion already mentioned. The handling of angry or aggressive behaviour provides a good illustration of many of the skills necessary for effective interaction and communication. Violence is often associated with a highly charged emotional state. As with other strong emotions, behaviour quite different to that normally exhibited may be apparent. The consequences may be extremely important, both for the individual concerned and for others. Indeed, it is not exaggerating to describe them as sometimes being a matter of life and death. And as with so many strong emotions, one effect may be the production of the same or other strong emotions in any individual drawn into such an episode. The present chapter is therefore largely concerned with the skills involved in dealing with the violent or potentially violent individual, primarily from the viewpoint of a one-to-one interaction.

It is essential that those likely to encounter such individuals be adequately prepared. Although it is tempting to put off consideration of such issues until the need arises, it is clear that by the time an angry or aggressive episode is under way, it is too late to start thinking about the best ways of dealing with such interactions. Anger and aggression have a way of escalating rapidly, particularly if handled badly. Moreover, the professional confronted with an angry client is also likely to undergo considerable emotional disturbance, with fear, anxiety or even panic clouding rational thought processes. The time to think about dealing with violent episodes is well before they occur, so that the essential issues can be considered, and the necessary skills rehearsed, well before the problems actually arise.

With many behavioural and psychological difficulties it is often possible to take a largely empirical approach, therapists and other professionals trying out different strategies until the problem begins to respond. In the field of aggressive behaviour such an approach carries a number of risks. In particular, the potentially serious consequences of aggression mean that every effort needs to be made to produce a rapid reduction or elimination of the problem. Unlike, say, the obsessional client who checks the window lock six times before going to bed, the angry or aggressive individual cannot be left with the problem until a solution is hit upon by chance. Moreover, it is the case that what may constitute a helpful course of action with one individual may prove quite counterproductive with another, resulting in escalation rather than alleviation of the violence. One consequence of such problems is the need for the skilled professional to have both a practical and theoretical grounding in the field of aggressive behaviour. It is appropriate, therefore, at this stage to look a little more closely at the processes involved in the generation of angry, aggressive and violent behaviour.

Anger and Violence: Theoretical Aspects

Freudian Theory

The problem of violent and aggressive behaviour has been a concern to psychologists, psychiatrists and psychoanalysts for decades. Even Freud, who produced such remarkable insights into so many areas of human behaviour, experienced considerable difficulty in the comprehension of humanity's aggression. Freud's views on the causes of violence are far too complex to be given full justice here, but a few points about his theory are worth noting.

His account of violence varied quite considerably throughout his life, although the central concept remained fairly consistent. Freud postulated, in addition to the libidinous energy or 'Eros' responsible for much of human behaviour, a destructive energy which he called 'Thanatos' and which produced a drive towards death and destruction. The organism, it was argued, existed in a constant state of tension resulting from its departure from a natural state of decay and disorganisation. The only way in which this tension could be discharged was through the death of the organism. Redirection of this energy, from being self-directed to being outwardly directed was, Freud believed, the key to human aggression. In this framework, an angry outburst would occur when the pressure of the aggressive energy rose to a level which the individual could no longer control. Aggressive or angry behaviour would produce a temporary discharge of the energy, after which the tension would again build up. One possible implication of this would be the potentially beneficial effect of cathartic activities like violent sports, through which some energy could be discharged in an acceptable fashion.

Inevitably, this account represents only an oversimplified description of a remarkably complex theory. It provides, however, sufficient outline to permit a few important considerations. It is important to note that the theory underwent considerable revision in Freud's lifetime, with, for example, the status of Thanatos as a totally independent source of energy from Eros often remaining unclear. Freud himself seems never to have been entirely happy with his analysis, a view which was shared by many of his followers. The prominent Freudian Stafford-Clark (1967), for example, has said of the concept of Thanatos that it has 'proved of far more use to artists and novelists than to clinicians'. Moreover, the therapeutic implications of a Freudian approach have not obtained support from research studies. In particular, procedures which might have expected to provide cathartic experiences have tended to be associated with increased rather than decreased likelihood of violence. In a detailed study of violent sports in different cultures, Sipes (1973) found evidence in direct contrast to that suggested by a Freudian perspective. An assessment of the amount of violent sport in various cultures was found to correlate positively with the level of violence in that culture. Rather than the violent sport providing an acceptable, cathartic alternative to violence, it seems that the cultures in which there are more 'outlets' for aggressive energy are nonetheless also the ones in which most violence occurs.

Personality Theories

As a result of considerations like these, Freudian theories have tended to fall rather out of favour, and subsequent research on violence has proceeded largely in other directions. A considerable amount of research, for example, has studied the relationship between different personality types and violence. Typically, such studies involve the adminstration of personality tests to groups of violent and otherwise similar non-violent individuals. Any differences in personality between the two are than taken as indicative of a significant role for the personality factors identified. Working within this kind of framework, various workers have suggested the role of specific personality factors. Eysenck (1983) for example, has suggested that those scoring high on neuroticism and extraversion scales are more likely to be violent and has linked this to a broader theory of criminal behaviour and the acquisition of internal morality through processes of conditioning.

However, many workers have raised serious objections to Eysenck's position, questioning the simplistic assumption of a Pavlovian conditioning process as producing the individual's sense of right and wrong, and calling into question the notion that all types of criminal behaviour, both violent and non-violent, stem from a single personality pattern. Certainly, it is worth noting that a considerable amount of the violence in modern society is not at all associated with other crime or even with any crime at all. Much is legitimised (for instance, the use of physical punishment with children, warfare and, in some cultures, the use of beatings and tortures) as part of the judicial system. A considerable amount of violence is also kept separate from the judicial system despite being illegal; examples include family violence, violence in institutions, between street gangs and so on. With so much violence being unassociated with crime, a theory which appears to treat crime and violence as synonymous is bound to be regarded with some scepticism.

Other personality theorists, however, have often concentrated specifically on aggressive behaviour. One such theory was proposed by Megargee (1966) who suggested that it was possible to identify two quite specific personality types in the study of extreme aggression. The first, or undercontrolled type, represented the individual who shows little restraint or inhibition in the use of aggressive behaviour, but who simply reacts in a violent manner to any or most provoking situations. If an individual is undercontrolled in this way, it is unsurprising that a high level of violence is the result. Perhaps of more interest is Megargee's second type. Here it is argued that the individual, far from being undercontrolled, is actually overcontrolled, unwilling to resort to violence even under strong provocation. While such an individual might show little history of violence, because of such overcontrol, it is apparent that some such individuals will eventually become exposed to provocations which defeat even their extreme self-control. The violent behaviour eventually occurs, and may be extreme. Various reasons have been given for the observation that such individuals may eventually show a quite disproportionately high level of aggression. These include the suggestion that such individuals may be more likely to experience extreme provocation than others (since the people around them have learned that they can be hostile without fear of reprisal) and the possiblity that, being unused to acting violently, they are unskilled at matching their own level of violence to the needs of the situation.

It should be remembered, however, that the suggestion that being overcontrolled may lead to violence needs to be treated with some caution. While several studies of extreme offenders have identified both over- and undercontrolled individuals among such groups (see, for example, Blackburn, 1968), it is important to remember that there may exist large numbers of overcontrolled individuals in the population at large, of whom the majority may show no violence at all. It is far from clear that overcontrol inevitably leads to extreme violence, and many such people may go through life showing no violence whatever. The relationship may be thought of as like that between slimming and anorexia nervosa; most anorexics will have been on a diet, but only a tiny percentage of women who go on a diet will become anorexic.

Besides the specific problems of individual theories, approaches to behaviour through the study of personality have also encountered wider problems. In particular, the recognition that situational determinants may be much more powerful than personality factors in determining an individual's behaviour has led to studies of the former falling into disfavour. Particularly influential here was the series of studies reported by Mischel (1967) in which he demonstrated the poor predictive power of personality tests relative to knowledge of the actual situation in which the behaviour occurred. In consequence, much of the research on aggression has shifted towards a study of the environmental factors involved in violence, with the experimental laboratory providing the setting for much current research.

Frustration Theory

Modern experimental work on aggressive behaviour can in fact be traced back at least as far as the first half of this century, with the so-called 'frustration aggression hypothesis' (Miller, 1941) having considerable influence. The cornerstone of this theory was summarised by the statement 'aggression is always a consequence of frustration' (Dollard, Doob, Miller, *et al.*, 1939). What this rather ambiguous statement meant was that if frustration occurred, aggression would always be the result, a conclusion supported at the time by much experimental work.

However, later studies have cast doubt on this conclusion; some workers, for example, reporting that regression rather than aggression may be a likely consequence. That is, the individual experiencing frustration may show generally rather immature behaviour rather than behaviour which is specifically aggressive. Other responses such as withdrawal from the situation and help-seeking behaviours have also been noted in response to frustration (Bandura, 1973). The frustration–aggression hypothesis is also limited in failing to encompass aggressive behaviour which has no relationship whatever to frustration, as when violence occurs for such reasons as direct personal gain.

Operant Conditioning and Reactive Aggression

Today, theorists in the field of aggression have generally found it necessary to consider at least two potentially independent processes in the explanation of aggression. At one level aggression may often represent nothing more than a 'means to an end'. In the society in which we live, there may be many payoffs associated with aggressive behaviour, including status, power, influence and even direct financial consequences. Such events will often reward the individual's violent behaviour, or, more technically, will be reinforcers of the behaviour (see Chapter 5).

The behaviour in such instances constitutes an example of what has been termed 'operant behaviour', behaviour primarily under the control of consequent reinforcement. Behaviour which is reinforced is more likely to be repeated than behaviour which is not. If the behaviour is necessary for reinforcement to be obtained, then we should not be surprised that the behaviour occurs. In this sense, aggressive behaviour to obtain, say, power, may be no different from an experimental animal pressing a lever to obtain food. Indeed, experimental studies have shown that aggressive behaviour can be produced in laboratory animals using food to reinforce successive approximations to such behaviour (see, for example, Reynolds, Catania and Skinner, 1963); a number of naturalistic studies of children have suggested similar processes occurring in their aggression (for example, Patterson, Cobb and Ray, 1967). Buss (1971) has pointed to a number of reinforcers by which society may currently (if unintentionally) reinforce aggressive behaviour in its members.

While recognition of such factors makes such aggressive behaviour unsurprising, it is, however, clearly inadequate to expect the process of operant conditioning to account for the whole of aggressive behaviour. Often, aggressive behaviour appears to be under neither direct nor indirect control of its consequences (like reinforcement), but rather seems to be a direct consequence of certain antecedents or prior stimuli. Because of this most theorists have found it necessary to suggest the operation of a second process in order to account for the whole of aggressive behaviour.

That aggressive behaviour may be produced without any form of reinforcement, but simply in response to a specific prior stimulus, has been widely demonstrated. In a now classic study, Ulrich and Azrin (1962) showed that if two rats were placed in an experimental chamber and given an electric shock, their immediate response would be to attack each other. Without the shock the rats showed no signs of hostility. Such a response was termed 'shock-induced fighting'. Since then it has become clear that other aggressive responses may also be produced by other kinds of aversive stimulus, and the terms 'reflexive aggression' or 'reactive aggression' may be more appropriate (Owens and Bagshaw, 1985).

In general, it appears that an increased likelihood of aggression is apparent when an individual is exposed to aversive stimulation from which escape is impractical. Since Ulrich and Azrin's original experiment the same sort of process has been demonstrated in a wide range of species (including humans) with a variety of aversive stimuli. It is important to note that the response may be obtained not only in response to intrinsically aversive stimuli but also to stimuli whose aversive properties have been conditioned. Thus if a laboratory animal has learned to associate some neutral stimulus (for instance, a light) with an aversive event, this stimulus will itself elicit the aggressive response (Vernon and Ulrich, 1966). Obviously, in these circumstances whether or not a response is obtained to the light will depend upon whether the animal has had the appropriate prior conditioning. Such differences in conditioning history may obviously be of relevance to the study of individual variations in aggression.

While it is recognised that the two basic processes outlined above — operant and reactive aggression — are conceptually independent, it is apparent that in practice the two often occur simultaneously. Thus, an individual may react violently to some aversive event, but this may be reinforced by the effect it has on others. In other situations the relationship may be quite complex. Aggression has, for example, been noted in association with the withdrawal of reinforcement, or 'extinction-induced aggression' (Kelly and Hake, 1970). Here the failure of reinforcement to occur is itself aversive and, in consequence, may produce its own aggressive behaviour.

It is also important to remember that many aggressive episodes involve considerable interaction between the two or more people involved. The aggressive behaviour of one individual may constitute an aversive stimulus for the other, who also acts aggressively in response and produces further aggression in the first. Under such circumstances aggression may rapidly escalate. Concurrent with this is the observation that aggressive behaviour is producing a strong effect on the other person, an observation which may provide reinforcement of such behaviour. Again, the possibility of rapid escalation is clear.

It is thus possible to think of aggressive behaviour as involving one or both of these two basic processes. Of course, the actions of these processes are themselves modified by a number of other factors. Alcohol and certain drugs, for example, seem to reduce the influence of aversive stimuli on behaviour. In consequence, the probability of reactive aggression may be reduced. However, if the threat of aversive consequences is serving to inhibit operant aggression, the role of the alcohol may be to increase the probability of such behaviour by removing the normal constraints. One implication of this is that any attempt at drug treatment of aggression needs to be made in the context of a thorough behavioural analysis.

In a similar way, other treatments for aggressive behaviour may also depend to a greater or lesser extent on the role of reactive and operant processes. Such dependence implies that therapists working with aggressive or potentially aggressive individuals need to appreciate the theoretical, as well as the practical basis of such treatments.

Dealing With the Aggressive Individual

Aggressive episodes will frequently involve a number of stages, from the initiation of aggressive or pre-aggressive behaviour, through a period of escalation, often to some violent expression of the conflict, resentment and finally to an eventual (if temporary) resolution. A consideration of the processes outlined in the previous section may clarify how such stages can arise. For example, some mild aversive event may cause one person to show mild hositility to another. This mild hostility then elicits a hostile response from the second person which, in conjunction with the initial aversive event, produces further, stronger hostility and a progressive escalation.

Such escalation may be accelerated by the signs of anger and annoyance in each person, reinforcing the hostile behaviour of the other. The escalation may have a number of outcomes. In some circumstances the behaviour of one person may eventually become so aversive that the other simply withdraws, leaving the situation. Alternatively, the escalation may lead to physical conflict such that one person is unable to continue playing a role in the escalation. At this point, aggressive behaviour may no longer be elicited from the victor in the conflict, whose anger may thereupon be replaced with remorse. Obviously, the possible routes to escalation may multiply where more than two people are involved.

It is important, too, to remember that escalation may take place over a considerable period of time. A person may, for example, frequently rely upon the use of aggressive behaviour to obtain acquiescence from others. If such behaviour is successful it will, according to the principle of reinforcement, continue to occur.

However, if the behaviour loses its effectiveness, perhaps because someone has decided to 'take a stand', the initial effect may be to produce an increase in aggression. In general, the discontinuing of reinforcement of a previously reinforced behaviour will produce an immediate temporary increase in the behaviour, followed by a gradual decrease (Skinner, 1938). If this increase is sufficiently frightening to the victim, the latter may after all back down, thus reinforcing a new, higher level of aggression. (In addition, of course, the removal of reinforcement, extinction, may itself produce aggressive behaviour through a reactive process.) Further escalation may occur if the victim later regrets backing down and decides again to resist, repeating the previous sequence of events and producing a new level of escalation. The whole process may take weeks, months or even years, with the aggressor systematically increasing the level of aggression while the victim periodically attempts to desist from giving in.

In dealing with the problem of aggression, most if not all workers in the field are agreed that intervention should occur at as early a stage as possible. Dealing with an individual who has been allowed to become angry is considerably more difficult than dealing with the same individual during a calmer moment. As with many other problems, anger and aggression are better prevented than cured. Clearly, on the basis of even the limited theoretical outline given above, violent incidents may vary considerably both in their form and in the underlying processes involved. As a result it is not possible to give simple, rigid guidelines on how to deal with a violent episode. Nevertheless, on the basis of what is known, together with consideration of the experience of those accustomed to dealing with violence (for example, Packham, 1978; Carney, 1979) it is possible to highlight certain general areas for consideration.

Acting Calmly

Totally to ignore aggressive behaviour, as might be recommended in dealing with other forms of problematic operant behaviour, is usually neither realistic nor advisable in the context of aggression. First, the very fact that extinction may produce aggresssion may mean that the risk is increased. While in general it is appropriate to avoid reinforcing aggressive behaviour, it is important to note that much aggressive behaviour, particularly in its early stages, may also contain a substantial non-aggressive component (for instance, a legitimate complaint). If this, too, goes unreinforced not only is the chance of positive, adaptive behaviour lost but further aggression may also be introduced as a consequence of the extinction.

Preferable in such circumstances is what has been described as 'calm normality'. This involves responding in a calm, positive manner to the non-violent aspects of the individual's behaviour, dealing with them as far as possible as one would deal with a non-violent individual with a similar problem. Such normality being close to what the individual encounters in day-to-day living is also unlikely to be extremely aversive and therefore unlikely to produce reactive aggression.

Indicating a Low Probability of Reinforcement

If behaviour is under reinforcement control, it is much more likely to occur if the individual can see that reinforcement is probable. Thus, any activity which increases the likelihood of an attack succeeding should be avoided. This may mean nothing more complex than avoiding turning one's back on an aggressor or avoiding giving them a weapon. Even such strategies may not be entirely simple, however. Giving someone a cup of coffee, for example, may look like a friendly gesture but may also equip the individual with a potentially scalding liquid.

Observing the Progress of An Incident

Many of the factors which influence the progress of an aggressive incident will be idiosyncratic to the aggressor involved. This makes it difficult to say in advance how an individual will react to any particular response. By observing what makes the individual angrier, and what less so, it is possible to make moment-to-moment adjustments in one's own behaviour in order to avoid the risk of a violent outburst. Obviously, related to this is the need to observe one's own reactions. It is particularly important in dealing with aggressive episodes that at least one of the people concerned stays calm. By observing one's own behaviour, any signs of anger in oneself can be detected at an early stage and efforts made to calm down and relax before things get out of hand.

Relaxing the Individual

Anger and relaxation are difficult to experience simultaneously. If, therefore, the angry individual can be relaxed, this may be sufficient to displace the anger. Again, it is important that the therapist or other professional retains an obvious air of calmness. Both anger and relaxation may be quickly picked up by clients, and when communicated may result in corresponding changes in their own emotional state. Put simply, dealing with angry people can make us angry, dealing with calm people can make us calm. It is up to the trained professional to be the one who sets the pattern for interpersonal interactions.

Relaxation, of course, may also make a physical attack difficult or impossible. At its simplest level, it is more difficult to launch into a vicious physical attack when sitting relaxed in an armchair than it is when one is upright and tense. By calming and relaxing the aggressive individual, a potentially violent attack may be totally diverted.

Dealing with a violent incident often involves treading a careful line between certain courses of action. Aggressive behaviour should not be reinforced, but at the same time legitimate elements of complaint should be given due consideration. Hostility towards the individual should be avoided, but at the same time it should be clear that aggression will achieve no useful end. The professional's manner should be calm and friendly but not patronising. Such a fine degree of skill may be difficult to learn, and organisations and institutions dealing with violent individuals should ensure that adequate training in such skills is available. Such training may include role-plays, theoretical training and practical experience. For many professionals specific training is available for dealing with the potentially violent individual. Nurses in England, for example, have the English National Board's course number 955, 'Care of the violent or potentially violent individual'. Courses like this, and others, are often open to a wide range of professions, and may provide much useful experience and training.

Much of the natural history of each aggressive episode depends a great deal on the reaction of the target of the aggression. To be confronted with an aggressive individual may produce a number of reactions in the inexperienced professional. There may be surprise that such aggressive behaviour occurs. There may be quite realistic fear of pain, injury or even death. There may be anxiety or even panic if the professional is unsure of how to deal with the aggression. While it is inappropriate for such professionals not to experience any reaction at all, it is critical that their emotional reaction be kept under control. Over-reaction may cloud the professional's judgement and lead to hasty reactions which are counterproductive. Attempts to prepare professionals for dealing with violent incidents might therefore include the following:

1. Self awareness, and in particular a rapid recognition of the signs of particular emotional reactions in oneself. As noted above, skilled professionals should be

able to detect the first signs of strong emotions in themselves and take action accordingly;

2. Self-control, and in particular the ability to relax. Once the signs of fear, anxiety, panic and so on are apparent the professional should be able to counter these with a deliberate attempt at relaxation;

3. Rehearsal, preferably in either role-play or real situations of progressively increasing difficulty. Familiarity with violent situations can do much to reduce the professional's tendency towards anxiety or anger. Moreover, a history of dealing successfully with problems of violence gives the professional a degree of confidence sufficient to prevent panic while still enabling overconfidence to be avoided;

4. Theoretical understanding, especially of the psychological processes involved. The professional who doesn't understand what is happening in a violent incident is much more likely to be afraid or bewildered. If the individual can recognise the processes going on in an aggressive episode, the feeling of familiarity with the situation is markedly increased.

Treating the Aggressive Person

For many professionals, however, the occurrence of any aggressive incident is undesirable, and the main efforts of such workers are directed towards helping the individual deal with anger and aggression in such a way as to prevent incidents arising. In this context, a number of treatment procedures have been devised aimed at helping the aggressive individual control angry outbursts.

Often, such treatment procedures are more appropriate to one or other process in aggression. Extinction procedures, for example, may be of value in certain cases of operant aggression but may have little relevance to dealing with reactive aggression; with other procedures, the converse may apply. A number of psychological procedures of value in the treatment of aggression have been outlined by Owens and Ashcroft (1985) and Goldstein, Carr, Davidson, *et al.* (1981). Among those of relevance to the treatment of anger problems are a number derived from conventional behaviour therapy procedures, including the following treatments.

Systematic Densenitisation

Widely used in the treatment of phobias, the procedures of systematic desensitisation have been adapted to provide individuals with alternatives to aggression in response to aversive stimuli. Basically, systematic desensitisation involves the individual practising some alternative response to the one which is problematic in the presence of stimuli of increasing difficulty. As the new response replaces the old with any given stimulus, the treatment proceeds to one of slightly greater difficulty, until the individual can reliably produce the new response to situations which would earlier have been too difficult to cope with.

In practical terms, the use of systematic desensitisation in anger control will usually involve the client first learning a suitable alternative response. Most common in this context is the learning of some kind of relaxation, for example, the progressive muscle relaxation procedure devised by Jacobsen (1938). Once the client is able to relax with ease the types of situation which normally give rise to an aggressive response are identified, usually by interview and recapitulation of previous aggressive incidents. The client then puts these in order from the ones where self-control and relaxation would be easiest to those where it would be most difficult. At this stage therapist and client may also devise hypothetical situations in order to produce a hierarchy of increasing difficulty. The client is then presented with the first situation, either in reality or in imagination, and learns to relax in such situations. When relaxation in the easy situation can be achieved reliably, the individual progresses to the next item and so on until all have been mastered. At this stage the individual is capable of reacting calmly, rather than angrily, to situations which would previously have resulted in aggression.

Numerous studies have indicated the value of such procedures in the control of aggressive behaviour (see, for example, Evans, 1970, Rimm, de Groot, Boord, *et al.*, 1971, Carr and Binkoff, 1981). In general, such studies stay close to the framework outlined above, although one author (Smith, 1973) has reported the use of laughter rather than relaxation as a response incompatible with aggression. Like many other procedures, systematic desensitisation is often used as a component in a broader 'package' of treatment routines.

Assertiveness Training

On first consideration, the notion of teaching aggressive individuals to be more assertive may appear paradoxical. Assertion training, however, distinguishes between an aggressive and an assertive response, in particular noting that the former is often purely egocentric with little or no consideration for the other person, and that the aggressive response is often excessive and socially unacceptable. In assertiveness training the individual is taught to behave in such a way as to obtain the required goals without generating hostility or some other undesirable response from others. (See Chapter 17 for a detailed discussion of assertiveness.)

Central concepts in assertiveness training are those of 'interpersonal empathy' and the 'minimal effective response'. The former reflects the emphasis in assertion training of appreciating the position, goals and rights of the other person, such that the aggressive individual goes beyond the self-centredness characteristic of aggressive behaviour. The minimal effective response refers to that response between an over-reaction which, while achieving the required goals, is excessive, and an under-reaction which while not generating hostility in others, fails to achieve the required objective. In essence, the client is taught to identify what would be the least that could be done in a situation in order to still achieve a positive outcome.

In practical terms, assertiveness training involves the therapist and client first identifying those areas where appropriate assertiveness needs to be learned, and the exploration and practice of alternative responses to those typically shown by the client. Various teaching procedures may be employed, including role plays, video feedback, direct instruction, gradual shaping and so on. It is not unusual for client and therapist to exchange roles at times, the therapist modelling both appropriate and inappropriate behaviour for the client to observe.

Assertiveness training has an obvious role in dealing with the problems of the 'overcontrolled' individual of the type described by Megargee (1966), but it should be remembered that the teaching of an appropriately assertive response may also be of benefit to those who habitually respond aggressively. The value of assertion training in dealing with aggression has been indicated by various studies (for example, Wallace *et al.*, 1973; Foy, Eisler and Pinkston, 1975), although it should be noted that assertion training has often been found to be highly specific, suggesting that successful training may require practice of a wide range of responses and situations.

A broader area, in which assertiveness training might appropriately be subsumed, is that of social skills training (SST). Here the individual is taught a wide range of skills appropriate to normal social interaction, such skills often including those of appropriate assertion. Such procedures are often conducted in groups, with the potential for highly cost-effective therapy. As with assertiveness training, however, SST has often experienced problems in generalisation, meaning that care must be taken to include a suitably wide range of situations and responses in the training programme.

Rational Emotive Therapy (RET)

First devised by Ellis (1962), the main assumption of RET is that an individual's irrational behaviour reflects underlying irrational thoughts or assumptions. The aim of RET, then, is to replace such assumptions with more rational thoughts and beliefs, the irrational behaviour then changing in consequence. Typically RET programmes involve a number of stages. First, the therapist explains to the client the rationale of the therapy, that the content of thoughts and beliefs can have a marked influence on behaviour. Second, the therapist and client collaborate on identifying irrational thoughts and beliefs which are causing the problem behaviour. Thus, an aggressive individual might appear to act in accordance with the belief 'I have to get my own way all the time or I won't be respected'. Such a belief may be challenged and replaced with a more realistic view. Finally, clients are encouraged to identify their own irrational beliefs and to challenge such beliefs for themselves.

As with assertion training, therapist and client may often switch roles, the client being asked to argue against some particular irrational belief while the therapist role plays the client holding such a belief. In general, applications of RET have extended well beyond the field of aggressive behaviour, although reports of its use specifically for aggression do exist (for instance, DiGiuseppe, 1977). It is important to remember that the irrational beliefs which are identified in therapy may not previously have been explicitly spelled out. Once they are brought into the open they will often be seen by clients, as well as by therapists, as irrational and without foundation.

Package Treatments

A number of workers have attempted to maximise the chances of success in dealing with problems of aggression by combining different treatment procedures into a single package. One of the most widely reported of such packages is the 'anger control' programme of Novaco (see, for example, Novaco, 1975). Such packages often include not only the types of procedure described above (systematic desensitisation, assertion training, RET) but also a number of other procedures including self-control skills, behaviour rehearsal and the explicit teaching of alternative responses.

A central feature of the package is that clients are taught to confront and prepare for difficult situations, rather than avoiding thinking about them until they arise. In this way the likely areas of difficulty can be identified and the client given the opportunity to practise appropriate ways to deal with such areas. The client is also taught to identify precursors of anger (for example, feelings of tension and annoyance) and to deal with these at the time (for instance, relaxation). Finally, the client is taught to go back over situations where the anger control fails, in order to identify what went wrong and to guard against making the same mistake again. The use of such packages has proved remarkably popular and been applied to a number of problem areas including the treatment of violent offenders, violence by those in authority (for example, police officers) and such problems as child abuse. A fuller account of the use of anger control procedures may also be found in Alves (1985).

There are, of course, many other approaches to the treatment of aggressive behaviour. A number of drugs and surgical treatments, for example, have been suggested as being of value in certain cases. But such procedures go beyond the general context of communication skills; moreover, their use may be limited to the short term (since the body may adapt to chronically administered drugs), may depend on a detailed behavioural analysis of the problem (since drugs may affect, say, reactive aggression while leaving operant behaviour undisturbed) and may involve numerous unwanted side-effects. A discussion of such procedures may be found in Owens and Ashcroft (1985). From the viewpoint of effective communication with the violent individual, however, it may still be of value to conduct a detailed behavioural analysis, particularly where the problem remains unresponsive to the types of technique outlined above. In the face of such analyses many problems may be resolved when the simple application of a technique is unsuccessful.

Functional Analysis of Aggressive Behaviour

The procedure known as functional analysis has come into increasing prominence within clinical psychology, being applied to a range of general problem areas (for instance, Ferster, 1967; Slade, 1982) and specific clinical problems (for instance, Owens and Ashcroft, 1982). Essentially, the functional analysis of a clinical problem attempts to identify the variables of which the problem is a function, and the specific nature of this functional relationship. Within psychology, the term has also come to acquire much the same meaning as it has within such subjects as biology and anthropology; a problem is seen as serving some particular function within the behavioural system as a whole, and is consequently maintained by that system. Thus an individual's aggressive behaviour may be seen to be a function of a consequent reinforcement such as power; similarly, the behaviour can be said to serve the function of making the individual more powerful within the social group.

Common to each of these uses of the term is the acknowledgement that, seen in the context of the variables of which it is a function, a seemingly bizarre behaviour can appear intelligible. That a person is extremely aggressive towards friends might appear odd, but in the context of an irrational belief that such aggression earns respect, might appear intelligible. Identification of the relevant variables, and their integration into a total model of the problem behaviour consititutes a functional analysis or formulation of the problem. Once adequately formulated, the system as a whole can be examined in order to determine what variables might be changed with a consequent change in the behaviour.

Typically, a functional analysis involves three stages, through which treatment moves on a cyclical basis. The initial stage is that of information-gathering or assessment; on the basis of information gathered a formulation is produced, and on the basis of that formulation the third stage, that of intervention, is developed. The process then reverts to the initial stage, that of assessment, on this occasion the assessment of the results (if any) of the intervention. This assessment of the intervention provides further information according to which the formulation can, if necessary, be further refined leading to the development of a new intervention and the cycle being repeated. Each of these stages merits a little further discussion.

Obtaining Information

In gathering information about a problem of aggression it is necessary to identify two specific aspects; what information is needed and how it is to be obtained. With respect to the former it has become customary to identify three main headings under which information is needed with the mnemonic A-B-C, in which the letters stand for antecedents, behaviour and consequences. That is, information is required regarding the behaviour itself, the circumstances and factors which lead up to the behaviour, and its consequences for the individual and others. With respect to the behaviour it will usually be convenient to know the form that the behaviour takes. This may have several aspects, for example an individual may show physical aggression towards other people, verbal aggression towards other people, physical aggression towards inanimate objects and so on. In addition, it will usually be desirable to know the frequency of each of these behaviours in order to assess the effectiveness (or otherwise) of later intervention.

In considering antecedents there is obviously a case for attempting to identify aversive events which act as triggers to reactive aggression. In identifying such factors it is also valuable to note that such aversive events may only elicit aggression where escape is impractical; it may also, therefore, be useful to identify the circumstances which prevent escape from the situation. Antecedents may, of course, also be significant in the analysis of operant aggression. Indicators of the availability of reinforcement (discriminative stimuli) may exert a great deal of control over operant behaviour. Thus the presence of a peer group who will be impressed by aggression may indicate to the individual that such behaviour will be reinforced. Aggressive behaviour may then be much more likely to occur when the peer group is present than when they are not.

Antecedents need not, of course, be immediate precursors of the behaviour. A set of instructions given one day may be of great significance in producing the behaviour at a later date. Finally, it should be noted that antecedents may compete with each other in their effects, and that combinations of antecedents may not relate in any simple way to their individual effects. An offensive remark by any one individual may produce an aggressive response, but if there are ten such individuals, such a response may be far more risky than leaving the situation.

Much of what has been said about antecedents will also apply to consequences. Here the obvious targets for identification are reinforcers and punishers. As with antecedents these may be immediate, but they may also be separated in time from the behaviour itself; in this context, however, it is worth remembering that, all other things being equal, immediate reinforcers will be more powerful than delayed ones. Reinforcers will also have an effect on the functional status of particular antecedents; if, for example, reinforcement is always delivered by a specific individual, that individual may become a discriminative stimulus for the behaviour to be reinforced. As with antecedents, combinations of reinforcers may not relate simply in their effects to the action of individual reinforcers, and two events which are individually reinforcing may turn out to be aversive in combination.

With both reinforcers and punishers it is clear that the effects of specific events may be quite idiosyncratic to the person in question. Thus an event which has a punishing effect on one person (for example, being shouted at) may have a reinforcing effect on another. Individual conditioning histories, states of deprivation and so on mean that two people may relate quite differently to the same physical event, and the effect of such events on behaviour should not be assumed in advance but, where possible, assessed empirically.

In specifying exactly how the necessary information is to be obtained, both direct and indirect sources of information can be identified. Some information regarding violent episodes may be obtained from direct observation; this may be particularly the case when the violence occurs in some institutional setting, like a prison, school or hospital. Usually, attempts at observing such behaviour will involve a 'sampling' of the individual's behaviour, observations being made at various intervals in time and an estimate of the frequency of aggressive behaviour being made.

While this type of procedure has commonly been used in a number of attempts to control problem behaviours, it is probably of limited value in the study of such things as angry outbursts. Since most violent behaviour occurs with a fairly low frequency, it is unlikely that a period of time chosen for the sampling of behaviour will coincide with a rare outburst. Moreover, when an angry outburst does occur, the people around will usually have far too much to do to permit careful assessment of the circumstances; dealing with the anger and violence themselves will usually be the first priority.

Because of these and similar factors, most of the information required in the analysis of aggressive or angry episodes will come from indirect sources. Of these, the most obvious is the person who is experiencing the anger. Most commonly, information is gathered by the clinical interview, judicious use of open-ended and relatively closed questions allowing both a broad assessment of the problem and more detailed investigation of specific areas. In conducting such interviews it is often useful to enquire not only what happened in particular circumstances but also why the individual thought it happened. While it would be a mistake to automatically assume that individuals always had an accurate assessment of the forces acting on their behaviour, most will have at least a partial analysis and will provide some useful starting points for further exploration.

Of course, the interview is not the only way in which relevant information may be gathered. Much of value may be obtained by the use of inventories, questionnaires and so on. Such procedures may include the use of formal personality tests, rating scales and, on occasion, the use of more general life histories. In the latter procedure clients are asked to write an account of their lives from the earliest point they can remember to the present time. Besides providing in convenient form much of the information which would be obtained from an interview, the life history often enables clients to identify for themselves important events leading to the development of their present problem. In addition, in some circumstances, there may be clues in the way certain items are phrased by clients, with particularly high value perhaps being placed on aggressive or dominant elements of behaviour.

Besides the information obtained from the client, it is often possible to obtain information from others who are in some way involved in the problem. Victims of angry outbursts may, like the client, be interviewed in the hope of obtaining further information regarding the antecedents, behaviour and consequences. Other individuals who may provide useful information include relatives, friends, those involved in dealing with the anger (police, hospital staff and so on) and others. Each may have a particular contribution to make. Relatives, for example, may be able to provide a good deal of historical information, friends can give information about recent important events in the client's life, and the victim about the actual circumstances of an episode.

In this context, however, it is important to take care in interviewing the victims of violence. Victims may respond to a violent episode in a number of ways. Reactions may include obvious ones like fear and anxiety, which may call for care in the interview procedure, to less obvious ones such as denial and guilt. Denial may affect the information gathered if the individual attempts to trivialise or dismiss an incident ('I don't want to talk about it; it wasn't that important and it's all over now'). Guilt may arise from the individual's attempt to make sense of the incident ('I must have done something to deserve it'). Obviously, reactions such as these will need to be handled with delicacy and tact.

In addition to the information which may be obtained from other people, it is also possible to gain considerable amounts of information from written records. Many aggressive individuals have a long history of problems such as temper control, with documentation of their difficulties in hospitals, schools and courts. Such information may be used to supplement information from other sources and may help to give a complete picture. In general, it is worth considering as wide a range of sources as possible in identifying the factors involved in a specific problem.

Inevitably, of course, each of these sources of information is less than perfect. Accidental inaccuracies may creep into any account of an incident, as people fail to achieve total recall. In addition, the information obtained may be subject to systematic bias. The client, for example, may distort information such as to minimise the seriousness of an outburst, or may overemphasise the role of others in the circumstances building up to loss of temper. Occasionally, information may be withheld of which the client is ashamed, particularly if the client cannot see that the information is relevant to the problem. A man may, for example, fail to tell his therapist about problems of impotence, seeing these as independent of anger control problems. Under such circumstances it may be necessary for the therapist to explain why such issues as sexual problems may be relevant, stressing the need for openness and honesty in giving information.

Other sources of information may also be subject to systematic distortion. A victim may intentionally or otherwise play down any contributory role in an angry outburst, particularly if compensation may be involved. Friends and relatives may attempt to paint the client in a positive light. Written records, of course, are subject to distortion in much the same way as other sources. In addition, it is important to avoid being impressed by the recurrence of specific factors in different records; often these reflect nothing more than the fact that each writer has already read, and been influenced by, the previous records. All this is not to say of course, that the information supplied is valueless, but rather that it should be treated with caution, due recognition being given to the problems presented by each particular source.

Formulations and Interventions

Having obtained as much information as is possible, it then becomes important to make sense of what has been learned. The mass of information obtained from the various sources described above needs to be organised and classified in such a way as to make it manageable and meaningful without losing more than is necessary. An obvious first step in the classification of the information obtained is to highlight likely factors involved in the problem. Anything which is in any way unusual in the information, and anything which might seem to fit in with a theoretical model of anger and aggression, should be noted. Such factors can then be roughly divided into antecedents, behaviours, and consequences.

While this kind of division may be relatively straightforward, being based primarily on temporal sequencing, it should be remembered that the distinctions may be blurred. Losing a fight may serve as a punishment for one aggressive outburst, but also be an important antecedent of the next. Behaviours which look similar to a casual observer may be markedly different in terms of the factors of which they are a function. Because of this any classification of factors, particularly in the early stages of an analysis, should be seen as tentative.

Futher classification of relevant factors may include the division of antecedents and consequences according to the behaviours to which they relate and the processes which they reflect. Some antecedents, for example, will be significant triggering aversive events in reactive aggression. Others will be important discriminative stimuli in operant aggression. Consequences, similarly may need subdividing, particularly into those which reinforce behaviour and those which punish. Here, of course, a distinction may become particularly blurred, the punishing consequence of one behaviour serving as the aversive trigger of another. In addition, antecedents and consequences may be important not because of a significant influence on the behaviour itself but because they moderate other antecedents and consequences which do have a direct influence. Besides psychological variables, these may include such factors as drugs and alcohol. The kinds of skill which permit effective interaction with a sober individual may be totally inappropriate when the same individual is intoxicated. The weakening of the effects of aversive events by alcohol, for example, may mean that reminding a person of past unpleasant consequences of anger (remorse, guilt), while effective normally, may do little to influence the person's behaviour when drunk.

As a last stage in the initial classification, it is often straightforward to subdivide factors into those whose role is purely historical, and which are no longer operating, and those which are still present and may be playing a part in the maintenance of the behaviour. The circumstances which lead to the development of a behaviour are not always those which later maintain its existence. A client may have first learned to be violent as part of some sporting activity like boxing or judo. Later this same behaviour may be triggered by aversive events with no relation to the original learning experience. An implication of this is that it may prove necessary to develop two formulations of the problem, one concerning its aetiology, the other concerned with its subsequent maintenance.

Having (provisionally) identified and classified the various factors thought to be involved in the aggression, it is necessary to map out the various relationships between them. Often some factors will be seen to serve broadly similar functions in the system as a whole; such factors may meaningfully be grouped together.

Some factors will relate simply and directly to a single behaviour, others may relate in a complex way to several behaviours and to other relevant factors. Often, the mapping out of the inter-relationships will indicate the existence of feedback loops in the behavioural system. Such 'vicious circles' will usually have the effect of stabilising the problem at some particular level, and may indicate particularly important points for intervention. By mapping out the various interrelationships in this way, the behaviour can be seen to 'make sense' in terms of the context in which it occurs. Anything which does not make sense indicates a need for the gathering of further information. Often, a formulation at this stage will be only one of many which are consistent with the information available. Nevertheless, such a tentative formulation may form a useful basis for an initial intervention.

Attempts at intervention, in the light of a formulation of the problem, will take the form of attempts to change the relevant factors, the relationships between them, or both. Thus the client who is involved in heated arguments with a spouse may do so partly as a reaction to the spouse's behaviour. Intervention here may take the form of changing the spouse's behaviour, changing the client's reaction to such behaviour (for instance, by such procedures as desensitisation), or both. The specific form of the intervention will thus depend on such factors as access to relevant variables (the first of the options just described may be impossible if the spouse is unwilling or unable to change) and their supposed role in the behavioural system as a whole.

Any variable involved in a feedback loop is likely to constitute a prime target for intervention, because of the risk that failure to disrupt such a loop will result in the behaviour restabilising at its old level. Finally, of course, it may be important to take into account not only the extent to which relevant variables may be changed in the individual's present environment, but also how realistically these may reflect the possible future environments. The patient in a psychiatric hospital whose behaviour is controlled by constant supervision is unlikely to encounter similar contingencies when eventually discharged to the wider community.

Evaluation Strategies

Once an intervention has been implemented on the basis of some formulation of the problem, it is necessary to conduct some form of evaluation in order to determine the effects (if any). A common basis for evaluation is a comparison of the frequency of the behaviour before and after the intervention. While such a procedure leaves open the possibility that any change may be due to coincidental changes, rather than the intervention, for most clinical purposes it will be all that is necessary. Even such a simple procedure, however, has a few complications. In particular, it is important that the behaviours assessed are carefully identified and subdivided. Simply counting the frequency of angry outbursts before and after some intervention, for example, may appear to show no change in behaviour. Yet dramatic changes may have taken place; for example, each individual outburst may have previously involved considerable physical violence but may now only involve mild verbal abuse. Thus, evaluation should be closely linked to the

formulation, close attention being paid to the different forms of behaviour identified by the formulation and the expected effects of any intervention.

In practice, direct observation will often be as problematic in evaluation as
it is when initially gathering information. As with the initital gathering of information it will be often be necessary to rely on indirect sources, in particular the
self-report of the client and information gathered from significant others. Inevitably
such information will be susceptible to error in evaluation just as it is in the initial
assessment, and due allowance will have to be made for this. The conduct of
such indirect evaluation is often facilitated by the use of formal measures, particularly when these are matched to the individual and permit comparison of pre-
and post-intervention problems. Such formal procedures may include the use of
rating scales and specific clinical evaluation (for instance, the Personal Questionnaire of Shapiro, 1964).

Where an intervention brings about a successful reduction in behaviour, there
will rarely, in most practical settings, be any need for more careful evaluation.
However, problems may arise when the evaluation shows no change in the level
of behaviour. At first glance such results may seem to carry the obvious implication that the original formulation was in error and is in need of revision. While
this may be true, it is not the only possible interpretation. Obviously, negative
results may reflect a failure not of the intervention but of the evaluation procedure,
and it may be necessary to check that the latter is indeed being adequately
conducted. In addition, negative results may reflect a failing neither of the
formulation nor the evaluation, but rather a failure in the way intervention is being
carried out. Communication failure between therapist and client may result in
the latter failing to implement an intervention procedure correctly, with a consequent failure to change the behaviour.

Often, however, failure of an intervention will mean that the original
formulation was, in fact, in error and is in need of revision. In producing such
revisions (and indeed in producing the original formulation) it may be beneficial
to enlist directly the help of the client. While few clients will be familar with
psychological jargon like 'reactive aggression', 'reinforcement' and so forth, it
will often be possible to communicate the general ideas in non-technical language.
Thus it may be possible to say to a client 'there seems a possibility that the things
which make you lose your temper are often to do with your feeling you're not
being treated with respect'. Such a translation of concepts is close enough for
most practical purposes and may permit rapid identification and validation of
hypotheses regarding the specific aversive stimuli involved. With a little practice
it is usually possible to translate the greater part of a formulation into non-technical
language which is accessible to the client.

Under such circumstances, the client's opinion regarding the plausibility of
either a total formulation or its individual elements may lead to rapid understanding
of the problem. This is not to say, of course, that the client will necessarily be
correct; but no harm is done if the error is irrelevant to successful intervention,
and if it relates to outcome the error will be revealed by the intervention's lack

of success.

The use of functional analysis, then, represents a cyclical process in contrast to the linear process characteristic of the application of specific techniques. Initial assessment leads to initial formulation, an attempt at intervention and further assessment. All is well if the intervention is successful, otherwise reformulation leads to further intervention, reassessment and the repetition of the cycle. Using such a strategy, the procedure may be continued until either the correct formulation reveals that the relevant factors cannot be changed or until all conceivable formulations have been exhausted. More often than not, success will be apparent before either of these occurs.

Methodological Issues

In closing, it is appropriate to comment on some of the methodological issues involved both in work with violence and, correspondingly, on work with other strong emotions. Such issues have implications both for clinical practice and for the conduct and evaluation of research. Perhaps the most obvious point for comment is that anger, like most strong emotions, is usually a relatively infrequent occurrence even in those for whom it is most problematic. While this may be good from the point of view of psychological well-being, it does present problems when such emotions are to be studied. In effect most studies of actual anger, clinical or otherwise, are studies of small samples of behaviour. Usually, they are studied under less than ideal conditions — if studied directly there will usually be considerable commotion, if studied indirectly by looking back on episodes, considerable error and distortion may be apparent.

The infrequency of such emotions constitutes a particular problem from the point of view of clinical intervention. If a problem like an angry outburst occurs only once every month, or even less often, it will take at least this long before any clue is obtained as to the success or otherwise of an intervention. The problem is compounded by the observation that, broadly speaking, it is the least severe episodes of anger which occur the most often. As a result, these present fewer problems for the therapist and intervention may be relatively straightforward. Unfortunately, it is in the severest form of anger and aggression that success is most important, and it is here that the therapist's hands may be tied by the unavailability of information resulting from low frequencies.

Moreover, the most serious of cases are the ones where it is most important to produce rapid results. Often this implies that insufficient time can be set aside for the gathering of data and the preparation of a detailed formulation; intervention will often have to be made on the basis of limited assessment not only of the problem but even of its severity. In consequence, both intervention and evaluation may be seriously impaired.

The seriousness of strong emotions is problematic, too, from a research point of view. While many behavioural processes may be investigated directly in the laboratory, the serious implications and consequences of strong emotions imply that their study must involve only limited analogues of the process of interest. Thus, much of what is believed about strong emotions and how to handle them is based on the study of other species, or the study of mild analogues of the problem. A theory invoked to explain a murderous outburst, for example, may be based on research in which aggression consisted of giving a certain type of response to a projective test. Obviously, information of this kind carries an unavoidable risk of error. As with the error involved in the assessment of individual problems, this is not to imply that the information gained in this way is valueless. Rather, it is to recognise that such information is often the best to hand, but at the same time to beware of placing too much faith in any single study. The study of anger and aggression, like the study of other strong emotions, is still in many ways uncharted territory. Unfortunately, the urgency of the problem forces us to set foot into such territory without the luxury of waiting for a more detailed exploration.

References

Alves, E. (1985) 'Anger Control Procedures' in E. Karas (ed.) *Current Issues in Clinical Psychology, Vol. 2*, Plenum, New York

Bandura, A. (1973) *Aggression: A Social Learning Analysis,* Prentice Hall, New Jersey

Blackburn, R. (1968) 'Personality in Relation to Extreme Aggression in Psychiatric Offenders', *British Journal of Psychiatry, 114*, 821–8

Buss, A.H. (1971) 'Aggression Pays' in J.L. Singer (ed.) *The Control of Aggression and Violence,* Academic Press, New York

Carney, M.W.P. (1979) 'Management of the Disturbed Patient', *Nursing Times,* November, pp. 1896–9

Carr, E.G. and Binkoff, J.A. (1981) 'Self-control' in A.P. Goldstein, E.G. Carr, W.S. Davidson II *et al.* (eds), *In Response to Aggression,* Pergamon, New York

DiGiuseppe, R.A. (1977) 'The Use of Behaviour Modification to Establish Rational Self-Statements in Children', *Rational Living, 10*, 18–20

Dollard, J., Doob, L., Miller, N., *et al.* (1939) *Frustration and Aggression,* Yale University Press, New Haven, Ct

Ellis, A. (1962) *Reason and Emotion in Psychotherapy,* Lyle Stuart, New York

Evans, D.R. (1970) 'Specific Aggression, Arousal and Reciprocal Inhibition Therapy', *The Western Psychologist, 1*, 125–30

Eysenck, H.J. (1983) 'Current Theories of Crime' in E. Karas (ed.) *Current Issues in Clinical Psychology, Vol. 1*, Plenum, New York

Ferster, C.B. (1967) 'A Functional Analysis of Depression', *American Psychologist, 28*, 857

Foy, E.W., Eisler, R.M. and Pinkston, S. (1975) 'Modelled Assertion in a Case of Explosive Rages', *Journal of Behaviour Therapy and Experimental Psychiatry, 6*, 135–8

Goldstein, A.P., Carr, E.G., Davidson, W.S. *et al.* (1981) *In Response to Aggression,* Pergamon, New York

Jacobsen, E. (1938) *Progressive Relaxation,* University of Chicago Press, Chicago

Kelly, J.F. and Hake, D.F. (1970) 'An Extinction-induced Increase in an Aggressive Response with Humans', *Journal of Experimental Analysis of Behaviour, 14*, 154–64

Megargee, E.I. (1966) 'Undercontrolled and Overcontrolled Personality Types in Extreme Anti-social Aggression', *Pscyhological Monographs, 80* whole no. 611

Miller, N. (1941) 'The Frustration-aggression Hypothesis', *Psychological Review, 48*, 337–42

Mischel, W. (1967) *Personality and Assessment,* Wiley, New York

Novaco, R.W. (1975) *Anger Control,* Lexington, Massachusetts

Owens, R.G. and Ashcroft, J.B. (1982) 'Functional Analysis in Applied Psychology', *British Journal of Clinical Psychology, 21,* 181–89

——— (1985) *Violence: A Guide For The Caring Professions,* Croom Helm, Beckenham

——— and Bagshaw, M. (1985) 'First Steps in the Functional Analysis of Aggression' in E. Karas (ed.), *Current Issues in Clinical Psychology, Vol. 2,* Plenum, New York

Packham, H. (1978) 'Managing the Violent Patient', *Nursing Mirror,* 22 June, pp. 17–20

Patterson, G.R., Cobb, J.A. and Ray, R.S. (1967) 'A Social Engineering Technology for Retraining the Families of Aggressive Boys' in H.E. Adams and I.P. Unikel (eds), *Issues and Trends in Behaviour Therapy,* C.C. Thomas, Springfield, Illinois

Reynolds, G.S., Catania, A.C., and Skinner, B.F. (1963) 'Conditioned and Unconditioned Aggression in Pigeons', *Journal of the Experimental Analysis of Behaviour, 6,* 73–4

Rimm, D.C., deGroot, J.C., Boord, P. *et al.* (1971) 'Systematic Desensitisation of an Anger Response', *Behaviour Research and Therapy, 9,* 273–80

Shapiro, M.B. (1964) 'The Measurement of Clinically Relevant Variables', *Journal of Psychosomatic Research, 8,* 245–54

Sipes, R.G. (1973) 'War, Sports and Aggression: An Empirical Test of Two Rival Theories', *American Anthropologist, 75,* 64–85

Skinner, B.F. (1938) *The Behaviour of Organisms,* Appleton Century Crofts, New York

Slade, P.D. (1982) 'Towards a Functional Analysis of Anorexia Nervosa and Bulimia Nervosa', *British Journal of Clinical Psychology, 21,* 167–79

Smith, R.E. (1973) 'The Use of Humour in Counter-conditioning of Anger Responses', *Behaviour Therapy, 4,* 576–80

Stafford-Clark, D. (1967) *What Freud Really Said,* Penguin, Harmondsworth

Ulrich, R.E. and Azrin, N.H. (1962) 'Reflexive Fighting in Response to Aversive Stimulation', *Journal of the Experimental Analysis of Behaviour, 5,* 511–20

Vernon, W. and Ulrich, R. (1966) 'Classical Conditioning of Pain-elicited Aggression', *Science, 152,* 668–9

Wallace, C., Tergen, J., Liberman, R. and Baker, V. (1973) 'Destructive Behaviour Treated by Contingency Contracts and Assertive Training: A Case Study', *Journal of Behaviour Therapy and Experimental Psychiatry, 4,* 273–374

17 ASSERTING AND CONFRONTING

Richard F. Rakos

> If not I for myself, who then?
> And being for myself, what am I?
> And if not now, when?
> — Hillel

These words by the ancient Sage Hillel, though discussing knowledge and meritorious behaviour in general (Goldin, 1957), also speak to the three critical issues germane to the effective use of assertion in contemporary interpersonal interactions: the right to express the assertive response, the social responsibilities attendant to assertive expression, and the decision to actually engage in such expression. In the past 15 years a plethora of research has coalesced into a corpus of information which nicely complements Hillel's philosophy: the Sage's words not only stand the test of time but also the shift in *Weltanshauung* from monotheism to secular humanism.

Though many of the complex and subtle aspects of assertion remain obscure, current understanding is nevertheless fairly sophisticated — certainly in comparison to early, nonempirical treatises which suggested that assertion was the panacea for interpersonal conflicts of all kinds (for example, Baer, 1976; Fensterheim and Baer, 1975) or an individual right to be expressed without constraints and perhaps even selfishly (for example, Smith, 1975). As a social behaviour emitted in an uncontrolled social world, appropriate assertion is no more or less than an adaptive skill. Thus, the purpose of this chapter is to succinctly summarise present understanding of the conditions under which assertive behaviour in conflict situations is both appropriate and useful.

Defining Assertive Behaviour

The first widely promoted definitions of assertion were fairly general ones emphasising the individual's right to express his/her desires while simultaneously respecting the rights of the other people involved (for example, Alberti and Emmons, 1978; Lange and Jakubowski, 1976). They were developed by clinicians from the pioneering formulations introduced by Salter (1949) and Wolpe (1969), and specified components (be direct and to the point, talk in a firm but respectful tone, maintain eye contact) derived from face or content validity. However, researchers found such conceptualisations unhelpful for guiding systematic theoretical and empirical inquiry, since content will vary with situational, individual and cultural factors. Instead, functional (contentless) definitions derived from the operant approach were advanced. For example, Rich and Schroeder (1976) proposed that:

> (Assertive behaviour is) the skill to seek, maintain, or enhance reinforcement in an interpersonal situation through the expression of feelings or wants when such expression risks loss of reinforcement or even punishment . . . The degree of assertiveness may be measured by the effectiveness of an individual's response in producing, maintaining, or enhancing reinforcement (p. 1082).

From this perspective, several critical conceptual features emerge. First, assertion is a *skill*, not a 'trait' that someone 'has' or 'lacks'. Research has demonstrated that assertive behaviour is primarily a function of the situation and the interaction of the person and situation, rather than a function of intrapersonal cross-situational dispositions or traits (Galassi, Galassi and Vedder, 1981; Heimberg and Becker, 1981; Schroeder and Rakos, 1983). Thus, an individual may behave assertively in one context (for instance, refuse a friend's request) but not in another (comply with a similar request from a co-worker). Furthermore, as a situation-specific skill, assertive responses are presumed to be learned through the same general modalities that other skills are acquired (primarily operant conditioning and modelling). Second, assertion occurs in an interpersonal context — it is a social skill. Third, it is an expressive skill, involving verbal and nonverbal responses. Fourth, assertion involves risk — there has to be some chance that the asserter will not 'get his/her way'. Finally, the extent of assertiveness is measured by outcome. Though most researchers concur that outcome is the 'ultimate criterion for evaluating performance' (McFall, 1982), more complex criteria are required to accommodate two observations: first, since assertion is 'risky' it is quite possible that even technically appropriate behaviour may fail to achieve reinforcement, and second, behaviour that is consensually evaluated as unskilled (for example, crazy talk: Curran, 1979) or antisocial (for example, physical assault: Arkowitz, 1981) may in fact be reinforced.

Appreciation of these possiblities necessitates expansion of evaluative criteria to include effectiveness and social acceptability (that is, social validity: Kazdin, 1977; Wolf, 1978). In the discussion that follows, it shall be seen that a sophisticated analysis of assertion must accommodate each of the issues raised by Rich and Schroeder's (1976) definition (situation-specific skill, interpersonal context, components of the expressive skill, assessment of risk and social competence and desirability).

Response Classes of Assertion

Assertive behaviour, in addition to being a situation-specific skill, encompasses several partially independent response classes; since individuals may be able to perform behaviours within one class but not another (Galassi *et al.*, 1981), a unified trait conceptualisation of assertion is further weakened. Schroeder, Rakos and

Moe's (1983) literature review identified four 'positive' response classes (admitting personal shortcomings, initiating interactions, giving and receiving compliments, expressing positive feelings), and three 'negative' or conflict ones (expressing unpopular or different opinions, requesting behaviour changes by other people, refusing unreasonable requests). Though the focus here will be on the conflict assertion skills, it is important to bear in mind that assertion also includes positive expressiveness.

Distinguishing Assertion from Aggression

Researchers and clinicians have generally assumed the existence of a single continuum encompassing nonassertive–assertive–aggressive behaviour (Galassi *et al.*, 1981). Since most studies find significant correlations between these behaviours, the assumption appears to be warranted. Conceptually, the single continuum highlights the appropriateness of assertiveness training for aggressive as well as nonassertive individuals but obscures the clear differentiation of conflict assertive behaviour from aggressive behaviour. This is a critical distinction since the lay population often labels conflict assertion as aggression (for example, Hull and Schroeder, 1979) thereby reducing the social acceptability and attractiveness of assertive response alternatives.

Rich and Schroeder's (1976) functional definition, by deliberately eschewing the specification of content (social values, goals, sanctioned behaviours), is too unspecific and abstract to distinguish between assertive and aggressive responses. Others have therefore returned to search for a useful but flexible content definition. Alberti and Emmons (1978) and Lange and Jakubowski (1976) stressed that appropriate assertion, unlike aggression, respects the other person's rights and dignity by being emitted in a nonhostile tone of voice and by avoiding attacking statements. Hollandsworth (1977) proposed that, in terms of objective behaviour, aggressive responses were distinguished by their use of a verbal threat specifying the future delivery on punishment. Rakos (1979) argued that this was unsatisfactory: after repeated nonthreatening assertions have failed, it may be appropriate to 'escalate' (Rimm and Masters, 1979) the assertion by including a threat as Hollandsworth defined it (for instance, 'If you do not refund my money, I will contact the Consumers Affairs Office and register a formal complaint against your policy'). Instead, Rakos suggested that assertion, which is generally viewed as a discrete behaviour and a personal right, should be considered as a chain of overt and covert behaviours encompassing rights and their antecedent and subsequent social responsibilities (obligations). Emission of the assertive right alone, without the social obligations, is 'expressive behaviour', and by itself, aggressive. Conflict assertion, on the other hand, involves the following social responsibilities (Rakos, 1979):

Antecedent (emitted prior to expressive behaviour):
1. Engaging in sufficient overt and covert behaviour to determine the rights of *all* participants;

2. Developing a verbal and nonverbal response repertoire which is intended to influence the other person's offending behaviour but not the evaluation of his/her 'worth';

3. Considering the potential negative consequences of expressive behaviour to the other involved persons.

Subsequent (emitted after expressive behaviour):

1. Providing a brief, honest explanation for expressive behaviour;

2. Providing alternate interpretations of expressive behaviour, and empathic communications concerning its implications, in an attempt to minimise any hurt, anger and unhappiness experienced by the other person;

3. Protecting the other person's rights if that person cannot;

4. Seeking a mutually acceptable compromise when legitimate rights conflict.

According to Rakos, the antecedent obligations are necessary prerequisites to expressive behaviour in all conflict interactions, while the subsequent ones are pragmatically important when continuing relationships are involved. From this perspective, the emission of the social obligation behaviours, in addition to the expressive behaviour, distinguishes assertion from aggression. Thus, simply saying, 'No, I do not want to work late tonight' to your boss — which is an assertive response according to both Rich and Schroeder and Hollandsworth — would be classified by Rakos' definition as an expressive response, and by itself aggressive. In a continuing relationship with a boss, the antecedent and subsequent obligations also define appropriate assertion. The obligation statements have the advantage of combining adequate specificity (they can be readily assessed and trained; Rakos and Schroeder, 1979) with flexibility (the exact content can vary according to situational, social and cultural norms and values).

In summary, the conceptualisation of assertion as a chain of behaviours proposes that expression of rights alone is aggressive; expression of rights and emission of antecedent social responsibilities is assertive in noncontinuing relationships; expression of rights and emission of antecedent and subsequent responsibilities is assertive in continuing relationships.

Conflict Assertion as an Adaptive Skill in Interpersonal Communication

The role of conflict assertive skills in interpersonal effectiveness and personal adjustment is suggested by data from several diverse research strategies.

Effects of Assertiveness Training

The acquisition or improvement of assertive behaviours has been associated with a variety of benefits, including increases in children's and/or adolescents' social competence (Joachim, 1981; Rotheram, Armstrong and Booraem, 1982), self-concept (Waksman, 1984a, b), and self-esteem (Stake, Deville and Pennell, 1983); enhancement of couples' perception of the clarity of communication (Epstein, Digoivann and Jayne-Lazarus, 1978) and level of trust and intimacy (Gordon and Waldo, 1984) in their relationships; decreases in women's sexual timidity (Hammond and Oei, 1982) and increases in their perceptions of their personal right to refuse intrusive demands (Kidder, Boell and Moyer, 1983); increases in the coping skills of adolescent diabetics (Johnson, Gross and Weldman, 1982); gains in alcoholics' interpersonal job-related skills (Foy, Massey, Duer *et al.*, 1979), and ability to refuse offers of alcohol (Foy, Miller, Eisler, *et al.*, 1976); and enhancement of the ability to resist peer pressure to use drugs by adolescents (Horan and Williams, 1982) and college students (Williams, Hadden and Marcavage, 1983).

Comparisons of Clinical and Nonclinical Populations

In studies comparing normal individuals with clinical populations, specific and/or pervasive assertive skill deficits have been manifested by depressed individuals (Barbaree and Davis, 1984), agoraphobics (Chambless, Hunter and Jackson, 1982), alcoholics (Twentyman, Greenwald, Greenwald, *et al.*, 1982), hypertensive and normotensive medical patients (Keane, Martin, Berler, *et al.*, 1982; Morrison, Bellack and Manuck, 1985), incarcerated offenders (Kirchner, Kennedy and Draguns, 1979), and overcontrolled hostile murderers (Quinsey, Maguire and Varney, 1983). In addition, Hamilton and Maisto (1979) found that alcoholics reported significantly greater discomfort than nonalcoholics when dealing with conflict situations, particularly when a familiar person was involved.

Correlational Data

Descriptive and correlational studies also indicate that assertiveness is related to adaptive functioning. Sanchez and Lewinsohn (1980) found a correlation of -0.5 between depression and assertiveness in 12 depressed outpatients over a 12-week period. Furthermore, they observed 'that the rate of emitted assertive behavior may indeed be better able to predict subsequent level of depression than level of depression can predict subsequent rate of emitted assertive behaviour' (p. 120), suggesting that acquisition of assertive skills may be an effective component of therapy for depression.

Assertive behaviour may also be important for maintaining and enhancing self-regulation (self-control). Miller and Eisler (1977) obtained a correlation of -0.63 between alcoholics' drinking behaviour and their conflict assertion abilities, which is consistent with Miller, Hersen, Eisler, *et al.'s* (1974) observation that alcoholics, but not social drinkers, increase alcohol consumption following exposure to interpersonal stress. Furthermore, interpersonal conflict and social pressure are two of the three primary precipitating events associated with relapse by individuals experiencing drinking, smoking, gambling, drug use or overeating problems (Cummings, Gordon and Marlatt, 1980; Marlatt and Gordon, 1980), accounting for 16 and 20 per cent of the relapses, respectively. The importance of assertive skills in self-regulation is also suggested by the strong relationships obtained between assertive capabilities and leadership abilities, lack of impulsivity and an orientation toward attainment of long-term demanding goals (Green, Burkhart and Harrison, 1979) as well as reduced social anxiety (Sundel and Lobb, 1982).

Assertion has also been found to be associated with adaptive functioning in nonclinical contexts. Two diverse examples will be mentioned. Cianni-Surridge and Horan's (1983) finding that certain assertive responses (but not others) enhance an employer's reaction to a job applicant reinforces the conceptualisation of assertion as a situation-specific skill rather than as a trait. The second example suggests the role of assertion in the lives of young children: nonassertive, compliant interpersonal problem-solving strategies emitted by kindergarten children correlate strongly with isolate play in kindergarten *and* first grade (Rubin, Daniels-Beirness and Bream, 1984). The implication of this finding for preventive intervention is clear.

Overall, the research compellingly indicates that adequate assertive conflict resolution skills are facilitative of, if not essential for, adaptive, rewarding psychological functioning and growth, at least in cultural contexts dominated by secular Western norms and values. Common sense also informs us that the ability to skilfully handle life's inevitable interpersonal conflicts will maximise attainment of short- and long-term reinforcement. Attention is now given to identifying the composition of these very important social skills.

The Skill of Conflict Assertion

Successful assertion and confrontation in interpersonal conflict situations requires emission of numerous overt and covert response components. These can be categorised as follows:

1. Content — the overt and covert verbal behaviour of the asserter, or what the individual *says* publicly to others and privately to him/herself;
2. Paralinguistic elements — how the asserter *sounds*;
3. Nonverbal behaviours — how the asserter *looks*;
4. Social interaction skills — how the asserter behaves in the *process* of the interaction, including timing, initiation, persistence, and stimulus control skills.

The identification of the specific components comprising these categories is limited, to a certain extent, by the conceptualisation of assertion as a learned social skill whose emission is largely dependent on situational determinants. Since every situation is likely to introduce unique considerations, the conclusions presented below are offered as general guides only, which must be flexibly modified to be congruent with the particular conflict context. This, by the way, is the author's basic view of the parent field of assertiveness training, namely behaviour modification: systematic integration of empirical data and common sense, flexibly applied so as to conform to the requirements of the individual(s) and the relevant natural environment.

Content of Conflict Assertion: Overt Components

The publicly observable verbal responses which constitute appropriate assertion in conflict situations can be conceptually divided into two major categories (Rakos, 1979): expression of the assertive right and emission of the attendant verbalisations required to place the expression of the right within the context of socially responsible and appropriate behaviour (these obligations will be referred to as 'elaborations' in the present discussion).

Expression of Rights. The core of any assertion, its *raison d'être,* is the expression of rights. In the early, overly enthusiastic days of the assertiveness training 'movement', it was the sole skill trained by researchers and the one that was popularised in self-help books (for example, Fensterheim and Baer, 1975; Smith, 1975). However, as discussed above, the rights statement is now generally recognised as necessary but not sufficient for resolving conflict in a way that maximises both short- and long-term rewards.

The specific content of the expression of rights will vary as a function of the response class but will include a statement of affect, desire, or opinion (Kolotkin, Wielkiewicz, Judd, *et al.,* 1984; Romano and Bellack, 1980) as in the following examples:

> *Refusal:* 'No, thank you, I am not interested in purchasing a ticket.'
> *Behaviour change request:* 'I am upset with the way you leave household chores for the last minute' (statement of conflict or negative feelings). 'I would like you to do them more promptly' (request for new behaviour).
> *Expressing an unpopular or different opinion:* 'I disagree with the Council's recommendation. I feel we definitely should not endorse the Mayor for a second term.'

Several important topographical features of these rights verbalisations require comment. First, they utilise 'I–statements', in which the speaker assumes responsiblity for his/her feelings, rather than 'you–statements', which attempt to attribute responsibility for personal feelings to the other person (Lange and Jakubowski, 1976; Winship and Kelly, 1976). Research indicates that 'I-statements' are indeed related to judgements of overall assertion, while 'You–statements' are associated with aggressive behaviour (Kolotkin *et al.,* 1984). Thus the statement, 'I lose my patience and get angry when you dawdle' would be considered to be assertive, but 'You make me impatient and angry when you dawdle' would likely be viewed as aggressive.

A second feature of the overt content is that it is both direct and respectful.

A *direct* expression of rights contains a clear, succinct statement describing one's feelings, desires and perceptions, though this may be preceded by an introductory 'orientating statement' indicating the topic to be discussed (Kolotkin *et al.*, 1984), as in the example of the expression of unpopular opinions. However, explanations or apologies are omitted; these latter verbalisations may be appropriate as elaborations of the rights statement (see below) but when intertwined with it, they tend to obscure the focus of the concern and reduce the impact of the assertion. A direct statement also completely eschews excuses, lies or any form of dishonesty. Furthermore, a *respectful* response expresses one's own concerns without blaming, attacking or demeaning the other person. Nonassertive statements are usually indirect; aggressive statements are usually disrespectful; and passive-aggressive ones are usually both indirect and disrespectful.

A third comment concerns behaviour change requests, which are assumed to require a statement of conflict or negative feeling followed by a request for new behaviour. While the specific request for new behaviour is a characteristic of assertive individuals (Eisler, Miller and Hersen, 1973; Pitcher and Meikle, 1980) and contributes to judgements of assertion by trained raters (Bordewick and Bornstein, 1980; Kolotkin *et al.*, 1984), lay people report that it adds little to the conflict statement (Mullinix and Galassi, 1981) and may even border on aggressiveness (Rose and Tryon, 1979). These conflicting data suggest that the specific request statement may be most useful when a desired response to the conflict statement alone is not forthcoming (escalation and persistence are discussed later).

Finally, noncompliance in response to unreasonable requests is an important component of assertive content. It is characteristic of assertive individuals (Eisler *et al.*, 1973; Pitcher and Meikle, 1980) and is highly correlated with judgements of overall assertion (Bordewick and Bornstein, 1980).

An extensive body of research has assessed the social response to the *standard assertion* (conflict assertion that involves only the expression of rights). A consistent pattern has emerged: standard assertion is judged to be equally potent to, and more desirable than, aggressive behaviour (Epstein, 1980; Hull and Schroeder, 1979; Mullinix and Galassi, 1981; Woolfolk and Dever, 1979). It is also judged to be more socially competent or effective, *but distinctly less likeable*, than nonassertive behaviour (Gormally, 1982; Hull and Schroeder, 1979; Keane, St Lawrence, Himadi, *et al.*, 1983a; Keane, Wedding and Kelly, 1983b; Kelly, Kern, Kirkley, *et al.*, 1980; Kern, 1982; Kern, Cavell and Beck, 1985; St Lawrence, Hansen, Cutts, *et al.*, 1985; Woolfolk and Dever, 1979). Thus, simply expressing one's rights appears to entail distinct risks of social rejection along with its potential rewards.

Expression of Elaborations. Research focused only on the expression of assertive rights until the late 1970s, when three studies finally produced data concerning the elaboration components. Woolfolk and Dever (1979) assessed the social response to a statement they called 'assertion plus extra consideration' and determined that the 'extras' (short explanation and acknowledgement of the other person's reality) enhanced the evaluation of the assertion without detracting from its potency. Romano and Bellack (1980) found that offering compromises and alternatives, acknowledging the feelings of the other person, and providing reasons or explanation for one's behaviour were considered by lay people to be important components of skilled assertion in refusal situations. Finally, Pitcher and Meikle (1980) observed that assertive individuals used more praise and apologies in conflict situations than did nonassertive individuals.

When elaborations such as explanations, compromises, praise and so on are emitted along with the expression of rights, the resulting *empathic assertion* is generally evaluated as equally potent to, but more likeable, desirable and appropriate than, the *standard assertion* which only expresses rights (Hollandsworth and Cooley, 1978; Hrop and Rakos, 1985; Kern *et al.*, 1985; Rakos and Hrop, 1983; Woolfolk and Dever, 1979). In fact, empathic assertions are evaluated as comparable to passivity in terms of likeability and desirability, but of course as more effective (Kern, 1982; Kern *et al.*, 1985; Woolfolk and Dever, 1979). Therefore, the interpersonally potent yet socially acceptable empathic assertion, comprised of elaborations that can be easily operationalised and reliably assessed (Bruch, Heisler and Conroy, 1981; Rakos and Schroeder, 1979) as well as successfully trained (Rakos and Schroeder, 1979), has emerged as the generally preferred training goal. The specific elaboration components can be summarised as follows, noting that as important interpersonal communications skills in their own right, they are discussed in detail in several chapters of this book:

1. A succinct, nondefensive, honest explanation for the necessity to emit the expression of rights (see Chapter 8);
2. A statement conveying empathy for, or understanding of, the effects on the other person of the expression of rights (see Chapters 6 and 18);
3. Praise or another positive comment directed toward the other individual (see Chapter 15);
4. A short apology, clearly indicating that it is directed toward the inconvenience or disappointment that will result from the expression of rights (for instance, 'I'm sorry you'll have to miss that concert') — rather than toward the *necessity* or *fact* of the expression of rights (for instance, 'I'm sorry I have to say no').
5. An attempt to identify a mutually acceptable compromise when legitimate rights conflict, recognising that the search for such a compromise may not be successful (the determination of legitimate rights will be discussed in the next section when covert content components are considered; also see Chapters 10 and 13).

Content of Conflict Assertion: Covert Components

Information-processing skills — the categorisation and conscious and automatic processing of data — are critical elements of competent social interaction (McFall,

1982; Meichenbaum, Butler and Gruson, 1981; Morrison and Bellack, 1981; Trower, 1982). Trower, for example, observed that conscious self-monitoring of one's behaviour can occur with reference to external standards (situational and interpersonal cues which generate social roles, norms and rules, as well as empirically based self-efficacy [competency] and outcome expectations) or to internal standards (idiosyncratic nonempirical beliefs, perceptions and expectations). Though both reference standards are undoubtedly utilised by most people, evidence suggests that the external situation–orientation is associated with social skill, while the internal self-focus is characteristic of unskilled individuals (Trower, 1982).

The ability to utilise the external orientation requires what Schroeder, Driver and Streufert (1967) call conceptual complexity, which permits the individual to: (1) make increasingly precise discriminations among situational cues, allowing consideration of broader and more varied viewpoints; (2) increase the use of internally but rationally developed standards for problem solving; and (3) integrate more information and increase tolerance for conflict. Not surprisingly, Bruch (1981; Bruch, Heisler and Conroy, 1981) has found that assertive individuals evidence greater conceptual complexity (CC) than nonassertive people and, further, that high CC individuals, compared to low CC ones, evidence a generally superior knowledge of assertive content, oral delivery skill and use of adaptive cognitions. In addition, high CC people perform more assertively and utilise elaborative statements to a greater extent in conflicts involving continuing relationships.

Such situations demand the greatest ability to utilise multiple perspectives and internal rational standards, since they generally require increased response flexibility and refined relationship–enhancing behaviours to produce an effective yet socially acceptable assertion. Conflicts involving noncontinuing relationships, on the other hand, can usually be handled in a straightforward manner indicated by social norms.

The specific cognitive abilities necessary to produce a sophisticated, rational, empirical analysis of the information pertaining to the social conflict can be categorised as knowledge, self-statements (self-instructions), expectancies, philosophical beliefs, problem-solving skills and social perception skills.

Knowledge. Nonassertive (as well as assertive) individuals can categorise passive, assertive and aggressive responses accurately (Bordewick and Bornstein, 1980), but the extent to which they have acquired the cognitive knowledge necessary to produce an appropriate assertive response remains unclear. Several studies have found that such individuals do not manifest deficits in relevant knowledge (Alden and Safran, 1978; Schwartz and Gottman, 1976), but more recent work has obtained contradictory data (Bruch, 1981; Heimberg and Becker, 1981). This issue remains unresolved, but it seems prudent to assume that many nonassertive individuals lack basic knowledge pertaining to the construction of appropriate assertion and therefore require exposure to the relevant information.

Self-statements (Self-instructions). Meichenbaum *et al.* (1981) emphasise 'negative internal dialogue' as a class of cognitions that interferes with competent social responding. A negative self-statement in response to an unreasonable request might be saying to yourself 'I will get embarrassed if I refuse' or 'He might not like me unless I say yes', while positive ones are exemplified by 'There doesn't seem to be any good reason why I should say yes' or 'I have the right to refuse' (Heimberg and Becker, 1981). The research demonstrates consistently that assertive individuals emit approximately twice as many positive as negative self-statements when confronted with social conflict, while nonassertive people emit approximately equal numbers of each (Bruch, 1981; Heimberg, Chiauzzi, Becker, *et al.*, 1983b; Pitcher and Meikle, 1980; Schwartz and Gottman, 1976). More recent work suggests that the absolute frequency of positive and negative self-statements is less important than the 'mix' (Blankenberg and Heimberg, 1984).

Therefore, an appropriate repertoire of adaptive positive self-statements appears to be important for enacting assertive behaviour. Regardless of whether the repertoire of self-statements is the crucial difference between assertive and nonassertive individuals (Schwartz and Gottman, 1976) or one of several (along with knowledge and performance skill deficits: Bruch, 1981), they merit close analysis when examining the source of an individual's unassertiveness. Indeed, direct training in appropriate self-instruction alone can increase assertive responding (Craighead, 1979; Glass, Gottman and Schmurak, 1976; Twentyman, Pharr and Conner, 1980).

Expectancies. Assertive individuals expect conflict assertion to produce more positive consequences and fewer negative ones than do nonassertive individuals (Blankenberg and Heimberg, 1984; Chiauzzi and Heimberg, 1986; Eisler, Frederiksen and Peterson, 1978; Fiedler and Beach, 1978; Kuperminc and Heimberg, 1983). Furthermore, the potential outcomes are evaluated differently: assertive individuals view the potential positive consequences of assertion as more desirable and the potential negative ones as more undesirable (Blankenberg and Heimberg, 1984; Kuperminc and Heimberg, 1983). Thus, assertive people have *outcome expectations* that differ from those of nonassertive individuals in terms of both probability of occurrence and subjective importance. In addition, *self-efficacy expectations* (Bandura, 1977), which refer to one's perceived ability to enact a specific response in a particular situation regardless of the actual outcome, are much stronger in conflict situations for assertive as compared to nonassertive individuals (Chiauzzi and Heimberg, 1986).

Finally, *situational efficacy expectations,* which describe the confidence a person has in his/her ability to generate any response to deal with a situation successfully, are greater for assertive individuals, but only in those situations where the other person's behaviour is judged to be highly unreasonable (Chiauzzi and Heimberg, 1986). Taken together, these data suggest that assertive individuals approach conflict situations with an adaptive appraisal of the situation and a realistic self-confidence in their ability to emit appropriate behaviours. Self-instruction training focusing on producing realistic expectations in the form of positive self-statements (Meichenbaum, 1977) and graduated successful performance in the actual or even role-play situation (Bandura, 1977) are two strategies for modifying the maladaptive expectations of nonassertive individuals.

Philosophical beliefs. Ellis' (1962) identification of eleven pervasive 'irrational beliefs' as impediments to psychological adjustment has stimulated research into their role in nonassertive behaviour. Five of them seem most directly related to assertion: demands for perfection in self and others in important situations; demands for universal approval from significant others; defining personal rights and self-worth by external achievement in subjectively important areas; catastrophising, or exaggerating the meaning of an undesired outcome; and viewing passivity as preferable to active intervention, believing things will eventually work out without 'rocking the boat'. The typical nonassertive person might be expected to think: 'I must assert myself without any mistakes or the assertion will fail (self-perfection), the other person will be hurt and angry (univeral approval), and that would be terrible (catastrophising), and would confirm that I'm just no good (self-denigration). Things will be better if I let it pass and see what happens (inaction). These belief statements may be prefaced by: 'I don't have the right to infringe or make demands on this other person' (self-denigration) and/or 'I should not have to even deal with this situation since the other person should not be acting this way' (other-perfection).

There is some evidence that endorsing these beliefs in general is related to nonassertive behaviour (Alden and Safran, 1978; Alden and Cappe, 1981). Furthermore, nonassertive people in conflict situations entertain the possibility of many more negative 'overwhelming consequences' (that is, catastrophising) than positive ones, while assertive individuals consider similar frequencies of both; as with self-statements, the 'mix' seems more critical than absolute frequency or intensity of extreme expectations (Blankenburg and Heimberg, 1984). Thus, rational alternatives to the irrational beliefs seem likely to facilitate the performance of assertive behaviour. They would have the following general content (Ellis, 1962; Rakos and Schroeder, 1980):

Imperfection: 'I am human and the world is very complicated; therefore I will make mistakes even when the situation is important to me. The other person is also human, lives in the same complex world, and will also make mistakes in important situations' (no self- or other blaming; acceptance of inevitable human imperfection and frailty);

Rejection: 'There is no way I can please everyone who is important to me all the time, *even if I always place their needs first,* because the world is too complicated and its operation too capricious' (acceptance of some inevitable rejection);

Noncatastrophising: 'Negative outcomes *are* unfortunate, inconvenient, unpleasant — but not terrible — and I will attempt constructive amelioration where possible, and live with them where change is not feasible. This must be my approach even when the unfavourable outcome involves an issue that is very important to me, because the world does not know or care what is important to me' (realistic understanding and acceptance of one's place in the large context);

Action: 'Since the world is not oriented toward fulfilling my desires, active attempts to influence it are the only ways for me to increase the likelihood that my desires will be achieved' (acceptance of responsiblity);

Self-worth: 'I am as worthy, and have the same basic human rights, as anyone else, regardless of how much or how little I or others have achieved. I have the basic right to assert myself and attempt to influence the situation to increase my rewards' (acceptance of basic self-worth and human rights).

The direct modification of irrational thinking has usually been a component of assertiveness training (Rich and Schroeder, 1976). 'Rational relabelling' or 'cognitive restructuring' involves first identifying the specific irrational thought emitted as a response to a particular situation. Nonassertive people have often learned the irrational thoughts so well that they don't actually think them, but behave 'as if' they think them. After identification of the actual or implicit thought, the individual is taught to challenge it and actively substitute a rational alternative, and evaluate its utility (Goldfried and Davison, 1976; Rakos and Schroeder, 1980). Research has demonstrated that such rational relabelling procedures can enhance conflict assertive behaviour (Alden, Safran and Weideman, 1978; Hatzenbuehler and Schroeder, 1982; Linehan, Goldfried and Goldfried, 1979), leading to the suggestion that a preponderance of irrational beliefs is the central characteristic of socially unskilled behaviour (Trower, 1982). However, the addition of the rational relabelling procedure to the standard behavioural training 'package' has consistently provided only limited added benefits (Carmody, 1978; Hatzenbuehler and Schroeder, 1982; Hammen, Jacobs, Mayol, *et al.*, 1980; Linehan *et al.*, 1979; Tiegerman and Kassinove, 1977; Wolfe and Fodor, 1977), supporting Bandura's (1978) contention that though performance may be fundamentally cognitively mediated, those cognitions are most efficaciously modified when the behaviours on which they are based are first changed. He therefore advocates performance-based interventions.

A final comment: since rational thoughts appear to be a component of assertive behaviour, rational relabelling procedures may prove to be more important in promoting generalisation of assertive responses to novel people and situations (Scott, Himadi and Keane, 1983) than in facilitating initial acquisition of the response.

Social Perception Skills. Two distinct cognitive skills are involved in interpersonal perception (Argyle, 1981): accurate perception and empathic role-taking. Accurate perception has been more thoroughly investigated, and the data strongly indicate that nonassertive individuals are deficient in this skill. They misjudge the amount of anger communicated by aggressive and assertive responses (Morrison and Bellack, 1981) and place exaggerated emphasis on the status of the other person and the degree of social norm transgression when analysing conflict situations (Rudy, Merluzzi and Henahan, 1982). A realistic assessment of social norms *per se* is appropriate, of course: they provide some of the data necessary to incorporate external criteria into a sophisticated analysis of the situation. Epstein (1980), for example, found that compliance with, anger toward and sympathy for an asserter making a request varied with how reasonable the request was perceived to be and the extent of sacrifice required to comply. However, nonassertive individuals perceive 'reasonableness', and therefore, the legitimate rights of the other person and social transgressions, differently from assertive individuals: the former judge requests as more reasonable (Blankenburg and Heimberg, 1984; Chiauzzi and Heimberg, 1986), especially ones that are consensually evaluated to be of low or moderate legitimacy. This inaccurate perception of conflict situations, particularly the ones most appropriate for assertion (those involving requests of questionable legitimacy) may be a major contributor to a decision to behave nonassertively.

Accurate perception appears to be particularly important in conflict situations of moderate legitimacy, in which both assertive and nonassertive individuals produce more thoughts, but fewer objective ones (Chiauzzi and Heimberg, 1983), and report decreased intention to assert and weakened specific self-efficacy beliefs (Chiauzzi and Heimberg, 1986). These findings suggest that ambiguous situations make the greatest demands on an individual in terms of determining the legitimate rights of all persons involved. Those persons with high conceptual complexity abilities will be better able to evaluate the situational considerations, make appropriate reasonableness determinations and synthesise the resultant increase in total positive and negative thoughts into adaptive, accurate discriminations. Accurate social perception skills are, therefore, necessary to assess the legitimate rights under contention, which is a prerequisite for effective, appropriate assertion (Heimberg and Becker, 1981; Rakos, 1979).

In addition to accurately perceiving the situation that is presented, the socially skilled person will be able to understand the perceptions of the other involved individuals, a skill called role-taking by Meichenbaum *et al.* (1981) and metaperception by Argyle (1981). The superior social evaluation of the empathic assertion relative to the standard one suggests the importance of this skill in conflict resolution. The issue in terms of social perception, however, is not one of empathic content but one of cue discrimination, that is, when would such a response facilitate social interaction? At present, only one study has investigated this skill: Fischetti, Peterson, Curran, *et al.* (1984) found heterosocially skilled and unskilled people differed in their ability to recognise when a vocal or gestural response from them would help a speaker continue to talk. Sixty per cent of the skilled but only 36 per cent of the unskilled people were good cue discriminators. These data may help explain earlier findings that skilled and unskilled individuals differ not in the frequency of their vocalisations or gestures, but rather in the timing or placement of them, and hence their reinforcing skill (Fischetti, Curran and Wassberg 1977; Peterson, Fischetti, Curran, *et al.*, 1981; see Chapter 5).

Interpersonal Problem-solving Skills. The ability to enact a systematic problem-solving strategy has been identified as a component of social competence (Meichenbaum *et al.*, 1981; Trower, 1982) and observed to be deficient in a variety of clinical populations (Schroeder and Rakos, 1983). The problem-solving sequence involves problem recognition, problem definition and formulation, generation of potential response alternatives, decision-making (assessment of response alternatives *vis-à-vis* expected outcomes and desired goals), and solution implementation and evaluation (D'Zurilla and Nezu, 1982). Chiauzzi and Heimberg (1986) investigated these abilities in relation to assertion, and found that nonassertive individuals exhibited deficits in the previously discussed perceptual skills of problem recognition and assessment and in their ability to select an appropriate response, but not in their ability to generate response alternatives, either in terms of number or quality. The analysis of the problem-solving skills involved in assertion is consistent with formulations that view assertion as a sequence of overt and covert skills, rather than as one discrete skill (Heimberg and Becker, 1981; Rakos, 1979), and should prove fruitful by providing a framework for operationalising and training the components of the conceptual complexity necessary for effective assertion in complex situations (Bruch *et al.*, 1981).

Paralinguistic and Nonverbal Components

The paralinguistic and nonverbal features of a verbalisation are critical components of effective communication (see Chapter 3) and social skill (Barlow, Abel, Blanchard, *et al.*, 1977; Conger and Farrell, 1981; Conger, Wallander, Mariotto, *et al.*, 1980; Trower, 1980). Assertion trainers also consider them essential for efficacious conflict assertion (Alberti and Emmons, 1978; Eisler and Frederiksen, 1980; Lange and Jakubowksi, 1976; Zuker, 1983). A synthesis of the research offers training guidelines which must be embraced cautiously, since cultural differences in communication styles (Cheek, 1976; Furnham, 1979) are not reflected in the research to date, which has been conducted primarily with white middle-class Americans.

Paralinguistic Characteristics

Voice volume, firmness and intonation, and response latency, duration and fluency have been presumed to be the important vocal dimensions involved in conflict assertion.

Latency. In studies evaluating actual behavioural samples, a short response latency emerges as a criterion component of effective assertion in some studies (Eisler *et al.*, 1973; Kolotkin *et al.*, 1984; Pitcher and Meikle, 1980; Rose and Tryon, 1979) but not in others (Bourque and Ladouceur, 1979; Romano and Bellack, 1980). Latency is longer in conflict situations than in positive ones (Eisler, Hersen, Miller, *et al.*, 1975; Pitcher and Meikle, 1980) and is influenced by specific situations and sex of the participants (Pitcher and Meikle, 1980; Rose and Tryon, 1979).

Pitcher and Meikle, for example, found that the longest latencies occurred with conflict assertions to males. These situational influences make intuitive sense: a socially skilled person, though able to emit an appropriate verbal response, might be expected to manifest a modest delay so as to utilise the various covert skills discussed previously, process the relevant situational information and then determine the constitution of an appropriate response. It seems reasonable to conclude that a moderately short response latency that is responsive to situational variables is a component of conflict assertion. In fact, those studies which failed to identify short latency as an important characteristic may have ignored situational influences (Galassi *et al.*, 1981).

Duration. Originally, researchers assumed that short response duration was an important feature of conflict assertion, probably noting the tendency for nonassertive individuals to include long explanations, excuses and apologies in their replies. However, since appropriate assertion involves verbalising elaborations as well as expressing rights, it is not surprising that response duration has failed to distinguish assertive responses from nonassertive ones (Bourque and Ladouceur, 1979; Pitcher and Meikle, 1980). However, duration is an important cue utilised by lay people when assessing conflict assertion (Romano and Bellack, 1980) and is consistently correlated with ratings of overall assertiveness (for example, Bordewick and Bornstein, 1980; Kolotkin *et al.*, 1984).

As with latency, duration is longer in conflict as opposed to positive situations (Eisler *et al.*, 1975; Pitcher and Meikle, 1980) and when the assertion is directed toward a male (Pitcher and Meikle, 1980). Thus, situational cues must be considered in determining appropriate response duration: the length of the assertion must be sufficient to communicate effectively in a given context. Mere verbiage in and of itself is neither assertive nor unassertive. In fact, Heimberg, Harrison, Goldberg *et al.* (1979) found a curvilinear relationship between assertiveness and response duration: moderately assertive individuals exhibited much shorter duration than either highly assertive or nonassertive individuals.

Fluency. Though consistently described as an important paralinguistic characteristic of conflict assertion, flueney has been infrequently investigated. Kolotkin *et al.* (1984) found it to be weakly related to judgements of overall assertion, and Pitcher and Meikle (1980) found that a 'paralinguistic rating' (volume, intonation, fluency) was similar for assertive and nonassertive individuals (superior in positive situations compared to conflict ones, and when responding to females as opposed to males). Nevertheless, trainers consistently emphasise the importance of a nonhesitant, fluent response (for instance, Eisler and Frederiksen, 1980; Lange and Jakubowski, 1976; Rakos and Schroeder, 1980).

Volume. Rose and Tryon (1979) found conflict assertions delivered at the 76dB level were consistently perceived as appropriately assertive, those at the 68dB level as marginally assertive and those at the 84dB level as aggressive. Other research has found that assertive individuals speak louder than nonassertive ones (Eisler *et al.*, 1973), and that volume increases in conflict situations (Eisler *et al.*, 1975). Appropriate volume is considered by lay people to be an important indicant of assertion (Romano and Bellack, 1980), and correlates strongly with judgements of assertion by trained (Bordewick and Bornstein, 1980; Kolotkin *et al.*, 1984) and untrained (Romano and Bellack, 1980) observers. Except for the Pitcher and Meikle (1980) study, which found the paralinguistic rating (volume, fluency, intonation) to be unrelated to judgements of assertive behaviour, the data here are consistent: effective conflict assertion statements are delivered in a moderately loud volume appropriate to the situation.

Intonation (Inflection). Lay people consider intonation to be an important feature of effective conflict assertion and one of the most important contributors to criterion ratings of such behaviour (Romano and Bellack, 1980). However, as with response duration, both highly assertive and nonassertive people evidence greater inflection than moderately assertive individuals (Heimberg *et al.*, 1979). Thus, inflection appears to be an important attribute of assertive responding, though it is not a distinguishing characteristic. As with many of the previous paralinguistic qualities, intermediate levels of inflection are judged to be most appropriately assertive (Rose and Tryon, 1979), and this is the quality that trainers emphasise.

Firmness (Affect). Increased firmness is highly correlated with judgements of assertion (Bordewick and Bornstein, 1980; Kolotkin *et al.*, 1984). However, while Eisler *et al.* (1973) found assertive psychiatric patients evidenced greater affect than nonassertive ones, Bourque and Ladouceur (1979) failed to obtain such differences between assertive and nonassertive college students. Affective qualities may be more diverse within a patient population and therefore more discriminatory. Situational variables may also influence the firmness of delivery: Eisler *et al.* (1975), again observing psychiatric patients, found that affect was greater in conflict situations than in positive ones. These meagre data suggest that affective quality is important, especially in conflict situations, and support the attention devoted in training to developing firm responses.

Summary of Paralinguistic Qualities: Firmness, intermediate levels of volume and intonation, and moderate response latency and duration seem to be important characteristics of conflict assertion. The benefits of a fluent response have little empirical support yet make intuitive sense. Firmness, latency and duration will vary according to the specific situation and persons involved (for instance, they are likely to increase when the assertion is directed toward a male). Appropriate conflict assertion therefore requires flexible paralinguistic abilities which demonstrate sensitivity to situational cues.

Nonverbal Characteristics

Research and clinical training have generally focused on the nonverbal responses of eye contact, facial expression, gestures and 'body language'. Overall, body cues have been found to convey a great deal of information about assertive behaviour (McFall, Winnett, Bordewick, *et al.*, 1982), as they do about communication skills in general (see Chapter 3). The specific responses have been extensively investigated allowing an examination of the contribution each makes toward judgements of assertion.

Eye Contact. Lay people consider eye contact to be an important component of conflict assertion (McFall *et al.*, 1982; Romano and Bellack, 1980) which correlates highly with ratings of overall assertiveness (Kolotkin *et al.*, 1984). The duration of eye contact is longer in conflict situations than in positive ones (Eisler *et al.*, 1975). However, the actual amount of eye contact may be only one of several contributors to skilful performance, since assertive and nonassertive individuals do not always engage in it for different lengths of time (Bourque and Ladouceur, 1979; Heimberg *et al.*, 1979). Eye contact must also be emitted flexibly and perhaps somewhat intermittently, rather than in a fixed stare, especially since it is engaged in by the listener and *not* by the speaker in general social conversation between caucasions (LaFrance and Mayo, 1976).

Facial Expression. Judgements of assertion are strongly influenced by overall facial expression (Romano and Bellack, 1980) as well as by specific mouth, eyebrow and forehead cues (McFall *et al.*, 1982). The latter researchers found that an uncontrolled fidgety mouth, wrinkled forehead and animated, constantly moving eyebrows communicated unassertiveness, and interestingly, provided more information about male asserters but were more influential in evaluating female asserters. They did not observe males and females utilising these cues differently in making judgements, but Romano and Bellack (1980) did: '(M)ales and females differed substantially in the number, pattern and valence of the cues used . . . female judges seemed to be sensitive to and made use of more behavioral cues . . .' (p. 488). In particular, they noted that smiles, which in general evidence a very minimal impact on the perception of assertiveness (Kolotkin *et al.*, 1984), strongly detracted from women's (but not men's!) evaluations of female asserters.

Facial expression, therefore, is an important component of assertion, particularly for women. Compared to males, females may be more astute at discriminating these cues in others, but as asserters they emit them in more subtle ways which nevertheless strongly influence the perception of their assertion. This suggests that it is important to not only teach appropriate facial expression to all trainees, but to also teach males to attend to these cues and interpret them accurately, particularly when emitted by females.

Gestures. When involved in a conflict interaction, socially competent individuals increase their use of gestures (Trower, 1980) and use their arms and hands differently than unskilled individuals (McFall *et al.*, 1982). In fact, arm movements that are smooth and steady while speaking and inconspicuous while listening, and hands that are not fidgety or involved in excessive manipulative activity, are the most important nonverbal contributors to judgements of male assertion (McFall *et al.*, 1982). They are also quite influential in the perception of female assertion, especially when judged by males: physical gestures enhance the evaluation while extraneous and restrained movements are viewed negatively (Romano and Bellack, 1980). In addition, arm and hand gestures may be most important when the conflict interaction involves opposite sexed participants (Rose and Tryon, 1979). Taken together, these data indicate clearly that the impact of an assertive response is enhanced when accompanied by an appropriate repertoire of gestures.

Body Language. While general body posture contributes little to experts' ratings of overall assertion (Kolotkin *et al.*, 1984), it is a significant factor in lay people's judgements (Romano and Bellack, 1980). Head, neck, shoulder and torso positions that are upright, exhibit little extraneous movement, squarely face the other person and involve purposive movement while speaking yet remain quiet while listening are associated with assertive behaviour (McFall *et al.*, 1982). Head and neck positions evidencing up-and-down nodding and side-to-side tilting, shoulders which are stooped, shrugging or hunched, and torso activity such as rotating, rocking and squirming communicate unassertiveness (McFall *et al.*, 1982). These cues contribute more to judgements of male as opposed to female asserters, but overall, are less important than the other non-verbal characteristics (McFall *et al.*, 1982; Romano and Bellack, 1980).

Finally, while meaningful posture shifts are appropriate (Trower, 1980), actually approaching the other person while asserting is perceived by lay people as aggressive (Rose and Tryon, 1979). These data suggest an important but relatively modest contribution by body cues to effective assertion, and indicate that some attention to them in training is warranted.

Summary of Nonverbal Responses. Eye contact, facial expression, gestures and, to a lesser extent, body language all influence judgements of conflict assertion. Facial expression for female asserters, and gestures for male asserters, may be particularly influential in the evaluation of such behaviour. As with the paralinguistic qualities of the response, the nonverbal components must be appropriate to the context. In general, effective conflict assertion requires steady but not rigid eye contact, a calm, sincere, serious facial expression, flexible use of arm and hand gestures, and a relaxed, involved body posture. Body movements should be fluid and purposeful when speaking but quiet and inconspicuous when listening (McFall *et al.*, 1982).

Process (Interactive) Skills

Since assertion is by definition a social skill, all the previous components are really 'interactive skills'. However, several behavioural capabilities comprised of the previously discussed overt and covert components merit individual discussion since they are intricately involved in the *ongoing* conflict interaction.

Response Timing. As noted earlier, socially unskilled individuals evidence inadequate timing of vocalisations and gestures (Fischetti *et al.*, 1977; Petersen et al., 1981), and must learn to respond more appropriately to situational cues (Fischetti *et al.*, 1984). Trower (1980), for example, found that skilled individuals not only spoke more than unskilled persons, but did so when the other person attended to the verbalisations, when the other person engaged in long periods of silence or when the situation required an assertive response. Skilled individuals also looked more when listening.

Initiation and Persistence. In the section discussing problem-solving skills, it is noted that a crucial step involves selection of the appropriate response, which may legitimately be passivity or compliance in certain circumstances as when the realistic risks of assertion are great or the offending individual's situation requires exceptional 'understanding' (Alberti and Emmons, 1978; Rakos and Schroeder, 1980). However, if the decision is made to assert oneself, the initial assertion should be one that is likely to be the *minimal effective response* (MER: Rimm and Masters, 1979). If the MER proves ineffective, and the decision is made to persist, *escalation* is appropriate. This involves increasing the intensity of certain paralinguistic qualities (voice volume, intonation, affect, response duration) and/or modifying the verbal content (providing further explanation, increasing empathy, suggesting additional potential compromises). Aversive consequences may also be specified as noted when distinctions between assertion and aggression were discussed. If a change in someone's behaviour is desired, and only a statement of the conflict has been emitted, the specific behaviour change request may be added. Identification of the MER is important because an escalated response emitted as an initial assertion (a common error by novices) will likely be evaluated as inappropriate and aggressive, which may result in negative consequences for the asserter and reinforce beliefs that such behaviour is indeed risky. For a simple example, imagine a salesman comes to the front door selling a product you do not want, but he does not respect your lack of interest. Appropriate assertion might involve the following:

MER: 'No, thanks, I'm not interested.'
Escalation 1: 'No, I told you I'm not at all interested. Good day.'

Escalation 2: 'I am *not* interested!' (Louder volume, firmer affect and intonation.)

Escalation 3: 'I told you I am not interested. If you do not leave immediately, I will contact your supervisor and register a complaint against you' (volume, affect, intonation maintained or increased slightly from previous response, and aversive contingency specified).

Effective persistence requires that the asserter maintain the conflict focus and resist manipulations (Rakos and Schroeder, 1980). This is particularly difficult to do when a continuing relationship is involved and when the novice asserter is starting to behave less submissively and thereby no longer meeting the expectations of others. Several examples will help clarify the skill of maintaining the focus.

Example 1:
Salesman, a stranger, says after two earlier refusals, 'But these encyclopedias are so helpful for school and I see you have two children. Surely you can appreciate how advantageous they will be in their education. I'm certain you are concerned about your children's education.'
Assertive response: 'I'm *not* interested in purchasing the encyclopedias.'

This response avoids the salesman's manipulative ploy of challenging the parent's commitment to his/her children's education, which is irrelevant to the current decision not to purchase the encyclopedias. If the parent defends him/herself, the focus will soon shift to education. Maintaining the focus in such a situation often means simple repetition *without qualification*. If one says, 'I'm not interested at this time', he/she may be asked to explain why not 'now', and then 'when', and if 'money' is the problem, how about an 'extended payment plan?'

Example 2:
Father, used to his child coming over for dinner every Sunday, says after the child indicates he/she has made other plans this week: 'You don't care about me anymore . . .' or 'So go and see your friends, if they are more important to you.'

Here we are dealing with an important continuing relationship, in which the child is initiating assertive behaviour, resulting in the father experiencing an unexpected loss of reinforcement and the feelings of hurt and/or anger that often accompany aversive consequences. Protecting the relationship and maintaining the focus in this situation generally requires: (1) increased empathic reflection of the underlying feelings (see Chapters 6 and 18); (2) repetition of the explicit explanation (see Chapter 8); and (3) a search for a mutually acceptable compromise (see Chapters 10 and 13), if conflicting rights are judged to be present. It is desirable, though often exceptionally difficult, to address these verbalisations to the *existence* of the feelings rather than to the *content* of the feelings:

> *Assertive response:* 'Dad, I hear how angry and disappointed you are that I will not be coming for dinner this week. I know how important the family dinners are to you, but as I said, I really want to go to this cocktail party. I hope you understand my feelings. I am free Wednesday evening — I can stop by then for a few hours. How does that sound?'

This response attends to the feelings but does not lose the focus and become defensive by debating the extent of 'caring' for parents or the relative 'importance' of different relationships. Caring, if present, can be demonstrated through the compromise. Sometimes, however, the interaction will continue and the content of the feelings will have to be addressed more directly, resulting in an increased probability of losing the assertive focus:

> *Assertive response:* 'Dad, I know how much you look forward to our Sunday dinners, and I enjoy them tremendously too, but sometimes I have other engagements which are also very important to me. I really do value our relationship, and care about you, and my missing the dinner has nothing to do with how I feel about you. I'm sorry you do not see this as I do. Anyway, as I said, I am free Wednesday evening, and I'd like to stop by then. Is that all right?'

If the other person continues to experience negative feelings as a consequence of the assertion, and the relationship is a valued one, an assertion directed at those feelings, either immediately or at a later, more planned time, may be necessary:

> *Assertive response:* 'Dad, I want to talk to you about our phone conversation last week — you sounded pretty hurt and angry, and seemed to feel that if I cared about you I would always make the Sunday dinner. I would like to talk about that because I don't see it quite the same way.'

Persistence increases the chances for a desired outcome but cannot guarantee it, since assertion is, by definition, risky. The car mechanic may not reduce unwarranted charges regardless of the extent of escalation. An assertion specifying a future contingency — '. . . therefore you will hear from my lawyer' — may be the best one can do, though that outcome is clearly unsatisfying.

Furthermore, persistence, even when successful as defined by outcome, may involve risk to the relationship: the other person may feel hurt, angry or disappointed. Skilful use of the covert components of assertion will be necessary to accurately assess the situation, avoid rationalisations which justify nonassertive behaviour, and decide, first, whether to assert and, second, the extent of escalation desirable given the importance of the conflict at issue, the realistic probability of various positive and negative outcomes, and the relationship involved. Acquiring the overt and covert assertive skills described in this chapter gives one the freedom and therefore the choice to assert — it is not a mandate to always assert (Alberti and Emmons, 1978; Rakos and Schroeder, 1980).

Stimulus Control Skills. Antecedent and consequent stimulus control skills facilitate effective, socially acceptable assertion by altering the context in which the assertion is emitted. Antecedent stimulus control refers to arranging the environment prior to asserting so as to maximise the possibility of a favourable outcome. These skills are generally assertive behaviours themselves: requests to move to a private room prior to a confrontation, requests for a delay prior to making a decision (which permits time to identify and rehearse appropriate responses) or inquiries to the other person regarding convenient times to set aside for the discussion of concerns. Conflicts that are discussed in private, without time pressures, and with prior deliberation are more likely to be resolved with mutual satisfaction.

Consequent stimulus control refers to reinforcing the other person (see Chapter 5) for listening to and/or complying with the assertion. Providing contingent verbal reinforcement for desired behaviour in response to the assertion is likely to encourage similar behaviour in the future and may also minimise negative perceptions of the conflict interaction (Levin and Gross, 1984; St Lawrence *et al.*, 1985).

Social Validity of Conflict Assertion

Throughout this chapter, it is stressed that the utility of assertion is determined by two outcomes: in addition to exerting social influence, the performance of assertive behaviours may have an enduring impact on the relationship of the participants. Since longitudinal studies assessing the course of 'assertive' versus 'nonassertive' relationships would be extraordinarily difficult to conduct, the burgeoning research has addressed the issue from the perspective of social validity (Kazdin, 1977; Wolf, 1978): what are the evaluations and perceptions of conflict assertive behaviour by participants or observers?

Social Evaluation of Conflict Assertion: General Findings

The social validity of *standard assertion* (expression of the assertive right without elaboration) in conflict situations has already been discussed in detail. Briefly, it is generally judged to be more socially competent, but less likeable, than nonassertive behaviour, and to be at least as potent as, and more favourably evaluated than, aggressive behaviour. *Empathic assertions,* which express rights and elaborations (explanatory, positive and conciliatory statements) are judged more favourably than standard assertions and comparably to nonassertion. The elaborations, moreover, do not detract from the potency of the assertion. (These findings have been discussed earlier.)

Only Mullinix and Galassi (1981) failed to obtain benefits with the addition of an empathic statement to behaviour change requests in the work environment. Since elaborations appear to be important components of both refusals and behaviour change requests (Pitcher and Meikle, 1980), this inconsistency may be a function of normative differences between business and nonbusiness situations (where the rest of the research was conducted).

Overall, the elaborative statements appear to be a powerful way to enhance the evaluation of standard conflict assertion without compromising its potency. In addition, similar benefits are obtained when experience with the asserter includes positive interactions as well as the conflict one, such as commendatory assertions like receiving thanks, compliments and requests or offers for help (Levin and Gross, 1984; St Lawrence *et al.*, 1985), social conversation (Delamater and McNamara, 1984), and those inherent in friendships (Lewis and Gallois, 1984). These additional interactions may provide a broader context for judging the conflict assertion, allowing positive qualities to be attributed to the asserter. Very possibly, then, the most socially effective conflict assertion may be produced by embedding an empathic assertion within other positive behaviours.

Gender Effects on the Social Response to Conflict Assertion

Sex role data (Broverman, Broverman, Clarkson, *et al.*, 1970) and early investigations of gender effects (Romano and Bellack, 1980) led to predictions that assertion by females would be perceived less positively than assertion by males. However, approximately 15 studies addressing this issue have now been conducted, and the overwhelming majority fails to identify any systematic biases in the evaluation of either standard or empathic assertion (Kern *et al.*, 1985) or the specific response classes (Hull and Schroeder, 1979; Lewis and Gallois, 1984; Schroeder *et al.*, 1983) as a function of gender of asserter or judge.

An alternate approach to investigating gender effects focuses on sex-role orientation, rather than sex *per se,* and may ultimately prove more fruitful. Masculine sex-role characteristics are attributed to asserters in conflict situations (Hess, Bridgewater, Bornstein, *et al.*, 1980), masculinity and conflict assertion abilities are significantly correlated (Nix, Lohr and Mosesso, 1984), and 'androgynous' and 'masculine' women are more assertive than 'feminine' women (Rodriguez, Nietzel and Berzins, 1980). Thus, it is not surprising that Kern *et al.* (1985) found that female asserters were devalued only by men *and* women holding traditional, conservative attitudes towards women's role in society.

These data suggest that, first, the pervasive assumption that assertion entails generally greater risks for women than for men (Kahn, 1981; MacDonald, 1982) in unjustified and, second, women should be taught the skills required to identify those individuals holding conservative attitudes towards women's role in society and the elaborative verbalisations necessary to decrease the probability of a negative reaction from such individuals when a decision is made to nevertheless assert (Kern *et al.*, 1985).

Social Evaluation of Assertive Response Classes

The studies assessing the perception of the different response classes of standard assertion have produced conflicting data. Schroeder and his colleagues (Hull and Schroeder, 1979; Schroeder *et al.*, 1983) determined that expressing unpopular opinions involved the greatest amount of assertiveness and refusals the least amount. Behaviour change requests were judged to be most socially desirable and expressing unpopular opinions were least acceptable. However, Lewis and Gallois (1984) obtained essentially contradictory results: behaviour change requests consisting of the conflict statement only were judged to be most assertive and least socially desirable, while expressing different opinions was perceived most favourably. Furthermore, expressions of different opinions by friends were more positively evaluated than such behaviour by strangers or refusals by friends, and refusals by strangers were more favourably perceived than refusals by friends or the conflict statement component of behaviour change requests by strangers.

The social response to the different response classes has important clinical implications, particularly for the selection of the initial behaviours targeted for training. The data to date permit only a few tentative recommendations. First, the common strategy of beginning training with refusals to strangers, which demands relatively modest amounts of behaviour, seems to be supported by the research. Second, expressing unpopular opinions to strangers is likely to be received negatively, and should be introduced after trainees have already experienced some success with other assertive behaviours. Unfortunately, methodological differences between the studies preclude additional suggestions. For example, the differential reaction to behaviour change request may be partly a function of the different response topographies utilised by Schroeder *et al.* (1983) and Lewis and Gallois (1984) (conflict statement plus specific request versus conflict statement only, respectively).

As a final comment, however, it should be noted that these investigations evaluated standard assertion only. Friends, as members of an ongoing relationship, might very well accept a difference of opinion without explanation, compromise or empathy, but are likely to expect those elaborations to accompany a refusal of a request. These data, then, are consistent with theoretical perspectives that stress the appropriateness of utilising the empathic assertion for resolving conflicts in continuing relationships (Rakos, 1979).

Effect of Level of Assertiveness of Evaluator on Judgements of Conflict Assertion

Although both assertive and nonassertive individuals can distinguish among assertion, aggression and nonassertion (Bordewick and Bornstein, 1980), they may evaluate these styles differently. Kern (1982) found that nonassertive individuals rated nonassertive behaviour in refusal situations as more likeable, desirable and competent than either standard or empathic assertions. The cognitive differences between assertive and nonassertive individuals which were discussed earlier may partially explain these results: lack of conceptual complexity, inaccurate evaluation of legitimacy of requests and irrational beliefs are major contributors to an unfavourable perception of assertion as a style of interpersonal conflict behaviour.

Therefore, trainees need to be sensitised to the potential negative reaction to assertion by nonassertive persons. Empathic assertions provide one way to partially minimise adverse reactions, since nonassertive individuals judge such behaviour more favourably than standard assertion (Kern, 1982). Nevertheless, they still view empathic assertion as less likeable than do assertive people. Other data suggest that emitting commendatory assertions along with conflict ones (Levin and Gross, 1984) or embedding the assertion within naturalistic social conversation (Delamater and McNamara, 1984) may attenuate or avoid a negative reaction by the nonassertive individual.

Racial and Cultural Variables in the Evaluation of Conflict Assertion

The behavioural and normative differences between the interpersonal communication styles of black and white Americans have raised concerns that current assertiveness training programmes may be inappropriate for blacks (Caldwell-Colbert and Jenkins, 1982; Cheek, 1976). Though blacks and whites evidence equal knowledge of standard assertion (Lineberger and Calhoun, 1983) and perform similarly on role-play interactions (Lineberger and Beezley, 1980), differences as a function of race have been obtained in more subtle measures. Blacks make extensive use of black English vernacular when writing out assertive responses, and inter-racial assertions by both blacks and whites are more aggressive than intra-racial ones (Lineberger and Calhoun, 1983). Furthermore, ratings of several content and paralinguistic components by trained black and white judges are influenced by race of the asserter (Turner, Biedel, Hersen, *et al.,* 1984).

These data, as well as the historical discrimination against blacks in the United States, suggest that the perception of assertion may indeed be influenced by racial variables. However, initial research has not supported this possiblity. Whites perceive standard assertion by blacks and whites similarly in terms of likeability and skilfullness (Kelly, St Lawrence, Bradlyn, *et al.,* 1982). In addition, blacks evaluate standard assertion involving two blacks as more competent but less likeable than nonassertion (Keane *et al.,* 1983a), a finding consistent with the general social perception research. While these two studies suggest that concerns about the appropriateness of cross-cultural application of assertiveness training may be exaggerated, conclusions drawn from them are limited in two respects. First, the findings indicating important differences between intra- and inter-racial interactions are not taken into consideration and, second, the superior social evaluation of empathic assertion, compared to standard assertion, has not been confirmed in the context of race of the participants.

A recent study by Hrop and Rakos (1985) addressed these shortcomings by having blacks and whites evaluate standard and empathic conflict assertions involving black-black, black-white, white-black and white-white participants. White observers were influenced by race of asserter but not by race of assertee. They felt more uncomfortable with either type of assertion by a black than with comparable behaviour emitted by a white. Furthermore, they evaluated the empathic assertion more favourably than the standard assertion when the asserter was white but not when he was black. These data suggest that the elaboration statements are appropriate training goals for whites asserting to whites, but that for blacks asserting *to* whites, training might deemphasise those components in favour of awareness of, and additional strategies for decreasing, whites' discomfort with black assertiveness.

Blacks, on the other hand, were affected by both the race of asserter and assertee. They perceived empathic assertion by whites to blacks as less positive than standard assertion in the same context, but reversed their judgement for black-to-black interactions, in which elaborative verbalisations significantly enhanced the evaluation of assertion. Therefore, different training goals for assertion *to* blacks may be indicated: standard assertion for white trainees, and empathic assertion for black trainees.

Generalisations about the appropriateness of assertiveness training for different cultural and ethnic groups must be made cautiously. For example, Hrop and Rakos (1985) emphasise that their results, obtained from college blacks in the United States, may not be representative of noncollege, inner-city American blacks. It appears that as a group's sociocultural similarity to dominant North American norms and values increases, its members' assertiveness approaches that of white Americans, with whom the vast bulk of the research has been conducted (for instance, Furnham, 1979; Hall and Beil-Warner, 1978; Kipper and Jaffe, 1976; McCormick, 1982). Thus it is critical to assess sociocultural variables when training conflict assertion skills:

> . . . the concept of assertiveness is culture bound, and particularly North American. In many other cultures, asserting oneself in the way that is normative in North America and parts of Europe is neither encouraged nor tolerated. Humility, subservience, and tolerance are valued above assertiveness in many other cultures, especially for women. Furthermore, the lack of assertiveness is not necessarily a sign of inadequacy or anxiety, though in instances it may be (Furnham, 1976, p. 522).

Perhaps the best caveat regarding the appropriateness of assertion is to maintain an awareness of what it actually is: a situation–specific learned social skill that may enhance an individual's adaptation within his/her environment. It is *not* an intrinsic quality of an individual which defines psychological health or adaptation.

Teaching Conflict Assertion Skills

Though a detailed description of the training procedures is beyond the scope of this chapter, a few germane comments are offered. Training can be categorised into five basic operations (Rich and Schroeder, 1976): response acquisition strategies (instructions, overt and covert modelling, bibliotherapy), response reproduction procedures (overt and covert behavioural rehearsal), response refinement techniques (shaping, coaching, feedback, reinforcement), cognitive restructuring procedures (rational relabelling, self-instruction training, problem-solving), and response transfer strategies (homework assignments, systematic naturalistic experimentation, covert modelling and rehearsal).

While research data indicate that each of the specific interventions can produce gains in assertive behaviour, the most common approach entails a comprehensive 'treatment package' offered to individuals or groups. Galassi *et al.* (1981) provide an excellent review of this research; unfortunately it is becoming somewhat dated.

Numerous resources are available to facilitate clinical intervention. Excellent trainer manuals have been developed by Eisler and Frederiksen (1980) and Lange and Jakubowski (1976). An empirically validated self-administered audio-cassette programme, which includes didactic instruction, role-playing and written exercises, is available as an adjunct to professionally guided intervention (Rakos and Schroeder, 1980). In addition, a plethora of commercially available self-help books permit the use of adjunctive bibliotherapy; Kelly (1979) provides detailed summaries of 24 of them. Target populations of these books include women, children, job employees and employers, as well as the general public. The pace of publication of these materials has slowed in recent years, but new ones still occasionally appear (for instance, Zuker, 1983, focusing on the work environment), and it would not be surprising if the next wave of self-help assertiveness books addressed specific ethnic or cultural populations. While these manuals lack empirical data regarding their efficacy (though data are available which describe their level of readability [Heimberg, Andrasik, Blankenberg, *et al.*, 1983a]), clinical experience suggests that the utilisation of appropriate bibliotherapy material can contribute to effective and efficient intervention.

Final Comment

Assertion in conflict situations has been the focus of hundreds of research studies and dozens of books over the past 15 years. The early investigations clearly established the effectiveness of assertiveness training interventions in facilitating the acquisition and performance of the target skills, and we are now at the point where more mature, sophisticated issues are being addressed. These include the identification of assertive deficits in various clinical and nonclinical populations, the role of assertion in adaptive psychological functioning, strategies for enhancing the maintenance and generalisation of assertive skills, and the main focus of the present chapter, the identification of the overt and covert response components that comprise effective and socially acceptable performance in various environmental contexts.

The field's concern has gradually shifted, therefore, from the training of specific overt responses in laboratory situations to the assessment and evaluation of skilful, competent performance in the natural environment. The present, rather comprehensive, summary of both the early and more mature research demonstrates that a great deal is known about conflict assertion in general, yet when questions are asked about specifics — such as the individual response classes, situational variables, type of relationship involved or demographic and cultural characteristics — it is quickly realised that knowledge is still limited. Consequently, conclusions must be tentative and, as always, open to revision.

References

Alberti, R. and Emmons, M. (1978) *Your Perfect Right: A Guide to Assertive Behaviour*, 3rd edn. Impact, San Luis Obispo, California

Alden, L. and Safran, J. (1978) 'Irrational Beliefs and Nonassertive Behavior', *Cog. Ther. Res.*, 2, 357–64

———— Safran, J. and Weideman, R. (1978) 'A Comparison of Cognitive and Skills Training Strategies in the Treatment of Unassertive Clients', *Behav. Ther.*, 9, 843–6

———— and Cappe, R. (1981) 'Non-Assertiveness: Skill Deficit or Selective Self-evaluation?' *Behav. Ther.*, 12, 107–15

Argyle, M. (1981) 'The Contribution of Social Interaction Research to Social Skill Training' in J. Wine and M. Smye (eds), *Social Competence*, Academic Press, New York

Arkowitz, H. (1981) 'Assessment of Social Skills' in M. Hersen and A. Bellack (eds), *Behavioral Assessment: A Practical Handbook*, 2nd edn., Pergamon Press, New York

Baer, J. (1976) *How to Be an Assertive (not Aggressive) Woman in Life, in Love, and on the Job*, Signet, New York

Bandura, A. (1977) 'Self-efficacy: Towards a Unifying Theory of Behavior Change', *Psychol. Rev.*, 84, 191–215

———— (1978) 'The Self-system in Reciprocal Determination', *Amer. Psychol.*, 33, 344–58

Barbaree, H. and Davis, R. (1984) 'Assertive Behavior, Self-expectations and Self-evaluations in Mildly Depressed University Women', *Cog. Ther. Res.*, 8, 153–72

Barlow, D., Abel, G., Blanchard, E., Bristow, A. and Young, L. (1977) 'A Heterosocial Skills Behavior Checklist for Males', *Behav. Ther.*, 8, 229–59

Blankenberg, R. and Heimberg, R. (1984) 'Assertive Refusal, Perceived Consequences, and Reasonableness of Request', paper presented at the annual convention of the Association for Advancement of Behavior Therapy, Philadelphia

Bordewick, M. and Bornstein, P. (1980) 'Examination of Multiple Cognitive Response Dimensions Among Differentially Assertive Individuals', *Behav. Ther.*, 11, 440–8

Bourque, P. and Ladouceur, R. (1979) 'Self-report and Behavioral Measures in the Assessment of Assertive Behavior', *J. Behav. Ther. Exper. Psychiat.*, 10, 287–92

Broverman, I., Broverman, D., Clarkson, F., Rosenkrantz, P. and Vogel, S. (1970) 'Sex-role Stereotypes and Clinical Judgements of Mental Health', *J. Consult. Clin. Psychol.*, 34, 1–7

Bruch, M. (1981) 'A Task Analysis of Assertive Behavior Revisited: Replication and Extension', *Behav. Ther.*, 12, 217–30

———— Heisler, B. and Conroy, C. (1981) 'Effects of Conceptual Complexity on Assertive Behavior', *J. Counsel. Psychol. 28*, 377–85

Caldwell-Colbert, A. and Jenkins, J. (1982) 'Modification of Interpersonal Behavior' in S. Turner and R. Jones (eds), *Behavior Modification in Black Populations*, Plenum, New York

Carmody, T. (1978) 'Rational-emotive, Self-instructional and Behavioral Assertion Training: Facilitating Maintenance', *Cog. Ther. Res.*, 2, 241–53

Chambless, D., Hunter, K. and Jackson, A. (1982) 'Social Anxiety and Assertiveness: A Comparison of the Correlation in Phobic and College Student Samples', *Behav. Res. Ther.*, 20, 403–4

Cheek, D. (1976) *Assertive Black . . . Puzzled White*, Impact, San Luis Obispo, California

Chiauzzi, E. and Heimberg, R. (1983) 'The Effects of Subjects' Level of Assertiveness, Sex, and

Legitimacy of Request on Assertion-Relevant Cognitions: An Analysis by Postperformance Videotape Reconstruction', *Cog. Ther. Res.*, 7, 555–64

—— and Heimberg, R. (1986) 'Legitimacy of Request and Social Problem-Solving: A Study of Assertive and Nonassertive Subjects', *Behav. Mod..* 10, 3–18

Cianni-Surridge, M. and Horan. J. (1983) 'On the Wisdom of Assertive Job-Seeking Behavior', *J. Counsel. Psychol.*, 30, 209–14

Conger, A., Wallander, J., Mariotto, M. and Ward, D. (1980) 'Peer Judgements of Heterosexual Social Anxiety and Skill: What Do They Pay Attention to Anyhow?' *Behav. Assess.*, 2, 243–59

Conger, J. and Farrell, A. (1981) 'Behavioral Components of Heterosexual Skills', *Behav. Ther.*, 12, 41–55

Craighead, L. (1979) 'Self-instructional Training for Assertive Refusal Behavior', *Behav. Ther.*, 10, 529–42

Cummings, C., Gordon, J. and Marlatt, G. (1980) 'Relapse: Strategy of Prevention and Prediction' in W. Miller (ed.), *The Addictive Behaviors*, Pergamon Press, Oxford

Curran, J. (1979) 'Social Skills: Methodological Issues and Future Directions' in A. Bellack and M. Herson (eds), *Research and Practice in Social Skills Training*, Guildford Press, New York

Delamater, R. and McNamara, J. (1984) 'Perceptions of Assertiveness of High- and Low-Assertive Female College Students', paper presented at annual convention of Association for Advancement of Behavior Therapy, Philadelphia

D'Zurilla, T. and Nezu, A. (1982) 'Social Problem-solving in Adults' in P. Kendall (ed.), *Advances in Cognitive-Behavioral Research and Therapy (Vol. 1)*, Academic Press, New York

Eisler, R., Miller, P. and Hersen, M. (1973) 'Components of Assertive Behavior', *J. Clin. Psychol.*, 29, 295–9

—— Hersen, M., Miller, P. and Blanchard, F. (1975) 'Situational Determinants of Assertive Behavior', *J. Consult. Clin. Psychol.* 43, 333–40

—— Frederiksen, L. and Peterson, G. (1978) 'The Relationship of Cognitive Variables to the Expression of Assertiveness', *Behav. Ther.*, 9, 419–27

—— and Fredericksen, L. (1980), *Perfecting Social Skills*, Plenum, New York

Ellis, A. (1962) *Reason and Emotion in Psychotherapy*, Stuart, New York

Epstein, N., Digoivann, I. and Jayne-Lazarus, C. (1978) 'Assertion Training for Couples', *J. Behav. Ther. Exp. Psychiat.*, 9, 149–56

—— (1980) 'The Social Consequences of Assertion, Aggression, Passive Aggression, and Submission: Situational and Dispositional Determinants', *Behav. Ther.*, 11, 662–9

Fensterheim, H. and Baer, J. (1975) *Don't Say Yes When You Want to Say No: How Assertiveness Training Can Change Your Life.* David McKay, Co. Inc, New York

Fiedler, D. and Beach, L. (1978) 'On the Decision to be Assertive', *J. Consult. Clin. Psychol.*, 46, 537–46

Fischetti, M., Curran, J. and Wassberg, H. (1977) 'Sense of Timing: A Skill Deficit in Heterosexual-Socially Anxious Males', *Behav. Mod.*, 1, 179–94

—— Peterson, J., Curran, J., *et al.* (1984) 'Social Cue Discrimination Versus Motor Skill: A Missing Distinction in Social Skill Assessment', *Behav. Assess.*, 6, 27–32

Foy, D., Miller, P., Eisler, R. and O'Toole, D. (1976) 'Social-skills Training to Teach Alcoholics to Refuse Drinks Effectively', *J. Stud. Alcohol.*, 37, 1340–5

—— Massey, F., Duer, J., Ross, J. and Wotten, L. (1979) 'Social Skills Training to Improve Alcoholics' Vocational Interpersonal Competency', *J. Counsel. Psychol.*, 26, 128–32

Furnham, A. (1979) 'Assertiveness in Three Cultures: Multidimensionality and Cultural Differences', *J. Clin. Psychol.*, 35, 522–7

Galassi, J., Galassi, M. and Vedder, M. (1981) 'Perspectives on Assertion as a Social Skills Model' in J. Wine and M. Smye (eds), *Social Competence*, Guilford Press, New York

Glass, C., Gottman, J. and Schmurak, S. (1976) 'Response Acquisition and Cognitive Self-statement Modification Approaches to Dating Skills Training', *J. Counsel. Psychol.*, 23, 520–6

Goldin, J. (1957), *The Living Talmud*, Mentor, New York

Goldfried, M. and Davison, G. (1976) *Clinical Behavior Therapy*, Holt, Rinehart and Winston, New York

Gordon, S. and Waldo, M. (1984) 'The Effects of Assertive Training on Couples' Relationships', *Amer. J. Fam. Ther.*, 12, 73–7

Gormally, J. (1982) 'Evaluation of Assertiveness: Effects of Gender, Rater Involvement, and Level of Assertiveness', *Behav. Ther.*, 13, 219–25

Green, S., Burkhart, B. and Harrison, W. (1979) 'Personality Correlates of Self-Report, Role-Playing, and *In Vivo* Measures of Assertiveness', *J. Consult. Clin. Psychol., 47*, 16–24

Hall, J. and Beil-Warner, D. (1978) 'Assertiveness of Male Anglo and Mexican-American College Students', *J. Soc. Psychol. 105*, 175–8

Hamilton, F. and Maisto, S. (1979) 'Assertive Behavior and Perceived Discomfort of Alcoholics in Assertion-Required Situations', *J. Consult. Clin. Psychol., 47*, 196–7

Hammen, C., Jacobs, M., Mayol, A. and Cochran, S. (1980) 'Dysfunctional Cognitions and the Effectiveness of Skills and Cognitive Behavioral Assertion Training', *J. Consult. Clin. Psychol., 48*, 685–95

Hammond, P. and Oei, T. (1982) 'Social Skills Training and Cognitive Restructuring with Sexual Unassertiveness in Women', *J. Sex Marital Ther., 8*, 297–304

Hatzenbuehler, L. and Schroeder, H. (1982) 'Assertiveness Training with Out-patients: The Effectiveness of Skill Training and Cognitive Procedures', *Behav. Psychother., 10*, 234–52

Heimberg, R., Harrison, D., Goldberg, L., Des Marias, S. and Blue, S. (1979) 'The Relationship of Self-Report and Behavioral Assertion in an Offender Population', *J. Behav. Ther. Exper. Psychiat., 10*, 283–6

———— Andrasik, F., Blankenberg, R. and Edlund S. (1983a) 'A Readability Analysis of Commerically Available Self-help Books for Assertiveness', *Beh. Couns. Comm. Interv., 3*, 198–204

———— and Becker, R. (1981) 'Cognitive and Behavioral Models of Assertive Behavior: Review, Analysis and Integration', *Clin. Psychol. Rev., 1*, 353–73

———— Chiauzzi, E., Becker, R. and Madrazo-Peterson, R. (1983b) 'Cognitive Mediation of Assertive Behavior: An Analysis of the Self-Statement Patterns of College Students, Psychiatric Patients, and Normal Adults', *Cog. Ther. Res., 7*, 455–64

Hess, E., Bridgewater, C., Bornstein, P. and Sweeney, T. (1980) 'Situational Determinants in the Perception of Assertiveness: Gender-related Influences', *Behav. Ther., 11*, 49–58

Hollandsworth, J. (1977) 'Differentiating Assertion and Aggression: Some Behavioral Guidelines', *Behav. Ther., 9*, 640–6

———— and Cooley, M. (1978) 'Provoking Anger and Gaining Compliance with Assertive Versus Aggressive Responses', *Behav. Ther., 9*, 640–6

Horan, J. and Williams, J. (1982) 'Longitudinal Study of Assertion Training as a Drug Abuse Prevention Strategy', *Amer. Educ. Res. J., 19*, 341–51

Hrop, S. and Rakos, R. (1985) 'The Influence of Race in the Social Evaluation of Assertion in Conflict Situations', *Behav. Ther., 16*, 478–93

Hull, D. and Schroeder, H. (1979) 'Some Interpersonal Effects of Assertion, Non-assertion and Aggression', *Behav. Ther., 10*, 20–9

Joachim, P. (1981) 'Training Self-reliance and Assertiveness with Orphanage Children: A Practice Report', *Praxis der Kinderpsychol. und Kinderpsychiat., 30*, 182–5

Johnson, W., Gross, A. and Weldman, H. (1982) 'Developing Coping Skills in Adolescent Diabetics', *Corrective Soc. Psychiat. and J. Behav. Technol., Meth. and Ther., 28*, 116–20

Kahn, S. (1981) 'Issues in the Assessment and Training of Assertiveness with Women' in J. Wine and M. Smye (eds), *Social Competence*, Guilford Press, New York

Kazdin, A. (1977) 'Assessing the Clinical or Applied Importance of Behavior Change Through Social Validation', *Behav. Mod., 1*, 427–52

Keane, T., Martin, J., Berler, E., Wooten, L., Fleece, E. and Williams, J. (1982) 'Are Hypertensives Less Assertive? A Controlled Evaluation', *J. Consult. Clin. Psychol., 50*, 499–508

———— St Lawrence, J, Himadi, W., Graves, K. and Kelly, J. (1983a) 'Blacks' Perception of Assertive Behavior: An Empirical Evaluation', *Behav. Mod., 7*, 97–111

———— Wedding, D. and Kelly, J. (1983b) 'Assessing Subjective Responses to Assertive Behavior: Data from Patient Samples', *Behav. Mod., 7*, 317–30

Kelly, C. (1979) *Assertion Training: A Facilitator's Guide*. University Associates, LaJolla, California

Kelly, J., Kern, J., Kirkley, B., *et al.* (1980) 'Reactions to Assertive Versus Unassertive Behavior: Differential Effects for Males and Females and Implications for Assertiveness Training', *Behav. Ther., 11*, 670–82

———— St Lawrence, J., Bradlyn, A., Himadi, W., Graves, K. and Keane, T. (1982) 'Interpersonal Reaction to Assertive and Unassertive Styles When Handling Social Conflict Situations', *J. Behav. Ther. Exper. Psychiat., 13*, 33–40

Kern, J. (1982) 'Predicting the Impact of Assertive, Empathic-assertive, and Nonassertive Behavior: The Assertiveness of the Assertee', *Behav., Ther., 13*, 486–98

———— Cavell, T. and Beck, B. (1985) 'Predicting Differential Reactions to Males' Versus Females' Assertions, Empathic Assertions, and Nonassertions', *Behav. Ther.*, *16*, 63–75

Kidder, L., Boell, J. and Moyer, M. (1983) 'Rights Consciousness and Victimization Prevention: Personal Defense and Assertiveness Training', *J. Soc. Issues*, *39*, 153–68

Kipper, D. and Jaffe, Y. (1976) 'The College Self-Expression Scale: Israeli Data', *Psychol. Rep.*, *39*, 1301–2

Kirchner, E., Kennedy, R. and Draguns, J. (1979) 'Assertion and Aggression in Adult Offenders', *Behav. Ther.*, *10*, 452–71

Kolotkin, R., Wielkiewicz, R., Judd, B. *et al.* (1984) 'Behavioral Components of Assertion: Comparison of Univariate and Multivariate Assessment Strategies', *Behav. Assess.*, *6*, 61–78

Kuperminc, M. and Heimberg, R. (1983) 'Consequence Probability and Utility as Factors in the Decision to Behave Assertively', *Behav. Ther.*, *14*, 637–46

LaFrance, M. and Mayo, C. (1976) 'Racial Differences in Gaze Behavior During Conversations: Two Systematic Observational Studies', *J. Pers. Soc. Psychol.*, *33*, 547–52

Lange, A. and Jakubowski, P. (1976) *Responsible Assertive Behavior*, Research Press, Champaign, Illinois

Levin, R. and Gross, A. (1984) 'Reactions to Assertive Versus Nonassertive Behavior: Females in Commendatory and Refusal Situations', *Behav. Mod.*, *8*, 581–92

Lewis, P. and Gallois, C. (1984) 'Disagreements, Refusals, or Negative Feelings: Perceptions of Negatively Assertive Messages From Friends and Strangers', *Behav. Ther.*, *15*, 353–68

Lineberger, M. and Beezley, D. (1980) 'Components of Assertive Behavior: Are There Black-White Differences?' paper presented at annual meeting of the American Psychological Association, Montreal

———— and Calhoun, K. (1983) 'Assertive Behavior in Black and White American Undergraduates', *J. of Psychol.*, *113*, 139–48

Linehan, M., Goldfried., M. and Goldfried, A. (1979) 'Assertion Therapy: Skill Training or Cognitive Restructuring', *Behav. Ther.*, *10*, 371–88

MacDonald, M. (1982) 'Assertion Training for Women' in J. Curran and P. Monti (eds), *Social Skills Training*, Guilford Press, New York

Marlatt, G. and Gorden, J. (1980) 'Determinations of Relapse: Implications for the Maintenance of Behavior Change' in P. Davidson and S. Davidson (eds), *Behavioral Medicine: Changing Health Lifestyles*, Brunner/Mazel, New York

McCormick, I. (1982) 'New Zealand Student Norms for the Rathus Assertiveness Schedule', *N. Zeal. Psychol.*, *11*, 27–9

McFall, M., Winett, R., Bordewick, M. *et al.* (1982) 'Nonverbal Components in the Communication of Assertiveness', *Behav. Mod.*, *6*, 121–40

McFall, R. (1982) 'A Review and Reformulation of the Concept of Social Skills', *Beh. Assess.*, *4*, 1–33

Meichenbaum, D. (1977) *Cognitive Behavior Modification: An Integrative Approach*, Plenum, New York

———— Butler, L. and Gruson, L. (1981) 'Toward a Conceptual Model of Social Competence' in J. Wine and M. Smye (eds), *Social Competence*, Guilford Press, New York

Miller, P., Hersen, M., Eisler, R. *et al.* (1974) 'Effects of Social Stress on Operant Drinking of Alcoholics and Social Drinkers', *Behav. Res. Ther.*, *12*, 67–72

———— and Eisler, R. (1977) 'Assertive Behavior in Alcoholics: A Descriptive Analysis', *Behav. Ther.*, *8*, 222–8

Morrison, R. and Bellack, A. (1981) 'The Role of Social Perception in Social Skill', *Behav. Ther.*, *12*, 69–79

———— Bellack, A. and Manuck, S. (1985) 'Role of Social Competence in Borderline Essential Hypertension', *J. Consult. Clin. Psychol.*, *53*, 248–55

Mullinix, S. and Galassi, J. (1981) 'Deriving the Content of Social Skills Training with a Verbal Response Components Approach', *Behav. Assess.*, *3*, 55–66

Nix, J., Lohr, J. and Mosesso, L. (1984) 'The Relationship of Sex-Role Characteristics to Self-Report and Role-Play Measures of Assertiveness in Women', *Behav. Assess.*, *6*, 89–94

Peterson, J., Fischetti, M., Curran, J. *et al.* (1981) 'Sense of Timing: A Skill Deficit in Heterosocially Anxious Women', *Behav. Ther.*, *12*, 195–201

Pitcher, S. and Meikle, S. (1980) 'The Topography of Assertive Behavior in Positive and Negative Situations', *Behav. Ther.*, *11*, 532–47

Quinsey, V., Maguire, A. and Varney, G. (1983) 'Assertion and Overcontrolled Hostility Among

Mentally Disordered Murderers', *J. Cons. Clin. Psy.*, *31*, 550–6

Rakos, R. (1979) 'Content Consideration in the Distinction Between Assertive and Aggressive Behavior', *Psychol. Rep.*, *44*, 767–73

———— and Schroeder, H. (1979) 'Development and Empirical Evaluation of a Self-administered Assertiveness Training Program', *J. Consult. Clin. Psychol.*, *47*, 991–3

———— and Schroeder, H. (1980) *Self-Administered Assertiveness Training*, BMA Audio Cassettes, New York

———— and Hrop, S. (1983) 'The Influence of Positive Content and Mode of Presentation on the Social Evaluation of Assertive Behavior in Conflict Situations', *Behav. Counsel. Comm, Interv.*, *3*, 152–64

Rich, A. and Schroeder, H. (1976) 'Research Issues in Assertiveness Training', *Psychol. Bull.*, *83*, 1084–96

Rimm, D. and Masters, J. (1979) *Behavior Therapy: Techniques and Empirical Findings*, 2nd edn, Academic Press, New York

Rodriguez, R., Nietzel, M. and Berzins, J. (1980) 'Sex Role Orientation and Assertiveness Among Female College Students', *Behav. Ther.*, *11*, 353–66

Romano, J. and Bellack, A. (1980) 'Social Validation of a Component Model of Assertive Behavior', *J. Consult, Clin. Psychol.*, *48*, 478–90

Rose, Y. and Tryon, W. (1979) 'Judgements of Assertive Behavior as a Function of Speech Loudness, Latency, Content, Gestures, Inflection and Sex', *Behav. Mod.*, *3*, 112–25

Rotheram, M., Armstrong, M. and Booraem, C. (1982) 'Assertiveness Training in Fourth and Fifth Grade Children', *Amer. J. Comm. Psychol.*, *10*, 567–82

Rubin, K., Daniels-Beirness, T. and Bream, L. (1984) 'Social Isolation and Social Problem-Solving: A Longitudinal Study', *J. Consult. Clin. Psychol.*, *52*, 17–25

Rudy, T., Merluzzi, T. and Henahan, P. (1982) 'Construal of Complex Assertion Situations: A Multidimensional Analysis', *J. Consult. Clin. Psychol.*, *50*, 125–37

Salter, A. (1949) *Conditioned Reflex Therapy*, Farrar, Straus and Giroux, New York

Sanchez, B. and Lewinsohn, P. (1980) 'Assertive Behavior and Depression', *J. Consult. Clin. Psychol.*, *48*, 119–20

Schroeder, H., Driver, M. and Streufert, S. (1967) *Human Information Processing*, Holt, Rinehart and Winston, New York

Schroeder, H.E. and Rakos, R. (1983) 'The Identification and Assessment of Social Skills' in R. Ellis and D. Whittington (eds), *New Directions in Social Skill Training*, Croom Helm, London

———— Rakos, R. and Moe, J. (1983) 'The Social Perception of Assertive Behavior as a Function of Response Class and Gender', *Behav. Ther.*, *14*, 534–44

Schwartz, A. and Gottman, J. (1976) 'Toward a Task Analysis of Assertive Behavior', *J. Consult. Clin. Psychol.*, *44*, 910–20

Scott, R., Himadi, W. and Keane, T. (1983) 'A Review of Generalisation in Social Skills Training: Suggestions for Future Research' in M. Hersen, R. Eisler and P. Miller (eds), *Progress in Behavior Modification, Vol. 15*, Academic Press, New York

Smith, M. (1975) *When I Say No, I Feel Guilty*, Dial, New York

Stake, J., DeVille, C. and Pennell, C. (1983) 'The Effects of Assertiveness Training on the Performance Self-Esteem of Adolescent Girls', *J. Youth. Adol.*, *12*, 435–42

St Lawrence, J., Hansen, D., Cutts, T., *et al.* (1985) 'Situational Context: Effects on Perceptions of Assertive and Unassertive Behavior', *Behav. Ther.*, *16*, 51–62

Sundel, M. and Lobb, M. (1982) 'Reinforcement Contingencies and Role Relationships in Assertiveness Within a General Population', *Psychol. Rep.*, *51*, 1007–15

Tiegerman, S. and Kassinove, J. (1977) 'Effects of Assertive Training and Cognitive Components of Rational Therapy on Assertive Behaviors and Interpersonal Anxiety', *Psychol. Rep.*, *40*, 535–42

Trower, P. (1980) 'Situational Analysis of the Components and Processes of Behavior of Socially Skilled and Unskilled Patients', *J. Consult. Clin. Psychol.*, *48*, 327–39

———— (1982) 'Toward a Generative Model of Social Skills: A Critique and Synthesis' in J. Curran and P. Monti (eds), *Social Skills Training: A Practical Handbook for Assessment and Treatment*, Guilford Press, New York

Turner, S., Beidel, D., Hersen, M. *et al.* (1984) 'Effects of Race on Ratings of Social Skill', *J. Consult. Clin. Psychol.*, *52*, 474–5

Twentyman, C., Pharr, D. and Conner, J. (1980) 'A Comparison of Three Covert Assertion Training Procedures', *J. Clin. Psychol.*, *16*, 520–5

————, Greenwald, D., Greenwald, M. *et al.* (1982) 'An Assessment of Skill Deficits in Alcoholics', *J. Behav. Assess., 4*, 317–26

Waksman, S. (1984a) 'Assertion Training with Adolescents', *Adolescence, 19*, 121–30

———— (1984b) 'A Controlled Evaluation of Assertion Training with Adolescents', *Adolescence, 19*, 277–82

Williams, J., Hadden, K. and Marcavage, E. (1983) 'Experimental Study of Assertion Training as a Drug Prevention Strategy for Use with College Students', *J. College Stud. Pers., 24*, 201–6

Winship, B. and Kelly, J. (1976) 'A Verbal Response Model of Assertiveness', *J. Counsel. Psychol., 23*, 215–20

Wolf, M. (1978) 'Social Validity: The Case for Subjective Measurement or How Applied Behavior Analysis is Finding Its Heart', *J. Appl. Behav. Anal., 11*, 203–14

Wolfe, J. and Fodor, I. (1977) 'Modifying Assertive Behavior in Women: A Comparison of Three Approaches', *Behav Ther., 8*, 567–74

Wolpe, J. (1969) *The Practice of Behavior Therapy*, Pergamon, Oxford

Woolfolk, R. and Dever, S. (1979) 'Perceptions of Assertion: An Empirical Analysis', *Behav. Ther., 10*, 404–11

Zuker, E. (1983) *Mastering Assertiveness Skills*, American Management Associations, New York

18 SHOWING WARMTH AND EMPATHY

Jerry Authier

How does one define warmth and empathy? The terms seem so general and perhaps even vague that the definition of these concepts is at the very least extremely difficult. At the same time the concepts go hand-in-hand and thus it is difficult to define one without some consideration being given to the other. Warmth has to be present if one is to convey compassionate understanding to another person and, conversely, some level of empathy needs to be present if one is to feel genuine warmth towards another. However, a key difference between warmth and empathy is the 'fact versus feeling' distinction. Warmth can be manifested towards another person even while solely considering the facts of their problematic situation, whereas empathy involves being attuned to the feeling component of the person's problematic situation. These terms are now defined more specifically.

Sometimes it is easier to define something by talking about what it is not. Warmth is not being exceptionally positive toward someone. Warmth is not being friendly, congenial, amiable or other adjectives that are used to describe 'a nice person'. That is, even though the layman may consider some of these descriptions as accurate descriptions of a person who is a warm person, warmth is far more. Rogers (1961) discussed warmth in terms of an 'attitude of deep respect and full acceptance for the client as he is' (p. 74). Rogers goes on to comment that 'warmth' is an attitude of acceptance that sufficiently conveys 'the most profound type of liking or affection for the core of the person' (Rogers, 1961, p. 65). Carkhuff (1969) talks about the highest level of respect as being an ability for the interviewer to 'care deeply or fully accept the client'. Behaviourally warmth is what McKay, Davis and Fanning (1983) might call 'total listening', or what Ivey (1971) might call 'effective attending'. Specifically as the present author defines it, warmth is basically a valuing of the other person and a communication of that attitude both verbally and nonverbally such that a genuine interest in him/her as a person and his/her problem has been conveyed.

Empathy involves more than demonstrating a genuine interest in the person and his/her problems. Specifically, empathy is defined as 'being attuned to the way another person is feeling and conveying that understanding in a language he/she can understand'. In layman's terms it is literally being able to put yourself in the other person's shoes so that you genuinely feel the way they are feeling with regard to their particular situation or problem. Empathy then is not sympathy for a person's plight. It is not premature reassurance or consolation with regard to a person's dilemma. It is not Roger's (1957) early definition of being 'as if you were in the other person's shoes'; it is, then, being in the other person's shoes. Roger's (1975) in his most recent definition of empathy probably conveys this experiential aspect of being empathetic better than anyone. Drawing on the concept of 'experiencing' as formulated by Gendlin (1962), Rogers has recently defined empathy as:

> The way of being with another person which is termed empathetic has several facets. It means entering the private perceptual world of the other and becoming thoroughly at home in it. It involves being sensitive moment to moment to the changing felt meanings which flow in this other person, to the fear or rage or tenderness or confusion or whatever that he/she is experiencing. It means temporarily living in his/her life moving about in it delicately without making judgments, sensing meanings which he/she is scarcely aware, but not trying to uncover feeling of which the person it totally unaware, since this would be too threatening. It includes communicating your sensing of his/her world as you look from fresh and unfrightened eyes at elements of which the individual is fearful. It means frequently checking with him/her as to the accuracy of your sensing and being guided by the responses you receive. You are a confident companion to the other person in his/her inner world. By pointing to the possible meanings in the flow of his/her experiencing you help the person to focus on this useful type of reference, to experience the meanings more fully, and to move forward in the experiencing. To be with another in this way means that for the time being you lay aside the views and values you hold for yourself in order to enter another's world without prejudice. In some sense you lay aside yourself and this can only be done by a person who is secure enough in himself that he knows he will not get lost in what may turn out to be the strange or bizarre world of the other, and can comfortably return to his own world when he wishes (p. 4)

Although for the most part, this author is in agreement with Rogers' (1975) definition of empathy, he does take exception to his point 'sensing meanings which he/she is scarely aware, but not trying to uncover feeling of which the person is totally unaware, since this would be too threatening'. The author has found through his clinical experiences that the uncovering of feelings of which the person is unaware, although possibly threatening to that individual, is perhaps the most powerful way of demonstrating empathic understanding.

One final point regarding the definition of empathy should be made. Recently, there have been attempts to view empathy as a multistage interpersonal process. Barrett-Lennard (1962), for example, theorises that empathy involves an empathy cycle consisting of three types of empathy: (1) empathic resonation (in which the empathiser responds emotionally to the other); (2) expressed empathy (the communicative act); and (3) received empathy (how the client responds).

Gladstein (1977), on the other hand, discusses cognitive empathy defined as intellectually taking the role or perspective of the other person, and affective empathy defined as responding with the same emotion to another person's emotion. Gladstein has proposed empathy as a multistage interpersonal process that can involve emotional contagion, identification and role-taking. Although all of these concepts may be useful in terms of further clarifying additional features of empathy, this chapter deals largely with the communicative act of the Barrett-Lennard (1962) empathy cycle. Moreover, it will be seen in later discussion that how one communicates empathic understanding involves essentially both Gladstein's cognitive and affective empathy.

Research

At the risk of covering old ground, it seems important at this juncture to discuss briefly the importance of someone conveying warmth and empathy during the helping process. Numerous earlier studies (for instance, Dickenson and Truax, 1966; Carkhuff and Truax, 1965; Rogers, Gendlin, Kiesler, *et al.*, 1967; and Truax, 1963) have presented evidence that accurate empathy and nonpossessive warmth are related to constructive change in patients. Furthermore, evidence has accumulated demonstrating that therapists low in these characteristics actually have detrimental effect on their clients. Moreover, Fiedler (1950, 1951) in two now classic studies found that a therapist's manifestation of the 'ideal therapeutic relationship' was based on his/her level of expertise rather than his/her theoretical orientation. Examination of the eight major factors comprising an 'ideal therapeutic relationship' which are presented below, makes it clear that warmth and empathy are central components of such a relationship:

1. The therapist is able to participate completely in the patient's communication;
2. The therapist's comments are always right in line with what the patient is trying to convey;
3. The therapist is well able to understand the patient's feelings;
4. The therapist really tries to understand the patient's feelings;
5. The therapist always follows the patient's line of thought;
6. The therapist's tone of voice conveys the complete ability to share the patient's feelings;
7. The therapist sees the patient as a co-worker on a common problem;
8. The therapist treats the patient as an equal.

These classic studies, then, along with those studies cited earlier clearly show the manifestion of high levels of warmth and empathy is crucial to providing effective therapy regardless of a therapist's theoretical orientation, the context of the therapy or the type of patient. As such, it appears that the evidence warrants the following conclusions:

1. Manifestations of empathy early in the relationship predicts therapeutic success (Barrett-Lennard, 1962; Tausch 1973);
2. The more experienced the therapist, the more likely he is to be empathic

(Fiedler, 1950, 1951; Mullen and Abeles, 1972);

3. Therapists who are integrated within themselves possess high degrees of empathy (Bergin and Jasper, 1969; Bergin and Solomon, 1970);

4. Therapists offer empathy definitively more than even helpful friends (Van der Vien, 1970);

5. Therapist level of offered empathy is correlated with self-exploration and process movement (Bergin and Strupp, 1972; Kurtz and Grummon, 1972; Tausch, Bastine, Friese, *et al.,* 1970);

6. Clients perceive therapists to possess more empathy in successful cases (Cartwright and Lerner, 1966; Van Der Vien, 1970);

7. Empathy in the therapeutic relationship is clearly related to positive outcome (for example, Aspy and Roebuck, 1975; Barrett-Lennard, 1962; Rogers *et al.,* 1967; and Truax, 1966).

It seems important to caution the reader about misinterpreting the above conclusions. These conclusions need to be tempered with consideration of the purpose and stage of the counselling relationship, the client preference for closeness within that relationship, particularly in light of cultural and ethnic considerations and, finally, the particular problem or issue being discussed. That is, counsellor manifestation of empathy is not a panacea nor is it something that should be offered universally; indeed, as will be seen later, there needs to be an ebb and flow between the manifestation of warmth and empathy such that effective communication is always enhanced. In fact, as has been alluded to, some studies have demonstrated that too much empathy may sometimes have an inhibitory effect on communication. In conclusion, although empathy can be helpful in some stages of the counselling process with most clients for certain goals, it is really the skill of the clinician that allows him/her to respond with the appropriate degree of empathy.

Specific Skill for Showing Warmth

Thus far, warmth has been described in such a way that the reader may still question how one goes about conveying warmth to his or her patient. Warmth as defined by Authier and Gustafson (1973) consists of three major dimensions: (1) communicating a willingness to listen; (2) communicating respect for the individuals worth, integrity and abilities; and (3) communicating an interest in facilitating the client in telling his or her own story.

Communicating a willingness to listen is conveyed largely through the microcounselling attending behaviours (Ivey, 1971; Ivey and Authier, 1978), particularly the non-verbal behaviours of eye contact, posture and gesturing. Additionally, if seating distance is such that it does not infringe on the patient's personal space, and if one rotates towards one's client and leans forward, these behaviours sometimes communicate an even greater willingness to listen on the part of the helper. Of course, these behaviours need to be individualised depending on the cultural, or ethnic background of the client and/or the topic or particular situation being discussed.

Communicating respect for the individual's worth, abilities and integrity can be accomplished in several ways. Using the person's name often puts him on the level of being a person in distress rather than a patient or client. Moreover, positive statements about the client's abilities can demonstrate a helper's appreciation for the person's assets. It is, of course, crucial to avoid stereotyped gestures and responses, and to use nonevaluative and nonabsolute language. Finally, by leaving the choice of which option the client implements to solve his or her problem to the client, a therapist demonstrates a respect for the integrity of the client of 'knowing' what, in the long run, is best and most suitable for him/her and his/her circumstances.

Communicating interest in facilitating the client telling his or her own story, in essence, involves many of the verbal skills that have been defined as attending behaviours as outlined by Ivey (1971) and Ivey and Authier (1978). Specifically, the microcounselling verbal skills of open invitation to talk, single questions, minimal encourages to talk and paraphrases; all are helpful facilitative skills that allow the client to tell his/her own story. Also, if these skills are accompanied by some of the nonverbal components that communicate that the therapist is willing to listen to the patient or client, then facilitation of the client's telling his or her own story is more likely to occur. It is especially important to avoid interrupting the client and that voice tone and facial expression convey a genuine interest in what the client is saying.

On the surface, it may seem that these behaviours are fairly straightforward and easily conveyed, and in many respects they are; however, often even the very effective interviewer does not include the total package of these behaviours when interacting with a client. Yet it is the contention of this author that optimal 'warmth' is demonstrated *only* when *all* of these behaviours are manifested by the interviewer. This is not to say that one cannot demonstrate warmth to his/her patient by mainfesting only some of these behaviours but rather to underscore the necessity of incorporating all of the behaviours into one's interviewing style if one is to convey optimal warmth toward his/her client. This notion is confirmed to some extent by McKay *et al.* (1983) who outlined six components of 'total listening'. These components which are very similar to the authors are as follows:

1. Maintaining good eye contact;
2. Leaning slightly forward;
3. Reinforcing the speaker by nodding or paraphrasing;
4. By clarifying and asking questions;
5. By actively moving away from distractions;
6. By being committed even if you are angry or upset to understanding what was said.

Although some of the verbal skills of showing warmth have been adequately explained in previous chapters, it seems important to define these skills as they are defined through the microcounselling paradigm. The definitions to follow, although perhaps overlapping with Chapters 4, 6 and 10, are designed to define the four key verbal skills that convey warmth such that counsellors utilising these skills will be able to establish a warm relationship with his/her client in the manner defined by this author.

An open invitation to talk is one of the main verbal behaviours allowing an interviewer to 'show warmth' to his/her client. This skill, which was developed by Phillips, Lockhart and Moreland (1969b), is specifically concerned with helping clients to talk and explore their thoughts and feelings through inviting them to talk openly via the open question. It is sometimes best to compare this skill with its respective opposite, that is, the closed question. An open question, as depicted by the example below, allows the client to answer in a way that he/she feels most comfortable, whereas a closed question essentially asks for a yes/no answer or a specific piece of factual information (see Chapter 4 for further information):

Open: How satisfied are you with your marital relationship?
Closed: Are you satisfied with your marital relationship?

It may be observed that the open question provides room for the client to express his/her view of marital satisfaction without the imposed view of the interviewer. An open comment allows the client an opportunity to explore himself with the support of the interviewer. A closed question, on the other hand, often emphasises factual content, sometimes implying a lack of interest in what the client has to say, and frequently attacks or puts the client in his place.

Crucial to the giving of open-ended questions is the concept of who is to lead the interview. While the interviewer does ask questions while using this skill, the questions are centred around concerns of the client rather than around concerns of the interviewer. A typical problem with closed questions is that the interviewer leads the client to topics of interest to the interviewer only. Too often an interviewer projects his/her own theoretical orientation onto the information he/she is trying to gather, thereby imposing an artificial structuring too early. If the interviewer relies on closed questions to structure his/her interview, he/she usually is forced to concentrate so hard on thinking up the next question that he/she fails to listen and attend to the client.

In summary, open invitations to talk are extremely useful in a number of different situations. For example:

1. They help begin an interview.
(a) What would you like to talk about today? How have things been since the last time we talked together? And so on;
2. They help to get the interviewee to elaborate on a point.
(a) Could you tell me more about that? How did you feel when that happened?
3. They help elicit examples of specific behaviour so that the interviewer is

better able to understand what the interviewee is describing.

(a) Will you give me a specific example? What do you do when you get 'depressed'? What do you mean when you say that your father is out of his mind?

4. They help focus the client's attention on his/her feelings.

(a) What are you feeling as you're telling me this? How did you feel then?

In addition to asking open questions it is important to ask single questions. When two or more questions are asked the second or one of the later questions is almost always a closed question. The tendency to ask several questions seems to be in response to one's own uncertainty about the other person's response. If he/she does not respond immediately or looks a little unclear, your response may be to try to clarify your question. The result, however, is often a multiple choice question and almost always involves a narrowing of the range of responses open to interviewees. If the other person is unclear about your question he/she will usually say so or it will be apparent from the answer. You can then ask a different open question. To avoid asking more than one question requires your trusting that either you asked the first question clearly and the delay in responding reflects some difficulty on the part of the client or that, even if you asked a poor or unclear question, you will have a chance to clarify it after giving the other person a chance to respond.

Minimal encourages to talk is a skill concerned with helping the client to keep talking once he/she has started. This skill, which was initially developed by Phillips, Lockhart and Moreland (1969a), is designed to help keep the client going. Examples of minimal encourages to talk include simple 'umms-hmms', repetition of one or two words from what the client has just said, one word questions, head nods and a variety of body postures and gestures. By using such minimal encourages, the interviewer is showing interest and involvement but at the same time is allowing the client to determine the primary direction of the interview. Minimal encourages also can serve to reinforce client behaviour and demonstrate the helper's interest and caring for the client.

As Philips *et al.* (1969a) stress, 'the successful useage of this technique presupposes that the interviewer has tuned into what the client is discussing.' As such, the minimal encourages help the client express him or herself more clearly and provide an avenue whereby the counsellor or interviewer can express an interest in the client as well as assist him/her in continued self-exploration. Minimal encourages to talk should follow directly from what the interviewee has just said. When used correctly, the interviewee, although maintaining control of the interview in that he is talking about what he wants to discuss, is forced to elaborate, explain and to take a more in-depth look at his/her problem. Often, the interviewer will want and need to talk more, and to direct or focus more actively the content of what the client is saying. However, this is an extremely useful technique whether it is used as an adjunct to other techniques or relied on primarily by itself. A few examples of the skills are listed below:

1. Oh? So? Then? And?;
2. The repetition of one or two key words;
3. Boy! Gee! Wow!;
4. How did you feel about that?
5. Yes, tell me more, go on,
6. What?
7. Umm-hmm.

Paraphrasing is another of the verbal skills by which the interviewer can convey warmth. This skill was initially developed by Ivey, Moreland, Phillips, *et al.* (1969) and was designed as a means to clarify confusing verbal content by highlighting issues which are being discussed by the client. In this vein the paraphrase serves three important functions: (1) to convey to the client that the interviewer is with him and/or trying to understand what he/she is saying; (2) to crystallise the client's comments by repeating what he/she has said in a more concise manner; (3) to check the interviewer's own perceptions to be sure that he/she really does understand what the client is describing (see also Chapter 6).

Utilisation of this technique then allows the interviewer to feed back to the client the essence of what the client has just said. In this manner the skill is extremely functional in clarifying confusing content, tying a number of recent comments together, highlighting issues by stating them more concisely and/or checking one's perceptions. Some examples of paraphrasing are presented below:

Helpee:	I don't know about him. One moment he's nice as can be, and the next he is a real bastard.
Helper:	He's pretty inconsistent then.
Helpee:	Every day there is something new to do. There must be ten different activities going on at one time around here.
Helper:	So there are lots of activities for you to choose from.
Helpee:	He is supposed to be an authority, yet he's mixed up all the time. He talks as if everything he says is true, but he's quite uncertain a lot of the time.
Helper:	You feel that if a man gives you the impression that he knows everything, then he should know everything.

Hopefully, this section has helped to clarify how a counsellor can develop a 'warm' relationship with a client by a willingness to listen and by valuing them as people. Moreover, utilisation of the verbal and nonverbal skills defined above allows a counsellor to facilitate the client's exploration of his/her problem. It has been emphasised that the better an interviewer can incorporate these behaviours into his/her interviewing style, the better he/she will be able to convey warmth.

Specific Skills for Showing Empathy

As has been alluded to, a person's ability to convey 'warmth' is the first step toward conveying an empathic understanding of the patient's situation or problem. That is, effective dynamic helping demands more than listening. Carkhuff (1969) talks about 'additive dimensions' of helping. In a similar vein, Egan (1975) discusses interviewing skills which help the helper to convey 'advanced accurate empathy'. Likewise, Ivey and Authier (1978) discuss the skills of interpersonal influence as 'additive dimensions'. These authors go on to outline a 'one, two, three pattern' which is described as a systematic format for creating an interactional relationship between the counsellor and client. This pattern, presented below, is a way for a counsellor to prevent the use of an influencing skill from being disruptive:

1. The helper must attend accurately and empathetically to the helpee and communicate this attention by the attending skills. Successful attending can result in Carkhuff's (1969) level 3 helping, Egan's (1975) primary empathy or the basic empathy described by Rogers (1975). Occasionally effective attending can lead to even higher levels of communication;

2. The helper then may, as appropriate, share him or herself via the influencing skills of directions, self-disclosure or interpretation. This additional dimension permits a higher level of empathy to develop involving not only the client's world but also the helper's world;

3. The helper then 'checks out the accuracy or reasonableness of attending or influencing skills' (for instance, 'How does that sound to you?'), thus allowing a mutual 'I–You' or 'I–Thou' exploration. Further, the tentativeness in the check-out allows for mutual growth (Ivey and Gluckstern, 1976).

It can be seen then, that empathy, while relying heavily on warmth for its foundation, involves more than being 'warm'. The author, based primarily upon his work with his close associate Gustafson (Authier and Gustafson, 1973), views empathy to be composed of two major dimensions: (1) a feeling-versus-fact dimension; and (2) a distance dimension. Drawing heavily from the literature in terms of theoretical descriptions and research-derived relationships, specific behaviours have been identified which are thought to be the behavioural components of empathy. These behavioural components of empathy are emphasised in the outline below:

1. Nonverbal behaviour — built on a basis of respect nonverbals but differ in intensity, congruence of vocal tone and pace and volume:
(a) Eye contact — longer;
(b) Seating distance — closer;
(c) Lean forward — more including possibly touching;
(d) Facial expression of more than interest;

(e) Degree of body tension communicating more involvement;
(f) Gestures towards self.

2. Verbal behaviour — the focus of comments and questions is on the *feeling content* rather than the event or fact content of the person's verbalisations:
(a) Reflecting the *current* feeling, particularly those expressed nonverbally and using words or expressions that actually express the intensity of the feeling;
(b) Make a statement rather than ask a question using tentative language;
(c) Confrontation;
(d) Self-disclosure.

At this juncture it seems important to clarify the feeling versus event or fact distinction which, as alluded to previously, is one major difference between being warm and being empathic. As noted from the outline, the primary focus of the interviewer is on the feelings of the client. Once helpers begin to focus on feelings, they will find themselves, almost of necessity, using many of the nonverbal skills of warmth in a more intense fashion. As such, the eye contact may be more intense though certainly not a stare, the seating distance may be closer and there may be more of a forward lean even to the point of touching the client. Two additional behaviours which help the counsellor to convey empathy are facial expression and tone of voice. Now, the helper appears genuinely concerned rather than merely interested and this is often conveyed by the facial expression and the tone of voice of the helper.

At this point it appears important to make clear that there is not a 'prescribed way' to convey high levels of empathy because this will vary with the style of each helper. However, generally speaking, the more intensely one manifests the underlying behaviours of warmth as one becomes attuned to feelings of the clients and attempts to convey this understanding in a manner that the client can understand, the greater the likelihood that the client will experience the helper as empathic. Additionally, the four major verbal skills depicted in the above outline (that is, reflection of feeling, making a question into a statement, confrontation of verbal and nonverbal inconsistencies in behaviour and self-disclosure) can help the counsellor to convey even higher levels of empathy. However, before turning to the specific verbal skills of empathy, the distance dimension requires further elaboration.

Distance can be considered literally in terms of physical space, time, abstractness, intensity or personal involvement. The importance of this dimension in each of these aspects will be emphasised in varying degree with each of the verbal behaviours of empathy to be discussed below. However, to clarify this dimension, consider that the topic of anger has in some way been raised by the client. In some ways the decision to focus on the feeling itself is a way of reducing the distance by demonstrating to the client that the counsellor is willing to discuss his/her anger openly and directly. In terms of abstractness, the counsellor can talk about anger as an emotion, man's anger, anger in the patient's family or specifically about the anger that the patient has just expressed. In terms of time, the counsellor can talk about angry feelings expressed as a child, the anger the patient had yesterday or his/her angry feeling right now.

In terms of intensity, the counsellor can focus on slight feelings of anger, such as annoyance, or intense anger such as rage. Moreover, while discussing the anger that the patient is feeling at that moment, if the counsellor has an appropriate seating distance, posturing, eye contact, facial expression and tone of voice, then all these behaviours enhance the use of the verbal skill, thus allowing the counsellor to be more empathic. As shall be seen, sometimes even the specific choice of which verbal skill to use has a way of reducing the distance. That is, the reflection of feeling or question into statement skill, although still empathic verbal skills do not allow one to decrease the emotional distance between the helper and the helpee as much as do either the confrontation or the self-disclosure skill. In general, decreasing the distance in any of these respects will tend to increase the counsellor's level of empathy. Therefore, the highest empathic response would reflect a decreased distance on several dimensions. That is, an extremely high empathic response would likely involve a close interpersonal distance, the exploration in the first person of the client's most personal and immediate feelings and reactions, while at the same time being attuned to his/her mood. Finally, an empathic response such as this will also help the client to realise and clarify aspects of the feeling in a nonthreatening manner even though it may help him/her to become aware of feelings that were actually out of his/her awareness.

Reflection of feeling involves reflecting the feeling the counsellor hears the client expressing. By using reflection of feeling, the interviewer conveys to the interviewee that he is trying to understand just how the client feels, thus reinforcing the client's free expression of feelings. The more quickly a client comes to see the interviewer as a person with whom it is safe to open up to, the sooner the client is able to utilise the interviewer's support to begin exploration of feelings regarding the problem. Reflection of feeling also serves as a good perception check in that, by reflecting feelings, the interviewer gets feedback on the accuracy of his/her perceptions. Concurrently, the interviewer is often able to crystallise more sharply, for the client, the client's own feelings, thus enabling him/her to deal more effectively with whatever feeling might be present. In general, the interviewer can determine if he/she is using this technique successfully by whether or not the client begins to express more feelings and to recognise the feelings he/she does express. The following are some examples of good reflections of feeling:

Helpee: I couldn't think of anything to say when he said that he liked my hair. (Blushes.)

Helper: You must have felt pretty happy, but also perhaps a little embarrassed.

Helpee: I'm so out of it; I can hardly operate. I can't do anything because the feeling is always there.

Helper: Like there is a terrible burden that you are carrying around.
Helpee: I could hardly believe it. That was probably one of the most wonderful things that ever happened to me.
Helper: You sound really ecstatic.
Helpee: After that I suggested that we all go out for some beer and pizza, but they all kept playing cards. (Low affect, sudden slouch in posture, etc.)
Helper: I sense that you are pretty disappointed and maybe even a little angry that no one responded to your suggestion.

At the risk of being redundant, it seems important to underscore the distance dimension as reflected by the four examples of the reflection of feeling skill. Note in the first example, although the focus is on the patient's feelings, they are 'then and there' feelings. Still there is an attempt to reduce the distance while focusing on whether or not there may be another feeling present other than the happiness that the patient expressed. In the second example, although not explicit, there is at least an implied focus on immediate feelings in the use of the feeling word that is a bit different than the patient is actually discussing. In the third example the helper homes in on the immediate 'here and now' feelings and is attempting to label the feeling as accurately as he/she possibly can. Finally, in the fourth example, the helper reduces the distance by using a personal pronoun, his/her own perception of the 'here and now' feelings that the client is experiencing. This last example is technically both a reflection of feeling and a question into statement since, as alluded to, the counsellor is taking the risk of adding his/her interpretation with regard to the client's feelings. To further clarify question into statement skill and how it can serve to reduce the distance, attention is now given to that particular skill.

Questions into statements also help the patient to explore his/her feelings. Often a client who is asked one question after another tends to feel as if he/she is being interrogated. Even if the questions are asked in a pleasant and nonthreatening manner, the impression that a series of questions can give is that one has some specific idea which one is unwilling to state openly, but is collecting evidence to support. The client's responses can be either to become quite guarded and give very little information or to try to give the answer which he/she thinks is being fished for. In either case, the danger is that the client's attention is taken from his/her concern by his/her trying to guess what the counsellor is getting at. Another possibility is that the client might try to defend against whatever he/she fears you may be tricking or forcing him/her to say. One way of preventing this from happening is for the counsellor to make some of the questions into a statement. Moreover, making a question into a statement has a way of reducing the 'distance' between the helper and helpee in several respects. A helper's statements of his/her opinion of what is being discussed shows the helper is listening. Such a statement can also help to strengthen the relationship in the sense that the helper is taking a greater risk. That is, by giving his/her opinion the helper is 'owning' his/her perception or impression of what is being discussed and in doing so risks being wrong, or in laymen's terms, 'putting his foot in his mouth'. The helpee's recognition of the helper taking a greater risk may then foster and/or reinforce the helpee taking greater risks in the relationship, possibly including opening up more.

The easiest way to make questions into statements is by the use of such phrases as 'it sounds like', 'it appears like', 'it looks like', 'I hear you saying', 'it's my impression'. These kind of tentative phrases also show the helpee that the counsellor is attempting to, or working at, understanding what he/she is saying. Thus, the main concept here really revolves around the counsellor giving his impression or opinions of what the client is saying. Since questions arise from the counsellor's impression or perception, the task is not as difficult as may be thought. However, since most counsellors are used to asking questions rather than giving opinions, it does call for an active effort on the counsellor's part. It might help for the counsellor to consider what he was about to ask, and then merely change the wording so that it comes out in the form of a statement rather than in the form of a question.

Some examples are listed below. Note that all the examples deal with the content of the helpee's statement. This does not mean that the question-into-statement skill cannot deal with feelings. In fact, making a question into a statement with regard to the helpee's feeling may be the most useful form of making a question into a statement. However, as has already been demonstrated through a previous example, technically, the counsellor is using both the reflection of feeling and the question-into-statement skill. The counsellor has already learned the former skill; consequently, the emphasis here will be on making questions into statements with regard to the content of the helpee's statement.

Helpee: Things at work are in a mess because I can't get along with my boss or my fellow employees.
Helper question: Aren't things going well at work?
Helper question into a statement: It appears as if things aren't going very well at work.
Helpee: I just couldn't get to sleep last night because of this headache I had.
Helper question: Do you usually have difficulty sleeping because of your headaches?
Helper question into a statement: It's my impression that your headaches must be fairly severe to cause you to have difficulty getting to sleep.
Helpee: I just can't seem to make up my mind about anything anymore.
Helper question: What do you suppose makes it so hard for you to make decisions?
Helper question into a statement: It sounds to me like you've been having trouble making decisions lately.
Helpee: My husband and I have more or less been going our separate ways for several months now.

Helper question: Why don't you and your husband get along?
Helper question into a statment: It seems to me that you and your husband may not be getting along very well since you've both opted to kind of go your separate ways.

As has been outlined earlier, confrontation consists of opening up for consideration contradictions or discrepancies in the client's behaviour by commenting on them. These comments differ from paraphrases and reflections of feeling in that the contrast is drawn from an external frame of reference (that is, the counsellor's) rather than the client's own statements and frame of reference. The purpose of the confrontation skill is to help the person break through defences which he/she has put up to avoid consideration of a conflictual area and to promote honest communication. Conflict-laden areas are usually important to approach but they are also very delicate in that they are often the areas with which the person is most afraid of dealing. Most often the person is not totally unaware of additional or conflicting feelings but is either unaware that he/she is sending conflicting signals or does not have the vocabulary and/or permission to explore those feelings effectively.

Effective use of the confrontation skill adds a note of 'reality' to the conflicts, since inconsistent messages are signs or signals suggesting the existence of these conflictual feelings. Perhaps most importantly, sometimes directly but often by implication, the counsellor sends a nurturing 'accepting, nonjudgemental' (that is, 'warm') message of permission that it would be understandable and all right if the person were to be feeling these conflicting emotions. This simultaneous conveyance of intense warmth and empathy allows the person to consider potentially very threatening material without feeling overwhelmed with fear. Obviously, the usefulness of pointing out contradictory behaviours depends primarily on how the comment is given. If the confrontation is felt as an attack, the result can be increased defensiveness and a weakening of the relationship. If the confrontation is successful then the result can be the exploration of formerly blocked areas and a building of the relationship by demonstrating that: (1) the counsellor is tuned in; (2) honest communication is valued; and (3) the counsellor cares, or else would not risk undermining the relationship.

It is important to remember that helpful confrontations are not always aimed at weaknesses and deficits and, in fact, can often be used to draw attention to strengths and assets. Timing and the nonjudgemental manner in which they are given are important factors in the client's being able to use the information conveyed. The use of this skill presupposes some level of trust in the interview relationship which has been built through the use of other skills. The counsellor's tone of voice, the way he introduces the confrontation, his posture and facial expression as well as other nonverbal cues are major factors in the client's acceptance of the confrontation, possibly because of reducing the emotional distance.

Two types of confrontation that allow a focus on feeling, particularly immediate feelings occurring during the helping interactive process, are those that focus on contradictions between the content of the client's statement (what he/she says) and his/her affect (the way he/she says it), and those that focus on inconsistencies with what he/she reports feeling in a particular situation and the way one would expect to react or feel in the same situation. An example of each of these two types of confrontation is presented below:

1. Verbal–nonverbal inconsistency:
   Helper: 'How are you today?'
   Helpee: 'Oh (sighs) things are just fine.' (Slow speech, slumped posture.)
   Helper: 'You're saying your fine but you look and sound kind of down.'
2. Personal frame of reference inconsistency:
   Helpee: 'It was really a nice thing that Jeanie married him after all.' (Smiling)
   Helper: 'I'm a little puzzled by your smile. If my fiancée married another man, I think I would be quite upset.'

Self-disclosure as this author defines it, refers to an interpersonal helping skill which, when used appropriately like the use of reflection of feeling, can serve to reinforce the true expression of feelings. Similarly, self-disclosure can serve to reinforce the expression of content areas that the client may not otherwise feel free to express. These assertions become clear when one realises that self-disclosure consists of more than the therapist merely relating his problem areas or feelings to the client. On the contrary, self-disclosure will not be effective unless the therapist is able to directly relate his/her personal experience to the client's current concerns. By using self-disclosure in this manner, the therapist is able to convey to the client that he/she can *really* appreciate what the client might be experiencing, or in layman's terms, the therapist is able to put him/herself in the client's shoes. Such a message can serve to facilitate the client's own self-exploration of his/her feeling by giving the person another view of a similar concern, by decreasing his/her feeling of isolation and uniqueness and by increasing his/her trust in the helper through a demonstrated interest and trust in the counsellor. (See Chapter 9 for a full discussion of self-disclosure.)

Three components are necessary for a therapist's use of self-disclosure to be effective: first, use of a personal pronoun; second, use of a personal experience and/or feeling that may have been connected with the experience; and, third, bringing back to the client the way the therapist thinks the client may have been affected by the experience. A caution concerning the latter point is for the therapist to be certain that he/she does not discount the client's feelings or prescribe how he/she thinks the client should be feeling. In conjunction with the above, the tone of voice, facial expression, posture and other nonverbal behaviours are crucial in conveying a genuine attempt to understand and encourage the client to express his/her feelings and what's really on his/her mind.

The most powerful type of self-disclosure is a 'here and now' self-disclosure because it both focuses on the client's feelings as well as reduces the distance in the relationship. This type of self-disclosure is one which allows the counsellor to tell the patient the impact that his/her behaviour is having on the counsellor at that moment. This is in opposition to a 'then and there' self-disclosure which relates to a past feeling that may have been similar to a patient's current concern. The 'then and there' self-disclosure can even take the form of past experiences that the counsellor has observed others to have rather than the counsellor's own personal experiences. The 'here and now' versus the 'then and there' self-disclosures relates then to the distancing effect discussed earlier. It takes a fairly sensitive counsellor to be able to 'feel' the impact of the client so deeply that he/she is able to convey this feeling and concern in the interview situation as a 'here and now' experience. For example, if a person is talking of his/her fears of allowing themself to get really close to someone, a 'then and there' self-disclosure might be one which would relate his/her feelings of reluctance or fears about getting too close that the counsellor may have felt in the past. A 'here and now' self-disclosure on the other hand, would be one in which the counsellor would discuss his own fears and concerns regarding getting too close in the helping relationship with that person, and the perception that the patient him/herself may be having difficulty allowing him/herself to get close as well.

It is readily apparent that the use of the self-disclosure skill needs to be genuine and not smack of insincerity or lack of concern as these feelings will discourage rather than encourage free expression of feelings. The key to sounding sincere is for the therapist to use experiences that are *real* for him/her.

The following are examples of self-disclosures which assume realness for the therapist and consequently are said in a genuine, sincere and concerned manner, manifested by an appropriate tone of voice, facial expression, posture and other nonverbal behaviours. The examples are broken into 'then and there' and 'here and now' self-disclosures as a means of trying to further clarify the distance dimension:

1. 'Then and there' self-disclosures:
   Helpee: (Crying) 'I'm so upset since my girlfriend left me.'
   Helper: 'I can appreciate what you must be feeling. Many of my patients have experienced a loss through the breakup of a relationship and they're usually quite depressed because of grieving about the loss. I'm wondering if that's how it is for you?'
   Helpee: (Crying) 'I'm so upset since my girlfriend left me.'
   Helper: 'I can appreciate what you must be experiencing. A few years ago my girlfriend left me and I really felt lonely and sad. I'm wondering if those are some of the feelings you are having?'
2. 'Here and now' self-disclosure:
   Helpee: 'When I want to make a point with my boss yet can't seem to get it across, it makes me totally frustrated just adding to the problems between us.'
   Helper: 'I think I understand what you feel. I sometimes become quite

frustrated when I am unable to make my point. However, I usually also find myself getting kind of angry too. I wonder if you have any of those kinds of feeling?'

Helpee: 'When I want to make a point with my boss yet can't seem to get it across it makes me totally frustrated just adding to the problems between us.'

Helper: 'I can appreciate some of how you feel. I sense that there are times when you get frustrated because you aren't able to make the point with me and at those times you feel that it adds to a problem in our communication. However, I must admit that sometimes I've even been frustrated with myself because I've felt I haven't made my point with regard to you. At those times I've found myself kind of getting angry at myself and perhaps a little angry with you because it doesn't sound like you're getting the point. I wonder if you've had similar feelings toward me?'

Hopefully, the descriptions and examples of the various verbal skills of empathy have served to clarify how appropriate use of these skills can help to convey empathic understanding on the part of the counsellor. Moreover, it should be readily apparent that use of the skills in such a way that there is a feeling focus and a reduction of the distance between the counsellor and his/her client allows for manifestation of even higher levels of empathy. Indeed, use of the verbal skills of empathy in this manner often reduce the distance thereby allowing the interviewer to explore feelings of which the client is unaware in a nonthreatening manner. Use of the skills in this way contributes to the author's notion that effective empathy often involves helping the patient to become aware of feelings that he/she may be defending him/herself against. Thus, contrary to Rogers (1975), empathy can involve exploring feelings of which the client is unaware.

Showing Empathy With Emotionally Distressed Patients

Although it is hoped that the reader now understands how to go about conveying warmth and/or empathy to his/her patients, it still may not be clear as to when it is appropriate to convey only warmth and when it is appropriate to convey more empathy. That is, with what patient, with what underlying personality structure, with what underlying problem, in what kind of situation is warmth enough? Or put another way, when does a certain patient, with a certain underlying personality structure and a certain problem require more than warmth thus warranting empathy? If it is not already clear, the fact-versus-feeling distinction can help to answer this question. At least as a general rule of thumb, warmth is enough if a person is dealing with a problem that is not causing him/her an undue amount of emotional distress. Thus, people with fairly routine problems who are merely seeking advice, such as someone seeking help from a guidance interviewer, someone visiting a physician with a routine medical problem, someone who is looking at ways to enhance his/her marriage or someone sorting through how he/she can best handle a job-related problem, may require the counsellor to only manifest warmth. Of course, it is readily apparent that if a person seeking help in any of these areas is emotionally distressed by the problem then that requires an empathic helper. Another rule of thumb with regard to the level of empathy that a counsellor would need to convey is that, generally, the more distraught the person seeking help, the higher the level of empathy needing to be conveyed by the helper. However, as indicated in a previous section, *too* much empathy either in terms of the level conveyed or the length of time that it is conveyed can sometimes be inhibitory with regard to client progress. Still other factors that need to be taken into account, in addition to the intensity of the emotional distress of the patient, are the actual purpose or goals of counselling, the stage of the counselling, the personality of the patient and the patient preference with regard to the relationship he/she wants to form with his/her counsellor.

Perhaps the best way to elucidate among situations calling for warmth, a moderate amount of empathy, or a high level of empathy, would be to take a certain problem and follow it through when the patient is displaying very little, a moderate amount, or a good deal, of emotional distress. For example, imagine three patients whose personalities are essentially within normal limits, who prefer a close emotional relationship between themselves and their physicians and who are seeking out patient evaluation for chest pain:

1. Problem A: Patient presents to the physician complaining in a matter-of-fact manner that he has noticed chest pain from time to time for the past week or so and he thought that 'just to be on the safe side' he would come in for a check-up. The doctor's facial expression conveys interest in the presenting problem and he maintains good eye contact while rotating toward the patient with the proper seating distance. He gathers the medical history by using open questions, minimal encourages to talk and paraphrases.

Patient: 'Doctor, I've been having chest pain for the past week or so and although it hasn't been very severe nor do I have any history of heart problem, nor is there any history of heart problems in my family, I thought just to be on the safe side I would come in and let you check it over.'

Physician: 'So you have been bothered with chest pain for about a week and thought it would be a good idea to get it checked out.' (Paraphrase.)

Patient: 'Yes'

Physician: 'How does your chest feel when you're having the pain? (Open invitation to talk.)

Patient: 'It's kind of a sharp jabbing pain that only lasts a few seconds.'

Physician: 'What seems to bring the pain on?' (Open invitation to talk.)

Patient: 'I haven't really been able to notice any specific thing that brings it on but the first time that I experienced it was after I'd been digging in my garden and it's been bothering me ever since.'

Physician: 'How unusual is it for you to do that kind of work?' (Open invitation to talk.)

Patient: 'Well, it's really quite unusual because I'm an accountant and typically don't do physical labour.'

Physician: 'It sounds as if you may have strained some muscles in your chest when doing that physical labour, but just to be on the safe side let's get an EKG to make certain that we aren't missing anything. How does that sound to you?' (Question into statement followed by open invitation to talk.)

Patient: 'Yes, I think I would like that. I think I would feel better knowing that there isn't any evidence of heart difficulty.'

2. Problem B: Patient presenting for chest pain for outpatient evaluation manifesting some anxiety about the chest pain he has been having for the past week or so.

Patient: 'Doctor, I thought I'd better come in and see you because I've been worried about some pains that I have been having in my chest.'

Physician: 'What kind of pains have you been having?' (Open invitation to talk.)

Patient: 'Dull pains that sort of feel like somebody is standing on my chest and sometimes I even feel some numbness in my left arm.'

Physician: 'What do you think might be causing this chest pain.' (Open invitation to talk.)

Patient: 'I'm afraid I might be having a heart attack.'

Physician: 'So you're frightened that the chest pain could actually be a heart attack.' (Reflection of feeling.)

Patient: 'Yes.'

Physician: 'You seem quite worried about this.' (Reflection of feeling.)

Patient: 'Yes, I am because my grandfather died of a heart attack and I'm afraid that I may have inherited his "bad heart".'

Physician: 'Many of my patients with chest pains are justifiably worried about it because after all if the chest pain is related to their heart it can be fairly serious.' (Then-and-there self-disclosure.)

Patient: 'Yes, I know that's why I thought I'd better come in and get it checked out.'

Physician: 'Yes let's do that. Let's go ahead and get an EKG to see what's going on and based on that result if need be even get a stress test. How does that sound to you?' (Open invitiation to talk.)

3. Problem C: Patient presents to emergency room at 9 o'clock in the evening because of being frightened by experiencing sudden outset of chest pains while out working in his garden.

Physician: 'I see from the nurse's notes that you've been having chest pain.' (Paraphrase of nurse's note.)

Patient: 'Yes, doctor. It just came on all of a sudden while I was out working in my garden.' (With a worried facial expression and a somewhat tremulous voice.)

Physician: 'You look really worried. What do you think it might be?' (Reflection of feeling followed by open invitation to talk.)

Patient: 'I'm afraid it might be a heart attack because my father died of a heart

attack when he was about my age.'
Physician: 'I don't blame you for being afraid. I think I'd be pretty frightened if I had chest pain knowing that my father died of a heart attack. Is that how you're feeling?' (Here-and-now self-disclosure.)
Patient: 'Yes, I'm very frightened.'

Although the above example regards an emotionally distressed medical patient, varying degrees of empathy would appropriately be conveyed with a vocational guidance client, psychiatric patient or practically anyone who is experiencing emotional distress. Likewise, although the patient is anxious, it is appropriate to be empathic with many types of emotional distress (for instance, anger, hurt, resentment, grief, depression, elation) that a person may be experiencing. Again the key, in terms of the amount of empathy that would be appropriate to be displayed, would be based on the amount of emotional distress the patient would be manifesting. At the risk of overstating the point, consider three patients who are experiencing various degrees of depression because of marital problems:

1. Problem A: A woman who has been married for ten years presents to a mental health professional with the following complaint.
Patient: 'My husband and I have been discussing our marriage and both of us agree that it is not as satisfying as it once was. Thus I made the appointment to get some ideas from you as to whether or not there might be something we could do to enhance our marriage.'
Doctor: 'What are some of the aspects of the marriage that don't seem as satisfying anymore.' (Open invitation to talk.)
Patient: 'Well, it just kind of seems like we go our separate ways and thus don't spend much time together.'
Doctor: 'Sounds like you're thinking if you could spend a little more time together that that might be a first step towards improving your marriage.' (Question into statement.)
Patient: 'Yes, I think that would be a big help.'
Doctor: 'What else have you noticed as a problem in the marriage?' (Open invitation to talk.)
Patient: 'Well, obviously since we don't see each other very much we don't communicate as much as we once did.'
Doctor: 'So your communication is not as good as it once was either.' (Paraphrase.)
Doctor: 'It's my impression that you're thinking that if you and your husband could find a way of spending more time together and during that time learn to communicate more effectively, that would be a couple of steps toward helping your marriage.' (Question into statement.)
Patient: 'Yes, I think it really would help.'
Doctor: 'What other areas have you noticed as possible problem areas in the marriage?' (Open invitation to talk.)
Patient: 'None doctor; we still get along in terms of us not arguing. Of course,

if we don't talk much I guess we can't argue.'

Doctor: 'How about your sexual relationship?' (Open invitation to talk.)

Patient: 'Although it is not as frequent as when we were first married, it's still very satisfying at least from my perspective but that might be something you might want to ask my husband about when I bring him in the next time.'

2. Problem B: Woman presenting for help with her marriage of ten years duration with a moderate amount of distress, manifested by a worried facial expression, her tone of voice and posturing, and the content of some of her verbalisations.

Patient: 'Doctor, I'm at my wits' end.'

Doctor: 'You seem very upset. What's wrong?' (Reflection of feeling followed by open invitation to talk.)

Patient: 'My husband and I just aren't getting along anymore.'

Doctor: 'That sounds like that would be really distressful. What seems to be the problem?' (Reflection of feeling followed by open invitation to talk.)

Patient: 'We've been married for ten years now and it just seems like in the last few years we never do anything together.' (Becomes tearful.)

Doctor: 'You seem very sad about the problem you are having in your marriage.' (Reflection of feeling.)

Patient: 'Yes, I am because I'm afraid we might get a divorce and I don't want to.'

Doctor: 'Afraid?' (Minimal encourager to talk — repetition of key feeling word.)

Patient: 'Yes. I'm afraid because we had a big argument last night and he threatened to leave me.'

Doctor: 'I don't blame you for being frightened and sad, I think if my spouse threatened to divorce me I'd feel frightened and sad too, however, I also think I would feel quite rejected and hurt. I wonder if you are having any of those feelings?' (Here-and-now self-disclosure.)

Patient: 'Yes, I love him very much and I never dreamed that he would actually want to divorce me.'

3. Problem C: Patient presenting with marital problem in a psychiatric outpatient unit seeing the doctor of the day at midnight. Patient is tearful, tremulous with a bruise and cut around her right eye and is sobbing as she walks into the doctor's office.

Doctor: 'You seem terribly, terribly, upset; what is going on?'

Patient: 'Doctor, my husband and I just had a big argument and he actually got so mad that he hit me and he's never done that before.'

Doctor: 'It sounds like he hurt you a good deal not only emotionally, but also physically.' (Reflection of feeling.)

Patient: 'Yes, doctor. I just cannot believe that he would do something like that.'

Doctor: 'I think if my husband would physically abuse me for the first time after ten years of marriage that I would really feel totally stunned. I wonder if that's how you're feeling?' (Here-and-now, self-disclosure.)

Patient: 'Oh yes, doctor, that's exactly how I am feeling, I feel like I just can't trust him anymore after doing something like this to me.'

Doctor: 'Yes, it sounds like you're feeling as if he's betrayed your trust in him.'

(Reflection of feeling.)

Patient: 'I just don't know how he could ever do such an awful thing.' (Angry tone of voice with clinched fists.)

Doctor: 'Although I think I can appreciate how you're feeling, I guess for me I would even feel some anger toward my spouse if I were in your shoes. I wonder if you are having any of those feelings?' (Here-and-now self-disclosure.)

Patient: 'No, doctor. I am not angry! I'm hurt and betrayed but I don't think I'm angry.'

Doctor: 'You say you're not angry but your tone of voice and clenched fists suggests that you might be.' (Verbal–nonverbal inconsistency confrontation.)

Patient: 'Yes, I guess I am. I just can't believe he could do such an awful thing.'

Although the above examples can in no way take into account *all* the variables that enter into whether or not conveying warmth or empathy is appropriate, it is hoped that they do make the point that the intensity of the emotional distress can be used as a rule of thumb, particularly in that initial contact with someone coming to the counsellor for help. Obviously, if one is getting into a later stage of counselling, particularly the action or termination stage, then less empathy might be warranted even in some of the situations as depicted above. Likewise, if the underlying personality of the client is such that being empathic may only serve to help the patient become more dependent upon the counsellor or foster his/her playing a 'poor me' game, then being empathic might not be appropriate. Moreover, if the client's preference is for only a neutral relationship with the counsellor, then again it may be inappropriate for the counsellor to convey empathic understanding. Note also that sometimes the particular setting plays a role in whether or not conveying warmth and/or empathy is warranted. That is, although certainly not always true, if one is presenting for help at an odd time of the day in a hospital or in an emergency room, then it may be more appropriate to display empathy with patients in these settings than if they are coming into the counsellor's office for a scheduled appointment.

It seems important to highlight how the focus in the above examples changes from being factual and content-oriented when a doctor conveys only warmth, to being feeling-focused when the doctor conveys empathy. As such, the open question is focused on feelings and the minimal encouragement to talk involves repetition of a key feeling word expressed by the patient. Additionally, the paraphrase changes to the reflection-of-feeling skill or the question-into-statement skill, two of the verbal behaviours of empathy. Moreover, it should be noted that both the self-disclosure and confrontation skills are included in some of the higher level empathy situations, thus in essence allowing the doctor to convey higher levels of empathy through these verbal behaviours. More subtle differences can also be seen, particularly as it pertains to the use of self-disclosure and the distance dimension discussed earlier. That is, note how the doctor's use of a personal pronoun and a 'here and now' self-disclosure rather than a 'then and there' self-disclosure allows him to convey a higher level of empathy by 'being with' the patient.

By way of summary, showing warmth involves essentially communicating a willingness to listen, communicating a respect for the individual's worth, integrity and abilities and facilitating the patient to tell his/her own story. Communicating a willingness to listen is accomplished essentially through nonverbal behaviours, including good eye contact, appropriate seating distance, a relaxed posture with appropriate gesturing, a facial expression of interest and a neutral tone of voice. Facilitating the patient to tell his/her own story is largely accomplished through the use of minimal encourages to talk, open questions and paraphrases. Finally, communicating respect for the individual's worth, integrity and abilities is accomplished largely through the use of the person's name, avoidance of interruptions, avoidance of judgemental statements or stereotype behaviours and leaving the options to the client.

Being able to show empathy, in addition to being warm, involves a focus upon the feelings that the patient is experiencing and being able to convey this understanding in a language that is commensurate with his/her cultural and educational background. Conveyance of empathy involves a more intense use of the nonverbal behaviours of warmth, plus the use of the minimal encourages to talk and open invitations to talk with a feeling emphasis. Additionally, reflections of feeling, questions into statements, confrontations and self-disclosure are four verbal behaviours that allow one to communicate even higher levels of empathic understanding to one's patient. Finally, empathy is further enhanced if these particular skills can be used in a nondistancing manner such that the communication is focused on 'here and now' feelings. The here and now confrontation and/or self-disclosure are particularly helpful in this regard, especially if it helps the counsellor to get the patient to become aware of underlying feelings that he or she may be denying or repressing.

Again, it is important to realise that there needs to be an ebb and flow of the conveyance of warmth and empathy depending on the purpose or goal of the encounter, the level of emotional distress being experienced by the patient, the underlying personality of the patient, along with whether or not they prefer their helper to be emotionally close or emotionally neutral and the stage of the counselling process itself. This ebb and flow of being warm and/or empathic is what the 'art of helping' is comprised. Hopefully, this chapter will serve to enhance the reader's understanding of warmth and empathy as well as provide skills to integrate into the therapeutic process, helping the reader to practise the 'art' of showing warmth and empathy.

References

Aspy, D. and Roebuck, F. (1975) 'From Humane Ideas to Humane Technology and Back Again, Many Times', *Education, 95*,3

Authier, J. and Gustafson, K. (1973) *Enriching Intimacy: A Behavioral Approach,* unpublished training manual, University of Nebraska Medical Center, Omaha

Barrett-Lennard, G.T. (1962) 'Dimensions of Therapist Response as Causal Factors in Therapeutic Change', *Psychological Monographs, 76,* 43, whole no. 562

Bergin, A.E. and Jasper, L.G. (1969) 'Correlates of Empathy in Psychotherapy: A Replication', *Journal of Abnormal Psychology, 74,* 477–81
—— and Soloman, S. (1970) 'Personality and Performance Correlates of Empathic Understanding in Psychotherapy' in J.T. Hart and T.M. Tomlinson (eds), *New Directions in Client-centered Therapy,* Houghton Mifflin, Boston
—— and Strupp, H.H. (1972) *Changing Frontiers in the Science of Psychotherapy,* Aldine-Atherton, Chicago
Carkhuff, R. and Truax, C. (1965) 'Training in Counselling and Psychotherapy: An Evaluation of an Integrated Didactic and Experiential Approach', *Journal of Consulting Psychology, 29,* 333–6
—— (1969) 'The Counselor's Contribution to Facilitative Process', mimeographed manuscript, Buffalo, State University of New York, 1968. Cited in R. Carkhuff *Helping and Human Relations,* Holt, Rhinehart and Winston, New York
Cartwright, R.D. and Lerner, B. (1966) 'Empathy, Need to Change, and Improvement in Psychotherapy' in G.E. Stollak, B.G. Guerney, Jr and M. Rothberg (eds), *Psychotherapy Research: Selected Readings,* Rand McNally, Chicago
Dickenson, W. and Truax, C. (1966) 'Group Counseling with College Underachievers: Comparisons With a Control Group and Relationship to Empathy, Warmth, and Genuineness', *Personnel Guidance Journal.*
Egan, G. (1975) *The Skilled Helper,* Brooks-Cole, Monterey
Fiedler, F. (1950) 'The Concept of an Ideal Relationship', *Journal of Consulting Psychology, 14,* 239–45
—— (1951) 'Factor Analyses of Psychoanalytic, Nondirective and Adlerian Therapeutic Relationships', *Journal of Consulting Psychology, 15,* 32–8
Gendlin, E.T. (1962) *Experiencing and the Creation of Meaning,* The Free Press of Glencoe, New York
Gladstein, G.A. (1977), 'Empathy and Counseling Outcome: An Empirical and Conceptual Review', *Counseling Psychologist, 6,* 70–9
Ivey, A., Moreland, J., Phillips, J., *et al.* (1969) *Paraphrasing,* unpublished manual, University of Massachusetts, Amherst
—— (1971) *Microcounseling: Innovations in Interviewing Training,* C.C. Thomas, Springfield
—— and Gluckstern, N. (1976) *Basic Influencing Skills: Leader and Participant Manuals,* Microtraining, North Amherst
—— and Authier, J. (1978) *Microcounseling: Innovation in Interviewing, Counseling, Psychotherapy, and Psychoeducation,* 2nd edn, Charles C. Thomas, Springfield
Kurtz, R.R. and Grummon, D.L. (1972) 'Different Approaches to the Measurement of Therapist Empathy and Their Relationship to Therapy Outcomes', *Journal of Consulting and Clinical Psychology, 39,* 106–15
McKay, M., Davis, M., and Fanning, P. (1983) *Messenger: The Communication Book,* New Horbinge Publications, Oakland
Mullen, J. and Abeles, N. (1972) 'Relationship of Liking, Empathy and Therapist's Experience to Outcome of Therapy', *Psychotherapy,* an Aldine Annual, Aldine-Atherton, Chicago
Phillips, J., Lockhart, J. and Moreland, J. (1969a) *Minimal Encourages to Talk,* unpublished manual, University of Massachusetts, Amherst
—— (1969b) *Open Invitation to Talk,* unpublished manual, University of Massachusetts, Amherst
Rogers, C.R. (1957) 'The Necessary and Sufficient Conditions of Therapeutic Personality Change', *Journal of Consulting Psychology, 21,* 95–103
—— (1961) *On Becoming a Person,* Houghton Mifflin, Boston
—— Gendlin, E.T., Kiesler, D.J., *et al.* (eds) (1967) *The Therapeutic Relationship and Its Impact. A study of psychotherapy with schizophrenics.* Madison, University of Wisconsin Press.
—— (1975) 'Empathic: An Unappreciated Way of Being', *Counseling Psychologist, 5,* 2–10
Tausch, R., Bastine, R., Friese, H. *et al.* (1970) 'Variablen und Ergebnisse bei Psychotherapie nit Alternieranden Psychotherapeuten', *Verlag fur Psychologie, 23,* Gottengen
—— (1973) *Personal Communication*
Truax, C.B. (1963) 'Effective Ingredients in Psychotherapy: An Approach to Unraveling the Patient-therapist Interaction', *Journal of Counseling Psychology, 10,* 256–63
—— (1966) 'Therapist Empathy, Warmth and Genuineness and Patient Change in Group Psychotherapy: A Comparison between Interaction Unit Measures, Time Sample Measures and Patient Perception Measures', *Journal of Clinical Psychology, 22,* 225–9
Van Der Vien, F. (1970) 'Client Perception of Therapist Conditions as a Factor in Psychotherapy', in J.T. Hart and T.M. Tomlinson (eds), *New Directions in Client-centred Therapy,* Houghton Mifflin, Boston

Part 5:
CONCLUSION

19 CONCLUSION

Owen Hargie

This book has incorporated a detailed analysis of a wide range of communication skills. While the focus throughout has been upon interactions between professionals and clients, it is obvious that many of the elements of communication focused upon also have direct applicability to everyday 'social' encounters. Thus, for example, while a knowledge of the skills involved in being assertive is important for most professionals in their work, such skills are also important in more general encounters. In this sense it is hoped the context of this text should be both interesting and very useful for the reader.

At the very least, the material contained herein provides a comprehensive language with which to analyse and evaluate interpersonal interaction. Without the necessary linguistic terminology to guide one's cognitive processes, one is unable to conceptualise and deal effectively with complex problems. Since social interaction is undoubtedly a complex process, it is essential to have a language with which to describe, analyse and attempt to understand this process. Thus, the reader should now be familiar with a wide glossary of interactional terms, pertaining to verbal and nonverbal communication in group and dyadic contexts, which can be employed when observing, describing and evaluating interpersonal communication.

An increased knowledge of the nature of communication should, hopefully, be followed by an increase in social competence. This competence encompasses both an ability to perceive and interpret accurately the cues being emitted by others, and a capacity to behave skilfully in response to others. Therefore, it is vital that the information contained in this book be *used* by the reader, who should be prepared to experiment with various social techniques until the most effective response repertoire is developed in any particular situation. It is anticipated that such experimentation will, for many professionals, occur in the context of a skills training programme. For this reason, it is useful to examine briefly the rationale for the skills approach to training, and some of the criticisms which have been levelled at this approach.

Training in Social Skills

As discussed in the Introduction to this book, many professionals now undergo some form of specialised social skills training as a preparation for practical experience. The most widely utilised method of training for professionals is the microtraining approach, which can be traced back to the development of microteaching in teacher education. Microteaching was first introduced at Stanford University, California, in 1963, when a number of educationists there decided that existing techniques for training teachers 'how to teach' needed to be revised. In recognising the many complexities involved in classroom teaching, the Stanford team felt that any attempt to train teachers should take place in a simplified situation (Allen and Ryan, 1969). Attention was turned to the methods of training used in other fields, where complicated skills were taught by being 'broken down' into simpler skill areas, and training often occurred in a simulated situation, rather than in the real environment.

Thus, actors have always had rehearsals prior to the presentation of a play, when various scenes are practised in isolation until judged to be satisfactory. The tennis player in training concentrates on specific aspects such as the serve, smash, lob, volley and backhand in order to improve his overall game. Similarly, the learner driver learns to use the various controls separately before taking the car on the road. The rationale in all of these instances is to analyse the overall complex act in terms of smaller component parts, train the individual to identify and utilise the parts separately and then combine the parts until the complete act is assimilated.

At Stanford this approach was applied to the training of teachers in a programme of training which comprised learning a number of teaching skills in a scaled-down teaching encounter termed microteaching. In microteaching, the trainee taught a small group of pupils (five to ten) for a short period of time (five to ten minutes) during which time the focus was on one particular skill of teaching, such as using questions. This 'microlesson', which took place in college, was video-recorded and the trainee then received feedback on the effectiveness of the questions used, in the form of a video replay coupled with tutorial guidance. This procedure was repeated for a number of teaching skills, and was designed to prepare students more systematically for actual classroom teaching practice.

Research in microteaching found this to be an effective method for training teachers (Hargie and Maidment, 1979). As a result, this training method was adapted by trainers in other fields to meet their own particular training requirements. All of these programmes now fall under the umbrella term of *microtraining,* wherein the core skills involved in professional interaction are identified and trainees are provided with an opportunity to acquire these skills in a safe training environment.

Hargie and Saunders (1983) have identified three distinct phases in microtraining, namely, preparation, training and evaluation. At the preparation stage, the skills necessary for effective professional communication are identified. Although most of the skills presented in this book will be relevant to all professions, there will be important differences in focus and emphasis. For example, a classroom teacher will use a great deal of overt verbal reinforcement during lessons, whereas a counsellor will usually rely more heavily on nonverbal reinforcers. Thus, the application of skills to contexts is an important task during preparation. The second phase is the actual training, during which time trainees will learn to identify and label the skills, will be given an opportunity to practise them, and will receive feedback on their performance. This phase therefore involves lectures, seminars and the use of video models, followed by simulated practicals with accompanying feedback from tutor, peers and, usually, close-circuit television (CCTV). The final element of microtraining is the evaluation of the programme in terms of changes in the performance of trainees and their ability to interact successfully in the professional situation. Although a large amount of formal evaluation has been conducted in this field, most trainers will evaluate their programmes informally, in terms of feedback from trainees, other tutors and fieldwork supervisors. Such information can then be used to guide future microtraining approaches.

This microtraining paradigm is clearly based on a 'reductionist' strategy for the study of social interaction. As was discussed in Chapters 1 and 2, this strategy for the study of social skill evolved from the study of motor skill where a similar approach had proved to be successful. Thus, it is argued, just as a motor sequence, such as driving a car or operating a machine, can be broken down into its component actions, so too can a social sequence, such as interviewing or teaching, be broken down into its component skills.

Criticisms of the Skills Approach

This reductionist approach to the study of interpersonal communication has met with some opposition from adherents of other theoretical perspectives. The opposition falls into two main areas. First, it is argued that the analysis of communication in terms of social skills simply does not make sense, since the study of such component skills is totally different from the study of the whole communication. Second, there is the viewpoint that by analysing social interaction in terms of skilled behaviour, the spontaneity and genuineness of human interaction will be lost. It is useful to examine each of these criticisms separately.

The Whole and the Parts

Advocates of Gestalt psychology would reject the notion that it is meaningful to isolate small segments of an overall sequence, and study these in isolation from the whole. Gestalt psychology (the psychology of form) originated in Germany in the early twentieth century, and emphasised the concept of structure. A central tenet of Gestaltism is that the whole is greater than the sum of the parts. Once an overall structure is broken down into smaller units, it is argued, the original meaning or form is changed accordingly. Thus, the study of each of the units in isolation is not equivalent to the study of the whole. For example, a triangle comprises three intersecting straight lines, yet the study of each of the lines in isolation is patently different from the study of the overall triangle.

Within Gestalt literature, however, there is confusion as to the nature of the relationship of component elements to the whole from which they are derived. Murphy and Kovach (1972) illustrate how, on the one hand, some Gestaltists argue that the component parts need to be studied in terms of their inter-relationships in order to understand the whole structure. On the other hand, however, there is the view that there are no component parts with separate attributes, and that structures can only be studied meaningfully as total entities. Taking this latter, more extreme interpretation, social interaction could be likened to a beautiful piece of pottery. The beauty and meaning of the pottery lie in its wholeness, and if the piece of pottery is smashed into smaller parts this beauty and meaning is lost forever. It does not make sense to study each of the smaller parts separately in order to understand the whole, and even if the parts are carefully put back together again, the original beauty is lost.

But is social interaction broken down in this sense, in microtraining? Proponents of microtraining would argue that the answer to this question is 'no'. Rather, social interaction is analysed in terms of clearly identifiable behaviours which are, at the same time, inter-related. Although emphasis is placed on one particular skill sequence of behaviours at a time during training, other skills will be present. Thus, for example, while the focus may be on the skill of questioning during microtraining, it is recognised that other skills will be operative when the skill of questioning is being used. No one skill is used in total isolation from other skills, and in this sense the 'parts' of social interaction differ from the 'parts' of a broken piece of pottery.

Obviously, each of the social skills studied can only exist in a social context. Social interaction, by definition, can never occur in a vacuum and this is recognised within the social skills model which underpins the 'micro' approach to the analysis of interpersonal interaction (see Chapter 2 for a discussion of this model). In practice, the microtraining method can be described as one of *homing in and honing up,* where one aspect of social interaction is focused upon at a time and trainees are encouraged to develop and refine their use of this particular aspect. Once the trainee has acquired a working knowledge of a number of skills of social interaction, the ultimate goal is to encourage the appropriate use of these skills in an integrated fashion.

It is also emphasised within the social skills model that the overall process of social interaction is affected by a large number of both situational and personal factors which may be operative at any given moment (see Chapter 2). The study of social skills *per se* is undertaken in order to provide some insight into this overall process of communication. It is recognised that not only should these elements be studied separately, but that consideration should also be given to the inter-relationship between elements. This line of thought is consistent with the view of those Gestaltists who hold that the study of parts should be undertaken in terms of their inter-relationships, in order to understand the overall structure.

Artificiality

Another objection which has been raised in opposition to microtraining, is that by teaching social skills to people, eventually social interaction will lose its natural beauty and become artificial and stilted. Everyone will become so aware of their own actions, and the actions and reactions of others, that this knowledge will inhibit their natural behaviour. In the final analysis, people will all end up behaving in the same fashion and individuality will be lost forever. This line of argument raises several important issues concerning the skills approach to training in communication.

Inevitably, in the teaching of social skills, those undergoing instruction will become aware of the nature, and function, of social behaviour — indeed, the development of such awareness is one of the main objectives of microtraining programmes. As a result of such awareness, social actions will become more conscious and seem artificial. This also occurs during the learning of motor skills. For example, when one is learning to drive a car, one is conscious of all of the motor skills necessary to perform the act, namely turning the ignition key, depressing clutch, engaging first gear, releasing clutch and depressing accelerator. When one is completely conscious of all of these motor skills the overall act becomes less fluent — thus the learner driver experiences the 'kangaroo petrol syndrome'! With practice and experience, however, the motor skills involved in driving a car become less conscious, and eventually the individual will perform the actions automatically. It is at this stage that the person is said to be skilled.

A similar phenomenon occurs in microtraining. Once the individual receives instruction in the use of a particular skill, the cognitive processes involved in the performing of this skill become conscious. At this stage, a 'training dip' may occur, where the awareness of the skill actually interferes with its implementation and social performance suffers accordingly. With practise and experience, however, the use of social skills will again become spontaneous, and the individual will lose any self-consciousness which may have affected him initially. This is a well-known phenomenon which occurs with trainees undergoing programmes of microtraining. Training dips are also encountered in the learning of motor skills. Thus, someone being coached in tennis may find that having to focus on, and practise separately, the serve, lob, smash or volley actually interferes with the overall performance. It is only when the tennis player has a chance to 'put it all together' that performance begins to improve.

During social interaction the individual may, at times, become aware of the effects of his behaviour, but for most of the time he will act at a subconscious level. It may be that it will be only when social interaction becomes strained that he will become aware of his actions. At such times prior training in social skills should bear fruit, with the individual being able to reflect quickly on the likely consequences of certain courses of possible actions, in relation to the reactions of the other person, or persons, involved. For example, if A finds that B is not very forthcoming, he may consciously decide to ask B an open question, pause and smile encouragingly in an attempt to persuade B to participate. Such conscious translations will usually be fairly rare, however, and the individual will interact without always having to think consciously about what he is doing.

The initial emphasis in microtraining has been on identifying social behaviours, and grouping these behaviours into social skills in order to facilitate the training process. In this respect, microtraining has been successful and, as illustrated in this book, advances have been made into the identification and classification of a large number of social skills in terms of their behavioural determinants. Once the behaviours have been mastered by the trainee, then the categorisation, by the individual, of these behaviours into more global skill areas seems to facilitate their utilisation during social interaction. As Hargie (1980) points out, such larger skill concepts can be assimilated more readily into the cognitive processes employed by the individual during social interaction. These skill concepts are used to guide the responses of the individual in that they provide various strategies for the individual to employ in the course of any interaction sequence (that is, ask *questions* to get information; provide *rewards* in order to encourage participation; be *assertive* to ensure that one's rights are respected; introduce *humour* to make the interaction more enjoyable). Once these skill concepts have been fully assimilated, behaviour will become smoother, and the individual will employ the concepts subconsciously. In other words, the person becomes more socially skilled.

As mentioned earlier, the study of social skills provides the individual with a language for interpreting social interaction. This is of vital import, since without such a language it would be extremely difficult to analyse or evaluate one's social behaviour. By studying social interaction in terms of social skills it is possible to discuss the nuances of social interaction with others, and give and receive feedback on social performance. It is also possible to reflect back on previous interactions in which one has been involved, and conceptualise these in terms of the appropriateness of the social skills employed, and how these could be developed or refined in any future encounters. Indeed, this process of self-analysis is one of the most important long-term benefits which accrue from training in social skills.

The argument that providing professionals with the opportunity to engage in social skills training will result in them all behaving in exactly the same way, can also be countered. This is analogous to arguing that by teaching everyone to talk, we will all eventually end up saying exactly the same things! Just as the latter state of affairs has not prevailed, there is absolutely no reason to believe that the former state of affairs would either. Individual differences will always influence the ways in which people behave socially. One's personality, home background, attitudes, values and so on will invariably affect one's goals in any given situation, and this will in turn affect how one behaves accordingly. Different professionals will develop different styles of behaviour in different contexts, and this is a desirable state of affairs. There is no evidence to suggest that, following instruction in social skills, everyone will conform to a set pattern of behaviour in any given situation. Rather, it is hoped that the individual will become more aware of the consequences of any particular behaviour in a given situation, and will be able to choose the behaviour he deems most suitable.

The emphasis during microtraining is to provide the individual with an understanding of social interaction, in terms of the effects of his own behaviour. Any controls on this behaviour should come from within the individual, in that he is always the decision-maker in terms of his own responses. It is hoped that the individual will become freer as a result of such training, since he will have a greater repertoire of social behaviours from which to choose. This is, in fact, evidenced by the finding that microtraining serves to increase the confidence of trainees in the professional situation.

Furthermore, this method has proved to be effective, in that research evidence indicates that the microtraining method, which examines social interaction in terms of component social skills, leads to improvements in the overall social performance of trainees who undertake this type of training. Hargie and Saunders (1983) in discussing this research, point out that:

> The general outcome from this research has been to demonstrate that microtraining is an effective method for improving the communicative competence of trainees; that it is often more effective than alternative training approaches; and that it is well received by both trainers and trainees alike.

Conclusion

This book has been concerned with a comprehensive analysis and evaluation of interpersonal communication, with particular reference to the work of professionals in terms of: providing an understanding of many of the nuances of social interaction; increasing their awareness of their own behaviour and of its effect upon others; interpreting and making sense of the behaviour of others; and generally contributing to an increased social awareness and interpersonal competence.

The theoretical perspectives discussed in Part 1 are essential in that they provide an underlying rationale for the analytic approach to communication adopted in the remaining chapters of the book. The core communication skills covered in Part 2 will have direct application, to a greater or lesser extent, to all professions. For those who spend a proportion of their work interacting in groups, the aspects covered in Part 3 will be of vital import. Finally, the dimensions of communication covered in Part 4 represent centrally important issues in the evaluation of social interaction, which will be of relevance to most professionals.

Overall, therefore, this book should be a useful handbook for many professionals, both pre-service and practising. Ideally, it can be employed as a course text during training programmes in communication, thereby facilitating the learning by trainees of interpersonal skills and dimensions. However, it can also be employed solely as a reference text by the interested, experienced professional. Either way, the coverage represents the most comprehensive review to date of communication skills. At the same time, it should be recognised that this is a rapidly developing field of study and, as knowledge increases, further skills and dimensions will be identified, and awareness of interpersonal communication expanded accordingly.

References

Allen, D. and Ryan, K. (1969) *Microteaching,* Addison-Wesley, Reading, Massachusetts

Hargie, O. (1980) 'An Evaluation of a Microteaching Programme', unpublished PhD thesis, University of Ulster, Jordanstown, N. Ireland

———— and Maidment, P. (1979) *Microteaching in Perspective,* Blackstaff Press, Belfast

———— and Saunders, C. (1983) 'Training Professional Skills' in P. Dowrick and S. Biggs (eds), *Using Video,* Wiley, London

Murphy, G. and Kovach, J. (1972) *Historical Introduction to Modern Psychology,* Routledge and Kegan Paul, London

INDEX